5

4

2 Farmhouse in Galicia
3 Looking out to sea, Cabo Finisterre
4 Gaudí's El Capricho, Comillas, Cantabria
5 Dusk, Picos de Europa

6 Nightlife, Calle Ancha, León
7 Townhouse, León
8 Local cheeses, Picos de Europa
9 Fresh seafood

Dana Facaros & Michael Pauls

NORTHERN
SPAIN

'Few places in Europe can boast
such a concentration of medieval
curiosities as this stretch of road,
where the mystic syncretism of the
Jews, Templars, pagans and pilgrims
was expressed in monuments with
secret messages that still tease
and mystify today.'

CADOGANguides

1 The meadows and rocky peaks of the Picos de Europa

10 El Palacio de Velarde, Santillana del Mar
11 Flower-filled balcony, Santillana del Mar
12 Cathedral, Burgos

10

11

12

13 Café, Burgos

14 Turret of Gaudí's Los Botines, León
15 San Isidora, León
16 Plaza Mayor, Burgos
17 Tiled cafe, Comillas

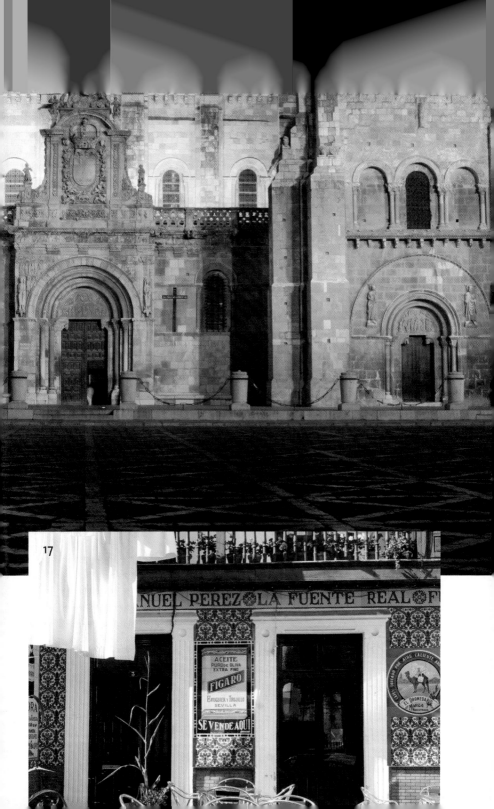

18

19

18 Shoreline, Cudillero, Asturias
19 Fishing boats, Cudillero, Asturias
20 Harbour, Cudillero, Asturias

21 León

About the authors

Dana Facaros and Michael Pauls have written over 40 books for Cadogan Guides, including all of the Spain series. They have lived all over Europe, but have now hung up their castanets in an old *presbytère* near the Lot.

About the updater

Mary-Ann Gallagher is a freelance travel writer and editor who has written and contributed to more than a dozen Cadogan guides. Her travels have taken her all over the world, but she is now happily settled in her favourite country – Spain.

Updater's acknowledgements

Heartfelt thanks to Josune García Yanguas and her family for wining, dining and entertaining me, as well as giving me the best restaurant tips in the whole region. Thanks to Dana and Michael who write the best travel guides on the planet, and to my eagle-eyed editor, Antonia, for all her hard work and patience.

Contents

Introducing

01
Introduction 1
A Guide to the Guide 4

02
History 5

03
Topics 19

04
Food and Drink 33

The Guide

05
Travel 43
Getting There 44
Entry Formalities 48
Getting Around 49

06
Practical A–Z 53
Children 54
Climate and
  When to Go 54
Disabled Travellers 54
Eating Out 55
Electricity 55
Embassies and
  Consulates 55

Entertainment and
  Nightlife 55
Festivals 56
Health and Insurance 57
Internet 59
Maps 59
Media 60
Money 61
Opening Hours 61
Photography 61
Pilgrim Facts 62
Police Business 62
Post Offices 62
Public Holidays 63
Sports and Activities 63
Telephones 64
Toilets 65
Tourist Information 65
Where to Stay 65
Women Travellers 68

07
**Navarra and
La Rioja 69**
Approaches from France:
  Down the Valleys of
  the Pyrenees 72
Pamplona (Iruña) 79
East of Pamplona:
  Sangüesa, Javier
  and Leyre 87
South of Pamplona
  to Tudela 91
Northwest of Pamplona:
  Aralar and San Miguel
  in Excelsis 94
Southwest of Pamplona:

the Camino de
  Santiago 96
Estella (Lizarra) 97
La Rioja 101
Logroño 102
Calahorra and
  La Rioja Baja 104
South of Logroño: Into the
  Sierra 107
Along the Pilgrim Route:
  West of Logroño 108
Wine Towns in
  Rioja Alta 114

08
**The Basque Lands
(Euskadi) 117**
An Introduction
  to the Basques 119
Along the Coast: France
  to San Sebastián 126
San Sebastián
  (Donostia) 127
Inland from
  San Sebastián 135
Along the Coast: San
  Sebastián to Bilbao 138
Ondarroa to Gernika 142
Inland: San Sebastián to
  Bilbao 147
Bilbao (Bilbo) 148
Vitoria (Gasteiz) 162
Álava Province 166

09
**Cantabria and the
Picos de Europa 171**

Bilbao to Santander: the
  Costa Esmeralda 174
Eastern Cantabria:
  Inland 177
Santander 178
South of Santander: the
  Heart of Cantabria 184
The Coast West
  of Santander 186
The Picos de Europa 193
The Asturian Picos
  de Europa 198
The Leónese Picos
  de Europa 201

10

Asturias 203
The Asturian 'Costa
  Verde': East to West 206
Gijón and Avilés 211
Oviedo 214
Southern Asturias 218
Western Coast 224

11

**Old Castile and
León 227**
Approaches to Burgos 230
Burgos 238
Southeast of Burgos 245
Along the Pilgrim Route:
  Burgos to Carrión de los
  Condes 251
Frómista 253
North of Frómista: the
  Románico Palentino 254
Along the Carrión River 257

Along the Pilgrims' Road
  to León 260
León 263
West of León 272
El Bierzo 277

12

Galicia 283
The Coast West of Asturias:
  As Mariñas de Lugo 286
The Galician Interior: the
  Road to Santiago 290
Lugo: a Detour off the
  Camino 293
Santiago de
  Compostela 297
Back to the Rías: the
  Golfo Ártabro 310
A Coruña 314
West of A Coruña:
  A Costa da Morte 317
Into the Rías Baixas 320
The Ria di Pontevedra 326
Pontevedra 327
The Ría de Vigo 330
Vigo 331
Up the Minho
  to Ourense 333
Ourense 338

Reference
Language 363
Glossary 366
Further Reading 367
Index 368

Maps
Northern Spain
  inside front cover
Chapter Divisions 2–3
Navarra and La Rioja 70
Approaches from
  France 72
Pamplona/Iruña 80
La Rioja 102
The Basque Lands
  (Euskadi) 118
San Sebastián
  (Donostia) 130–1
San Sebastián to
  Bilbao 139
Bilbao/Bilbo 150–1
Vitoria/Gasteiz 163
Cantabria 172–3
Santander 182–3
The Picos de Europa 193
Asturias 204–5
Old Castile and León
  228–9
Around Burgos 231
Burgos 237
León 268–9
West of León 273
Galicia 284
As Mariñas de Lugo 286
Santiago de
  Compostela 298–9
Golfo Ártabro and
  Costa da Morte 311
The Rías Baixas 321
Colour Touring Maps
  end of guide

Cadogan Guides
2nd Floor, 233 High Holborn
London WC1V 7DN
info@cadoganguides.co.uk
www.cadoganguides.com

The Globe Pequot Press
246 Goose Lane, PO Box 480, Guilford,
Connecticut 06437–0480

Copyright © Dana Facaros and Michael Pauls
   1996, 1999, 2001, 2003, 2006

Photographs by ©OLIVIA
Maps © Cadogan Guides, drawn by
   Maidenhead Cartographic Services Ltd
Art Direction: Sarah Rianhard-Gardner
Managing Editor: Natalie Pomier
Editor: Antonia Cunningham
Editorial Assistant: Nicola Jessop
Proofreading: Caroline Alexander
Indexing: Isobel McLean

Printed by Legoprint
A catalogue record for this book is available
   from the British Library
ISBN 10: 1-86011-312-5
ISBN 13: 978-1-86011-312-3

The author and publishers have made every effort
to ensure the accuracy of the information in this
book at the time of going to press. However, they
cannot accept any responsibility for any loss,
injury or inconvenience resulting from the use of
information contained in this guide.

Please help us to keep this guide up to date. We
have done our best to ensure that the information
in this guide is correct at the time of going to press,
but places and facilities are constantly changing,
and standards and prices in hotels and restaurants
fluctuate. We would be delighted to receive any
comments concerning existing entries or
omissions. Authors of the best letters will receive a
copy of the Cadogan Guide of their choice.

Introduction

A Guide to the Guide **4**

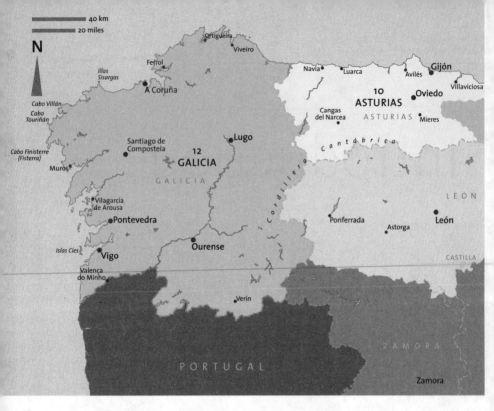

The north is the alternative Spain, the 'Green Spain', where all national stereotypes collapse, or at least those stereotypes we acquire on the Med. Northern landscapes can be just as spectacular, and beaches just as plentiful, with blue and emerald colours in the ocean and along the estuaries that bite into the coast; the mountains – the western Pyrenees, the Cordillera Cantábrica and the Picos de Europa – are endearingly lovely and inviting to linger and walk in, unlike much of the austere, dry *meseta* to the south. Here are sheep in the meadows, cows in the corn and storks on every spire – the biggest colony of these, over a hundred, live atop Calahorra cathedral. The northwest is as rich and lush as the rest of Spain is traditionally hard and dry; here you'll find Spain's finest cheer: Galician seafood, La Rioja wine, Asturian cider, Cantabrian cheese, Navarrese garden vegetables, Castilian sucking-pig and roast lamb, and the chefs with the best reputation for putting it all together – the Basques. Of course much of the north's luxuriance comes from the fact that no matter how Eliza Doolittle pronounces it, the rain in Spain does not fall mainly in the plain, but rather right on its head.

Northern Spain has the knack of acquiring a plethora of 'firsts' and then discreetly retiring into the background. The earliest settlers in Iberia found it convivial and left one of the world's great Palaeolithic masterpieces, at Altamira; the Basques, the oldest race in Europe, found it just as cosy and have called it home almost since the beginning of time. After the conquest of the Moors, the embryo of modern Spain, its architecture and language – Castilian – were formed in the mountains of Asturias

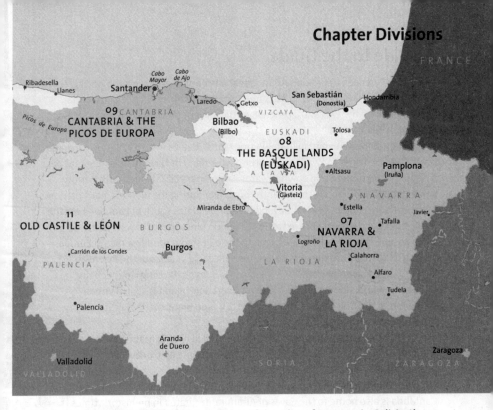

and crystalized in Burgos. With the discovery of the relics of St James in Galicia, the northwest became the forerunner of European tourism, inventing the pilgrimage to Santiago de Compostela, now in its second millennium. Even though Spain's centre of gravity gradually moved south to Madrid, the cities and countryside of the north have been adorned with a generous helping of magnificent architectural treasures, from the Visigothic to the most florid Baroque, not to mention a few works by the great Catalan *modernista* master Antoni Gaudí.

The Spaniards, especially the *Madrileños*, have in the past few decades guarded the northwest as a secret for themselves, although they only come in July and August, when it rains less. But even then you have to look hard to find beaches blighted by Benidormish excess (Laredo and Zarautz are the only ones that come close); tourism in northern Spain is more low key, and by the nature of its short 'season' is probably destined to remain so.

To let the threat of a shower or two keep you away would be to miss out on the best preserved and most idiosyncratic corners of old Europe, a place that has kept a sense of place in the face of creeping homogeneity, one full of unexpected pleasures: a Roman bridge over a brook, the fishmarket in A Coruña, a tableland in northern Castile abruptly cut away by a canyon filled with eagles, a spontaneous party that lasts until dawn in an outdoor *sidrería*, old women herding their cows home by twilight, the walls of stained glass in León, a Basque tug-of-war match, and a sunset at Finisterre, the end of the world.

A Guide to the Guide

From the Pyrenees to Galicia's Atlantic seaboard, our guide covers the northern sliver of Spain (Navarra, La Rioja, Euskadi, Cantabria, Asturias, Castile and Galicia), broadly tracking the westward progress of the ancient pilgrimage route to Santiago de Compostela.

Navarra, where we begin, spills down from the Pyrenees in lush valleys of pine and beech forest, an area known locally as the 'Switzerland of Navarra'. It is here that we pick up the pilgrimage trail down towards Pamplona, a city speared with narrow lanes through which bulls charge and crowds jeer during the world-famous madness of the Los Sanfermines festival. Beyond the barren plains south of Pamplona are the fertile banks of the River Ebro in **La Rioja**, a region pinstriped with vineyards.

The Basque Lands (Euskadi) are home to the oldest and proudest race in Europe. Among its features are the remote, unpronounceable villages of the Pyrenean lowlands, the golden bay of San Sebastián and Bilbao's dazzling Guggenheim museum – worldwide symbol of urban regeneration. Inland is stylish Vitoria, an industrial town that hosts the Fiesta de la Virgen Blanca, a six-day Spanish blowout with parties till dawn.

In the following chapter, we move from the rural idyll of **Cantabria**, where a common sight is a clog-clad farmer's wife driving home an ox-cart piled high with grass – Cantabria has the highest density of cows in Europe – to the peak-packed **Picos de Europa**, a haven for hikers and the most beautiful mountains in Spain. Cantabria is also home to the Caves of Altamira, decorated in prehistoric times with exuberant works of artistic genius.

Then there is the rugged beauty of **Asturias**, its coastline pockmarked with beaches, its tumbling mountain rapids and gentle lowland streams teeming with trout, salmon and eel; if you're lucky you might just catch a glimpse of the elusive Cantabrian bear, recently saved from extinction by the Asturian Wildlife Protection Fund. Inland, around Oviedo, you'll find a scattering of unusual pre-Romanesque churches, which have stood proud since the 9th century and are now protected by UNESCO as part of the 'Patrimony of Humanity'.

Old Castile and León comprise the rolling scrub-pocked plains of the *meseta*, a land of straggling hamlets and the most tortuous stretch of the *camino de Santiago*. We track down ancient hermitages in the Valley of Silence, and describe the diaphanous beauty of Gothic cathedrals in Burgos and León, built half of stone, half of light and air.

Galicia, Spain's sea-battered northwestern corner, is a place of its own, for many years removed from the mainstream of Spanish life and history. Its estuaries (*rías*) offer up a feast of sea creatures, which Galician cooks kindly whip up in a thousand different ways, while its jagged shoreline (dubbed 'coast of death') presents hundreds of coves, cliffs and sandy beaches to explore. Moss-stained Santiago de Compostela, the original European tourist destination, stands proud as the culmination of the pilgrim's journey, and the tail end of our guide.

History

25,000 BC–AD 409 **6**

409–711 **7**

711–800 **8**

800–1000 **10**

1000–1218 **11**

1218–1516 **12**

1516–1931 **14**

1931–the Present **16**

25,000 BC–AD 409
In which a cultural early bird slows down and gets carved up for lunch by Romans and Carthaginians

Along with southwestern France, this corner of Spain can claim itself as home to the world's oldest known culture. About 25,000 BC, in the Palaeolithic age, the peninsula's many caves began to fill up with Palaeospaniards (or perhaps the ancestors of the Basques, *see* p.120), living well enough off herds of bison and deer to create impressive works of art on cave walls from Cantabria to the western Pyrenees and Périgord. Scholars generally divide these people into the earlier Aurignacian and later Magdalenian cultures. The latter reached their height around 15,000 BC and created some of the Stone Age's finest art, notably in the caves of Altamira near Santander.

It's a long dull stretch from the Palaeolithic masters to the next interesting period in Europe, the Neolithic age. Neolithic culture, with settled farming, trade and megalithic building, may have come to Spain as early as 5500 BC, and it enjoyed a long and relatively peaceful reign over the peninsula, lasting until roughly 2000 BC. This culture, extending from Spain to Scandinavia, distinguished itself by creating Europe's first architecture, with its dolmens, other burial chambers, standing stones and stone circles. Neolithic peoples, though probably a matriarchal society, were sailors and traders, and liked to live near the coasts, including the northern coasts; large concentrations of megalithic monuments are found in the Basque country and Galicia. The latter seems to have been unusually prosperous; dolmen burials here included plenty of gold jewellery, rare for the time.

About 2000 BC, many of the peoples of Iberia learned the use of bronze and started using it to make weapons, while spending their spare time building fortresses to protect the bronze. In an Iberia increasingly turned towards the Mediterranean, the northern coast seems to have been spared most of this progress, and people carried on in their sweet old Neolithic way. About 800 BC, the native Iberians were joined by other peoples, notably the Celts from over the Pyrenees. These got along well enough with the Iberians; in many cases they gradually merged with some tribes, creating a new people, the Celtiberians, who occupied much of the centre and north of the peninsula. The heritage of the Celts everywhere is the *castro*, or as it is called in France and sometimes here too, the *oppidum*. Asterix's lot didn't care much for towns, but wherever there was some trade to be conducted, or treasure to be guarded, the Celts would have a sort of tiny urban centre, perched on a hilltop and surrounded by walls – more a castle than a town.

Meanwhile, the Phoenicians were making their presence felt in the south. Their traders and colonists began taking over parts of coastal Andalucía *c.*1200 BC, but evidence is lacking and it remains an open question just how much time the Phoenicians spent in the north. Several of the port towns have a height called *Atalaya*, believed to be a Phoenician word meaning 'tower', while *Spain* is another Phoenician word, meaning 'land of rabbits'. We can imagine that the northern coast was part of a fairly busy trade route, monopolized by Phoenician ships, bringing tin from Cornwall to make bronze in the Mediterranean – the Phoenicians were understandably secretive about the world they discovered outside the Pillars of Hercules, and they probably made up all the stories of sea monsters and such to scare off potential competitors.

Overlordship of Iberia fell to Rome in 202 BC, the big prize for the victory over Hannibal and Carthage in the Second Punic War. But just as the Carthaginians had never really controlled the wild northwest, Roman rule here was mostly a vain boast for another two centuries. The Romans found the region inhabited by a people they called the *Vascones*, the Basques, and further west the Celtiberian *Cantabri*, *Asturi* and *Gallæci*. Unlike the Carthaginians, the Romans couldn't bear a messy map, and they spent those two centuries methodically grinding down Celtiberians and Basques alike. One highlight of the endless campaigns was the epic siege of Numancia, a Celtiberian stronghold in what is now northern Castile (near Soria). After beating off Roman attacks for nineteen years, the Numancians escaped the dishonour of final defeat by burning the town with themselves inside it. To subdue Spain Rome had to send its best – Cato, Pompey, Caesar and Augustus were all commanders in the Spanish conquest – and the job was not finished in some isolated areas until 20 BC.

The rest of Spain had metal ores to make it worth the trouble, and even in the far northwest Rome probably broke even, thanks to the gold mines of El Bierzo. Only a few towns were founded: *Pallantia* (Palencia) was probably the biggest, followed by *Clunia* (an abandoned site near Aranda de Duero), *Pompaelo* (Pamplona), *Asturica Augusta* (Astorga), *Brigantium* (A Coruña), and *Lucus Augusti* (Lugo). Nor did the Romans break the bank building roads here, although the most important one, linking Zaragoza to León, would one day become the *camino de Santiago*. No town ever managed a population of more than about five thousand. So while the rest of Spain got a good washing and a Latin grammar to study, the peoples of the north were pretty much left alone. Compared to the rest of the western Empire, relatively few wealthy villas have been discovered here, a sign that the Roman élite had barely penetrated the region.

Throughout most of the imperial era, the north was a forgotten corner of the province of Tarracona, with its capital on the Mediterranean, modern Tarragona. In one of the reforms of Diocletian, this sprawling province was split up, the far western part gaining the name of *Gallaecia* after its Gaulish inhabitants – the future Galicia. Christianity spread quickly in Spain, at least among the officials and landlords in the south, so much so that the peninsula held its first Church council in 313. The only representative from the north was a bishop of a little town called Lanobriga (León).

409–711

In which the northwest dozes fitfully through a depressing parade of barbarian hordes

The first Germans had found their way into Iberia during the great barbarian raid of the 260s, though the legions gradually recovered and threw them out again. When the Rhine frontier collapsed in 407, some of the Germans storming westwards were probably already thinking of Spain. Vandals, Alans and Suevi all made it over the pass at Roncesvalles by 409, and they separately ranged the peninsula looking for land and swag. To try and restore order, what was left of the Empire sent in another horde, the Visigoths, as allies to sort their cousins out. They smashed the Alans and Vandals, but let the Suevi keep the remote northwest. Rome, now worrying that the cure might be worse than the disease, talked the Visigoths into crossing the Pyrenees again to have some fun in southern Gaul. In the resulting vacuum, a new horde of Vandals (the Siling Vandals) broke in in 422. They did what Vandals will do, seven years of it, before crossing the Straits of Gibraltar in search of richer lands and towns in Africa.

That left the field clear for the Suevi (or Swabians – their stay-at-home relations gave the name to a region of southwestern Germany). Under their chief Rechila, they made a little kingdom for themselves, centred at Astorga, and by 448 controlled much of the peninsula. In 456, however, the Visigoths came back and defeated them near Astorga, bottling the remnant up in remote Galicia. The Visigoths thought they were just adding some Iberian possessions to their kingdom of southern Gaul – but when the Franks in turn defeated them at the great Battle of Vouillé in 507 and chased them over the Pyrenees, they found themselves in a position they would have to be content with – as rulers of Spain.

As Teutonic barbarians go, the Visigoths were a cut above the rest. They did not drink out of skulls, like the Lombards, or smear bear grease all over their bodies, like the Franks. The line of their kings went back to Alaric I, the Goth who had sacked Rome. For the next two centuries, the Visigoths ruled their Spanish kingdom from Toledo, building churches and inventing a rather blunt code of laws in vulgar Latin; in the northwest, they engaged in endless desultory fighting with the Suevi until 585, when the great King Leovigild finally put an end to their kingdom.

Meanwhile, up in their mountains, the Basques lapsed into *de facto* independence, meeting in democratic assembly around the oak of Gernika to make their own laws. They were expanding in all directions, and especially present in what is now Navarra – peacefully colonizing lands wasted by too many hard times and too many armies. The kings sent frequent expeditions north to try and squeeze some tribute money out of them, with occasional success. Asturias and Galicia proved just as hard to control, and the Visigothic kingdom probably had no more influence here than the Romans had.

711–800

In the middle of the Dark Ages, Spanish history records one of its most frantic centuries ever

At the dawn of the eighth century, it seemed that the Visigothic kingdom had truly established itself: a stable state, by the standards of the time, with a strong Church and some modest cultural achievements (in architecture and literature especially, Spain was more than holding its own). In fact, riven with clan feuds and religious bigotry, the kingdom was a plum waiting to be picked. Of all the luck, this happened to be the first century of Islam, with the explosive bursts of the Arab armies across the Middle East and North Africa. After they had digested North Africa, Spain was the only place to go on Islam's western front, and the first small force under Tariq ibn-Zayad landed at Gibraltar in 711. The last Visigothic king, Roderick, was defeated and killed in a great battle near Toledo, and within three years the Muslims were in control of the entire peninsula – except, as you might have guessed by now, parts of the north.

The Arabs surged across the Pyrenees, only to be defeated and driven back by the Franks at Poitiers in 732, but what really kept them from consolidating their hold over northwest Spain was a short but intense revolt of the Muslim Berber troops in 740 against their Arab leaders. To hear the Spaniards tell the story though, the turning of the tide came with a legendary prince of Asturias named Pelayo, who defeated the Moors at the 'Battle of Covadonga' in 718 and kept Asturias free and Christian. Now, there seems to have really been a historic Pelayo, a Visigothic baron, but no reliable record of such a battle is preserved anywhere, and Asturias like the rest of the region was still largely pagan. Spanish history and national mythology are becoming inextricably intertwined; a little inconsequential skirmish in the mountains that Iberia's new masters didn't even notice would some day, in retrospect, appear as the beginning of a national history. Nearly forty years after the Battle of Covadonga, the *Chronicle of 754*, written by a Christian in al-Andalus, does not mention either the battle or the new Christian 'kingdom' in the north.

Later legends in Cantabria and Asturias spoke of the 'Foramontanos', who fled into the mountains from the Moors and 'returned to repopulate Castile'. And it seems likely that a number of die-hard Visigothic nobles took refuge up in the more inaccessible parts of Asturias. But the romantic legend of the last few defenders of the faith, heroically holed up in the Asturian mountains – the seed from which Spain would grow – is only partially true.

The records say that, only four years after the invasion began, the Moors were pretty much in control of Asturias and most of the rest of the northwest. Gijón, on the coast, fell to the Muslims in 715 and had an Arab governor for years afterwards, as did Pamplona. Galicia too was in Arab hands for some time.

While all this was happening, other neglected fringes of the Iberian world were beginning their careers, including the little state of Navarra. Pamplona freed itself from Muslim rule in the Berber revolt of 740, and the Basques were independent once again. Once again, though, they had to fight to stay that way. After beating the Moors at Poitiers, the self-confident Franks soon came over the Pyrenees looking for new lands to conquer. One of their raids gave birth to the famous legend of Roland and Oliver. These famous knights of Charlemagne perished at the hands of the Basques in an ambush at the pass of Roncesvalles in 778.

800–1000

The northern mountain boys tweak the moustaches of a powerful Emirate, and then found some kingdoms

The endless conquests and confusions of the 8th century set the pattern for centuries of Spain's history to come. The new Emirate of al-Andalus developed a policy of insulating itself from the wild north by a band of marches – no-man's-lands with military governors. At the beginning, these included what is now León, Castile and much of Aragón. The emirs might raid them every few years, but they could not keep Christian settlers from gradually filling in the empty spaces, laying the ground-work for the Reconquista.

While the Emirate (Caliphate after 929) was developing a brilliant Spanish-Muslim civilization in the middle of the Dark Ages, the northern kingdom was prospering and growing too, while economically and culturally drawing closer to Christian Europe. Not only was Asturias slowly and gradually expanding, but new centres of power appeared as well. In 800, the year Charlemagne was proclaimed emperor, the first written mention is made of the County of Castile, the 'Land of Castles'. The north may not have been so backward at all, comparatively speaking. The sophisticated and urbanized society of al-Andalus had a constant need for raw materials and food, and it spread prosperity and learning beyond its borders. One of the surprises of the Christian north was its pre-Romanesque architecture, as expressed in the famous 9th- and 10th-century churches around Asturias and Cantabria, built at a time when the rest of Europe was hardly building anything in stone. Design and clothing, however, were still heavily influenced by the latest fashions in Moorish Córdoba, Granada and Sevilla, and such educated princes as there were would more likely know Arabic than Latin.

In the 9th century, Muslim al-Andalus entered the golden age of its prosperity and power. Campaigns against the Christians in the north were frequent though incon-clusive: Pamplona was taken again in 842, and León in 848, but neither could be held for long. Under ineffectual caliphs such as Abd Allah, the late 9th century was a time of civil strife and confusion in the south, and it permitted the new kingdom of Asturias to take its first steps on the way to the Reconquista – the retaking of all Iberia for Christianity that had already been predicted, against all odds, in a Christian work called the *Prophetic Chronicle*.

Christians began to resettle and hold lands south of the Cantabrian mountains; they also managed to found or refound a number of towns in the no-man's-land of the Duero Valley, notably Burgos (884). The reign of Alfonso III (866–910) was a water-shed for the northerners, in which they pushed their boundaries into Portugal and resettled much of northern Castile (for convenience' sake historians call Asturias the 'Kingdom of León', after that city was taken in 913, though interestingly for centuries the kingdom had no name at all, and such kings as could write would sign docu-ments simply *Yo, el Rey*).

As for the Basques, by 824 Pamplona had chased the Franks out once and for all, forming the county of Navarra under a leader named Jimeno Aritza and his descendants. The Basques seem to have got on well enough with the Moors, and were often in alliance with them against the famous clan of the Banu Qasi – rene-gade Visigoths who had turned Muslim, and who held Zaragoza and much of Aragón not for the Emirate, but for themselves. Later, Basques would provide many of the favourite women in the palace harem at Córdoba, and consequently more than a few of the emirs were at least half Basque.

The reign of Abd ar-Rahman III (912–961), who declared himself Caliph, marked the high point of the power of al-Andalus, and a setback for the northerners, though the caliph could do little to stop the resettlement of the new northern lands. Abd ar-Rahman's notable contemporary in the north was Fernán González, *El Buen Conde*, the 'Good Count' of Castile (923–970) who, despite continuous war with the Moors, made his land into a kingdom independent of Asturias. More troubles for the north came with the rule in al-Andalus of al-Mansur, 'the Victorious', an ambitious vizier who had locked the weak young caliph Hisham II away in the palace at Córdoba and pulled all the strings himself. Al-Mansur defeated the Asturians and sacked León in 988, and Burgos in 1000. He forced most of the northerners to pay tribute, and on one raid his armies even occupied Santiago de Compostela, carrying off the church bells as a prize for the Great Mosque of Córdoba.

1000–1218
The northerners persist, and find that constant bellicosity brings big rewards

The Muslims definitely still held the real power in the peninsula, but the same al-Mansur who had won so many battles for them was unwittingly to be the downfall of the caliphate. By assuming personal power, he removed the main prop of the legitimacy of the state. When he died, his sons attempted to carry on in his place, leading to a revolution in 1009 that put an end to the political unity of al-Andalus forever, leaving a collection of small states quarrelling amongst themselves.

That was all the opportunity the warriors of the north needed. Especially under Alfonso VI (1065–1109) they extended their boundaries ever farther; Alfonso crowned a long string of victories with the capture of Toledo in 1085, securing permanent control of the central *meseta*. Alfonso was the first Castilian king to mint coins (instead of using Moorish currency); he collected tribute money from the little kings of al-Andalus, and he began calling himself 'Emperor of All Spain', but he never would have done it without the help of the Castilian adventurer El Cid, Rodrigo Díaz de Vivar.

The new millennium had definitely got off to an auspicious start for Christian Spain. But for a while it looked as if the big victor among the Christian states would be little Navarra. Still Basque but becoming increasingly hispanicized and feudalized, Navarra had reached its zenith under Sancho el Mayor (1000–35), capturing all of La Rioja and even much of Castile. But like so many of the transient empires formed in the free-for-all of the Reconquista, Sancho's proved to be only a house of cards, and Alfonso VI cut Navarra down to size in the 1070s. In fact, every Christian state was taking advantage of al-Andalus's disarray to expand its boundaries: León/Castile (united by marriage), Navarra, Portugal and Aragón. Aragón and León/Castile eventually emerged as the main rivals for dominance in the new Spain that was building. Under Alfonso I, *El Batallador*, Aragón emerged as a major power; in the 1110s Alfonso briefly controlled parts of Castile, including Burgos.

The new states could afford such rivalry; the new frontier life created by conditions on the *meseta* gave the Christians one particular military advantage: a class of hard men doing well enough to afford heavy armour and a horse. The Spanish cavalry was small in number, but they could cover ground quickly, raid everywhere and often carry the day in pitched battles against Moorish forces that were numerically superior. Another advantage was the spirit of the Crusader, both in reinforcing morale and attracting fresh blood; early on, the popes had declared Spain a legitimate sphere of Crusading activity, as much as was the Holy Land.

Al-Andalus, however, was not finished yet. Before the Christians could completely swallow it up, the various little states were swept away by the new Almoravid (Murabit) empire. Originally an Islamic fundamentalist movement among the Berbers, dominated by a few powerful tribes, this grew into an emirate that controlled all of Morocco. After the fall of Toledo the Almoravids were invited into Spain, where they stopped the Christian tide – and added al-Andalus to their dominions. They lasted until 1147, falling into decay and being replaced by a nearly identical African sectarian empire, that of the Almohads (Muwahhid).

Although Muslim art and culture continued to shine, the Almohads suffered the same decay of reforming zeal as had the Almoravids, once introduced to the pleasures of Córdoba and Sevilla. The great disaster for al-Andalus came in 1212: the Battle of Las Navas de Tolosa, where a Christian alliance led by Alfonso VIII of Castile destroyed the Almohad power forever. The great cities of the south were gobbled up soon after, leaving the Muslims only the little kingdom of Granada, which held out by careful diplomacy and heavy tributes until 1492. Six years after Las Navas de Tolosa, in 1218, León and Castile merged once and for all under Ferdinand III el Santo.

1218–1516

In which medieval Spain creates a fat and happy civilization, and pride goes before a fall

It's the great historical paradox of the Reconquista, one of the examples of Cervantean irony that Spain is always bountiful in providing: the northwest, previously little more relevant to Spain's history than Novgorod or Baluchistan, suddenly takes centre stage in creating a new Spain, and then with success finds itself left behind on the periphery again with nothing to do. After Las Navas de Tolosa, all the money was to be made in the centre and south, in *New* Castile around Madrid, and in al-Andalus – now Spanish Andalucía.

Castile had tripled in size, and its kings, now by far the most dangerous ones on the chessboard, began spending much more of their time in central towns such as Toledo and Valladolid, and less in León or Burgos. For simple geographical reasons, the northwest would never be the real heartland of a nation. But for the time being it managed to share fully in Western Europe's blossoming during the 12th and 13th centuries.

Particularly striking was the growth of towns. Trade came back in the Atlantic in a big way, for the first time since the Romans, and little ports from A Coruña to San Sebastián reawakened from 600 years' slumber. Increasingly, they sent wool to England, France and Flanders. That was the big-money commodity of the age, and the northern plains were perfectly suited for raising sheep. Run under a sophisticated sort of royal cooperative called the *mesta*, this trade fuelled most of medieval Castile's remarkable prosperity, and the annual fair at Medina del Campo became one of the biggest in Europe. Many of the northern cities at least doubled in size in the 12th century, the biggest boom in all history for places such as León and Burgos. Though doomed never to make a rôle for themselves as capitals or great trade centres, both these cities took advantage of the good times to create notable monuments, including the finest Gothic cathedrals in Spain. León began its in 1205, and Burgos followed in 1221.

With money came increasing power for the growing towns, and nearly all of them in this period were able to gain a high degree of independence from the kings, bishops or nobles who had formerly bossed them around. All over Spain, the towns were organizing themselves into *comunes*, as in the rest of Europe. A good example of the new type of medieval *comune* is Vitoria-Gasteiz, founded by King Alfonso VI of Navarra in 1181, soon after he had conquered the territory from Castile. Alfonso wanted a loyal town to consolidate his hold, and to keep the new settlers' loyalty, he granted it a charter of *fueros* (literally 'outsides', or exceptions to royal law) that gave the town rights of self-government and exemptions from some taxes and feudal responsibilities. This story was repeated literally hundreds of times across Christian Spain.

The *fueros* gave Spain a less oppressive government than most countries. They were made possible by the good example of the Basques. It was a good time for this incurably industrious people too, as they began to turn their talents to the sea. In 1296 a kind of Hanseatic league of Basque ports was founded, the *Hermandad de las Marismas*; shipping Vizcaya's iron and Castile's wool northwards, the *Hermandad* grew to control a disproportionate share of the Atlantic trade. But as in Navarra, the Basque language and culture were being pushed further into the background, in a world increasingly dominated by Spanish-speaking nobles and merchants. Navarra, condemned by geography to lose out in the Reconquista land grab, was now in full decline. French involvement in the kingdom dated from 1284, when an heiress of the kingdom, Juana I, married King Philip the Fair of France. Members of the Capetian dynasty ruled Navarra as a quaint Pyrenean Ruritania from then on.

Throughout the 14th and 15th centuries, the peninsula occupied itself with consolidating the gains of the Reconquista and trying to make some sense out of all the commotion that had occurred. Burgos and León got their tremendous cathedrals finished, but economically and culturally the northwest was increasingly left on the periphery of a Spain that was growing very large and complex. And already, some of the forces that would make this Spain go to pieces were in their larval forms – the big winners of the Reconquista, a bloated nobility and a dangerous but morally decayed Church, both exempt from taxes and loaded with privileges. On the whole, the experience of the Reconquista coarsened the life of Castile, creating a pirate ethos where honest labour was scorned, and wealth and honour were things to be snatched from one's neighbours.

The climax of unification came in 1469 with the marriage of *los Reyes Católicos*, Ferdinand of Aragon and Isabel of Castile. Under their reign Spain's borders were rounded out. Not only did they finally conquer the kingdom of Granada, the last remnant of al-Andalus, but Ferdinand's campaigns put an end to that medieval relic up north, the kingdom of Navarra. Spain was also embarking on its career as a grand imperialist, invading Italy and colonizing the Americas. All this cost a good deal of money, which Ferdinand and Isabel's ministers extorted out of the towns and cities of Castile. They whittled away at the communal lands and the *fueros*, and towns that had run their own affairs for centuries now found their assets carved up little by little among the crown and the local nobles. The religious bigotry of the 'Catholic Kings', Isabel in particular, put a perverse twist on Spanish life that was to last a long time. Under their reign the Inquisition was reintroduced, and the Jews expelled.

1516–1931
The north's history is dissolved into that of united Spain, and it isn't a pretty story

Worse was still to come. Whatever cash and valuables were left in Old Castile were soon relentlessly sucked out by Ferdinand and Isabel's grandson, the Habsburg Carlos I. Better known to history as Charles V, his title as Holy Roman Emperor, this rapacious megalomaniac gained the throne by declaring the rightful queen, his mother Juana, insane, and locking her up in a windowless cell for the next forty years. Charles and his Flemish minions then started squeezing Spain dry, to raise the gargantuan bribes that were necessary for an Imperial election in those days (even though there were only seven voters!). To accomplish the looting of his new country, Charles rescinded or ignored most of the remaining municipal *fueros*, wrecked the trade fairs and invented new taxes everywhere. The church and nobles jumped in for a share of the spoils, and Spain embarked on a rather remarkable and ultimately successful attempt to destroy its own economy.

A national financial collapse came in 1519, and an outraged Castile finally rose up in rebellion. The Comunero Revolt, a brave last attempt of the *comunes* to defend their purses and their liberties, began in 1520 and quickly spread through the towns of Old Castile. Charles' foreign troops put it down the following year, and though the king took a conciliatory line towards the rebels, there was no doubt now about who was boss. Castile was finished, its trade ruined and its once-thriving towns condemned to be the backwater relics they remain today.

Ripping out the heart of his country meant relatively little to Charles, who now had gold and silver flowing in from America to finance his endless aggressions across Europe. For a final note on one of history's bigger rotters, we see Charles after his abdication in 1556, living in a monastery at Yuste, in Extremadura, praying for his soul and gorging himself continually on eel pies. His favourite recreation in the later days was rehearsing his funeral, and at one practice session he caught a chill and died.

For Spain, still worse was yet to come. Under Charles's neurotic son Philip II, Spain reached the height of its book- and heretic-burning frenzy, while the economy stayed wrecked and military defeats piled up on every side. A particular blow against the northwest, motivated by corrupt ministers, was Philip's decision in 1573 to allow Sevilla to monopolize trade with the New World. The northern ports dwindled, and all the poor souls whose prospects had been ruined even had to find their way to the south to catch a boat just to emigrate.

This state of affairs lasted until 1788, by which time the northern towns had already undergone a steep decline along with the rest of Spain. Nevertheless, the northwest found ways to wring a penny from the Americas. The enterprising Basques, for example, created the *Compañia Guipuzcoana de Caracas*, which wangled a monopoly over the chocolate trade and brought a lot of money home to the Basque country. For generations, Basques and Spaniards alike contributed their share to Spain's colonial adventures. Sons who went overseas to make their fortunes were called *indianos* – and *indianos*, or *casas de indianos*, is also the name for the houses built by the lucky ones who came home well off; you'll see them everywhere in the northwest, as early as 1650 and as late as 1920.

If little good happened in these centuries, at least the north was usually spared the curse of armies and wars. That is, until Napoleon crossed the Pyrenees in 1808. French occupation led to a spontaneous national revolt – the Spaniards call it their 'War of Independence'. The British pitched in to fight their mutual nemesis, at first catastrophically as their army under Sir John Moore, pursued by Maréchal Soult, beat a desperate retreat across the northwest to flee from A Coruña. When the British returned under Wellington, it was their turn to chase the French from Cádiz to Paris, the result as much a disaster for Napoleon as his winter in Moscow. Wellington is well remembered by the Spanish for kicking the French out (they made him a duke too), but his boys dealt with conquered land far worse than Napoleon or any contemporary army would have dreamed, distinguishing themselves notably at the sack of San Sebastián. The French had been content with simply looting all the gold crucifixes and a lot of bad paintings.

But as the great chef Escoffier later expressed it, the only worthwhile thing France got out of the Peninsular War was the recipe for pheasant *à la Alcántara*. That did not stop the French from sending their army down again in 1823, with the blessing of the English and Austrians, to stamp out a democratic revolt against the despotic Bourbons. Nineteenth-century Spain became quite a wild place, often the very image of the banana republics that had just gained their independence from it in Latin America. The Basques, especially those of Navarra, did their best to keep the pot boiling. Supporting the claims of the pretender Don Carlos, they sided with the Church and reactionaries in the Carlist Wars of 1833–39 and 1872–6. Many Carlists only took up the cause in defence of what was left of their *fueros*, which liberal reformers in Madrid were trying to abolish. The generals of Isabel II put down both revolts, though there were some close moments, as in the Second Carlist War when the insurgents briefly besieged Bilbao.

Isabel II presided over the confusing height of the banana monarchy where rival generals and politicians could compete for her favours while issuing *pronunciamientos* and plotting backstage coups. But while the country as a whole was becoming an increasingly inconsequential backwater in Europe, some signs of life were stirring in unlikely places – not in the moribund Castilian centre, but on the periphery. Along with the Catalans, the Basques were doing their best to give the country a boost into the Industrial Revolution. Bilbao became a noisy boom town around its ironworks and shipyards, while a small echo was heard from tiny Asturias, which grew into Spain's most important mining region.

1931–the Present
The northerners choose sides, fight it out, and most finally conclude that pluralism isn't so bad after all

Along with industrialization came political change. The Basque Nationalist Party, or PNV, appeared to speak up for Basque concerns at the Cortes in Madrid, while Asturias with its strong unions became increasingly radicalized. The boom years of the First World War, provided by Spain's neutrality, were followed by a steep depression that brought social problems to a head, especially after the Second Republic was proclaimed in 1931. One famous event of the time, a prelude to the Civil War, was the bloody revolt of the Asturian miners in 1934, crushed by army troops under a general named Franco.

When the Civil War broke out in July 1936, the Basques and Asturians sided enthusiastically with the Republic, while Old Castile supported Franco. Until the end of the war the Nationalists kept their capital at Burgos. Most Galicians took the Nationalist side too – Franco was after all a native son, from Ferrol – and so did the Navarrese, whose politics still revolved around Carlism. Franco's armies soon reduced Republican territory in the northwest to a chain of small pockets along the coast. The Basques held out until 1937, when they succumbed to a campaign distinguished by the terror bombing of Guernica, performed by Franco's Nazi allies.

After the war the Basques suffered more than anyone for their loyalty to the Republic. As in Catalunya, the government suppressed even the casual use of the native language, forbade most festivals and cultural manifestations, and sent thousands of intellectuals to prison or exile. State industrial schemes were consciously planned in a way to bring in large numbers of Spanish job-seekers to dilute the Basque population. The Basque response was the growth of the terrorist ETA, beginning in the 1950s. As the only active resistance to the dictatorship, the ETA attracted widespread sympathy within Spain and elsewhere, especially in 1973 when they blew the car of Franco's hand-picked successor, Admiral Carrero Blanco, over the roof of a Madrid church.

In striking contrast, plenty of Navarrese, mostly Carlists, found posts in Franco's army and government until the end of the regime in 1975 (the Spanish fascists even borrowed the Carlists' yoke-and-arrows symbol for their own party). There are Carlists to be found even today, although the current pretender, Prince Hugo de Borbón, has tacitly acknowledged King Juan Carlos by paying him a social visit. Navarra remains the most politically reactionary part of Spain, maybe of all Europe; Pamplona, its bright and prosperous capital, is the Mecca of the Opus Dei, the sinister, secret Catholic organization that in Franco's later years attempted to gain control of the Spanish government by insinuating its members into high positions.

In Galicia, Cantabria and Castile, politics remain quietly Neanderthal; these are the only parts of Spain where you're still likely to see statues and streets named after Nationalist heroes. Since the restoration of democracy in 1977, the most dramatic change in Spain has been the reversal of centuries of centralization, with the creation of autonomous regional governments throughout the country, including Galicia, Asturias, Cantabria, the Basque country (Euskadi), Navarra and Old Castile – the latter the only part of Spain where a majority didn't want autonomy, and had it forced upon them by Madrid. The Basques got a special autonomy statute, and they have made the most of it, with their own schools, television and police force.

This wasn't enough for the die-hards of the ETA, who still demand total independence, and who have continued their murders and bombing campaigns, almost always in other parts of Spain. The surprise truce declared in September 1998 brought 15 months of peace to Spain and the Basque lands during which it was hoped that a peaceful solution could be found. Unfortunately, the ETA found its marginalization in peace worse than the disgust it inspired when it was active, and in December 1999 the organization resumed the terror. The most spectacular loser in the May 2001 regional elections was Euskal Herritarok (ETA's political wing), which lost half of its 14 seats. Indeed, the record turnout of nearly 80 per cent of eligible voters gave a clear message to the rest of Spain: terrorism no, nationalism yes.

The message seemed to reach deaf ears when two days after the election, Basque journalist and anti-violence campaigner Gorka Landaburu lost part of his hand when a packet bomb sent to his home exploded.

Then, in August the same year, a Municipal Councillor in Leiza died when a bomb exploded beneath his van. Ten hours later an officer with the Basque police force was shot dead with a sub-machine gun as he parked his car in Tolosa. A further deadly attack took place in Madrid with the car bomb assassination of a national police office. A subsequent poll showed that terrorism had moved even further ahead of unemployment as the main concern of Spaniards.

Until the summer of 2002, most ETA attacks had taken place either in the capital or the Basque country. Tourism seemed to be the target that year when, during the height of the season, two car bombs exploded in Fuengirola on the Costa del Sol and a few weeks later in a resort near Alicante, resulting in the death of a child.

The Spanish government responded definitively on the 26 July by applying the newly devised 'Ley de Partidos' to Batasuna, the political wing of the ETA, effectively making the party illegal, on the grounds of its 'carrying out politics in connivance with terror' and for 'encouraging generalised intimidation' among other points. The group's offices were closed by the Basque police and its accounts frozen. Meanwhile the party moved to Bayonne, France where it is registered as an association.

In a further development approximately three months later, the president of the (recognized) Basque government, Juan José Ibarretxe, put an end to the political ambiguity in the region and placed his cards clearly on the table, proposing that the European Union grant the Basque Country the status of free state, associated to Spain with shared sovereignty, a plan that no one except the Basques takes seriously.

This was still a key issue in the Basque elections of April 2005, which Ibarretxe's party won – but only just. They lost their overall majority, and much of their bargaining power with it.

Meanwhile, Aznar's hard-line Partido Popular (PP) were ousted from government in the dramatic Spanish general election of 2004, when the Spanish people expressed their anger at the PP's deliberate attempts to implicate ETA in the terrible bombings at Madrid train stations on 11th March 2004.in which almost two hundred people were killed. The attacks were claimed by Islamic fundamentalists in retaliation for Spanish involvement in the Iraq war (opposed by more than 90 per cent of Spaniards)

In early 2005, the new Socialist goverment under José Luís Rodríguez Zapatero promised to open peace talks with ETA if the group laid down its arms, but the announcement was followed by a series of car bombings in Madrid. These were widely perceived to be a gesture of defiance from ETA, and the government responded by arresting Arnaldo Otegi, the leader of the (still outlawed) Batasuna party, and by threatening to limit some areas of the Basque Country's current autonomy. For now, the Basque Country and all Spain remain on tenterhooks hoping that this time, finally, a peaceful solution will be found.

Meanwhile, the real story in Euskadi is not this relic of a troubled past, but the surprising rebirth of Bilbao as a symbol of the Basques' future. Long known only for industrial obsolescence and rust, the city has pulled itself up with such projects as Frank Gehry's Guggenheim Museum, a state-of-the-art metro and a huge riverfront redevelopment plan; in only a few years Bilbao has emerged from nowhere to become one of the most exciting cities in Spain, and the showcase for a small, ancient nation that in the past has always been able to absorb new ideas, innovate and prosper. The Basques, in spite of their troubles, seem poised to do it again.

Topics

The Pilgrimage to Santiago 20
The Official History **20**
A Field of Stars **22**
The Wild Goose Chase **23**
Of Racial Purity and Pork 25
The Spanish Distemper 27
Home on the Range **27**
El Cid Campeador **28**
Reconquista Man **29**
The Saving Grace 30

03

The Pilgrimage to Santiago

The Official History

No saint on the calendar has as many names as Spain's patron – Iago, Diego, Jaime, Jacques, Jacobus, Santiago or, in English, James the Greater. James the fisherman was one of the first disciples chosen by Jesus, who nicknamed him Boanerges, 'the son of thunder', after his booming voice. After the Crucifixion, he seems to have been a rather ineffectual proselytizer for the faith; in the year 44 Herod Agrippa in Caesarea beheaded him and threw his body to the dogs. But Spain had another task in store for James: nothing less than posthumously leading a 700-year-old crusade against the peninsula's infidels.

In fact, the evidence suggests that it was really the French who put him up to it: the first mention of the Apostle's relics in Spain appear in an 830 annex to the *Martirologio de Florus*, written in 806 in Lyon; after the fright of 732, when the Moors invaded as far as Poitiers and settled a good portion of France's Mediterranean coast, the French were ready to pull out all the stops to encourage their old Christian neighbours to rally and defeat the heathen. A new history of James emerged, one with links to Spain. First, before his martyrdom, he went to Zaragoza to convert the Spaniards and failed. Second, after his martyrdom, two of his disciples piously gathered his remains and sailed off with them in a stone boat (faith works wonders). The destination was Iria Flavia in remote Galicia, and the disciples buried Boanerges in the nearby cemetery of Compostela. In 814, a shower of shooting stars guided a hermit shepherd named Pelayo to the site of James's tomb; the bones were 'authenticated' by Bishop Theodomir. Another legend identifies Charlemagne (who died in 814) with the discovery of James's relics: in the Emperor's tomb at Aachen you can see the 'Vision of Charlemagne', with a scene of the Milky Way, the Via Lactea, a common name for the pilgrims' road.

In 844, not long after the discovery of the relics, James was called into active duty in the battle of Clavijo, appearing on a white horse to help Ramiro I of Asturias defeat the Moors. This new role as Santiago Matamoros, the Moor-Slayer, was a great morale booster for the forces of the Reconquista, who made 'Santiago!' their battle cry. In the churches along the Camino, James is portrayed either as a humble pilgrim himself or as a mighty warrior trampling the Moors underfoot. Ramiro was so pleased by his divine assistance that he made a pledge, the *voto de Santiago*, that ordained an annual property tax for St James's church at Compostela.

Never mind that the bones, the battle and the *voto* were as bogus as each other; the story struck deep spiritual, poetic and political chords that fitted perfectly with the great cultural awakening of the 10th and 11th centuries. The medieval belief that a few holy bones or teeth could serve as a hotline to heaven made the discovery essential. After all, the Moors had some powerful juju of their own: an arm of the Prophet Muhammad in the Great Mosque of Córdoba (possession of it was Abd ar-Rahman's justification for declaring himself Caliph in 929). Another factor in the early 9th century was the Church's need for a focal point to assert its doctrinal control over the newborn kingdoms of Spain, especially over the Celts in Galicia, stubborn followers of the Gnostic Priscillian heresy (*see* p.296). A third factor must have been the desire to reintegrate Spain into Europe – and what better way to do it than to increase human, commercial and cultural traffic over the Pyrenees? Pilgrimages to Jerusalem and Rome were already in vogue; after the long centuries of the Dark Ages, the Church was keen on re-establishing contacts across the old Roman empire it had inherited for Christianity.

The French were the great promoters of the Camino de Santiago (the Way to Santiago), so great in fact that the most commonly tramped route became known as the *camino francés*. The first official pilgrim was Gotescalco, bishop of Le Puy, in 950; others followed, including Mozarab Christians (those living under Moorish rule) from Andalucía, who emigrated north and put themselves under the protection of Santiago, founding some of the first churches and monasteries along the road in the province of León.

In the next century, especially once the frontier with the Moors was firmly pushed back to the south bank of the Duero, the French monks of the reforming abbey of Cluny did more than anyone to popularize the pilgrimage, setting up sister houses and hospitals along the way. Nor were the early Spanish kings slow to pick up on the commercial potential of the road; Sancho the Great of Navarra and Alfonso VI of Castile founded a number of religious houses and institutions along the way and invited down French settlers to help run them. It was at this time too that the French stuck another oar in with their *Chanson de Roland*, which made Charlemagne something of a proto-pilgrim, although his adventure into Pamplona happened decades before the discovery of James's relics.

The 12th century witnessed a veritable boom along the *camino francés*: the arrival of new monastic and military orders, including the Templars, the Hospitallers, and the Knights of Santiago, which all vowed to defend the pilgrim from dangers en route. In 1130, the Abbey of Cluny commissioned Aymery Picaud, a priest from Poitou, to write the *Codex Calixtinus*, the world's first travel guide, chock-full of prejudices and practical advice for pilgrims: he describes the four main roads through France and gives tips on where not to drink the water, where to find the best lodging, where to be on guard against 'false pilgrims' who came not to atone for crimes but to commit them. The final bonus for Santiago de Compostela came in 1189, when Pope Alexander III declared it a Holy City on equal footing with Jerusalem and Rome, offering a plenary indulgence – a full remission from Purgatory – to pilgrims on Holy Years (if you're planning a trip the next will be 2010; other years you'll only get half time off). The favourite song they would sing along the way was the Ultreya:

Dum Pater familias, rex universorum
donaret provincias ius apostolorum
Jacobus Hispanias lux ilustrat morum
Primus ex apostolis, martyr Jerosolimis
Jacobus egregio, sacre et martyrio.
Herru Sanctiagu, grot Santiagu
e ultreia e suseia, Deus adiuva nos

(Our father, King of the Universe/Concede the land to apostolic right/Santiago of Spain is the light illuminating tradition/First among the Apostles, martyr of Jerusalem/Distinguished Santiago, holy and martyred/Lord Santiago, Great Santiago!/And Forward! and Onward! God help us!)

The Tour de Saint-Jacques in Paris was a traditional rallying point for groups of pilgrims (there was more safety in numbers); from there the return journey was 1,280km (800 miles) and took a minimum of four months on foot. It was not something to go into lightly, but for many it was more than an act of faith, a chance to get out and see the world. By the time of Aymery Picaud the French had been joined by pilgrims from across Europe. Many were ill (hence the large number of hospitals), hoping to complete the pilgrimage before they died. Not a few were thieves, murderers and delinquents condemned by the judge to make the journey for penance. Sometimes dangerous cons had to do it in chains. To keep them from cheating or stealing someone else's indulgence (the Compostellana certificate), pilgrims had to have their documents stamped by the clergy at various points along the route, just as they do today (as a nice touch, the old stamps and seals have recently been revived).

An estimated half a million people a year made the trek in the Middle Ages (out of a European population of about 60 million) and, even in the 18th century, the so-called century of Enlightenment, the pass at Roncesvalles still counted 30,000 pilgrims a year. But in the 19th century numbers fell dramatically; most of the monasteries and churches were closed for ever with the confiscation of church lands in 1837; many were converted into stables or simply pillaged for their building stone. In the 1970s, just when it seemed as defunct as a dodo, the pilgrimage made a remarkable revival, due to a number of factors – the modern world's disillusionment with conventional religion; the search for something beyond what overorganized day-to-day life and church attendance can offer and, more prosaically, the growth of ecological and alternative tourism. In 1982 John Paul II became the first Pope ever to visit Santiago; in 1985, UNESCO declared it the 'Foremost Cultural Route in Europe', helping to fund the restoration of some of the Romanesque churches that punctuate the trail. Although modern roads have changed the face of the pilgrimage for ever, efforts have been made to create alternative paths for pedestrians, marked every 500m with a stylized scallop shell; new inexpensive *hostales* have sprouted along the way for walkers or cyclists. The pilgrims' quest is back in business.

A Field of Stars

In the Middle Ages it took real courage to leave home and make such an arduous, perilous journey west to Finisterre; back then, as today, there was more to it than just picking up an indulgence to deposit as credit in the Bank of Grace. The pilgrimage was one of the few opportunities for the average Middle Ager to attain a consciousness and understanding beyond the strict limits of Church dogma. All the humbuggery over the 'discovery' of the Apostle's relics in the far northwest corner of Spain would never have caught the popular imagination so powerfully had it not been for the deep mythopoeic resonances already present; especially for the Celts, the far west was the abode of souls that pass on. It was an ancient Indo-European belief that a star appears in the Milky Way whenever a mortal is born, and shoots towards the west when they die, towards the realm of the dead in, as for example the Celts conceived it, the Castle of the Goddess Arianhrod (the constellation Corona Borealis). Similarly, in Plato, the dead go to the celestial west, to the spot where the Milky Way meets the circle of the Zodiac – towards the real 'Compostela' (*campus stellae in finis terrae*), the field of stars at the world's end. To make the journey to the end of the world while still alive was to come to terms with our ultimate destiny, to vanquish and harrow hell, to understand the mystery in a unique way with both the body and mind. There were certainly plenty of miracles and mysteries for the pilgrims to ponder as they followed the setting sun, both in legends and in the subject matter chosen by the sculptors who decorated the portals and capitals of the churches along the way. Much of their symbolism is enigmatic in the extreme. With the destruction, deterioration and ham-handed restoration of so many pilgrim churches and hospitals, many important clues left by the itinerant guilds of builders were lost, but the remains include Celtic and other pagan symbols, man-eating lions, eagles and snakes, two-headed monsters, jovial eroticism, labyrinths, figures from the zodiac or from the 'labours of the months', and much more, along with a wide range of orthodox and unorthodox depictions of scenes from scripture.

Aymery Picaud's *Codex Calixtinus* divided the *camino francés* into 13 days or stages. Some are rather long hauls, possible only with a fresh horse, others are short and walkable; some of the stages are to famous towns like León and Burgos, others to dusty one-horse nowheres, apparently chosen arbitrarily, which existed on their reputation only as long as the *Codex Calixtinus* was consulted. The number 13 has its own deep resonance, going back to the proto-pilgrimages of ancient Egypt, when a journey down the Nile was a living re-enactment of the journey made by an Egyptian after death. Egypt itself was a metaphor for the heavens, while the Nile was divided into 12 parts representing the Zodiac, as a lunar year is 12 or 13 months. As if to prove such ideas reached Spain, a curious 9th-century BC Egyptian alabaster burial urn, found at Almuñécar and displayed in the Casa Castril in Granada, has hieroglyphs that suggest such a pilgrimage:

> *I have arrived from my foreign land. I have passed through countries and have heard about your being, you of the primordial state of the two lands, you who has engendered what exists. In you your two eyes shine. Your Word is the way of life that gives breath to all throats. Now I am in the horizon, flooded by the happiness of the harija oases and I speak to it like a friend. In me there is a source of health, of life, beyond your shores.*

The Wild Goose Chase

One theory has it that the Goose Game, a favourite children's pastime in Spain and most continental countries, is a playful memory of the pilgrimage, the medieval path of initiation. The Goose Game first became popular at the time of Philip II, the age when anything faintly outside church dogma was likely to lead to an auto-da-fé. In the Goose Game, the board has a path of 63 squares set in a spiral, leading inwards to the goal, with a picture of a goose in the centre, a total of 64. Twelve of the 63 squares also have pictures of geese, which are invariably good to land on; another nine have obstacles (the bridge, the inn, the dice, the well, the labyrinth, the prison, death, and the gateway to the goal). Players roll dice to move their markers around the board. A number of writers on Compostela, beginning with Louis Charpentier who wrote *The Mystery of Compostela* (1973), have remarked on the persistency of the word 'goose' in the place names along the Camino de Santiago. *Oca* is Spanish for goose, *Ganso* is the Visigothic German, *Anser* the Latin, and a look at the map reveals that northwest Spain has far more than its share of goosey names: El Ganso, the Montes de Oca, Rio Oja, Puerto de la Oca, the river Anso.

Goosiness permeates the other side of the Pyrenees too. In France, *dévider les jars*, 'to spin the ganders', meant to speak in argot, the secret language of the builders' confraternities. The mysterious, now vanished *agotes* (or *cagots* in French), an outcast race who lived on either side of the Navarrese Pyrenees, were often forced to wear a goose foot around their necks. Basques had a race of lovely but goose-footed fairies, the *laminak*, and Toulouse was the home of the famous Visigothic queen Ranachile, wife of Theodoric II. Better known as *La reine pédauque*, the 'goose foot', her story inspired the legend of goose-footed Berthe, Charlemagne's mum, a rather domestic queen who told children stories by her spinning wheel (French fairy tales customarily begin with 'In the time when good Queen Berthe spun'). Andrew Lang found the first reference to Mother Goose, *La Mere d'Oye*, in 1650.

So why choose, of all God's creatures, a goose as the key? One guess is that the goose is only a European adaptation of the Egyptian ibis, the bird sacred to Isis that destroyed the eggs of the Nile crocodile and annually battled winged serpents from Arabia (geese are pretty handy with serpents too, as every farmer knows). The figure of Isis distantly haunts the whole *camino*, which is littered with miraculous, usually dark-faced statues of the Virgin, her Christian equivalent. The Universal Way to Compostela, the Milky Way, the Starry Stairway to heaven, was a path of initiation into the mysteries of life and death and unity of all things. A wild goose chase, for those who understood the cosmic joke. Why else would the figures Master Mateo carved on the cathedral of Santiago laugh so merrily?

To the insufficiently pious, the real revelation of the pilgrimage to Santiago is that when you get to the end, there's simply nothing there – just a corpse that could be a mythical character's or anybody's. In the Goose Game, the square just before the goal is the Tomb, and if you land here you're dead and have to start again from the beginning. To those who see the pilgrimage as containing a secret teaching for a few, that's just the point. Once you have made it to Santiago de Compostela, it would hardly make sense not to go all the way to land's end. It isn't far, and the trail meets the sea at Noia, a place that intriguingly enough was a holy site long before Compostela, with Neolithic dolmens, and a churchyard full of mysterious tombstones from the Middle Ages, carved with signs and motifs that no one has ever explained.

Of Racial Purity and Pork

Spanish history is shot through with tragicomic implosions. One of the most destructive was the mania for *limpieza de sangre* (purity of blood), a doctrine that so undermined the national economy in the 15th–17th centuries that all the loot from the Americas couldn't patch the gaping wound. Purity of blood meant pure Christian ancestry, something probably only a few Asturian and Basque hillbillies could claim with a clear conscience. But as the Reconquista swept south, Castile, more than any of the other kingdoms of the northwest, began to define itself as a nation by religious segregation. Many Jews and Moors tried to conform by converting and, although at first they were accepted without stigma, bigotry raised its ugly head in the 1400s, just as the Christians achieved total control.

The Jews were the first to go. In Spain since the Diaspora, they were an educated and useful minority, many of them doctors and moneylenders (two of the few professions they were allowed to exercise). They were the subject of the first purity of blood law, the 1449 Toledo decree, issued in spite of opposition from the king of Castile and the pope: 'We declare that the so-called *conversos*, offspring of perverse Jewish ancestors, must be held by law to be infamous and ignominious, unfit and unworthy to hold any public office or benefice within the city of Toledo.' Many cities followed suit. In 1480, Isabel and Ferdinand refounded the Inquisition to institutionalize discrimination against *conversos*: any of them suspected of backsliding in the faith – or often anyone merely accused of it – would have their property confiscated by the state, and would probably be burned at the stake. In 1492, Isabel celebrated the conquest of Granada by booting the Jews out of Spain. The kings of Navarra took them under their wing, at least until 1514, when Navarra itself was gobbled up by Ferdinand. Not satisfied with this, the Inquisition after 1530 began posting in the cathedrals the names of everyone who had any dealings at all with the Holy Office, so that people suspected of 'tainted blood' could always be readily identified – and not hired for any important post. In response, books of family trees were published, to prove one's own purity or to disparage someone else's. *Limpieza de sangre* contributed more than anything to the prevailing atmosphere in 16th-century Spain, which could be described as raging, surreal paranoia. The economic result was more concrete: by bankrupting and expelling the Jews and *conversos*, the perennially broke kings of Spain had to borrow money from Genoese bankers at calamitous rates. The annual silver fleet from the Americas would sail into Sevilla only to be sucked up whole by the Italians.

Muslims who refused to convert were given their walking papers in 1502. Those who did convert, the *moriscos*, were robbed and booted out a century later. The *moriscos* were excellent farmers, experts in irrigation, and willing to perform jobs no pure-blooded Spaniard would touch. Although the usual mafia of aristocrats, especially the Count of Lerma, picked up a tidy bundle from the sale of their confiscated lands, the *moriscos*' departure left many parts of Spain not far from Skid Row. Philip III, imbecile spawn of many generations of Habsburg family incest, was the king who allowed the *moriscos* to be put out. Philip, incidentally, died from sitting too close to the fire – so weighty was his concept of his own nobility that he couldn't imagine getting up and moving away from the flames on his own.

The blood obsession was becoming increasingly kinky. In Spain, a true aristocrat would bleed 'blue', while his younger brothers, poor *hidalgos* (and Christ himself, profusely, in a thousand horror-show Spanish statues) bled red, and everyone else bled 'plain blood' unless they were Moors, Jews or Lutheran heretics, whose blood was said to be 'black'. The *hidalgos* (from *hijo de algo*, 'son of somebody'), once the backbone of medieval Castile, were by now a mentally deranged caste of haughty layabouts. Located at the bottom of the noble ladder, with neither land nor vassals, they came to be the class most obsessed with blood and honour. It was their sole capital, all that they had from the ancestors who achieved the Reconquista. Many of them went to America as *conquistadores*, but most stayed, impoverished and futile like Don Quixote, guarding the iron-bound coffers where they kept their letters patent, attesting to their arms, rank, and privileges that exempted them from direct taxation and debtors' prison, all the time depriving Spain of productive men and poisoning society with their attitude.

> *My father was afflicted by a disgrace which he passed on to all his sons like*
> *original sin. He was a hidalgo. This is not unlike being a poet, for there are*
> *few hidalgos who escape perpetual poverty and continuous hunger. He possessed*
> *letters patent of his nobility so ancient that even he was unable to read them,*
> *and no one cared to touch them for fear of getting their fingers greasy from*
> *the bedraggled knots and ribbons of the tattered parchments. Even the mice*
> *took care not to gnaw them lest they were stricken with sterility.*
>
> Estebanillo González (1646)

Short of resorting to being bled by a barber to see what colour of *sangre* leaked out, there were two sure-fire ways to tell a true Christian Spaniard: he hardly ever washed (monks in particular never bathed, and called the inevitable result 'the odour of sanctity'), and he ate lots of pork. Bathing was Jewish, Moorish and effeminate: one of the first acts of Isabel and Ferdinand after the conquest of Granada was to close the baths. If a suspect hadn't bathed recently, the second test was to offer him a bit of pig meat. Now this was perhaps a more honest vetting; Spain has been known for pork since ancient times; and even a serious historian like Diodorus Siculus could rave about Iberian 'hams transcendently superlative' in the 1st century AD.

We can suppose that making the pig into a badge of the True Faith could not happen without some distortion of the national psyche. Pigs and Spanish strange- ness went hand in hand, sometimes in the most uncanny ways. Extremadura was long Spain's hog heaven, and the best, most exquisite porkers there were fed on vipers. Like so many *conquistadores*, the great, unspeakable Pizarro came from there; he was suckled by a sow, and started his career as a swineherd. The Spanish national psychosis of the old days, a witches' brew of *limpieza de sangre*, lust for gold, vicious imperialism, hatred and bigotry, found its reflection in the kitchen, in an obsession with pork that can be disconcerting, even today.

The Spanish Distemper

Home on the Range

If you want to see the best-preserved early medieval frescoes in Spain, you'll have to go to Gaceo, a dusty nowhere off the road from Vitoria to Pamplona. It's an unpromising spot, but if you can find the man with the key, there is a wonderful cartoon vision of heaven and hell – a rare relic from a lost world. So often in Spain, the real treasures are hidden in out-of-the-way places. Gaceo is a somewhat special case – a Roman road, later the Camino Real (now the N1), once ran through it. Still, it would be only natural to ask why such a huge expenditure, by medieval standards, of money and talent should have been lavished on tiny Gaceo. That question itself is a key to understanding Spain.

All over Castile, in scores of cities and even villages, you will sense there were great expectations long ago, and greater disappointments afterwards. A dusty hamlet will sport an arcaded Plaza Mayor that never quite grew into a stone one like Vitoria's or Madrid's. Similarities with provincial American towns are obvious: a half-built feeling, streets ludicrously too wide for the traffic, laid out anticipating a boom that never came, and a couple of Plateresque palaces, sticking out from the humble tile roofs like the grand Victorian business blocks amidst the car parks of wasted American city centres. Like America, and unlike any European country save Russia, Spain has a heritage as a frontier society. Nearly every valley and plain south of the Cordillera Cantábrica knows a history of reconquest from the Moors and Christian resettlement. Romans, Vandals, Alans, Suevi, Byzantines, Franks, Visigoths and Arabs had all done their part to make Spain's central plateau into an empty waste. From the 800s, when the Asturians and others began to cross the mountains, to the final victory over the heathen Moor in 1492, the wave of the Reconquista spread gradually southwards; at one time every part of it was the scene of pioneers reclaiming land and founding villages and towns. And as in the American West, the money that fuelled the expansion came largely from livestock – sheep, not cows, though. The biggest ranchers were the *hidalgos*, and they dominated frontier political life by influence and force; the towns found themselves constantly on the defensive against the *hidalgos'* attempted land grabs and extortions (and sadly the towns usually lost).

Few frontier expansions in history ever came off quite like this one, though. The people that started America's push west arrived logically from behind the frontier; many of Spain's, bizarrely enough, came from beyond it. The northwest was hardly overflowing with population at the beginning of the Reconquista, and the numbers were largely supplied by Mozarab Christians from Muslim-ruled Spain, from al-Andalus, looking for free land and a Christian atmosphere. Few facts were ever recorded about this trickling exodus, but it is reasonable to assume that Mozarabs with the gumption to pack up and move into the lonesome *meseta* were also likely to be the most fanatical supporters of Christianity and the new Christian states. And instead of half-naked Indians without towns or technology, the heathen enemy of the new Spanish frontiersmen happened to be probably the most delightful and sophisticated civilization in the Western world, led by caliphs whose greatest joys were writing lyrical poetry and planting pleasure gardens with tinkling fountains. Such irony can weigh on a nation's soul.

The pioneer warriors of the north had a secret weapon in their fight against the Moors – utter ruthlessness. Organized in highly mobile raiding parties, they could extort tributes from the Muslim lands simply by threatening to girdle their irreplaceable olive trees. Destroying crops and villages was another key tactic. The Christians expanded their boundaries by making the lands beyond it uninhabitable. It all worked brilliantly, and behind the lines the new Spain gradually took shape. What happened in the end to all hopes of the frontiersmen can be read in Spain's sad history. The boom did come, fitfully and unequally, but nearly every village and town of Castile enjoyed at least a few decades of dizzying prosperity, enough to at least begin some grandiose projects. The woebegone church at Villalcázar de Sirga comes to mind. Santa María looks to have been planned to match the size of Burgos cathedral, and thrown up in a hurry. Sadly it never got more than a third finished, and the dust blows around it today. As always, after the boom came the bust, and what a bust it was. Castile has been busted ever since.

El Cid Campeador

In the Spanish pantheon El Cid Campeador comes in a close second to Santiago himself, but unlike Arthur, Siegfried, Roland and other heroes of national medieval epics, the Cid, Rodrigo Díaz de Vivar (1043–99), was entirely flesh and blood. Born in Vivar near Burgos, his unique title is derived from the Arabic *sayyidi* ('my lord'), and *Campeador*, which means 'Battler'. His fame spread widely among both Moors and Christians (in his career he served both Alfonso VI of Castile and the Emir of Zaragoza); even before his death ballads celebrated his prowess. The greatest achievement of his life, the capture of Valencia from the Moors in 1095, took place when he was already 52 years old.

Through modern eyes, Rodrigo was little better than a gangster, but for the warrior class of the Reconquista, he served as a model of virtue – fearless, with an exaggerated sense of honour, devoutly Catholic yet wholly pragmatic, a generous conqueror, devoted to his family, who paid his debts and always kept his word. The Cid was the perfect man for his time, living in the frontier society among Christians, Moors and Jews, where a king's powers were limited, and the main issues of the day were the simple pleasures of turf and booty.

For all that, 'O Born in a Happy Hour' – Rodrigo's other nickname – would not have had such a long shelf life, inspiring such diverse spirits as Corneille and Hollywood (where he was played, inevitably, by Charlton Heston), if there wasn't something more to his character. This comes through in the epic *Poem of the Cid*, composed around 1140, less than half a century after his death. For 500 years the actual poem was lost, until 1779 when the royal librarian, through some literary detective work, located a copy from 1307, appropriately enough in Vivar, the Cid's hometown. Not a single ounce of the magic or marvellous touches the text; the Rodrigo Díaz that emerges lies and cheats, but has a rustic sense of humour and a certain generous charm, always ready to praise another, happy to have his wife and daughters present to watch him 'earn his bread' fighting the Moors. You can't help liking the guy. His saga, though somewhat repetitive to read, is also the first known example of the Spanish gift for realism that would reach its climax in Cervantes' *Don Quixote*. Actually, even more realism would have been in order, for life on the frontier was not always the stuff of poetry.

Reconquista Man

Here he comes. Slouching in a rough woollen tunic, García Gómez is riding out of the sorrowful wilderness of the Cantabrian mountains and into history. García Gómez may look the Arkansawyer redneck of the American frontier, the sort that proverbially 'never had nothin', never learned nothin', and don't want nothin', but he is a man on the make. He's got himself an iron sword, while his daddy had to get by with a big stick that he cut himself, like Little John – he carried it around, and anyone that gave him any lip was likely to get a taste of it with iron; such encounters are fewer but a little more dangerous. Of course being a Castilian, he is a *hidalgo*, really *hijo de algo*, a 'son of somebody'; we're all *muy noble y muy leal*, ain't we boys? At least as much as the big shot who owns the castle – he just came and nicked it from the former proprietor. Nicked his wife too.

The first thing to do is clear some land. And as you can see from the Castilian landscape today, there was something in García Gómez that didn't love trees. They used to say that a squirrel could go from Portugal to the Pyrenees, if he wanted, without touching ground. Juan José and his sons will do their best to blot out the offending forests, and the coup de grâce will be administered by the Habsburgs, who as we remember were always building Armadas, and also creaming the profits off the timber trade for themselves and sending them home to Germany. Next thing to do is wrestle all the stones out of the fields, and build a dry-stone house. Piece of cake. In a generation or two, with a lot of luck and an eye constantly on the main chance, the family will be able to afford a little showplace – one of the hundreds of rude hilltop castles that gave Castile its name.

Unlike the settlers of the American west, García Gómez did not come over the mountains with his Bible in his hand. He couldn't really read it, and anyhow the Church doesn't exactly hand them out – a little later, when Ferdinand and Isabel bring in the Inquisition, a man could get himself incinerated just for reading one in Spanish. It might give him ideas. But García Gómez is content to let the learned clerics tell him what to believe. The mysteries of faith, all conducted in Latin of course, are too subtle for him, and the Church supplies the insistent, shrill propaganda that shapes his life: the triumph of the only faith over the godless Moors and Jews. Every now and then fire-eating preachers like St Peter Martyr do the circuit, rousing the fools in the towns against the heathens, and our man will ride into town for the show; afterwards the good townspeople usually let off some steam, and any resident heathens are happy to escape with their lives. The towns are mostly of the one-horse variety (León, the biggest, counted a thousand souls at most in the early 11th century, maybe ten times that while they were building their extravagant cathedral) and they are not there to show a Gómez a good time. They're full of suspicious merchants, officials and monks, and though they'd usually let him through the gate when he and the town weren't feuding, García Gómez hardly ever has reason to go.

Status in this neck of the woods is a horse. Being able to afford one of these most prized commodities ensures García Gómez's position as one of the mounted warriors in the local count's retinue, ready to form an army for the king or a springtime expedition south to fight the Moors and grab some booty. A horse was the most significant investment the average man could have, but the men of the Reconquista knew how to make it pay. Then as now, Arabian blood was prized most of all – it was mainly through Spain that Arabian horses first came into Europe. The profits to buy the beast came from sheep. Gómez has a nice little spread, and a village of malodorous tenant farmers to kick in a little rent. They pay taxes and tithes, as do the townspeople. Gómez, being a *hidalgo*, does not.

Keep your eye on this boy, for he is blessed by the gods. Tucked away on a peninsula at the extremity of Europe, the *hidalgo* has nobody to bang away against except the hapless Moors, and eventually he will have all their land and goods. By 1500, flushed with ill-gotten wealth, he will be troubling the peace of Europe, and soon after he and his sword will be tramping around the Andes, up into Kansas and down the Amazon. And finally, before he rides off into the sunset he will burn himself out completely, tilting at windmills on the plains of La Mancha.

The Saving Grace

For all the sound and fury of the Reconquista, all the waste and futility, was anything left that would last? There are people capable of conjuring up beauty and delight in any age, and at the beginning of the Middle Ages, Europe had the cash to do it in stone for the first time since the late Roman Empire. 'So it was,' wrote an 11th-century chronicler, 'as though the world had shaken herself and cast off her old age, and were clothing herself everywhere in a white garment of churches.' Spain shared fully in this flowering of Romanesque architecture and art; indeed the little Christian kingdoms of the north were the unlikely vanguard of the movement.

Where did the Romanesque come from? Unlike most parts of western Europe, northern Spain had very few Roman buildings left to serve as models. But from scattered examples around Europe and the Middle East, it is easy to see a continuous progression everywhere from late Roman architecture through the Dark Ages. The real homeland of Romanesque seems to be Syria, where Greek Christians built elegant basilican churches with plenty of rounded arches, windows and blind arcading up until the 7th-century Muslim conquest. Syrian monks, including most likely the architects and painters, spread across Christendom after that as refugees, taking the style with them. In this age buildings of any kind are few, and records almost nonexistent, and while early Romanesque works in Armenia, northern Italy and Asturias may show some striking similarities, it is impossible to say too much about how they got that way. Europe's first Romanesque churches appeared in the hills of Asturias in the 9th century, practically the only important architecture anywhere in Europe from that dark time. These showed classical elements, pediments, columns and arches, as well as considerable borrowings from the Muslim south: notably delicate double windows called *ajimeces*, divided by a column, and horseshoe arches, a native Spanish style that the Moors had adapted from the Visigoths.

In the sudden, explosive burst of energy and economic expansion after the magic year 1000, the impulse to build and create spread across Europe; in Spain, as elsewhere, the Romanesque churches were the symbol of the new civilization that had emerged from the chrysalis of the Dark Ages. One of the oldest Asturian buildings, San Miguel de Lillo at Oviedo, has carvings of what seems to be a circus scene, setting the tone for the wild imaginative freedom that characterizes all Romanesque art. The greatest charms of most churches are the carved portals, capitals and cloisters, on which you will see not only scriptural scenes, but legions of fantastical monsters, legendary heroes from Hercules to Roland, mermaids, farting monks, droll-looking insects, intricate floral designs and arabesques, demons, house cats, camels and leopards, spirals, labyrinths, hunting scenes, whales – everything in God's good creation, along with many things God never thought of, boiling up from the depths of the medieval unconscious. Unlike every age of religious art that followed, the Romanesque was never constrained by any narrow Church dogma; perhaps the most striking example is the number of frankly erotic scenes, as on the portal of the country church at Cervatos in Cantabria. Anything at all that could be experienced, or imagined, was a fit subject to decorate the House of God.

Expressive freedom in the Romanesque was hardly limited to stone carving. The buildings themselves show a wide variety of ideas. Every province of Europe had its own distinct style and, within each, builders were often free to follow their fancy; eccentricities in northern Spain range from the octagonal churches at Eunate and Torres del Río in Navarra, modelled after the Holy Sepulchre in Jerusalem (these were either built or inspired by the Templars), to the outlandish Santa María del Sar at Santiago, built with the columns and walls of the nave tilted precariously outwards, or the Basque church of San Miguel de Arratxinaga in Markina, built over a huge dolmen – many early churches, most perhaps, replaced pre-Christian holy sites. What ties all the disparate Romanesque works together is a simple theory of proportions. Instead of the classical 'orders', medieval builders employed a new system of sacred architecture based on constructive geometry. Anyone with a mathematical bent will enjoy looking over the buildings, seeing how every point in them can be proved with a compass and straightedge, just as their builders designed them. Later ages of religious building may be more showy, more technically sophisticated, but none has the same hold over the imagination. The Romanesque is the art of springtime, of a new world where rules were few and fancy could wander where it liked.

The pilgrimage trail to Santiago is also a pilgrimage through some of medieval Europe's finest creations, from rustic one-aisled village churches to the great basilica of Santiago de Compostela, the biggest and most ambitious Romanesque work in Spain. Some of the other major attractions include Santo Domingo de Silos, south of

Burgos, with the most beautiful Romanesque cloister in Spain; Estella, with a wealth of Romanesque buildings; San Martín at Frómista, west of Burgos; and the remote area called the 'Románico Palatino', north of Frómista, with the biggest concentration of Romanesque country churches in Europe.

Food and Drink

Fish Soup and Pig's Ear 34
Rioja, *Sidra* and Other Tipples 36
Practicalities 38
Learning to Eat the Spanish Way **38**
Menu Reader **40**
What to Drink Where **41**

Fish Soup and Pig's Ear

The massive influx of tourists has had its effect on Spanish kitchens, but so has the Spaniards' own increased prosperity and, perhaps most significantly, the new federalism. Each region, each town even, has come to feel a new interest and pride in the things that set it apart, and food is definitely one of them. Northern Spain, with its markedly different personalities, is a special treat in this regard.

Seafood is undoubtedly the star of the show in the areas along the northern coast. The Atlantic has much more and better seafood than has the Mediterranean, and the ardent fishermen of this region are perfectly positioned to nab the best of it. They have plenty of practice cooking the stuff – archaeologists have found remains of sea urchins in settlements 10,000 years old. The bounty of the sea finds expression in famous fish soups from the western *caldereta Asturiana* to the Basque *ttoro*, and there are any number of prized delicacies in every region: surprising things, such as *kokotxas*, 'cheeks' of the hake, or the Galician *vieiras de Santiago*, scallops cooked with almonds. On the whole, though, Spaniards try to keep their seafood simple. Galicians like to cook fish with potatoes and garlic; Basques do it with simple garlic and parsley sauces.

By popular acclaim, the champion cooks of northern Spain – really of all Spain – are the **Basques**, who coincidentally are also the most legendary eaters. Like the Greeks, the well-travelled Basques take their culinary skill with them everywhere. Basque restaurants turn up in unlikely places all over France, and it isn't unusual to drive through a dusty, one-horse town out in the American West where the only restaurant serves up good Basque home cooking.

Marseilles may have its *bouillabaisse*, among a score of other exotic and treasured fish stews of southern Europe, but the Basques stoutly maintain their version, called *ttoro* (pronounced tioro), is the king of them all; naturally there is a solemn confraternity of the finest *ttoro* chefs. A proper one requires a pound of mussels and a mess of crayfish and congers, as well as the head of a codfish and three different kinds of other fish. Basque cuisine relishes imaginative yet simple sauces, including the legendary *pil pil* (originally named for the sound it made while frying), where somehow olive oil, garlic, and chillies magically meld with the cooking juices of salt cod. Another delight is fresh tuna cooked with tomatoes, garlic, aubergine and spices and *chipirones* (squid) – reputedly the only kind in the world that are all black, and better than they sound.

Each Basque chef knows how to work wonders with elvers (*angulas* or *txitxardin*) in garlic sauce, salmon and the famous *txangurro* – spider crab, flaked, seasoned, stuffed and served in its own shell. Gourmets especially recommend *kokotxas a la Donostiarra*, hake cheeks with a garlic and parsley green sauce, clams and slightly piquant red *guindilla* peppers. These peppers are another icon of the Basque kitchen; housewives still hang strings of them on the walls of their houses for drying (and for decoration). Peppers turn up everywhere: in omelettes, in sauces for seafood, or in the common stewed chicken. Basques like to wash it down with *txakoli*, a tangy green wine produced on the coast with just a modicum of sunlight.

The **Galicians** too have their talents in the kitchen, with the best of the best seafood, including some delicacies found nowhere else in the world. Throughout Spain Gallego restaurants command as much respect as Basque. The estuaries are rich in an extraordinary array of seafood, from the famous scallops of Santiago and lobster to some creatures unique to Galicia such as *zamburiñas* scallops, lobster-like *santiaguiños*, and ugly *percebes*, that have no names in English. Quantity is matched by quality: Galician seafood is considered the best in the world and preparation is kept as simple as possible. Another favourite served in every town are *empanadas*, large flat flaky pies filled with eels or lamprey (the most sought after; try it before you knock it), sardines, pork, or veal. Turnip greens (*grelos*) are a staple, especially in *caldo gallego*, a broth that also features turnips and white beans; in winter, the heartier *lacón con grelos*, pork shoulder with greens, sausages and potatoes, holds pride of place. Galicia produces Spain's best veal and good cheeses, such as Roquefort-like *cabrales* and *gamonedo*, both mainly from cow's milk mixed with smaller quantities of ewe's or goat's milk; birch-smoked pear-shaped *San Simón*; or mild, soft *ulloa* or *pasiego*. A tapas meal to make a Gallego weep includes grilled sardines, *pulpo gallego* (tender octopus with peppers and paprika), roasted small green peppers (*pimientas de Padrón*), with chewy hunks of bread and lightly salted breast-shaped *tetilla* cheese, washed down with white Ribeira wine. For dessert try *tarta de Santiago* (almond tart), and to top it all off, a glass of Galician fire water, *aguardiente* – served at night after a meal to ward off evil spirits – properly burned (*queimada*), with lemon peel and sugar.

Inland, though you'll still find plenty of seafood, the cuisine is an entirely different world. Cooking can be heavy, almost medieval, with plenty of roasts and chops, stews and game dishes – partridge and pheasant are special favourites. Local dishes include *cochinillo asado* (roast suckling-pig), the most prized speciality of **Castile**, *chuletas de cordero a la navarra* (lamb chops), *truchas con jamón* (trout stuffed with ham) or, for something out of the ordinary, *liebres con chocolate* (hare with chocolate), washed down by the good strong wines from Tudela and Estella. **Asturias** and **Cantabria** are the dairylands of Spain, and produce a number of cheeses, notably the *Cabrales* of Asturias, made from cow's, sheep's and goat's milk all mixed together. Asturias has its famous dishes too, including hake in *sidra* (the ubiquitous local cider) or *fabada*, an enchanting mess of beans usually served with pork.

You would do well to sharpen your taste for **pork** before venturing into Castile. Here not much of the pig gets thrown away. Besides the famous ham, the bacon, chops and such, Castilians take what's left to make endless sausages, smoked sausages, blood sausages, tripes and puddings. Castilians make the somewhat extravagant claim that pork 'spiritualizes the stomach' (back in the days of the Reconquista and Inquisition, eating it also confirmed one's status as a Christian), and the less expensive pig parts are the staple of cooking; big chunks of pig meat get thrown into all the heavy stews and casseroles that Castilians love. The apotheosis of the porker in Spain is *cochinillo asado*, roast suckling-pig, and its capital is Segovia, where top *asadores* wear medals and cover their restaurant walls with parchment certificates that look like papal bulls, proclaiming their culinary achievements. *Cochinillo* can be a genuine treat, though from here the attractiveness of the cuisine drops off rather sharply.

Another favourite is the famous *botillo* of El Bierzo (*botillo del Bierzo*), which can include minced pork, sausages, fat, lips and ears. Wrap all this up in a pig's intestine, hang it in the chimney for two or three months, and there you are.

One of the symptoms of pork abuse is a permanent craving for pulses on the side. Red beans, white beans, chick peas and lentils, the Spaniards' real staples are all those spirit-laden dried delights that Pythagoras and other philosophers warned us against (of course any Pythagoreans in Spain would have been tidied away by the Inquisition long ago). The 'musical fruit' adds much to the, let us say, expansive nature of much traditional cooking, as in the countryman's *olla podrida*, praised by Cervantes, or the 'Maragato stew' with chick peas, pig's ears and trotters, and a few inches of blood sausage. Pork and beans is wagon cooking, the simple food of pioneers – pig-farming pioneers – and the presence of such a humble cuisine is another of the curious phenomena bobbing in the wake of Spain's curious history. It is the cuisine of the frontier experience.

Rioja, *Sidra* and Other Tipples

There are 55 areas in Spain under the control of the *Instituto Nacional de Denominaciones de Origen* (INDO), which acts as a guide to the consumer and keeps a strict eye on the quality of Spanish wine (DO, or *denominación de origen*, is the same as French AOC). **La Rioja** is the best known and richest area for wine in Spain, producing a great range from young whites to heavy, fruity reds; it is divided into several sub-districts, including the Rioja Alavesa, in the Basque province of Álava north of the Ebro. East of Logroño, there is an extension of the La Rioja wine belt in Navarra.

Rioja tastes like no other: soft, warm, mellow, full-bodied, with a distinct vanilla bouquet; its *vino de gran reserva* spends three years ageing in American oak barrels, and then another in bottles, before release to the public. The Phoenicians introduced the first vines, which after the various invasions were replanted under the auspices of the Church; the first law concerning wine was decreed by Bishop Abilio in the 9th century. The arrival of masses of thirsty pilgrims proved a big boost to business, much as mass tourism would do in the 1960s and 1970s.

Despite a long pedigree, the Rioja we drink today dates from the 1860s, when growers from Bordeaux, their own vineyards wiped out by phylloxera, brought their techniques south of the border and wrought immense improvements on the native varieties. By the time the plague reached La Rioja in 1899, the owners were prepared for it with disease-resistant stock. During the First World War, when the vineyards of Champagne were badly damaged, the French returned to buy up *bodegas*, sticking French labels on the bottles and trucking them over the Pyrenees. Rioja finally received the respect it deserved after Franco passed on to the great fascist parade ground in the sky. In the last 20 years, *bodegas* have attracted buyers from around the world and prices have skyrocketed. La Rioja's growing area covers 48,000 hectares, comprising three zones: Rioja Alta, home of the best red and white wines, followed by

Rioja Alavesa (on the left bank of the Ebro in Alava province) known for its lighter, perfumed wines, and the decidedly more arid Rioja Baja, where the wines are coarse and mostly used for blending – a common practice in La Rioja. The varieties used for the reds are mostly spicy, fruity Tempranillo (covering some 24,000 hectares alone), followed by Garnacha Tinta (a third of the red production, a good alcohol booster) with smaller portions of Graciano (for the bouquet) and high-tannin Mazuela (for acidity and tone). Traditional Rioja whites are relatively unknown but are excellent, golden and vanilla-scented like the reds: Viura grapes are the dominant grape, with smaller doses of Malvasía and Garnacha Blanca. Unlike French wines, Riojas are never sold until they're ready to drink (although of course you can keep the better wines even longer). DOC rules specify that La Rioja's Gran Reserva, which accounts for only 3 per cent of the production, spends a minimum of two years maturing in American oak barrels (six months for whites and rosés) then four more in the *bodega* before it's sold. *Reservas* (6 per cent of the production) spend at least one year in oak and three in the *bodega*. *Crianzas* (30 per cent of the production) spends at least a year in the barrel and another in the bottle. The other 61 per cent of La Rioja is *sin crianza* and labelled CVC (*conjunto de varias cosechas*, combination of various vintages): this includes the new young white wines and light reds (*claretes*) fermented at cool temperatures in stainless steel vats, skipping the oak barrels altogether and losing most of the vanilla tones.

Of course you'll find plenty of **other Spanish wines** in the region. Euskadi is known for its very palatable young 'green' wine called *Txacoli* (in 1994 made a *denominación de origen*), which is poured into the glass with bravura from a height like cider. *Txakoli* is made along the coast, around Getaria and Zarautz, as well as in small regions in Vizcaya and Álava provinces. In addition, there is a small, recently declared DO region around León, El Bierzo, with light and fruity reds (Casar de Valdaiga is a good one). Galicia's excellent Ribeíro (west of Ourense), made from aromatic Albarino grapes, resembles the delicate *vinho verde* of neighbouring Portugal; other good wines from the region are *Rías Baixas* (areas on the coast near Pontevedra, and south of Vigo on the Portuguese border) and *Valdeorros* (east of Ourense) – pleasant light vintages that complement the regional dishes, seafood in particular.

Much of the inexpensive wine sold throughout the country comes from La Mancha or the neighbouring Valdepeñas DO regions. And then there is Jerez, or what we in English call **sherry**. When a Spaniard invites you to *tomar una copa* (glass) it will nearly always be filled with this Andalucían sunshine. It comes in a wide range of varieties: *manzanillas* are very dry, *fino* is dry, light and young (the most famous is Tío Pepe); *amontillados* are a bit sweeter and rich; *olorosos* are very sweet dessert sherries, and can be either brown, cream or *amoroso*.

North of the Cordillera Cantábrica in Asturias, where apples grow better than vines, they produce hard **cider**, or *sidra*, which can come as a shock to the tastebuds for the first five minutes, then it goes down just fine. Cider means as much to Asturians as milk to babies; Basques are fond of good hard cider too. They claim to have taught the more famous cider makers of Normandy and Asturias their secrets, and back in the 1500s Basque fishermen used to trade the stuff with the American Indians for furs.

Spanish **brandy** (mostly from Jerez too) is excellent; the two most popular brands, *103* (very light in colour) and *Soberano*, are both drunk extensively by Spanish labourers and postmen at about 7am (they throw a shot into their breakfast coffee and call it a *carajillo*). *Anís* (sweet or dry) is also quite popular. *Sangría* is the famous summertime punch of red wine, brandy, mineral water, orange and lemon with ice, but beware – it's rarely made very well, even when you can find it. Each region has its wine and liqueur specialities and nearly every monastery in Spain seems to make some kind of herbal potion or digestive liqueur that tastes more or less like cough syrup. In the Basque country, look for *Izarra*, a potent mix of Pyrenean herbs with exotic spices, which comes in either green or the less potent yellow; for something more unusual you can top off your meal with a tipple of deadly Basque hooch, *pacharán* (sloe brandy).

Practicalities

Learning to eat the Spanish Way

Going to Spain, you may have to learn to eat all over again; dining is a much more complex affair here than in many countries. The essential fact to learn is that Spaniards like to eat *all day long* – this scheme spreads the gratification evenly through the day, and it facilitates digestion, which in Spain can be problematic. Give it some consideration. Start out with a big coffee, a *doble*, and a pastry (mostly poor French clones, with extra sugar) or find a progressive-looking bar where you might find a more fitting breakfast – a glass of wine or brandy, and a salami sandwich or *pincho*, or a glazed American doughnut. These bars will be around all day, their piles of treats under the glass cases on the bar growing by the hour, an eternal alternative to a heavy sit-down dinner. Ask around for the one that does seafood tapas. As if the bars weren't enough, there are *pastelerías* in the towns with all sorts of savoury pastries, *merenderos* (snack stands) in the countryside, and ice cream everywhere. You will never be more than a hundred feet from ice cream in a Spanish town. For a mid-morning or mid-afternoon energizer, there are sweet 'n' greasy *churros* (those inscrutable fried things that look like garden slugs) sold in bars and *churrerías*, dipped in thick cups of rich chocolate, for most non-Spaniards a once in a lifetime gut-gurgling experience.

The best **restaurants** are almost always those specializing in regional cuisine, though at the upmarket end of the scale you'll find plenty of new restaurants with innovative dishes heavily influenced by what the Basques call their *cocina nueva* – as with French *nouvelle cuisine* expect a lot of surprising combinations, peculiar sauces and an obsession with appearances. There are still thousands of old-fashioned restaurants around – and many of the sort that travellers have been complaining about for centuries; Spanish cooking still usually comes a bit on the heavy side. The worst offenders are often those with the little flags and ten-language menus in the most touristy areas, and in general you'd do better to buy some bread, Cabrales cheese and a bottle of Rioja red and have a picnic. But the regions along the northern coast have a repertoire of traditional dishes as gratifying as any in the country, and seafood is undoubtedly the star of the show.

In any coastal town or village, the best seafood restaurants will be around the harbour. The fancier ones will post set menus, while at the rest you'll find only a chalkboard with prices listed for a plate of grilled fish, or prawns or whatever else came in that day. It's a convivial arrangement; just choose a plate, or negotiate a full dinner with the waiter. Don't expect seafood to be a bargain though; a plate of prawns in garlic all by itself usually costs about €8–10.

If you dine where the locals do you'll be assured of a good deal if not necessarily a good meal. Almost every restaurant offers a *menú del día*, or a *menú turístico*, featuring an appetizer, a main course, dessert, bread and drink at a set price, always a certain percentage lower than if you had ordered the items *à la carte*. These are always posted outside the restaurant, in the window or on the plywood chef by the door; decide what you want before going in if it's a set-price menu, because these bargains are hardly ever listed on the menu the waiter gives you at the table. Unless it's explicitly written on the bill (*la cuenta*), service is *not* included in the total, so tip accordingly. Spaniards will just round up the bill by a few euros – 10 per cent is considered ludicrous, and 3–5 per cent is generous – but in tourist areas, there are different expectations of visitors.

If you are travelling on a budget you may want to eat one of your meals a day at a **tapas bar** or *tasca*. Tapas (*caxuelitas* in Basque, though this is very unusual) means 'lids', and they started out as little saucers of goodies served on top of a drink. They have evolved over the years to form a main part of the world's greatest snack culture. Bars that specialize in them have platter after platter of delectable titbits, from shellfish to slices of omelette or mushrooms baked in garlic or vegetables in vinaigrette or stews. All you have to do is pick out what looks best and order a *porción* (an hors d'oeuvre) or a *ración* (a big helping) if it looks really good. It's hard to generalize about prices, but on average €10-15 of tapas and wine or beer will really fill you up. You can always save money in bars by standing up; sit at that charming table on the terrace and you'll find prices can jump considerably.

Another advantage of tapas is that they're available at what most Americans or Britons would consider normal dining hours. Spaniards are notoriously late diners; in the morning it's a coffee and roll grabbed at the bar, a huge meal at around 2 or 3pm, then after work at 8pm a few tapas at the bar to hold them over until supper at 10 or 11pm. After living in Spain for a few months this makes perfect sense, but it's exasperating to the average visitor. On the coasts, restaurants tend to open earlier to accommodate foreigners (some as early as 5pm) but you may as well do as the Spaniards do. Galicians are the early diners of Spain (8 or 9pm); Basques do it from 9 to 11 – if you can find a restaurant at all. In quieter non-touristy areas they will be inconspicuous and few. Just ask someone, and you will find a nice *comedor* with home cooking tucked in a back room behind a bar – if you hadn't asked you never would have found it.

Such *comedores* (literally, dining-rooms), where the food and décor are usually equally drab but cheap, are common everywhere, along with *cafeterías*, those places

Menu Reader

Fish (*Pescados*)

acedías small plaice
adobo fish marinated in white wine
almejas clams
anchoas anchovies
anguilas eels
ástaco crayfish
bacalao codfish (usually dried)
bogavante lobster
calamares squid
cangrejo crab
centolo spider crab
chanquetes whitebait
chipirones baby squid
... en su tinta ...in its own ink
dorado, lubina sea bass
escabeche pickled or marinated fish
gambas prawns
langosta lobster
langostinos giant prawns
mariscos shellfish
mejillones mussels
merluza hake
mero grouper
navajas razor-shell clams
ostras oysters
percebes barnacles
pescadilla whiting
pez espada swordfish
platija plaice
pulpo octopus
rape anglerfish
trucha trout
veneras scallops
zarzuela fish stew

Meat and Fowl (*Carnes y Aves*)

albóndigas meatballs
asado roast
buey ox
callos tripe
cerdo pork
chorizo spiced sausage
chuletas chops
cochinillo suckling pig
conejo rabbit
corazón heart
cordero lamb
faisán pheasant
fiambres cold meats
hígado liver
jabalí wild boar
jamón de York raw cured ham
jamón serrano baked ham
liebre hare
lomo pork loin
morcilla blood sausage
pato duck
pavo turkey
perdiz partridge
pinchitos spicy mini kebabs
pollo chicken
rabo/cola de toro bull's tail with
    onions and tomatoes
salchicha sausage
salchichón salami

that feature photographs of their *platos combinados* (combination plates) to eliminate any language problem. Dinner will go for between €12 and €15, and you'll find as many good ones as real stinkers. *Asadores* are restaurants that specialize in roast meat or fish; *marisquerías* serve only fish and shellfish. Visit one in the countryside on a Sunday lunchtime when all the Spanish families go out to eat and make merry.

There are also many Chinese restaurants in Spain which are fairly good and inexpensive (though all pretty much the same), and American fast-food outlets in the big cities and resort areas; while Italian restaurants are 98 per cent dismal in Spain, you can usually get a reasonable pizza. Don't neglect the rapidly disappearing shacks on the beach – they often serve up barbecued sardines that are out of this world. Vegetarians are catered for in the cities, which always manage to come up with one or two veggie restaurants, usually rather good ones too. In the countryside and away from the main resorts, proper vegetarians and vegans will find it hard going, though

sesos brains
solomillo sirloin steak
ternera veal
   Note: *potajes, cocidos, guisados, estofados, fabadas* and *cazuelas* are kinds of stew.

Fruits and Vegetables (*Frutas y verduras*)
alcachofas artichokes
apio celery
erenjena aubergine (eggplant)
cebolla onion
champiñones mushrooms
ciruela plum
col, repollo cabbage
coliflor cauliflower
endibias endives
espárragos asparagus
espinacas spinach
fresas strawberries
garbanzos chick peas
judías (verdes) French beans
lechuga lettuce
lentejas lentils
manzanas apple
naranja orange
patatas potatoes
   (fritas/salteadas) (fried/sautéed)
   (al horno) (baked)
pomelo grapefruit
puerros leeks
remolachas beetroots (beets)
setas Spanish mushrooms
zanahorias carrots

Desserts (*Postres*)
arroz con leche rice pudding
bizcocho/pastel/torta cake
blanco y negro ice cream and coffee float
flan crème caramel
galletas biscuits (cookies)
helados ice creams
pajama flan with ice cream
pasteles pastries
queso cheese
requesón cottage cheese
tarta de frutas fruit pie
turrón nougat

Miscellaneous
pan bread
mantequilla butter
huevos eggs
tortilla omelette
arroz rice
azucar sugar
aceite oil
vinagre vinegar
sal salt
pimienta pepper
ensalada salad
desayuno breakfast
almuerzo/comida lunch
cena dinner
cuenta bill
carta/menú menu
menú del día set meal

See p.341 for more restaurant vocabulary.

tapas make it easier to get your nutrition than in some other southern European countries. Navarra, perhaps the best producer of fruit and vegetables in Spain, is particularly good for veggies. Fish-eaters will manage just about everywhere.

What to Drink Where
   No matter how much other costs have risen in Spain, wine has remained refreshingly inexpensive by northern European or American standards. What's more, the north produces much of Spain's best – the famous reds of La Rioja and a number of good whites from Galicia. A restaurant's *vino del lugar* or *vino de la casa* is always your least expensive option while dining out; it usually comes out of a barrel or glass jug and may be a surprise either way. Anyone with more than a passing interest in wine will want to visit a *bodega* or two. A good place to start would be Haro, the growing and marketing centre for the wines of Rioja Alta, with a clutch of bodegas near the train station (*see* p.114).

Northern Spain is not all wine though. One bottle of Asturian cider, or *sidra*, is usually enough if you mean to do any walking afterwards; if not, the ritual of drinking it can make your evening. In any proper restaurant the waiter will hold the bottle over his head and pour it into a pint glass held behind his hip. The ones with the most *duende* do it without looking, splashing the stuff all over you, the floor, themselves, and people at three or four adjacent tables. This is done to air the stuff out; for the same reason they never put more than an inch in the glass, but it's a point of honour among them never to let your glass stay empty longer than fifteen seconds. In most bars they'll just leave the bottle (green, without a label and returnable) on the table and let you try it yourself. *Sidrerías* are the social centres of every Asturian town and village (there are also quite a few in Euskadi); to find one just follow your nose. In summer they migrate out onto the streets, and whole families gab around them until one in the morning, with small children bicycling between the tables.

Many Spaniards prefer beer, which is generally nondescript. The most popular brand is San Miguel, but try Mahou Five Star if you see it. Imported whisky and other spirits are pretty inexpensive, though even cheaper are the versions Spain bottles itself, which may come close to your home favourites. Coffee, tea, all the international soft-drink brands and the locally-made *Kas* round off the average café fare. Spanish coffee is good and strong and if you want a lot of it order a *doble*; one of those will keep you awake even through the guided tour of a Bourbon palace. In summer look for the bars that make *blanco y negros* – coffee and ice cream treats that quickly become addictive in the hot sun. Ground almonds whipped to create *horchata de chufa* are also refreshing in summer.

Travel

Getting There 44
By Air from the UK 44
By Air from the USA 44
By Sea 44
By Rail 46
Specialist Tour Operators 46
By Bus or Coach 48
By Car 48
Entry Formalities 48
Getting Around 49
By Air 49
By Rail 49
By Bus 50
By City Bus and Taxi 51
By Car 51

05

Getting There

By Air from the UK

There are many flight options to Spain these days, especially from the UK. In the face of stiff competition from the budget airlines, even the national carriers, Iberia and British Airways, often feature special promotions which can bring prices down as low as £59 for a return flight.

It's worth checking out the low-cost airlines, although they don't always offer the cheapest flight options unless you book well in advance. For the very best deals, shop around online: the website *www.opodo.co.uk* is particularly useful for price comparisons on all the major national carriers, while *www.cheapflights.co.uk* is good for finding the cheapest deal on budget airlines. You can usually save by going off-season, while APEX fares, purchased at least two weeks in advance, offer a discount, especially if you're travelling mid-week. Low-cost airlines like easyJet sell one-way tickets, so there's no need to stay over a Saturday night to get the best deals. There are also discounts for domestic flights and for children (usually under 12 or 14, depending on the carrier). Infants under 2 usually travel free.

Students and those under 26 have the option of special discount charters, departing from the UK, but make sure you have proof of student status. An STA Youth card costs £7; there is also a GO-25 card.

There are international airports in Bilbao, Santander, Santiago de Compostela and Oviedo (Aviles), For national airports, *see* p.49 (Getting Around By Air).

British Airways has a daily flight to Bilbao from London Heathrow (code-sharing with Iberia).

easyJet operates twice-daily flights to Bilbao from London Stansted, and daily flights to Asturias.

Air Berlin flies daily to Bilbao from London Stansted.

Iberia flies direct to Bilbao from London Heathrow daily, and to Bilbao via Barcelona, Málaga or Madrid from Manchester. There are connections with major UK cities via London Heathrow. There are also direct flights to Santiago de Compostela and flights to Santander, Vitoria, Pamplona, Vigo, San Sebastian and A Coruña (via Madrid or Barcelona).

Ryanair has flights to Santander and Santiago de Compostela from London Stansted.

By Air from the USA

There are no direct flights to Bilbao or other airports in Northern Spain from the USA and Canada, but numerous carriers fly direct to Madrid and a few to Barcelona A high-season return will cost around US$1,100–2,000. **Iberia**, the national airline, offers fly-drive deals and you can use their toll-free line, **t** (800) 772 4642, from anywhere in the USA. Alternatively, it may be cheaper to fly to London and pick up an onward flight to Spain from there, especially off-season (October–April).

If you are flying on to Spain from London on the same day, be careful to check the flights are to and from the same airport. It's a long trek across London from Heathrow to Gatwick or Stansted. If you do need to make the direct connection, the trains to Stansted go from London, King's Cross St Pancras station which can be reached from Victoria (where the Gatwick Express comes into London) by taxi (about £15) or via the Tube on the Victoria line (£2 per adult). If you come in to Paddington on the the the Heathrow Express, the taxi fare will be similar or you can make the connection by Tube on the Circle or Hammersmith and City lines. For train times to Stansted airport from King's Cross ring **t** 08457 484950.

By Sea

P&O Ferries, t 08705 980 333 (UK), **t** 902 02 04 61 (Spain), *www.poferries.com*. Sailing from Portsmouth to Bilbao, P&O's *Pride of Bilbao* is the UK's largest ferry, with accommodation for 2,500 passengers and 600 cars. It also offers several restaurants, a cinema, sauna and swimming pool, and has cabins for all passengers. The service is year-round and usually departs from Portsmouth on Tuesday and Saturday at

Airline Carriers

UK

British Airways, t 0870 850 9850,
www.britishairways.co.uk
easyJet, t 0871 244 2366, www.easyjet.com
Iberia, t 0870 609 0500, www.iberia.com
Ryanair, t 0871 246 0000,
www.ryanair.com

USA and Canada

Air Canada, t 1-888 2712 7786,
www.aircanada.ca
American Airlines, t 1-800 433 7300,
www.aa.com
British Airways, t 1-800 247 9297,
www.britishairways.com
Continental Airlines, t 1-800 231 0856,
www.continental.com
Delta, t 1-800 221 1212, www.delta.com
Iberia, t 1-800 772 4642, www.iberia.com
United Airlines, t 1-800 864 8331,
www.ual.com

Discounts and Special Deals

UK and Ireland

CIE Tours International, t (01) 703 1888,
www.cietours.ie
Joe Walsh Tours, t (01) 241 0800,
www.joewalshtours.ie
Trailfinders, t 08450 58 58 58,
www.trailfinders.com
Flightbookers t 0870 814 0000,
www.ebookers.com
www.cheapflights.co.uk
www.expedia.com
www.lastminute.com

USA and Canada

CAir Brokers International USA t 800 883 3273,
www.airbrokers.com

Last Minute Travel Club USA t 800 527 8646,
Canada t 877 970 3500, www.lastminute
club.com. Payment of an annual membership fee gets you cheap standby deals;
there are also special rates for the major
car rental companies in Europe, and for
train tickets.
Spanish Heritage Tours, 200 Broadacres Drive,
Bloomfield, NJ 07003, t 1-800 456 5050,
www.shtours.com
www.traveldiscounts.com. Members get
special discount rates on flights, hotels
and tours.
www.orbitz.com. Cheap flights, hotels and car
rental companies.

Student Discounts

Students and those aged under 26 are
eligible for considerable reductions on flights,
train fares, admission fees to museums,
concerts and more. Agencies specializing in
student and youth travel can help you apply
for the correct ID cards, as well as filling you in
on the best deals.
Europe Student Travel, 6 Campden St, London
W8, t (020) 7727 7647
STA Travel, www.sta-travel.com. Has over 400
branches all over the world, including more
than 50 in the UK. Check the website for
more info, or call intersales on 0870 1600
599 (UK) or 1-800 777 0112 (US).
Travel Cuts, 187 College St, Toronto, Ontario
M5T 1P7, t (416) 979 2406, www.travelcuts.
com. Canada's largest student travel
specialists.
usit, Aston Quay, Dublin 2, t (01) 602 1600,
www.usitnow.ie. Also: Belfast, t (028)
90324073; Cork, t (021) 270 900; Galway,
t (091) 524 601; Limerick, t (061) 332 079;
Waterford, t (051) 872 601.
Youth Travel, t 0870 887 0135, www.youth-
travel.com. Online travel agency specialising
in youth and student fares, ideas for gap
years, international student cards, working
abroad programmes, etc.

8pm, returning from Bilbao on Monday and
Thursday at 12.30am. Although fares vary
throughout the year, at the time of writing,
a high-season return for two adults, one
child and a car in an economy 4-berth
cabin was around £1,100. Note that the

Spanish terminal is at the port of Santurzi,
13km from the centre of Bilbao. In Bilbao,
contact Ferries Golfo de Vizcaya, Cosme
Echevarrieta 1, t 94 423 44 77.
Brittany Ferries, t 08705 360 360, www.
brittanyferries.co.uk. Ferries from Plymouth

to Santander, west of Bilbao; prices and services are comparable to the P&O ferry.

If you prefer to cross the Channel to France, **Brittany Ferries** sail from Portsmouth to Caen and St-Malo, Poole to Cherbourg and St-Malo, and Plymouth to Roscoff; **P&O** can transport you from Dover to Calais and from Portsmouth to Le Havre and Cherbourg; **P&O Stena, t** 08705 980 333, sail from Dover to Calais, Southampton to Cherbourg and Newhaven to Dieppe. A good price-comparison website is *www. ferrysmart.co.uk.*

Hoverspeed Fast Ferries, t 0870 240 8070, *www.hoverspeed.com*, goes from Newhaven to Dieppe in 2hrs. Prices range from £30 return for a foot passenger to £140 return for a vehicle with two passengers (during high season). Cheaper fares are available if you book in advance, e.g. £60 return for a car and five passengers.

Speed Ferries, t 0870 22 00 570, *www. speedferries.com*, offer a high-speed service that runs between Dover and Boulogne.

Prices start at £25 one-way for a car and five passengers.

By Rail

From London to San Sebastián it's a full day's trip, changing in Paris and again at Bordeaux or Hendaye in the small hours of the morning. The **TGV service** from Paris to Bordeaux speeds things up. The other option is to take a direct train from Paris to Vitoria, and take a bus or local train to your final destination from there. For Bilbao, you will have to change at San Sebastián for the slow, but scenic, Euskotren service which takes two-and-a-half hours.

Time can also be saved by taking the **Eurostar (t** 08705 186 186, *www.eurostar.com*) through the Channel Tunnel to Paris (2hrs 40 mins). Fares are lower if you book tickets at least 14 days in advance, and range from around £59 (if booked more than two weeks in advance) to £300 for a standard return. You must check in at least 30 minutes before

---

Specialist Tour Operators

General
CV Travel, Thames Wharf Studios, Rainville Road, London W6 9HA, **t** 0870 606 0802, *www.cvtravel.net*. Small luxury hotels and up-market villas on the coast and inland.

First Choice, t 0870 900 2128, *www.firstchoice.co.uk*. One of the biggest package holiday providers.

Totally Spain, Barrio Zoña 39193 Castillo, Cantabria, **t** 942 637 358; in the UK phone, **t** 0709 229 6272, *info@totallyspain.com*, *www.totallyspain.com*. Organizes tailor-made and themed holidays in Bilbao and the Spanish Basque lands, as well as tours and city breaks.

Unicorn Holidays Ltd, 2–10 Cross Road, Tadworth, Surrey KT20 5UJ, **t** (01737) 812 255, *www.unicornholidays.com*. Tailor-made fly-drive and self-drive touring holidays featuring the *paradores* and many other excellent hotels.

Cultural Tours
Martin Randall, Voysey House, Barley Mow Passage, London W4 4GB, **t** (020) 8742 3355,

f (020) 8742 7766, *www.martinrandall. com*. Lecturer-accompanied cultural tours of the region.

NRCSA (National Registration Center for Study Abroad), PO Box 1393, Milwaukee, WI 53201, **t** (414) 278 0631, **f** (414) 271 8884, *study@nrcsa.com*. Organizes language and cultural course programmes in San Sebastián.

Page & Moy Ltd, 136–140 London Road, Leicester LE2 1EN, **t** 08708 33 40 12, *www. page-moy.com*. Cultural guided tours throughout Spain.

Plantagenet Tours, 85 The Grove, Moordown, Bournemouth BH9 2TY, **t** (01202) 521895, *www.plantagenet-tours.com*. Historical tour every spring of Castile, Galicia and Asturias.

Prospect Music and Art Tours Ltd, PO Box 4972, London W1A 7FL, **t** (020) 7486 5704, **f** (020) 7486 5868, *sales@prospecttours. com*. Fully-escorted tours led by art historians.

Walking Tours
Alternative Travel Group, 69–71 Banbury Road, Oxford OX2 6PE, **t** (01865) 315 678, *www.*

departure, or you will not be allowed on to the train.

Bookings and Passes

If you plan to take some long train journeys, it may be worth investing in a rail pass. The good-value **Euro Domino** pass entitles EU citizens (or anyone resident in the EU for at least six months) to unlimited rail travel through Spain for three to eight days in a month for £84–£195, or £71–£145 for 12–25-year-olds.

There's also the **Inter-Rail** pass (which is available to anyone who has been resident in Europe for at least six months). This offers 16, 22 days' or one month's unlimited travel in Europe (countries are grouped into zones), plus discounts on trains to cross-Channel ferry terminals and returns on Eurostar from £59. Inter-Rail cards are not valid on trains in the UK.

Visitors from North America have a wide choice of passes, including **Eurailpass**, **Europass**, and the **France 'n Spain pass**, which can all be purchased in the USA. A one-month Eurailpass costs around $615/946 for those aged under/over 26 years.

For long-distance train travel, **bicycles** need to be transported separately, and must be registered and insured. They can be delivered to your destination, although this may take several days. On Eurostar you need to check in your bike at least 24 hours before you travel, or wait 24 hours to receive it at the other end.

Rail Europe handles bookings for all services, including Eurostar and Motorail, and sells rail passes.

UK, Rail Europe, 179 Piccadilly, London W1V 0BA, **t** 08708 371 371, *www.raileurope.co.uk*. Calls cost 50p a minute.

USA, **t** 1 877 257 2887 (USA) or **t** 1 800 361 RAIL (Canada), *www.raileurope.com*.

Note that rail passes are not valid on Spain's numerous narrow-gauge (FEVE) lines; you will also have to pay supplements for any kind of express train.

---

atg-oxford.co.uk. Offers pilgrimages to Santiago de Compostela on foot, and also other walking tours.

Exodus, Grange Mills, Weir Road, London SW12 0NE, **t** 0870 240 5550, *www.exodus.co.uk*. Offers walking and activity tours throughout Spain.

Explore Worldwide Ltd, 1 Frederick St, Aldershot, Hants GU11 1LQ, **t** 0870 333 4001, *www.explore.co.uk*. Offers small-group exploratory holidays and treks in the Picos de Europa.

Pico Verde, 792 Wilmslow Rd, Didsbury, Manchester, M20 6UG, **t** 0161 773 5335, *www.picoverde.com*. Walking holidays in northern Spain, including the Atlantic Pyrenees.

Ramblers Holidays, Box 43, Welwyn Garden City, Herts AL8 6PQ, **t** (01707) 331 133, *www.ramblersholidays.co.uk*. Walking tours in the Pyrenees.

Sherpa Expeditions, 131a Heston Road, Hounslow, Middlesex TW5 0RD, **t** (020) 8577 2717, *www.sherpaexpeditions.com*. Guided walks in the Picos de Europa.

Waymark Holidays, 44 Windsor Road, Slough, SL1 2EJ, **t** (01753) 516 477, *www.waymark*

holidays.com. Guided walks along the Camino de Santiago.

Special-interest Holidays

Arblaster & Clarke Wine Tours, Clarke House, Farnham Rd, West Liss, Liss GU33 6JQ, **t** (01730) 893 344, *www.winetours.co.uk*. Tours to the Rioja region, escorted by a wine expert, with lunches and visits to *bodegas*.

Cobblestone Tours 757 St Charles Av, Suite 203, New Orleans, LA 70130, **t** 800 227 7889, **t** (504) 522 7888, **f** (504) 525 1273, *www.cobblestonetours.com*. Small group culture tours in the Basque country, including Bilbao and a visit to the Guggenheim; also offers a wine and gastronomy tour.

Euro Adventures, C/Velázquez Moreno 9, Vigo, Pontevedra, Galicia, **t** 98 622 13 99, *www.euroadventures.net*. Gastronomic tours, walking tours, and tailor-made holidays.

Exsus Travel, **t** 020 7292 5050, *www.exsus.com*. Tailor-made tours of the Basque region.

Pyrenean Experience, **t** 0121 711 3428, *www.pyreneanexperience.com*. Beginners' Spanish and walking holidays, painting holidays and tailor-made holidays in the Spanish Pyrenees.

Spanish Consulates

Australia: Level 24, St Martin's Tower, 31 Market St, Sydney NSW 2000, t (02) 61 24 33.

Canada: 1 West Mount Square, Montreal H3Z 2P9, t (514) 935 5235; 200 Cross Street West, Toronto, Ontario t (416) 977 1661.

France: 165 Blvd Malesherbes, 75840 Paris, t 01 44 29 40 00.

Germany: Steinplatz 1, Berlin t (30) 315 09 251/315 09 251.

Ireland: 17a Merlyn Park, Ballsbridge, Dublin 4, t (1) 283 8227.

Italy: Palacio Borghese, Largo Fontanella di Borghese, 00186 Roma, t 06 687 82 64.

Netherlands: Frederiksplein 34, 1017 XN Amsterdam, t (20) 620 3811.

New Zealand: 345 Great South Rd, Takanini, Auckland, t (09) 299 6019.

UK: 20 Draycott Place, London SW3 2RZ, t (020) 7589 8989; 1a Brook House, 70 Spring Gardens, Manchester M2 2BQ, t (0161) 236 1262, f (0161) 228 7467; 63 North Castle Street, Edinburgh EH2 3LJ, t (0131) 220 1843.

USA: 545 Boylston Street, Boston, MA 02116, t (617) 536 2506; 180 North Michigan Avenue, Chicago, IL 60601, t (312) 782 4588; 2655 Le Jeune Road, 203 Coral Gables, Florida, t (305) 446 5511; 5055 Wilshire Blvd, Suite 960 Los Angeles, CA 90036, t (323) 938 0158; 150 East 58th Street, New York, NY 10155, t (212) 355 4080; 2375 Pennyslvania Avenue NW, Washington, DC 20009, t (202) 728 2330.

For information on Spanish trains, see Getting Around p.49.

By Bus or Coach

Eurolines offers departures several times a week in the summer (once a week out of season) from London to Spain (although most require a change, usually in Paris or Tours), along the east coast as far as Alicante, or to Algeciras via San Sebastián and Burgos. From either San Sebastián or Burgos, it will be easy to find further connections to any other town in the northwest. Journey time from London to San Sebastián is 21 hours . The fare goes from £86–139 return, or to Vitoria and Burgos from £105–132. Look out for regular promotions, usually offered in low season.

There are discounts for anyone under 26, senior citizens and children under 12. The national coach companies operate services that connect with the continental bus system. In summer, the coach is the best bargain for those over 26; off-season you'll probably find a cheaper flight.

Information and booking: t 08705 143219, www.eurolines.co.uk, or www.eurolines.com.

By Car

From the UK via France you have a choice of routes. If you get the ferry or train (see below) to Calais you may face going through or around Paris on the abominable périphérique, a task best tackled on either side of rush hour. To avoid it, you can get a ferry from Portsmouth to Cherbourg, Caen, Le Havre or St-Malo (see above). From any of these ports, the most direct route takes you to Bordeaux down the western coast of France, past Biarritz to the border at Irún, and on to San Sebastián and Bilbao. For ferry information, see p.44.

You may find it less tiring to try the ferry from Plymouth to Santander (see above), which cuts out driving through France and saves expensive autoroute tolls.

For something a little different, opt for one of the routes the old Santiago pilgrims followed over the Pyrenees, through Puigcerdà and Somport-Canfranc, or through Roncesvalles and the Vall d'Aran – you can get warmed up for Spain by inspecting the French Basque country along the way (see the Cadogan Guides to Gascony & the Pyrenees and Bilbao & the Basque Lands).

Entry Formalities

Passports and Visas

Holders of full EU, US and Canadian passports can enter Spain freely without any kind of visa for stays of up to three months, just by showing the passport. If they intend to stay longer, EU citizens are required to register with the Foreign Nationals Office (Officina de Extranjeros) at the local police station and obtain a community resident's card (*tarjeta de residente comunitario*). Non-EU citizens who wish to stay for more than three months should apply for a special visa at a Spanish consulate before leaving home.

Customs

Duty-free allowances have been abolished within the EU. For those arriving from outside the EU, duty-free limits are one litre of spirits or two litres of fortified wine (port, sherry, brandy), plus two litres of wine and 200 cigarettes.

Much larger quantities – up to 10 litres of spirits, 90 litres of wine, 110 litres of beer and 800 cigarettes – bought locally, can be taken through customs provided you are travelling between EU countries, and if you can prove that they are for private consumption only.

For more information, US citizens can phone the US Customs Service, **t** (202) 354 1000, or consult *www.customs.gov*.

If you are travelling from the UK or the US, don't bother to pick up any alcohol in transit; it's cheaper to buy drink off the supermarket shelves in Spain.

Getting Around

By Air

Internal flights in Spain are with Iberia (*see* box p.45), **Spanair** (*www.spanair.com*), **Air Europa** (*www.air-europa.com*) and the budget airline **Vueling** (*www.vueling.com*). You'll find airports in the following cities: Oviedo, Bilbao, A Coruña, León, Logroño, Pamplona, Santander, Santiago de Compostela, Vigo and Vitoria. Some of these, including Oviedo (Aviles), Santander and Santiago de Compostela also offer international flights with budget airlines (see Getting There By Air, above). Bilbao, the largest city, is logically the main air hub, with about seven daily flights to Madrid and four to Barcelona, as well as a daily flight to Santiago and three a week to Vigo. More typical is Oviedo/Gijón's airport, with several daily flights to Madrid and one or two a week to Santiago, Vitoria and A Coruña.

Airline Information in Spain

Iberia,t 902 400 500, *www.iberia.es*.
Air Europa, t 902 401 501, *www.air-europa.como*
Spanair, t 902 13 14 25, *www.spanair.com*
Vueling, t 902 33 39 33, *www.vueling.com*

Prices are inexpensive compared to most of Europe, and if you shop around and are willing to travel at night on slow days you can pick up some bargains, especially if you're going on a round trip.

By Rail

If you're using public transport, there is usually an even choice between the bus and train. Buses are usually cheaper, and often faster, and are often the only way to reach smaller towns and villages. However, for long distances, trains are usually faster.

Democracy in Spain has made the trains run on time, but western Europe's most eccentric railway, **RENFE**, still has a way to go. The problem isn't the trains themselves; they're almost always clean and comfortable, and do their best to keep to the schedules. Steam engines, country families picnicking on *chorizo* sandwiches in the aisles, and drunken conductors are now only items for nostalgia, but the new efficient RENFE remains bewildering for visitors.

There are no fewer than 13 varieties of train, from the luxury **TEE** (Trans-Europe Express) to the excruciating *semi-directo* and *ferrobús*. Watch out for these; they stop at every conceivable hamlet to deliver mail.

Iberia Information

A Coruña: A Coruã, **t** 98 118 72 54.
Bilbao: C/Ercilla 20, **t** 94 424 19 35; Sondika airport, **t** 94 471 14 56.
Gijón: C/Alfredo Truán 8, **t** 98 517 6049.
León: León Airport, **t** 98 787 77 18.
Oviedo: C/Gil de Jaz 16, **t** 98 526 68 53.
Santander: Paseo pereda 18, **t** 94 222 97 04.
Santiago de Compostela: C/general Pardiãs 36, **t** 98 157 20 24.
Vitoria: Avda Gasteiz 84, **t** 94 522 82 50.

Watch out for these; they stop at every conceivable hamlet to deliver mail. The best are the **Talgo** trains, speedy, stylish beasts in gleaming stainless steel, designed and built entirely in Spain; the Spaniards are very proud of them. **TER** trains are almost as good. There are basically four kinds of train service: the high-speed inter-city trains; the slower and less expensive *regionales*, which link major towns and cities; *cercanías*, which are local services connected to a major hub like Bilbao; and the two narrow-gauge railways, the FEVE, which runs from Bilbao to Oviedo via Santander, and the **Eusko Tren** (Basque Railways) connects Bilbao and San Sebastián by way of Zarautz and Zumaya. Though slow and more expensive than the bus, both these narrow-gauge lines show off rural Spanish life and scenery at their best.

Every variety of train has different services and a different price. There are discounts for children (under 4 years old, free; 4–12 pay 50 per cent), large families, senior citizens (50 per cent) and regular travellers, and 25 per cent discounts on *Días Azules* ('blue days') for round trip tickets only. 'Blue days' are posted in the RENFE calendars in every station – really almost every day. If you buy a single ticket, hang on to it, because if you decide to return you are still elegible for a discount. There is a discount pass for people under 26, the *tarjeta joven*, and BIGE or BIJ youth fares are available from TIVE offices in larger cities.

Every city has a **RENFE travel office** in the centre, and you can make use of these for information and tickets. Alternatively, call their centralized information/reservations telephone number t 902 24 02 02, or check the website *www.renfe.es* (also in English). Always buy tickets in advance if you can; one of RENFE's little tricks is to close ticket offices 10 minutes before your train arrives; if you show up at the last minute, you could be out of luck. Other stations don't open ticket-windows until the train is a couple of minutes away. Don't rely on the list of trains posted; always ask at the station or travel office. There may well be an earlier train that makes an obscure connection. Fares average €10 for every 100km (63 miles) – €16 first class – but there are supplements on the faster trains that can raise the price by as much as 80%.

RENFE has plenty of services you'll never hear about – like car transport to all parts of Spain.

Rail Excursions

FEVE has inaugurated a series of special trains especially designed to attract tourists. One of these, the **Transcantábrica**, takes in some of the loveliest parts of northern Spain, including the Picos de Europa. The Basque Railways narrow-gauge line maintains an electric train from the 1920s with wooden carriages, and runs it in summer for excursions around San Sebastián; ask at the Eusko Tren station there for details.

Left Luggage

Most large Spanish stations have left-luggage facilities, although some closed after the bombings in Madrid in 2004. Almost all now screen luggage before allowing you to place it in the lockers, and some stations which don't have screening facilities have simply withdrawn luggage services. Always check in advance. The word in Spanish is *consigna*.

By Bus

With literally hundreds of companies providing services all over Spain, expect confusion. Most bus stations have an information point (although it is unlikely you will find an English-speaker) which will provide you with schedules and fare information. Buy tickets from the window dedicated to the company providing the service. Tourist information offices are the best sources of information. They almost always know every route and schedule.

Like the trains, buses are cheap by northern European standards but no memorable bargain; if you're travelling on the cheap you'll find that transport is your biggest expense. Usually, whether you go by train or bus will depend on simple convenience: in some places the train station is a long way from the centre, in others the bus station is out of town.

Small towns and villages can normally be reached by bus only through their provincial capitals. Buses are usually clean and dependable, and there's plenty of room for baggage in the compartment underneath. On the more luxurious buses you even get air conditioning and a movie (Kung Fu, or sappy Spanish flicks from the Franco era).

By City Bus and Taxi

Every Spanish city has a perfectly adequate system of public transport. You won't need to make much use of it, though, for even in the big cities nearly all the attractions are within walking distance of each other. **City buses** usually cost around €1; if you intend to use them often there are books of tickets called *abonamientos* or *bono-Bus* or *tarjeta* cards to punch on entry, available from tobacco shops (*estancos*). Bus drivers will give change if you don't have the correct amount, but will only accept bills of 10 euros or less. In many cities the bus's entire route will be displayed on the signs at each stop (*parada*).

Taxis are still cheap enough for the Spaniards to use them regularly. The average fare for a ride within a city is €5–8. Taxis are metered, and the drivers are usually honest; they are entitled to certain surcharges (for luggage, night or holiday trips, to the train or airport, etc.) and if you cross the city limits they can usually charge double. It's rarely hard to hail a cab from the street, and there will always be a few around the stations. If you get stuck where there are none, call information for the number of a radio taxi. If you call a radio taxi, be aware that the fare will start as the taxi-driver makes his way to you: in practice, this rarely comes to more than two or three euros.

By Car

This is probably the most pleasurable way of getting about, though the convenience is balanced by a considerable cost; petrol is as expensive in Spain as anywhere else in Europe (except the UK). In cities, parking is often difficult and only a few hotels – the more expensive ones – have parking. Spaniards may still have a reputation as hotheads behind the wheel, but you will find that northerners potter about rather serenely, and on the whole they are as careful as you could wish.

Spain's highway network is in good repair, and many major cities are now linked by dual carriageways. The government is investing trillions of Euros on a full-scale highway system, much of which is already up and running. A proper road has been built along the northern coast from Bilbao to beyond Gijón, when it peters out. Oviedo sits at a motorway hub, which links it with Bilbao to the east, and Le'on and Madrid to the south, with another motorway linking A Coruña and Vigo with Porto and Lisbon. In some rural areas in western Asturias or Galicia, the road will suddenly disappear, leaving you stranded on a hellish road little better than a mule track, crammed with heavy trucks. The other motorist's nightmare is the Bilbao area; even if you're passing through, you'll probably get good and lost among the endless roadworks and bizarre topography. Be warned that tolls on the motorways (*autopistas*) are sheer highway robbery.

Drivers must carry registration and insurance papers. If you're coming from the UK or Ireland, the dip of the headlights must be adjusted to the right (you can buy patches to stick on the headlights). Carrying a warning triangle is mandatory, and it should be placed 50m (55 yards) behind the car if you have a breakdown. Seat belts are mandatory. Drivers with a valid licence from an EU country, Canada, the USA or Australia don't need an international licence for Spain.

Car Rental

This is slightly cheaper than elsewhere in Europe. The best deals can usually be found online, but you should also ask your airline if they offer any discounts on car rental. The big international companies are expensive, but firms such as Holiday Autos (*www.holidayautos. com*), Auto Europe (*www.autoeurope.com*) and ATESA (*www.atesa.es*) offer better rates. Prices for the smallest cars begin at about €150 (£105) a week with unlimited mileage, but insurance can add to the costs. Local firms may offer a better deal, but these should be treated with some caution. Local firms also rent **mopeds** and **bicycles**, especially in tourist areas. **Hitchhiking** involves a long wait; few Spaniards ever do it.

Car hire companies

Auto Europe in UK t 0800 169 97 97, US t 1 800 223 5555, *www.autoeurope.com*

Avis in UK t 0870 60 60 100, Spain t 94 344 37 00, *www.avis.com*

Budget in USA t 800 527 0700, in UK t 08701 56 56 56, *www.budget.com*

Europcar in UK t 0870 607 5000, USA t 877 940 6900, Spain t 91 343 45 12, *www.europcar.com*

Hertz in UK t 08708 44 88 44, in France t 01 39 41 919 525, Spain t 917 499 069, *www.hertz.com*

Holiday Autos in the UK t 0870 400 4461, Spain t 902 448 449, *www.holidayautos.com*

Practical A–Z

Children 54
Climate and When to Go 54
Disabled Travellers 54
Eating Out 55
Electricity 55
Embassies and Consulates 55
Entertainment and Night Life 55
Festivals 56
Health and Insurance 57
Internet 59
Maps 59
Media 60
Money 61
Opening Hours 61
Photography 61
Pilgrim Facts 62
Police Business 62
Post Offices 62
Public Holidays 63
Smoking 63
Sports and Activities 63
Telephones 64
Toilets 65
Tourist Information 65
Where to Stay 65
Women Travellers 68

Children

Spaniards love children, and they'll welcome yours almost everywhere. Baby foods etc. are widely available, but don't expect to find babysitters except at the really smart hotels. Spaniards always take their children with them, even if they're up till 4am. Nor are there many special amusements for kids – though these are beginning to spring up with Spain's new prosperity, for better or for worse; traditionally Spaniards never thought of their children as separate little creatures who ought to be amused. Ask at a local tourist office for a list of attractions geared towards children.

Climate and When to Go

You get just one guess to figure out what makes the north coast of Spain so luxuriantly green. The Cordillera Cantábrica stops all the weather fronts coming over the Atlantic and squeezes out all the precipitation; the coast gets between three and four inches of rain in August – and the real rainy season doesn't start until September. Galicia seems to get a bit less rain than the coastal regions to the east, and the high Castilian plains are climatically another world – hot and dry most of the year, chilly and strange in winter. La Rioja enjoys a more reasonable climate between the two extremes, which is very good for the vines. For the coast as a whole, rain is spread around the calendar; plenty of it falls from September–January, with July the most reliable month (only an inch or two, if you're lucky). The rain champion is the Basque coast, which can get seven or eight feet a year, as much as Wales or the west of Ireland.

Spring and summer are the best times to visit; the winter can be pleasant, though damp and chilly. Most Spanish homes – and hotel rooms – are not made for the winter. High season is between June and September, when the ocean is warm enough for water sports, the fiesta calendar is in full swing and everything is open.

Disabled Travellers

Facilities for disabled travellers are limited in Spain, and public transport is not particularly wheelchair-friendly, though RENFE usually provides wheelchairs at main city stations. Many are slowly being upgraded to provide services for the disabled (lift acess to platforms, etc). You are advised to contact the Spanish Tourist Office, which has compiled a two-page fact sheet and can give general information on accessible accommodation, or any of the organizations that specifically provide services for people with disabilities.

Specialist Organizations in Spain
ONCE (Organización Nacional de Ciegos de España), C/ José Ortega y Gasset 22-24, **t** 91 577 37 56, *www.once.es*. The Spanish association for blind people; they offer a number of services, including maps in Braille.
ECOM, Gran Via de les Corts Catalanes 562 Principal, Barcelona, **t** 93 451 55 50, *www.ecom.es*. The federation of private Spanish organizations offering a range of services for disabled people.

Specialist Organizations in the UK
Holiday Care Information Unit, 7th Floor, Sunley House, 4 Bedford Park, Croydon, Surren CR0 2AP, **t** 0845 124 9971, *www.holidaycare.org.uk*. Information on accessible hotels and attractions.
RADAR (The Royal Association for Disability and Rehabilitation), Unit 12, City Forum, 250 City Road, London EC1V 8AF, **t** (020) 7250 3222, *www.radar.org.uk*. Has a wide range of travel information.
Royal National Institute for the Blind, 105 Judd St, London WC1H 9NE, **t** (020) 7388 1266, *www.rnib.org.uk*. Information for blind travellers.

Specialist Organizations in the USA
American Foundation for the Blind, 11 Penn Plaza, Suite 300, New York, NY 10001, **t** (212) 502 7600; toll free **t** 800 232 5463, *www.afb.org*. This is the best source of information in the US for visually-impaired travellers.

Average Maximum Temperatures in °C

	Jan	April	July	Oct
San Sebastián	15	27	34	24
A Coruña	16	25	27	26

Average Monthly Rainfall in mm

	Jan	April	July	Oct
San Sebastián	142	84	92	142
A Coruña	125	78	35	135

Mobility International USA, 451 Broadway, Eugene, OR 97440, **t** (541) 343 1284, *www.miusa.org*. Offers a service similar to that of its sister organization in the UK.
SATH (Society for Accessible Travel & Hospitality), Suite 610, 347 5th Avenue, New York, NY 10016, **t** (212) 447 7284, *www.sath.org*. Travel and access information; also details other access resources on the web.

Other Useful Contacts

Access Travel, 6 The Hillock, Astley, Lancashire M29 7GW, **t** (01942) 888844, *info@access-travel.co.uk, www.access-travel.co.uk*. Travel agent for disabled people: special air fares, car hire and wheelchair accessible accommodation.
Alternative Leisure Co, 165 Middlesex Turnpike, Suite 206, Bedford, MA 01730, **t** (718) 275 0023, *www.alctrips.com*. Organizes vacations abroad for disabled people.

Eating Out

Spaniards are notoriously late diners; in the morning it's a coffee and roll grabbed at the bar, a huge meal at around 2 or 3pm, then after work at 8pm a few tapas at the bar to hold them over until supper at 10 or 11pm. On the coasts, restaurants tend to open earlier to accommodate foreigners (some as early as 5pm), while Galicians are the early diners of Spain (8 or 9pm); Basques do it from 9 to 11. Note that in non-touristy areas restaurants will be inconspicuous and few. Just ask someone, and you should find a nice *comedor* with home cooking tucked in a back room behind a bar. A wide array of snacking establishments will help fill in the gaps in your day, wherever you are.

If you dine where the locals do you'll be assured of a good deal if not necessarily a good meal. Almost every restaurant offers a *menú del día*, or a *menú turístico* (usually only available on weekdays, as they are designed to cater for local workers), featuring an appetizer, a main course, dessert, bread and drink at a set price, always a certain percentage lower than if you had ordered the items *à la carte*.

Unless it's explicitly written on the bill (*la cuenta*), service is *not* included in the total, so tip accordingly.

Restaurant Price Categories
Prices are based on a three-course meal with drinks, per person.
expensive over €40
moderate €20–40
budget under €20

In the Eating Out sections in this book, restaurants have been priced according to the categories in the box above.
See also **Food and Drink** pp.33–42.

Electricity

The current is 225AC/220V, the same as most of Europe. Americans will need converters, and the British will need two-pin adapters for the different plugs. These are easily available from ironmongers/hardware stores (*ferreterías*) and department stores.

Embassies and Consulates

Australia: Plaza Descubridor Diego Ordaz 3, Madrid, **t** 91 353 66 00.
Canada: C/Núñez de Balboa 35, Madrid, **t** 91 423 32 50, *www.canada-es.org*.
Ireland: C/Bartell Abogados, Bilbao, **t** 94 423 04 14.
New Zealand: Plaza de la Lealtad 2, Madrid, **t** 91 523 02 26.
UK: Alameda Urquijo 2, Bilbao, **t** 94 415 76 00, *www.ukinspain.com*.
USA: Calle Serrano 75, Madrid, **t** 91 587 22 00, *www.embusa.es*; consular office for passports, around the corner at Paseo de la Castellana 52.

Entertainment and Nightlife

Bars and **cafés** soak up most of the Spaniards' leisure time. These are wonderful institutions, where you can eat breakfast or linger over a glass of beer until 4 in the morning; in any of them you could see an old sailor delicately sipping his camomile tea next to a young mother, baby under her arm, stopping in for a beer break during her shopping. If you aren't familiar with a town, walking into any of them can be an adventure. Some bars put on

Parisian airs; others, including the *chigres* (another word for *sidrerías* in Asturias) are resolutely proletarian. Some have great snacks, or tapas, some have pinball machines or digital one-armed bandits, doling out electronic versions of *La Cucaracha* whenever they get lonely. Some keep the music on, while others have no tape player and are dedicated to serious snacking, newspaper reading and coffee. Where there's music, you may hear gormless, saccharine Spanish rock, but then again you may hear Django Reinhardt or Camarón or Celia Cruz or arias from the *zarzuela* (operettas from the Madrid stage). Out along the highways you will find hundreds of truck-stop bars where you can eat a factory-made doughnut accompanied by a Coke and pretend you're in Oklahoma.

At night, some bars will have live music – jazz, rock or flamenco, or maybe salsa in the styles of Colombia, Cuba and New York, an increasingly popular genre here. Many night-time bars and clubs are totally invisible in the day, exploding into blue-light noise palaces punctually from midnight until 6am. This is the twilight world of *la marcha*, the all-night pub crawl of Madrid and Barcelona that finds a reflection in any Spanish city, especially if it has a university. Spots that stay open late tend to congregate in one area of the city centre, accompanied by a few restaurants to satisfy nocturnal binges. Cities that can nourish a proper *marcha* include Santander, San Sebastián, Oviedo, Santiago, A Coruña, Pontevedra, Pamplona and León. Industrial, hard-working Bilbao does its best, while Burgos and Vigo are a little too staid to try very hard at all.

Discos and **night clubs** are easily found in the big cities and tourist spots; most tend to be expensive. Ask around for the current favourites, which change as quickly as those in New York or Paris. Watch out for posters for **concerts** and **ballets**; every year brings more acts to the touristy cities. Santander and San Sebastián in particular are known for their music festivals.

Beyond the slot machines in the bars and petrol stations, there will be plenty of other opportunities to lose money pointlessly. Every Spaniard is a gambler; there seem to be an infinite number of lotteries run by the State (the *Lotería Deportiva*), for the blind (ONCE), the Red Cross, or the church, and there are casinos in major resorts.

Festivals

One of the most spiritually deadening aspects of Francoism was the banning of many local and regional fiestas. These are now celebrated with gusto, and if you can arrange your itinerary to include one or two you'll be guaranteeing an unforgettable holiday. Besides those listed on pp.57–60, there are literally thousands of others, and new ones spring up all the time.

The big holidays celebrated throughout Spain are *Corpus Christi* in late May; Holy Week (*Semana Santa*), the week preceding Easter; 15 August (the Assumption of the Virgin) and 25 July (the feast day of Spain's patron, Santiago). No matter where you are, there are bound to be fireworks or processions on these dates, especially for *Semana Santa* and *Corpus Christi*.

Beware that dates for most festivals tend to be fluid, flowing towards the nearest weekend; if the actual date falls on a Thursday or a Tuesday, Spaniards 'bridge' the fiesta with the weekend to create a four-day whoopee. If there's a fiesta you want to attend, check the date at the tourist office in advance.

Many village patronal fiestas feature *romerías* (pilgrimages) up to a venerated shrine. Getting there is half the fun, with everyone in local costume, riding on horseback or driving covered wagons full of picnic supplies. Music, dancing, food, wine and fire-works are all necessary ingredients of a proper fiesta, while the bigger ones often include bullfights, funfairs, circuses and competitions. In the Basque lands and Navarra, summer fiestas often feature a loose bull or two stam-peding through the streets – an *encierro*. 'Giants' (10ft-tall dummies of Fernando and Isabel and a Moor) and 'fat-heads' (comical or grotesque caricatures) pirouette through the throngs and tease the children.

Semana Santa is a major tourist event, though not as much as in southern Spain; unless you're prepared to fight the crowds to see the *pasos* (ornate floats depicting scenes from the Passion), carried in an excruciatingly slow march to lugubrious tuba music, and accompanied by children and men decked out in costumes copied by the Ku Klux Klan, you may want to skip it; the real revelry takes place after Easter.

Calendar of Events

January

1 Enormous livestock fair, Betanzos (near A Coruña).
6 *Los Reyes* (the three Magi) procession, Baiona (Pontevedra).
15 San Mauro, big fiesta with fireworks, Villanova de Arousa (Pontevedra).
19–20 San Sebastián's *Tamborrada*, marches of the Basque pipe-and-drum corps.
3rd Sunday San Vicente, bachelors' party at Los Arcos (Navarra).
22 Fiesta at San Vicente de la Barquera (Cantabria).
28 San Tirso, with dances and the burning of a papier-mâché *falla*, in Villafranca del Bierzo (León).
30 San Lesmes, patron of Burgos.
End January Ituren and Zubieta (Navarra), dances of the *ioaldunak* with pointed hats, fur vests, and big bells.

February

Carnival (Feb/early March) A big affair anywhere in Spain. Some of the biggest are in Bilbao, San Sebastián, Vitoria and Tolosa. The entire week before Lent, Asturias puts on the biggest show in the northwest: at Avilés on Saturday and Tuesday; at Gijón on Monday; and in Oviedo on Tuesday, or Mardi Gras, the day before Ash Wednesday.

March

1 Fiesta de San Rosendo, Celanova (Ourense).

Two Sundays (after the 4th) The *Javierada*, two important pilgrimages for St Francis Xavier at Javier (Navarra).

April

Palm Sunday Procession at Monte San Tecla, A Garda (Pontevedra).
Semana Santa (Holy Week) In the north, it's the Castilians who really get into the processions, especially at León and Covarrubias (Burgos). Good Friday brings *Los Picaos*, medieval-style self-flagellants, San Vicente de la Sonsierra (La Rioja); Descent from the Cross, Vivero (Lugo); mystery play, Balsameda (Vizcaya), processions in Hondarrabia and Segura (Guipúzcoa). In Avilés (Asturias), Easter and Easter Monday are celebrated with the Fiesta del Bollo, with folklore groups, cake eating and regattas.
19 Festival of Santísimo Cristo, Finisterre (A Coruña).
1st Sunday (after Easter) San Vicente de Barquera's La Folia, where the sailors transport an image of the Virgin at night in an illuminated maritime procession (Cantabria). Festivities for San Telmo, including bull running on the beach, Zumaia (Guipúzcoa).
2nd Sunday (after Easter) Fiesta de San Isidoro, in León.
2nd Monday (after Easter) Fiesta de San Telmo, Tui (Pontevedra).
25 San Marcos, Noia (A Coruña).
End April Wine Festival, Ribadavia (Ourense); tasting and judging of the local Reibero, as

---

The Calendar of Events above is hardly complete: during the summer every village has its own special fiesta, with a wheezing brass band to serenade the statue of the patron saint on his or her annual airing through the streets, a few bulls or heifers to chase the young bloods in the street, a market and fun fair (with the volume of the latest disco or techno hits turned up full blast), food and dancing into the night and perhaps even some fireworks if the Ayuntamiento's pot is full of euros.

Note that many of the dates are subject to change (to fit weekends, etc.); a call ahead to the tourist office is always a good idea.

Health and Insurance

The E111 forms for EU nationals have been replaced by the European Health Insurance Card (EHIC) that will give the bearer access to the state health care scheme and public hospitals in all EU countries. Like the old system, the card is available for UK residents for free at post offices or can be ordered online at *www.ehic.org.uk* or t 0845 606 2030. Unlike the E111 forms, however, you'll need to apply for a card for every member of the family (you'll need passports and national insurance numbers). The EHIC must be stamped and well as music and *artensania* from Galicia and Portugal.

May

10–15 Saint's day and parades, Santo Domingo de la Calzada (La Rioja).

22 Santa Rita, Vilagarcía de Arousa (Pontevedra).

23 Anniversary of the battle of Clavijo (La Rioja).

Corpus Christi Usually falls at the end of May or early June (Thursday after Trinity Sunday), initiating four days of festivities. Also, *Procesión del Olé*, with dances, Frómista (Palencia); Flower carpets in the streets, Ponteareas (Pontevedra). On the first day after Corpus Christi, Los Corpillos dances and celebrations at Las Huelgas, Burgos; Maragato festivals, Astorga (León) and surrounding areas.

June

11 San Bernabé, with the distribution of grilled fish, Logroño (La Rioja).

12 San Juan, with *encierros*, giants and Maragato bagpipers, Sahagún (León).

21–24 San Juan, bonfires and fishwives' festivities in Laredo (Cantabria); La Magdalena, with Basque sports, Bermeo (Vizcaya), followed by a nautical *romería* to the isle of Izaro. For midsummer's day, 'bonfires of San Juan' in many Basque villages. León celebrates St John's Day with parties and bull fights, bonfire in Plaza Alfonso II, Oviedo (Asturias).

24 Vueltas de San Juan, Nájera (La Rioja); Fiesta de San Juan, Laguardia (Álava).

26 Fiesta de San Pelayo, Zarautz (Guipúzcoa).

End of June San Felices de Bilibio at Haro (La Rioja), pilgrimage and drunken 'wine battles'. Cudillero (Asturias), *La Amuravela*, satirical poems on the year's events in the local dialect and lots of drink.

29 Wine battle, Haro (La Rioja).

29 Burgos, San Pedro, beginning of two weeks of International Folklore Feria. Fiesta de San Pedro, Orio and Zumaia (Guipúzcoa).

30 *El Coso Blanco*, processions and fireworks, in Castro Urdiales (Cantabria); fiesta of San Marcial, Irún (Guipúzcoa).

July

All month Santander holds its International Music Festival.

First Sunday *Rapa das Bestas* (Gallego wild horse round-ups, races and shearings), Viveiro and San Lorenzo de Sabucedo (Lugo). At La Estrada (Pontevedra), another *Rapa das Bestas*, with big festivities from Saturday till Monday.

5–9 Getxo Jazz Festival, Getxo (Vizcaya); both international and national bands.

7–14 Pamplona (Navarra) the famous running of the bulls and mad party for San Fermín.

11 San Benitiño de Lérez, with river races and pagentry, Pontevedra (Galicia).

14–16 International Celtic Festival, Ortigueria (A Coruña).

15 Comillas (Cantabria), 'catch the goose' and other country fair-type festivities and humour. Avilés (Asturias) has dances, entertainment and bullfights.

Last half Historical sound and light pageant, Nájera (La Rioja).

---

signed to be valid, and the card must be renewed annually.

This card enables you to claim free treatment from an INSS doctor. In an emergency, ask to be taken to the nearest *hospital de la seguridad social*.

Before resorting to a *médico* (doctor) and his fat fee (ask at the tourist office for a list of English-speaking doctors), go to a pharmacy and tell them your woes. Spanish *farmacéuticos* are highly skilled and if there's a prescription medicine that you know will cure you, they'll often supply it without a doctor's note. (*El País* and the other national newspapers list *farmacías* in large cities that stay open all night, and most pharmacies post a rota card in the window with the addresses.)

No inoculations are required to enter Spain, though it never hurts to check that your tetanus jab is up-to-date if you want to venture on into Morocco. The tap water is safe to drink but at the slightest twinge of queasiness, switch to the bottled stuff.

Travel insurance, available through most travel agents, is highly recommended – not least because it avoids the tortuous bureaucracy of the Spanish health service. For a small monthly charge, not only is your health insured, but your bags and money as well. Be sure to save all doctor's receipts (you'll have to pay cash on

16 Virgen del Carmen with boat processions, Muros and Concubión (A Coruña).
Third week Jazz festival, Vitoria.
Last 10 days International Jazz Festival, the biggest in Spain, San Sebastián.
22 Anguiano (La Rioja), fiesta with the dance of the *Zancos*, down the streets and steps on stilts; Bermeo (Vizcaya), boat races, Basque sports and dancing. Fiesta de Santa María Magdalena, Rentería (Guipúzcoa).
24 Tudela (Navarra), music and dancing for a week for Santa Ana.
25 Santiago de Compostela, great celebrations for Santiago – national offering to the saint, the swinging of the *Botafumeiro*, burning of a cardboard replica of Córdoba's Mezquita, fireworks and more; Romería de Saniaguiño do Monte, with bagpipes and a sardine and pepper feast, Padrón (A Coruña); Cangas de Onís (Asturias), shepherds' festival. Also Vitoria and Bilbao's saint's day, Santiago.
Last Sunday Fiesta de la Playa, Langosteira (Finisterre); Fiesta de los Vaqueros, La Brana de Aristebano, by Luarca (Asturias).
29 Luarca (Asturias), Vaqueiro festival, mock wedding and dances; Santa María de Ribarteme (Pontevedra), pilgrimage made in coffins by people who narrowly escaped death the year before. Octopus-eating festival, Villanova de Arousa (Pontevedra) Fiesta de San Pedro, Mundaka (Vizcaya).
31 Fiesta de San Ignacio, Getxo (Vizcaya) and Azpetia (Guipúzcoa).

August
Throughout International Music Festival, Santander.

3–9 Estella (Navarra), ancient fiesta, with giants and the only *encierro* where women can run with the bulls.
First Saturday Arriondas-Ribadesella (Asturias), great kayak race on the Río Sella.
First Sunday Gijón, Asturias Day celebrations, with lots of folklore. Festival of Albariño wine, Cambados (Pontevedra); Santa Cruz, at Ribadeo (Lugo).
5–10 Vitoria, giants, music, bonfires and more for the Virgen Blanca – one of Spain's best parties (*see* p.162).
6 Fiesta de San Salvador, Getaria (Guipúzcoa).
10 San Juan Dantzak, procession and traditional dancing at Berástegui (Guipúzcoa). Cudillero, International Celtic Music Festival.
9–11 Foz (Lugo), San Lorenzo festivities, folklore and kayaking.
Second Sunday Cabezón de la Sal (Cantabria), Mountain Day folklore, song contests; Carballino (Ourense), octopus-eating festival and bagpipe music. Romería to the Ermita de Oca, Villafranca de Montes de Oca (La Rioja).
15–16 Assumption of the Virgin and San Roque festivities at Sada (A Coruña), with a big sardine roast, also fiesta de San Roque at Gernika (Vizcaya); Llanes (Asturias), bagpipes and ancient dances; on the Saturday after the 15th, Bilbao has its *Aste Nagustia* ('Great Week'), with Basque sports and races; International Fireworks festival, San Sebastián; *El Rosario*, fisherman's fiesta, Luarca (Asturias).
15–19 Battle of flowers at Betanzos (A Coruña).
Third week San Zoilo, Carrión de los Condes (Palencia).

the spot), pharmacy receipts, and police documents (if you're reporting a theft).

Internet

Getting online is easy and cheap in Spain. Every city of any size will have several places scattered around, while heavily visited towns are likely to be infested with 'cibers', as the Spanish call their Internet cafes. Even the most unlikely and out-of-the-way one-horse towns sometimes have Internet facilities – if you can get past the hordes of local youths indulging their aggression on digitized baddies. Average

price from Bilbao to Santiago is €2 an hour; coastal resorts tend to be more expensive, rising to an inflated €4 in places like Zarautz.

Maps

Cartography has been an art in Spain since the 12th-century Catalans charted their Mediterranean Empire in Europe's first great school of map-making. The tourist offices give out detailed maps of every town. Unfortunately, for rural areas you will not find the detail you need for serious exploration of the countryside and signposting isn't all it could be.

25 San Ginés, Sangenxo (Pontevedra).
26 Festa da Istoria, Ribadavia (Ourense); the whole village celebrates its origins with street pageantry and markets.
Last Week Gijón (Asturias); cider festival with free tasting and pouring competitions.
Last Sunday Vivero (Lugo), pilgrimage and music; *encierro*, Calahorra (La Rioja).
31 Loiola (Guipúzcoa), St Ignacio de Loiola Day; Battle of Flowers, Laredo (Cantabria).

September
First week San Sebastián, Basque food festival.
2 Lekeitio (Vizcaya), Basque 'goose games', including contest to pull the head off a goose with a greased neck.
6–10 Fiestas del Portal, Ribadavia (Ourense).
7–10 Pilgrimage of Nostra Señora da Barca, Muxía (A Coruña).
7–8 *Encierro*, Ampuero (Cantabria).
8 Fiesta of the Virgin of Guadalupe, Hondarrabia (Guipúzcoa); Fiesta de la Virgen de la Encina, Ponferrada (León); pilgrimage at Cebreiro (Lugo); San Andreu, Cervo (Lugo).
8–10 Fiesta of Santa Eufemia at Bermeo (Vizcaya).
8 Virgin's Birthday with celebrations in many places.
12 San Sebastián, International Film Festival.
2nd week Zarautz (Euzkadi), Basque fun and games.
16 Folk festival, Llanes (Asturias).
19 Oviedo, big Americas Day celebration, with floats and bands from all over Latin America; Logroño has the *Vendimia* wine festival of La Rioja.

Third weekend Americas Day, celebrating the many immigrants to the Americas from Asturias, Oviedo.
Last weekend San Cosme y San Damián, with antique dances, Covarrubias (Burgos).
27 Theft of the saints procession, Arnedo (La Rioja).
29 Fiesta de San Miguel, Oñati (Guipúzcoa); traditional Basque dancing at Markina (Vizcaya).

October
First Sunday *Las Cantaderas*, with medieval song and a sacred dance, León.
Second Sunday Shellfish festival, O Grove (Pontevedra).
13 Fiesta de San Fausto, Durango (Vizcaya).
18–20 Mondoñedo (Lugo), *As San Lucas*, big horse fair dating from the Middle Ages.

November
11 Fiesta de San Martín, Bueu (Galicia).
19 Fiesta de San Andrés, Estella (Navarra).
Last Sunday Oyster festival, Arcade (Pontevedra).

December
6 San Nicolás Obispillo, Segura (Guipúzcoa).
13 Santa Lucía fair, Zumárraga (Guipúzcoa).
21 Santo Tomás fair, with processions, San Sebastián, Bilbao, Azpeitia.
Last week *O Feitoman*, handicrafts fair, Vigo (Pontevedra); *Olentzero* processions in many Basque villages.
31 The National Offering to the Apostle – a major religious ceremony with the *bota-fumeiro* in Santiago de Compostela.

The maps available in Britain and America aren't very good, and you won't find much better general maps in Spain. On most, the road system in particular will be out of date, thanks to Spain's ambitious road improvement programmes.

Topographical maps for hikers and mountaineers can be obtained from CNIG (Centro Nacional de Información Geográfica), part of the Instituto Geográfico Nacional (IGN). There are shops in all provincial capitals, and their maps are usually available in larger bookshops. You can buy maps and travel books online from the Spanish travel bookshop Altaïr at *www.altair.es*.

If in the UK, visit Stanfords at 12 Long Acre, WC2, for the biggest selection. There are other branches at 29 Corn St, Bristol, t (0117) 929 9966; 39 Spring Gardens, Manchester t (0161) 831 0250, or you can buy online at *www.stanfords.co.uk*.

Media

The Socialist *El País* is Spain's biggest and best national newspaper, closely followed by the centre-right *El Mundo*, though circulation for both is low. Spaniards don't read newspapers; *¡Hola!* – the Spanish version of *Hello!* – and the little magazine with television listings and scandals are by far the best-selling periodicals.

Films are cheap, and the Spaniards are some of the world's great cinema-goers; though half of the great cinemas have been converted into discos, others are still magnificent. There are also lots of cheap outdoor cinemas in the summer. Look for films by Carlos Saura (*Carmen*, *Blood Wedding*, *El Dorado*), who is regarded as Buñuel's natural successor, Victor Erice or, most incredibly, Marx Brothers movies dubbed in Spanish. Another bright light is director Pedro Almodóvar (*Women on the Verge of a Nervous Breakdown* and Oscar-winning *All About My Mother*).

Major British newspapers are usually available in all tourist areas and big cities; the American New York *Herald Tribune*, the *Wall Street Journal*, and the awful *USA Today* are harder to find. Most hit the newsstands a day late; issues of *Time* and *Newsweek* often hang about, fading in the sun, til they find a home.

Money

Spain is one of the 12 European Union countries to use a single currency, the **euro** (€). Euro notes and coins, issued on 1 January 2002, replaced the *peseta*. Coins are issued in denominations of 1, 2, 5, 10, 20 and 50 cents and 1 and 2 euros. Notes are issued in denominations of 5, 10, 20, 50, 100, 200 and 500 euros. You can no longer use *pesetas*.

Beware of private exchange offices in tourist areas, which can be a rip-off despite the 'no commission' sign. You can sometimes change money at travel agencies, fancy hotels, restaurants and big department stores like El Corte Inglés. There are 24-hour *cambios* at most of the big train stations.

Wiring money from overseas entails no special difficulties; just give yourself two weeks to be on the safe side, and work through one of the larger institutions (Banco Central, Banco de Bilbao, Banco Español de Crédito, Banco Hispano Americano, Banco de Santander, Banco de Vizcaya). All transactions have to go through Madrid.

Credit cards are widely accepted at most shops and restaurants although, naturally, not bars. For purchases, you will have to show some ID (a passport or identity card) when using a credit card. Smaller hotels, pensiones, restaurants and cafés, particularly in rural areas, won't accept credit cards. Museums and monuments almost never have credit card facilities. The handiest way to keep yourself in cash is by using the automatic bank tellers that you'll find on street corners in most towns; they gorge out thousands of euros, so long as you can remember your PIN number.

Travellers' cheques, if they are from one of the major companies, will be simple to cash at most bank exchanges.

For bank opening hours, *see* **Opening Hours**.

Opening Hours

Most **banks** are open Mon–Fri 8.30–2 and Sat (mainly in winter) 8.30–1.

Most of the less important **churches** are always closed. Some cities probably have more churches than faithful communicants, so many churches are unused. If you're determined to see one, it will never be hard to find the *sacristán* or caretaker. Usually they live close by, and would be glad to show you around for a tip. Don't be surprised when cathedrals and famous churches charge for admission – just consider the cost of upkeep.

Shops usually open from 10am. Spaniards take their main meal at 2pm and, except in the larger cities, most shops close for 2–3 hours in the afternoon, usually from 1pm or 2pm. In the evening, most stay open until 7pm or 8pm.

Museums and historical sites tend to follow shop opening hours too, though abbreviated in the winter months; nearly all close on Mondays. We have tried to list the hours for the important sights. Seldom-visited ones have a raffish disregard for their official hours, or open only when the mood strikes them. Don't be discouraged: bang on doors and ask around.

Photography

Film is quite expensive everywhere; so is developing, but in any city there will be plenty of places where you can get processing done in a hurry. Serious photographers must give some consideration to the strong sunlight and high reflectivity of surfaces (pavements and buildings) in towns. If you're there during the summer, use ASA 100 film.

Pilgrim Facts

To be considered a pilgrim you have three choices of transport: foot, horse or bicycle. By foot, if you're reasonably fit and can clock off 30km (19 miles) a day, expect a journey of six weeks from Roncesvalles to Santiago; to enjoy the experience and take in all the monuments along or just off the way, give yourself two months. To get the Compostela certificate in Santiago (and the time off purgatory that goes with it) genuine pilgrims are expected to bring a letter of accreditation from their parish priest, from one of the world-wide confraternities, including the Confraternity of Saint James UK (for members only), c/o Marion Marples, 27 Blackfriars Rd, London, SE1 8 NY, www.csj.org.uk. The 'credential letter' (credencial in Spanish) must be stamped along the way in order for pilgrims to qualify for the Compostela certificate (you must complete 100km on foot, or 200km by bicycle). The credential letter also entitles you to stay free or very cheaply in the refugios run by towns, churches or monasteries along the way, although the accommodation is often little more than a place to lay a sleeping bag; note that they can have fairly early curfews. The footpath is well marked, though bear in mind that in most parts of the trip, especially in Castilla y León, you won't have a footpath at all, but a dusty verge along a busy highway. July and August may have the best weather for the trip, but also bring the most traffic. Spanish organizations devoted to helping pilgrims and answering questions include the Federación Española de Asociaciones de Amigos del Camino de Santiago, C/Ruavieja 3, Logroño-La Rioja, t 941 24 56 74, www.caminosantiago.org. There are numerous useful websites, including www.jacobeo.net (Spanish only), www.csj.org.uk (in English), and www.americanpilgrims.com (in English). The Spanish tourist offices can also provide basic information.

Police Business

Crime is not really a big problem in Spain, and Spaniards talk about it perhaps more than is warranted, though there are signs that the country is gradually catching up with the rest of us. Pickpocketing and robbing parked cars are the specialities; except for some quarters of the largest cities, walking around at night is no problem – partly because everybody does it. Crime is also spreading to the tourist areas; even there though, you're generally safer in Spain than you would be at home: the national crime rate is roughly a quarter of that in Britain.

Note that in Spain less than 8 grams of marijuana is legal; anything else may easily earn you the traditional 'six years and a day'. In Galicia, the traditional smuggling business has created a growing drug problem at home, along with some fierce vigilante efforts by locals to stop it.

There are several species of **police**, and their authority varies with the area. Franco's old goon squads, the Policía Armada, have been reformed and relatively demilitarized into the Policía Nacional, once known as 'chocolate drops' for their brown uniforms, but now they wear blue and white; their duties largely consist of driving around in cars and drinking coffee. They are respected more than the Policía Armada, at least since their first commander, Lt General José Antonio Sáenz de Santa María, ordered his men to surround the Cortés to foil Tejero's attempted coup in 1981, thereby proving that they were strongly on the side of the newly-born democracy.

The Policía Municipal (Udaltzainzoa in Basque) in some towns do control crime, while in others they are limited to directing traffic. Mostly in rural areas, you will see the Guardia Civil, with green uniforms. The Guardia is now most conspicuous as a highway patrol, assisting motorists and handing out tickets (ignoring 'no passing' zones is the easiest way to get one). Most traffic violations are payable on the spot; the traffic cops have a reputation for upright honesty.

The Basques don't want anything to do with any of these and have set up their own police force, the Ertzantza. You'll see them looking dapper in their red berets, waiting by the roadsides for motorists in a barely legal hurry.

Post Offices

Every city has one main post office (correos) and several smaller branches which are usually impossible to locate. The main post offices are usually open 8am–9pm and 9–1 on Saturdays. They are always crowded, but unless you have packages to send, you may not need ever to visit one. Most tobacconists sell stamps (*sellos*) and they'll usually know the correct postage for whatever you're sending. Post everything air mail (*por avión*) and don't send postcards unless you don't care when they arrive. Mailboxes are bright yellow and scarce.

There is also, of course, the poste restante (general delivery). In Spain this is called *lista de correos*, and it is as chancy as anywhere else. Don't confuse post offices with the *Caja Postal*, the postal savings banks, which look just like them.

Public Holidays

The Spanish, like the Italians, try to have as many as possible. Everything closes on:

1 January New Year's Day
6 January Epiphany
Holy Thursday (March/April)
Good Friday (March/April)
1 May Labour Day
May/June *Corpus Christi*
25 July *Santiago Apóstol* (St James's Day)
15 August *Asunción* (Assumption)
12 October *Día de la Hispanidad*
(Columbus Day)
1 November *Todos los Santos* (All Saints' Day)
6 December *Día de la Constitución*
(Constitution Day)
8 December *Immaculada Concepción*
(Immaculate Conception)
25 December *Navidad* (Christmas Day)

Smoking

A new law banning smoking in offices, shops, schools, hospitals, cultural centres and on public transport was introduced on 1 January, 2006.

Sports and Activities

Football has pride of place in the Spanish heart, though you will not often find Athletic Club de Bilbao or any of the other northern teams except A Coruña challenging the dominance of Real Madrid and Barcelona.

Bullfighting and **cycling** vie for second place; all are regularly shown on television which, despite a heavy fare of dubbed American shows, everyone is inordinately fond of watching. Euskadi has its own stations, and on some rainy night in your hotel you may have the treat of seeing John Wayne dubbed into Basque.

Cycling

Cycling is taken extremely seriously in Spain and you don't often see people using a bike as a form of transport. Instead, Lycra-clad enthusiasts pedal furiously up the steepest of hills on weekends, causing dire traffic hazards while they strive to reach the standards set by Miguel Indurain, the Navarrese winner of the Tour de France for three years running. If you want to bring your own bicycle to Spain, you can make arrangements by ferry or train; by air, you'll almost always have to dismantle your bike to some extent and pack it in some kind of crate. Each airline seems to have its own policy.

In summer the moderate climate of the Basque lands, Cantabria, Asturias and Galicia, with their greenery and network of coastal secondary roads, make them perfect spots for cycling. It's probably the current transport of choice among pilgrims to Santiago; pedalling across the frying pan of northern Castille in August is appropriately a lot like purgatory.

Fishing and Hunting

Fishing and hunting are long-standing Spanish obsessions, and you'll need to get a licence for both. Freshwater fishing permits (*permisos de pesca*) are issued from the Consejería de Agricultura y Pesca (Agriculture and Fishing Council), which has an office in each of the the provincial capital cities. A maritime recreational fishing licence (1st and 3rd Class) is required for fishing from the shore or from a boat near the coast; get it from the Delegación Provincial de la Consejería de Agricultura y Pesca, which also has an office in each provincial capital city (tourist information offices can provide addresses). For more **information contact** the Spanish Fishing Federation (Federación Española de Pesca y

Casting), Navas de Tolosa 3, 28013 Madrid, t/f 91 532 83 52, *www.fepyc.es*

Deep-sea fishermen need to obtain a 5-year licence from the provincial Comandancias de Marina. **Information** on the best fishing waters and boat rentals can be obtained from the Directorate General of Sea Fishing, Subsecretaria de la Marina Mercante, Ministerio de Comercio, Calle Ruiz de Alarcón 1, Madrid.

You may bring sporting guns to Spain, but you must declare them on arrival and present a valid firearms certificate with a Spanish translation bearing a consulate stamp. **Hunters** (boar and deer are the big game, with quail, hare, partridges and pigeons, and ducks and geese along the coasts in the winter) are obliged to get a licence (*permiso de caza*) from the local autonomous community, presenting their passports and record of insurance coverage.

Information: the Spanish tourist office, or Spanish Hunting Federation (Federación Española de Caza), C/Francos Rodríguez 70, 28039 Madrid, t 91 311 14 11, *www.fedecaza.com*.

Golf

English settlers built Spain's first golf course at the Rio Tinto mines in Andalucía in the 19th century, and since the advent of Severiano Ballesteros (whose home course is the Real Golf de Pedreña in Santander) Spaniards too have gone nuts for the game. The sunny warm winters, combined with greens of international tournament standard, attract golfing enthusiasts from all over the world throughout the year. Any real-estate agent on the coast hoping to sell villas to foreigners, especially Scandinavians and the latest newcomers, the Japanese, stands little chance of closing a deal unless his property is within 10 minutes of a golf course.

Most places hire out golf clubs. Green fees have taken a leap in recent years, however, and even the humblest clubs will charge at least €20 in low season. Many hotels cater specifically for the golfer and there are numerous tour operators specializing in golf packages. **Information**: any Spanish tourist office, or the Royal Spanish Golf Federation, Capitán Haya 9–5, 28020 Madrid, t 91 555 26 82, *www. golfspainfederation.com*.

Hiking and Mountaineering

Spain's sierras attract thousands of hikers and mountaineers. Los Picos de Europa and the Pyrenees are by far the most popular, though there are also some lovely hikes in El Bierzo of western León and Os Ancares of eastern Galicia.

The tourist office or the Spanish Mountaineering Federation provide a list of *refugios*, which offer mountain shelter in many places. Some are well equipped and can supply food. Most, however, do not, so take your own sleeping bags, cooking equipment and food with you.

Hiking boots are essential, as is a detailed map of the area, issued by the Instituto Geográfico Nacional, or the Servicio Geográfico Ejército. **Information**: Federación Española de Deportes de Montaña y Escalada, C/Floridablanca 84, Barcelona, t 93 426 4267, *www.fedme.es*.

Tennis

There is equal fervour in Spain for tennis as for golf, inspired by recently retired international champion Arantxa Sánchez Vicario, and current favourites like Conchita Martínez, Carlos Moya, Felix Mantilla and Alex Corretja. Every resort hotel has its own courts; municipal ones tend to be rare or hard to get to. **Information**: Royal Spanish Tennis Federation, Avenida Diagonal 618, 08021 Barcelona, t 93 201 08 44, *www.rfet.es*.

Telephones

Emergency numbers:

Emergencies: t 112 (this is a pan-European number for all emergency services).
Police, t 091.
Fire Brigade t 080

Calls within Spain are expensive (€0.25–0.80 for a short local call), and overseas calls from Spain are among the most expensive in Europe: calls to the UK cost about €2 a minute, to the USA substantially more. Most tobacconists sell PIN number phonecards that make international phone calls much cheaper.

Public phone booths have instructions in English and accept phonecards, available from newsstands, tobacconists and post offices. In some Spanish phone booths, there will also be a little slide on top that holds coins.

In every big city (and many smaller ones) in Spain there are calling centres (*locutorios*), where you call from metered booths. They offer cheap international calls, but national calls or calls to mobiles are expensive . They open and close with alarming frequency and can usually be found around bus and train stations. Expect to pay a big surcharge if you do any telephoning from your hotel or any public place that does not have a coin slot. Cheap rate is from 10pm–8am Monday–Saturday and all day Sunday and public holidays.

For calls to Spain from the UK, dial 00 followed by the country code (34), the area code and the number. For international calls from Spain, dial 00 and then the country code, etc. Spanish telephone codes are incorporated into the telephone numbers: all numbers in this guide are listed as they must be dialled.

Toilets

Apart from bus and train stations, public facilities are rare in Spain. On the other hand, every bar on every corner has a toilet; don't feel uncomfortable using it without purchasing something – the Spaniards do it all the time. Just ask for *los servicios* and take your own toilet paper to be on the safe side.

Tourist Information

After receiving millions of tourists each year for the last four decades, no country has more information offices, or more helpful ones, or more intelligent brochures and detailed maps. Every city will have an office, and you will almost always find someone who speaks English except in rural areas. Sometimes they'll be less helpful in the big cities in the summer. More often, though, you'll be surprised at how well they know the details of accommodation and transportation.

Many large cities also maintain **municipal tourist offices**, though they're not as well equipped as those run by the Ministry of Tourism, better known as **Turismo**. Hours for most offices are Monday to Friday, 9.30–1.30 and 4–7, Saturday mornings only and closed on Sundays.

Where to Stay

Hotels in Spain are no longer the bargains they once were. However, overall rates are still pretty reasonable (above all by comparison with Britain), and there are still some great bargains to be had. For those travelling on a

Accommodation Price Ranges

Note: Prices listed here and elsewhere in the book are for a double room with bathroom.

luxury over €180

expensive €130–180

moderate €80–130

inexpensive €50–80

budget under €50

tight budget, there are plenty of *hostales* (generally one- or two-star places), rooms over bars, and rooms in private homes. One thing you can still count on is a consistent level of quality and service; the Spanish government regulates hotels more intelligently, and more closely, than any other Mediterranean country. Room prices must be posted in the hotel lobbies and in the rooms, and if there's any problem you can ask for the complaints book, or *Libro de Reclamaciones*. No one ever writes anything in these; any written complaint must be passed on to the authorities immediately. Hotel keepers would always rather correct the problem for you.

The prices given in this guide are for double rooms with ensuite bathrooms (unless stated otherwise) but do not include VAT (IVA) charged at 7 per cent in hotels. No VAT is charged on other categories of accommodation. Prices for single rooms will average about 60% of a double, while triples or an extra bed are around 35 per cent more. Within the price ranges shown, the most expensive are likely to be in the big cities, while the cheapest places are always in provincial towns.

On the whole, prices are surprisingly consistent. No government could resist the chance, however, to insert a little bureaucratic confusion, and the wide range of accommodation in Spain is classified in a complex system. Look for the little **blue plaques** next to the doors of all *hoteles*, *hostales*, etc. which identify the classification and number of stars.

If you're travelling around a lot, a good investment would be the government publication *Guía de Hoteles*, a great fat book with every classified hotel and *hostal* in Spain, available in many bookshops (€10). The government also publishes similar guides to holiday flats (*apartamentos turísticos*) and campsites.

Local tourist information offices will have a complete accommodation list for their province, and some can be very helpful with finding a room when things are tight.

Paradores

The government, in its plan to develop tourism in the 1950s, started this nationwide chain of classy hotels to draw some attention to little-visited areas. They restored old palaces, castles and monasteries for the purpose, furnished them with antiques and installed fine restaurants featuring local specialities. *Paradores* for many people are one of the best reasons for visiting Spain. Not all *paradores* are historic landmarks; in resort areas, they are as likely to be cleanly designed modern buildings, usually in a good location with a pool and some sports facilities. As their popularity has increased, so have their prices; in most cases both the rooms and the restaurant will be the most expensive in town.

Paradores are classed as three- or four-star hotels, and their prices range from €95 in remote provincial towns to €135 and upwards for the most popular. They are open all year round and offer substantial off-season discounts. There are also discounts for the over-60s and the under-30s (but these must be booked in advance, more information under 'offers and promotions' on their website). There is also a good-value pass called the Five-night Card, which offers five nights in any parador for a substantial discount. If you can afford a *parador*, there is no better place to stay. We've mentioned most of them throughout this book.

Advance Booking

Spain: Head office, C/Requena 3, 28013, Madrid **t** 91 516 66 66.

UK: Keytel International, 402 Edgware Road, London W2 1ED, **t** (020) 7616 0300, www.keytel.co.uk.

USA: Marketing Ahead Inc., 381 Park Ave South, Suite 718, New York, NY 10016, **t** 800 223 1356, *www.marketingahead.com*.

More information at *www.parador.es*. Look out for their special offers.

Hotels

Hoteles (H) are rated from one to five stars, according to the services they offer. These are the most expensive places, and even a one-star hotel will be a comfortable, middle-range establishment. *Hotel Residencias* (HR) are the same, only without a restaurant. Many of the more expensive hotels have some rooms available at prices lower than those listed. They won't tell you, though; you'll have to ask.

You can often get discounts in the off-season but will be charged higher rates during important festivals. These are supposedly regulated, but in practice hoteliers charge whatever they can get. If you want to attend any of these big events, be sure to book your hotel as far in advance as possible.

Hostales and Pensiones

Hostales (Hs) and *Pensiones* (P) are rated with from one to three stars. These are usually more modest places, often a floor in an apartment block; a two-star *hostal* is roughly equivalent to a one-star hotel, but not always. *Pensiones* may require full- or half-board; there aren't many of these establishments, only a few in resort areas. *Hostal Residencias* (HsR), like *hotel residencias*, do not offer meals except breakfast, and not always that. Of course, *hostales* and *pensiones* with one or two stars will often have cheaper rooms without private baths.

Some cheap *hostales* in ports and big cities can be crummy and noisy beyond belief – as you lie there unable to sleep, you can only marvel at the human body's ability to produce such a wealth of unidentifiable sounds, coming through the paper-thin walls of the room next door. Don't worry too much though: the vast majority will be clean, welcoming places run by nice families that go out of their way to keep up the place.

Fondas, Casas de Huéspedes and Camas

The bottom of the scale is occupied by the *fonda* (F) and *casa de huéspedes* (CH), little different from a one-star *hostal*, though usually cheaper. Off the scale completely are hundreds of unclassified cheap places, usually rooms in an apartment or over a bar and identified only by a little sign reading *camas* (beds) or *habitaciones* (rooms). You can also ask in bars or at the tourist office for unidentified *casas particulares*, private houses with a room or two. In fact, in most towns and resorts you will

not have to look at all. Someone will probably find you in the bus or train station, and ask you if you need a room. Almost all of these will be pleasant enough. Prices are usually negotiable (before you are taken to the place, of course). Always make sure the location of the place suits you – 'five minutes away' can mean five minutes on foot, or ten minutes in a car with a hell-bent Spanish driver.

In many villages these rooms will be the only accommodation on offer, but they're usually clean – Spanish women are manic housekeepers. The best will be in small towns and villages, and around universities. Occasionally you'll find a room over a bar, run by somebody's grandmother, that is nicer than a four-star hotel – complete with frilly pillows, lovely old furnishings, and a shrine to the Virgin Mary. The worst are inevitably found in industrial cities or dull modern ones. It always helps to see the room first.

In cities, the best places to look are right in the centre, not around the bus and train stations. Many inexpensive establishments will ask you to pay a day in advance.

Alternative Accommodation

Youth hostels exist in Spain, but they're rarely worth the trouble. Most are open only in the summer; there are the usual inconveniences and silly rules, and often hostels are in out-of-the-way locations. Worst of all, they are usually full of noisy school groups. You'll be better off with the inexpensive *hostales* and *fondas* – sometimes these are even cheaper than youth hostels – or ask at the local tourist office for rooms that might be available in **university dormitories**.

If you fancy some peace and tranquillity, the national tourist office has a list of 64 **monasteries** and **convents** that welcome guests. Accommodation and meals are simple and guests can usually take part in the religious ceremonies.

Camping

Campsites are rated from one to three stars, depending on their facilities, and in addition to the ones listed in the official government handbook there are always others, rather primitive, that are unlisted. On the whole camping is a good deal, and facilities in most first-class sites include shops, restaurants, bars, laundries, hot showers, first aid, swimming pools, telephones and, occasionally, a tennis court. Caravans (campers) converge on all the more developed sites, but if you just want to pitch your little tent or sleep out in some quiet field, ask around in the bars or at likely farms.

Camping is forbidden in many forest areas because of fears of fire, as well as on the beaches (though you can often get close to some quieter shores if you're discreet). If you're doing some hiking, bring a sleeping bag and stay in the free **refugios** along the major trails.

Information: the government handbook *Guía Oficial de Campings* can be found in most bookstores and at the Spanish tourist office. For further details contact the Camping and Caravan Club, Greenfields House, Westwood Way, Coventry CV4 8JH, **t** (024) 7669 4995 (membership necessary, £24–28) or Federación Española de Empresarios de Campings, San Bernardo 97–99, Edificio Colomina, 28015 Madrid, **t** 91 448 12 34, where reservations for sites can also be made.

Private Homes, Self-catering Accommodation and *Casas Rurales*

With the rise in hotel prices, self-catering accommodation has become an increasingly popular way of vacationing in Spain. *Casas rurales*, rural accommodation in farms or country houses, has become extremely popular and is a wonderful way to enjoy the spectacular countryside of northern Spain. Some are rented whole, while others offer B&B accommodation. Provincial tourist information offices have full lists of *casas rurales* and other self-catering properties. A very useful website is *www.toprural.com*, which lists all kinds of rural accommodation throughout Spain and is also in English. This type of accommodation is also called *Agriturismo*, or *Turismo Rural*, or in Basque (wait for it) *Nekazalturismoa*

There are also numerous private firms offering self-catering accommodation. These can be anything from modern bungalows to the bottom floor of a traditional half-timbered cottage; some places are simply large, purpose-built houses with a number of rooms. Kitchen facilities may or may not be available. Prices generally fall in the range of €25–80 per day for a double room. Here are a few firms that arrange self-catering holidays in the north:

In the UK
Casas Cantabricas, 31 Arbury Road, Cambridge, CB4 2JB, **t** (01223) 328 721, *www.casas.co.uk*. Holiday houses and small hotels.

Individual Travellers, Manor Court, Bignor, Pulborough, West Sussex, RH20 1QD, **t** 08700 780 194, *www.indiv-travellers.com*. Village and rural accommodation in farmhouses and cottages.

Keytel International, 402 Edgware Road, London, W2 1ED, **t** (020) 7616 0300, *paradors@keytel.com*, *www.keytel.co.uk*.

Magic of Spain, 227 Shepherd's Bush Road, London W6 7AS, **t** 0800 980 3378, *www.magictravelgroup.co.uk*. Apartments and hotels along the coast.

Travellers' Way, The Barns, Hewell Lane, Tardebigge, Bromsgrove, Worcs B60 1LP, **t** (01527)573700, *www.travellersway.co.uk*. Self-catering and hotels along the coast, in mountain villages and in the cities.

In the USA
The Spanish Tourist board in Spain (*www.okspain.org*) has a list of tour operators in the USA which specialise in travel to Spain.

EC Tours, 12500 Riverside Drive, Suite 206 Toluca Lake, CA 91602, **t** 800 388 0877, *www.ectours.com*. Hotels, flights, accommodation in hotels, villas and apartments.

Spain4Rent, *www.spain4rent.com*. Online villa rental company, with properties throughout northern Spain.

Women Travellers

On the whole, the horror stories of sexual harassment in Spain are a thing of the past – unless you dress provocatively and hang out by the bus station after dark. All Spaniards seem to melt when they see blondes, so if you're fair you're in for a tougher time.

Even Spanish women sunbathe topless these days at the international resorts, but do be discreet elsewhere, especially if you are near small villages.

Apart from in resorts on the coast, it often tends to be the older men who comment on your appearance as a matter of course. Whether you can understand what is being said or not, it is best to ignore them without being rude.

Navarra and La Rioja

Approaches from France:
  Down the Valleys of the Pyrenees 72
Pamplona (Iruña) 79
East of Pamplona: Sangüesa, Javier and Leyre **87**
South of Pamplona to Tudela **91**
Northwest of Pamplona:
  Aralar and San Miguel in Excelsis **94**
Southwest of Pamplona: the Camino de Santiago **96**
Estella (Lizarra): Town of the Star **97**
La Rioja 101
Logroño **102**
Calahorra and La Rioja Baja **104**
South of Logroño: Into the Sierra **107**
Along the Pilgrim Route: West of Logroño **108**
Wine Towns in Rioja Alta **114**

Navarra & La Rioja

Highlights

1 Running of the Bulls, at the Los Sanfermines festival in Pamplona
2 Atmospheric Estella, 'Town of the Star'
3 Chickens in church, Santo Domingo de la Calzada
4 Wine bodegas of Rioja Alta
5 Thousands of dinosaur footprints around Préjano

Europe's traditional front door to Spain, Navarra is also a good introduction to the Spanish plurals, the 'Spains' combining a sizeable, often nationalistic Basque minority up in the misty western Pyrenees and a conservative, non-Basque Navarrese majority tending the sunny vineyards and gardens of the Ebro valley flatlands to the south. The combination (in Spain both sides are known as tough cookies lacking polish) hasn't always been comfortable, and only now that much of the population has abandoned the countryside have tensions between the two groups loosened up.

As everyone must know by now, much of this 'loosening up' is concentrated in Pamplona, the capital both groups share, into an ecstatic week-long bacchanalia of inebriated recklessness, bull running and partying known as 'Los Sanfermines'.

Roads from Navarra – most importantly, the Camino de Santiago – flow naturally southwest into the autonomous *comunidad* of La Rioja, celebrated far out of proportion to its size for its red wine with the distinctive vanilla flavour. Historically coveted by the two whales on either side of it – Navarra and Castile – this shrimp has blossomed in the new federal Spain, as evidenced by the brash new *bodegas* that have sprouted up along every wine road.

Navarra: A Potted History

To understand the standoffish, weird James Dean role Navarra traditionally plays, you need a bit of Spanish history, which is full of the phrase 'except Navarra'. Even in 'the nation of nations' the region has stood apart ever since 605, when the Franks tried to harness it as part of the Duchy of Vasconia, a huge untenable territory that extended from the Garonne to the Ebro. Charlemagne himself came down in 778, either to discipline the unruly duchy or to force it to join his fight against the Moors, and after razing the walls of Pamplona he went stumping back to France – except for his rear guard, which the furious Basques of Pamplona ambushed in 778 at the pass of Roncesvalles ('Valley of the Thorntrees').

Charlemagne taught the Navarrese that owing nothing to nobody was the way to go, and within a few years of his passing they created the independent kingdom of Navarra. Its most talented king, Sancho III 'the Great' (1004–34), firmly established the *camino francés* through Navarra and controlled much of French Basque country and Galicia, and pocketed Castile and León after the death of its last count, setting up his son Ferdinand I as the first to take the title of 'King of the Spains'. The centre was too precocious to hold, and by the time of Sancho IV (1054–76) Navarra was once again a fierce rival of Castile, but avoided entanglements – marital or martial – by playing the French card. 'The Flea between Two Monkeys', as it became known, was ruled by three different French dynasties between 1234 and 1512, when Ferdinand the Catholic slyly demanded that Navarra let his armies march through to France. His demand, as he anticipated, was refused and he used the refusal as an excuse to grab Navarra south of the Pyrenees. France was left with only Basse Navarre, a thimble-sized realm but one that gave her a long line of kings, with the accession of Henri IV (1589–1610). Ferdinand kept the Navarrese happy by maintaining their *fueros* (or privileges), which in practice gave the region an independence enjoyed by no other in Spain; it was ruled by a viceroy, minted its own coins and had its own government. Napoleonic and Liberal attempts to do away with the *fueros* in the cause of central unity turned the Navarrese into fierce reactionaries and the most ardent of Carlists (supporters of the pretender, Charles III). In the 1930s Navarra rejected the Republic's offer of autonomy; instead, the Navarrese Carlist *requetés* in their distinctive red berets became some of Franco's best troops, fighting for their old privileges and Catholicism – just as the Basques were, only on the Republican side. Franco rewarded Navarra by leaving the *fueros* intact, making it the only autonomous region in Spain until his death.

Approaches from France: Down the Valleys of the Pyrenees

The Navarrese Pyrenees don't win altitude records, but they're green, wooded and shot through with legends, many lingering in the mists around Roncesvalles, for centuries the pass most favoured by French pilgrims. Much of Navarra's Basque population is concentrated in the three valleys of Roncal, Salazar and Baztán where seemingly every house in every hamlet is emblazoned with a coat of arms – for the Basques have traditionally considered themselves all equal and therefore all noble.

The Eastern Valleys: Valle del Roncal and Valle de Salazar

Like many Pyrenean valleys, the Roncal was so remote for centuries that the central authorities were content to let it run its own show. Time has changed a few things: timber logged on its thickly forested slopes now travels by truck instead of careering down the Esca River, and the valley's renowned sheep's cheese, *queso de Roncal*, is now made in a factory (but according to farm traditions). Mist often envelops **Isaba**, the Valle del Roncal's biggest town, gathered under its fortress church of **San Cipriano** (1540). Every 13 July since 1375, at stone frontier marker no.262, the mayor of Isaba and his colleagues don traditional costume, march up to meet their counterparts from the Valle de Baretous in France and ask them three times for the 'Tribute of the Three Cows', in exchange for the right to graze their herds in the Valle del Roncal in August – something both sides used to kill for before the annual tribute was agreed on. Isaba

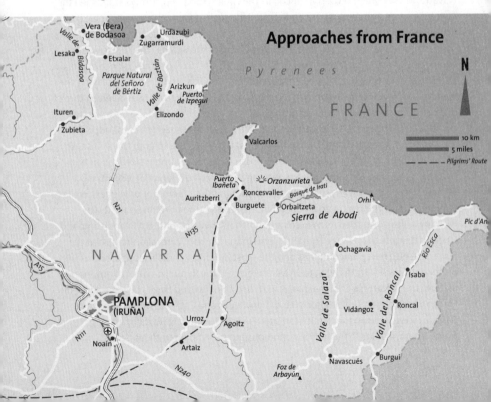

provides an excellent base for exploring the magnificent mountain scenery: hike up
the region's highest peaks, **Pic d'Anie** (8,200ft) and **Mesa de los Tres Reyes** (7,900ft), or
make the most beautiful walk of all, into the Parque Natural Pirenáico to the **refugio
de Belagua** (*t 948 394 002*), set in a stunning glacial amphitheatre.

Roncal, once the capital of the valley, is a pretty village surrounded by pine forests. The
great, amiable Basque tenor Julián Gayarre (1844–90) was born here and lies buried
in a suitably high operatic tomb just outside town; the **Casa-Museo Julián Gayarre**
(*open Apr–Sept Tues–Sun 11.30–1.30 and 5–7; Oct–Mar Sat–Sun 11.30–1.30 and 4–6;
adm*) contains costumes and photos from his glory days. **Burgui**, south, has a Roman
bridge, and two roads that cut over to the Valle de Salazar: an easy one westward to
Navascués and a narrow one northward by way of the remote village of Vidángoz.

The sparsely populated **Valle de Salazar** is much less visited but just as lovely,
abubble with trout streams, beech forests and old, white stone, Basque chalet-like
caserónes with their pompous coats of arms. The best line the riverfront and cobbled
lanes in **Ochagavía**, the local metropolis and another good base for walks. An easy
one is up to the 13th-century chapel of **Santa María de Muskilda**, topped by an
unusual square tower with a round roof: its *romería* on 8 September is celebrated
with some of Navarra's most ancient dances.

To the north, a road twists through the Sierra de Abodi to the snow-white hermitage
of Nuestra Señora de las Nieves (1954): from here, trails of varying length and difficulty
lead into the vast beech and ancient yew **Forest of Irati**, the largest primeval forest in
Spain, with majestic Mt Orhi (6,618ft) as a backdrop. This is one of the richest wildlife
habitats in the Pyrenees, full of red squirrels, deer and wild boar, with lesser populations
of wild cat and beech marten. The area also contains a couple of real rarities: the white-
backed woodpecker, found only where there are plenty of insect-ridden beech trees; and
the endemic Pyrenean Desvan, a kind of aquatic shrew with a nose like a dragon's snout.
Besides the usual Basque fairy folk, the forest is haunted by the ghost of Jeanne d'Albret,
queen of Navarra and mother of Henri IV, a nasty, diehard Protestant fanatic. Poisoned
in 1572, Jeanne tours her old domain on windy nights escorted by Basque *lamias* or
nymphs, with whom she never would have been caught dead while still alive. On the
other side of the forest the picturesque village of **Orbaitzeta** makes a good base for
explorations; nearby, a dolmen called **Azpegi I** is surrounded by a circle of 123 stones.

To the south, the spectacular 1,000ft sheer-sided limestone gorge, the **Foz de Arbayún**,
extends for 10km below the road, home to Spain's largest colonies of rare griffon vultures
(*buitres leonados*) with their 8-ft wingspan, and an assortment of smaller eagles; you
can nearly always spot them floating majestically around the roadside belvedere
between Navascués and Lumbier. Manmade wonders, Leyre and Sangüesa, are just
south (*see* pp.87–91).

Roncesvalles (Orreaga)

Of all the passes over the Pyrenees, introverted Roncesvalles was the most renowned
in the Middle Ages. French pilgrims would mumble verses from the *Chanson de Roland*
as they paid their respects to the sites associated with Charlemagne and his nephew
Roland, then say their first prayer to another gallant knight, Santiago. From Roncesvalles'

Getting Around

By Bus

There are no trains here; and in most cases the buses from Pamplona go only once a day.

La Tafallesa: t 94 870 203. Serves the Valle del Roncal, stopping at Yesa, near the lake, and 4km from the monastery of Leyre (*see* below).

Roncalesa: t 94 830 02 57. Also serves the Valle del Roncal.

Río Irati: t 94 822 14 70. For the Valles de Salazar and Aezkoa; one bus daily to Ochagavía, and one to Orbaizeta.

La Montañesa: t 94 821 15 84. For Roncesvalles, you can go as far as Burguete and walk 3km.

La Baztanesa: t 94 822 67 12. Serves the Valle de Baztán.

Artieda, t 94 830 02 87. Has twice-daily services (one on Sat and none on Sun) from Pamplona to Roncesvalles.

Tourist Information

Ochagavía: t 94 889 06 41, *oit.ochagavia@cfnavarra.es*

Roncal: Calle Iriartea s/n, **t** 94 847 52 56, *oit.roncal@cfnavarra.es*.

Where to Stay and Eat

Navarra as a whole has made efforts to improve reasonably priced accommodation. Traditional houses have been restored as *casas rurales*, or bed and breakfasts: write to the Pamplona tourist office for their *Guía de Alojamientos de Turismo Rural*, or see *www.navarra.es*, which has a comprehensive list (Spanish only)

Valle del Roncal ✉ 31680

***Isaba, C/Bormapea 51, Isaba, **t** 94 889 30 00, *hotelisaba@ctv.es, www.husalamontana.com* (*moderate*). Modern, luxurious and with every imaginable facility, including sauna and gym.

*Hs Lola, Mendigatxa 17, Isaba, **t** 94 889 30 12, *www.hostallola.com* (*moderate*). Welcoming little place with comfy rooms and a decent, reasonably priced restaurant.

*Hotel Ezkaurre, Garagardoia 14, Isaba, **t** 94 889 33 03, (*inexpensive*). Tucked away down a back street, this classic mountain *hostal* has comfortable rooms and a cosy top-floor sitting room, complete with fireplace and stunning mountain views.

Colegiata it's 781km (485 miles) to Compostela, a distance the fittest pilgrims could cover in 20 days. The Colegiata had a sad, has-been look back in the 1970s, when the medieval floods of pilgrims had dried to a trickle of eccentrics. No one predicted that in the 1990s the number of pilgrims who stopped to have their documents stamped would grow by the thousands each year, especially in the last Holy Year, 2004.

The three main pilgrims' routes from France converged at Saint-Jean-Pied-de-Port and then continued up to the busy frontier town of **Valcarlos**, the 'carlos' in its name referring to Charlemagne, who was camped here when he heard the dying Roland's horn blast. From here the road winds up through lush greenery to Roncesvalles, where the 12th-century church of **Sancti Spiritus** (the 'Silo de Charlemagne') is said to have been first built as Roland's tomb. According to legend, by the time the emperor arrived not only were Roland and the peers dead, but so were all the Saracens; since he couldn't tell who was who (poor Charlemagne – his legends always make him seem as thick as a pudding), he asked heaven for a sign to make sure he gave all the Franks a Christian burial, and all at once the Christian corpses looked up to heaven, with red roses sprouting from their lips. Equally unlucky pilgrims were laid in the 7th-century **ossuary** underneath; according to Aymeric Picaud, author of the first guide to the Camino de Santiago, many of these were done in by 'false pilgrims', most

*Hs Zaltua, Castillo 23, Roncal, t 94 847 50 08
(*inexpensive*). A pleasant, if basic, *hostal* in
the centre of town.
Pensión Begoña, C/Castillo 118, Roncal,
t 94 847 50 56 (*inexpensive*). Spic and span,
near the centre.
Pensión Txiki, Mendigatxa 17, Isaba, t 94 889
31 18 (*inexpensive*). This place offers
reasonable half-board above a restaurant
and bar.
Pensión Txabalkua, Izargentea 16, Isaba,
t 94 889 30 83 (*budget*). One of the cheapest
options for half-board rates.
Tapia, Bormapea 23, Isaba, t 94 889 30 13
(*budget*). Serves regional dishes and *platos
combinados*, all reasonably priced and
reliably good.
In Roncal itself choose between:
There are several *casas rurales* in and around
Roncal: visit the website (Spanish only)
www.roncal-salazar.com for full details or
contact the tourist office. The website
www.toprural.com is available in several
languages.

Ochagavía ✉ 31680

Most accommodation in the Salazar valley is
in *casas rurales (see above for websites)*.

**Hs Salazar, C/Mayor s/n, t 94 889 00 53,
f 94 889 03 70 (*moderate*). In Oronz, just
south of Ochagavía, with a swimming pool
and pretty views.
Auñamendi, Pza Gurpide 1, t 94 889 01 89,
auniamendi@jet.es (*moderate*). Some of
the smaller rooms are *inexpensive*; serves
trout with ham and a good asparagus and
prawn pudding. *Closed mid-Sept–mid-Oct.*
Casa Ballent, t 94 889 03 73 (*inexpensive*).
One of the best, with just 3 cosy bedrooms,
a welcoming owner and views from the
terrace over the Pyrenees and the
communal vegetable patch.
*Hs Orialde, C/Urrutia 6, t 94 889 00 27
(*budget*). A 12-bedroom place featuring
Basque cooking in the kitchen. *Open
July–Oct.*

Orbaitzeta ✉ 31670

There are no hotels here, and only a handful
of *casas rurales*.
Casa Mujurdin, t 94 876 60 46 (*budget*). Has
just two rooms with shared bath in a classic
Basque stone house.
Casa Sastrarena, t 94 876 60 93 (*budget*).
Offers rooms with private bath and a pretty
garden, for a marginally higher price.

of them Navarrese, 'expert in all deeds of violence, fierce and savage, dishonest and
false, imperious and rude, cruel and quarrelsome' and worse. Adjacent, the tiny
church of Santiago (*open daily 10–2 and 3.30–5.30; adm, combined adm with Silo
available, see above*) is a plain Gothic chapel from the 13th century.

Set back from the road, the **Colegiata de Roncesvalles** is a French-style Gothic church
consecrated in 1219, replacing the first Colegiata, built up at Puerto Ibañeta in 1127;
after five ghastly winters the frostbitten monks moved down to the foot of the pass.
What was originally the front of the church caved in under the snow in 1600 (hence
the incongruous corrugated zinc roof on the rest) and was replaced by a **cloister**, from
where you can pop into the 14th-century chapterhouse to see the stained glass (1960)
showing a scene from the 1212 battle of Las Navas de Tolosa, where Sancho VII the
Strong led the Navarrese to their greatest victory over the Moors. The chains in the
chapel are among those that bound 10,000 slaves at the ankle and wrist, forming a
human shield around the emir's tent, a scurvy tactic that failed to prevent the Christians
from leaping over and carrying off the tent as booty. The chapterhouse holds the **tomb
of Sancho the Strong**. Apparently in life the king was exactly as tall as his 7ft 4in effigy:
pilgrims used to think that his battle maces, now in the museum, belonged to Roland.
Sancho financed the Colegiata, which over time has been stripped of its costly gifts,

Roland the Rotter

All over the Pyrenees, you'll find memories of Roland – from the *Brèche de Roland* in the High Pyrenees, hewn with a mighty stroke of his sword Durandal, to a menhir on Monte Aralar that he tossed like Obelix. From here, his fame spread across the whole of Europe, remembered in everything from Ariosto's Renaissance epic *Orlando Furioso* to the ancient, mysterious statue of 'Roland the Giant' that stands in front of Bremen city hall.

But who is this Roland really? Outside of the *Chanson de Roland*, information is scarce. The chronicler Eginhardt, writing *c.* 830, mentions a certain Roland, Duke of the Marches of Brittany – who perished in Charles the Great's famous ambush in the Pyrenees in 778 – without according him any particular importance. Two hundred years later this obscure incident had blossomed into one of the great epics of medieval Europe.

Here is the mighty hero, with his wise friend and companion-in-arms Oliver. Here is the most puissant knight in the army of his uncle Charlemagne, come down from the north to crusade against the heathen Muslims of Spain. Charlemagne sweeps all before him, occupying many lands south of the Pyrenees and burning Pamplona to the ground before coming to grief at an unsuccessful siege of Zaragoza. On their return, Roland and Oliver and the peers of the rearguard are trapped at the pass of Roncesvalles, thanks to a tip from Roland's jealous stepfather Ganelon. Numberless hordes of paynims overwhelm the French; though outnumbered, they cut down Saracens by the thousands, like General Custer or John Wayne against the savage Injuns. Finally Roland, cut with a thousand wounds, smites his sword Durandal against the rock, meaning to keep it from the hands of the infidels (although in the *Chanson* he ends up heaving it in the air, whereupon it finally ends up stuck in the cliff at Rocamadour, a major site on the pilgrims' road in southwest France). He then sounds his horn Oliphant to warn Charlemagne, who alas is too far away to rescue them, puffing so hard that he blows his brains out as Michael and Gabriel appear to escort his soul to heaven, the archetypal warrior victorious in defeat. History says it wasn't a Muslim horde at all, but rather the Navarrese Basques who did Roland in. And why shouldn't they get their revenge on these uncouth Franks who were devastating their land, trying to force this democratic nation to kneel before some crowned foreign thug who called himself their king? We might excuse a people who did not even have a word in their language for 'king' if they were not much impressed with Charlemagne.

How this affair metamorphosed into an epic at the turn of the millennium or how the caterpillar Roland of history re-emerged as the mythological butterfly in the *Chanson* is murky, but as with most epics it involved a modicum of propaganda. The immediate source of the *Chanson* is said to have been a famous vision of Roland given to an 11th-century archbishop of Pamplona, which transformed Basque farmers into infidel knights (just in time for the Crusades). For the French there was another bonus: glorification of Carolingian imperialism provided poetic justification for the expansionist dreams of the Capetian kings.

Tourist Information

Roncesvalles: Antiguo Molino, **t** 94 876 03 01, *oit.roncesvalles@cfnavarra.es*.

Where to Stay and Eat

Roncesvalles ✉ 31650

If you have no luck at the places listed, try one of several *casas rurales* in the vicinity.

***Hotel Loizu**, Burguete (3km from Roncesvalles), **t** 94 876 00 08, *hloizu@cmn. navarra.net* (*moderate*). A good choice *hostal* with plenty of atmosphere for reasonable rates.

***Hs Casa Sabina**, **t** 94 876 00 12 (*moderate*). Situated by the monastery entrance, with six pleasant rooms and tasty Navarrese cooking. Very popular with pilgrims, so book ahead.

****Hostal Burguete**, Auritz, **t** 94 879 0488, *hburguete@auritz-burguete.org* (*inexpensive*). Whenever Hemingway decamped to the Pyrenees he stayed here; though its elegance is mostly faded, this antique-bedecked old place is still a great choice for slumming it in style.

****Hs La Posada**, **t** 94 876 02 25 *www.laposadaderoncesvalles.com* (*budget*). A charming choice, with spacious rooms in the Colegiata, and a fine restaurant (*moderate*).

with the exception of a much-revered 13th-century image of the Virgin under her baldachin. Its jumbled, anachronistic, pious legend tells how, after the battle at the pass, Charlemagne founded a monastery up at Ibañeta. When the Moors poured through to attack France in 732 the monks hid the statue, and it remained hidden until 1130 when it was revealed to a Basque shepherd by a red stag with a star shimmering between its antlers. The fascinating **museum** (*open daily 11–1.30 and 4–6; adm*) contains such rarefied medieval treasures as the emerald which fell from the Emir's turban when giant King Sancho burst into his tent at Las Navas de Tolosa (surely it was a sight enough to scare the emerald off anybody); an 11th-century *pyx*, or golden box used to hold the Host; and a reliquary of gold and enamel called 'Charlemagne's chessboard' (*c.* 1350) for its 32 little cases, each designed to hold a saintly fingertip or tooth. Among the paintings there's an excellent 15th-century Flemish triptych and a *Holy Family* by Morales, and two books on Confucianism, purchased in India in the time of St Francis Xavier.

An easy and beautiful path from the monastery leads up in half an hour to the **Puerto Ibañeta** (3,150ft) where the Basques, hidden on Mounts Astobizkar and Orzanzurieta, dropped boulders on the heads of the Franks. A modern chapel replaces the monastery of San Salvador, where the monks would toll a bell to guide pilgrims through the mists and snow storms. Heading south, the pretty villages of **Burguete/Auritz** and **Espinal/Auritzberri** were the pilgrims' next stops and are still good places to stay.

Western Valleys: Valle de Baztán and Valle de Bidasoa

Frequent rains off the Atlantic make the valleys west of Roncesvalles so lush that they're called the 'Switzerland of Navarra'. Both are dotted with well-preserved, unspoiled white Basque villages, trout streams and quietly beautiful scenery.

The **Valle de Baztán** once had Spain's largest *agote* population (*see* p.89) and perhaps not entirely coincidentally a legendary colony of witches in the early 17th century, who based their activities in **Zugarramurdi**, a pretty place just in from the French frontier. Just outside the village, carved out of the mountain by the *Infernuko Erreka* (Hell's

Where to Stay and Eat

Urdazubi/Urdax ✉ 31711

Hostal Irigoienea, C/Salvador, t 94 859 92 67, www.irigoienea.com (*inexpensive*). A white-washed, Navarrese farmhouse, this is a charming place to stay.

Menta, on the Dantxarina road, t 94 859 90 20 (*moderate*). Situated opposite a busy shopping centre that attracts the French. You can feast on a superb mix of French and Navarrese dishes, with game dishes in season; good wine list too. *Closed Mon eve and Tues*.

Elizondo ✉ 31700

★★★Baztán, on the main road, t 94 858 00 50, hotelbaztan@tsai.es (*moderate*). Modern with panoramic views, a swimming pool and a garden. *Closed Dec–Mar*.

Señorío de Ursúa, Caserio Ikazatea, Arizkun, t 948 45 35 00, www.hotelursua.com

(*moderate*). Sumptuous rooms and a fine restaurant in this beautifully renovated 17th-century Basque farmhouse (4.5km from Elizondo).

★★Hs Saskaitz, M. Azphilikueta 10, t 94 858 04 88, f 94 858 06 15, hotelelizondo@biazpe.net (*inexpensive*). Cosy enough, and in the centre of town.

Pensión Eskisaroi, t 94 858 00 13 (*budget*). A cut-price option that also provides *inexpensive* dinners.

Casa Rural Urruska, 10km away in Barrio de Bearzún, t 94 845 21 06 (*inexpensive*). Simple but solid, tasty home cooking is served to guests at this friendly casa rural.

Casa Galarza, C/Santiago 1, t 94 858 01 01 (*budget*). A rival to Roncal's offerings, this haven of traditional Baztánian cuisine and cheese serves *txuri-tabeltz*, a stew of lamb's tripe for which Elizondo is famous. *Closed Tues*.

Stream), the vast **Cuevas de Zugarramurdi** (*t 94 859 91 70; open daily 9–7; adm*) were the scene of black sabbaths, or *akelarres*, in which the participants smeared themselves with an unguent made of human brains and bones, mixed with belladonna, toads, salamanders and snakes – at least according to the 31 people imprisoned and 'put to the question' by the Logroño inquisition in 1609; of those condemned, 13 died under torture and six survived to be burned alive at an *auto-da-fé*. On the summer solstice the locals still gather in the caves for a feast and a dance. Even older magic was built into the **cromlechs of Mairuillarrieta**, dedicated to the Basque goddess Mairu or Mari, reached by a path from the village. There are other caves, the lovely stalactite **Cuevas de Urdax** just south at Urdazubi/Urdax, where Basque nymphs or *lamias* once frolicked in the stream; guided tours run roughly every 20 minutes in the summer.

Elizondo, one of the prettiest villages in the Baztán valley, has an informal tourist office in C/Jaime Urrutia (*t 94 858 12 79*), where you can pick up a map that pinpoints the historic houses: those along the river are especially impressive. **Arizcun**, 7km west, has the fortified stone house of one of Spain's busiest conquistadores, Pedro de Ursúa, leader of the search for El Dorado up the Amazon in 1560. The parish church has a striking Baroque façade. Further south a road turns east to France by way of the spectacular **Izpegui pass** (*summer only*).

Navarra's westernmost Pyrenean valley, the Valle de Bidasoa, embraces streams filled with salmon and trout and, more prosaically, the main San Sebastián–Pamplona road. Bus services in the area offer a chance to visit charming old Basque villages such as **Vera (Bera) de Bidasoa**, only a couple of miles from the French frontier, where the former home of the anarchistic Basque novelist Pío Baroja (1872–1956; author of *Memorias de un hombre de acción*) is now an **ethnographic museum** (*t 94 863 00 20 for an* *appointment*). Lesaka, equally pretty, claims one of the best-preserved fortified feudal houses in Navarra. Tiny Etxalar/Echalar, a hamlet that time forgot, is on a stream on the pretty, seldom-used road to Zugarramurdi – seldom used except in October, during the annual wild pigeon and woodcock holocaust. The church at Etxalar is surrounded by 100 Basque funerary steles with their distinctive star discs.

Further south, the **Parque Natural del Señorío de Bértiz**, a former private estate, has foot, cycle and horse-riding paths through thousands of acres of chestnut, beech and oak forests; the gardens near the manor boast over 120 species of exotic trees (*Visitors' centre open winter daily 10–1.30 and 4–5.30; summer 10–1.30 and 4–7.30. Botanic garden open Oct–Mar 10–2 and 4–6, Apr–Sept 10–2 and 4–8; adm. Natural Park open Oct-Mar 10–6, Apr–Sept 10–8*). Note the coat of arms of the lord of Bértiz, showing a mermaid holding a mirror and comb; Charles III had her placed there in 1421 in honour of the persuasive powers of his ambassador, Micheto de Bértiz. Two villages west of here, **Zubieta** and **Ituren**, are famous for a carnival ritual to usher in spring that could have been invented by Dr Seuss: men called the *joaldunak* dress up in striped dunce's caps and lacy smocks, and tie a pair of *polunpak* (giant bells) to their backs with an intricate network of laces. Thus arrayed, the *joaldunak* make a *zanpantzar*, a group of 20 or so who march from village to village, their *polunpak* smacking and jangling.

Pamplona (Iruña)

Whether you call it Pamplona, the town founded by Pompey in 75 BC, or by its older name Iruña, which means simply 'the city' in Basque, the capital of autonomous Navarra sits on a strategic 1,400ft pimple on the beautiful fertile plain, its existence as inevitable as its nickname, the 'Gateway of Spain'. For a few years in the 730s, the Arabs used it in reverse, as the gateway to France, until their dreams of Europe were hammered at Poitiers. Over the next decades the Vascones regained control of Pamplona, clobbered Charlemagne after he burnt their walls, and set up their own king. In 918 the Moors razed Pamplona to the ground again. To encourage rebuilding, Sancho III the Great invited his subjects in French Navarre to come and start trades in what became the two new districts of Pamplona, San Cernín and San Nicolás. The fact that the three districts of the city were practically independent and had their own privileges led to violent rivalry, so much so that in 1521 the French Navarrese unsuccessfully besieged Pamplona in an effort to regain San Cernín and San Nicolás. Wounded while fighting for Castile was a certain Captain Íñigo López de Recalde, who convalesced in Pamplona, got religion in a militant way and founded the Jesuits.

Pamplona seems to have been naturally conducive to that sort of thing, with a reputation for being crazily austere, brooding and puritanical. For anyone who knows the city only for throwing the wildest party in Europe, this comes as a shock of *desfase* or maladjustment, a word that means (and gleefully celebrates) the unresolved contradictions that coexist in post-Franco Spain. Stern Catholicism is part of the city's fabric. 'From the top to the bottom of Pamplonese society, I have found the whole place poisoned by clerical alkaloid,' grumped Basque philosopher Unamuno. 'It oozed

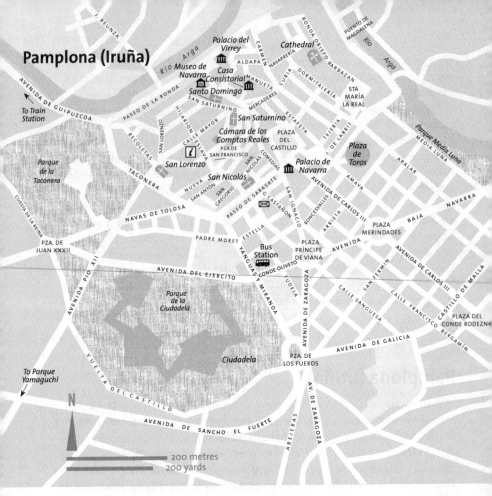

out of every corner...one drop in the eye is enough to infect you forever.' In the 1950s, the secretive Opus Dei, Christianity's ultra-conservative fifth column, chose Pamplona to build their Universidad de Navarra. In the 1960s the city's new tennis club still built separate swimming pools for men and women. Forty years later, a new Pamplona prides itself on setting up Spain's first shelter for battered women, the first city workshops for training disadvantaged youths and the first urban rubbish recycling programme. 'Pamplona is a city that gives much more than it promises', said Victor Hugo. It certainly will if you come the second week of July for the Sanfermines, but expect it to take as well: your money, your watch, your sleep and a lifetime's supply of adrenalin.

A Walk through the Casco Viejo

Pamplona was squeezed in a tight girdle of walls until the early 1900s, when the city spread in all directions and accumulated around 185,000 inhabitants in the process. But for all its 20th-century flab, the vital organs in the historic Casco Viejo remain intact, curled tightly around the city's heart, the spacious **Plaza del Castillo**. Off the southwest corner extends the **Paseo de Sarasate**, populated by stone kings and

Getting There and Around

By Air
Pamplona's airport (t 94 816 87 00) is 6km south of the city, with daily connections to Madrid and Barcelona. The cheapest way to get to the airport is to take no.16 bus from the bus station (every half-hour) to Noaín, which drops you eight hundred metres from the airport.

By Train
Pamplona's **train station** is 2km out of town on Avda San Jorge. Bus no.9 makes connections from the centre every 10mins, t 94 813 02 02; tickets and information can also be had at the railway office in town at C/Estella 8, t 94 822 72 82, or call the centralized RENFE information service t 90 224 02 02 for all timetable information and reservations.

By Bus
The **bus station** is in town, near the citadel, at C/Conde Oliveto 8; for information t 94 822 38 54. Besides provincial connections, there are ten buses daily to Vitoria, six to Bilbao, ten to San Sebastián (plus five slower services) and six to Zaragoza. There are fewer services at weekends, particularly on Sundays.

Tourist Information
C/ Eslava 1, Plaza San Fransisco, t 94 820 65 40, f 94 820 70 34, *oit.pamplona@cfnavarra.es*. A **booking service** is run for *casas rurales* throughout Navarra, t 902 196 462 (*daily 11–4*). For information on Los Sanfermines and events, see *www.sanfermin.com*.
Cultural/historical **walking tours** of the city are organised by Erreka, C/Curia 18, t 94 822 15 06, *info@erreka.net*, and by Estafeta Tours, C/Estafeta 45, t 948 225 768.
The **post office** is at Paseo de Sarasate 9, t 948 207 217; **internet access** is available at

Naveganet, Trav. de Acella 3, t 94 819 92 97 (*open 10.30–1.30 and 3.30–10.30*).
There is a **market** Mon–Sat morning at the Mercado de Santo Domingo, Plaza de los Burgos.

Where to Stay

Pamplona ✉ 31300
During San Fermín, hotel prices double and often triple, supplemented by scores of overpriced rooms in *casas particulares*, and advertised weeks ahead in the local newspapers, *Navarra Hoy* or *Diario de Navarra*. If you end up sleeping outside, any of the gardens along the walls or river are preferable to the noisy, filthy, vomit-filled citadel. Keep a close eye on your belongings (petty criminals, unfortunately, go into overdrive along with everyone else during the fiesta) and check in what you don't need at the *consigna* in Plaza San Francisco next to the tourist office; everyone else does too, so get there early. Two free campsites are set up along the road to France, but again, don't leave anything there you might really miss. If you stay outside Pamplona and drive into town, beware that breaking into cars is epidemic.

Luxury–Expensive
****Iruña Palace Los Tres Reyes**, Jardines de la Taconera, t 94 822 66 00, *www.hotel3reyes.com*. Conveniently located a short walk from the old town, this big modern hotel pampers its well-heeled guests with every possible convenience including an indoor heated pool and tennis courts.
***Yoldi**, Avda San Ignacio 11, t 94 822 48 00, *www.hotelyoldi.com*. A modern, business hotel which has long been the favourite of *toreros* and bullfighting *aficionados*.

queens and the overwrought **Monumento a los Fueros**, erected by popular subscription after Madrid tried to mess with Navarra's privileges back in 1893. The bronze allegory of Navarra holds a copy of the *Ley Foral*, or Fueros' Law, surrounded by the broken chains from the battle of Las Navas de Tolosa, symbolizing freedom; these also feature on Navarra's coat of arms. Historical frescoes decorate the neoclassical

Moderate

★★★**Europa**, C/Espoz y Mina 11 (just off Pza Castillo), t 94 822 18 00, www.hreuropa.com. Flower-filled balconies, some overlooking the *encierro* action in Estafeta, and attractive, traditional rooms. The restaurant, one of the city's finest, is run by the same management as the Alhambra's (*see* below).

★★★**Maisonnave**, C/Nueva 20 (next to Pza San Francisco), t 94 822 26 00, www.hotelmaison nave.es. Offers comfort and prestige and a peaceful garden at the back.

★★★**NH El Toro**, at Berrioplano (5km from Pamplona on the Guipúzcoa road), t 94 830 22 11, nhtoro@nh-hotels.es. Quiet rooms in a traditional-style mansion, overlooking a statue group of the *encierro*.

★**Arriazu Hostal**, C/Comedias 14, t 94 81 02 02, www.hostalarriazu.com. Gem of a new *hostal* in prime locale, with plush furnishings and good-size rooms.

Inexpensive

★★**Eslava**, Pza Virgen de la O 7, t 94 822 22 70, f 94 822 51 57. www.hotel-eslava.com. Small and friendly. Some functionally furnished rooms; views over the walls of Pamplona.

★★**Hostal Navarra**, C/Tudela 9, t 94 822 51 64, www.hostelnavarra.com. Next to the bus station, this offers immaculate rooms and all the conveniences. Five minutes' walk from the Casco Viejo. Prices leap to €200 during Sanfermine, when you'll find better deals elsewhere.

★★**Hs Príncipe de Viana I and II**, Avda Zaragoza 4, t 94 824 91 47, f 94 824 91 46. Clean but faded rooms with baths.

★**Hs Bearán**, San Nicolás 25, t 94 822 34 28, f 94 822 43 02. One of the few decent *hostales*, where all doubles have bath, TV and air con.

Pensión Lambertini, C/Mercaderes 17, t 94 821 03 03 (*inexpensive–budget*). Has a comfy living room stuffed with books and knick-knacks, and balconies overlooking the route

of the *encierro*. Ask for one of the lovely rooms at the back, which boast extensive views across the Cuenca de Pamplona.

Budget

Cheaper *hostales* and *fondas* are mostly on C/San Gregorio and C/San Nicolás.

★**Pensión Casa García**, C/San Gregorio 12, t 94 822 38 93. Offers very plain double rooms without bath, and an adequate *menú del día* in its restaurant.

Casa Otano, San Nicolás 5, t 94 822 70 36. Popular for its nice rooms with baths, and a good, *budget* restaurant-bar.

Pensión Santa Cecilia, C/Navarrería 17, t 94 822 22 30. Located in an 18th-century palace, and providing one of the nicest cheap sleeps under lofty ceilings in huge rooms.

Pensión Sarasate, Paseo de Sarasate 30, t 94 822 30 84. Small and personal; decent but unspectacular rooms with baths.

Excaba, t 94 833 03 15. The nearest campsite, 7km to the north.

Eating Out

Alhambra, C/Bergamín 7, t 94 826 11 62 (*expensive*). Look out for the imaginative dishes at this fashionable place, a favourite with local gourmets: potatoes stuffed with truffles and scampi and homemade desserts. *Closed Sun and mid-July to early Aug.*

Europa, C/Espoz y Mina 11, t 94 822 18 00 (*expensive*). Indulges diners with refined service and classic Navarrese meat and game dishes; try the stewed breast and thigh of pigeon, smothered in rich gravy. It's popular for weddings and other big events. *Closed Sun.*

Hartza, C/Juan de Labrit 19, t 94 822 45 68 (*expensive*). Famous for its *bonito encebollado* (tuna with onions), hake dishes and good home-made desserts. *Closed Sun eve, Mon, and 1–24 Aug.*

Palacio de Navarra, also in the Paseo; the archives contain one of the best caches of medieval documents in Spain and the garden boasts a massive sequoia. It now hosts temporary art exhibitions (check with tourist office for times).

Off the east end of Plaza del Castillo, the narrow streets jammed with shops and bars were once the *Judería*, where Pamplona's Jews, 'a gentle and reasonable race'

Josetxo, Pza Príncipe de Viana 1, t 94 822 20 97 (*expensive*). Has been a local gourmet institution in Pamplona for 50 years. Try to book one of the small Belle Epoque dining rooms upstairs, and choose between delicacies such as *ajo arriero con bogavante* (seafood casserole with lobster) or the chef's prize *solomillo a la broche con salsa de trufa* (steak fillet on a spit with truffle sauce). *Closed Sun and Aug.*

Rodero, C/E Arrieta 3, t 94 822 80 35 (*expensive*). Currently considered the best restaurant in the city, serving modern variations on Navarrese, Basque and French recipes prepared with the finest seasonal ingredients. *Closed Sun, Mon eve and Aug.*

Asador Olaverri, C/Santa Marta 4, t 94 823 50 63 (*moderate*). Come here for a big grilled meat and wine feast. Good value and great atmosphere. *Closed Sun eve and mid-July–mid-Aug.*

Baserri, C/San Nicolás 32, t 94 822 20 21 (*moderate*). Hard to beat for *cocina en miniatura*; its fine creations have walked away repeatedly with top honours at Pamplona's annual Concurso de Pinchos. You can try a selection of them, as well as delicacies such as fresh rocket and smoked cod salad. They also offer a choice of more than 80 wines.

Bodegon Sarria, Estafeta 52, t 94 822 77 13 (*moderate*). Fronted by a wonderful old bar (with some of the best tapas in town) with black-and-white pics of Hemingway and bulls, the restaurant dishes up solid, traditional fare.

Chalet de Izu, Avda Baja Navarra 47, t 94 822 60 93 (*moderate*). Situated near Parque Media Luna, with plenty of swish atmosphere and good *menús*. It's another popular spot for weddings.

Erburu, C/San Lorenzo 19, t 94 822 51 69 (*moderate*). Serves Navarrese-style seafood and excellent beef. There's also a popular tapas bar. *Closed Mon and last two weeks of July.*

Casa Manolo, C/Garcia Castañon 12, t 948 22 51 02 (*moderate*). Traditional, welcoming and good value, with a range of set menús offering fine local cuisine.

San Fermín, C/San Nicolás 44, t 948 22 21 91 (*moderate*). This is one of the best places to try Navarra's famous vegetables, all freshly prepared. They also offer tasty meat and fish dishes, and there's a lunch menú for €12.

Sarasate, C/San Nicolás 19, t 94 822 57 27 (*cheap*). For the best vegetarian meals in Pamplona. *Closed Sun and evenings, except Fri and Sat.*

Cafés and Bars

As well as elegant cafés, Pamplona had some 700 bars at the last count, or one for every 280 inhabitants, many of whom seem to be always in them, day and night. Favourite late-night bar-crawling zones in the Casco Viejo are C/San Nicolás and San Gregorio, San Lorenzo and Jarauta, and Navarrería, the latter still popular with the Basques and alternative Pamplonese.

Café Iruña, Plaza del Castillo. You can tuck into *cheap* light meals until 2.30am at this famous 1888 *modernista* place, with etched glass and chandeliers. It also boasts the best terrace in the city.

Fiterro, C/Estafeta 58. this is the very best tapas bar on legendary Estafeta, with a fine array of mouthwatering pinxos.**Letyana**, Travesia de Bayona 2. Excellent, award-winning pinxos, a great atmosphere and it's also a good spot for breakfast or a coffee break.

Mesón del Caballo Blanco, Rincón del Caballo Blanco (behind the cathedral). An atmospheric old stone house with a terrace – a delightful place to linger; in winter sandwiches are served around the fireplace.

El Molino, Avda Bayona 13. A much-loved classic, with fabulous *pinxos* and a regular crowd of locals.

according to the King of Navarra, lived unmolested until Navarra was gobbled up by the Castile of Ferdinand and Isabel. Behind these, tucked up near the ramparts, the gracious 14th–15th-century Gothic **Cathedral** (*entrance on C/Dormitalería, open Mon–Fri 10–1.30 and 4–7, Sat 1–1.30; adm, includes cloister and Museo Diocesano*) hides behind a dull-witted, neoclassical façade, slapped on in the 18th century by a

Pamplona's Annual Meltdown: Los Sanfermines

Before Hemingway there was Fermín, son of a Roman senator and first bishop of Pamplona. His family had been converted by San Saturnino (Sernin, or Cernín) of Toulouse, who was martyred in the 3rd century AD by being dragged around town by a bull. Fermín, for his part, travelled as a missionary to the Gauls and was beheaded in Amiens for his trouble. Some time between then and 1324, when Pamplona held its first fiesta, Fermín decided to take bullfighters under his saintly cape; by 1591 his festival had found its current dates and form. Although it's the running of the bulls that has made Los Sanfermines world-famous, this insanely dangerous activity is only a tiny portion of the nine days of nonstop revelling when 'Pamplona becomes the world capital of happiness', a state of hyper-bliss fuelled by three million litres of alcohol each year.

There is some order to the madness. The Sanfermines officially open at noon on 6 July, when thousands of Navarrese in their festival attire (white shirts and white trousers or skirts, red sashes and red bandanas) gather in front of the town hall to hold their bandanas aloft as a rocket called *El Chupinazo* is fired off the balcony and a city councillor cries in Spanish and Basque: 'People of Pamplona! Long live San Fermín!' The city explodes with a mighty roar while tens of thousands of champagne corks pop (and bottles are smashed on the pavement, usually causing the first casualties).

In the afternoon the giants and big heads (*gigantes y cabezudos*) – as essential to the fiesta as the bulls – leave their 'home' in the bus station. The eight 13ft plaster giants supported by dancers date from 1860 and represent kings and queens, whirling and swirling the minuet, their sweeping skirts flowing in the air. They are accompanied by the *cabezudos* and *kilikis*, big-headed figures in tricorn hats, with names like Napoleon and Patata, who wallop children on the head with foam rubber balls tied to bats. This is also the prerogative of the *zaldikos*, the colourfully dressed men wearing cardboard horses around their waists; all are accompanied by dancers, *txistularis* (Basque flutes) and *gaiteros*.

At four o'clock a massive scrum, the *Riau Riau*, begins when members of the Corporación de San Fermín dressed in all their finery try to proceed 400m down the Calle Mayor to the chapel of San Fermín at San Lorenzo's for vespers, but everyone else tries to prevent them in a gung-ho defiance of authority, to the extent that it's often late at night before the Corporación achieves its goal. The mayor of Pamplona has tried for several years to ban the chaotic *Riau Riau*, but it seems to be unbannable. After a first night of carousing and dancing in the streets, the dawn of 7 July and every following day is welcomed with the *dianas*, a city-wide wake-up call performed on screeching pipes.

Traditionally the *encierro* started at 7am (so that festivities kicked off on the seventh hour of the seventh day of the seventh month), though nowadays the bulls begin their daily charge at 8am. If you want a good place to watch, wedge yourself into a spot along the route – Cuesta de San Domingo, Mercaderes and Estafeta – at least an hour earlier. Before running, the locals sing a hymn to Fermín and arm themselves with a rolled-up newspaper to distract the bull's attention, since the animals – 1,200lbs of muscle and fury – charge at the nearest moving object, ideally at a flung newspaper instead of a falling runner. A rocket goes up as the first bull leaves the corral; a second rocket means that all are released; and a third signals that all have made it to the bullring – on a good run the whole *encierro* only lasts three minutes. The most dangerous moments are when the runners and bulls have to squeeze into the runway of the bullring, or when a bull gets loose from his fellows and panics. People (and not all of them tourists) get trampled and gored every year; if you run you can hedge your bets by running on weekdays, when it's less crowded, and by avoiding the *toros* of the Salvador Guardiola ranch, which have the most bloodstained record.

The spirit of abandon is so infectious that, even if you come determined not to run, you may find yourself joining in on a self-destructive spur of the moment impulse. Women do defy the authorities and run, although the police try to pull them out. During the *encierro* the lower seats of the bullring are free (again, arrive early), except on Sunday; from here you can watch the bulls and runners pile in and, after-wards, more fun and games as heifers with padded horns are released on the crowd in the ring. The traditional breakfast is huge (bull stews, lamb's sweetbreads, ham and eggs in tomato sauce, washed down with gallons of chilled rosé and *pacharán*).

The bullfights themselves take place daily at 6.30 in the evening – tickets sell out with the speed of lightning and are usually only available from scalpers. The *sombra* seats are for serious *aficionados*, while members of the 16 *peñas* (clubs devoted to making noise and in general being as obnoxious as possible) fill up the *sol* seats and create a parallel fiesta if the action in the ring isn't up to snuff, or create pandemo-nium if it is. Afternoons also see other bull sports that are bloodless (for the bull, at any rate): the dodging, swerving *concurso de recortadores* or leaping *corrida vasca-landesa*.

Between the bullfights there are concerts, *jotas* and Basque dances, processions of the relics of San Fermín and other religious services, parades and activities for young children and senior citizens. At night fireworks burst over the citadel and the *toro de fuego* or 'fire bull', carried by a runner and spitting fireworks, chases children down the route of the *encierro*. Then there's the midnight *El Estruendo de Irún*, led by an enormous drum called the *bomba*, in which hundreds of people – just about anyone who can lay their hands on anything that makes a sound – gather and let loose in an ear-bashing sonic disorder.

At midnight on 14 July Pamplona winds down to an exhausted, nostalgic finale, a ceremony known as the *Pobre de mí*; everyone gathers in front of the town hall (or in the Plaza del Castillo for the livelier, unofficial ceremony), with a candle and sings 'Poor me, poor me, another San Fermín has come to an end'. As the clock strikes twelve everyone removes their red scarves and agrees, like Hemingway, that it was 'a damned fine show' and promises to do better and worse next year. Diehards party on until 8am the next day, and perform one last feat, the *encierro de la villavesa*: the bulls are all dead, so they run in front of a bus.

misguided do-gooder; a shame because the original front, according to travellers' descriptions, was as lusty as the one at Cervatos (*see* p.186). When completed, it was the second-largest cathedral in Spain after León's, and suitable shelter for the beautiful alabaster tombs of the cathedral's sponsors, big-nosed Charles III 'the Noble' and his big-nosed queen Leonora de Trastámara, sculpted in the 15th century by Jean de Lomme of Tournai. The kings of Navarra were crowned before the Romanesque *Virgen del Sagrario* on the high altar. The delicacy of the Gothic **cloister** (1280–1472) approaches gossamer in stone and reaches a climax of decorative bravura in the justly named **Puerta Preciosa** (1325), carved with a superb *Dormition of the Virgin*. Off the cloister, the **Museo Diocesano** occupies the kitchen and refectory, where pilgrims once dined: the refectory is filled with sweet-faced 12th–15th-century carvings of the Madonna and Child, while the kitchen is mainly remarkable for its enormous chimneys, one in each corner with a huge lantern-chimney in the middle. The Cillería (behind the ticket desk) contains two contains two remarkable reliquaries – the 1258 *Relicario del Santo Sepulcro* and the 1401 *Relicario del Lignum Crucis*, adorned with precious stones.

The narrow old lanes around the cathedral belong to the **Navarrería**, the original Basque quarter, populated in the Middle Ages by cathedral builders and farmers who tilled the bishop's lands. Here on the promontory you'll find the most impressive part of the surviving **walls** built by Philip II, with a reputation for impregnability so powerful that no one challenged their reputation until the French tried to hole up here against Wellington; the views stretch for miles over the plain. Just west, the 13th-century **Palacio del Virrey**, once the royal palace and now houses the local military government.

Continuing past the attractive **Portal de Zumalacárregui** (16th-century, but renamed after the Carlist hero), the **Museo de Navarra** (*t 94 833 2074, www.cfnavarra.es; open 9.30–2 and 5–7, Sun and hols 11–2, closed Mon; adm*) occupies a huge 16th-century hospital and contains everything from Navarrese prehistory to contemporary art, with Roman mosaics, Gothic wall paintings, carved capitals from Pamplona's original Romanesque cathedral (minus any of the naughty bits), an ivory coffret from Leyre made in Córdoba in the 11th century and a fine portrait of the Marqués de San Adrián by Goya. A pretty courtyard, with Roman mosaics, offers views of a stretch of the old city walls. Just below the museum, wooden barricades remind you that this is the beginning of the *encierro*; the bulls leave their corral near Plaza Santo Domingo and head up C/Mercaderes and Estafeta. Follow their route and you'll come to Plaza Consistorial and the colourful Baroque **Casa Consistorial**, topped with jaunty allegorical figures. Pamplona's nobles built their finest escutcheoned palaces just off this square, along C/Zapatería and C/Mayor. Plazas de Consejo and San Francisco, set diagonally opposite each other, are also worth a look, the latter with a *modernista* hotel converted into a bank. Nearby in C/Ansoleaga, the well-preserved Gothic **Cámara de los Comptos Reales** (*open Mon–Fri 8–3*), the kings' mint in the 12th century, has a magnificent porch opening on to a vault and patio with some original decorations intact.

The not always tremendously popular *francos* (Gascons, mostly), invited to Pamplona by Sancho the Great, lived just to the south in their two rival quarters named after, and defended by, 13th-century churches that doubled as fortresses when their fellow citizens went on the war path. These are **San Saturnino** (or San Cernín) in C/San

Saturnino and **San Nicolás** in lively, bar-lined C/San Nicolás; a plaque by the former marks the site where the first Pamplonans were converted by San Saturnino. Further west, **San Lorenzo** is best known for its chapel dedicated to San Fermín, built by the city in 1717, where his bust reliquary quietly resides 51 weeks of the year, presiding over weddings; so many Pamplonese want to be married under his protective eye that there's a two-year waiting list (*all churches open 8.30–12 and 6.30–7.30*).

Pamplona is well endowed with parks that are good for naps during the fiesta. The oldest, the French-style **Parque de la Taconera**, closes out the west end of the Casco Viejo and has one of the city's nicest cafés, the **Vienés**, in a charming old kiosk. Just south, the star-shaped **Ciudadela**, built on the orders of Philip II, is now a green park inside and outside the steep walls. The immaculate **Parque Yamaguchi** is named after Pamplona's Japanese 'twin', and has a neat Japanese garden complete with lakeside wooden house for the tea ceremony. Also here is one of Pamplona's newer attractions, a tall, fat, red-and-blue tower containing the **Planetario** (*t 94 826 00 04, www.pamplonetario.org; open Aug–Sept 11.30–1.30 and 6–9, Oct–June 9.30–1.30 and 5.30–9; adm, closed July*). The prettiest garden, **Parque Media Luna**, lines the river east of the city and has a path ending at the medieval bridge used by the pilgrims. The park in front of the **Plaza de Toros** – the third largest in the world – was renamed Paseo Hemingway and has a grizzled bust of the writer whose *The Sun Also Rises* (1926) made Pamplona a household word.

The celebrated sculptor Jorge Oteiza (1908–2003) is remembered in a sleek new museum, the **Museo Oteiza**, located 9km from Pamplona close to the village of Navarra de Alzuza (*www.museooteiza.com, t 948 4332074, open Oct–May Tues–Fri 10–3, Sat–Sun and hols 11–7, June–Sept Tues–Sun 11–7; adm, free on Fri*). The collection includes more than 1600 sculptures, along with sketches and designs, from the prolific and charismatic sculptor, who was one of the most influential Spanish artists of the 20th century

East of Pamplona: Sangüesa, Javier and Leyre

Pilgrims from Mediterranean lands would cross the Pyrenees at Somport in Aragón and enter Navarra at Sangüesa, home of one of the very best Romanesque churches and one of the craziest palaces in all Spain, but these days, if the wind's wrong, the pong of the nearby paper mill hurries visitors along; note that if you go by bus from Pamplona (*La Veloz Sangüesina, t 94 822 69 95*) there are only three a day and you'll be stuck with the stink longer than you might like. If you're driving, there's enough interest in the area to make a day's excursion.

Aoiz (Agoitz)

The region due east of Pamplona, crossed by the Río Irati, gets few tourists but, if you're driving, the undulating landscapes and nearly deserted villages make an interesting alternative to the more direct N240 to Sangüesa. Aoiz itself has fine old houses, a medieval bridge and the 15th-century church of **San Miguel Arcángel**, worth a look for its excellent *retablo mayor* (1580) by Basque master Juan de Achieta and its unusual 12th-century painted stone font. Romanesque connoisseurs should go out of their way to **Artaiz**, a tiny blip to the southwest (due south of Urroz), where the church of **San Martín** has the finest sculpture in rural Navarra.

Sangüesa

Sangüesa was a direct product of the pilgrimage, purposely moved from its original hill-top location in the 11th century to the spot where the road crosses the River Aragón. In 1122 Alfonso el Batallador, king of neighbouring Aragón, sent down a colony of *francos* to augment Sangüesa's population, and ten years after that ordered the Knights of St John to build a church well worth stopping for: **Santa María la Real**. This possesses one of the most intriguing and extraordinary portals on the whole Camino (unfortunately the street in front is quite busy, so you have to look at it between the cars), so strange that some writers believe that its symbols (knotted labyrinths, mermaids, two-headed beasts symbolizing duality, etc.) were sculpted by *agotes* or by a brotherhood of artists on to something deeper than orthodox Catholicism; even the damned are laughing in the *Last Judgement* on the tympanum, presided over by a Christ in Majesty with a secret smile and vigorous Evangelists almost dancing around the throne. Below, the elongated figures on the jambs show stylistic similarities to

Tourist Information

Aoiz: C/Francisco Indurain 12, t 94 833 65 98.
Javier: t 94 888 03 42.
Sangüesa: t 94 887 14 11, *oit.sanguesa@cfnavarra.es*. Guided visits – a good way of ensuring the monuments are open – are organised by the tourist office.

Where to Stay and Eat

Aoiz ✉ 31430
*Hs Beti Jai, Santa Agueda 4, t 94 833 60 52 *www.beti-jai.com* (*inexpensive*). Has 14 rooms and an excellent restaurant (*moderate*), mixing the best regional traditions with modern techniques; the hake in langoustine sauce is especially good. *Closed Mon.*

Sangüesa ✉ 31400
**Yamaguchi, on the road to Javier, t 94 887 01 27, *www.hotelyamaguchi.com* (*inexpensive*). A modern hotel with a pool, *frontón*, and nice restaurant.
**Hs Las Navas, C/Alfonso El Batallador 7, t 94 887 00 77 (*budget*). A handful of basic but spotless rooms for a very low price.

Mediavilla, C/Alfonso El Batallador, t 94 887 02 12 (*moderate*). A Basque *asador* serving delicious chargrilled fish and meat with excellent local wine. *Closed Mon.*

Javier/Leyre ✉ 31411
****Hotel Señorio de Monjardín, Ctra de Leyre s/n, t 94 888 41 88, *www.hotels enoriodemnojardin.com* (*expensive*). A large, modern 3km from Leyre on the N240, with some luxurious suites and a restaurant featuring Navarrese cuisine and seasonal game dishes.
***Xabier, 35 Plaza de Javier, t 94 888 40 35, *www.hotelxabier.com* (*moderate*). You can stay and eat next to the castle at this charming and historic hotel-restaurant.
**Hospedería de Leyre, t 94 888 40 11, *www.hotelhospederiadeleyre.com* (*moderate*). This charming former pilgrims' hostel at Leyre is the perfect antidote to stress; its restaurant specializes in traditional Navarrese cuisine. *Open Mar–Nov.*
*El Mesón, t 94 888 40 35, (*moderate*). Also next to the castle but rather more basic.

Chartres cathedral, although again the subjects are unusual: on the left the three Marys (the Virgin, Mary Magdalene and Mary Solomé, mother of St James), on the right Peter, Paul and Judas, hanged, with the inscription *Judas Mercator*. The upper half of the portal is by another hand altogether, crossed by two tiers of Apostles of near-Egyptian rigidity and another Christ in Majesty surrounded by symbols of the four Evangelists. If the church is open, ask the sacristan to show you the capitals in the apse, hidden behind the Flemish Renaissance *retablo*. Note the well in the corner: not something you find every day inside a church. Walk around to see the beautiful carved corbels on the apse and the octagonal tower.

When Aragón and Navarra went their separate ways, the kings of Navarra made Sangüesa one of their several residences. Sangüesa's arcaded Rua Mayor is lined with palaces, including the **Casa Consistorial**, built over the old royal patio of arms, today a charming leafy square; behind this is the austere 12th-century, twin-towered Palacio del Príncipe de Viana. The 12th-century church of **Santiago** has a huge battlemented

Europe's Untouchables: The *Agotes*

Some of Europe's best-known outcasts, the *agotes* (*cagotes* in French) lived in the valleys of Navarra and especially across the Pyrenees in Basse Navarre and Gascony. Apartheid-style laws forced them to live separately and only marry other *agotes*; to enter church only by a certain door and hear Mass in a special corner; to dress differently, with a goose foot sewn on to the backs of their coats; to play castanets at all crossroads and other public places to warn passers-by of their presence. Trades were forbidden them – except as builders and carpenters, a craft they excelled at to the extent that they were often called 'the Master Carpenters' instead of *agotes*.

Guesses as to who the *agotes* actually were and how they came to be pariahs varies in the extreme: some say they were dwarves, or albinos covered with a blond down, or Visigoths who failed to give up their Arian heresies and took refuge in the mountains when the Moors invaded. A strong tradition linking the *agotes* to leprosy suggests that they were descended from a colony sent to live up in the remote valleys; but leprosy is not hereditary, and the *agotes* who lived in Sangüesa and other towns were not lepers, although the stigma may have remained. In the Middle Ages, their ranks may have been swollen by all the loose ends of Europe who landed up along the road to Santiago. Or it may have been that the *agotes* were only symbolic lepers, kept at a distance for the stigma of their heresies (curiously, they were also *Crestias*, or Christians, as if emphasizing that they were still, really, in the fold). This heresy may have been a highly contagious kind of universal mysticism practised by the Templars or the Order of the Knights of St Lazarus, an order founded in the East before the Templars, and devoted to the care of lepers, using Lazarus as their symbol of death within life. Whatever the real reason for their pariah status, it was forgotten by the 16th century, when the fed-up *agotes* petitioned the pope to give them the same rights as other citizens. The pope agreed, but it was only in the 20th century, after a long civil rights struggle, that the *agotes* were fully integrated into society, intermarrying with non-*agotes* and vanishing without trace.

tower and carved capitals and conserves a large stone statue of St James, discovered buried under the floor in 1965. The slightly later, Gothic **San Salvador** has a pentagonal tower and a huge porch, sheltering a carved portal; its Plateresque choir stalls come from Leyre. Just around the corner in C/Alfonso el Batallador, the brick **Palacio Vallesantoro** catches the eye with its corkscrew Baroque portal and the widest, most extraordinary wooden eaves in Spain, carved with a phantasmagorical menagerie that makes the creatures on Santa María look tame.

Javier and Leyre

Sangüesa is the base for visiting two of Navarra's holy sites. **Javier**, 13km away, is topped by a picturesque if over-restored battlemented castle, the birthplace in 1506 of St Francisco de Javier (Xavier), Jesuit apostle of the Indies and Japan. Though the castle is now a Jesuit college, you can take the tour (*open 9–1 and 4–7; adm*) and learn a lot about both St Francis Xavier and castles – this one dates back to the 11th century, was wrecked in 1516 by Cardinal Cisneros' troops, and was restored after 1952. Perhaps most fascinating is the fresco *Dance of Death*, a grim reminder that the Pyrenees were especially hard hit by the plague.

Just north of Javier, at **Yesa**, the Río Aragón has been dammed to form the vast **Yesa Reservoir**. A road from Yesa leads up into the beautiful Sierra de Leyre and the **Monasterio de San Salvador de Leyre** (*www.monasteriodeleyre.com, open daily 10.15–2 and 3.30–7; adm*). Its foundation predates the Moors, and in the 8th century its most famous abbot, San Virila, so constantly prayed to heaven for a peek into infinity that he was granted his wish by the lovely warbling of a bird. To the abbot, the vision was a sublime moment, but when he went down to tell his monks about it he found that all had changed – his eternal second had lasted 300 years.

Leyre essentially dates from the 11th century when Sancho the Great declared it 'the centre and heart of my realm'. The first kings of Navarra were buried there, and the abbot of Leyre served as the bishop of Pamplona. Abandoned in the 19th century, the monastery was reoccupied in 1950 by the Benedictines, who began a restoration programme that unfortunately obscures much of the older building. Visits begin in the 11th-century pre-Romanesque **crypt**, where the first impression is that the church is sinking into the ground: the columns are runty little stubs of unequal height weighed down by heavy block capitals, carved with simple geometric designs that stand at about chest level. Above, the church, harmonious, light and austere, provides the perfect setting for the Benedictines' beautiful Gregorian matins and vespers (*t 94 888 42 30; Mon–Fri 7.30am, 9am, 7 pm – in summer, Thurs at 7.30pm – and 9pm, Sun and hols 9am [there are other masses, but not with Gregorian chant]*). The bones of the first ten kings of Navarra lie in a simple wooden casket behind a fine grill; the 13th-century statue of the Virgin of Leyre sits on the altar. The west portal, the **Porta Speciosa**, is finely carved with a mix of saints and monsters. If Rip Van Winkle legends don't faze you, it's a 10-minute walk up to the **Fountain of San Virila** for a magnificent view of the artificial lake and Navarrese countryside that the abbot contemplated during his prayers, although the warbling birds have been replaced by hang-gliding Spaniards. Nature is a main attraction in eastern Navarra. The Sierra de Leyre divides the Roncal and Salazar valleys (*see* pp.72–3), but there are two splendid gorges close at hand. The **Foz de Lumbier**, formed by the Irati river, has a pleasant riverside trail for walking or cycling, and is a breeding site for griffon vultures and the rare red-beaked variety of chough. The even more spectacular, sheer-sided, 6km **Foz de Arbayún** (*see* p.73) lies further to the north along the Río Salazar, with more griffon and a few Egyptian vultures; both gorges are accessible from Lumbier.

South of Pamplona to Tudela

The green valleys of the Pyrenees are a distant memory south of Pamplona; here the skies are bright and clear, the land arid and toasted golden brown after the last winter rains, except for the green swathes of vineyards of La Ribera, cradle of Navarra's finest, freshest rosés.

Tafalla and Olite

In the 17th century, a Dutchman named E Cock described Tafalla and Olite as the 'flowers of Navarra' and both have determinedly crowed Cock's sweet nicknames ever since. Old **Tafalla** has wilted a bit over the centuries and grass grows between the cobbles, but it still has an impressive main square (Plaza de Navarra) and claims one of the finest and biggest *retablos* in the north: a masterpiece by Basque artist Juan de Ancheta tucked away in the austere church of **Santa María**. West of Tafalla, **Artajona** has the air of an abandoned stage set: majestic medieval walls with startlingly intact crenellated towers (known as 'El Cerco') defend little more than the 13th-century fortress church of **San Saturnino**. This has a tympanum showing the saint exorcising the devil from a woman, watched by Juana de Navarra and Philip the Fair of France, while the lintel shows Saturnino's martyrdom with the bull. The Hispano-Flemish *retablo mayor* dates from 1515. This is the second church on the site; Artajona's walls, redone in the 1300s, were first built between 1085 and 1103 by the Templars and canons of Saint-Sernin (San Saturnino) of Toulouse, at a time when the Counts of Toulouse were among the chief players in Europe, leading the First Crusade and fighting side by side with the Cid. Near Artajona, the **Ermita de la Virgen** shelters a lovely bronze and enamel 13th-century Virgin holding a bouquet of roses, and has two megalithic gallery tombs nearby.

Olite, a fabulous medieval town south of Tafalla, is dwarfed by its bewitching, lofty-towered **Palacio Real de Olite** (*open winter 10–2 and 4–6; summer 10–2 and 4–7, also July and Aug until 8; adm*), built for the king of Navarra in 1407. Each of its 15 towers and turrets has its own character, and restorers have made the whole thing seem startlingly new. Inside, the décor is *mudéjar*; hanging gardens were suspended from the great arches of the terraces, and there was a *leonera* or lion pit, and a very busy set of dungeons; the Navarrese royal families led messy, frustrated lives. At night the whole complex is illuminated with a golden light, creating a striking backdrop to performances in the summer Festival of Navarra. The castle's Gothic chapel, **Santa María la Real** (*open 9.30–12 and 5–8*) has a gorgeous 13th-century façade and a sweet-faced Virgin from the same period above the altar. The Romanesque church of San

Getting Around

By Train and Bus

Most trains between Pamplona and the main junction of Altsasu stop at Huarte-Araquil; trains linking Pamplona and Zaragoza call at Tafalla, Olite and Tudela. Conda buses (t 94 822 10 26, www.conda.es) stop at Tafalla, Olite and Tudela on the way to Zaragoza.

Tourist Information

Olite: Plaza Carlos III, t 94 874 17 03, oit.olite@cfnavarra.es.

Tudela: C/Juicio 4, t 94 884 80 58, www.tudela.com. The new tourist office has exhibits on local history, arts, crafts and food.

There are **markets** in Tafalla on Plaza Navarra on Friday; in Olite in Paseo del Portal on Wednesday; in Fitero in Plaza San Raimundo on Tuesday and Friday.

Where to Stay and Eat

Tafalla ✉ 31300

✭✭Hs Tafalla, on the Zaragoza road, t 94 870 03 00, www.hostaltafalla.com (moderate).

Modern roadside hotel, with comfortable rooms and delicious food (especially anything involving asparagus, lamb and hake). Closed Fri.

Túbal , Plaza de Navarra 2, t 94 870 08 52 (expensive). Chef Atxen Jiménez draws in diners from Pamplona and beyond with her delicious variations on classic Navarrese themes. Countless well-deserved gourmet awards mean you should book well in advance. Closed Sun eve, Mon and late Aug.

Olite ✉ 31390

✭✭✭Parador Príncipe de Viana, t 94 874 00 00, olite@parador.es (moderate). Next to the Castle of Charles III in the converted 13th-century Castillo de los Teobaldos. A garden, air conditioning and beautiful furnishings make castle-dwelling a delight, as do delicious Navarrese gourmet treats in the dining room.

El Joyosa Guardo, C/Medios 23, t 94 874 13 03, www.lajoyosaguardo.com (moderate). Chic new hotel in a renovated mansion with a stylish mix of antiques and contemporary furnishings, and a very elegant restaurant.

✭✭Hotel Merindad de Olite, Rúa de la Juderia 11, t/f 94 874 07 35 (inexpensive). In a restored old building, which incorporates part of the

Pedro (same hours) has an octagonal tower and portal adorned with two large stone eagles, one devouring the hare it has captured (symbolizing force) and the other more friendly, representing gentleness.

East of Tafalla and Olite, the little wine-producing village of S**an Martín de Unx** has a superb crypt under its 12th-century church and a string of bodegas. From here a byroad branches south for the spectacularly lovely medieval village of **Ujué**, set on a hill corrugated with terraces, where a shepherd, directed by a dove, found the statue of the black Virgin now housed in the powerful 13th-century Romanesque-Gothic church of Santa María. The doorway has finely carved scenes of the Last Supper and the Magi and the altar preserves the heart of King Charles II of Navarra. Every year since 1043, on the first Sunday after St Mark's day (25 April), the Virgin has been the object of a solemn pilgrimage that departs from Tafalla at 2am.

Tudela

Founded by the Moors, Tudela, the second city of Navarra and capital of La Ribera region, was the last town in Navarra to submit to Ferdinand the Catholic, and it did so most unwillingly. Before the big bigot, Tudela had always made a point of welcoming Jews, Moors and heretics expelled from Castile or persecuted by the Inquisition, and it

12th-century walls. Good restaurant serving traditional fare.

**Casa Zanito, Rúa Mayor 16, t 94 874 06 44, (*inexpensive*). A modern hotel with a good restaurant (*moderate*) serving classic dishes.

Ujué ✉ 31390

Accommodation in this area is restricted to *casas rurales*.

Casa El Chofer I and II, t 94 873 90 11 (*budget*). Simple rooms with private bath.

Mesón las Torres, t 94 873 90 52 (*moderate*). This has long been *the* place to dine, with Navarrese taste treats and Ujué's special candied almonds. *Lunch only.*

Tudela ✉ 31500

**Hs Remigio, C/Gaztambide 4, t 94 882 08 50, (*budget*). A simple hostal, not far from the Plaza de Fueros, decorated with an old-fashioned rusticity.

*Hs Nueva Parrilla, Carlos III el Noble 12, t 94 882 24 00 (*budget*). A friendly, basic choice with functional rooms.

Casa Ignacio, C/Cortaderos 11, t 94 882 10 21 (*moderate*). Try the famous *menestra de verduras*: delicious asparagus, artichokes, peas, celery and lettuces. Book a table here to taste them at their freshest. *Closed Mon eve, Tues and 15 Aug–15 Sept.*

Restaurant 33, C/Capuchinos 7, t 94 882 76 06 (*moderate*). Widely regarded as the best restaurant in Navarra when it comes to the preparation of the celebrated local produce - they even offer a *menú* entirely of vegetable dishes. Carnivores will be more than satisfied with the local lamb dishes and country stews.

Iruña, Calle Muro 11, t 94 882 10 00 (*moderate*). Another great place to try the local *menestra de verduras. Closed Thurs.*

Bar Aragon, Plaza de los Fueros 2 (*budget*). Low-key café/restaurant on the square, with good *tapas* such as *habitas salteados con jamón* (baby broad beans and ham). Livens up at night.

Cintruénigo ✉ 31592

Hotel Restaurante Maher, C/La Ribera 19, t 94 881 11 50 (*expensive–moderate*). The best reason to stop here is to dine here, at one of Navarra's best restaurants. Delicious Navarrese dishes with an imaginative *nouvelle cuisine* touch are on the menu.

---

was no accident that its tolerant environment nurtured three of Spain's top medieval writers: Benjamin of Tudela, the great traveller and chronicler (1127–73); the poet Judah Ha-Levi of the same period; and Dr Miguel Servet (1511–53), one of the first to write about the circulation of the blood.

Don't be disheartened by Tudela's protective coating of dusty, gritty sprawl, head straight for its picturesque, labyrinthine Moorish-Jewish kernel, around the elegant 17th-century **Plaza de los Fueros**; the decorations on the façades recall its use as a bull ring in the 18th and 19th centuries. The Gothic **Cathedral** (*open Tues–Sat 10–1.30–1 and 4–7, Sun 10–1.30; adm*) was built over the Great Mosque in the 12th century and topped with a pretty 17th-century tower. It has three decorated doorways: the north and south portals have capitals with New Testament scenes, while the west portal, the Portada del Juicio Final, is devoted to the Last Judgement, depicted in 114 different scenes in eight soaring bands. The delightful choir, behind its Renaissance grille, is considered the finest Flamboyant Gothic work in Navarra, carved with geometric flora, fauna and fantasy motifs; note, under the main chair, the figures of two crows picking out the eyes of a man – the dean who commissioned the work but refused to pay the sculptors the agreed price. The main altar has a beautiful Hispano-Flemish *retablo* painted by Pedro Díaz de Oviedo and yet more chains from Las Navas de Tolosa; there's an ornate

Gothic *retablo* of Santa Caterina and a chapel of Santa Ana, patroness of Tudela, with a cupola that approaches Baroque orgasm. The cool, plant-filled 13th-century cloister, with twin and triple columns, has capitals on the life of Jesus and other New Testament stories, while the Escuela de Cristo, off the east end of the cloister, has *mudéjar* paintings and decorations. The square, pedestrianised and filled with a sea of tables spilling out from terrace cafés, is a favourite with locals.

Among the best palaces are the **Casa del Almirante** near the cathedral and, in the C/de Magallón, the lovely Renaissance **Palace of the Marqués de San Adrián**. An irregular, 17-arched, 13th-century bridge spanning the Ebro still takes much of Tudela's traffic, with help from a new ultra-modern suspension bridge.

Around Tudela

Just east of Tudela is a striking desert region straight out of the American Far West known as the **Bárdenas Reales** (the website *www.bardenasreales.es* has lots of useful practical information), , where erosion has sculpted steep tabletops, weird wrinkled hills and rocks balanced on pyramids. The best way to see it (and not get lost) is by the GR 13 walking path, crossing its northern extent from the Hermitage of the Virgen del Yugo. South of Tudela, **Cascante** is known for its wines and the lofty church of the Virgen del Romero (Our Lady of the Rosemary Bush), built in the 17th century and reached by way of an arcaded walkway from the village below.

The small spa town of **Fitero** (the waters are used in treating tuberculosis) grew up around the 11th-century Cistercian **Monastery of Santa María la Real**, whose abbot, San Raimundo, founded the famous Order of the Knights of Calatrava in 1158. Don't miss the Romanesque Sala Capitular, a monumental *retablo* from the 1500s, the ornate 18th-century chapel of the Virgen de la Barda and, among the treasures, a 10th-century ivory coffer from the workshop of the Caliph of Córdoba. **Cintruénigo** and **Corella** just north are important producers of DO Navarra wine, with a good dozen *bodegas* in the environs.

Northwest of Pamplona: Aralar and San Miguel in Excelsis

Navarra's magic mountain, **Aralar**, now a natural park, is a favourite spot for a picnic or Sunday hike, gracefully wooded with beech, rowan, and hawthorn groves. It has been sacred to the Basques since neolithic times, when they erected 30 dolmens and menhirs in the yew groves around Putxerri, the biggest concentration of neolithic monuments in all Spain. On top is Navarra's holy of holies, the **Sanctuary of San Miguel in Excelsis** (*open 9.30–8*), on a panoramic north–south road (NA–7510) that climbs over Aralar between Uharte–Arakil and Lekunberri.

The gloomy stone chapel, built by the Count of Goñi, was consecrated in 1098. Guarded traditionally by mastiffs (we didn't see any), the chapel has had an empty air ever since French Basques plundered it in 1797, when they knocked off St Michael's head (or so say apologists who find the crystal head too weird); the hands of the desecrators were chopped off before they were put to death and nailed over the chapel door. You can

The Knight, the Dragon and the Archangel

In the 9th century, Count Teodosio de Goñi went off to fight the Saracens with his Visigothic overlord King Witiza. He was returning home when he met a hermit (the devil in disguise) who warned him that his wife was unfaithful. Seething with rage, the knight stormed into his castle, saw two forms lying in his bed and without hesitation slew them both. When he ran out he met his wife returning from Mass, who told him, to his horror, that she had given his own aged parents the bed.

Horrified, Teodosio went to Rome to ask the pope what penance he could do. After three nights the pope dreamt that Teodosio should wear heavy chains in solitude until God showed his forgiveness by breaking them. Binding himself in chains, Teodosio went to the top of Mt Aralar and lived as a hermit for years, when one day, when he was sitting next to a cave a scaly green dragon emerged, smoke billowing from its nostrils. Teodosio implored the aid of St Michael, who suddenly appeared with his sword in hand, and spoke to the dragon in perfect Basque: '*Nor Jaunggoitkoa bezaka*?' ('Who is stronger than God?'). The dragon slunk back into its cave, and the archangel struck off the knight's chains and left a statue of himself – an angelic figure with a large cross on its head and an empty glass case where the face ought to be.

Every year between March and August the figure goes on a fertility-blessing tour through a hundred Navarra villages; on Corpus Christi pilgrims walk or cycle up to the chapel to pay their respects.

see the chains worn by Teodosio de Goñi and the hole through which the dragon appeared; pilgrims still stick their heads into it, although no one remembers why. A high-tech alarm system protects the recently stolen, but, fortunately, recently rediscovered, enamelled Byzantine *retablo*, showing the Virgin on a rainbow in a mandorla with the Christ Child; the only comparable work in Europe is the great altarpiece in St Mark's in Venice. Tentatively dated 1028, it is likely that it was originally stolen from Constantinople by a Crusader and sold to Sancho the Great, who donated it to the chapel.

Around Aralar

Of the villages under the mountain, **Lekunberri** is the most orientated to tourism, but **Leitza**, just north, is a prettier choice, besides being the home of Basque legend Iñaki Perurena, the *arrejazotzale* or champion heavy-stone weightlifter. Along the road to Tolosa, **Betelu** not only bottles Navarra's mineral water, but has a fun little roadside swimming hole with slides where the stream has been dammed. **Zudaire**, south of Aralar, is the head town in a broken terrain called **Las Améscoas**, the refuge of the Carlists and delight of speleologists: most of the caves are located above Zudaire around Baquedano with its craggy ravine and streams.

Aralar is hardly the only mountain in Europe dedicated to heaven's Generalissimo: there's Mont-Saint-Michel in France, St Michael's Mount in England, and Monte Sant'Angelo in Italy to name a few. In art Michael is often shown with a spear, not slaying as much as *transfixing* dragons to the earth: the spots where he does this are said to be sources

Tourist Information

Lekunberri: Plazaola 21, t 94 850 72 04, oit.lekunberri@cfnavarra.es.

Where to Stay and Eat

**Hs Ayestarán II, C/Aralar 22, in Lekunberri, t 94 850 41 27 (*moderate*). Has a pleasant old-fashioned atmosphere, tennis, children's recreational facilities, a pool and garden; *menús* feature home-cooked stews, stuffed peppers and codfish with almonds.

*Hs Basa Kabi, Alto de Leitza, t 94 851 01 25, *basakabi@jet.es* (*inexpensive*). Sleep and eat reasonably at this rural hotel in the hills 5km from Leitza. Good, local restaurant.

Asador Epeleta, Aralar s/n, Lekunberri, t 948 50 43 57 (*expensive–moderate*). Possibly the finest roast meats in Spain, along with good seafood. Book well in advance. *Closed Mon, second fortnight of June.*

Venta Muguiro, Autopista A15 (exit 123), t 948 50 41 02 (*moderate*). An old-fashioned 19th-century inn, with country cooking and plenty of atmosphere despite the nearby motorway.

of underground water. And sure enough, the Sierra de Aralar is so karstic as to be practically hollow; under the sanctuary there's an immense subterranean river that makes moaning dragonish sounds, feeding an icy lake under a domed cavern.

Southwest of Pamplona: the Camino de Santiago

Few places in Europe can boast such a concentration of medieval curiosities as this stretch of road, where the mystic syncretism of the Jews, Templars, pagans and pilgrims was expressed in monuments with secret messages that still tease and mystify today.

From Pamplona to Estella

A short turn off the N111 (about 15km from Pamplona) leads to the old village of **Obanos**, and 1.6km beyond that village to a lonely field and **Santa María de Eunate** (*open Jan–Feb and Nov 10.30–2.30; Mar–June and Oct 10.30–1.30 and 4–7; July–Sept 10–1 and 4.30–7, closed Mon and Dec*), a striking 12th-century church that was built by the Templars. The Templars often built their chapels as octagons, but this one was purposely made irregular, and is surrounded by a unique 33-arched octagonal cloister – hence its name 'Eunate' (the Hundred Doors). Many knights were buried here, and it's likely that its peculiar structure had deep significance in the Templars' initiatory rites. There are only a few carved capitals – some little monsters, and pomegranates on the portal, which, oddly, faces north. During the chapel's restoration, scallop shells were discovered along with the tombs – the church served as a mortuary chapel for pilgrims. The lack of a central keystone supporting the eight ribs inside hints that Arab architects were involved in the building, and the Romanesque Virgin by the alabaster window is a copy of the one stolen in 1974.

The *camino francés* from Roncesvalles (*see* p.73) and the *camino aragonés* converged at the bridge, which dated from the 11th century, in pretty **Puente la Reina**. This hasn't changed much since the day when pilgrims marched down the sombre Rúa Mayor, where many of the houses still preserve their coats of arms. The pilgrims traditionally entered Puente la Reina through the arch of another Templar foundation, El Crucifijo, a church with scallops and Celtic interlaced designs on the portal and two naves. The smaller one was added to house a powerful 14th-century German crucifix left by a pilgrim, where the Christ is nailed not to a cross but the trunk and branches of a Y-shaped tree.

Towards the bridge, the church of **Santiago** has a weathered Moorish-style lobed portal and inside, two excellent polychrome 14th-century statues. From Puente la Reina, the path (although not the road) continues up to atmospheric old **Cirauqui** propped on its hill, where the church of San Román has another multi-foiled portal framed in archivolts with geometric designs. The ancient road to the west of Cirauqui, paved with Roman stones, predates even the pilgrims.

Estella (Lizarra): Town of the Star

Estella, known as Estella la Bella for its beauty, was a much anticipated stop along the pilgrimage route. It owes its foundation in 1090 to a convenient miracle: nightly showers of shooting stars that always fell on the same place on a hill intrigued some shepherds, who investigated and found a cave hidden by thorns, sheltering a statue of the Virgin. Returning from the siege of Toledo the same year, King Sancho I founded Estella on the opposite bank of Río Ega from the old settlement of Lizarra (coincidentally the Basque word for 'star') and populated it with *francos*, or freemen: artisans, merchants and others who owed allegiance to no feudal lord (although confusingly, most of these *francos* were Franks from Gascony, who fought in the Reconquista for pay or piety's sake). Thanks to them, Estella has numerous fine medieval buildings; if many have been cropped, thank the Grand Inquisitor of Castile, Cardinal Cisneros, whose troops literally cut Navarra down to size in 1512.

The most exciting time to visit Estella is the Friday before the first Sunday in August, when it holds the only *encierro* where women are welcome, even if the bulls are really heifers with padded horns.

The arcaded **Plaza Fueros** is the town's bustling main square, full of terrace cafés, and overlooked by the Gothic church of San Juan with a dour early 20th-century façade and ear-splitting bells which ring out on the hour. To the west is the **Basílica de Nuestra Señora de Puy**, a must on the pious pilgrim route which was built on the overlook where the stars fell on Navarra that night. The 14th-century Virgin is still there, but the old basilica was replaced in 1951 with a concrete and glass star-shaped church and a *mirador* offering lovely views across the old town. South of Plaza de Santiago, the highlight for art pilgrims is 12th-century **San Miguel**, the parish church of the *francos*, set on a craggy rock atop its original set of steps (which lead up from C/Chapitel). Don't hesitate: march right up them for the magnificent portal, where Christ in majesty holds pride of place among angels, Evangelists and the Elders of the Apocalypse. On the left St Michael pins down the mighty dragon and weighs souls; on the right an angel shows the empty tomb to the three Marys. The top, sadly, fell to the Cardinal's tower-bashing squad, but the brackets are good, especially the man-eating wolf.

Getting Around

By Bus

La Estellesa buses (t 94 821 32 25, www.laestellesa.com) from Pamplona stop at Puente la Reina and Estella (with a fancy neo-Moorish station) en route to Logroño five times a day.

Tourist Information

Estella: San Nicolás 1, t 94 855 63 01, oit.estella@cfnavarra.es.
Puente la Reina: Plaza Mena s/n t 94 834 08 45.
Los Arcos: In the Ayuntamiento t 94 844 11 42.
Viana: Plaza de los Fueros, t 94 844 63 02.

Where to Stay and Eat

Puente la Reina ✉ 31100

★★★★**Hotel El Peregrino**, on the Pamplona road, t 94 834 00 75, www.hotelelperegrino.com (*expensive*). This stone and timber place isn't as old as it looks, but it has cosy, air-conditioned rooms and a pool, and serves up excellent meals with a French gourmet touch in a split-level dining room. *Closed Sun eve and Mon.*

★★★**Hotel Jakue**, C/Irunbidea, t 94 834 10 17, www.jakue.com (*moderate*). At the northern end of town, this modern, functional hotel has decent, comfortable rooms and a surprisingly good restaurant.

Estella ✉ 31200

Estella isn't known for its dining – consider a picnic by the banks of the river.

★★★**Irache**, in Ayegui (3km away on the Logroño road), t 94 855 11 50, f 94 855 47 54, www.gsmhoteles.es (*moderate*). The largest

and most comfortable hotel, set in a 1970s urbanización, offering air con and a pool.

★**Hs Cristina**, C/Baja Navarra 1, t 94 855 07 72 (*inexpensive*). A simple place run by a kindly woman; may be noisy on Saturday night.

★**Pensión San Andrés**, C/Mayor 1, t 94 855 04 58 (*inexpensive*). Excellent value, clean and central, with family-size rooms overlooking the square (ask for rooms on the top floor).

Fonda Izarra, C/Caldería 20, t 94 855 06 78 (*budget*). The doubles here are the cheapest in Estella.

La Navarra, Gustavo de Maeztú 16, t 94 855 00 40 (*expensive–moderate*). A good bet, perhaps more for its medieval atmosphere than food, which is good if a bit pricey. *Closed Sun eve and Mon.*

La Cepa, Pza Fueros 15, t 94 855 00 15 (*moderate*). Specializes in Basque and Navarrese cuisine, with a reasonable *menú degustación* and terrace. *Closed Sun eve.*

Los Arcos ✉ 31210

★★**Hotel Monaco**, Pza del Coso 22, t 94 864 00 00, www.monacohotel.net (*inexpensive*). Recently refurbished modest hotel in the centre, with crisp modern rooms..

★★**Hs Ezequiel**, La Serna 14, t 94 864 02 96, t 94 864 02 78 (*budget*). A friendly, family-run hotel, with large restaurant and bar.

Viana ✉ 31230

Borgia, Serapio Urra, t 94 864 57 81 (*expensive–moderate*). Avant-garde décor is the setting for Aurora Cariñanos' temple of personal, imaginative cuisine, where you can dine delectably on dishes such as *pochas con caracoles al tomillo* (fresh haricot beans with snails and thyme), accompanied by an excellent cellar. *Closed Sun eve and Aug.*

Casa Armendariz, Navarro Villoslada 19, in the centre, (*moderate–inexpensive*). A mix of traditional and modern cuisine at this good-value *sidrería*.

Near San Miguel you'll find a faithful 19th-century copy of Estella's medieval bridge, which pilgrims crossed to the Lizarra side to visit the 12th-century **San Sepolcro,** with a fascinating façade added in 1328 but again truncated by Cisneros. The tympanum has an animated Last Supper, Crucifixion, Resurrection and what looks to be the harrowing of hell; statues of the 12 apostles flank the door – one of them appears to be holding a stack of pancakes. To the right of the bridge is the piquant centre of old Lizarra, with churches and palaces bearing proud coats of arms, most now occupied by antique shops, along Calle de la Rúa ('Street of the Street'). The finest palace is the Plateresque brick **Casa Fray Diego**, now used as the Casa de Cultura (*open Tues–Sat 6.30-8.30, Sat–Sun 12–2*). Off to the left was the Judería, or Jewish ghetto, its 12th-century synagogue converted into **Santa María de Jus del Castillo**, where the apse is decorated with a rich assortment of Romanesque modillions. The church is dwarfed by the adjacent and wonderfully austere 13th-century monastery of **Santo Domingo**, recently converted into a retirement home. Further up, near the new bridge, a 16th-century fountain under a canopy of linden trees in **Plaza de San Martín** makes a delightful place to linger for a while.

A curving flight of the stairs leads up to the 12th-century **San Pedro de la Rúa** (*open for guided visits, see tourist office for information, or for mass only*), defended by a skyscraper bell tower. The Moorish-inspired foiled arch of the portal is crowned by a relief of St James in a boat with stars, blessed by a giant hand emerging from the water. Inside, the church has its share of curiosities: a unique column made of three interlaced 'serpents' and the black Virgin de la O, a cult figure of the masons, who left their marks all over the church. The Baroque chapel to the left houses St Andrew's shoulder blade; the story goes that the Bishop of Patras took it with him for good luck while making the pilgrimage in 1270. Luck failed him in Estella, where he died and was buried in San Pedro's cloister, along with his relic. The apostle's shoulder blade wasn't going to have any of this, and made itself known by a curious light that appeared over the tomb; in 1626, the day when Andrew was proclaimed patron of Estella, a burning vision of his X-shaped cross hovered over the church. Of the cloister, only two galleries survive, reconstructed after the castle above was blown up in 1572 and crashed on top of it. The capitals are especially good, carved with the lives of the saints and the Apocalypse: the twisted column is a copy of the one in Santo Domingo de Silos in Burgos.

Over the years Estella became a favourite residence of the kings, whose 12th-century **Palacio de los Reyes de Navarra**, opposite San Pedro, is one of the best-preserved civic buildings from the period. Prominent at street level a capital bears the oldest known depiction of Roland, clad in scaly armour, fighting the equally scaly giant Ferragut; further up, another capital shows devils and animal musicians, including a donkey playing a harp. The palace now houses the **Museo Gustavo de Maeztú** (*t 94 854 60 37; open Tues–Sat 11–1 and 5–7, 11–1.30; adm*), devoted to works by Estella's best-known painter (1887–1947). At the tourist office next door, have a look at the model showing the evolution of Estella between 1090 and 1990.

Around Estella

Estella is an important producer of DO Navarra wine, and the most interesting *bodega* to visit just happens to be the Benedictine **Monasterio de Irache**, 2km west at Ayegui (*monastery open winter Tues 10–1.30, Wed–Sun 10–1.30 and 4.30–6; summer Tues 10–1.30, Wed–Fri 10–1.30 and 5–7, Sat–Sun 9–1.30 and 4–7; wine museum open Sat–Sun 10–2 and 4–8pm*). First recorded in 958, it later received a generous endowment from Sancho the Great, who helped finance one of the very first pilgrims' hospitals here. In 1569

Philip II moved Sahagún's university of theology here, where it remained, enjoying the same privileges as Salamanca until it closed down with the expropriation of monasteries in 1824. The complex is a handsome mix behind an eclectic façade. The entrance is through an elegant Plateresque door, and leads into an austerely beautiful Romanesque church with three apses under a Renaissance dome, stripped of centuries' encrustation of altarpieces: the original Romanesque north door is decorated with hunting scenes. The sumptuous Plateresque cloister has grotesque and religious capitals. The small wine museum preserves Irache's 1,000-year-old custom of offering free drinks to pilgrims.

Twelve kilometres up the San Sebastián road in Abarzua, the **Monasterío de Iranzu** *(open daily summer 10–2 and 4–8; winter 10–2 and 4–6; adm, to arrange guided visits call 94 852 00 47)* was founded in the 11th century by Cistercians, who chose to live in a dramatic ravine true to their preference for remote settings in the wilds. It was recently restored by the government of Navarra and given to the Theatine order. The monks will show you around their medieval kitchen and Romanesque-Gothic cloister with a hexagonal fountain and church. South of Estella on the Ebro, **Lodosa** is famous for its *appellation contrôlée* red peppers, *pimientas del piquillo*, that are dried in long garlands over the white façades of the houses; its church San Miguel has an immense rococo *retablo*.

Los Arcos and Sorlada

After Estella, the pilgrims walked to **Los Arcos** where, tucked off the N111, is an arcaded plaza and a 16th-century church, Santa María, with a pretty cathedral-size Gothic cloister, carved choir stalls and frantic Baroque *retablos*. Seven kilometres north of Los Arcos at **Sorlada**, a grand 18th-century Baroque basilica belongs to **San Gregorio Ostiense**, a once immensely popular saint who lost much of his influence to modern fertilizers. His story is told in the basilica's naïve paintings: back in 1039 locusts plagued the region so badly that a group of farmers walked to Rome and asked the pope for help. The pope had a dream that Cardinal Gregory of Ostia was the man for the job, and off he went to Navarra, where he preached and dispersed the locusts, an exertion that killed him after five years. He was buried at Sorlada and forgotten, until a light redirected farmers to his tomb. Remembering his good juju against the locusts (and their ancestral Celtic head cult) they would cart his skull reliquary around their fields, pouring water through the hole which made it into 'holy Gregory water'. Philip II had gallons of it sent down to water the orchards of the Escorial. West of Los Arcos, **Torres del Río** has a striking tall octagonal church, **Santo Sepolcro**, built by the Knights of the Holy Sepulchre; like Santa María Eunate, it may have been a mortuary chapel for pilgrims. The cross-ribbed vaulting is exactly like that in the churches built in Córdoba under the Caliphs; if restoration work has been completed, don't miss the shadowy interior.

Viana: Where Cesare Borgia Bit the Dust

Just before La Rioja, **Viana** fits a lot of monumentality into a small space. Founded by King Sancho VII the Strong in 1219 to defend his frontier with Castile, it became the hereditary principality of the heir to the throne of Navarra in 1423. Although its once proud castle fell to Cardinal Cisneros' demolition programme, nobles and courtly hangers-on stayed on and built themselves splendid mansions with big coats of arms and the elegant 17th-century **Casa Consistorial**, crowned with an escutcheon the size of an asteroid, and the 13th–14th-century church of **Santa María**, hidden by a magnificent concave Renaissance façade, based on a triumphant arch with a coffered ceiling designed and carved by Juan de Goyaz (1549). Inside, the Gothic interior is quite airy and lovely, culminating in an intricate gilded Baroque retable. The façade could be considered the tombstone of Cesare Borgia (1475–1507), whose memorial, all that is left of his desecrated remains, lies buried under the marker in front of the church.

Now how did Pope Alexander VI's son and Machiavelli's hero end up in Viana? With the papacy and central Italy in his pocket by 1502, married to Charlotte, the King of Navarre's sister, and supported by France, Cesare had embarked on a brilliant career as a ruthless Renaissance prince-assassin. When his father pulled the rug out from under him by dying suddenly in 1503, Cesare himself was too ill to get to the Vatican and influence the conclave to elect a Borgia candidate; according to Machiavelli's *The Prince*, it was the only political mistake he ever made. It proved to be fatal. Once Julius II, archenemy of the Borgias, was elected in late 1503, Cesare's conquests in Italy were frittered away in anarchy, the French turned against him, and he went from being on top of the world to a man whose life was in danger. He fled to Aragón, the cradle of the Borgias, only to be imprisoned by Ferdinand. Navarra proved to be his only refuge, and he died in a skirmish in Viana, fighting Castilian rebels.

La Rioja

La Rioja may be named after the river Oja, one of the seven tributaries of the Ebro, but to most people it means wine, wine and more wine. The banks of the Ebro are frilly with vineyards and pinstriped with rows of garden vegetables on the flat, tremendously fertile plains of Rioja Baja around Calahorra.

In the Sierra de la Demanda in the southwest, mountains are high enough to ski down; in the gullies of Rioja Baja, dinosaurs once made the earth tremble, or at least left their curious tracks in the squodge of a prehistoric bog, which hardened and petrified for posterity.

Wedged up against the Ebro between Navarra and Castile, who once so hotly contested its fields and vineyards, the *comunidad* of La Rioja is now the smallest autonomous region in Spain (5,000 sq km) – not that there is any distinctive Riojan language or race, although in the 11th century a king, one of the four sons of Sancho the Great of Navarra, sat in Nájera. This was a brief but marked period of independence, when Riojans began the history of Castilian Spanish as a written and poetic language and contributed to the invention of Santiago, with a first sighting of the battling Son of Thunder at Calvijo and more than one miracle and saint along its stretch of the pilgrimage road.

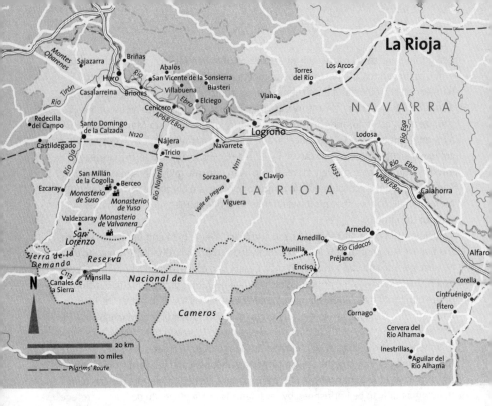

Logroño

More than half of all the 250,000 Riojans live in Logroño, their shiny, up-to-date capital famous not only for wine but also coffee caramels. It began under the Visigoths as *Gronio*, The Ford, but really bloomed only with the advent of the pilgrimage, when a stone bridge was built over the Ebro by San Juan de Ortega, one of La Rioja's two building saints. A prosperous modern agricultural centre, it nonetheless contains a pleasant little historic centre huddled around the graceful cathedral.

A Walk Around Logroño

Logroño is a big long sausage of a town, but the interesting bits are concentrated in a small area near the Ebro. Barely an arch survives of San Juan's first bridge, which was replaced in the 1800s by the **Puente de Hierro**, or iron bridge. Just off this the pilgrims would pass in front of the 16th-century fountain and lofty Gothic **Santiago**, the oldest church in town. This was rebuilt in 1500, with a single nave a startling 53ft wide and still standing, in spite of the fact that its architect had no confidence in his handiwork and left town as soon as it was completed. It has a Renaissance *retablo*, and at the front a mighty 18th-century statue of Santiago Matamoros ('St James Moor-killer') who rides a steed with *cojones* as big as beach balls. The sculptor of the equestrian statue of General Espartero (in Logroño's central park, the **Espolón**) took them into consideration and equipped the mortal general's mortal horse a few degrees less generously.

Getting Around

By Train
Several trains a day link Haro, Logroño, and Calahorra on the Bilbao–Zaragoza route. The RENFE station is at Plaza Europa: timetable and ticket information from t 902 24 02 02, or www.renfe.es.

By Bus
Logroño's bus links are faster and more frequent than train services. Several buses a day run to Burgos (via the towns on the pilgrims' route), Zaragoza, Vitoria, Pamplona and Rioja's villages.

In Logroño the bus station is at Avda de España 1, t 94 123 59 83, and the train station (with a left luggage office) is nearby in Piazza de Europa.

Tourist Information

Paseo del Espolón, t 94 129 12 60, www. logroño.org (for city information) or www. larioja.org/turismo (this website covers all tourist offices in La Rioja).

There is a **market** for country produce and products at Mercado del Campo, Marqués de la Enseñada 52. Open Tues and Fri 8–2.

Where to Stay

Logroño ✉ 26000
Logroño has a surprising number of luxury modern hotels, but few of them possess much charm.

****Gran Hotel AC La Rioja, C/Madre de Dios 21, t 94 127 23 50, www.ac-hotels.com. The only 5-star hotel in Logroño, this is modern and geared towards business travellers – but it offers guests every necessary convenience.

****Carlton Rioja, Gran Vía del Rey Juan Carlos I 5, t 94 124 21 00, f 94 124 35 02, www.pretur.es (expensive–moderate). Glassy modern block located on the edge of the Casco Antiguo.

***Ciudad de Logroño, C/Menéndez Pelayo 7, t 94 125 02 44, f 94 125 43 90, www.pretur.es

(moderate). Central, modern and comfortable, with views over a park.

***Hotel Marqués de Vallejo, Marqués de Vallejo 8, t 94 124 83 33, f 94 124 02 88, www.hotelmarquesdevallejo.com (moderate–inexpensive). A handsome place near the cathedral, with a sleek contemporary interior hiding behind a historic façade.

***Hotel Murrieta, Marqués de Murrieta 1, t 94 122 41 50, f 94 122 32 13, hotels@ pretur.es (inexpensive). A bland, modern hotel, but central and offering guests free Internet access.

Residencia Daniel, C/Juan 21, t 94 125 29 48 (inexpensive). Has spotless rooms amid the bustle of the casco viejo.

**Hs la Numantina, C/Sagasta 4, t 94 125 14 11 (budget). Modest, but attractively priced hostal in the centre.

Eating Out

For tapas, try C/Laurel and C/San Juan.

El Cachetero, C/Laurel 3, t 94 122 84 63 (expensive–moderate). A popular choice for four generations, Logroño's best restaurant serves mouth-watering menestras and local delicacies such as pigs' trotters stuffed with mushrooms, capers and paté; book ahead. Closed Sun and Wed eve and last week of Aug.

El Rincón del Vino, Marqués de San Nicolás 136, t 94 120 53 92 (expensive–moderate). As well as a vast selection of the promised vino, they have a fine asador serving delicacies like sirloin steak with wild mushroom stuffing. Closed Sun eve, Mon and Aug.

Las Cubanas, C/San Agustín 17, t 94 122 00 50 (budget). Come here with the locals for a delicious menestra; the place owes its popularity to excellent regional cuisine, its friendly atmosphere and good value. Closed eves.

Los Gabrieles, C/Bretón de los Herreros 8, t 94 122 60 80 (budget). Grand traditional restaurant off the main square with dishes like cazuela de pimientos (pepper stew) and pisto riojana (Rioja-style ratatouille) on the menu.

The skyline of Logroño is stabbed by church towers, including two slender 18th-century Churrigueresque towers by Martín de Beratúa that frame the magnificent Baroque façade of the cathedral, **Santa María de la Redonda** in Plaza del Mercado, a front that belies the Gothic-inspired gloom inside (*open Mon-Sat 8–1 and 6.30–8.30, Sun 9–2 and 6.30–8.30*); the rotundity of its name (the first Romanesque church was octagonal) is recalled in an exuberant round rococo altar. Near here, in a high-security strongbox, is the *Tabla de Calvario*, supposedly painted by Michelangelo for his friend and muse Vittoria Colonna. Logroño's most distinctive landmark is its nubby pyramidal 'Needle', the 149ft 13th-century spire atop the lantern of **Santa María de Palacio**, in C/Marqués de San Nicolás, a church said to have been founded by no one less than Emperor Constantine. If it's open, pop in to see the Renaissance choir stalls, the 13th-century *Nuestra Señora de la Antigua*, and what remains of the Gothic cloister. Another tower, brick 11th-century *mudéjar* this time, looks over **San Bartolomé** with a ruggedly carved, time-blackened 14th-century Gothic façade; the smooth white interior, recently restored, has lovely shallow choir vaults.

The 17th-century Palacio del General Espartero in Plaza San Agustín now holds the **Museo Provincial de La Rioja** (*open Tues–Sat 10–2 and 4–7, until 9 in July and Aug, Sun and hols 11.30–2; adm*), full of art from disappeared churches (14th-century painting from San Millán and *San Francisco with Brother Lion* by El Greco), Flemish coffers and orphaned academic 19th-century paintings from the Prado's storerooms. There is a number of wine cellars in the area, including **Bodegas Marqués de Murrieta**, at Ygay (*www.marquesdemurrieta.com, Ctra de Zaragoza, kilometre 403, t 94 127 13 70*), founded in 1852 and famous for its 35–40-year-old *Gran Reservas*.

Calahorra and La Rioja Baja

Down the Ebro, east of Logroño, La Rioja Baja is flat, fertile, well watered and endowed with a sunny Mediterranean climate. Olive oil and wine are the two main-stays of the economy, with the kind of peppers the Spanish devour by the kilo coming in a close third. Few tourists pass through here, and those who do are mostly dinosaur fanciers: it's one thing to see a pile of dusty old bones in a museum, but quite another to walk along and find their splayed footprints at your feet.

Calahorra

Despite its down-at-heel appearance, Calahorra has an interesting history. In fact, it has been inhabited for so long (since Palaeolithic times) that St Jerome speculated that it was founded by Tubal, grandson of Noah.

It first makes history as Kalauria, an important Celtiberian fortress town under Carthaginian sway that, thanks to the Ebro, traded with the Greek colonies on the Mediterranean coast. In 187 BC the town was grabbed by Rome; then, in a dispute between Pompey and Sertorius in AD 72, it held out against Pompey until all its defenders were dead through starvation, a fanaticism that gave rise to the expression 'Calagurritan hungers'. The Romans rebuilt it, and Calahorra returned the favour by

Tourist Information

Calahorra: C/Ángel Olivan 8, t 94 114 63 98, www.ayto-calahorra.es.
Arnedo: Palacio de la Baronesa, C/Carrera 9, t 94 138 39 88, *www.arnedo.com*.
There are **markets** in Calahorra on Pza del Raso on Thursdays; in Alfaro on Fridays; in Cervera de Río Alhama on Fridays; and in Arnedo on Mondays and Tuesdays.

Where to Stay and Eat

Calahorra ✉ 26500

****Parador de Calahorra, t 94 113 03 58, f 94 113 51 39, *calahorra@parador.es* (*moderate*). A modern, red-brick parador near the scanty Roman ruins of Calagurris, with good views, newly renovated rooms and air conditioning. It has a good restaurant serving regional and international cuisine.
**Chef Nino, C/Padre Lúcas 2, t 94 113 20 29 (*inexpensive*). A modest hotel, which boasts the best restaurant (*moderate*) in town, serving an excellent Basque-Rioja *menú*.
*Hostal Teresa, C/Santo Domingo 2, t 94 113 03 32 (*budget*). The budget option, central but with very basic rooms.
Casa Mateo, Pza del Raso 15, t 94 113 00 09 (*moderate*). Delicious fresh produce, including the local vegetables for which the region is famed, make this restaurant an excellent choice.
La Taberna de la Cuarta Esquina, Ctra Esquinas 16, t 94 113 43 55 (*moderate*). Calahorra's best-know restaurant is justly renowned for its well-prepared fish, game and vegetable dishes and reasonably priced wines. *Closed Tues eve, Wed and July.*

Bar La Bodega, Doctor Castro Viejo 12 (*budget*). Excellent for tapas washed down with local crianza wine.

Arnedo ✉ 26580

***Victoria, Pso de la Constitución 97, t 94 138 01 00 (*expensive*). Recent and comfortable, offering good value with a pool and tennis court, plus the best restaurant in town.
***Molino de Cidacos, Ctra de Arnedo km 14, Arnedillo (14km from Arnedo), t 94 139 40 63, *www.pegarrido.com* (*moderate*). A lovingly restored 17th-century flour mill now houses one of the prettiest hotels in the region.
**Virrey, Pso de la Constitución 27, t 94 138 01 50 (*moderate*). Despite the ultra-modern façade, this is a welcoming place closer to the centre; one of the few hotels in the *comunidad* with facilities for the disabled.
**Hospedería Las Pedrolas, Plaza F'elix Merino 16, t 94 139 44 01 (*inexpensive*). An enchanting and stylish little inn in a whitewashed 18th-century building next to the church in the lovely spa town of Arnedillo (15km from Arnedo).
Picabea, C/Virrey Lezana 1, t 94 138 13 58 (*budget*). Serves good seafood and almond-filled pastries, or *fardelejos*, for which Arnedo is famous. *Closed Sun and Mon eve.*

Enciso ✉ 26580

Posada de Santa Rita, Ctra de Soria 7, t 94 139 60 71 (*inexpensive*). This little red 19th-century house is a cosy place to stay, with a small library devoted to dinosaurs.
La Fábrica de Harinas, Ctra de Soria 10, t 94 139 60 51 (*budget*). Offers delicious meals based on game dishes, served in an atmospheric old flour mill. *Open daily in summer, otherwise weekends and holidays only.*

giving Rome Marcus Fabius Quintilian (42–118), the first salaried professor of rhetoric in Rome and author of *Institutio Oratoria*, the empire's textbook on the fine art of talking. In the Middle Ages Calahorra was a prize craved by both Aragón and Castile; in a famous incident in the romance of *Las Mocedades del Cid* (and in the film *El Cid* (1961, starring Charlton Heston), the Cid fought one to one for the city against Aragón's champion, vowing to lose not only the town but his head if he were defeated, but gaining both Calahorra and the hand of his beloved Jimena if he won. Which of course he did.

Calahorra has been an episcopal see since the 5th century, but the **Cathedral** has been fussed with frequently. Behind a fruity, floral neoclassical façade pasted on in 1700, the nave with graceful star vaulting is a product of 1485. The furnishings are equally eclectic: the Gothic *Cristo de la Pelota*, 'Christ of the ball', is part of a Deposition from the Cross, the alabaster statues of the saints are 17th century, and there are paintings attributed to Titian and Zurbarán. The Plateresque cloister houses the **Museo Diocesano** (*open Sun and hols only, 12–2*) with a 12th-century Bible and 15th-century Custodia called *El Ciprés*, made of gold and silver, donated to the cathedral by Henri IV.

Just over the Río Cidacos, note the unusual 13-spout fountain. Near the cathedral, the church of Santiago and its *retablo* of St James is considered the finest neoclassical work in La Rioja. Nearby, the **Museo Municipal**'s archaeological collection (*open Tues–Sat 12–2 and 6–9, Sun 12–2*) stars the serene Roman bust of the Dama Calagurritana, symbol of the city. Just north of this, the church of San Andrés has a Gothic portal illustrating the triumph over paganism, and the Arco del Planillo is the only gateway surviving from the Roman walls of Calagurris; other Roman bits are further up, along panoramic Camino Bellavista.

East of Calahorra: the Alhama Valley

Down the Ebro holding down the east end of La Rioja, **Alfaro** was known as Ilurcis in the 5th century BC but kept its Arab name even after the Reconquista. Its chief monument is the enormous twin-towered **Colegiata de San Miguel** (*currently closed for restoration*), built in the 16th and 17th centuries and reminiscent of colonial churches in South America. The Colegiata's chief claim to fame, however, are its lodgers: it has more stork nests on its generous roof than any other in Spain, a colony of some 250 birds.

Further south, **Cervera del Río Alhama** long had an Arab majority and still has a Moorish feel to it: villagers speak *cerverano* (the town website, *www.riojainternet.com/cervera*, has a great little dictionary), with hundreds of words that are a last relic of the lost language of the Mozarabs, or Christians living in Moorish Spain. Between **Aguilar del Río Alhama** and **Inestrillas**, the Celtiberians, fleeing after the conquest by Mantis Acidinus (181 BC), holed up from the Romans for a hundred years at **Contrebia Leucada**, built on terraces, defended on one side by the river and the others by a vast ditch. It is a rare surviving example of Celtiberian town planning and water systems, and is currently being excavated.

La Rioja's Dinosaurs

South of Calahorra, **Arnedo** is a shoe-making town with a **Museo de Calzado** (shoe museum) to prove it (*C/Palacio 10, t 94 138 16 44; open Tues–Sat 10–1 and 4–8, Sun 11–2; adm*). Every 27 September the town's patron saints Cosme and Damián are honoured in the usual Spanish effigy procession, only here the parade is combined with a scrum: villagers from Navarra come in to attack the procession and make three bold attempts to make off with the saints' statues, claiming that the Riojans stole them centuries ago.

South of Arnedo, **Arnedillo** has been La Rioja's most important spa since 1847, with hot salty water good for rheumatic arthritis and stress. This is all recent history compared to the main attraction in these parts. 'When there is no trace of Spielberg left,' reads the tourist brochure, 'the dinosaur tracks will still be here.' Take that, Hollywood! La Rioja Baja has 5,000 footprints – Europe's largest concentration of dinosaur tracks, or ichnites as they're called – dating back 120 million years when La Rioja was lush, warm and wet and the denizens of the Cretaceous (post-Jurassic) period stomped through the marshes.

Somehow conditions for preserving their prints in these broken hills were better than most places: a different kind of mud filled in the tracks, preserving the impression after the mud was turned to stone. In the Middle Ages, the ichnites were said to be the hoofmarks of Santiago's horse or prints left by giant chickens that lived in the time of the Moors.

The best places to find them are in **Préjano** just east of Arnedillo and the Los Cayos gully at **Cornago. Enciso** has the largest number, especially at the Valdecevillo bed, and also houses the **Museo Paleontogólico** (*open winter Mon–Sat 11–2 and 3–6, Sun 11–2; summer daily 11–2 and 5–8; adm*), a significant collection of bones and other prehistoric relics. Other sites are just north in **Munilla** in a gully called Peñaportillo; **Igea** has more tracks and petrified plants, including a tree trunk.

South of Logroño: Into the Sierra

Dry history and misty legend are often one and the same in three-digit years in northwest Spain. Although the western bit of La Rioja was reconquered by Alfonso I of Asturias back in the 8th century, the Christians' hold on the land was tenuous and often lost for long periods to the Moors, whose Caliph made the Christians pay a tribute of a hundred maidens into their harem in return for the right to worship. This humiliating loss of young womanhood was the source of the legendary Battle of **Clavijo**, where Santiago Matamoros made his famous debut on his white horse to lead Ramiro and the Christians to victory. In gratitude, Ramiro decided to donate to Santiago a measure of wine and wheat for every *yugada* of land he reconquered, in a document known as the *Voto de Santiago* dated May 844 – a 13th-century forgery by the monks of guess where. The hamlet of Clavijo is on a dead-end road south of Logroño under a rocky outcrop and a ruined castle, with crenellations that look like a witch's teeth. The end of the tribute is celebrated on the third Sunday in May in the village of **Sorzano**, just west of the N111, when a hundred girls dressed in white carrying holly and flowers make a pilgrimage to the Hermitage del Roble. The N111 ascends through the forested **Valley of Iregua**, which narrows between the sheer cliffs and buttes of the Sierra de Cameros, dotted with old, now partly abandoned villages of shepherds, who still follow the old transhumance paths to Extremadura in the winter. There are especially lovely views of the square-cut natural gorge, the Peñas de Islallana, and the Vega del Iregua below it from the heights of **Viguera**.

Two kilometres away, in Castañares de las Cuevas, the 12th-century hermitage of **San Estéban** has frescoes of the Apocalypse and more good views. **Torrecilla en Cameros** has an attractive old centre and another church with frescoes, the 16th-century Nuestra Señora de Tómalos.

Along the Pilgrim Route: West of Logroño

Beyond Logroño, the segment of the Camino de Santiago that crosses La Rioja is short but choice and full of interest, even though only a fraction of the monuments a 12th-century pilgrim would have known remain intact. A nearly obligatory detour remains: the famous pair of monasteries at San Millán de la Cogolla.

Navarrete

Eleven kilometres west of Logroño, **Navarrete** is known for its ceramics and rosé wine. In the Middle Ages it made pilgrims comfortable in its hospital of San Juan de Arce. Of this, only the gate survives, doing duty as the entrance to the cemetery. It has lively capitals – the carvings showing St Michael and the dragon, a pair of picnicking pilgrims, and Roland grappling with the giant Ferragut; a pile of rocks, known as the *Poyo de Roldán*, marks the spot where Charlemagne's nephew floored the big bully with a boulder. The older houses in Navarrete look narrow and poky but are actually quite spacious (due to a tax on façade sizes). The 16th-century church of the **Asunción**, sometimes attributed to Philip II's architect Juan de Herrera, contains an elaborate Churrigueresque *retablo* and a triptych (in the sacristy) by Rembrandt's student Adrian Ysenbrandt.

Nájera: the Residence of Kings

Arabic *Náxara*, or 'between two hills', Nájera is a bustling furniture-making town with an illustrious pedigree. It str addles both banks of the trout-filled Najerilla, where the Moorish giant Ferragut was defending the bridge like the troll in *Three Billy Goats Gruff* when Charlemagne's knights tried to cross it. Ferragut picked them up by the armour and gathered them under his arm – at least until Roland arrived on the scene and gave him what for.

After the Moors flattened Pamplona in 918, the kings of Navarra chose to live in Nájera, mainly to keep an eye on the ambitious upstart kingdom of Castile. The first *Rex Hispaniorum*, Sancho III the Great (1004–35) held his court in both Nájera and Pamplona; in 1020 he diverted the Camino de Santiago to pass through Nájera's centre, assuring it of a good income. When he divided his kingdom between his sons, one took Pamplona and another, García III, made Nájera his capital and reconquered Rioja Baja, creating a buffer between Castile and Aragón. His grandsons were squeezed by these two medieval powerhouses, and in 1076 Nájera was snatched by Alfonso VI of Castile and the Cid. The Cid's daughter, Doña Elvira, made a happy second marriage with the son of the last king of Nájera and their son, García V, became King of Navarra in 1134.

Tourist Information

Nájera: C/Constantino Garrán 8, t 94 136 00 41, www.aytonajera.es
San Millán: Monesterio de Yuso, t 94 137 32 59
Santo Domingo: C/Mayor 70, t 94 134 12 30.
Ezcaray: C/Sagastía 1, t 94 135 46 79, www.ezcaray.org

Where to Stay and Eat

Nájera ✉ 26300

****Hostería Monasterio de San Millán**,
t 94 137 32 77, hosteria @sanmillan.com
(moderate). Situated in the monastery itself,
with a good restaurant.
***San Fernando**, Pso San Julián 1, t 94 136
37 00 (moderate). A modern hotel on the
Najerilla river with recently renovated
rooms.
***Hs Hispano**, La Cepa 2, t 94 136 29 57,
hispano@najera.net (inexpensive). A good
choice, plus restaurant.
La Parra (casa rural), La Canal 4, Campróvin
(8km from Nájera), t 94 136 16 11 (budget).
Simple B&B accommodation in a pleasant
family house.
El Mono, C/Mayor 42, t 94 136 30 28
(moderate). Nájera's favourite for local
dishes like roast lamb, or leek and prawn
tart. Buzzy bar at the entrance.
Los Parrales, C/Mayor 52, t 94 136 37 35
(budget). A few doors down, this family-run
restaurant has an excellent, good-value
menu, plus a summer terrace.

Santo Domingo ✉ 26250

****Parador de Santo Domingo de la Calzada**,
Pza del Santo 3, t 94 134 03 00,
santodomingo@parador.es (moderate). This
elegant parador occupies the pilgrim's
hostal built by Santo Domingo; the restaurant serves a delicious, if pricy menu.
***Hospedería Cistercisense**, C/Pinar 2,
t 94 134 07 00, www.cister-lacalzada.com
(inexpensive). A pleasant guesthouse run by
Cistercian nuns.
***Hs Río**, Echegoyen 2, t 94 134 00 85 ((budget)).
Try this for something (budget)er.
El Peregrino, C/Zumalacárregui 18, t 94 134
02 02 (budget). Local dishes are served in a
garden . Closed Mon.
El Rincón de Emilio, Pza de Bonifacio Gil 7,
t 94 134 09 90 (moderate). A well-known
restaurant specialising in the regional
cuisine. It does a wonderful set menu
featuring organic produce (€35). Closed Tues
eve and three weeks in Feb.

Ezcaray ✉ 26280

*****Echaurren**, C/Héroes del Alcázar 2,
t 94 135 40 47, f 94 142 71 33, info@
echaurren.com (moderate). Since the
beginning of the 20th century, this has
been the place to sleep and eat; recently it
has been renovated. It's usually essential to
book a table at the hotel's restaurant
(expensive), known for its spectacular,
contemporary cuisine. Closed Nov and Sun
eve in winter.
*****Hostería Valle del Oja**, Ctra Posadas-
Ezcaray, t 94 142 74 16 (moderate). In a
beautiful riverside setting 6km from
Ezcaray, this converted mill has comfortable
rooms, a pool and tennis.
***Iguareña**, C/Lamberto Felipe Muñoz 14,
t/f 94 135 41 44 (inexpensive). A good
choice; quiet, with a moderately priced
Basque restaurant.

In 1052 García III was hunting on the banks of the Najerilla when he saw a dove fly
past over the thick woods on a hill. He sent his falcon after it and followed the birds
through the trees into a cave, from which a bright light emanated; inside he found
the dove and falcon cooing side by side and a statue of the Virgin and Child, a jar of
fresh lilies, a lamp and a bell. To celebrate the miracle, García founded an order of
knights, the Caballeros de la Terraza (the Knights of the Jar – a mystic receptacle like
the Holy Grail) and the church, which was rebuilt in the 15th century as the
monastery of **Santa María la Real** (open Tues–Sat 10–2 and 5–8; adm) and restored

after 1895 by the Franciscans. The entrance is through a beautiful Flamboyant Gothic door, the **Portal of Charles V**, crowned with the emperor's coat of arms. Through here waits the serene and lovely Gothic-Plateresque **Claustro de los Caballeros**, with 24 arches half-veiled by intricate sculpted screens carved to imitate lace: no two are alike. Cloister chapels hold the elegant effigy tomb of a 13th-century Queen of Portugal. From here a Plateresque walnut door leads into the solemn 15th-century **church**. The original Flemish *retablo mayor* was sold for a piece of bread when the monastery was dissolved in 1835, but the 17th-century wowser in its place still holds the miraculous 11th-century statue of Santa María la Real. Originally she wore a large ruby. This was pinched by Pedro the Cruel in 1367 to pay the Black Prince and the English for whipping the French-supported army of his brother Enrique de Trastámara in a battle near Nájera. The ruby now glows on the State Crown of England, but it cost the Black Prince his life – from a Spanish fever.

Near the high altar are the tombs of the Dukes of Nájera, King Ferdinand of Aragón's right-hand men, who gave Ignatius of Loyola his first job as a soldier. At the entrance of the holy cave are 16th-century tombs of the 10th–12th-century dynasties of Pamplona and Nájera, among them the original sarcophagus of Sancho III's 21-year-old wife Blanca. This is the finest Romanesque Spanish tomb to come down to us, with a Christ in Majesty, the Massacre of the Innocents (note how, unusually, everyone seems to be smiling), the death of the queen and mourning of the king. Behind the kings is the holy cave; up the spiral stair is the remarkable Isabelline Gothic choir (1493–95), believed to have been carved by Jewish conversos (note the Hebrew letters on chair 23), a masterpiece of grace, detail and fantasy. The armour-clad King García figures on the main chair and Gothic paintings of kings and queens around the top create a charming trompe l'oeil effect. History buffs may want to check out the town's **archaeological museum** on Plaza de Nájero (*open Mon–Sat 10–2 and 5–8, Sun 10–2; adm*) in the centre.

Just outside Nájera, hill-top **Tricio** was an important Roman town known as *Tritium Megalon*. Its small mortuary temple was converted wholesale in 1181 into the **Basilica Nuestra Señora d'Arcos** (*open Tues–Sat 10.30–1.30 and 4.30–7.30, Sun 10.30–1.30*) to house a miraculous dark-skinned statue of the Virgin; mellow Roman columns support Visigothic arches covered with Baroque stuccoes that at first glance seem to be made of white icing. Traces of Romanesque paintings (the only ones found so far in La Rioja) remain on the walls: scenes of the Last Supper, the Passion and Jerusalem.

San Millán de la Cogolla: Yuso and Suso

From Nájera it's a 17km detour south into the Sierra de la Demanda and **San Millán de la Cogolla**, a village that grew up around two ancient monasteries, Yuso ('The Lower' in old Castilian) and Suso ('The Upper'); *Cogolla* was a nickname for the monks' habit. San Millán (473–574) spent much of his 101 years living in the caves on the hill, his sanctity attracting numerous male and female anchorites.

In the 7th century the anchorites built the first monastery at **Suso**, signposted up a 2km narrow road (*open daily summer 10.30–1.30 and 4–6.30, winter 10.30–1 and 4–6;*

The Cradle of Spanish

When the Arabs invaded Iberia, the Christians who fled into the mountainous regions of the north were isolated for several centuries. Latin speakers and Visigoths found themselves among pagan speakers of Iberia's pre-Roman languages, cut off from the Moors and from each other. Several languages developed in addition to the Stone Age tongue of the Basques: Catalan, Gallego, Babel and Aragonese.

From Babel, the first language of the Reconquista, evolved the tongue that would dominate: Castilian, or *castellano*, or what most people know simply as Spanish. The predominance of Castilian owes as much to Castile's conquering role in history as to the fact that the language is one of the most efficient means of communication ever devised. The Visigoths endowed it with aspirates and a stricter framework than any other Romance language, 'a dry, harsh, stone-cracking tongue', according to VS Pritchett, 'a sort of desert Latin chipped off at the edges by its lipped consonants and dry-throated gutturals...and each word is as distinct and hard as a pebble.' It was the first modern language to have a grammar written for it. When a copy was presented to Queen Isabella in 1492, she understandably asked what it was for. 'Your Majesty,' replied a perceptive bishop, 'language is the perfect instrument of empire.'

In the centuries to come, this concise, flexible and expressive language would prove just that, an instrument that would contribute more to Spanish unity than any laws or institutions, while spreading itself effortlessly over much of the New World.

In 1870, the aforementioned Emilian gloss long held in Yuso was carted off to the Royal Academy of History in Madrid, and La Rioja still wants it back. But Yuso has another feather in its cap: Gonzalo de Berceo, the shepherd-priest born in the nearby village of Berceo in 1198 and educated as a choirboy at San Millán, who took Castilian out of the margins and made it into poetry. Gonzalo's verses on the lives of local saints have a simple, sweet quality and, as befits a good Riojan, were inspired by a draught of wine. His *Vida de San Millán* ends:

> *Quiero fer una prosa en román paladino,*
> *en cual suele el pueblo fablar con su vecino,*
> *ca non so tan letrado por fer otro latino;*
> *bien valdrá, como creo, un vaso de bon vino.*

> (I want to make a verse in the clear Romance
> used by the people to speak with their neighbours,
> those who aren't so lettered in real Latin;
> it's well worth, I think, a cup of good wine.)

adm), and soon became known for their literary efforts when the 7th-century monk San Baudelio wrote the *Life of San Millán*. Carved out of a wooded hill, the shadowy little church has a cloister at the entrance, containing the tombs of three queens of Navarra and those of the Seven Infantes de Lara and their tutor Nuño Salido, who met a tragic end after a game played at their uncle's wedding went wrong and a member of the bride's family was accidentally killed. Poet Gonzalo de Berceo, the first to write in Spanish, loved to sit and write in the Visigothic portico. The church was heavily damaged by Al Mansour in the Reconquista and rebuilt in the 10th and 11th centuries, with Romanesque arches on one end and Mozarabic and Visigothic down the second aisle. Because of the lack of security, Suso's treasures – notably its golden Flemish diptych – have been removed.

Even the 11th-century tomb with its recumbent alabaster effigy of San Millán is empty, not due to any 20th-century security precautions, but rather because in 1053 King García III decided that San Millán's relics belonged in Nájera. The bones were loaded onto a cart, but the oxen, once they reached the bottom of the hill, refused to budge another inch. Realizing that 'the saint didn't want to leave his lands', García built a new, more splendid, monastery on the spot where the oxen stopped. This is **Yuso** (*www.monasteriodeyuso.org; open winter Tues–Sun 10.30–1 and 4–6, summer daily 10.30–1.30 and 4–6.30; adm*), known as the 'Escorial of La Rioja' after it was rebuilt on a grand scale in the 16th century, its main entrance crowned by an equestrian relief of San Millán in the guise of Santiago Matámoros.

In the Middle Ages Yuso continued Suso's reputation as a literary centre: the monastery is proudest of its one anonymous monk who, in the 10th century, was writing a commentary in the margins of his Latin text or, to be precise, on folio 72 of the *Emilian 60 Codex*, when for 43 words he lapsed into the vernacular – the first known use of Castilian. It's engraved on stone along with other exhibits (mostly portraits of kings) in the **Salón de Reyes**. Interestingly, Yuso also has the first known example of written Basque; under the Kings of Navarra, both languages were current in medieval La Rioja.

The Renaissance church has weighty ogival vaulting and a 16th-century *retablo* on the life of San Millán; you can learn more about him in the paintings along the upper cloister, built in 1572. The library has hundreds of old codices and manuscripts, if not the precious Emilian gloss, while the small **museum** contains Yuso's prizes: the ornate wooden reliquary chests of San Millán and San Felices de Bilibio, commissioned in 1063, covered with ivory plates, gold and precious jewels. They were stripped of their gold and jewels by Napoleon's plundering troops, who fortunately had no eye for medieval ivories.

There are two other important religious houses in the vicinity. Just north of San Millán and Berceo, **Santa María de Cañas** was founded in 1169 and has a fine tall Gothic church with two floors of windows filling the nave with light. Off the cloister, the chapterhouse has the superb 14th-century tomb of the abbess-daughter of the founder, Doña Urraca López de Haro, decorated with nuns, ladies, bishops and abbots, as well as a benevolent 13th-century statue of St Anne, holding her daughter Mary and grandson Jesus on her lap. The nuns have long been famous for their engraved ceramic work.

South of San Millán, 15km from Anguiano in the verdant foothills of the Sierra de la Demanda, the 12th-century Benedictine **Monasterio de Valvanera** (*open daily 10–8*) was built to shelter its much-venerated Virgin, the patroness of La Rioja, discovered in a hollow tree by a thief named Nuño who became a saint. On her knee baby Jesus in regal robes is turned to the left, to avert his gaze, they say, ever since a couple forni-cated in the church, a sin that led the monks to erect a circle of white crosses, which no woman was allowed to cross, around the church. Other works of art were pillaged by the French or lost when the monks abandoned the monastery in 1839. They returned in 1885 and have been distilling their herbal Valvanera liqueur ever since, plucking the herbs according to the phases of the moon.

Further south, on the C113, **Mansilla** has an artificial lake and the impressive ruins of a 12th-century church dedicated to St Catherine, while the hamlet of **Canales de l a Sierra** is overlooked by the church of San Esteban, with strange composite monsters on its capitals.

Santo Domingo de la Calzada and its Chickens

As they made their way across La Rioja, pilgrims especially looked forward to **Santo Domingo de la Calzada**, a delightful walled village, now famous for its *muebles* (furniture) but that owes its name and existence to the first road saint. Born a shepherd, Domingo (1019–1109) applied for a monkish career at Valvanera and San Millán. Rejected, he devoted his life to building bridges and making the pilgrims' way easier, clearing paths with a magic sickle just like a druid, making him the patron saint of engineers and public works, hence *de la Calzada* ('of the causeway'). His village grew up by a complex of his works: a long stone bridge over the Río Oja, a hospital (now a *refugio*), a guest-house (now a *parador*) and a church. The local people call him their *abuelito*, or little grandfather. His church, now the **Catedral de Santo Domingo** (*open Mon–Sat 10–1.30 and 4–6.30; adm, includes adm to cloister and museum*) was founded on land donated in 1098 by King Alfonso VI. Reconstruction began in 1158 and took centuries to finish: the first tower was destroyed by lightning in 1450; the second one, completed in 1750, sagged menacingly, and was torn down in 1760; the third, 243ft high, freestanding and neoclassical to match the façade, was built by Basque tower-master Martín de Beratúa in 1762 on boggy ground, shored up with sand, limestone and a ton of cow horns.

The Gothic interior is simple but lavishly decorated, but what everyone remembers best are the rooster and hen, cackling in their own late-Gothic henhouse. Their presence recalls the miracle that took place in Santo Domingo's hostal: a handsome 18-year-old German pilgrim named Hugonell, travelling with his parents, refused the advances of the maid, who avenged herself by planting a silver goblet in his pack and accusing him of theft. Hugonell was summarily hanged by the judge while his parents sadly continued to Compostela. On the way back, they passed the gallows and were amazed to find their son still alive and glad to see them, telling them it was a miracle of Santo Domingo. They hurried to the judge and told him; the judge, about to dig into a pair of roast fowl, laughed and said their son was as alive as the birds on his table, upon which both came to life and flew away. Since then, a white hen and cock have been kept in the church, and are replaced every month; pilgrims would take one of their feathers and stick it in their hats for good luck. Under the window you can even see a piece of the gallows.

Opposite the henhouse is the magnificent tomb of Santo Domingo, designed by Felipe de Vigarni (1517–29); the saint's recumbent statue suggests he could be a starter in heaven's basketball league. On the high altar, the huge Plateresque *retablo* (1540) is the last and best work of Damián Forment, one of Spain's finest Renaissance painters. The carved choir is another excellent, detailed Plateresque work (1530s), decorated with painted scenes on the life of St Domingo, while the chapels are equally beautiful and ornate, especially the screen of the **Capilla de la Magdalena**. The Gothic-*mudéjar* cloister is now used as a museum (*same hours as cathedral*).

Outside the cathedral, take a look at its ornate Romanesque apse, at the nearby walls, erected by Pedro the Cruel, and at the handsome, arcaded plaza, with a stately 16th-century **Casa Consistorial**. At the west end of town, the Renaissance **Convento de San Francisco** was built by Philip II's favourite architect, Juan de Herrera, to house the elaborate tomb of the king's confessor, Fray Bernardo de Fresneda.

South of Santo Domingo, the most dramatic of La Rioja's seven valleys, the Oja, slices through the lofty Sierra de la Demanda up to the handsome stone village of **Ezcaray**. Ezcaray made its fortune on merino wool but now serves as a centre for mountain excursions, with the ski resort of **Valdezcaray** (ski info at *www.valdezcaray.es*) on Mt San Lorenzo (7,451ft), and picnic tables in the beech and pine forests. Don't miss a trip up to the **Ermita de la Virgen de Allende**, site of recent archaeological digs and where some delightful paintings by a well-meaning artist show St Michael dressed up like an 18th-century *generalísimo*, his avenging sword replaced by a harquebus. The Virgin is celebrated on the 24th and 25th of September, with traditional dances and parades and a pilgrimage to the hermitage.

Wine Towns in Rioja Alta

To the north along the Ebro lies the Rioja Alta, a lush region of abrupt natural features rising above rolling hills, carpeted with vineyards and roads lined with brash spanking new wine *bodegas* that speak of La Rioja's rising reputation, and just might lose their sharp kitsch edge over the next 200 years.

Haro

At the confluence of the Ebro and Tirón, Haro is a working wine town built around a large arcaded square. Its chief monuments are a handful of noble houses, the attractive **Casa Consistorial** (1775) and the 16th-century church of **Santo Tomás** up in Plaza Iglesia, bearing a handsome, recently restored Plateresque façade with sculpture and reliefs in several registers, paid for by the Condestables de Castilla. Haro is the growing and marketing centre for the wines of Rioja Alta, with a clutch of *bodegas* near the train station. While most *bodegas* welcome visitors, they usually require advance notice (the tourist office has a useful booklet listing them all). An exception is **Bodegas Bilbaínas** (*Barrio de la Estación 3*, *t 94 131 01 47*, *www.bodegasbilbainas.com*), with a pretty façade in *azulejos*, usually open mornings and late afternoons. Nearby, you'll find one of the newest – and already among the most praised – wine-producers: **Bodegas Roda** (*www.roda.es*, *t 94 130 30 01*). Along Costa del Vino, you'll find the celebrated cellars of the **CUNE**, or CVNE (*t 94 130 48 00*), home of a fine bubbly; Chilean-owned **López de Heredia** (*www.lopezdeheredia.com*, *t 94 131 02 44*), makers of one of the best Riojas, *Viña Tondonia*; and the vast, French-founded **Rioja Alta** (*Avda Vizcaya*, *t 94 131 03 46*), with 25,000 barrels. The even larger **Federico Paternina** (*Avda de Santo*

Tourist Information

Haro: Plaza Hermanos F. Rodríguez,
t 94 130 33 66.
There is a **market** on Tuesdays and Saturdays
on Arco de Santa Bárbara.

Where to Stay and Eat

Haro ✉ 26200

****Ciudad de Haro, Ctra N124, Km 41, t 94 131
12 13, f 94 131 17 21,
www.hotelciudaddeharo.com (*expensive*).
Along the highway, overlooking Haro, this
modern hotel has been newly restored and
enlarged. Well-equipped rooms, extensive
gardens and a swimming pool.

****Los Agustinos, Plaza de San Agustín 2,
t 94 131 13 08, f 94 130 31 48 (*moderate*).
Superbly restored, occupying a former
Augustinian monastery that later served as
a prison: note the graffiti carved into the
columns of the garden cloister. Rooms are
quiet, air-conditioned and equipped with
satellite TV.

*Hs Aragón, La Vega 9, t 94 131 00 04 (*budget*).
Basic, but the better of the couple of
hostales on this street.

Beethoven I and II, C/Santo Tomás 3–5 and
Pza de la Iglesia 8, t 94 131 11 81 (*moderate*).
Traditional mushroom, fish and vegetable
dishes are the prizes at these two good
dining establishments across the street
from each other.

Briñas ✉ 26200

***Hospederia Señorio de Casalarreina,
Plaza Santo Domingo de Gúzman 6,
Casalarreina (5km from Haro), t 94 132
47 30, *infocasalarreina@hotelesconen
canto.org* (*expensive*). A charming rural
hotel in part of the 16th-century monastery,
with luxurious rooms (with Jacuzzi) and
a swimming pool.

***Hospederia Señorio de Briñas, Travesía de
la Calle Real 3, t 94 030 42 24, f 94 130 43 45,
brinas@hotelesconencanto.org (*moderate*).
Has some unique split-level rooms in a
carefully-restored mini palace, tastefully
decorated with antiques.

*El Portal de La Rioja, Ctra De la Vitoria, km 42,
t 94 130 34 86 (*inexpensive*). As well as
rooms with baths, there is an excellent
restaurant serving chops grilled on vine
cuttings (*chuletas al sarmiento*), a craft
shop and a wine museum with century-
old bottles.

Domingo 1, *t 94 131 05 50*), founded in 1896 by the Plaza de Toros, houses four million
bottles, and welcomes visitors daily except for Monday. Another, **Martínez Lacuesta
Hnos** (*C/Ventilla 71, t 94 131 00 50, www.martinezlacuesta.com*) is in the old gas company
that became obsolete back in 1891, when Haro became the first city in Spain to have
public electric street lighting – hence the slogan '*Ya se ven las luces, ya estamos en
Haro*'. Among the shops, **Selección Vinos de Rioja** (*Pza Paz 5, t 94 130 30 17*) offers tastings and a wide variety of different Riojas.

Since 1892, Haro's **Estación Enológica**, C/Bretón de los Herreros 4 (just behind the
bus station), has tested new wine-making techniques and varieties; its excellent
Wine Museum (*t 94 131 05 47; open Mon–Sat 10–2 and 4–8, Sun 10–2; adm*) offers
detailed explanations of the latest high-tech processes used in La Rioja. For a far less
serious initiation, or rather baptism, in Rioja, come on 29 July when **San Felices** is celebrated with a Batalla del Vino. Everyone dresses in white and, after the Mass, fortified
with *zurracapote* (Rioja sangría, made with red wine, citrus fruit and cinnamon) and
armed with every conceivable squirter, splasher and sprayer, opposing groups douse
one another with 100,000 litres of wine. This Dionysian free-for-all takes place 3km
from Haro at the Peña de Bilibio, below the striking rock formation and pass of the
Conchas de Haro, 'the Shells of Haro', where Felices, a hermit-follower of San Millán,

lived in a cave. Archaeologists have recently discovered a 10th-century church and the ruins of a Roman town, Castrum Bilibium, or Haro la Vieja, just under the rocks.

Around Haro: the Sonsierra

There aren't many landmarks around Haro, but a handful of villages are worth a look if you're trawling about looking for that perfect bottle. A good place to start is the Sonsierra, a pocket of La Rioja on the left bank of the Ebro. **Briñas**, just north of Haro, has a number of noble escutcheoned manors left over from the days when it was the playground of the Haro nobility. These days wine is the be-all and end-all; there's even a *bodega* under the church. Don't confuse Briñas with **Briones** to the east, where there is a nubbly church tower and a bridge to **San Vicente de la Sonsierra**, a village best known in La Rioja since 1499 for its Guild of Flagellants, *Los Picaos*, headquartered at **Ermita de Vera Cruz**. During Holy Week, clad in anonymous hoods, the *Picaos* whip themselves across the shoulders, then pique the bruises with wax balls full of crystal splinters until the blood runs. Just outside San Vicente, the curious 12th-century Romanesque church **Santa María de la Piscina** was founded by Ramiro Sanchez, son-in-law of the Cid, who allegedly brought back a piece of the True Cross from the Crusades. Over the door there's a shield carved with mysterious numbers and symbols. Paintings inside represent the *piscina probática* (waters of the flock) of Jerusalem and the Holy Grail. Just east, **Abalos** has one of the oldest cellars in Spain, the **Bodegón Real Divisa** (*t 94 125 81 33*,), owned by descendants of the Cid, and a 16th-century church, San Esteban Protomártir, decorated with dragons. In **Elciego**, 9km southeast of Abalos, you'll find the *bodega* of the Marqués de Riscal (*t 94 160 60 00, www.marquesderiscal.com*), a famous producer who helped establish the reputation of Riojas in the 19th century. The vineyard has a reputation for knowing just how to age wines, and some 30,000 barrels patiently sit in the cellars here, some for as long as 50 years. An added attraction is a new complex designed by none other than Frank Gehry, architect of the Guggenheim Museum in Bilbao. Gehry has once again used titanium for the undulating roof of the building, which now houses a shop, museum and Basque restaurant. It will also house a much-anticipated luxury hotel, due to open in July 2006.

Back on the south bank of the Ebro, **Cenicero**, in spite of jokes about its name (it means 'ashtray' – apparently shepherds once came here to gather around huge bonfires), is another important wine town which has proudly borne the sobriquet the 'Humanitarian' since the 1920s, when the inhabitants went out of their way to care for victims of a train wreck. It has some of Rioja's grandest *bodegas*: ultra-modern **Berberana** (*t 94 145 31 00*), and **Amezola de la Mora** (*t 94 145 45 32*), on the San Asensio road, a fine example of old *bodega* architecture, ideal for its *crianzas* and *reservas*. West of Haro, **Sajazarra** boasts a well-preserved 13th-century castle, and **Cellórigo**, 'the Pulpit of La Rioja', has views as far as Logroño and an 11th-century castle under the sharp-pointed crags of Peña Lengua. **Casalarreina** is a little Renaissance hamlet around the Renaissance convent of La Piedad (1508); 2km east in **Cihuri** the Río Tirón is crossed by a pretty Roman bridge.

The Basque Lands (Euskadi)

An Introduction to the Basques **119**
Along the Coast: France to San Sebastián 126
San Sebastián (Donostia) 128
Inland from San Sebastián **135**
Along the Coast: San Sebastián to Bilbao 138
Ondarroa to Gernika **141**
Inland: San Sebastián to Bilbao 146
Bilbao (Bilbo) 148
Vitoria (Gasteiz) 162
Álava Province 168

08

The Basque Lands (Euskadi)

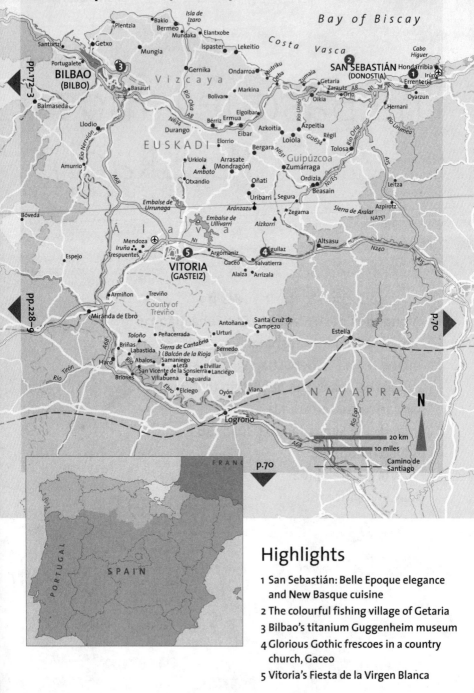

Highlights

1 San Sebastián: Belle Epoque elegance and New Basque cuisine
2 The colourful fishing village of Getaria
3 Bilbao's titanium Guggenheim museum
4 Glorious Gothic frescoes in a country church, Gaceo
5 Vitoria's Fiesta de la Virgen Blanca

The Basque lands, known in the Basque language as 'Euskadi' ('Collection of Basques'), contain, according to the autonomy agreement of 1981, the three provinces of Vizcaya, Guipúzcoa and Álava. To the Basques themselves, however, 'Euskadi' means all lands inhabited by Basques – the 'Seven Provinces' that include Labourd, Haute-Navarre and the Soule in France and the northern part of Navarra. When it isn't raining, Euskadi is one of the most charming corners of Spain – rural for the most part, lush and green, crisscrossed by a network of mountain streams that meander every which way through steep, narrow valleys in their search for the sea. Great stone country houses resembling Swiss chalets dot the hillsides and riverbanks – though the next valley over may have a grotty little town gathered about a mill. Spain's industrial revolution began in Euskadi, and even today the three Basque provinces are among the most industrialized and wealthy in the country. But in most of Euskadi, industry and finance seem remote. Basque nationalism, on the other hand, is ever present; every bridge, underpass, and pelota court has been painted with the Basque flag and slogans of the *Euskadi Ta Askatsuna* ('Freedom for Basques'), the notorious ETA, the small but violent minority that has given this ancient people a bad press.

An Introduction to the Basques

Nomansland, the territory of the Basques, in a region called Cornucopia, where the vines are tied up with sausages. And in those parts there was a mountain made entirely of grated Parmesan cheese on whose slopes there were people who spent their whole time making macaroni and ravioli.

The Decameron, VIII

When did the inhabitants of Basqueland become Basques? Wild stories like Boccaccio's have often been told about the Basques and their inscrutable ways, but the conclusions reached by many scholars are almost as hard to believe. It seems likely that the Basques are no less than the aborigines of Europe, the descendants of Cro-Magnon hunter-gatherers and painters, having survived in their secluded valleys during the great Indo-European migrations of peoples from the east thousands of years ago. This theory has had a big boost from the discovery that the Basques have the highest proportion of type O blood in the world, as do other people pushed long ago into Europe's corners – the Irish, the Scots, and Cretans.

Yet even more peculiarly, the Basques also have the world's highest incidence of Rh negative blood, a factor characteristic of the indigenous prehistoric European race. Other clues are the slight but telling physical differences between the Basques and their neighbours: they have long noses and long earlobes, are bigger and stronger, and the distinct shape of their skulls is matched only by those of their ancestors, buried under dolmens in 2000 BC.

One doesn't visit the Basque country to see the sights, which are few and far between. The real attraction is the Basques themselves, a taciturn though likeable lot, and their distinctive culture and way of life. The setting also helps to make the trip worthwhile; emerald landscapes well tended by the same people for millennia (and so should they be emerald; the Basque country gets as much rain as the west of Ireland).

History

'The Basques are like good women; they have no history.' So runs the old saying. Another of their jokes is that, when God created the first man, he got the bones from a Basque graveyard. No one knows for sure just how far back they go – only that someone, incredibly, must have been around even before them. For the areas around the Pyrenees are one of the oldest inhabited places on earth, and one of the cradles of human culture. The first European yet discovered, 'Tautavel Man', parked his carcass in a cave at the western end of the chain some 450,000 years ago. Traces of habitation in the Basque lands go back at least 100,000 years, and somebody was painting pictures on cave walls as early as 35,000 BC. While the most famous examples yet discovered are in southwestern France and Cantabria, the Cro-Magnons in the Basque provinces were no slouches, as the painted caves at Santimamiña and elsewhere show.

Genetic research, perhaps less subjective than phrenology, has confirmed a unique persistence of the European Palaeolithic DNA markers in the ethnic Basque population. Even the Basque language, with no known relatives, offers its hints of extreme antiquity; practically every word for common tools, for instance, comes from the ancient root *haiz*, meaning stone, even *haiztur*, scissors.

Sheep, not native to Basqueland, arrived around 5000 BC, followed by horses and cattle, part of the Neolithic agricultural and cultural revolution that spread across western Europe. Today scholars believe that those with farming know-how migrated slowly out of Turkey, and hunter-gatherer traditions slowly disappeared through intermarriage. This is when the ancestors of the Basques remained aloof. But if they didn't mingle, they did learn agriculture, the domestication of animals, and building – their lasting monuments include dolmens, *tumuli* and menhirs.

About 800 BC, Celtic peoples started moving through the region, probably inter-marrying with the original people as well as conquering them. Again the ancestors of the Basques, for some reason remained unassimilated while picking up tips from the newcomers, on metal-working and cultivating wheat. When the Romans came, they found a nation they called the Aquitanians or Vascones, speaking a non-Indo European language and occupying much of the land between the Ebro and the Garonne.

The Romans never really exercised much control over the Basques' mountain fast-nesses, and the Visigoths and Franks who followed found the Basques a permanent headache. Charlemagne pacified the inhabitants of the plains by 781, but the mountain Basques held out, and taught the aggressive emperor a costly lesson in the legendary battle of Roncesvalles (*see* p.76). As the medieval states that claimed Basque property – Navarra, Asturias/Castilla, England, Béarn and France – grew in wealth and power, there was increasingly little chance that an event like Roncesvalles could be repeated. This was a world dominated by a feudal aristocracy, one made up of foreigners, the descendants of Germanic invaders and Roman landowners, and with such bossy neighbours it is not surprising that the Basques never coalesced into a nation. The

Basques at this time are practically invisible, their language merely the *patois* of countrymen, and nobody paid much attention to them. All through the Middle Ages, the Basque boundaries shrank gradually but inexorably as the natives were either pushed out or assimilated by Spaniards, Gascons and Catalans. Many place names, especially in the eastern Pyrenees, give clues of a Basque origin, but by the 1300s the Basque lands had contracted roughly within the boundaries they retain today.

Despite the decline, the Basques survived as a nation throughout. When they finally did agree to recognize the suzerainty of Castilla it was on their own terms, retaining *fueros* (privileges) and ancient laws, one of which was that every king, once crowned, should come to Gernika and swear under the sacred oak tree to uphold their laws. Since then, Basques have always played an important role in Spanish affairs, far out of proportion to their numbers. They were great sailors and explorers, shipbuilders and whalers, *conquistadores* and pirates, and nowadays they run most of Spain's banks. The Basques organized the first whale fishery, in the Middle Ages. At first they only took whales that came too close to the shore, but as the whales got wise the Basques began chasing them farther out to sea. Without much evidence, the Basques say they landed in the Americas long before Columbus (who took a Basque pilot along); Basque sailors helped the English conquer Wales, built the Spanish Armada, and founded a number of Spanish colonies, including the Philippines, as well as cities like Buenos Aires. The *conquistadores* Lope de Aguirre (so well portrayed by Klaus Kinski in Herzog's film *Aguirre, the Wrath of God*) and Pedro de Ursúa were Basques; the Basque captain Sebastián Elcano became the first man to sail around the world. Two of Spain's most important saints, St Ignatius of Loyola and St Francis Xavier, were also Basque.

In the 19th century, the Basque lands suffered as much as any other part of France or Spain from rural poverty and depopulation. Young Basques from the mountain uplands went in great numbers to the Americas, especially to Argentina and the United States, where the Basque connection goes back to the 1,500 sailors (many of them veterans of the corsairs) who came to join Lafayette and fight for American independence. Simón Bolívar, liberator of Venezuela and Colombia, was of Basque descent. In the bayous of Louisiana and east Texas, and on the Argentine pampas, Basques became some of the first cowboys in the 1840s, setting the model and contributing much to the image (*lariat*, among other cowboy terms, is a Basque word, and exotic *cinema locales* such as Durango, Colorado and Laredo, Texas were named after Basque villages). Later in the century they moved further west, taking lonely jobs as shepherds in the Rockies. There are still large Basque communities in Idaho, Utah, California and other states. Throughout history, the Basques have wanted only to be left alone, and they always support any politics that promise to uphold their ancient rights and liberties. In modern times, this has meant adventures with both the far right and the far left. In the 19th century, when progress meant doing away with quaint relics like Basque culture and *fueros*, the Basques remembered their pious nature and took the side of Fernando VII's reactionary brother Don Carlos in the second Carlist war (1876), and lost the *fueros* as a result. At the same time Euskadi with its iron deposits and port towns began to industrialize, and while many prospered, the majority of workers, seeing their traditional society threatened on all sides, flocked to the banner of Basque Nationalism.

Nationalism is hardly a recent phenomenon. It started in the 18th century, with a community of liberal bourgeois in Bilbao and the other outward-looking port cities; these supported Enlightenment thinkers such as Manuel de Larramendi, who developed a concept of Basque nationhood based on language and tradition. Throughout the 19th century, nationalist thought and the development of Basque culture proceeded apace in Spain, while, at least on the political side, it ran into a stone wall in the much more repressive climate of France. French Euskadi thus became a sideshow to main events, while in Spain, the PNV, the first Basque nationalist party, controlled a majority of the region's parliamentary seats from 1917 on. In 1931, when supporters of a republic offered the Basques autonomy in exchange for support, they jumped at the chance, despite reservations about the new Second Republic's secularism. When the Civil War broke out, they remained loyal to the Republic and even the priests fought side by side with the 'Reds'. To break their spirit, the German Condor Legion practised the world's first saturation bombing of a civilian target at Gernika (*see* p.144–5).

Franco later took special pains to single out the Basques for reprisals of all kinds, outlawing their language and running the region as a police state, so that even the thousands of Castilians who immigrated to Euskadi to work in the factories felt oppressed enough to sympathize with Basque Nationalist goals. Franco's rule was a catastrophe for the Basques: there were over 100,000 prisoners and 200,000 exiles after the Civil War, including the entire intelligentsia and political leadership. Resistance groups did not start forming until 1952, and the grim atmosphere of Francoist repression determined the equally poisonous nature of the antidote. The ETA (*Euskadi Ta Askatsuna*, or Freedom for Basques) was founded in 1959. Its bombing campaign near the end of Franco's reign was singularly effective – notably when they blew the car carrying Franco's anointed successor, Admiral Carrero Blanco, over the roof of a Madrid church.

The repression of the Basques during the Franco years caused the Spanish state to lose any claims to legitimacy in the eyes of many, and when called upon to ratify the new constitution in 1978, most Basques abstained from the ballot box; those who voted, voted no. Although they regarded the autonomy imposed on them as second rate, they have made the best of it, and today Euskadi has the greatest autonomy of any region in Spain. Taxes are collected by local governments, and local rule covers education, culture, industry, health services, police, agriculture and fishing etc. Most parents, even Spanish, choose to have their children educated in Basque and Spanish. The Basque government at Gasteiz (Vitoria) is held up in Spain as a model of efficiency and progressiveness.

Today 70 per cent of Basques vote for nationalist parties, mostly for the moderate PNV and the more nationalist but still peaceful Eusko Alkartasuna (Basque Solidarity); on the whole they are progressive-left on most issues, strongly anti-nuclear and anti-NATO. The left wing opposition, Herri Batasuna (now *Euskal Herritarok*), the only party to openly support ETA, regularly gets some 15 per cent of the vote; their garish posters on every wall. Terrorist ETA has gone steadily downhill since its failure to make an impression during Spain's year of celebrations in 1992. Widespread disgust with terror tactics has made the ETA fall out of favour, though support for a totally independent Euskadi remains considerable. Most people, however, are in no hurry for it, and would rather see independence brought about as part of a peaceful and evolutionary process.

Language

Speaking the local language is an art! The Basques point out with great pride that their language is not only Europe's oldest, but also the most difficult; the only language ever found to have any similarity to it is Berber. There are four distinct dialects, and in each the grammar is Kafkaesque, to put it mildly. Verbs, for example, can vary according to the gender of the person you are addressing. The vast number of grammatical tenses includes not only a subjunctive, but two different potentials, an eventual, and a hypothetical. But grammatical complexity permits beauty and economy; you can express anything in Basque in fewer words than in most other languages.

Basque is maddeningly, spectacularly indirect. For example, 'I am spinning', comes out as '*Iruten ari nuzu*', or literally, 'In the act of spinning doing you have me!' Or try out this proverb: '*Izan gabe eman dezakegun gauza bakarra da zoriona*'... 'Having without, give (*Izan gabe eman*) we can (*dezakegun*), one thing only is (*gauza bakarra da*), happiness (*zoriona*)' – 'Happiness is the only thing we can give without having.' Pronunciation, thank heavens, is not such a problem; it's phonetic, and there are only a few letters you need to know: e as long a; u as oo; j as ee; s as something halfway between s and sh; tz or z, as s; and x as sh. Pronounce all the vowels, and don't make any soft consonant sounds; practise on the village of Azcoitia (ahs-ko-IT-ee-ah).

Peculiarities of the language include the habit of doubling words for effect, unknown to any European tongue but common among the Polynesians, and some entertaining onomatopoeia. In Basque, something very hot is *bero-bero*, and when a Basque walks on all fours it is called *hitipiti-hatapata*. Looking at a menu in a Basque restaurant (they have the best cuisine in Spain, so you'll want to do this often), you may well be *keko-meko* (undecided); if you choose *birristi-barrasta* (carelessly), you might get *ttattu* (little cat), a supposed speciality in Bilbao in the 19th century. Basques can put it away; other Spaniards accuse them of *mauka-mauka* (gluttony). Like eskimos, who know no generic word for 'ice', the Basques have no word for 'tree' or 'animal'. And being the democratic folk they are, there's no word for 'king' either – they had to borrow one from the French and Spanish potentates they were forced to pay taxes to.

Due to the severe cultural oppression under Franco, the percentage of Basque speakers is higher on the French side, according to a recent survey: 64 per cent in Basse-Navarre, 54 per cent in the Soule, and 26 per cent in Labourd, as opposed to 45 per cent in

A Basque Outline

Very few Basque words have made it into English, although one, 'silhouette', is derived in a most roundabout way from a Basque word, *zuleta*, which means 'many holes'. The surname Zulueta or Zuloeta was probably given to a family who lived among the holes, or caves. One branch of the Zulueta family in France adopted the spelling Silhouette. Their most famous member, Etienne de Silhouette (1709–67), was a writer and politician who held the powerful post of controller-general. He wasn't very good at it and didn't keep his office long, and his meagre policies cast but a shadow (according to one explanation), although others say Silhouette himself liked to draw portraits in outlines and hang them on the walls of his château.

Guipúzcoa, 18 per cent in Vizcaya, 10 per cent in Navarra, and only 9 per cent in Álava. However, for the first time, the numbers are rising in a revival that has touched all aspects of Basque culture. In Euskadi, the language is now mandatory in school, and in the past decade 100,000 adults have learned to speak it. Basque TV and radio are broadcast on both sides of the border; there are Basque newspapers, including *Gara* and *Berria* , and over 1,000 books of all kinds published annually, a remarkable statistic for a population of only a million potential readers: one novel, *Obabakoak* (1989), by Basqueland's best-known living writer, Bernardo Atxaga, is the first ever to be translated into English. Equally encouraging is the continuing popularity of the *bertsulari*, poets (often scarcely literate shepherds) who have memorized a vast repertoire of traditional pieces and are especially skilled at complex improvisations at festivals and competitions. One is the hero of a Basque cartoon series for kids.

Note that both the Spanish and Basque names for towns and provinces are official, and both are used on road signs: San Sebastián/Donostia, Bilbao/Bilbo, Vitoria/Gasteiz etc.

Folklore

The Basques are not alone. In fact, their long intimacy with their land has forced them to share it with an unreasonably large number of gods, demons, spirits and fairies, creatures of one of the richest mythologies of Europe.

Many tales are connected to the dolmens and other Neolithic monuments that grow so thickly on the mountains here; often their names connect them to Mari, the ancient Basque great goddess. The dolmens were built by the *jentillak*, the race of giants that once lived side by side with the Basques. The *jentillak*, often a great help to their neighbours, invented metallurgy and the saw, and introduced the growing of wheat. One day a strange storm cloud appeared from the east, and the wisest of the *jentillak* recognized it as an omen and interpreted it as the end of their age. The giants marched off into the earth, under a dolmen still visible in the Arratzaran valley in Navarra. One was left behind, named Olentzero, and he explained to the Basques: 'Kixmi [Jesus] is born and this means the end of our race.'

Olentzero lives on today, as the jolly fat doll or straw figure seen prominently in the Basques' celebrations of Christmas and New Year's Day, the leader of all the processions. You will find Olentzero in Basque homes and even in the churches, often bearing an unusual resemblance to the Michelin man; he'll probably be surrounded by food because, of course, being one of the *jentillak*, Olentzero likes to eat all day.

Other familiar creatures include the *laminak*, originally small female fairies with a capacity to help or harm, now a sort of leprechaun, which get blamed for everything that goes wrong. And where mythology fades off into nursery-lore, we have the 'man with the sack' who comes to carry off naughty children, and a large bestiary with jokes like the elusive *dahu*, a kind of lizard with legs that are shorter on one side – the better to walk the mountain slopes. Along with the myths goes a remarkable body of pre-Christian religious survivals, including rituals that lasted well into the 20th century; many old Basques in isolated villages can remember festivals with midsummer bonfires in their childhood, and in some villages the custom is coming back, just as it is in the Catalan Pyrenees. (Any excuse for a party.)

Basques are passionately fond of music, whether it's choral music at Mass (which they do extremely well), Basque rock (rare, fortunately), or traditional tunes played by village bands. Dozens of traditional dances are still current, and small groups in many villages keep them up; you'll have a chance to see them at any village fête – especially in Guipúzcoa, where you can tour the villages on a Sunday morning and usually find a couple with traditional dances going on in the square. Traditional Basque instruments include the *txistu*, a three-holed flute played with one hand, the other hand beating the rhythm on the tambour; another is the *dultzaina*, a primitive bagpipe. When they're in the mood, the Basques dance some of the most furiously athletic dances in the world, especially the *Bolant Dantza* ('Flying Dance') or *La Espata Dantza* ('Sword Dance').

The real monument of Euskadi is the *etxe*, a word that means much more to a Basque than just 'house'. In the old days, it was the heads of households who met to make laws at the assemblies, and it is common to find families whose home has been on the same site for over a thousand years. The cemeteries have been around even longer. Basques have distinctive 'discoidal' or round-headed tombstones. Archaeologists have dug up models 4,500 years old, and they've been using the same style ever since. The earliest ones often had human figures, sun symbols or other symbols carved on them; since the coming of Christianity the stones usually show crosses. You will see them in any churchyard, usually turned south so that the sun shines on the carved face all day.

Basque Diversions

Basques definitely know how to eat. Go into a village restaurant at 9am on a market day, and watch the boys tuck into their three-course breakfasts – soup, tons of meat, fish and potatoes, with a gallon or so of wine for each. Fortunately for them, the Basques also know how to cook. Their distinctive and world-renowned cuisine will be one of the delights of your visit to the Basque country (*see* **Food and Drink** pp.33–42).

The real national sport, of course, is smuggling sheep over the border. But the Basques love to play, and over the millennia they have evolved a number of outlandish games that are unique in the world. Many of these are based on pure brute strength, a major element of the national mystique. Even today, especially strong, tall people are said to be descendants of the *jentillak*. One can imagine them, back in the mists of time, impressing each other by carrying around boulders – because that's what they do today, in a number of events generally called the *harri altxatzea*, literally 'stone-lifting'. In one, contestants see how many times they can lift a 500lb stone in five minutes; in others, they roll boulders around their shoulders. Related to this is the *untziketariak*, in which we see how fast a Basque can run with 100lb weights in each hand. They're fond of the tug-of-war too; they probably invented it. You will also see them at the village festivals pulling loaded wagons, racing with 200lb sacks on their shoulders, or chopping huge tree trunks against the clock. Don't fool with these people.

The miracle is that at the same time they could develop a sport like *pelota*, the world's fastest ball game. Few sports in the world can offer an image as beautiful and memorable as the *pelotari* in his traditional loose, pure white costume, chasing down the ball with a long, curving *chistera*. *Pelota* takes a wide variety of forms, but the basic element is always the ball: a hard core, wrapped tightly with string and covered with hide – like a baseball, only smaller and with much more bounce; in a serious match it can reach speeds of 150mph. The oldest form of the game is *rebot*, played without a wall. This is done bare-handed; other versions, played in an outdoor *frontón*, may be bare-handed, with a leather glove (*pasaka* or *joko garbi*), or with the *chistera*, made of leather and osier, which enables a player to scoop up the ball and fling it back in the same motion.

Whatever the game, it usually requires teams of two players each. The ground in front of the wall is marked off in *cuadros* every 4m from it; to be in, a ball bounced off the wall must hit between the 4th and 7th *cuadros*, if it is not returned on the fly. Games are usually to 35 points. Every Basque village has a *frontón*, usually right in the centre. On some village churches from as far back as the 1600s, you can see how the architects left one smooth, blank wall to accommodate the game. It may also be played in a covered court, or on one with another wall on the left side, a *jaï-alaï*, when the game is called *cesta punta*, the fastest and most furious form of *pelota*. Thanks to Basque immigrants this is now a popular sport around the Caribbean and some areas of the USA.

Along the Coast: France to San Sebastián

If you are driving in from France, there is a choice of routes: the A8 (also signposted, confusingly, as the E5/E70 and E80) motorway which is expensive though occasionally dramatic, or the old routes through Hendaye and Hondarribia, built up around the ford of the Río Bidasoa, which has endowed it with a spacious, protected sandy beach. **Hondarribia** (Fuenterrabía in Spanish) gets overlooked with all the border confusion, but this is one of the most agreeable destinations on the coast; the village glows with colour – in its brightly painted houses, especially along Calle San Nicolás, or Calle Pampinot, in its flower-loaded balconies and in its fishing fleet that has taken on France in the EU's battles over fishing rights. The town has had its share of sieges – you can still see the ancient walls and a **castle of Charles V**, now a *parador* – and every summer sees an

Border Anomaly

In the Río Bidasoa between Hendaye and Hondarribia there is a small island called the Isla de la Conferencia, or Ile des Faisans. This was a traditional meeting place for French and Spanish diplomats since the 1400s. In 1659 the Treaty of the Pyrenees was signed here, ending the long wars between France and Spain; the following year representatives of both sides returned to plan the marriage of Louis XIV and the Spanish infanta. A special pavilion was erected for the occasion, and the King of Spain sent his court painter, Velázquez, to decorate it. Unfortunately the artist caught a bad cold here that eventually killed him. The last big meeting in the area was the one in 1940 between Hitler and Franco (not on the island, but in the Führer's private rail car in Hendaye station). Even today the island is owned jointly by both countries, and there is a solemn agreement in a cabinet somewhere that details how the Spanish police shall look after it from April to October, and the French for the other six months. But really, there isn't anything to watch over; the island at present is uninhabited and completely empty.

Getting Around

It's only 20 minutes by bus from San Sebastián to Irún or Hondarribia on the frontier; connections are frequent by bus and train and not a few people watching their euros stay in Irún (or in France) rather than in the more pricey capital. If you're not in a hurry, take the narrow-gauge Eusko Tren for a leisurely ride through some fine scenery.

Tourist Information

Irún: Puente de Santiago (Barrio de Behobia s/n), t 94 362 26 27, and in the train station, t 94 361 67 08.

Hondarribia: Javier Ugarte 6, t 94 364 54 58, f 94 364 54 66, *www.bidasoaturismo.com* (website has information for Hondarribia, Irún and Hendaia/Hendaye.)

Where to Stay and Eat

Hondarribia ✉ 20280

In the moderate and inexpensive ranges there are few choices. Rooms are a better bargain across the border in Hendaye, though Hondarribia makes a more pleasant stay.

★★★**Parador de Imperador Carlos V**, Pza de Armas 14, t 94 364 55 00, f 94 364 21 53, *hondarribia@parador.es* (*luxury*). Prettily situated in an ancient castle that housed so many kings and dukes on French business over the centuries.

★★★**Hotel Obispo**, Pza del Obispo, t 94 364 54 00, *www.hotelobispo.com* (*expensive*). Another ancient mansion, this one in the old residence of the Bishop of Hondarribia, with sumptuously refitted rooms and splendid views.

★★★**Pampinot**, Nagusia 5, t 94 364 06 00, *www.hotelpampinot.com* (*expensive–moderate*). Smaller, but just as noble as the two mentioned above, with eight rooms in a restored 15th-century mansion in the heart of the old quarter.

★★**Hostal Álvarez Quintero**, C/Alvarez Quintero 7, t 94 364 22 99 (*moderate*). This is one of a small number of *hostales* and is dependable and relatively good value. It even has a small pool.

★★**San Nikolas**, Pza de Armas 6, t 94 364 42 78 (*inexpensive*). This has very attractive rooms right on the plaza.

Restaurant Sebastian, C/Nagusi Kalea 7–9, t 94 364 01 67 (*expensive*). Offers intimate dining in an ancient grocery store; try the wonderful pheasant stuffed with wild mushrooms. *Closed Sun eve, Mon and Nov.*

Arraunlari, Butroi Pasealekug 3, t 94 364 15 81 (*moderate*). This is the best restaurant in the region serving imaginative and award-winning New Basque cuisine with a strong local flavour. *Closed Sun eve and Mon.*

Restaurant Danontzat, C/Las Tiendas 6, t 94 364 56 63 (*budget*). Budget snack/tapas bar downstairs with tasty *platos combinados* for under €8.

Irún ✉ 20300

Cheaper rooms in Irún are no longer the bargain they once were and very little is available for under €36.

★★★**Alcazar**, Avda Iparralde 11, t 94 362 09 00, *hotelalcazar@euskalnet.net* (*expensive*). Offers 48 rooms in the centre of town, 5km from the beach. This is at the top of the price range.

★★**Lizaso**, C/Aduana 5–7, t 94 361 16 00 (*inexpensive*). Possibly the best deal in Irún, with decent rooms.

Ramon Roteta, Villa Ainara, Irún 1, t 94 364 16 93 (*expensive*). Offers gracious dining in a lovely villa with a garden; grand cuisine and superb desserts. *Closed Sun eve and Thurs.*

Larretxipi, Larretxipi 5, t 94 363 26 59 (*moderate*). Has excellent fish, though a number of places nearby are cheaper.

Bar Oiarso, C/Mayor 17 (*budget*). Best place for tapas, *bocadillos* and kebabs.

invasion of French tourists (the local defensive measure of raising prices has had little effect in repelling them). In the evening, head out towards the lighthouse on **Cabo Higuer** – the northeasternmost corner of Spain – for views of the sunset over the bay.

Irún, on the French border, is further up the Bidasoa. It was bombed to bits by Franco and his german friends in the Civil war and has little to recommend it. Inland you can climb **Monte San Marcial** for a memorable view over the Bay of Biscay (there is a road to the top), or else flee the bustling coast for the serene Valley of Oyarzun, one of Euskadi's rural beauty spots, with the pretty villages of Oyarzun, Lesaka and Vera de Bidasoa. There are Neolithic monuments all through this region, on both sides of the border; the spot where the Pyrenees meet the sea was a holy spot. A site called Oianleku, off the main road near Oyarzun, includes some small stone circles among the dolmens.

If you're driving you can take the coastal road from Hondarribia along Monte Jáizkibel, offering superb views over the **Bay of Biscay**, the French coast and the Pyrenees. Just east of San Sebastián, the long ribbon town of **Pasajes de San Juan** (Pasai Donibane) lines the east bank of an estuary, where there are several more picturesque old houses. Victor Hugo lived in one for a while, and the Marquis de Lafayette lodged in another before sailing off to aid Britain's American colonists in their revolution. Philip built part of the Invincible Armada here, although now all such business affairs are handled by San Juan's ugly stepsister across the estuary, **Pasajes de San Pedro**.

San Sebastián (Donostia)

At the beginning of the 21st century, it is difficult to imagine that a place like San Sebastián (*Donostia* in Basque) could ever exist. The Belle Epoque may be a hundred years ago, but in San Sebastián the buildings are still made of ice cream, with florid brass streetlights and trim in Impressionist colours; many people still dress up instinctively for the evening *paseo* around the Playa de la Concha. It's a movie set when the sun's shining, which is most of the time.

San Sebastián has probably been around as long as the Basques, but the first know reference to it is as a Roman port called *Easo*. It resurfaces in the Middle Ages; in the 12th century when the Navarrese controlled this part of the coast they built the first fortress on Monte Urgull, one that has been rebuilt and reinforced many times since. The first recorded tourist came rather against his will: François I, King of France, who was locked up in the fortress for a time by Charles V after he captured him at Pavia in 1527. But long before there were any '*costas*', wealthy Spaniards were coming to spend their summers bathing at San Sebastián. In the 1850s it was blessed by of Queen Isabel II, who brought the government and the court with her in summer (*see* p.178); also in her reign San Sebastián was made capital of the province, and the Paris–Madrid railroad was completed, making the city convenient to holiday-makers from both capitals.

Queen Regent María Cristina again made San Sebastián the rage in 1886 – following the example of Empress Eugénie of France, who had popularized nearby Biarritz. Despite being the sister city of Reno, Nevada, it's been a classy place to go ever since; a lovely, relaxed seaside resort in a spectacular setting, built around one of the peninsula's most enchanting bays, the oyster-shaped **Bahía de La Concha**, protected from bad moods of the Atlantic by a wooded islet, the **Isla de Santa Clara**, and by **Monte Urgull**, the hump-backed sentinel on the easternmost tip of the bay.

Playa de la Concha and the Comb of the Winds

Sheltered within the bay is the magnificent golden crescent of the **Playa de La Concha**, San Sebastián's centrepiece and its largest beach; on its western end stands a promontory topped by the mock-Tudor **Palace of Miramar of María Cristina**, now owned by the city and used for receptions and special exhibitions. A tunnel under the Miramar leads to the **Playa de Ondarreta**, a traditional society retreat. Ondarreta itself meets a dead end at seaside Monte Igueldo, crowned by a **Parque de Atracciones**. You can get to the top by road or by the delightful, rickety old funicular from the end of the beach, and the reward is a spectacular view over San Sebastián, the **Bay of Biscay** (*Bizkaiko Golkoa* in Basque) and the Cantabrian mountains. Back on the shore, beyond the beach and the funicular stands one of the most talked-about monuments of modern Spanish sculpture, Eduardo Chillida's **Peine de los Vientos**, the 'Comb of the Winds'. The work is a series of terraces, built into the rocks that guard the entrance to the bay, decorated with cast-iron constructions, the 'teeth' of the comb that smooths the winds coming from the sea towards the city. Chillida was a native of San Sebastián (he was once goalie for the local football side), and his house is on the cliffs above the monument. Nearly all the city behind these beaches dates from the 19th century; San Sebastián is an ancient place, but it has been burnt to the ground 12 times in its history, lastly by Wellington's drunken soldiery, who celebrated the conquest of the town with their accustomed murder and mayhem. The city was rebuilt and even expanded soon after, in a neat neoclassical grid with the **Catedral del Buen Pastor**, completed in the 1880s, at its centre.

A promenade-lined river, the **Urumea**, divides 19th-century Sanse (as the city is affectionately known) from the newer quarter of **Gros**, the working men-student-bohemian enclave, a lively place full of cheap bars and endowed with its own beach, the **Playa de Gros**, which is less crowded but lies outside the sheltered bay, subject to the wind, waves and filthy debris. The beachfront landscape here has just received a new adornment: a rather fearsome, angular convention centre called the **Kursaal**, of which guided tours are inexplicably offered. Of the three charming bridges that span the Urumea, the one named after María Cristina (near the station) most resembles a cream pastry.

La Parte Vieja and Monte Urgull

Most of the action in town takes place beneath Monte Urgull in the narrow streets of La Parte Vieja, or 'The Old Town' (also known as the Casco Viejo). From **La Concha** beach, its entrance is guarded by a beautiful square, the **Parque de Alderdi Eder**, and the enormous 19th-century **Ayuntamiento**, or town hall, formerly the casino that María Cristina built (the new one is on Calle Mayor). What remains of the city's fishing fleet may be seen in the harbour behind the Ayuntamiento, an area rimmed by souvenir shops, pricey tourist restaurants, and a pair of salty museums. Nearby, the **Museo Naval** (*open Tues–Sat 10–1.30 and 4–7.30, Sun 11–2; adm*), is set in the 18th-century Consulate, and is devoted to the Basques' proud naval history and, at the far end of the port, the **Aquarium** (*open July–Sept daily 10–10, rest of the year 10–8; adm*), stuffed

N

150 metres
100 yards

Monte Igueldo

Parque de
Atracciones

Funicular

Peine de los
Vientos

Isla de
Santa Clara

Aquarium

PASEO DE IGUELDO

AVENIDA DE SATRUSTEGUI

INFANTA CRISTINA

Playa de Ondarreta

Bahía de la Concha

AVENIDA DE ZUMALACÁRREGUI

CALLE MATIA

PASEO DE HERIZ

Palace of Miramar

Playa de la
Concha

PASEO DE LA CONCHA

ALTO DE MIRACONCHA

PASEO DEL DUQUE DE BAENA

CUESTE DE ALDAPETA

CAMINO VIEJO DE ALDAPETA

To
Palacio
Aiete

San Sebastián (Donostia)

Mar Cantábrico

PASEO NUEVO

British Cemetery

Monte Urgull

Castillo de Santa Cruz

Museo Naval

Museum of San Telmo

Santa María del Coro

PLAZA DE LA TRINIDAD

CALLE 31 DE AGOSTO

San Vicente

PASEO DE SALAMANCA

LA PARTE VIEJA

PUERTO

CALLE MAYOR

SAN JERONI

MIWINI

IÑIGO

ALDAMAR

PLAZA DE LA CONSTITUCIÓN

CALBETÓN FERMÍN

El Muelle

MARI

Playa de Gros

Playa de Zurriola

Palacio de Congresos Kursaal y Auditorio

PUENTE DE ZURRIOLA

AVENIDA DE LA ZURRIOLA

ALAMEDA DEL BOULEVARD

Ayuntamiento

PASEO REPÚBLICA ARGENTINA

CALLE OQUENDO

Parque de Alderdi Eder

PEÑA FLORIDA

PLAZA DE GIPÚZKOA

CALLE ANDÍA

PASEO DE COLÓN

CALLE DE ZABALETA

BERMINGHAM

C. NUEVA

CALLE DE SAN FRANCISCO

GEN. ARTECHE

CALLE MIRAMAR

CENTRO ROMÁNTICO

AVENIDA DE LA LIBERTAD

PUENTE DE SANTA CATALINA

PLAZA DE EUSKADI

GROS

SECUNDINO ESNAOLA

CALLE MIRACRUZ

PLAZA DE CERVANTES

CALLE LOIOLA

CALLE DE SAN MARCIAL

FUENTERRABÍA

ETXAIDE

PASEO DE LA CONCHA

PLAZA DE ZUBIETA ZARAGOZA

CALLE DE SAN MARTÍN

Mercado de la Brecha

PASEO DE FRANCIA

PASEO DE LOS FUEROS

PASEO DEL DUQUE DE MANDAS

CALLE DE SAN BARTOLOMÉ

CALLE DE EASO

CALLE DE URBANETA

Catedral del Buen Pastor

CALLE URDANETA

CALLE REYES CATÓLICOS

CALLE DE PRIM

PUENTE DE MARÍA CRISTINA

Estación del Norte

PLAZA EASO

CALLE MORAZA

PASEO DEL ÁRBOL DE GUERNICA

Estación de Amara

Río Urumea

Parque de Cristina Enea

To Bus Station

Río Urumea

Getting There and Around

By Air

San Sebastián's airport to the east, near Hondarribia, **t** 94 365 88 00, *www.aena.es*, has connections to Madrid and Barcelona. The bus to the airport, Hondarribia and Irún departs from Pza Guipúzkoa, **t** 94 364 13 02, every 12 minutes – note that this is really the bus for Hondarribia, and lets you off across the road from the airport.

By Train

RENFE trains depart from the Avda de Francia, in Gros, from Estación del Norte, **t** 90 224 02 02. There are frequent connections with Irún and Hendaye, and less frequent trains to Barcelona, Pamplona, Salamanca, Vitoria, Zaragoza, Paris, Burgos, and León. *Talgos* whizz all the way to Madrid, Málaga, Córdoba, Algeciras, Valencia, Alicante, Oviedo and Gijón.

Euski Tren (**t** 90 254 32 10) has services to Hendaye and Bilbao from Amara station on Plaza Easo: trains stop everywhere along the way (journey time to Bilbao is 2 hrs 45 mins).

By Bus

A bewildering number of small bus companies leave from the station on Pza de Pio XII on the southern end of town, a block from the river. The ticket office is nearby on C/Sancho el Sabio 33, though some lines have their offices on Paseo de Vizcaya. There are five buses daily to Oviedo, seven to Burgos and five to Galicia. Within Euskadi buses depart every half-hour to Bilbao and Vitoria and up to ten times a day to Pamplona. There are 20 bus lines in San Sebastián itself (**t** 94 328 71 00); no.16 goes to Igueldo and the funicular (*runs daily in summer 10–10, every 15 minutes*).

By Bike

Cycling is a great way to explore San Sebastián, especially along the 12km sea front promenade; it's possible to get from one end of the city to the other without having to cross a road. Bikes can be **hired** from several places around town including Paseo de la Zurriola 22, **t** 94 329 08 54.

By Motor Boat

Make excursions out to the Isla de Santa Clara every hour from the port (*summer only*), where you can also rent a rowing boat to go yourself.

Tourist Information

Municipal: on the river, C/Reina Regente, **t** 94 348 11 66, *www.sansebastianturismo. com*. They sell the San Sebastián Card, which offers free public transport plus discounts on museums and attractions, and is valid for two days (€10).
Walking tours: Guidatour, **t** 90 244 24 42, run walking tours daily June–Sept, weekends only Oct–May (€6) as well as bike tours, and pinxo tours. The tourist

---

with ships' models, the skeleton of a Basque whale that went belly-up in San Sebastián's port and, downstairs, tanks of fish and other sea creatures from various oceans around the world.

From here you can stroll along the outer edge of **Monte Urgull** on the Paseo Nuevo, a splendid little walk between turf and surf. In the late afternoon, when the light is best, stroll up one of the numerous paths to the summit of the rock; Monte Urgull is really the city's park, closed to traffic – and includes surprises along the way such as a British cemetery from Wellington's campaign, and some of the old bastions and ancient cannon of the city's defences. Up at the top is the half-ruined **Castillo de Santa Cruz de la Mota** (16th century), with a small but excellent museum of local history inside. Nearby an ungainly kitsch statue of Christ (from the Franco era) called the **Sagrado Corazón** keeps an eye on the holiday-makers on La Concha beach below.

office also rent out audio guides for self-guided visits, www.euskaltrip.com, (€10).

Tour bus: A guided tour bus departs from in front of the tourist office every hour, picking up and dropping off at all the major sights, t 69 642 98 47 (mobile).

Post office: on C/Urdareta behind the cathedral.

Internet access: Cyber Sare, Aldamar 3, t 94 343 08 87; Cyber Frudisk C/Miracruz 6, in Gros (book and music store with Cyber café); Ciber Networld, C/Aldamar 3, t 94 343 08 87.

Shopping

Along with the usual types of tourist shops in the Parte Vieja there are some original places that sell a range of items from surf-punk paraphernalia to exquisite home-made chocolates. The Centro Romántico has a wide range of fashionable boutiques, from chains like Zara and Mango to chic individual establishments selling Spanish designers.

Barrebnetxe, Plaza de Guipúzkoa 9, t 94 342 44 82. Fabulous Basque pastries, cakes, and chocolates, as well as wonderful bread. Also has a small café area.

Hontza, C/Okendo 4. If you're inspired by all the sumptuous seafood, this place sells books on Basque cooking in English.

Casa Ponsol, C/Narrica 4. An institution in the world of Basque berets, in business since 1832.

Where to Stay

San Sebastián ✉ 20000

San Sebastián is certainly not the best place to look for bargains; many of the cheaper *hostales* and *fondas* are packed with university students throughout the year. As a general rule, however, the further back you are from the sea, the less expensive the accommodation will be.

Luxury–Expensive

*****María Cristina, Oquendo 1, t 94 343 76 00, *www.westin.com*. For a touch of Belle Epoque elegance, this old grande dame is one of Spain's best hotels; it looks onto the Río Urumea's promenade, a short walk from La Concha.

****Gudamendi Park, Pza de Gudamendi Barrio de Igueldo, t 94 321 40 00, *gudamendi@saranet.es*. Quiet and comfortable, with attractive décor; located halfway up Monte Igueldo: best rooms have sea views.

****Hotel Londres y Inglaterra, Zubieta 2 (on La Concha beach), t 94 344 07 70, *www.hlondres.com*. The city's other most luxurious address, with splendid views from the rooms, first-class service, and plenty of charm, as well as one of the city's best restaurants.

Moderate

San Sebastián is a posh resort; many of the *hostales* fall into the moderate price category.

The centre of La Parte Vieja is the arcaded **Plaza de la Constitución**; within a few blocks of this local centre of Basque nationalism stand San Sebastián's three best monuments – the hyper-ornate façade of **Santa María del Coro** (18th century) on Vía Coro, the fine Gothic **church of San Vicente** on San Vicente and, nearby, the old Dominican **monastery of San Telmo**, now the fascinating **Museum of San Telmo** (*open Tues–Sat 10.30–1.30 and 4–7.30, Sun 10.30–2*), currently being expanded and modernised. The monastery's church is adorned with golden murals by the Catalan artist Josep Sert (1930) and are based on the history of the Basque people. Old Basque tombstones, with round heads adorned with geometric patterns, are lined up in the cloister; upstairs the museum contains three El Grecos, two bear skeletons, Basque lucky charms and amulets, Basque sports paraphernalia, the interior of a Basque cottage and more.

***La Galeria**, C/Infanta Cristina 1–3, **t** 94 321 60 77, *www.hotellagaleria.com*. A couple of minutes from Playa Ondarreta on a lovely quiet street, this French-inspired turn-of-the-century *palacete* has rooms full of antiques and individuality.

Pensión Bikain, C/Triunfo 8, **t 94 345 43 33, *www.pensionbikain.com*. Has top-notch facilities at a very good price, close to the beach and the *parte vieja*; spotless rooms, parking facilities, and a very helpful owner.

Inexpensive

The best you'll find will be at the higher end of the inexpensive range. There are a fair number, in the *parte vieja* and in the centre.

Pensión Alameda, Alameda del Boulevard, **t 94 342 64 49. The charming new owners of this central pensión have kitted out the newly decorated rooms with all kinds of thoughtful extras including hair-dryers, free WiFi Internet access, and complimentary mineral water.

Adore Plaza, Plaza Constitución 6, **t** 943 42 22 70, *www.adoreplaza.com*. Right on the beautiful plaza in the centre of the Casco Viejo, this new pensión offers rooms with or without ensuite facilities (those without are *budget*).

Budget

*Pensión Amalur, 31 de Agosto 44, **t** 94 342 96 54. Covered in flowers, this is a charming little spot in the Casco Viejo, with simple rooms, some with pretty balconies. A little noisy, but a good choice all the same..

Pensión San Lorenzo, C/San Lorenzo 2, **t 94 342 55 16. A very popular budget choice, with brightly decorated rooms (which come with fridge and kettle) and friendly owners.

La Sirena, **t** 94 331 02 68, *www.paisvasco.com/albergues*. A youth hostel situated at the end of Ondarreta beach, at the foot of the road up Monte Igueldo; it's the cheapest place in town.

Camping Igueldo, Paseo Padre Orkolaga 69, **t** 94 321 54 02, *www.campingigueldo.com*. Close to the Ondarreta beach and Monte Igueldo (5km from the centre), this large campsite is open year-round.

Eating Out

As eating is the local obsession, it's not surprising that the city can claim three of Spain's most renowned, award-winning restaurants – cathedrals of Basque cuisine. If you are after something cheaper, follow the crowds through the tapas bars of the *parte vieja*. There are several along C/31 de Agosto including La Cepa, Ormazábel and Gaztelu.

Akelarre, Paseo Padre Orkolaga (in the Barrio de Igueldo), **t** 94 331 12 09 (*expensive*). Combines exquisite meals with a beautiful setting and views over the sea. *Closed Sun eve and Mon*.

Arzak, Alto de Miracruz 21, **t** 94 327 84 65 (*expensive*). This is often described as the

The main attraction of La Parte Vieja is its countless bars, where the evening crowds devour delectable seafood tapas and Basque goodies. Eating is the city's greatest obsession, and there are societies (for some reason, all male) devoted to the preparation and consumption of huge Basque meals. A fun excursion is to gather some good food and row it out to **Isla de Santa Clara** for a picnic (*in summer there is a regular ferry to the island from El Muelle, the dock behind the Ayuntamiento; boats run from 10–8*).

About 8km from town, the open-air **Chillida-Leku Museum** is devoted to the works of San Sebastián's favourite son (*take the N1 from San Sebastián and turn off onto the 612132 to Hernani, **t** 94 333 60 06, www.museuochillidaleku.com; open July–Aug Mon, Wed–Sat 10.30–7, Sun 10.30–3; Sept–June 10.30–3; adm*).

finest restaurant in Spain and offers a constantly changing menu of delights. Make sure you book in advance. *Closed Sun eve, Mon, from Jan-June also closed Tues, two weeks in June and three weeks in Nov.*

Casa Nicolasa, Aldamar 4, t 94 342 17 62 (*expensive*). Another culinary shrine, founded in 1912, specializes in classic Basque cookery and offers a large choice of dishes. *Closed Sun, Mon, three weeks end–Jan/Feb, 10 days in Oct.*

Martín Berasategui, C/Loidi 4, Lasarte (8km from San Sebastián), t 94 336 64 71 (*expensive*). Although some may murmur that Berasategui has spread himself a little too thin with his countless enterprises in the Basque lands, his own restaurant remains a temple to New Basque cuisine at its finest. the menú de degustación is a hefty €112, but this is a dining experience you won't forget.

Rekondo, Pso de Igueldo 57, t 94 321 29 07 (*expensive*). A superb choice, specializing in grilled fish and meat and with a huge wine cellar; come here for elegant dining at around €36.

Urepel, Pso de Salamanca 3, t 94 342 40 40 (*expensive*). Another of San Sebastián's notable restaurants serving fine Basque food at reasonable prices.

Bodegón Alejandro, C/Fermín Calbetón 4, t 94 342 71 58 (*moderate–inexpensive*). This is where famed chef Martín Berasategui started out, and offers excellent traditional cuisine with innovative touches. The house speciality is a succulent *marmita de bonita*

(tuna stew), and there's a great lunch time deal at €12.

Makrobiotika, C/Intxaurrondo Kalea 52 (*budget*). San Sebastián's only macrobiotic restaurant, serving a variety of cereal-based dishes. Take bus 13 or 24 from the centre as it's a bit of a trek.

Portaletas, Puerto 8, t 94 342 42 72 (*budget*). Fronted by a tapas bar, this serves superb, good-value traditional cuisine. Try the *pastel de verduras* (a kind of layered vegetable cake) topped with sweet pepper sauce.

Entertainment and Nightlife

The centre of the serious party action is the streets of the Parte Vieja. You will find late-night bars and clubs around the end of Ondarreta beach.

Bataplán, Miraconcha 6, *www.bataplandisco.com*. Hugely popular seafront disco, with outdoor terrace, electro-pop and dance music.

Be Bop, Paseo de Salamanca 5, t 943 42 98 69. One of several bars in the area with live music. This one's a jazz venue.

Casino Kursaal, C/ Mayor 1, t 94 342 92 14. The place to hit if you fancy a flutter.

La Kabutzia, Paseo de la Concha, *www.lakabutzia.com*. The sleek Real Club Náutico is the setting for this crowd-pleasing disco, which offers a bit of everything - from salsa to pop.

Inland from San Sebastián

Tolosa

Guipúzcoa, San Sebastián's province, is the most densely populated rural part of the Basque country, where plenty of fat villages bear unpronounceable, unimaginable names. There being only one fast route through the area, from San Sebastián to Tolosa, you'll have to invest a lot of time on some lovely, lazy back roads if you want to see any of them. Despair will probably set in at a corner with signs pointing you to Aizarnazabal, Azpeitia, Azkoitia, Azkarate, or Araiz-Matximenta; you'll begin to think the Basques are doing this just for you.

One of the first Basque towns to join the industrial revolution, **Tolosa** (named after Toulouse) is still fairly industrialized and the largest town on the River Oria, thriving on paper mills (which explain the aroma), along with the manufacture of wicker *cestas* for *pelote*, and sweets, especially *tejas* (almond biscuits) and *delicias*. You can learn all about them in the **Museo de Confitería** at Lechuga 3, next to the Plaza del Ayuntamiento, or taste them in Tolosa's *pastelería* of renown: Gorrochategui, in C/Arbol de Gernika. Dining out is the other main reason to stop (*see below*), as the town itself is fairly drab.

Oñati

Southwest of Tolosa on the N1, there's the pretty mountain village of **Segura**, its main street lined with the palaces of a locally powerful family, the Guevaras, and other nobles. Segura lay on the original pilgrim route. Up in the mountains beyond Zegama bits of the original Roman road to Vitoria are still visible, but today there's no road at all, and this valley has become something of a dead end. Before Segura at Beasain, the main route branches westwards for **Oñati**, capital of the Pretender Don

Tourist Information

Tolosa: C/Nafarroa Etorbidea, t 94 365 49 72, f 94 365 05 79, *tolosaldeatour@euskalnet.net*.
Oñati: Foru Enparatza 11, t 94 378 34 53, f 94 378 30 69, *www.gipuzkoa.net/onati*.
There is a **market** in Tolosa on Saturdays in Plaza del Tinglado.

Where to Stay and Eat

Tolosa ✉ 20400

★Oria, Oria 2, t 94 365 46 88 *www.hoteloria.com* (*inexpensive*). Modern, central and comfortable. The nearby Oria 2 is in a pretty turn-of-the-20th-century villa.
Hs Oyarbide, Plaza Gorriti 1, t/f 94 367 00 17 (*inexpensive*). Functional rooms equipped with a sink are available here.
Casa Julián, Santa Clara 6, t 94 367 14 17 (*expensive*). Tolosa's oldest restaurant, and still one of the best, specializing in grilled steaks, *pimientos del piquillo* and *tejas de Tolosa*, with a good list of Rioja wines. *Closed Sun*.
Nicolás, Zumalacárregui 6, t 94 365 47 59 (*moderate*). Does delicious things with fresh and dried cod, as well as charcoal-grilled steaks. *Closed Sun and Aug*.

Azpeitia ✉ 20730

★★Loiola, Inazio Hiribidea, t 94 315 1616, *www.hotelloiala.com*

(*moderate*). The smartest choice, a crisp modern hotel with its own garden
Larrañaga, Ctra Urrestilla, t 943 81 11 80 (*budget*). For heaped plates of great home-cooking, follow the locals to this popular haunt.
Juantxo, Loiola Blde 3, t 94 381 43 15 (*moderate*). A welcoming, old-fashioned spot with an excellent reputation for its fine traditional cuisine made with market-fresh local produce, washed down with a pungent local *txakoli* wine. The home-made desserts are especially good. *Closed Sun, eves from Mon–Thurs, Aug*.

Oñati ✉ 20400

★★Etxe Aundi, Torre Auzo 10, t 94 378 19 56, *www.etxeaundi.com* (*moderate*). Traditional, stone-built hotel with charming rooms and a fine local restaurant.
★Etxeberria, Kale Barria 19 14, t 94 378 04 60 (*budget*). A reliable cheapie with very basic rooms above a bar/restaurant in the middle of town.
Hospedería de Aránzazu, t 94 378 13 13 (*budget*). A large place for pilgrims at the Sanctuary of Aránzazu, 9km east of town, with simple doubles with bath.
Txopekua, Barrio Uribarri, 94 378 05 71 (*moderate*). A good restaurant in a Basque homestead, situated on the road to Aránzazu.

Carlos in the Carlist wars. This was one of the few towns in Euskadi to be ruled by a noble, and it retained a sort of independence until 1845. For many years the town had the only Basque **university**, founded in 1540; its building, Oñati's landmark, has a beautiful Plateresque façade and a *mudéjar*-style arcaded courtyard (*Universidad Sancti Spiritus, open Mon–Thurs 9–5, Fri 9–2; adm, includes guided visit*). Oñati is known also for its number of well-preserved medieval palaces, one of which saw the birth of conquistador Lope de Aguirre, the deranged 'Wrath of God' in the film by Werner Herzog. The 15th-century parish church **San Miguel** contains a number of treasures, including the alabaster tomb of the university's founder, Bishop Zuázola de Ávila, attributed to Diego de Siloé, and an attractive Plateresque cloister. Other note-worthy buildings include the Baroque, rococo-style **Ayuntamiento** and the Franciscan **Convento de Bidaurreta**, but perhaps the greatest charm is the town's setting in a rich, rolling valley, dominated in the distance by the bluish pointed peaks of Mount Amboto and Udalaitz. A scenic road up from Oñati climbs in 9km to the **sanctuary of Arantzazu** (*open daily 10–6.30*). Here, in 1469, a shepherd found an icon of the Virgin by a thorn bush and a cow bell; the Virgin of Aránzazu became the patron saint of Guipúzcoa. The church that houses it has been rebuilt innumerable times since, lastly in 1950. Usually filled with tour buses and pilgrims, this is a curious temple of Basque modernism in a lonely and rugged setting, its two towers covered with a distinctive skin of pyramidal concrete nubs, creating a waffle-iron effect – a reference to an eccentric Renaissance conceit popular in Spain, seen in many buildings from Salamanca to Naples. The main doors are the work of Eduardo Chillida.

The only town of any size in the region has two names: Basques call it **Arrasate**, Spaniards Mondragón. Though a nondescript industrial town these days, Arrasate used to be a spa – a Spanish prime minister, Antonio Cánovas del Castillo, was murdered here by an anarchist in 1897 while taking a cure. Arrasate still has some of its medieval walls and gates, along with the 14th-century Gothic church of San Juan. Nevertheless, it's under the name of Mondragón that the town has made its mark, synonymous with one of the most successful and innovative cooperative ventures in the world, founded in the early 1960s and now employing a fifth of all workers in the southern Basque country. Farther north, the pretty village of **Bergara** has a number of palaces, churches and other monuments from the 16th and 17th centuries; note the Palacio Arrese, with its cut-out corner window in the best Spanish Renaissance style. If it were not for Bergara, you might be reading this by candlelight: a professor at the former Real Seminario Patriótico Bascongado here, in the 18th century, discovered tungsten, the element used in the filaments of light bulbs. West of Bergara, near the village of Zumárraga, is the unusual 15th-century fortress church of **Santa Maria**, popularly known as La Antigua. The hewn oak interior is rustic and spartan with carved geometric patterns running along the balustrades and beams, punctuated by the occasional female bust.

Loiola: St Ignatius's Home Town

Just south of Tolosa the twisting GI2634 branches westwards into the mountains, passing first Régil, a pretty mountain town with beautiful views from the Col de

Régil, the 'Balcón de Guipúzcoa'. This picturesque road continues to the ancient village of **Azpeitia** and the nearby hamlet of **Loiola** (Loyola), home of the **Sanctuary of St Ignatius** (*t 94 315 1616, open daily 10–1 and 3–7; free, audio guide €3*). Ignatius, or Íñigo López de Loyola, was born here in 1491, the last of 13 children of a noble family, who became the founder of those intellectual stormtroopers of Christ, the Jesuits. The actual house, built by the saint's grandfather after a four-year exile among the Moors, is a fortress-like *mudéjar* structure, redesigned inside as a museum (*open daily 10–1 and 3–7*) with solemn chapels and over-the-top gilded ceilings. Next to it stands the **basilica** (*open daily 10–1 and 3–7*), one of the outstanding Baroque works in all Spain. Carlo Fontana, a student of Bernini who had worked on many of the great Baroque building projects in Rome, was the main architect, and the costs were paid by a Habsburg queen of Austria; her family's coat of arms in stone hangs over the main door. Begun in 1689, this circular temple with its 211ft-high dome took almost 50 years to complete. To give an Italian building the proper Spanish touch, the ornate church rotunda is flanked by two plain, broad wings of monastery buildings, making a façade almost 500ft wide – creating the sharp contrast of vast, austere surfaces and patches of exuberant decoration that marks so many of the best Spanish buildings. At the entrance, a monumental stairway guarded by very stylized lions leads up to a porch under three arches; in it are five niches with statues of early Jesuit heroes, including St Francis Xavier, another Basque who met martyrdom, proselytizing the Japanese. Nothing on the exterior, though, prepares you for the overwrought stone carving that covers every part of the dome inside, designed by a group of masters that included Joaquín de Churriguerra, one of the three brothers whose taste for ornament gave Spanish architecture the word *churrigueresque*. As in most Jesuit monuments, no expense was spared, from the fine Carrara marble frieze around the rotunda to the elaborate pavement in coloured stone. Over the main altar, a life-size statue of St Ignatius is covered with silver contributed by the Basques of Caracas, Venezuela.

Along the Coast: San Sebastián to Bilbao

West of San Sebastián, the coastal cliffs keep all roads inland as far as **Orio**, a venerable fishing village that looks like an industrial town, at the mouth of the Río Orio, one of the most polluted rivers in Spain. Although the beach by Orio's very popular camp ground is clean enough, rough seas can bring out the no-swimming flags. If you're planning a picnic, drive up to the lush hill-top **Parque de Pagoeta**, signposted along the N634.

These same waves and a mile and a half of sand draw surfers to nearby **Zarautz**. Whaling and shipbuilding in the Middle Ages put Zarautz on the map, while more summering royalty – this time Belgium's King Baudouin and Queen Fabiola – inaugurated its international reputation as a resort. Now the second biggest resort in Euskadi after San Sebastían, Zarautz is especially popular among well-to-do Basque nationalists – hence summer courses in Basque language and folklore events, to go with the golf course, riding stables, and good food (with some harder-to-swallow prices).

In the historic centre of Zarautz, look for its trio of tower houses, especially the **Torre Luzea** in Calle Mayor and the one incorporated into the 16th-century **Palacio de Narros**. The most important church, **Santa María la Real**, has a half-Plateresque, half-Renaissance retablo; the campanile was added atop yet another medieval tower house in the 18th century.

Getaria (Guetaria)

Zarautz's shipbuilders built the *Vitoria*, the first ship to circumnavigate the globe, while the next fishing town to the east, **Getaria**, produced the man who captained it, Juan Sebastián Elcano: approaching from the east, a massive stone monument in his honour will be your introduction to this petite and utterly charming resort.

From the coastal road, you wouldn't think there was much to Getaria at all. Only pass through the old gate next to the monument, and you will find one of the loveliest villages of Euskadi, hugging the steep slope down to the harbour. Whenever the Getarianos go to Mass in the **church of San Salvador**, in the centre of the old town, they step on his grave, located just inside the door. Elcano was lost in the Pacific in 1526, so there probably isn't much of him in there anyway. Once beyond Elcano's tomb, this church has other surprises. Founded in the 13th century, it was rebuilt in 1429 in a curious off-kilter fashion: the wooden floor lilts as if on rough seas, and the choir vaulting is just as tilted. No one knows why. Along the right wall, near the suspended *ex-voto* of a ship, is something you rarely see in a church: a menorah. A double flight of stairs rises in the back, and the crypt and another chapel lie along the alley descending to the port. The crypt contains the remains of the ancestors of the same Queen Fabiola who made nearby Zarautz a resort. Getaria doesn't mind; although it has two small beaches of its own, it picked up all of Zarautz's fishing business. From the port, with its brightly painted boats and seafood restaurants, a path leads up to the top of Mouse Island, a pretty wooded natural area with flitting birds and fine views.

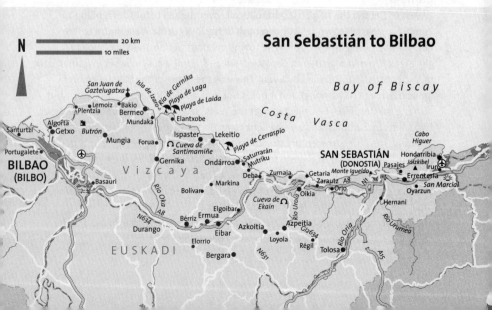

San Sebastián to Bilbao

Getting Around

The coast is served by frequent buses from San Sebastián; the narrow-gauge **Eusko Tren** line stops four or five times a day at Zarautz, Zumaia, Deva and Durango on the way to Bilbao.

Tourist Information

Zarautz: Nafarroa Kalea, **t** 94 383 09 90, **f** 94 383 56 28, *www.turismo.zarautz.com*
Getaria: Parque Aldamar 2, **t** 94 314 09 57, *www.paisvasco.com/getaria. Open summer only.*
Zumaia: Pza Zuloaga 1, **t/f** 94 314 33 96, *www.zumaia.net. Open summer only.*

Where to Stay and Eat

Orio ✉ 20810

Itsas Ondo, C/Kaia Kalea 7, **t** 94 313 11 79 (*moderate*). Has good, up-to-date, reasonably priced cuisine.
Joxe Mari, C/Erriko Enparantza s/n (in the town square), **t** 94 383 00 32 (*moderate*). Good food at a typical *asador. Closed Mon.*

Zarautz ✉ 20800

Zarautz can be as pricey as San Sebastián.
★★★★Karlos Arguiñano, Mendilauta 13, **t** 94 313 00 00, *www.hotelka.com* (*luxury–moderate*). A lavish mock castle on the beach owned by the eponymous celebrity chef. Its restaurant is one of the best dining places along this stretch of coast, with sophisticated seafood dishes and a warm, welcoming atmosphere (*closed Sun eve and Mon*).
Pensión Txiki-Polit, Musika Plaza s/n, **t** 94 383 53 57, *www.zarautz.com/txikipolit* (*inexpensive*). A good, central budget option, in a modern building in the heart of the old town. Spacious rooms and a good, cheap restaurant.
Pensión Lagunak, C/San Francisco 10, **t** 94 383 37 01 (*budget*). Basic but adequate, a little further from the action.
Camping Talai-Mendi, Monte Talai-Mendi, **t** 94 383 00 42 (*inexpensive*). A quiet campsite on a hillside with sea views (open summer only).
Aiten-Etxe, Elkano 3, **t** 94 383 25 02 (*expensive*). This may not win prizes for elegance, but it does offer fine, uncomplicated seafood accompanied by magnificent views along Zarautz's main beach. *Closed Sun eve.*

Zumaia

West of Getaria the N634 rises dramatically over the sea before descending to **Zumaia**, a pleasant town set at the mouth of the River Urola. A kilometre before Zumaia itself, keep an eye out for the town's chief attraction, the **Villa Zuloaga** (*t 94 385 2341, open mid-March–mid–Sept Wed–Sat 4–8; adm*), a cosy villa set in a small park of ancient trees, surrounded by a wall. This was the home of the Basque painter Ignacio Zuloaga (1870–1945), and it holds not only a selection of his own works, but also the masterpieces he collected over the years: several El Grecos, Goyas, Moraleses, two saints by Zurbarán and an excellent collection of medieval statues and *retablos*. Adjacent, the little 12th-century **church and cloister of Santiago Etxea** was a stop for pilgrims taking the coastal route to Compostela. Below stretches the pine-rimmed beach named after the painter, **Playa Zuloaga**. There's more art in the middle of Zumaia, in the 15th-century **church of San Pedro**: two triptychs on either side of the altar, the one on the right Flemish, and a dark, Gothic St Christopher on the back wall. There's another beach to the west at **San Telmo**, a dramatic swathe of sand under sheer red cliffs, known for the strength of its pounding surf.

Getaria ✉ 20808

★★Pensión Iribar, C/ Nagusia 34, t 94 314 04 06 (*inexpensive*). Four simple rooms in a great location on the quiet street leading down to the port. It also has a good restaurant (*moderate*).

★★Hs San Prudencio, t 94 314 04 11 (*budget*). A charming, rustic hotel just out of town, with a hilltop position and stunning views. It also has an excellent, inexpensive restaurant with a much sought-after terrace.

★★Pensión Guetariano, C/Herrerieta 3, t 94 314 05 67 (*budget*). In the cheerful green and yellow house at Getaria's main crossroads; a friendly place with magazines in the lounge and comfortable rooms with bath.

Kaia, Gral. Arnao 10 (upstairs), t 94 314 05 00 (*expensive*). Spectacular Basque seafood, elegant surroundings, charming staff and beautiful harbour views, Kaia is quite simply fabulous. Try the *kokotxas*, which melt in the mouth, or the extraordinary local anchovies, and follow with the grilled fish of the day. The ground floor has a cheaper grillhouse (Kai-Pe), where you can dine outside on spectacularly fresh local seafood.

Elkano, Herrerieta 2, t 943 14 06 14 (*inexpensive*). This traditional *asador* serves superb fish and meat grilled over charcoal and is justly considered one of the finest restaurants in the the Basque Lands.

Itxas-Etxe, Kaia 1, t 94 314 08 02 (*inexpensive*). Prime position on the harbour. Has daily menu of mainly 'catch of the day' fish, and a great lunch menú for €13.

Zumaia ✉ 20808

Some of the bars in the main square have *inexpensive* rooms, and cheaper food can be found on C/Erribera.

★★★Zelai, Itzurun s/n, t 94 386 51 00, *www.talasozelai.com* (*expensive*). A modern thalassotherapy centre with comfortable rooms in an unbeatable location high up on the cliffs. The restaurant is very good and offers beautiful sea views.

Agroturismo Jesuskoa, in Zumaia's Barrio de Oikia, t 94 386 17 39, *rjesuskoa@terra.es* (*inexpensive*). Six rooms in a restored farmhouse just outside town; it also has an apartment for rent, good for families.

Asador Bedua, Barrio Bedina, t 94 386 05 51 (*expensive*). Although a bit pricey, serves excellent grilled surf-and-turf in a friendly atmosphere. The *angulas* (in season) are justly famous.

Marina Berri, Puerto Deportiv o, t 943 865 617 (*restaurant expensive, otherwise moderate*). Elegant restaurant, café-bar and *sidreria* in one, with splendid port views. Excellent *menú del día* for under €10.

The coastal scenery between Zumaia and **Deba** is considered the best in Euskadi, with cliffs arcing gracefully from a choppy ocean in great vertical bands of pink and golden sandstone. A good way to explore it is by walking the cliff-top path that links Zumaia with **Mutriku** and Deba, passing through green fields and tiny hamlets and affording magnificent views. Mutriku is a quiet village set back on a narrow inlet 3km from the quiet beach at **Saturrarán**. Deba, a favoured resort at the turn of last century, nowadays lies happily in the shadows of the other coastal centres. The local church, **Santa Maria la Real**, is of late Gothic construction and has a spectacular painted portal; less elaborate, but somewhat older, are the Paleolithic scratchings in the nearby **Cueva de Ekain** (*only accessible to groups with prior appointment*).

Ondarroa to Gernika

Crossing into Vizcaya province at **Ondarroa** used to mean paying duty at the provincial customs house near the medieval stone Puente Vieja. The village is another pretty

The First Man to Sail around the World

In the great age of discovery, no Spanish or Portuguese captain worth his salt would set out without a Basque pilot, the heirs of centuries of experience in whaling boats off Europe's westernmost shores – they may have actually found the American coast in medieval times, and kept the knowledge secret. Columbus took a Basque pilot, and Elcano had the post of second-in-command to Magellan. In 1519, Charles V backed the Portuguese navigator Ferdinand Magellan's attempt to find a quick western route to the Indies by sailing southwest around the newly discovered continent of America to the Molucca islands, then cutting back to Spain around the Cape of Good Hope. Charles gave Magellan five ships, and in August they set forth from Seville. One ship turned back before attempting the Straits that took Magellan's name (October 1520). If already dismayed by the distances involved just crossing the Atlantic, Magellan must have been appalled at the extent of the Pacific. Even worse, by the time his little fleet made it to what is now the Philippines in 1521, a civil war had just broken out, which through tragic accident numbered Magellan among its victims. Elcano took over the helm and reached the Molucca islands before sailing halfway around the world to Seville in the only surviving ship. He arrived in October 1522, the holds stuffed to the brim with spices. In spite of his singular feat, Elcano was destined to remain forever in Magellan's shadow – except of course in the eyes of his fellow Getarianos. Besides the aforementioned monument, they erected a statue of Elcano just outside the gate of the old town, and stage a historical re-enactment of his homecoming every four years. Below the monument lies Getaria's port, sheltered by a peninsula and an islet known for its shape as El Ratón, the mouse.

fishing port, one of Vizcaya's busiest and a popular spot on sunny weekends, but most people press on west to **Lekeitio** (Lequeitio), with its promenade flanked by restaurants and lovely beaches, **Isuntza** and **Carraspio**, further out. Isabel II preferred the beaches here to San Sebastián; she was holidaying in Lekeitio when rebellion broke out under Marshal Prim in September 1868, deposing the dynasty and forcing Isabel into exile in France. The well-preserved palaces in Lekeitio's old quarter stand as testimony to its Belle Epoque popularity, but the elegant old port still catches more fish than tourists. Don't miss the early 16th-century Gothic **church of Santa Maria** and its impressive Flemish *retablo mayor*, an intricate explosion of gilded wood and polychrome carvings.

Lekeitio is famous for its *antzareguna*, which takes place during the San Antolines festival in early September. This goose rodeo, however, is not an event for the faint-hearted – although now, thankfully, they use a dead goose. A rope is stretched over the port, held on either side by strong tug-of-war veterans. In the middle a goose, liberally smeared in grease, is suspended by its feet over the port. Competitors, not allowed to weigh more than 70kg, are rowed up under the goose. One by one they attempt to grab the slippery bird by the neck, and tuck its head under their armpit.

From Lekeitio a detour off the main road leads northwards to **Elantxobe**, huddled beneath sheer cliffs, an immaculate little fishing village that funnels down to a bijou harbour. Geographical challenges have helped Elantxobe retain its remote atmos-

Getting Around

The coast is served by frequent Bizkaibus **buses** from Bilbao's Paseo del Arena. The narrow-gauge **Eusko Trenbideak** line runs out of Bilbao to Bermeo via Gernika (get off at Gernika, the stop after Gernika-Lumo) and Mundaka.

Tourist Information

Lekeitio: Independentzia Enparantza, **t** 94 684 40 17, *www.learjai.com*. *Open in summer only*.

Mundaka: Pza Lehendari Agirre, **t** 94 617 72 01, *www.mundaka.org*.

Bermeo: C C/Lamera s/n, **t** 94 617 91 54.

Gernika: C/Artekale 8, **t** 94 625 58 92, *www.gernika_lumo.net*.

There are **markets** in Gernika every Monday and Bermeo every Tuesday.

Where to Stay and Eat

Lekeitio ✉ 48280

★★★Emperatriz Zita, C/Santa Elena Etorbidea s/n, **t** 94 684 26 56, *ezita@aisiahoteles.com* (*moderate*). A plush modern palace of a place built over the ruins of the home of the last Austro-Hungarian empress.

★★Beitia, Avda Avda Abaroa 25, **t** 94 684 01 11 (*inexpensive*). Good value, adequate accommodation in a modern block.

Piñupe, Avda Abaroa 10, **t** 94 684 29 84 (*budget*). Simple rooms, but a really handy location, just 5 mins from the beach.

Meson Arropain, Ctra Marquina Ispaster, **t** 94 684 03 13 (*expensive*). A friendly restaurant 5km from Lekeitio; serves excellent fish dishes smothered with bubbling *salsas*, and has good *txakoli* to wash it all down with.

Zapirain, Igualdegui 3, **t** 94 684 02 55 (*moderate*). Serves abundant fish dinners.

Gernika ✉ 48300

★★Gernika, Carlos Gangoiti 17, **t** 94 625 03 50 (*inexpensive*). Good location, but there's little charm at this plain but recently renovated hotel.

Boliña, C/ Barrenkalle 3, **t** 94 625 03 00, *www.hotelbolina.net* (*inexpensive*). In the heart of the pedestrian area, this offers simple rooms with or without bath and a good restaurant (*moderate*).

Zallo Berri, C/ Juan Calzada 79, **t** 94 625 18 00. A delightful restaurant (*moderate*) serving fine regional cuisine with innovative touches (excellent value *menú del día*).

Baserri Maitea, Ctra. B1635 (near Forua, on the way to Bermeo), **t** 94 635 34 08 (*moderate*). A wonderful restaurant in a 300-year-old farmhouse with wooden beams; the fish is particularly good. Book in advance.

Mundaka ✉ 48360

★★Atalaya, Itxaropen Kalea 1, **t** 94 617 70 00, *www.hotel-atalalya-mundaka.com* (*moderate*). This is one of the loveliest hotels in the region, located right on the river in one of those glorious Basque buildings of a century ago with glass galleries all around. Small but comfortable rooms and a large terrace restaurant.

★Mundaka, Florentino Larriraga 9, **t** 94 687 67 00, *www.hotelmundaka.com* (*moderate*). A bit more down-to-earth yet with bar and internet facilities.

★El Puerto, Portu Kalea 1, **t** 94 687 67 25, *www.hotelelpuerto.com* (*inexpensive*). Bright and breezy rooms with views over the port and estuary.

Asador Zaldua, Sabino Arana 10, **t** 94 587 08 71 (*moderate*). Serves a wonderful array of fresh fish and succulent steaks, grilled to perfection. *Lunch only Nov–Jun*.

Bakio ✉ 48130

Gaztelu-Begi, San Pelaio Auzoa 86, **t** 94 619 49 24 (*inexpensive*). Delightful hotel and restaurant on a rocky headlan.

Hotel Joshe Mari, C/Bentalde 31, **t** 94 619 40 05, *joshemari@bakio.com* (*inexpensive*). Unusual hotel with only a handful of rooms, decorated with local antiques; the restaurant has good food in a relaxing atmosphere.

phere – there's only one way in, down the serpentine main street – and traditional fishermen's houses adorn the narrow lanes that wind down to the little port. Above loom the cliffs of Cabo Ogoña, tallest on the Basque coast.

Gernika (Guernica)

Beautifully set in the Mundaka valley, the ancient, sacred city of the Basques is mostly rebuilt now, and most of the inhabitants are too young to remember the horror that occurred one market day in 1937, when some 1,645 people were killed in a concentrated three-hour aerial bombardment by state-of-the-art German aircraft.

The **Tree of Gernika**, the seedling of an ancient oak, by the 19th-century Parliament building (*Las Casas Juntas*) is the symbol of Basque democracy; under it the representatives of the Basque provinces met in assembly from the Middle Ages, and here the laws were proclaimed. Later, the kings of Castille came here to swear to uphold Basque *fueros* and ancient laws. When the tree died in 1860, it was replanted with a sapling from one of its acorns; remnants of its 300-year-old trunk can be seen under a nearby pavilion. The young tree survived the bombing and its descendant serves as a potent symbol of freedom and hope, and not only for the Basques – Gernika shocked the world because it was the first time modern technology was used as a tool of terror, a prelude to our own greatest nightmares.

However, the hilltop area near the Tree of Gernika survived the onslaught relatively unscathed and the regal 18th-century Palacio Alegría, built on the remnants of an older fortified mansion, now contains the **Museo Euskal Herria** (*open Tues–Sat 10–2 and 4–7, Sun 10–3; adm*), dedicated to the history of the Basque Country from prehistoric times. It's an engaging little museum with plenty of models, audio-visuals and film clips describing Basque language, customs and traditions. Behind the museum is the **Parque de los Pueblos de Europa** (*open daily 10–7, until 9 in summer*), a shady green expanse with a pretty wooden bridge. Cross it to find a pair of modern memorials to commemorate the bombing: *Gure Aitaren Etxea*, 'our father's house', an eloquent contribution by Chillida, dedicated to peace, and an amorphous work by Henry Moore, *Large Figure in a Shelter*. Behind, another palace contains the information centre on the Urdaibai Biosphere Reserve (*see below*). Near the entrance to the park, there's a ceramic copy of Picasso's masterpiece; the Basques, who not surprisingly feel that they are the rightful owners, have been lobbying Madrid to send them the original to hang in the Guggenheim.

Down the hill, on the edge of the tiny pedestrianised old quarter full of chic cafés and boutiques, you'll find Gernika's newest memorial to peace, the **Museo de La Paz** (*Foru Plaza 1, t 94 627 02 13, open Tues–Sat 10–2 and 4–9, Sun 10–2; adm, guided visits available, call in advance to arrange visits in English*) which focuses on the bombing on the 26 April 1937. The centrepiece is a moving audio-visual exhibit (also in English) recounted by a local woman musing on her life just before her home is reduced to rubble. A gallery contains documents, uniforms, and shocking photographs relating to the bombing, and there are several exhibits related to peace around the world, highlighting the absurdity of the destruction that continues in other lives and cities worldwide.

Surrounding Gernika is the 220-square-kilometre **Urdaibai Biosphere Reserve**, created in 1984 to prevent the destruction of fragile habitats in the Ría de Mundaka.

The First Victim of Saturation Bombing

In 1937 Gernika became the kind of symbol for its times that Sarajevo was for the 1990s, a civilized little place that some thugs had chosen to flatten. Almost as soon as it happened, the Nationalist propaganda machine began sending out stories that the Communists had really destroyed the town by placing bombs in the sewers. It may have been the only time in his life that Francisco Franco was actually embarrassed. Just how much responsibility the Generalísimo had for Gernika will probably never be known, but there is nothing in his long shabby career that suggests he was capable of such a stunt – Franco could massacre prisoners and fill prisons with priests and professors, but Gernika was evil on a Nazi scale.

Hitler had sent his 'Condor Legion' to Spain not only to give Franco a hand, but to test the new Luftwaffe's theories of terror bombing, and his commanders coldly determined Gernika to be the site of the first lesson (on a market day too). Though the town had no military significance whatsoever, as a symbol of Basque nationhood it was the perfect spot for a bombing designed especially to destroy the enemy's morale – by breaking their hearts, perhaps. While Gernika had little effect on the war – the isolated Basque pocket was bound to fall anyhow – the Nazis were pleased enough with the results and the notoriety they gained from them to make such bombing the centre of their strategy; after Gernika came Warsaw, Rotterdam and Coventry among many others.

Picasso's great painting, resting safely in New York during the Franco years, did as much as the bombing itself to catch the world's attention. Since 1981 it has been proudly displayed in the Reina Sofia in Madrid, perhaps the ultimate exorcism of the War and the General. The *Guernica* that seemed so mysterious and revolutionary in its time now seems quite familiar and eloquent to us, so much have our ways of seeing changed since that distant age. The black and white gives it the immediacy of a newspaper photo. Picasso's preliminary sketches show that the central figures in the painting, the fallen horse and rider, were in his mind from the beginning. We can see in them the image of Gernika's destroyers: the eternal bully on horseback, the *caudillo*, the conqueror. In a way Guernica may have been Picasso's prophecy – with such an atrocity as this, the man on horseback may finally have gone too far.

The reserve is hardly a pristine wilderness – besides Gernika it counts 18 towns within its boundaries – but the sympathetic interaction between the area's inhabitants and their environment has led it to be considered an embodiment of that most elusive of eco-ideals: sustainable development. Farms and factories share Urdaibai with wetlands and lush oak forests; greenshank and bar-tailed godwit stalk the mud flats, while lucky observers may get a glimpse of the nocturnal genet, an odd mixture of raccoon and tabby cat with enormous eyes. About 5km east of Gernika, the **Cueva de Santimamiñe** (*guided tours Mon–Fri, 10, 11.15, 12.30, 4.30 and 6 – note that due to the fragility of the art, only 15 people at a time are allowed in, so get there early*) has Euskadi's best Palaeolithic art: two rooms with engravings of bison, horses, arrows, a bear and a deer, and geometric designs although they are rather fain. It is said that these caves are also the home of the Beigorri, a huge hairy red bull with a militant stare, the protector of the goddess Mari. A path leads from the cave entrance into the **Forest of Oma**, where local artist Agustín Ibarrola has fused art with nature by painting luminous multicoloured bands on the trees, achieving an array of perspective tricks.

Along the Coast to Bilbao: the Castle of Butrón

Just north of Gernika the Río Oka becomes a broad flat estuary (Ría de Gernika), snaking towards the Cantabrian Sea. Near the mouth lie the pretty beaches of **Laida** and **Laga**; there are others on the western shore at **Pedernales** and **Mundaka**, the latter famous among surfers for having the longest left-hand break in Europe. In Mundaka, enjoy wandering through labyrinthine alleys and soaking up the views from its charming waterfront promenade. In the mputh of the estuary the tiny island of Izaro used to be home to a band of hardy monks. Continuing round the coast, **Bermeo** is Euskadi's largest fishing port, a colourful, working town that makes few concessions to tourism. The long history of Basque seafaring is celebrated in the **Museo del Pescador** (*open Tues–Sat 10–1.30 and 4–7.30, Sun 10–1.30*), which relates stories of whaling expeditions from the Bay of Biscay to Newfoundland.

Further towards Bilbao lies **Bakio**, another *txakoli*-producing new town tucked into a little bay. Nearby, the hermitage-topped islet of **San Juan de Gaztelugatxa** is linked to the mainland by a bridge and offers magnificent views along the dark coastal cliffs. In the old days the isle supported a castle; the best one remaining in the vicinity is the 11th-century **Castillo de Butrón**, rebuilt in fairy-tale style in the 19th century and located in the wooded hills (take the BI634 west of Gatika). Butrón really deserves a visit (*open winter Wed-Fri 10.30–5.30, Sat 11–6; summer Mon–Sat 10.30–8; adm*); it's the Disneyland castle on a bad trip, an incredible pile of towers and corbelled ramparts in a gloomy dark stone, done in a style that other countries in the Victorian era generally saved for prisons and asylums. If you aren't careful you may end up on a guided tour; the place is kitted out with props and dummies in costume to better evoke the fantasy medieval atmosphere.

Inland: San Sebastián to Bilbao

Along the coast, the narrow twisting roads will take you nearly a day. The more common route west is the A8 motorway, with its exorbitant tolls, and the slower, parallel N634, both of which cut inland near Deba and follow some of the more somnolescent landscapes of Euskadi. If you avoid the tolls and follow the latter you'll get an object lesson in the life of the average Basque, passing through tidy, grey little industrial splotches like Eligobar and **Eibar**, a typically peculiar Basque factory town stuffed in a narrow valley, with plenty of tall apartment blocks around Spain's biggest sewing machine plant. Ermua, the next village up the road, is much the same.

Further south, on the BI2632, **Elorrio** is an attractive village of grand palaces and impressive little squares, adorned with a set of unique crucifixes from the 15–16th centuries. The façade of the Ayuntamiento bears a curious verse from Matthew 12:36:

'I tell you, on the day of judgment men will render account for every careless word they utter.' From the centre it's a lovely walk out to the **hermitage of San Adrián de Argiñeta**, where you can see the 9th- and 10th-century tombs of Argiñeta, carved out of rock, some adorned with pinwheel-like stars or Latin inscriptions. Nobody knows to whom these sarcophagi belong; some speculate they are the tombs of some leftover Visigoths.

It's another 6km to the biggest town in the area, **Durango**, a name that conjures up cowboys and Westerns in the New World (besides the Durango in Colorado, there is another in Mexico, which in colonial times was capital of the province of 'Nueva Vizcaya': there must have been a lot of Basques about). The original has nothing to detain you long, though there is an attractive Baroque centre behind its **Portal de Santa Ana**, an ornate survival from the old walls. In the centre, note the brightly painted Ayuntamiento, and the stone mosaic maze under the portico of Santa María de Uribarri. The most unusual single monument is the 19th-century **Kurutziaga Cross**, just outside the centre in a neighbourhood of the same name.

South of Durango, the Duranguesado massif juts abruptly out of rolling green hills, creating Vizcaya's most dramatic mountain scenery. Protected as the **Parque Natural Urkiola**, the range offers plenty of opportunities for sweaty assaults on the high peaks, or leisurely ambles through birch forest (the park's name means 'place of birch trees' in Basque). Local legends tell that the goddess Mari haunts these hills; earthly residents include goshawk, peregrine falcon and merlin, all of which can be spotted regularly.

Getting Around

Durango and Elorrio are both served by BizkaiBus from Paseo del Arenal in Bilbao, and slow but scenic EuskoTren services between Bilbao and San Sebastián call in Durango.

Tourist Information

Durango: C/ Asktatasun Ebordiea 2, t 94 603 39 38, www.durango-udala.net.
Alto de Urkiola: Caserío Toki-Alai, t 94 682 01 64.

Where to Stay and Eat

Unlike the coast, this is definitely not tourist country, and you'll tend to find only simple accommodation anywhere near the A8.

Durango ✉ 48200
****Gran Hotel Gran Durango, Gasteiz Bidea 2, t 94 621 75 80, www.granhoteldurango.com (expensive). An elegant 19th-century mansion, sumptuously converted into a smart hotel with pool, gardens and restaurant.
***Hotel Kurutziaga, C/Kurutziaga 52, t 94 620 08 64, www.kurutziaga.com (moderate). An 18th-century mansion converted into a modern business hotel, with a restaurant.
**Hs Juego de Bolos, San Agustinalde 2, t 94 681 10 99 (inexpensive). Durango's one hostal, with good restaurant downstairs.
Pedro Juan, C/ San Antonio 1, in Bérriz, t 94 682 6246 (moderate). In a lovely stone house, this serves fine regional dishes and fabulous home-made desserts. Lunch menú €8.

Markina ✉ 48200
**Vega, Abesúa 2, t 94 680 615 (inexpensive). You can get a good night's sleep at this central place, with large, airy rooms (with or without bath) overlooking the main plaza.
Niko, San Agustín 4, t 94 616 75 28. Good cooking with a bargain menú (downstairs from the Hotel Vega).

North of Durango, in the heartland of old Basque traditions, is the minute village and valley of **Bolívar**, where the family of the great Liberator of South America, Simón de Bolívar, originated (he was born in Venezuela in 1783). His Art Deco monument dwarfs the village square, and down the village's one lane, the site of his ancestral house has been fixed up as a **Museo Bolívar** (*t 94 616 4114, open Tues–Fri 10–1, Sat and Sun 12–2; July and Aug also 5–7; closed Mon*). Near the old parish **church of Santo Tomás** you can see the 'cattle trial yards' and the huge stone weights hauled by oxen at festivals.

Markina (Marquina), further north, is nicknamed the 'University of Pelota'; its historic *frontón* has produced champions who have made their mark around the world. On the right bank of the Río Artibay, stands the uncanny, hexagonal **church of San Miguel de Arretxinaga**, built around an enormous altar constructed by the giant *jentillak* (or, according to some, fallen from heaven) that consists of three massive rocks propped against one another. Probably a work of Neolithic times, it now shelters a statue of St Michael. There is another 'cattle trial yard' next to the church.

Bilbao (Bilbo)

Tucked in the lush clefts and folds of Euskadi's coastal mountains, and stretched along the Nervión, once a notorious industrial by-product resembling chocolate milk and now clean enough to support a few fish as it discharges its last effluents into the flushing tide, you'll find **Bilbao**. The name is Bilbo in Basque, but its inhabitants lovingly call it the *botxo*, the Basque word for hole, or orifice.

The orifice was originally a scattering of fishing hamlets, huddled on the left bank of a deep *ría* where the hills offered some protection from the Normans and other pirates. In 1300, when the coast was clear of such dangers, the lord of Vizcaya, Diego López de Haro, founded a new town on the right bank of the Ría de Bilbao. It quickly developed into the Basques' leading port, its main link to northern Europe, exporting Castile's wool to Flanders and the swords Shakespeare called 'bilbos'. In 1511 the merchants formed the *Consulado de Bilbao* to govern their affairs, an institution that survived and thrived until 1829.

The 19th century had other treats in store: the indignity of a French sacking in 1808 and sieges by the Carlists in both of their wars; Bilbao was the 'martyr city' of the Liberal cause. But this century also made Bilbao into a city. Blessed with its tremendous iron mines, forests, cheap hydraulic power and excellent port, Bilbao got a double dose of the Industrial Revolution. Steel mills, shipbuilding and other associated industries sprang up, quickly followed by banks and insurance companies and all the other accoutrements of capitalism to finance them. Workers from across the country poured into the tenements, and smoke clogged the air. It was Spain's Pittsburgh, and just as full of worker misery and exploitation. Franco punished it crushingly for its support of the Republicans, then in the 1960s whipped it forward as the industrial centre of Spain.

Of late, the rusting machinery has been removed and the once-seedy dock area gentrified. Meanwhile Greater Bilbao/Bilbo/botxo, with its population of over a million, the fourth city of Spain and its greatest port, not to mention the sister city of Boise, Idaho, is not twiddling its thumbs awaiting obsolescence. Thanks to banking, insurance and such less obviously dirty business, the economy is doing pretty well, and the city has embarked on an ambitious redevelopment programme, reclaiming vast areas of the centre formerly devoted to heavy industry. The hugely popular Guggenheim Museum, which opened in October 1997, has by itself significantly boosted the city's economy, attracting almost a million and a half visitors in its first year.

Other new projects include cleaning up the Nervíon (it even has a few fish now), a concert hall and convention centre (completed in 1998), and a library, park, hotel, offices and residential buildings all to be built on the site of the old shipyards. The new 'passenger interchange' at San Mamés has put local and international bus and train services under one huge roof, and the metro, with sleek modern stations designed by Sir Norman Foster, was completed in 1995 and has since been extended up the left bank of the river. The airport got an elegant new terminal designed by Santiago Calatrava in 2000, and the port is being given a boost as part of a vast harbour expansion project which includes an excellent Maritime Museum (opened 2004). Bilbao is shaping up to become one of the cities of Europe's future; come back in a few years and see.

The Casco Viejo

The Casco Viejo, the centre of the city from the 15th to the 19th century, is a small, snug region on the east bank of the Nervión; tucked out of the way across the Puente del Arenal from the bustling centre, it remains the city's heart. The bridge leaves you in **Plaza de Arriaga**, known familiarly as *El Arenal* from the sand flats that stood here long ago. Fittingly for a Basque city, its monuments are both musical, the opera house, or **Teatro Arriaga**, and a glorious Art Nouveau pavilion in steel and glass (*concerts every Sunday afternoon*). Adjacent to the Arenal is arcaded, enclosed **Plaza Nueva**, now a bit down-at-heel, but in its day the symbol of Bilbao's growth and prosperity.

Philosopher Miguel de Unamuno was born on nearby Calle La Ronda, not far from the **Museo Vasco** on La Cruz 4 (*open Tues–Sat 11–5, Sun 11–2; adm*). Located in an old Jesuit cloister, this offers for your perusal a scale-model of Vizcaya, a reconstruction of the rooms of the Consulate, the old merchants' organization, as well as tools, model ships and Basque gravestones. In the middle of the cloister, the ancient Idolo de Mikeldi is the museum's treasure – it looks like a primitive depiction of the cow that jumped over the moon.

Around the back of the museum, the **Catedral de Santiago** sends its graceful spire up over the centre of the Casco Viejo. Begun in the 1200s, most of this understated but elegant grey stone church is 14th–15th-century Gothic (though the façade was added in the 1880s). It matches its setting perfectly; everything to the south is the calm grey world of the 'Seven Streets', the core of Bilbao when it was still a village. All the colour and animation is concentrated in the 1929 **Mercado de la Ribera** on the river front, the largest covered market in Spain.

Nearby, the **Diocesan Museum of Sacred Art** (*open Tues–Sat 10.30–1.30 and 4–7, Sun 10.30–1.30; adm*), occupying the former Convento de la Encarnación, displays over

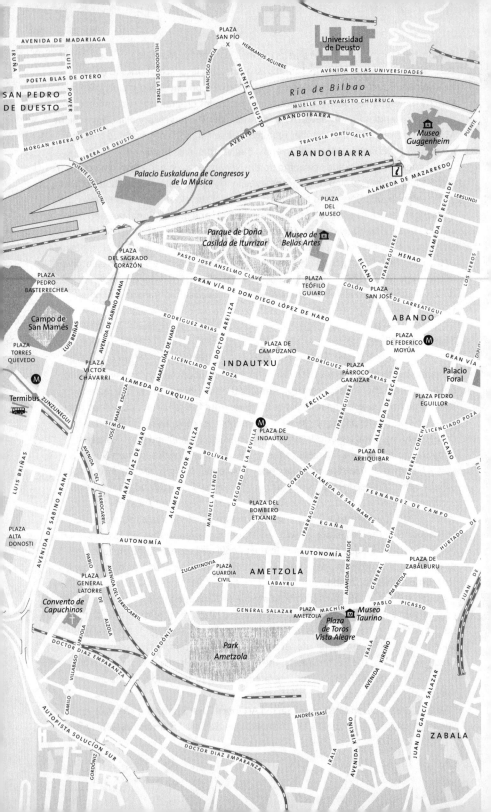

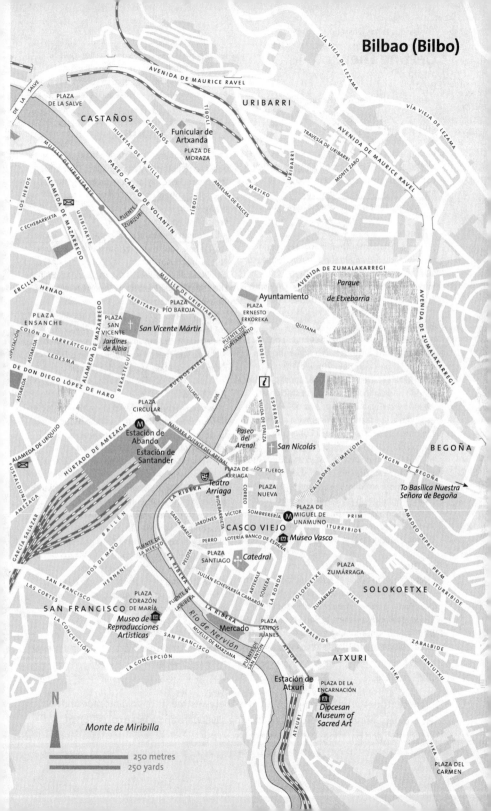

Bilbao (Bilbo)

CASTAÑOS
URIBARRI
PLAZA DE LA SALVE
AVENIDA DE MAURICE RAVEL
VÍA VIEJA DE LEZAMA
VÍA VIEJA DE LEZAMA

PLAZA DE LA SALVE
Funicular de Artxanda
PLAZA DE MORAZA
TRAVESÍA DE URIBARRI
AVENIDA DE MAURICE RAVEL
MONTE ZARO

HUERTAS DE LA VILLA
CASTAÑOS
TIBOLI
ANSELMA DE SALCES
MATIKO
URIBARRI

LOS HEROS
C ECHEBARRIETA
ALAMEDA DE MAZARREDO
URIBITARTE
PUENTE ZUBIZURI
MUELLE DE URIBITARTE
PASEO CAMPO DE VOLANTÍN
TIBOLI

MUELLE DE URIBITARTE
URIBITARTE
AVENIDA DE ZUMALAKARREGI
Parque de Etxebarria
AVENIDA DE ZUMALAKARREGI

ERCILLA
HENAO
PLAZA ENSANCHE
COLÓN DE LARREÁTEGUI
DIPUTACIÓN
ASTARLOA
LEDESMA
ALAMEDA DE MAZARREDO
BERASTEGUI
URIBITARTE
PÍO BAROJA
PLAZA SAN VICENTE
Jardines de Albia
San Vicente Mártir
Ayuntamiento
PLAZA ERNESTO ERKOREKA
PUENTE DEL AYUNTAMIENTO
QUITANA
SENDEIA

DE DON DIEGO LÓPEZ DE HARO
ASTARLOA
ALAMEDA DE URQUIJO
EUSKALDUNA
AMEZAGA
BUENOS AIRES
VILLARÍAS
RIVA
PLAZA CIRCULAR
NAVARRA PUENTE DEL ARENAL
Paseo del Arenal
San Nicolás
PLAZA DE LOS FUEROS
ESPERANZA
VIUDA DE EPALZA
i
BEGOÑA
VIRGEN DE BEGOÑA

GARCÍA SALAZAR
HURTADO DE AMEZAGA
Estación de Abando
Estación de Santander
LA RIBERA
BIDEBARRIETA
Teatro Arriaga
PLAZA DE ARRIAGA
CORREO
PLAZA NUEVA
CALZADAS DE MALLONA
PLAZA DE MIGUEL DE UNAMUNO
To Basílica Nuestra Señora de Begoña
AMADEO DEPRIT

BAILÉN
DOS DE MAYO
HERNANI
PUENTE DE LA MERCED
SANTA MARÍA
JARDINES
PERRO
VÍCTOR
SOMBRERERÍA
CASCO VIEJO
Museo Vasco
PRIM
ITURRIBIDE
PRIM
ITURRIBIDE

SAN FRANCISCO
LAS CORTES
LA CONCEPCIÓN
PLAZA CORAZÓN DE MARÍA
SAN FRANCISCO
Museo de Reproducciones Artísticas
PELOTA
PUENTE DE LA RIBERA
LARRIBERA
LA RIBERA
Río de Nervión
Mercado
JULIÁN ECHEVARRÍA CAMARÓN
ARTEKALE
SOMERA
LA RONDA
LOTERÍA BANCO DE ESPAÑA
PLAZA SANTIAGO
Catedral
PLAZA ZUMÁRRAGA
ZUMÁRRAGA
FIKA
SOLOKOETXE
SOLOKOETXE
ZABALBIDE

LA CONCEPCIÓN
SAN FRANCISCO
MUELLE DE MARZANA
PLAZA SANTOS JUANES
PUENTE DE SAN ANTÓN
ATXURI
ATXURI
FIKA
SANTUTXU
ZABALBIDE

N
Monte de Miribilla
Estación de Atxuri
PLAZA DE LA ENCARNACIÓN
Diocesan Museum of Sacred Art
FIKA

250 metres
250 yards

PLAZA DEL CARMEN

Getting There

By Air

Bilbao's Loui airport is the busiest in northwest Spain, with daily flights from London, Brussels, Frankfurt and Milan, and to most airports in Spain, including Santiago and Vigo (for information, t 94 453 23 06, www.aena.es). The airport is 10km north and approximately a €20-25 taxi ride from the centre; a bus service (route number A-3247) runs roughly every 30 minutes to the airport from Plaza Moyúa.

By Ferry

The P&O Portsmouth–Bilbao ferry operates twice weekly, arriving in the suburb of Santurzi, 13km from the centre of town. There is an information and bookings office on C/Cosme Echevarrieta 1, t 94 423 44 77, in the centre.

By Train

Bilbao has several train lines and about a dozen stations, although as a non-suburban commuter you only need three of them. The main RENFE station, with connections to France, Madrid and Galicia is known as **Estación de Abando**, Pza Circular (t 90 224 02 02). Next door at Bailén 2, but facing the river with a colourful tile front, is the **Estación de la Concordia**, where scenic, narrow-gauge FEVE trains come and go to Santander and Oviedo (t 94 423 22 66). The pretty little **Estación Atxuri**, at Atxuri 6 in the Casco Viejo, is used by the Basque regional line, Eusko Trenbideak (t 94 433 95 00) for connections to San Sebastián by way of Durango, Zarautz and Zumaia. A separate line serves Gernika, Mundaka and Bermeo.

By Bus

All interurban bus lines arrive and depart from **Termibus (t 94 439 42 00, www.termibus.com)** near San Mamés stadium in the Ensanche. There are hourly services to San Sebastián, Vitoria, and Santander, and several buses a day to Pamplona, Madrid, Barcelona, Galicia and Castilla-León. BizkaiBus (t 902 22 22 65, www.bizkaia.net) serves destinations within Vizcaya, including Durango, Gernika and the coastal villages from a separate terminal on **Paseo del Arenal**, near the Casco Viejo.

Getting Around

Bilbao's complex topography makes it a beast to negotiate by car; miss one turn, and you may have to circle 40km (no exaggeration!) back and around, only to end up in a field of orange barrels called Asua Crossroads from which few have ever returned.

If you make it to the centre, **parking** is just as frustrating; you'll find city-run garages at Plaza Nueva, Instituto Correos, Plaza del Ensanche and Plaza de Indautxu. If the car you parked in the street vanishes, call the Grúa Municipal (towing), t 94 420 50 98.

Nearly all of Bilbao's attractions are within walking distance of each other in the centre; the efficient **city bus** line (Bilbobus) and **Metro** will take you there if you're elsewhere. For a radio **taxi**, call t 94 410 21 21 or t 94 480 09 09.

By Metro

The metro consists of two lines: a main line, L1, from Etxebarri to Plentzia and a branch line, L2, which splits off at Sarriko to head up the left bank of the river to Setsao. The metro is the easiest way to the beaches at Getxo and Plentzia; there are stations at the Casco Viejo, Abando (for long-distance trains), Plaza Moyúa (closest to the Guggenheim), Indautxu and San Mamés (for Termibus). A single costs €1.15–1.40 depending on the distance travelled. There is also a €3 ticket that gives one-day, unlimited metro travel, or you can buy a Creditrans card. Metro services run about every 5 minutes in the centre, and every 20 minutes to Plentzia.

For information call t 94 425 40 25, or visit the website www.metrobilbao.com.

By Tram

A new tram system fills the last gap in inner Bilbao's public transport network. The line

eight centuries' worth of religious art and finery; vestments of gold brocade and embroidery; hundreds of pieces of glittering silverware and a large collection of sculptures and paintings by Basque artists.

runs alongside the Nervión, connecting Estación Atxuri with San Mamés via Abando, the Guggenheim and Abandoibarra. Trams run every 12–15 minutes and you can buy tickets from machines at tram stops, or use the Creditrans card (see above). Date-stamp your ticket before boarding.

By Taxi

To continue around the coast from Plentzia without your own transport, take a taxi to Mungia (€14) from where buses go to Bermeo.

Tourist Information

Tourist offices: The main offices are at Paseo del Arenal 1, t 94 479 57 60, in front of the Guggenheim at Abandoibarra 2, and in the Teatro Arriaga, Plaza Arriaga s/n, on the edge of the Casco Viejo. There is also an airport office, t 94 453 23 06, near the luggage carousel; go before you leave the luggage hall as it isn't accessible once you have passed through customs.

Post office: Alameda de Urquijo 19.

Internet access: Unlike the rest of Spain many hotels and hostales throughout the Pais Vasco have WiFi access: ask when you book your accommodation. Otherwise try Laser Center, C/Sendeja 5, t 94 445 35 09 (open Mon–Fri 10.30am–2.30am), near Abando station in the centre, and Cyberc@fé @ntxi, C/Briñas Luis 13, t 944 41 94 48 (open Mon-Fri 10.30-am–10.30pm), near the San Mamés stadium and transport interchange station.

Walking tours: The tourist information office offers two walking tours, one around the Casco Viejo (departures from the tourist information office at the Teatro Arriaga) and the other around the Ensanche (departures from the tourist office in front of the Guggenheim). Both tours last around 11/2 hours and cost 3 euros. For times and more information, call 94 479 57 60 or email bit@ayto.bilbao.net. Bilbao Paso a Paso, t 94 415 38 92, www.bilbaopasoapaso.com, organizes

walking tours around the city, including the Casco Viejo, as well as guided visits of the Guggenheim, gastronomic tastings and special trips into the surrounding hills. Phone for prices and timetable information.

Shopping

There's no shortage of opportunities to spend money in Bilbao. The Siete Calles are a good place to start, particularly C/Bidebarrieta and C/Correo, with plenty of upmarket clothing and shoe shops, and tacky souvenir places knocking out interminable ceramic Puppys.

For something slightly funkier try C/Somera, where youthful fashions dominate and subversive 'grow shops' line the street.

The trendiest boutiques are in the Ensanche, mostly south of the Gran Via around Plaza Indautxu; C/Ercilla is a good place to start.

La Casa del Libro, Colón de Larreategui 41. Sells a wide range of maps and books, including a good selection in English.

Urretxindorra, C/Iparraguirre 26. A good place to browse, with more of the same, including Basque cookbooks in English and one of the best selections of Basque music.

Mercado de la Ribera. Head here when it's time to buy the ingredients.

Where to Stay

Bilbao ✉ 48000

The 'Guggenheim Effect' has filled Bilbao's hotels to the brim with the kind of educated, culture-seeking tourist other cities dream of, so book in advance. The average visitor would probably prefer to stay in the Casco Viejo.

Luxury

Bilbao has several luxury hotels, catering for the businessmen who pass through; some of these offer discounts of up to 50 per cent at weekends. The following are centrally located and popular:

The Seven Streets being closely hemmed in by cliffs, Bilbao's centre spread over the bridge as the city grew, while garden suburbs were on the cliffs. Behind the large **church of San Nicolás**, off El Arenal, an elevator ascends to the upper town, from where it's a

*****Gran Hotel Domine Bilbao**, Alameda de Mazarredo 61, **t** 94 425 3300, *www.granhotel dominebilbao.com*. Currently the hottest place to stay in town, with a fabulous location right opposite the Guggenheim.

*****Lopez de Haro**, Obispo Orueta 2, **t** 94 423 55 00, *lh@hotellopezdeharo.com, www.hotellopezdeharo. com*. This classically elegant hotel has one of the city's finest restaurants.

****Carlton**, Pza Federico Moyúa 2, **t** 94 416 22 00, *www.aranzazu hoteles.com*. This plush 19th-century hotel has lodged famous bullfighters, along with Hemingway, Ava Gardner and Lauren Bacall.

Expensive

****Ercilla**, C/Ercilla 37–39, **t** 94 410 20 00, *www.hotelercilla.es*. A concrete monster, this grand, business-oriented hotel has a fine restaurant, Bermeo.

****Hotel Indautxu**, Pza Bombero Etxaniz, **t** 94 440 004, *www.hotelindautxu.com*. Has all the necessary comforts in a good quiet location; the house restaurant, **Etxaniz**, does delicious things with fish and lobster (*expensive*).

****NH Villa de Bilbao**, Gran Vía 87, **t** 94 441 60 00, *www.nh-hotels.com*. This sleek, modern hotel is particularly geared towards business people.

Moderate

***Conde Duque**, C/Campo Volantin 22, **t** 94 445 60 00, *www.hotelcondeduque.com*. Across the river from the Guggenheim, at the low end of this category.

Estadio, C/J Antonio Zunzunegui 10, **t** 94 442 50 11. On the other side of town, handy for Termibus, but a little overpriced.

Inexpensive

Most of the inexpensive rooms will be found in the Casco Viejo.

Hotel Iturrienea Ostatua, C/Santa Maria 14, **t** 94 416 15 00. Definitely the choice in the

Casco Viejo; great care and attention have gone in to equipping the rooms with a mix of antique and new furniture, while hosts of flowering plants trail from the balconies.

Hotel Ripa, C/Ripa 3, **t** 94 423 96 77, *www.hotel-ripa.com*. On the river front just opposite the Casco Viejo, with nice recently renovated rooms.

Hotel Zabalburu, C/PM Artola 8, **t** 94 443 71 00, *www.hotelzabalburu.com*. Pleasant rooms in a modern setting, with parking facilities.

Hs Hostal Gurea, C/Bidebarrieta 14, **t** 94 416 32 99. Has nice simple rooms (with bath).

*Arriaga**, C/Ribera 3 (off Plaza Arriaga), **t** 94 479 00 01. Comfortable modern rooms with parking, an important consideration in this crowded town.

*Plaza San Pedro**, C/Luzarra 7, **t** 94 476 31 26. Small hotel near the Guggenheim; good facilities for the price.

Budget

Hotel Artetxe, Camino de Berriz 95, **t** 94 474 77 80, *www.hotelartetxe.com*. A delightful option, this is a traditional Basque house on a hill above the city. Best if you have your own transport. Good restaurant and they also rent apartments in an annexe.

Don Claudio, C/Hermógenes Rojo 10, **t** 94 490 50 17. A good bet, although away from the centre.

Pensión Martínez, C/Villarias 8, **t** 94 423 91 78. A good clean cheapie in the centre of town.

Getxo ✉ 48990

Artaza, Avda Los Chopos 12, **t** 94 491 28 52, *hotelartaza@euskalnet.net* (*expensive*). Offers comfort with elegance in a refined mansion surrounded by tranquil parkland, a short walk from Neguri Metro station.

***Gran Hotel**, María Díaz de Haro 2, Portugalete, **t** 94 401 48 00, *www.granhotel puentecolgante.com* (*moderate*).Newish hotel in a sumptuous historic building at the foot of the Vizcaya Bridge. Excellent value.

short walk to the Viscayans' holy shrine, the 16th-century **Basílica de Begoña** with its unusual (later) spire. Inside, there is a venerated statue of the Virgin and huge paintings by Luca Giordano, who was very popular in his day. There are fine views of the old town.

***Hotel Igeretxe**, Playa Areaga, t 94 491 00 09 (*moderate*). This Belle Epoque hotel overlooks the estuary and pampers guests with saltwater therapy and algae baths.

Pensión Areeta, C/Mayor 13, t 94 463 81 36 (*inexpensive*). Has clean, comfortable rooms with bath.

Plentzia ✉ 48630

*****Hotel Kaian**, C/ Areatza 38, t 94 677 54 70 (*moderate–inexpensive*). A charming, peach-painted villa in its own little garden on the seafront, with just a handful of spacious rooms.

*****Hotel Uribe**, C/Erribea 13, t 94 677 44 78, www.hoteluribe.com. The choice place to stay, set in a restored mansion overlooking the *ría*; some of the rooms boast luxurious glassed-in balconies.

*****Hostal Palas**, C/Ribera 42, t 94 677 08 36 (*budget*). Has pleasant rooms with shared bath and a funky café.

Eating Out

This city may not get as wild about cuisine as San Sebastián, but eating is still a pleasure. For the purest Basque cuisine, look for the strangest names. Note that many restaurants close the week before, or after *Semana Grande* (the week before the 15th August).

Bermeo, C/Ercilla 37, t 94 470 57 00 (*expensive*). Traditional and sumptuous; if it's on the menu, this is the place to try one of the ultimate Basque treats, *kokotxas* – the 'cheek and throat' of a hake in a garlic and parsley sauce. *Closed Sat lunch, Sun eve and Aug; open Semana Grande*.

Goizeko-Kabi, C/Particular de Estraunza 4–6, t 94 441 11 29 (*expensive*). Has the right-sounding name and, sure enough, offers excellent cooking to match.

Gorrotxa, Alameda Urquijo 30, t 94 443 49 37 (*expensive*). Offers spectacular Basque food in a refined setting. Reservations essential. *Closed Sun and first two weeks Sept*.

Guría, Gran Vía 66, t 94 441 57 80 (*expensive*). Another old favourite serving traditional Basque fare. They also run the cheaper but excellent El Bistrot (same address) with a good lunch *menú* (€16). *Closed Sun eve*.

Jolastoki, Avda Leioa, in Neguri, t 94 491 20 31 (*expensive*). Has a reputation for elaborate fish and fowl dishes; choose between the posh dining-room and the sunny patio, and feast on delicately grilled turbot with saffron oil or chicken stuffed with truffles.

Víctor, Plaza Nueva 2, t 94 415 16 78 (*expensive*). In business for over 40 years, with an enviable reputation as one of the Casco Viejo's best restaurants; the *bodega* boasts over 1,500 different wines. *Closed Sun, last week in Aug and first in Sept*.

Zortziko, Alameda de Mazzarredo 17 (near Plaza de España), t 94 423 97 43 (*expensive*). You can splurge at this, the city's finest restaurant, where the quirky décor and fine service prepare you for innovative and immaculately presented treats from the kitchen: green almond soup and *estofado* of wild pigeon, washed down with the finest of Rioja wines. *Closed all day Sun, Mon eve, last week in Aug and first 2 weeks Sept*.

Guggenheim, Guggenheim Museum Bilbao, t 94 423 93 33 (*expensive–moderate*). Full of light, organic lines, and furniture designed by Frank Gehry; the food is an excellent snapshot of some of the best of Basque cooking. There are three *menú degustacións* on offer between €45 and €54, and a good-value lunchtime *menu del día* at €18.

La Granja, Plaza de España (*moderate*). An old, attractive café and tapas bar on the plaza.

Harrobia, C/del Perro 2, t 94 679 00 90 (*moderate*). Buzzy new restaurant serving *nueva cocina vasco* in elegant surroundings.

Metro Moyúa, Gran Vía 40, t 94 424 92 73 (*moderate*). A good menu offering *nouveau Basque cuisine* can be found here.

El Puerto, Aretxandra 20, in Getxo, t 94 491 21 66 (*moderate*). This old-time portside restaurant keeps things simple, serving

The Ensanche

Nobody in the 19th century had a sharper sense of urban design than the Spaniards, and wherever a town had money to do something big, the results were impressive.

mighty portions of fresh fish and seafood out on a big breezy terrace.

Amboto, C/Jardines (*budget*). A seafood place off Plaza Arriaga that specializes in *merluza* (hake) in a delicious sauce made from crabs.

Café Boulevard, Arenal 3, **t** 94 415 31 28 (*budget*). First opened in 1871, giving cultured society a meeting place before going to the opera, this café was revamped 50 years later, restoring its its elegant Art Deco interior. Pop in for an afternoon iced coffee, an early evening *copa* or tango lessons every Friday at 11pm.

La Deliciosa, C/Jardines (*budget*). A pretty, stylish, white-painted café-restaurant which attracts a hip young crowd and offers an excellent lunch menú for €8.50.

Guggen, Alameda de Rekalde 5 (*budget*). Perhaps the best of those restaurants cashing in on their proximity to the Guggenheim, with a good, varied menu.

Vegetariano, C/Urquijo 33, **t** 94 444 55 98 (*budget*). Has great value *menús* full of innovative vegetable-based dishes. *Open Mon–Fri lunch only.*

Pintxos/Tapas

Within Bilbao there are three main tapas areas to head for to stave off those hunger pangs until dinner. However, most of the early evening action takes place in the Casco Viejo, where there are plenty of good *taperias* to test out.

Berton, C/Jardines 11. Filled with locals at weekends, this bar is brimming with a zillion varieties of hefty pieces of heaven.

Café Iruña, C/Jardines de Albia 5. Across in the Ensanche the streets around C/Ledesma keep going until a bit later, centred around this legendary and beautiful *mudéjar*-style café that comes alive with the evening crowd.

Victor Montes, Plaza Nueva 8. Boasts a vast array of delectable *pintxos*, and plenty of

crianzas and *reservas* to wash them down. The arcaded central Plaza Nueva has numerous other great old *taperias*, with tables outside and elegant dining rooms for full-blown meals. *Closed Sun eve.*

Nightlife

One cultural form of which the city is especially fond is **opera**, and there are regular performances throughout the year. Bertolt Brecht and Kurt Weill fans will be disappointed to learn that 'Bill's Ballhaus in Bilbao' was only a figment of their imagination. Less highbrow culture is generally limited to weekends, in the streets of the Casco Viejo.

C/Barrenkale is a busy place with a number of clubs, while C/Somera has friendly and funky bars that are very popular with the Basque Nationalist community. In the Ensanche, there are more bars on C/Pérez Galdós and C/Licenciado Poza.

Conjunto Vacío, C/Muelle de la Merced 4. Big, popular *discoteca*.

The Cotton Club, C/Gregorio de la Revilla 25. Occasional live jazz and blues acts are staged here.

Distrito 9, on C/Ajuriagerra. Largely but not exclusively gay, with drag shows.

Kafé Antzokia, C/San Vicente (by the Jardines de Albia), www.kafeantzokia.com. Set in a former cinema and is a Basque-speaking café by day, bar and club by night with DJs all kinds of live performances from music to theatre.

Palacio Euskalduna de Congresos y de la Música, Avda Abandoibarra 4, **t** 94 403 50 00. Also puts on plays and musicals, and sometimes big-name foreign acts.

Teatro Arriaga, Plaza de Arriaga 1, **t** 94 416 33 33. Regular performances of opera, theatre and comedy. Full details of forthcoming shows are available from the box office or tourist office.

Like Barcelona, Bilbao in its industrial boom years had to face exponential population growth, and its mayors chose to plan for it instead of just letting things happen. The area across the river from Bilbao, the '**Anteiglesia de Abando**', was mostly farmland in the 1870s when the city annexed it. A trio of planners, Severino de Achúcarro, Pablo de

Alzola and Ernest Hoffmeyer, got the job of laying out the streets for what came to be known as the **Ensanche**, or 'Extension', and they came up with a simple-looking but rather ingenious plan, with diagonal boulevards dividing up the broad loop of the river like orange segments. The Ensanche begins across from El Arenal; just over the bridge from the old town, a statue of Bilbao's founder, Diego López de Haro, looks benignly over the massive banks and circling traffic in the **Plaza Circular**. This has become the business centre of the city, with the big grey skyscraper of the Banco Bilbao Vizcaya, built in the 1960s, to remind us who is the leading force in the city's destiny today. The RENFE station occupies one corner of the square; you'll have to walk around behind it on the river front to see one of the city's industrial age landmarks: the tiny **Bilbao–Santander rail station**, a charming Art Nouveau work with a wrought iron and tile façade, designed by Severino de Achúcarro. South of the stations, Plaza Zabálburu marks the beginning of Bilbao's less salubrious quarters. On the cusp lie the Vista Alegre bull ring and the **Museo Taurino** (*open Mon–Fri 10–1 and 4–6; adm*), which holds mementos from over 250 years of bullfighting history; the highlight is a magnificent embroidered cape by Goya, created for the Enlightenment-era matador Joaquin Rodriguez.

From Plaza Circular, the main boulevard of the Ensanche extends westwards: the **Gran Vía de Don Diego López de Haro**. A block to the north, the façade of the Corte Inglés department store is one vast high relief mural evoking the industry and history of Bilbao. The centre of the Ensanche scheme is Plaza de Federico Moyúa, better known as **La Elíptica**. The Hotel Carlton here, still one of the city's posh establishments, served as the seat of the Basque government under the Republic and during the Civil War. From La Elíptica, C/Elcano takes you to the **Museo de Bellas Artes** (*Plaza del Museo 2; open Tues–Sat 10–8, Sun 10–2; adm*), on the edge of the large and beautiful Parque de Doña Casilda Iturriza. It contains a worthy collection ranging from Flemish paintings (Metsys' *The Money Changers* is one of the best) to Spanish masters like Velázquez, El Greco, Zurbarán and Goya, to modern art by Picasso, Gauguin, Léger and the American Impressionist Mary Cassatt, and efforts by 19th- and 20th-century Basques. Overflow from the Guggenheim has brought more visitors, and the museum has been elegantly enlarged to accommodate them. The park itself is an agreeable place to spend an hour or two, with exotic trees carefully labelled, a lagoon, and a new light-and-colour bauble called the 'Cybernetic Fountain'.

Along the Nervión

When Bilbao's urban planners embarked on post-industrial regeneration in the late 1980s it was inevitable that the river bank would be the project's linchpin. The significance of the Nervión (which becomes the Ría de Bilbao) to Bilbao is as much symbolic as practical; for years it has been synonymous in Spain with massive industrial pollution, but clean-up efforts since 1981 have succeeded in making the river habitable to fish for the first time in nearly a century. Major developments have taken place above water too, as several kilometres of old rusting jetties and dock installations have been torn out to make room for a riverside park, stretching down-stream from Arenal bridge to the Guggenheim museum. Bilbaínos have taken to the development with gusto – thousands of them pour on to the river banks every evening to walk their dogs and eat ice cream – and when the trees grow, and the estuarine pong disappears, it's likely to be a very pleasant space. Halfway along, the new glass-floored **Zubi Zuri** ('White Bridge' in Basque) was one of the first additions to the riverfront landscape; its nautical theme – the bridge billows out like a great sail – has become a widespread motif in the architecture of New Bilbao. Across the river a funicular glides up to the hill-top park on **Monte Artxanda** (*runs every 15 minutes, 7.15–10pm, until 11pm in summer, www.funicularartxanda.com; adm*), where there are several restaurants and extensive views of the Casco Viejo, the Guggenheim and, on really clear days, the sea, 16km to the north. For an authentic cultural experience go up on a weekend, when half of Bilbao squeezes into the rattling cars and hangs out on the mountain, picnicking, chattering and enjoying the view.

The Guggenheim Museum

Downstream from Zubi Zuri a 60ft tower of steel and golden limestone heralds the presence of Bilbao's new art Mecca, and the centrepiece of its biggest riverfront redevelopment, Frank O Gehry's **Museo Guggenheim** (*Avenida Abandoibarra 2, t 94 435 90 80, www.guggenheim-bilbao.es; open Tues–Sun 10–8, daily in July and Aug; adm*). Gehry's titanium clipper ship occupies the Abandoibarra flats, until 1987 home to Bilbao's biggest shipyard and now a worldwide symbol of successful urban renewal; the museum fits in to the landscape perfectly, looking utterly futuristic and yet in keeping with the city's industrial past. Its massive popularity and high public visibility have helped to spawn an economic boom, the so-called 'Guggenheim Effect', which has been felt throughout the Basque lands and shows no sign as yet of slowing down.

A major part of the museum's success is due to its innovative design, which continues to attract universal curiosity – most visitors spend as much time wandering around the exterior, comparing opinions and examining angles, as they do looking at the artwork inside. Like the three blind men and the elephant, your interpretation will depend on which part of the building you are looking at: ships' hulls, truncated fish bodies, and palm trees all protrude from the bulging mass, the juxtaposition of natural forms and 21st-century technology suggesting a new genre of 'bio-architecture'. Some of the best views are to be had from the Puente de la Salve, a classic lump of 1960s concrete that Bilbao would rather have forgotten but which Gehry's design embraces, by way of the aforementioned limestone tower. One of his skylights looms up towards the bridge, looking for all the world like a giant open-mawed basking shark.

The **interior** spaces are no less remarkable. Access to the museum is by a broad flight of steps sweeping down from Avenida Abandoibarra through the entrance bottleneck and into the building's heart, a 150-foot-high atrium of white light and swooping curves. This is in every sense the museum's centre – galleries radiate from it on all sides, and you'll inevitably pass through time and again at different levels – but it is also a sculptural work of art in itself, Frank Gehry's contribution to the Guggenheim legend. Light floods in through glass curtain walls, and cascades down from skylights in the roof. Whatever the interpretation, Gehry's atrium is a worthy successor to Frank Lloyd Wright's legendary spiral design; watch out for his cheeky nod of the head to Frank

Puppy, or Life Imitates Art, Again

Before you even get a chance to step through the doors you'll be mugged by the Guggenheim's first (and biggest) exhibit, a 40ft mountain of flowers and love created by kitsch guru Jeff Koons and answering to the name of *Puppy* (pronounced 'poopy'). *Puppy*, presumably a West Highland terrier, is a familiar sight at galleries worldwide – he's made appearances in New York and Sydney, amongst others – a kind of vegetarian version of the Littlest Hobo, who wanders from city to city lending his support wherever art exhibitions need him, before turning tail and trotting off into the sunset. But, like the Littlest Hobo, eventually the time came to settle down, and *Puppy* has put down his roots firmly in Bilbao, to the delight of almost everyone. He's been adopted as the city's *de facto* mascot, his image decorating everything from T-shirts to Vizcaya governmental literature.

Puppy's meteoric rise to mass adulation no doubt amuses his creator. When Koons came across the dog, it was no more than a tacky porcelain souvenir, a mass-produced piece of commercial crassness. Having based a career on taking just this kind of tat and elevating it to the status of High Art, Koons saw potential in *Puppy*; a couple of months, one CAD programme and a few thousand begonias later and, *voila!*, a star was born. Yet just as junk can be made into art, art can be made into junk, and before long the poor pooch was back where he came from: cuddly *Puppys* are the hot souvenir in Bilbao.

senior. Outside the atrium, the Nervión is incorporated into the museum's design by way of an ingenious raised walkway, rising and curving and creating a union between river and water garden. The architect has also created some unique gallery spaces, especially the cavernous 'Fish Gallery', 420ft long by 100ft wide with whalebone-like ribs supporting the ceiling, designed to hold the biggest and heaviest works of modern art. *Snake*, a heavy iron sculpture designed especially for the gallery by Richard Serra, throws down the gauntlet to future artists; too heavy to move and too big to fit anywhere else, it's one of the few exhibits that's guaranteed to be on show. *Snake* has recently been augmented with Serra's seven-part sculpture *A Matter of Time* (2005), seven huge (they even dwarf the Snake itself) swirls of steel that were also created specifically for this space. A meditation on time, both physical and experiential, a journey to the centre of these swaying steel ellipses and spheres is curiously dislocating – walls appear and fall away when you least expect them to.

Don't underestimate the Guggenheim's popularity. Attendance rates have vastly exceeded those projected, and long queues to get in – up to an hour – have become frequent, especially at weekends. Once you're through the door it's easy enough to wander round the galleries independently; alternatively, audioguides can be hired for €4, with recorded information on the key works. Free guided tours cover each installation daily, in English, but there's a definite skill to getting on one – spaces are limited to 20 people and you can't sign up more than 30 minutes in advance.

The Collection

After Gehry's architectural fireworks, and Koons' giant dog, the collection itself has a hard act to follow; whether or not it succeeds will depend on when you go. Thanks to its links with major galleries in New York, Venice and Berlin, the Guggenheim has access to more masterworks of 20th-century art than a museum of its tender age has any right to. Yet the shifting nature of its exhibits means there's no guarantee that the piece you're desperate to see will be on show. In any event, the site-specific works by Koons and Serra will be there, as will Jenny Holzer's *Installation For Bilbao* (1997), a characteristically spiky LED monologue carrying implications of abuse, obsession and violation, scrolling upwards into a reflective ceiling via nine vertical columns.

If the permanent collection is up, look out for a good selection of European Avant Garde art: there's a pivotal work by Miró, *The Tilled Field* (1923–4); a selection of Kandinskys; some elongated heads by Modigliani; and scattered works by Picasso and Klee, mostly on permanent loan from the Guggenheim in New York. Underpinning these is Bilbao's own distinguished collection of Abstract Expressionism: Robert Motherwell's stark assessment of the Civil War, *Elegy to the Spanish Republic LV* (1955–60), takes pride of place here, complemented by a swirling late-period Pollock (*Ocean Greyness*, 1953) and De Kooning's forceful *Composition* (1955), a gestural riot of primary colours. The polychromatic chaos is balanced by a tranquil Rothko (*Untitled*, 1956) and Yves Klein's *Large Blue Anthropometry* (1960), which the artist created by smearing naked women in paint (the famously-patented *International Klein Blue*) and dragging them across the canvas while a 20-piece orchestra played his own *Symphonie Monotone*, a single note sustained for 10 minutes alternating with ten minutes' silence. There's a fairly patchy collection of Pop Art, perhaps best represented by Lichtenstein's unusually subdued *Interior With Mirrored Wall* (1991), some fine pieces by Schnabel, Dubuffet and Basquiat, and a moving monographic exhibition devoted to Anselm Kiefer. This juxtaposes the historically laden works of his early period – the notorious faces of Nazi Germany which glare down from *The Paths to Worldly Wisdom: Hermann's Battle* (1982–3). In *Sun Ship* (1994–5) a dried sunflower glides over devastated landscapes of ash and fallen trees, heading off to a brighter future, a future perhaps realized in the cracked desert colours of *Alone With Wind, Time and Sound* (1997).

Elsewhere, there's a small collection of works by Basque and Spanish artists – sculptures by Chillida and Cristina Iglesias, and a few textural paintings by Tapiés – which the museum's directors have pledged to augment with future purchases.

Temporary Exhibitions

Nothing draws the crowds to Bilbao like a big new exhibition – until the collection matures, they're the best guarantee of seeing a really strong body of work – and the Guggenheim has achieved a few stunning successes. Temporary features in the past have included a major exhibition of photographs by German cult cinematographer Wim Wenders, wide-ranging retrospectives of Chillida and Iglesias, and an assemblage of photography and sculpture by the likes of Picasso, Degas and Rodin. But nothing so far has been able to compete with the runaway success of 2000's 'The Art of the Motorcycle' exhibit, featuring highly-polished machines from an 1894 Hildebrand and Wulfmüller to turn of the millennium superbikes, with a floor plan designed by Frank Gehry in the shape of a Scalextric track. All of a sudden, half the Basque country was in gallery 104, dribbling over the lusty iron horse, and for a time leather, long hair and big beards shared the halls of high culture. Massive public demand bought the exhibit a three-month stay of execution, while art critics wrung their hands and prophesied doom, or at least the conversion of the Guggenheim into a transport museum.

The Guggenheim Effect

The Guggenheim's success has spawned an ambitious series of restoration projects throughout Bilbao, none of which are bigger than the transformation taking place on the Abandoibarra flats. Acres of railway sidings and container trucks have disappeared, making way for a new development under the direction of Argentinian architect César Pelli; office blocks, a hotel, shopping malls and a 30-storey tower block is sprouting up alongside the Guggenheim. An extensive park area is unfolding, completing the 'green corridor' between Parque de Doña Casilda Iturriza and Paseo del Arenal. The thick-set Palacio de Congresos y de la Musica, already in place a few hundred metres downstream, completes the project, its massive hulk evoking the days when rusty freighters churned up the waters of the Nervión.

More tangible reminders of the old trade are now housed in a spectacular new museum devoted to Bilbao's maritime history, the **Museo Marítimo Ría de Bilbao** (*Muelle Ramón de la Sota 1, t 90 213 10 00, www.museomaritimobilbao.org; open Tues-Sun 10–8, adm*). The permanent collection traces the history of the city's maritime history with restored fishing boats, sailing ships, cranes, historic nautical instruments and maps, along with film-clips, and all kinds of high-tech interactive exhibits (both in the immense indoor galleries and out in the docks). You can also investigate the old lock system which once operated on the river, The excellent temporary exhibitions – like the recent hugely popular Titanic exhibition which included a partial reconstruction of the doomed liner – are always huge crowd-pullers. Plenty of child-friendly activities and a café with a large terrace make this a great place to bring the kids.

Around Bilbao

Only a third of Bilbao's million-odd souls live within the city itself. Bilbao is the heart of a sprawling conurbation that lines the Nervión for 32km, with factories and tower blocks squeezing in wherever the terrain permits. The fancier suburbs are found near the coast, where there are dramatic cliffs and a number of beaches. The most distinguished of these is **Getxo** (Neguri, Algorta and Bidezabal Metro stations), a combination suburb, marina and beach resort whose waterfront is lined with lovely villas. Getxo claims one of the youngest populations in Vizcaya, and the closest beaches to downtown Bilbao, yet retains a distinctly refined atmosphere;

signs politely request that swimming costumes are not to be worn on the beachfront promenade. Traces of the town's more earthbound past continue to linger, especially in the graceful old fishing port of **Algorta**, which cascades down the cliffs from a defiantly modern *urbanisación*. Look out for 19th-century, late neoclassical **San Nicolas de Bari**, where stoups made of giant clam shells prop up the walls by the main door.

Almost everything else in Getxo was built in the 20th century, including the grandiose villas that line the waterfront between Ereaga and Las Arenas beaches. New money from iron and the shipyards paid for these mansions; it couldn't guarantee good taste, but at least in the 1920s it bought a nice view. Nowadays, however, the crumbling old castles look across to the proletarian suburbs of Bilbao's superport, sprawling along the left bank of the estuary from Santurtzi to Portugalete.

The *ría*, and a social chasm, are bridged at the Nervión's mouth by one of Vizcaya's great industrial age landmarks, the **Puente Colgante**, or 'Hanging Bridge' (Areeta Metro station, *open daily 10am-sunset, t 94 463 88 54, adm*); the name refers to a system (unique in its day) of transporting people and goods across the river by way of a suspended gondola, allowing free passage to tall ships without the palaver of swinging or raising the bridge. This is Bilbao's proudest monument from the 19th century – locals like to call it 'the Eiffel Tower of Vizcaya' – and was as much a symbol of a vigorous economy in its day as the Guggenheim is now. Modern-day visitors can take a lift to the uppermost span, for a commanding view of the port and estuary.

The beaches continue eastwards along the coast. Though they're jam-packed with Bilbaínos on weekends, they can be fun; both the beaches and the water are surprisingly clean. Two of the most popular are at Sopelanas and Plentzia; the latter is an agreeably sleepy town on weekdays, with a handsome medieval quarter. Plentzia lacks any real sights, but it's a good place to wander when the beach scene gets too frantic; the main monuments are Gothic Santa María Magdalena and the 16th-century town hall, now home to a small Museo Municipal, which has exhibits on Plentzia's fishing history.

If you are spending much time in Bilbao, might we recommend (though not for the faint-hearted) a ride around the mountains that hem in the city. On **Monte Artxandamendia**, or in the hills above Erandio or Portugalete, you will see incredible landscapes of steel mills perched on mountain tops, grazing sheep, Victorian castles, shantytowns and roads on stilts – scenes from some surrealist comic book.

Vitoria (Gasteiz)

Vitoria has style. It also has the air of a little Ruritanian capital – because it is one. The seat of the inland province of Álava, and since 1980 the capital of autonomous Euskadi, Vitoria has grown to be one of Spain's modern industrial centres, a phenomenon that has so far done little harm to one of the most surprisingly urbane cities in the nation. Although Wellington soundly defeated the forces of Joseph Bonaparte here in 1813, Vitoria's name has nothing to do with victory, but recalls the height (*Beturia* in Basque) on which the city was built. In the Middle Ages this was a hot border region between the kingdoms of Navarra and Castile. Navarrese King Alfonso VI founded a fortress

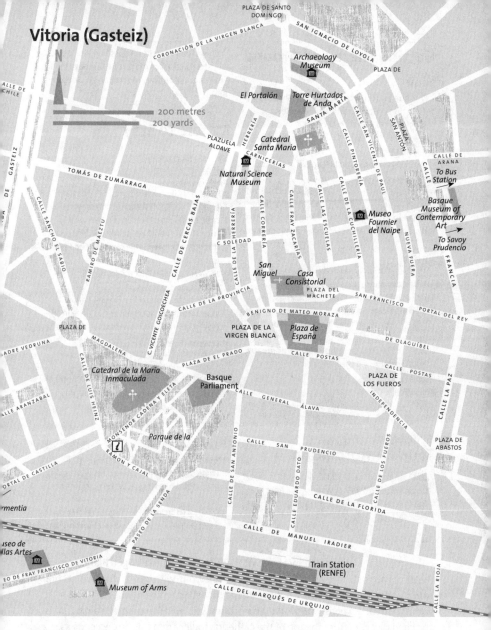

Vitoria (Gasteiz)

N

200 metres
200 yards

PLAZA DE SANTO DOMINGO

CORONACIÓN DE LA VIRGEN BLANCA

SAN IGNACIO DE LOYOLA

PLAZA DE

CALLE DE CHILE

ALLE DE CHILE

DE GASTEIZ

Archaeology Museum

El Portalón

Torre Hurtados de Anda

PLAZA DE SAN ANTÓN

TOMÁS DE ZUMÁRRAGA

PLAZUELA ALDAVE

HERRERÍA

Catedral Santa María

SANTA MARÍA

CALLE SAN VICENTE DE PAUL

CALLE PINTORERÍA

CALLE DE ARANA

To Bus Station

CALLE SANCHO EL SABIO

CALLE DE CERCAS BAJAS

CALLE CORRERÍA

CALLE DE LA HERRERÍA

C SOLEDAD

CALLE FRAY ZACARÍAS

CALLE LAS ESCUELAS

CALLE DE LA CUCHILLERÍA

Museo Fournier del Naipe

Basque Museum of Contemporary Art

To Savoy Prudencio

RAMIRO DE MAEZTU

Natural Science Museum

San Miguel

Casa Consistorial

PLAZA DEL MACHETE

SAN FRANCISCO

NUEVA FUERA

FRANCIA

PORTAL DEL REY

PLAZA DE

MAGDALENA

C. VICENTE GOICOECHEA

CALLE DE LA PROVINCIA

BENIGNO DE MATEO MORAZA

PLAZA DE LA VIRGEN BLANCA

Plaza de España

DE OLAGUÍBEL

ADRE VEDRUNA

Catedral de la María Inmaculada

CALLE DE LUIS HEINZ

MONSEÑOR CADENA Y ELETA

PLAZA DE EL PRADO

Basque Parliament

CALLE POSTAS

CALLE POSTAS

PLAZA DE LOS FUEROS

CALLE LA PAZ

CALLE GENERAL ÁLAVA

INDEPENDENCIA

RAMON Y CAJAL

Parque de la

CALLE DE SAN ANTONIO

CALLE SAN PRUDENCIO

CALLE DE EDUARDO DATO

CALLE DE LOS FUEROS

PLAZA DE ABASTOS

LLE ARANZABAL

ORTAL DE CASTILLA

PASEO DE LA SENDA

CALLE DE LA FLORIDA

CALLE DE MANUEL IRADIER

CALLE LA RIOJA

mentia

seo de las Artes

EO DE FRAY FRANCISCO DE VITORIA

Museum of Arms

Train Station (RENFE)

CALLE DEL MARQUÉS DE URQUIJO

and town here in 1181, but the Castilians managed to snatch it away from them soon after. Like everything else in medieval Castile, Vitoria boomed, and extended itself logically in concentric rings of streets – oddly enough, a plan exactly like Amsterdam's, without the canals. Hard hit by the wars and plagues of the 1300s, Vitoria stagnated for centuries, and began its recovery only with the industrial boom of the 1890s. It has preserved itself beautifully throughout, probably an important factor in getting Vitoria named the Basque capital in the autonomy agreement of 1981.

Getting There and Around

By Air
Foronda airport, 9km west of Vitoria, has connections with Madrid and Barcelona (**t** 94 516 35 00, *www.aena.es*).

By Train
Vitoria's station is at the top of C/Eduardo Dato (**t** 90 224 02 02 for centralized timetable information and reservations), six blocks from the old town. Trains between San Sebastián and Madrid pass through Vitoria; Salvatierra is a stop along RENFE's Vitoria–Pamplona run.

By Bus
The bus station is at C/Los Herran 50, **t** 94 525 84 00, a short walk east of the old town. There are regular services to San Sebastián, Bilbao and Logroño, as well as to the provincial villages. Because of the city's position on the main route north from Madrid, you can get a bus to nearly anywhere from here – Bordeaux, Paris, Germany and even London.

By Car
Most of the centre is a closed-off pedestrian zone, and parking spots are difficult to find.

Tourist Information

Plaza General Loma s/n, **t** 94 516 1598, *www.vitoria-gasteiz.org/turismo*. There is a Basque regional office at Parque de la Florida, **t** 94 513 1321.

There is a **market** on Thursdays, in Plaza de Abastos; also a flea market on Sundays in Plaza Nueva, and a clothes market on Wednesdays and Thursdays in C/Arana.

Where to Stay

Vitoria ✉ 01000

Expensive
★★★★**Hotel Ciudad de Vitoria**, Portal de Castilla 8, **t** 94 514 11 00, *www.hotelciudaddevitoria. com*. More character than most, with friendly staff and an indoor garden; good discounts are available on weekends and in summer.
★★★★**NH Canciller Ayala**, Ramón y Cajal 5, **t** 94 513 00 00, *www.nh hoteles.com*. Modern tower hotel next to the Florida Park with standard chain hotel décor but little in the way of charm. Still, it's central and offers good deals on the website.
★★★**General Álava**, Avda Gastéiz 79, **t** 94 522 22 00, *hga@jet.es*. **t** 94 521 5000, *www.hga.info*. Another of the large hotels in the new part of town, with modern, comfortable rooms geared towards business travellers.

Moderate
★★★**Almoneda**, C/Florida 7, **t** 94 515 40 84, *www.hotelalmoneda.com*. This welcoming little hotel has simple, tasteful rooms and a pleasant lounge full of eclectic antiques.
★★★**Hotel Palacio de Elorriaga**, C/Elorriaga 15, **t** 945263616, **f** 945 268 951. A charming hotel

---

The important thing to know about Vitoria is the **Fiesta de la Virgen Blanca**, on the 4th of August. It's a typical six-day Spanish blowout, with lots of champagne, fireworks, and parties until dawn, but the image that sticks in the mind is *Celedón*, a dummy wearing a beret and workman's clothes who holds an umbrella aloft that is attached to a wire from the top of the cathedral tower; from this he descends as gracefully as Mary Poppins, gliding across the plaza to start the festival. On the morning of the 10th he glides up again and pops back into the bell tower, and it's all over for another year.

El Casco Viejo
The old city, with its old core of neat, concentric streets, begins with **Plaza de la Virgen Blanca**, a delightful example of asymmetrical medieval town design. Adjacent, the

on the outskirts of the city, set in an elegant 17th-century mansion surrounded by gardens. The rooms are decorated in a mixture of traditional and contemporary styles.

Inexpensive

Vitoria offers a wide range of inexpensive choices, mostly catering for businessmen.

**Dato 28, C/Dato 28 (near the rail station), t 94 514 72 30, *www.hoteldato.com*. Conveniently located, with imaginative Art Deco furnishings and more rooms available on a parallel street.

*Achuri, C/Rioja 11, t 94 525 58 00. Comfortable, if smallish, rooms in a modern *hostal* close to the train station.

Budget

Hostal Nuvilla, Fueros 29, t 94 525 91 51. Old-fashioned house with wardrobes and sinks in all rooms.

Pension Araba, C/Florida 25, 1st floor, t 94 523 25 88. Bright and breezy *hostal* in the centre, with rooms with or without ensuite bathrooms.

Eating Out

Most of the good bars and restaurants in Vitoria are in the old town.

El Portalón, Correría 151, t 94 514 27 55 (*expensive*). Especially good, with tables on three floors of a 16th-century building and traditional Basque food. *Closed Sun.*

Zaldiarián, Avda de Gasteiz 21, t 94 513 48 22 (*expensive*). Smart restaurant serving award-winning traditional cuisine; book early as this is universally considered the best in town.

Mesa, Chile 1, t 94 522 84 94 (*moderate*). Serves typical local dishes, including game and mushrooms in season. *Closed Wed.*

Olarizu, Beato Tomas de Zumarraga 54, t 94 524 77 52 (*moderate*). Creative, elegant cuisine based on old Alavesa recipes.

Zabala, Mateo de Moraza 9, t 94 523 00 09 (*moderate–budget*). Old-fashioned and good. *Closed Sun and Aug.*

Oleaga, C/Adriano VI 15, t 94 522 3310 (*budget*). One of the best and most popular bars in town, with counters heaving with pintxos and a dining room serving good home-coooking at bargain prices.

Nightlife

Vitoria has its share of nightlife, mostly in the Parte Vieja, though C/Dato near the station can also be noisy after hours. Some of the clubs, a few on C/San Prudencio, for example, stay open until 6 or 7 in the morning.

Azkena, C/Coronacion de la Virgen Blanco 4, t 94 514 54 26. Big venue for live concerts, mainly rock and blues.

Café Caruso, C/Enrique de Eguren 9. A coffee house which has occasional concerts and exhibitions.

Odile, C/Manuel Iradier 58, t 94 528 31 64. Big, popular disco playing all the latest sounds.

---

enclosed and symmetrical **Plaza de España** provides a perfect contrast; this grand neoclassical confection was built in the 1780s, at the height of Spain's flirtation with the Enlightenment and now houses mostly city offices. Plaza de la Virgen Blanca is the centre of Vitoria's big party on 4 August, and it takes its name from the statue in the niche over the door of **San Miguel**, the 14th-century church that turns a graceful portico towards the top of the square. An 18th-century arcade called **Los Arcillos**, reached by a stair, runs under some graceful old glass-front buildings to connect Plaza de la Virgen Blanca to yet a third connected square on the slope of the hill: **Plaza del Machete**, named after the axe over which city officials would swear their oaths of office.

Behind San Miguel, Calle Fray Zacarías leads into the medieval streets; this was the high-status street for palaces, as evidenced by two 16th-century Plateresque beauties, the **Palacio Episcopal**, and the **Palacio Escoriaza-Esquivel**, built by a local boy who became physician to Charles V; this one has a Renaissance courtyard with a marble loggia. At the top of the street is the 14th-century **Catedral Santa Maria** (*t 94 525 51 35, www. catedralvitoria.com; currently undergoing an extensive restoration programme; guided tours in English; book in advance through the tourist office*). There is a beautifully carved western doorway and impressive central nave, the aisles lined with the tombs of notables from medieval times. Recent excavations in the Cathedral have unearthed remains of an ancient fortified church and other relics from the 13th century.

A couple of streets west of the cathedral on C/del Herrería, the **Torre de Doña Otxanta** is a defensive tower of the 15th–16th centuries. Italian early Renaissance cities, with their skylines of skyscraper-fortresses, set a fashion that found its way to other countries – fortresses like these were private castles in town, and city officials had to fight hard to keep their owners from acting like rustic barons on their manors, bossing everyone around and generally disturbing the peace of the neighbourhood. Now fully restored, the tower is home to the province's **Natural Science Museum** (*open Tues–Fri 11–2 and 4–6.30, Sat 10–2, Sun 11–2*). Another conspicuous tower nearby, the **Torre Hurtados de Anda**, lurks just to the north on C/Correría: this is a blank-walled fort with a half-timbered house on top – a proper urban castle.

Continuing northwards on C/Correría, a rambling brick and timber structure called **El Portalón**, built in the early 1500s, is one of the oldest buildings in town, and it gives an idea of what most of Vitoria must have looked like at the time. Just across the street at Correría 116, the **Archaeology Museum** (*open Tues–Fri 11–2 and 4–6.30, Sat 10–2, Sun 11–2*) occupies a lovely half-timbered house containing Roman finds and Basque 'star' tombstones, as well as some fascinating medieval finds, such as the exceedingly strange 'Relief of Marquinez'. There are over a hundred artificial caves in the province of Álava, and exhibits recount the story of the religious hermits who occupied many of them a thousand years ago.

The House of Cards

Palaces are fewer in the eastern quarter of old Vitoria, across C/Las Escuelas; the houses here are generally plainer, though older, especially those in the former **Judería**, the medieval Jewish neighbourhood that covered much of this area. On C/Cuchillería, in the Plateresque Palacio Bendaña, Spain's biggest manufacturer of playing cards (an old Vitoria speciality) has opened the **Museo Fournier del Naipe** (*open Tues–Fri 11–2 and 4–6.30, Sat 10–2, Sun 11–2*). The Fournier Company thinks their collection is the best anywhere; it includes the oldest surviving card (from the 1300s), as well as card-making machinery and paintings. The collection includes plenty of Tarot decks too; originally there was no difference between the cards for fortune telling and those for playing games.

Just east of here, at C/ Francia 24, is Vitoria's exciting new **Artium** (Basque Museum of Contemporary Art, *open Sun, Tues–Thurs 11–8, Fri–Sat 11–8.30pm; adm, 'you decide' on Weds*), with a permanent collection of more than 1,600 contemporary paintings, sculptures, drawings and photos by Basque and Spanish artists.

The New Cathedral and the Museum

The tourist information office shares the pretty **Parque de la Florida**, Vitoria's monumental centre, with the stern, no-nonsense **Basque Parliament** building (*t 94 524 78 00, if you want to sit in the gallery and watch them deliberate*) and the remarkable 'new cathedral', the **Catedral de la María Immaculada**. Here, the Basques showed their devotion to the Middle Ages by building a completely 'medieval' building, by medieval methods, beginning in 1907. Most of it is already finished, though there is enough decorative work undone inside to last them another century or two. The style seems to be part English Gothic, part Viollet-le-Duc, though the most endearing feature is the rows of comical modillions around the cornices – lots of satirical and monster faces, including caricatures of the architects and masons. It contains the Museo Diocesano de Arte Sacro (*open Tues–Fri 11–2 and 4–6.30, Sat 10–2, Sun 11–2, closed Mon*), with an appealing collection of medieval Madonnas, over-the-top Baroque religious paintings, and lavish church plate and ornaments.

Vitoria is a city of unexpected delights; one example, completing the park's monumental ensemble, is one of the most resplendent Art Deco petrol stations in all Spain, just behind the cathedral. Another, a few blocks east on Calle Eduardo Dato, is the fantastical **RENFE station**, done in a kind of Hollywood Moorish style with brightly coloured tiles. The city has just finished constructing a new embellishment: **Plaza de los Fueros**, a square just east of Plaza de la Virgen Blanca designed and decorated by Eduardo Chillida. It's a strange space – part Roman amphitheatre, part basketball court – that the locals haven't quite worked out what to do with yet; it seems to get most use after the bars have closed. At one end, an untitled Chillida sculpture is enclosed within angular walls.

The wonderful Parque de la Florida, laid out in 1855, retains much of the Romantic spirit of its times, with grand promenades, hidden bowers and overlooks. It was the centre of the city's fashionable district, and a shady walkway from the southern end of the park, the Paseo de la Senda, takes you to the elegant **Paseo de Fray Francisco de Vitoria**, lined with the Hispano-Victorian mansions of the old industrialists. One of these houses, the **Museo de Bellas Artes** (*open Tues–Fri 11–2 and 4–6.30, Sat 10–2, Sun 11–2*), features a well-displayed collection ranging from early paintings to Picasso and Miró, with a handful of great Spanish masters in between, all in a beautifully restored space with original features such as a Tiffany-style stained-glass skylight.

Some of the finest works are of the type *Escuela Hispanoflamenca*, paintings from the early 16th century, when the influence from the Low Countries was strong here; most are anonymous, and it is impossible to tell which country the artist was from. One of the finest works, a triptych of the Passion by the 'Master of the Legend of Santa Godelina', shows the same sort of conscious stylization as an Uccello; the longer you look at it, the stranger it seems. There are a number of medieval painted carved wood figures, and three paintings by Ribera, including a Crucifixion. As in all Basque museums, Basque painters are very well represented. Here you'll find some surprises such as a great early 20th-century landscapist named Fernando de Anarica, or his contemporary Ramon Zubiaurre, whose *Autoridades de mi Aldea* shares the not-quite-naïve sensibility of

Rousseau or Grant Wood. The façade of a 13th-century hermitage has been reconstructed in the garden. Up the Paseo at No.3, the **Museum of Arms** (*open Tues–Fri 11–2 and 4–6.30, Sat 10–2, Sun 11–2*) houses suits of armour, medieval weapons, dioramas and displays on Wellington's victory at the Battle of Vitoria.

Seeing the last of Vitoria's secrets means a pleasant 20-minute walk to the south-west (from the Paseo de Fray Francisco, take Paseo de Cervantes and Avenida de San Prudencio; this is part of the *camino francés*, one of the Santiago pilgrimage routes), to the **Basílica of San Prudencio**, in Armentia, a village swallowed up by the city's suburbs. The church was built at the end of the 12th century, with a fine doorway and curious reliefs and capitals carved inside.

West of Vitoria, you can visit Roman ruins including a long, 13-arched bridge at **Trespuentes**, near the remains of a town, the **oppidum of Iruña** (*open summer Tues–Sat 11–2 and 4–8, Sun 11–3; winter Tues–Sat 11–3, Sun 10–2; adm*). Two kilometres away at Mendoza, near the airport on the A 3302, a 13th-century defensive tower with great views over the countryside has been restored to house the **Museo de Heráldica** (*open May–Oct 11–2 and 4–8, Sun 11–3; Nov–Apr Tues–Fri 11–3, adm*), Spain's only museum dedicated to the origins and graphic styles of heraldic escutcheons; the exhibits give special attention to the histories of the great families of the Basque country.

Álava Province

Just because the Basque capital is located here, you might think that Álava (*Araba* in Basque) is the Euskadi heartland. In fact speakers of Basque make up precisely 4 per cent of the population, by far the lowest in the 'seven Basque provinces'. One senses that, having lost ground to the Spaniards for centuries during their long economic decline, the Basques purposely planted their Parliament here as part of a careful plan to reclaim the soil. Álava is home to the historical oddity of the County of Treviño, an enclave of Castilian Spaniards smack in the middle of the province. They are quite happy being part of Castile, just as they were in the Middle Ages, making Álava the only province in Spain, maybe in the world, that is shaped like a doughnut.

Gaceo and Alaiza

There aren't a lot of sights here, but for anyone interested in things medieval the province offers something truly outstanding – and almost totally unknown outside the area. The miniscule village of **Gaceo**, on the N1 east of Vitoria, offers nothing less than one of the finest ensembles of Gothic fresco painting anywhere in Europe. These are in the simple church of San Martín de Tours (*unfortunately, you can currently only enter the church on a private – and expensive – guided visit, summer only; contact the Salvatierra/Agurain tourist office for up-to-date information. Otherwise you can attend Sunday mass.*); covered in plaster, they were not rediscovered until 1966.

Research places these works between about 1325 and 1450. The style, a bit archaic with its Romanesque attention to flowing draperies, is distinctive enough for scholars to speculate about an obscure 'Basque-Navarrese' school of artists, perhaps centred in

Tourist Information

Antoñana: Cuesta de Lavadero, t 94 541 02 26 (*summer only*).

Laguardia: Abarca s/n, t 94 560 08 45, *www.laguardia-alava.com*.
There is a **market** in Laguardia on Sundays.

Where to Stay and Eat

Argómaniz ✉ 01192

★★★Parador de Argómaniz, N1 km 363, t 94 562 12 00, *argomaniz@parador.es* (*expensive*). One of the smaller and simpler *paradores*, but still very charming, with some rooms set in the original building, a 17th-century mansion with iron balconies. Tiny Argómaniz is 10km east of Vitoria, near the paintings of Gaceo. Great restaurant.

Laguardia ✉ 01300

This is definitely the place to stop over if you are passing through La Rioja Alavesa.

★★Antigua Bodega de D.Cosme Palacio, Ctra Elciego, t 94 562 11 95 (*moderate–inexpensive*). A delightful little hotel with a fine restaurant in the original bodega of this renowned wine-producer. Each room is named after a grape, and all are prettily decorated with rustic furnishings.

★★Posada Mayor de Migueloa, C/Mayor de Migueloa 20, t 94 562 11 75 (*moderate*). In a 17th-century mansion with antique furnishings; also has an excellent restaurant and wine cellar.

Hotel Castillo El Collado, Paseo El Collado, t 94 112 12 00, *www. euskalnet.net/hotelcollado.com* (*moderate*). The pick of places to stay in Laguardia, this is a 1920s' palace full of antiques and luscious fabrics, with an incredibly welcoming owner; if you're lucky he'll tell you the story of the 'Love and Madness' suite. The restaurant (*expensive*) serves excellent Basque and Navarrese dishes, including magnificent goat roasts.

★Marixa, C/Sancho Abarca 8, t 94 560 01 65. For the best dining experience in town, with *moderate* rooms and *expensive* meals. You might try an unlikely local favourite – *acelga rellena* (stuffed Swiss chard) – which is much better than it sounds.

★Pachico Martinez, C/Sancho Abarca 20, t 94 160 00 09, *www.pachico.com* (*inexpensive*). Has been in the same family since 1806 and is still doing fine today.

Vitoria; Byzantine influence is also strongly present, though details like the gnarled rugged cross are uniquely Spanish (such a cross was the symbol of the 19th-century Carlist rebels). Thanks to the plaster most of the paintings are well preserved though, oddly, many of the faces have vanished, as in the *Trinity*, with a figure of God enthroned, supporting Jesus on the cross, painted on the apse over the altar. True frescoes require that the plaster underneath the paintings, applied fresh each morning for an artist's day's work, is absolutely right in composition and application. The secrets were just being rediscovered in the 14th century in Italy; artists elsewhere hadn't got it quite right.

The figures around the Trinity on the apse seem to be arranged to represent the commemoration of All Saints' Day: various scenes of *Los Bienaventurados*, The Blessed – apostles, martyrs, confessors, virgins and more, all arranged neatly by category. On the right, note the conspicuous figures of St Michael, weighing souls at the Judgement Day, and Abraham, gathering the fortunate to his bosom. The choir vault too is entirely covered in frescoes, stock images of the Life of Christ divided by charming borders of trompe l'oeil designs and fantasy architecture. At the bottom right is something no medieval mural picture-book could be without: the souls of the damned getting variously swallowed up in the mouth of hell or cooked in a big pot.

Gaceo is not such an illogical spot for art as it seems. The modern N1 that connects Vitoria to Burgos and Pamplona roughly follows the course of the main northbound Roman road. Enough of it survived in medieval times to keep it an important route, used by pilgrims on their way to Compostela. Perhaps no one ever imagined Gaceo growing into a metropolis; it may have been that the village was a popular pilgrim stop, and that some pious person paid for the paintings to edify the sojourners' spirits, and give them something to think about as they made their way westwards.

While you're out in Gaceo you might as well carry on a little further and see some quite different paintings at another tiny hamlet, **Alaiza** (from the N1, take the A3100 south from Salvatierra). The Iglesia de la Asunción here is a barn-like 13th-century building; it too has a painted apse and choir, but the contrast with Gaceo's is like day with night. Instead of flowing Gothic draperies, Alaiza has one-colour cartoons so weird and primitive they might have been done by a Palaeolithic cave artist on a bad day. The central work, on the apse, shows soldiers besieging a castle, while on the choir vault and walls bizarre hooded figures joust, murder, or indulge in bodily functions not often seen on church walls. There is a contrastingly precise inscription underneath in Gothic letters, but no one has ever managed to decipher it. The best guess the Spaniards can come up with for this singular work is that these scenes were done *c.* 1367, while Alaiza was under the control of some rough English mercenary soldiers; one of them might have done it.

The closest village of any size in this region, **Salvatierra** is a pleasant old village of warm stone within striking distance of two of Euskadi's best dolmens – **Aizkomendi** at Eguilaz, visible in a little roadside park off the N1, and **Sorginetxe** in Arizala. North of the city, the biggest features on the landscape are the big dams and lakes of **Urrunaga** and **Ullivarri**. The lakes have become popular spots for fishing and water sports; Ullivarri even has a nudist beach. Further north, on the road to Durango, **Otxandio** was the original Basque iron town, a fact commemorated by a statue of the god Vulcan in the main square.

South of Vitoria: the Ebro Valley

Some of the best Rioja vines actually come from the province of Álava, a region known as **La Rioja Alavesa**, along the Ebro river facing the real La Rioja across the way. Perched high over the river, the key wine town here is walled, medieval **Laguardia** (Biasteri) where you can learn all about local wines and their production at **La Casa del Vino**, and visit more *bodegas*. Don't miss the 14th-century apostles carved in the portal of Laguardia's Gothic **Santa María de los Reyes**. Near Laguardia, an Iron Age village is still being excavated: the **Poblado de la Hoya**. Although the site is not open to the public, you can visit the adjacent small museum (t 94 518 19 18, *open May–Oct Tues–Fri 11–2 and 4–6.30, Sat 10–2, Sun 11–2; Oct–Apr Tues–Sat 11–3, Sun 10–2*), with a model of what La Hoya may have looked like and finds from the site; explanations are entirely in Castilian and Basque.

As for the **County of Treviño**, though this forgotten fief looks strangely compelling on the map, in reality there's plenty of oak woods and good farmland, but unhappily no greater attractions.

Cantabria

and the Picos de Europa

Bilbao to Santander: the Costa Esmeralda **174**
Eastern Cantabria: Inland **177**
Santander 178
South of Santander: the Heart of Cantabria **184**
The Coast West of Santander 186
The Picos de Europa 193
The Asturian Picos de Europa: Cangas and Covadonga **198**
The Leónese Picos de Europa **201**

Cantabria

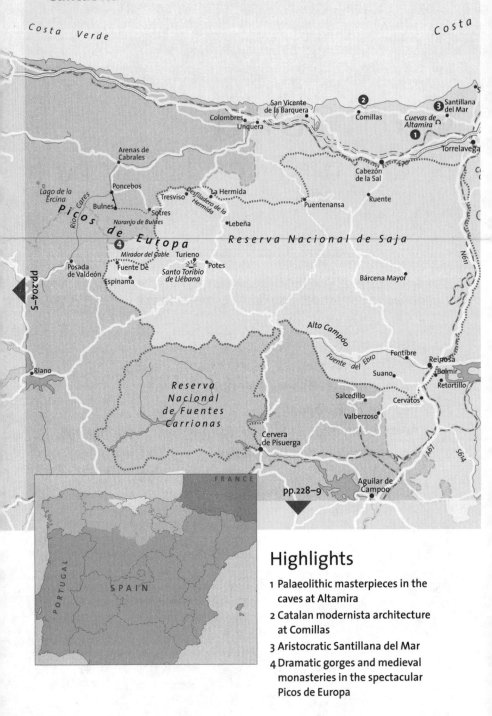

Highlights

1 Palaeolithic masterpieces in the caves at Altamira
2 Catalan modernista architecture at Comillas
3 Aristocratic Santillana del Mar
4 Dramatic gorges and medieval monasteries in the spectacular Picos de Europa

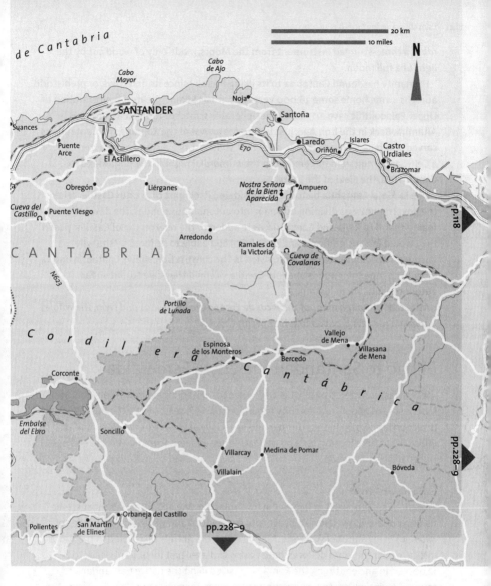

Spain's steep emerald-green dairy-land, Cantabria is wedged between the extraordinary Picos de Europa, the Cordillera Cantábrica and a coastline of scenic beaches. Santander, the capital and only large city, is a major summer resort and, while there are a handful of other tourist spots (Laredo, Comillas, and the medieval Santillana del Mar), much of Cantabria is serenely rural, claiming to have the highest density of cows in Europe. The majority of the bovine population lives indoors, and in the evening the most common Cantabrian sight is the farmer or his wife, often wearing wooden clogs, driving home an ox-cart laden with grass that they have cut from their several Lilliputian plots of land scattered over the hills. On rainy winter evenings in the more remote areas they gather to hear the strains of the *rabel*, a three-stringed instrument from the Moors, made only of wood cut by the light of a full moon.

Humanity has found Cantabria to its liking literally since its first cows, or prehistoric aurochs, came home some 38,000 years ago. It has Spain's greatest concentration of Upper Palaeolithic cave art, from indecipherable scratches to the masterpieces in Altamira. Back in the Iron Age, just before the arrival of the Romans, the Cantabrians carved star reliefs on large stone discs that still mystify everybody: were they part of a Celtic astral cult, remembered from the primordial night in the pilgrimage to Compostela, the Field of the Stars?

Like La Rioja, Cantabria historically considered itself part of greater Castile. When the government was dividing up Spain into autonomous regions, the devolutionists feared that if La Rioja and Cantabria were added to the new region of Castilla y León, they would feel insignificant and peripheral and liable to be lured by the wily Basques into joining Euskadi. A provision in the constitution allows Cantabria and La Rioja to change their minds and join Castilla y León if they care to, but so far autonomy suits them just fine.

*Note that although areas of the **Picos de Europa** are in Asturias and León, the whole mountain range is grouped together in this chapter.*

Bilbao to Santander: the Costa Esmeralda

If this eastern stretch of coast is all you see of Cantabria, you may think what you have just read about rural serenity is pure fiction. This seems to be the busiest coast in all northern Spain in the summer and especially at the weekend, when half of Bilbao is out here looking for a bit of beach; they all seem to end up on the endless sweep of sand at Laredo.

Castro Urdiales

Just half an hour west of Bilbao, Castro Urdiales is one of Cantabria's most scenic fishing ports, endowed with a beach and seafood restaurants that draw hordes of *bilbaínos* every summer weekend. Magdalenian-era graffiti, discovered in the 1960s in a cave near the Plaza de Toros, date Castro Urdiales' first inhabitants back to 12,000 BC. In ancient times, the Romans muscled in on the native Cantabrians to found *Flavióbriga*, located where the castle stands today.

A stronghold of the Templars in the Middle Ages, the town declined in the 14th century as Pedro I and Enrique II de Trastámara fought for this stretch of coast. It suffered even more grievously in 1813 when the French punished Castro's resistance in the War of Independence by burning most of it to the ground. Only a few streets near the harbour escaped the flames, beyond the 18th-century **Ayuntamiento**, at the top of the Paseo Marítimo.

From here, walk up to the fortress-like church of **Santa María de la Asunción** (*open June–Sept daily 10–1 and 4–6, rest of the year 4–6 only*), a magnificent Gothic temple with massive buttresses and pinnacles. Constructed almost entirely in the

Getting Around

By Train

The two daily FEVE trains between Santander and Bilbao stop at Treto (5km from Laredo); Pza de las Estaciones s/n, **t** 94 221 3350.

By Bus

Several Turytrans buses a day run along the coast between Santander and Bilbao; from Santander they depart from Pza de las Estaciones s/n, **t** 94 221 16 85.

Tourist Information

Castro Urdiales: Avda de la Constitución 1, **t** 94 287 15 12, *www.castro-urdiales.net*.
Laredo: Alameda de Miramar s/n, **t** 94 261 10 96.
Santoña: Palacio Manzanedo, **t** 94 266 00 66, *www.aytosantona.org*.
Noja: Avda del Ris 79-81, **t** 94 263 15 16.

There are **markets** in Castro Urdiales on Thursdays; in Laredo at the Mercado Municipal, daily except Sundays.

Where to Stay and Eat

Castro Urdiales ✉ 39700

Castro is a more pleasing place to stay than Laredo, though inexpensive places are hard to find (ask at a bar). Bars are concentrated along C/de la Rúa and the Paseo Marítimo.

****Las Rocas, Paseo de la Playa s/n, **t** 94 286 04 00, *www.lasrocashotel.com* (*expensive*). This luxurious, tranquil place overlooks the beach. Prices outside August are *moderate*.
***Miramar, Avda de la Playa 1, **t** 94 286 02 04 (*moderate*). A smart, modern hotel on the beach with attentive service.
La Sota, C/La Correría 1, **t 94 287 11 88, (*inexpensive*). Light and attractive *pensión* two blocks from the harbour, with sea views from most rooms.
*Hs Alberto, Avda de la República Argentina 2 (near the park), **t** 94 286 27 57 (*budget*). The bathless doubles are fine. *Open Mar–Sept only.*
Mesón El Marinero, Correría 23 (in the Casa de los Chelines, by the port), **t** 94 286 00 05 (*moderate*). The place to go for heaped plates of fresh seafood at reasonable prices. For less

than the typical €30 meal, feast on a wide selection of tapas at the bar.
El Segoviano, La Correría 19, **t** 94 286 18 59 (*moderate*). Castro's second culinary shrine, close by. Come here for roast suckling-pig or a seafood grill.
El Faro de Castro, La Plazuela 1, **t** 94 286 72 32 (*budget*). A good tapas place with tables overlooking the harbour. Locals flock here for the fried *calamares* at weekends.

Islares ✉ 39798

Hs Arenillas, **t 94 287 0900 (*budget*). A quiet and pleasant *hostal* near the beach.
Camping Playa Arenillas, **t** 94 286 3152. A large and comfortable campsite, by the beach.

Laredo ✉ 39770

Hotels here are small and quite expensive, and reservations are essential in the summer.
****Parador de Limpias, Fuente del Amor s/n, Limpias, **t** 94 262 89 00, *limpias@parador.es* (*expensive–moderate*). A new (2004) parador, 10km from Laredo (on the FEVE line), in a 19th-century palace surrounded by extensive parkland. Gym, tennis and pool.
***Risco, C/La Arenosa 2, **t** 94 260 50 30, *www.hotelrisco.com* (*moderate*). Good rooms with views over the protected bay and beach; the restaurant (*moderate*) is Laredo's top seafood palace, offering elaborate dishes such as a *capricho* of lobster, chicken and figs.
***Miramar, Alto de Laredo s/n, **t** 94 261 03 67, **f** 94 261 16 92 (*inexpensive; moderate in high season*). Modern, mid-size, with huge windows to take in the huge sea views.
Hotel Cortijo, C/Gonzalez Gallego 3, **t** 94 260 56 00 (*moderate*). Plush marble decor at this modern hotel, not too far from the beach. Ask for a room with a terrace to enjoy the view.
Montecristo, C/Calvo Sotelo 2, **t 94 260 57 00 (*inexpensive*). One of the better mid-priced beach hotels in town. *Open mid-Apr–mid-Oct*
*Pensión Salomón, C/Menéndez Pelayo 11, **t** 94 260 50 81 (*inexpensive*). With immaculate rooms and wooden floors, this is the best deal in the centre.
Casa Felipe, Travesía José Antonio 5, **t** 94 260 32 12 (*moderate*). Deliciously fresh seafood and shellfish and a wonderful range of local cheeses are on offer at this welcoming spot.

13th century, its Templar touches are most obvious in the unusual symbolism of the figures carved in the lovely frieze wrapped around the top of the church – rabbits kissing oxen, dragons devouring serpents devouring birds and more, although to see them properly you'll need binoculars. Inside there's a 13th-century sculpture, the *Virgen Blanca*, and a series of Gothic woodcarvings. You can also see the *Santa Cruz*, or 'Holy Cross', the Christian standard at the battle of Las Navas de Tolosa (1212). A Roman milestone remains in place in front of the church, while over the striking Roman/medieval bridge, most of the walls of Castro's pentagonal **Templar castle** have survived and now shelter a lighthouse.

Castro Urdiales' beach, **Playa Brazomar**, is at the other end of town, and fills up so quickly that a new artificial beach, the **Playa de Ostende**, has been created at the western end of town. If you want a top-to-toe tan, there's also a naturist beach just outside town at **El Pocillo** (but you have to scramble down the cliffs). The best beach, however, is 8km west up to **Islares**, a small village with a magnificent strand of sand under the cliffs, interspersed with shallow lagoons ideal for young children. Just west of Islares, at **Oriñón,** there's another beach worth stopping off at, and a campsite.

Laredo

Cantabria's biggest resort has little in common with its namesake on the Río Grande. The scenery in fact isn't too different, but on its streets there is hardly a cowboy alive or dead to be seen. This Laredo does have an old town, hidden somewhere among the *urbanizaciones*, but you'll remember it mostly as a haphazard Legoland of modern apartments with a frightening dearth of shops, restaurants and bars.

Laredo was the Roman *Portus Luliobrigensium*, the place where the Romans finally subdued the last diehard Celtiberians in a great sea battle. The medieval **Puebla Vieja** over the harbour was walled in by Alfonso VIII of Castile to safeguard the region from pirates; its 13th-century church **Santa María de la Asunción** has five naves (rare for the period) and curiously carved capitals. In the sacristy note the two eagle-shaped lecterns, donated by Charles V, who landed here on his way to his retirement at Yuste.

The late-Renaissance **Ayuntamiento** in Plaza Cachupín is said to mark the location of the harbour quay that the megalomaniac Emperor actually stepped on; behind it is the attractive tiled market building erected in 1902. Not really glossy or chic, Laredo especially attracts families, who cover its splendid beach and fill the scores of cafés, bars and discothèques in the Puebla Vieja. *Urbanizaciones* have almost reached the tip of Laredo's wide, sheltered pride and joy: **Playa de Salvé**, a gentle 5km-long crescent of sand.

From Laredo to Santander

West of Laredo the beaches continue: **Santoña** is another fishing-port resort and home town of Juan de la Cosa (b.1460), the cartographer who accompanied Columbus on his second voyage to America (1493) and is remembered with a suitably large monument. Santoña also claims that its shipbuilders made the *Santa María* for Columbus.

Another lovely area, **Noja**, has another stretch of fine, sandy beaches and a considerable villa and apartment *urbanización* along the shore – which seems to grow daily.

Local legend says that the village takes its name from Noah, whose Ark, they say, washed up on one of the mountains nearby. The rest of the way to Santander there are plenty of unexploited beaches, reachable on back roads off the main coastal route: the **Playas de Arnuero**, near the lighthouse at Cape Ajo, and the **Playas de Barayo**, west of Ajo.

Eastern Cantabria: Inland

This corner of the *comunidad* can offer absolutely nothing but scenery, but it is some of the sweetest and greenest cow country you'll ever see. Villages are tiny and the roads little more than paved mule tracks, meandering exasperatingly up and down the mountains, in and out of the eternal fog and mists. Almost all the houses are the lovely traditional Cantabrian type, with carved and painted wooden balconies on the front.

Small Nowheres and Secret Caves

South of Laredo the N629 for Burgos heads into the rugged and empty valley of the Soba. Near Ampuero you can visit one of the major sanctuaries of Cantabria, **Nuestra Señora de la Bien Aparecida**, a 17th-century chapel commemorating a miraculous appearance of the Virgin. Near **Ramales de la Victoria**, on the borders of Euskadi, there are a number of Palaeolithic painted caves, although only the **Cueva de Covalanas** is open to the public (*t 94 264 65 04 to arrange a visit; open summer Wed–Sun 10–1 and 4–7.30, winter Wed–Sun 10–2; adm, EU citizens free*).

The area directly south of Santander is an odd region. Once it was one of the biggest mining areas in the north, but it is finally being allowed to recuperate; there are mineral springs everywhere, and a small, modern spa resort, **Liérganes**, the biggest village in the area.

Tourist Information

Liérganes: Pso del Hombre Pez, t 94 252 80 21, *www.aytolierganes.com*.
There is a **market** in Solares on Wednesdays.

Where to Stay and Eat

Liérganes ✉ 39800 j

Liérganes is a thermal spa, and consequently the most dependable place to look for a hotel in these little-touristed parts.

★★★Gran Hotel Balneario, C/José Antonio s/n, t 94 252 8011, *www.grupocastelar.com* (*expensive*). The most luxurious of the spa hotels, with every modern facility.

★★★Posada del Sauce, C/José Antonio s/n, t 94 252 80 23, *www.grupocastelar.com* (*moderate–inexpensive*). A century-old stone inn with attractively decorated rooms, a pool and a good restaurant.

★★★Casona El Arral, C/Convento 1, t 94 252 84 75, *www.calidadcantabria.com* (*moderate*). A charmingly converted 19th-century mansion surrounded by gardens on the river.

★★El Cantábrico, Pso del Hombre Pez 8, t 94 252 80 48 (*inexpensive*). A modern and relatively luxurious place.

Ramales de la Victoria ✉ 39800

This village is the unlikely setting for one of Cantabria's best restaurants:

★★Río Asón, Barón de Adzaneta 17, t 94 264 61 57 (*expensive*). The restaurant's daily three-course menu is an excellent bargain, with game dishes, grilled meats with cèpes and a rarity – fresh salmon from the nearby Asón; it also has nine rooms and one suite. *Restaurant closed Sun eve and Mon*.

El Hombre Pez

In Liérganes, you might note the unusual name of the main street, the Paseo del Hombre Pez, which commemorates a wonderfully strange story from the 1700s. The 'Fish Man' was a native of this village, Francisco de la Vega Casar, who went off to Bilbao to work as a carpenter. One day he went out for a bathe in the river and never returned; his friends and family assumed he'd drowned. Nine years later some fishermen trawling in the Bay of Cádiz, way down in Andalucía, pulled up their nets and found an odd sort of fish inside, a damp and chilly man with scales covering most of his body. When they brought him back to Cádiz, a Cantabrian who had known him recognized him by a birthmark. The fish-man had lost the power of speech, but he understood enough to agree that he was in fact Francisco de la Vega Casar of Liérganes. He lived on land for nine more years, and it seems that he was exploited as a curiosity. De la Vega stayed chilly and damp until the end, and never accepted any food but raw fish. Needless to say, the people who were looking after him never let him get anywhere near the water. One day he simply slipped away and was never seen again.

Now, all this happened in the middle of the Age of Enlightenment, and Spain was full of learned sceptics, including the famous writer Fray Benito Feijóo, who couldn't let a chance like this slip by without looking into the common belief in the miraculous. The Hombre Pez's career was thoroughly investigated and plenty of witnesses confirmed all the details of the case. So did it really happen, or was it simply one of the most successful carnival tricks of all time?

Santander

The capital of Cantabria, Santander has a lot in common with San Sebastián – a large city beautifully situated on a protected bay, popularized by royalty as a summer resort. The story has it that Queen Isabel II first came down in the 1860s in the hope that the sea air would help with a bad dose of the clap (which she probably got from General O'Donnell, the prime minister, or another up-and-coming politician). Again, after the First World War, it was *the* fashionable place to go for Madrileños, especially with the founding of an international summer university (named after Menéndez Pelayo, Santander's favourite son and Spain's greatest antiquarian), offering holiday-makers highbrow culture to complement its wide beaches. Still, despite this and its widely acclaimed International Music Festival in August, Santander lacks the excitement and *joie de vivre* of San Sebastián.

On the other hand, Santander has been a great town for disasters. Two of the most recent were the explosion of a ship full of dynamite in 1893, killing 500 and clearing most of the harbour area, and the fire of 1941, which started in the Archbishop's Palace and destroyed most of the old centre. No city in northern Spain shows a more striking split personality. At the centre it's a gritty, workaday town rather like Bilbao without the smokestacks, but stray a few streets to the other side of the peninsula and you'll be in what seems to be a Belle Epoque dream resort, casino and all. The Santander of the festivals shows a bright and modern face to the world, but the real

Getting There and Around

By Air
Santander's airport is 7km away at Maliaño (no buses), with daily connections to Barcelona and Madrid with Iberia (t 94 220 2156) and to London Stansted with Ryanair (t 94 220 2412. Airport information *www.aena.es*, t 94 220 2100.

By Ferry
From Santander, Brittany Ferries sail to Plymouth twice-weekly from mid-March to mid-November. For information in Santander, call t 94 236 06 11, *www.brittanyferries.es*, or visit the ticket office at the Estación Marítima.

By Train
The train stations are both on Pza de las Estaciones s/n. RENFE, t 902 240 202 for information, has connections with Madrid, Palencia, Reinosa, Segovia and Valladolid. The narrow-gauge FEVE, t 94 221 33 50, *www.feve.es*, has trains to Bilbao, Oviedo, Torrelavega and Unquera; unfortunately they miss out the coastline towns east of Santander, which are served instead by buses.

By Bus
The central bus station is conveniently opposite the train stations on Navas de Tolosa, t 94 221 19 95, *www.santandereabus.com*. Connections from here include: **Continental Auto** to Burgos, Madrid and Ontaneda-Vejores; **Turytrans** to nearly all the coastal towns and resorts, and also to Bilbao, Zarauz, San Sebastián, Llanes, Oviedo, Gijón, Vitoria and Pamplona; **Intercar** to Galicia, Asturias and Euskadi; **Fernández** to León and **Autocares de Cantabria** to Logroño.

The main line up to the Picos de Europa is **Palomera**, with runs to Potes and Fuente Dé. Within Santander itself there are frequent buses and trolleys (nos.1, 2 and 7) that run from the centre to El Sardinero, just 20 minutes away.

By Boat
Lanchas Reginas, t 94 221 6753, runs a service to the beaches across the bay, with boats leaving every 15 minutes from 10.30am to 8.30pm from the Muelle de Ferrys, two blocks from the cathedral. They also offer tours of the bay and excursions around the Río Cubas. Call for details.

By Taxi
For a radio taxi, t 94 233 33 33.

Tourist Information

Regional: Pza de Velarde 5, t 94 231 07 08, f 94 231 32 48.
Municipal: Jardines de Pereda (in the city centre, facing the port), t 94 220 30 00, *www.ayto-santander.es*, at the beach in El Sardinero, t 94 274 04 14, and in the bus station opposite the train stations on Navas de Tolosa. They offer free guided walking tours of the city.

The **post office** is on the corner of Avda Alfonso XIII and C/Calvo Sotelo. Ciberlope, C/Lope de Vega 14, t 94 203 7910, offers Internet access.

There are **markets** in Plaza de la Esperanza behind the Ayuntamiento on Tuesdays, Wednesdays, Fridays and Saturdays for food; Mondays and Thursdays for clothes; in Plaza de México on Mondays, Wednesdays, Fridays and Saturdays for food; Tuesdays and Fridays for clothes (by the bullring at the end of Calle de San Fernando).

Shopping
Santander is a good city for shopping and it is very easy to while away an afternoon strolling along streets such as C/San Francisco in the city centre and others in the vicinity. A former covered market on C/General Mola is also now an upbeat shopping centre with bars and boutiques.
Lucio Herrezuelo, C/Calvo Sotelo 23. A good place for quality shoes and leather goods.
El Oso Goloso, C/Marqués de la Hermida 12. Gourmet deli selling goodies like chestnuts and goat's cheese.
Reigadas, C/Peña Herbosa 23. A wide selection of wines and liqueurs.
Libreria Estudio, C/Calvo Sotelo 21. Has a good selection of maps and books, including a number of walking guides to the Picos de Europa.

Where to Stay

Santander ✉ 39000

July to September are the busy (and expensive) months here, especially the first two, when the music festival and International University are in full swing. Prices are as high as in San Sebastián, though there are plenty of *casas particulares* to preserve your budget. Hang around the bus and train stations and someone will probably lead you to one.

Luxury

Santander's most elegant hotels are all found on the back side of town by the beaches. There are countless expensive chain hotels, with lots of amenities but little charm.

*****Hotel Real**, Pso de Pérez Galdós 28, t 94 227 25 50, *www.hotelreal.es*. A lovely Belle Epoque-style hotel located near the Playa de la Magdalena offering marvellous bay views, fine rooms and a well-kept garden.

****Hotel Bahía**, Avda de Alfonso XIII 6, t 94 220 50 00, *www.gruposardinero.com*. Stately modern hotel towering like a lighthouse between the old town and the port.

Expensive

****Castelar**, C/Castelar 25, t/f 94 222 52 00, *www.grupocastelar.com*. In the city centre, with sea views and all mod cons.

****Rhin**, t 94 227 43 00, *www.gruporhin.com*. Enjoys a smart location on Avda Reina Victoria, the main street facing the beaches.

****Hotel Hoyuela**, Avda de los Hoteles 7, t 94 228 2628, *www.gruposardinero. com*. Perhaps the prettiest hotel overlooking El Sardinero's beach, in a turn-of-the 20th-century mansion.

Moderate

***Hotel Central**, General Mola 5, t 94 222 24 00, *www.elcentral.com*. Good summer choice with spacious terraces and sea views.

***Hotel Sardinero**, Pza de Italia 1, t 94 227 11 00, *www.gruposardinero.com*. Popular and near the beaches of Sardinero and the casino.

HR Paris, Avda de los Hoteles 6, t 94 227 23 50. Elegantly-furnished rooms in a rambling old queen of a building near the casino.

Piñamar, C/Ruiz de Alda 15, t 94 236 18 66. Modern, functional and located near the train station.

Inexpensive

The cheaper hotels have gained a notoriety for being either dreary or rip-offs. If the price you are quoted seems ridiculously high, find out what it includes: a common sting, especially among the *pensiónes* around El Sardinero, is to include a 'secret' breakfast for which you will be charged even if you don't know about it. An official room-only price list should be posted somewhere near the front door.

Hs La Mexicana, C/Juan de Herrera 3, t 94 222 23 54. Good value choice in the centre, with friendly management and comfortable rooms. Big enough to have space when others in this price range are full. *Budget out of season.*

HR San Glorio, C/Ruiz Zorilla 18, t 94 231 29 62, *www.sanglorio.com*. Centrally located, with simple rooms and a restaurant.

Budget

Hs Rocamar, Avda de los Castros 41, t 94 227 72 68, *www.hostalrocamar.com*. Classic 1960s style-hostal located on a street in El Sardinero where there are several other inexpensive places to choose from.

*Hs Gran Antilla**, C/Isabel II 8, t 94 221 31 00. Well worn, but still a good deal in this over-priced town.

*Pensión La Porticada**, C/Mendez Nuñez 6, t 94 222 78 17. Sparkling rooms with balconies set in a building that speaks of vanished glory. Cheaper rates are available with shared bathroom.

Camping Cabo Mayor, t 94 239 1542, *www.cabomayor.com*. Located by the Cabo Mayor lighthouse.

Eating Out

Unlike San Sebastián, Santander is hardly known for its cuisine. The seafood, however, is always good, and the traditional place to get it is at the rather piquant Barrio Pesquero, an area rebuilt after the fire, just behind the train stations. Around the beaches, restaurants tend to be more elaborate.

El Serbal, C/Andrés del Río 7, t 942 22 25 15 (*expensive*). The swankiest restaurant in town, with elaborate contemporary cuisine in elegant surroundings. Winner of numerous awards, it is always worth booking in advance.

Restaurante Cañadio, C/Gómez Oreña 15, t 94 231 41 49 (*expensive-moderate*). For that special seafood moment – one of the best in town. Try the *croquetas de bacalao* (croquettes filled with cod) as a taster at the bar.

Bodega Cigaleña, C/Daoiz y Velarde 19, t 94 221 30 62 (*moderate*). A typical, dark *bodega* which harbours a wine museum; come here to get a feel for traditional fare. *Closed Sun.*

La Sardina de Plata, Glorieta del Dr Fleming 3 (in El Sardinero), t 94 227 10 35 (*moderate*). A fashionable place in a very pretty setting, offering imaginative renderings of traditional dishes such as *bacalao* with red peppers. *Closed Feb, Sun eve and Mon, except in summer.*

Zacarías, C/General Mola 1, t 94 221 23 23 (*moderate*). Offers a total '*mar y montaña*' Cantabrian culinary experience, including the region's excellent cheeses.

Bar del Puerto, Hernán Cortés 63 (in the Puerto Chico), t 94 221 30 01 (*budget*). The seafood here is worth stopping off for.

Bodega del Riojano, Río de la Pila 5 (north of the Jardines de Pereda), t 94 221 67 50 (*moderate–budget*). One of Santander's typical *bodegas* in the old quarter, offering healthy servings of tapas. Specialities are *rabo de buey* (oxtail), *morcillo estofado* (a blood sausage stew), and stuffed peppers. *Closed Sun eve and Mon.*

El Diluvio, General Mola 14, t 94 221 85 63 (*budget*). One of the best bars in town for mouthwatering canapés and tapas, always packed with locals.

La Gaviota, C/Marqués de la Ensenada, t 94 222 11 32 (*budget*). A favourite in the *barrio*, where you can try the seafood *menú del día* for under €10 or, for a little more, you can order a plate of whatever delicacy has come home with the fishermen.

Restaurante Modena, C/Eduardo Benot 6, t 94 231 33 71 (*budget*). A rare Italian restaurant with the usual pizza/pasta selection plus a few surprises, like crêpes.

Entertainment and Nightlife

Nightlife in Santander is concentrated in two places: first the proper *marcha* grounds in the old town, with a vast number of bars and clubs around C/de la Pila and Pza de Cañadío. This is the place where you're most likely to find live music and a raucous good time. Somewhat more staid entertainment can be had around El Sardinero; the Pza de Italia attracts the older set, while the overdressed young in search of fun head for the numerous bars and discothèques in Calle Panamá.

Festival Internacional de Santander. Since 1951, this August festival has showcased an extraordinary variety of music, dance and spectacle from around the world. Along with all the big-league culture, popular Spanish and Latin American song, dance, magic shows and fireworks take place every night throughout August at the Auditorium and the Finca Altamira.

For information contact the Oficina del Festival, Palacio de Festivales de Cantabria, C/Gamazo s/n, 39004, t 94 221 05 08, *www.festivalsantander.com*. Tickets are on sale in advance from the ticket booth at the Palacio de Festivales, from any branch of the Caja Cantabria bank, or from the special Festival booth in the Jardines de Pereda, near the library, t 94 231 33 42 (*open 11–2 and 5–8*).

Casa La Montaña, C/Vargas (the park boulevard northwest of the Renfe and Feve train stations). A typical wine *bodega*, with restaurant, full of big old barrels.

Canela, Plaza de Cañadío. One of many bars on this buzzy, late-night square, where there's always plenty going on.

La Conveniente, C/Gómez Oreña 9. An 18th-century bodega resurrected into an evocative cavernous bar, lined by 8,000-plus bottles, with live piano nightly. *Closed Sun.*

Gran Casino, Plaza de Italia s/n, t 94 203 0500. You can risk your euros from 7pm to 4am at this lavish night-haunt (dress up and bring your passport).

La Luna, C/General Mola 35. A classic place for those wanting to avoid the strictly young scene.

Rocambole, C/Hernán Cortés 10. An especially popular venue, which offers plenty of space to party until the rosy-fingered aurora appears in the sky.

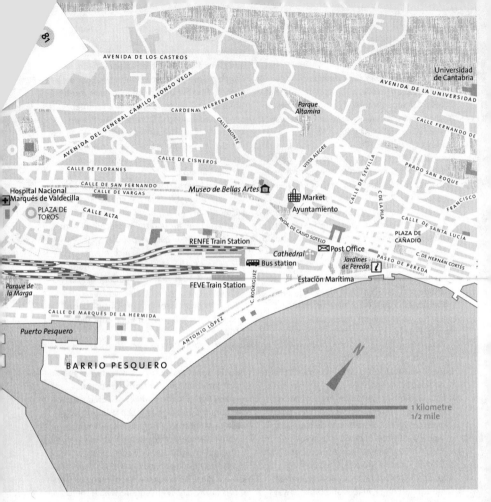

atmosphere of the place is still best represented by the pigeon-spattered statue of Franco in the centre (currently one of only three in the whole of Spain, although the local government have promised to dismantle it), and the grey streets still named after Nationalist hoodlums of the Civil War.

The Cathedral and Museums

In the centre, Santander's much-altered and rebuilt **Cathedral** (*next to the Diputación Regional on C/Casmiro Sainz 4; open daily 10–1 and 4–7.30*) is interesting mostly for its early Gothic crypt; this now forms the separate church of **Santísimo Cristo** (*open June–Sept, daily 8–1 and 4–8; rest of year open daily 8–1 and 5–8*), where a glass floor has been installed over the remains of a Roman building.

The **Museo de Prehistoria y Arqueología** (*open Tues–Sat 10–1 and 4–7, Sun 11–2; adm*), has exhibits devoted to Cantabria's prehistoric cave-dwellers, including tools, reproductions of their art, and two disc-shaped star tombstones the size of tractor tyres made just before the Roman conquest, discovered in the valley of the Buelna.

The best parts of old Santander lie to the north of the fishing port and the railway station, across the main Avda Calvo Sotelo. Near the Ayuntamiento, the **Museo de Bellas Artes** (*C/Rubio 6; open Mon–Fri 10.30–1 and 5.30–8, Sat 10.30–1; adm*) has, besides a contemporary art collection of dubious merit, a good Zurbarán and several Goyas, including a portrait of Ferdinand VII, commissioned by the city to flatter the king.

Nearby, the **Casa Museo de Menéndez Pelayo** (*open Mon, Wed and Fri 9–2, Tues and Thurs 9–2 and 4–9, Sat 9–1; adm, guided tours available*) has an extensive collection of books, many of them by great Catalan writers, which were donated to the city by the scholar himself. Behind the Ayuntamiento, the iron and glass **market** is the most colourful sight in Santander, especially the pride of the town: the glorious fish market.

On the way out to the beaches, Avenida Reina Victoria passes Santander's new **Museo Marítimo del Cantábrico** (*open May–Sept daily 10–0, Oct–Mar daily 10–7; adm*), which has an array of model ships, exhibits in the local maritime tradition and an aquarium.

dinero

The 1941 fire destroyed most of Santander's character but it spared the suburb of **El Sardinero**, with its fine twin beaches, imaginatively named **Primera** (First) and **Segunda** (Second), backed by the enormous Belle Epoque **casino**, recently refurbished in an effort to revive some of the city's lost panache.

El Sardinero is separated from the working end of the city by the beautiful **Peninsula de la Magdalena**, a city park fringed by two more splendid beaches, the **Playa de la Magdalena** and the **Playa del Promontorio**. The Tudor-style **Palacio de la Magdalena** at the end of the peninsula was a gift from the city to Alfonso XIII; when the king accepted it, Santander's return to fashion as a summer resort was guaranteed. Today it is part of the university.

Besides the beaches in the city, there are several miles of golden dunes across the bay at **Somo**, **El Puntal** and **Pedrena**, linked every 15 minutes by boat from the centre of town; **Playa las Atenas** nearby is a naturist beach. Just west of Santander at Liencres, there is another fine and very popular beach, **Valdearenas**, a huge expanse of sand bordered by pine woods. And if you have children in tow you will probably be visiting the **Parque de la Naturaleza de Cabárceno** (*www.parquedecabarceno.com; open daily summer 9.30–8, winter 9.30–6; adm*), 10km south of the city at Obregón, where a bit of land wasted by strip mining has been recycled into an attractive and enormous zoo, with more than 400 species from ape to zebra.

South of Santander: the Heart of Cantabria

South of the capital the land gradually rises to the Montañas de Santander, a pretty, hilly region that supports only a handful of villages. There are plenty of wide open spaces along these high roads of the old County of Castile, but there are a few attractions besides the solitude: caves of prehistoric art, untouched forests, the source of the Ebro and one of the sexiest churches in Europe.

The Caves of Puente Viesgo

If you haven't made an appointment in advance to see the caves of Altamira, you can at least get into Cantabria's second most spectacular set of prehistoric grottoes at **Puente Viesgo**. There are five caves altogether, but the only one open to the public is the Cueva del Castillo (*open May–Sept Wed–Sun 10–1 and 4–7.30; Oct–Apr Wed–Sun 9.30–4; adm, EU passport holders get in free; children under 12 strictly not admitted*). Decorated with graceful line drawings of stags, horses and other animals, this ensemble is believed to predate the even more eloquent art at Altamira.

Reinosa, on the rail line and just off the A67 motorway, is the main hub in this part of the Cantabrian mountains, with most of the area's hotels and restaurants. The source of northern Spain's longest river, the **Nacimiento del Ebro**, is signposted to the northwest in **Fontibre**; you can clamber down in the trees to stick your toes in the stream gurgling out of the ground. The river has barely begun when, just on the other side of Reinosa, it is dammed to form the massive **Embalse del Ebro**, the grass on its jagged

Getting Around

Reinosa's **bus station**, at the south end of town, is served from Santander by García, **t** 94 221 0960, and Alsa, **t** 902 42 22 42; Alsa goes to Bilbao (summer only, **t** 94 275 28 13). Donato, **t** 94 275 1432, links Reinosa to Espinilla and La Lomba in the Alto Campóo.

Tourist Information

Torrelavega: Ruíz Tagle 6, **t** 94 289 29 82, *www.aytotorrelavega.es*.
Reinosa: Avenida Puente Carlos III 23, **t** 94 275 52 15, *www.ayto-reinosa.es*.
There is a **market** in Reinosa on Mondays.

Where to Stay and Eat

Puente Arce ✉ 39478

One of the best restaurants in Cantabria can be found at this village, which lies 12km inland from Santander on the road to Torrelavega:

El Nuevo Molino, Barrio Monsignor 18, **t** 94 257 50 55 (*expensive*). In an old mill on the river, this long-established restaurant has been overhauled by the energetic management of El Serbal in Santander. (*see* p.180). It's the perfect place to treat yourself, with exceptional cuisine, a superb wine list, and great service. *Closed Sun eve and Tues.*

Puente Viesgo ✉ 39478

★★★Gran Hotel Balneario, C/Manuel Perez Mazo s/n, **t** 94 259 80 61, *www.balneariodepuenteviesgo.com* (*luxury–moderate*). If you have come to

see the caves, you can stop at this sumptuous modern establishment connected to a spa that's good for your rheumatism and neurological troubles; swimming pool, sauna and all the amenities. Great online deals available.

★★★Casona Azul de Toranzo, C/General Díaz de Villegas 5, Corvera de Toranzo, **t** 94 259 6400, *www.casonaazul.com* (*moderate–inexpensive*). A pair of elegant *Indiano* villas 3km from Puente Viesgo have been converted into a stylish small hotel set in gardens with a croquet lawn.

★★Pensión Carrion, at neighbouring Alceda, **t** 94 259 40 16 (*inexpensive*). A more realistic alternative in town.

Mesón El Cazador, Ctra General s/n, **t** 94 259 42 50 (*moderate–budget*). A good country restaurant in San Vicente de Toranzo, south of Puente Viesgo; offers boar, pheasant and other game dishes.

Reinosa ✉ 39200

★★★★Casona de Naveda de Campoo, Plaza del Medio Lugar 37, **t** 94 277 95 15 (*moderate*). An immaculate country hotel in an old stone house, with elegant rooms and friendly staff who can organise all kinds of activities.

★★★Vejo, Avda Cantabria 83 (in the newer part of town), **t** 94 275 17 00, *hvejo@ceoecant.es* (*moderate*). The most comfortable place in town, with a garden, bar and good restaurant.

★La Casona, in Nestares, **t** 94 275 17 88 (*inexpensive*). This old inn on the Reinosa–Cabezón de la Sal road is a scenic place to stay if you're driving.

shore cropped by horses and dairy cows, following the outline of a prehistoric lake. **Corconte**, on the eastern end of the lake, bottles mineral water next to an old spa.

The most beautiful part of the region lies west of Fontibre, in the virgin valleys of the **Saja National Reserve**, where beech, oak and birch forests follow the courses of clear streams. Real explorers can make for **Suano** and the **Población de Suso**, villages that figure on few maps, but can claim a large number of dolmens, a huge cromlech and the ruins of a Templar castle. The region's most important ski installation, **Alto Campoo**, lies to the west in the village of Hermandad Campoo de Suso (*see www.altocampoo.com for ski resort information*).

A Trinity of Romanesque Churches

South of Reinosa you'll find good Romanesque churches – in **Bolmir** and more significantly in **Retortillo**. Retortillo is near the scanty remains of the Roman city of **Julióbriga** (*open Wed–Sun 10.30–12.30 and 4–7; adm*) once the most important city of Cantabria. Set amidst the low walls is the church, with a unique sloping stair leading up to its campanile. Over the door note the carving of two animals shaking hands.

But the most extraordinary Romanesque church of all is south in **Cervatos**: the singular 12th-century **Colegiata**, at the top of a newly cobbled lane. It has a tympanum with an oriental design, a frieze of lions and, carved on to the corbels and capitals in the apse, unabashedly erotic figures that a respectable guidebook hesitates to describe. This unique, medieval tantric temple probably survived clerical prudishness over the centuries because of its remote location and the explanation that such sexual exhibitionism was meant to frighten, rather than tempt, parishioners with the horrors of sin.

South of Cervatos, the narrow CA272 soon meets up again with the Ebro. It's a lovely road, with lots of trees and local swimming holes by tiny villages. One of the largest is **Polientes**, with a roadside statue of a spotted dog and one of Cantabria's 'rupestrian churches' in a cave, although here little old ladies have set up a table by the altar to play cards. Follow the road and Ebro east to an even more remote region and the 12th-century church at **San Martín de Elines**, with a lofty cylindrical tower, keyhole windows, more fascinating modillions and carvings by the same school as Cervatos but without any bawdy flashers and sexual contortionists. The kindly caretaker lives in the house nearest the church and will take you around the cloister, with a 9th-century wall and tombs excavated from the garden in the centre; the most impressive is the fancy sepulchre of a pilgrim who died along the route.

The Coast West of Santander

This lush and lovely seaside stretch has been spared any Laredo toadstools, and what tourist development there is remains fairly discreet. When the summer hordes have vanished and the little windy roads belong to you alone, it is haunting and strange in a fairylike way. Even in the rain.

Santillana del Mar

Jean-Paul Sartre, who had always wanted to be a guidebook writer but couldn't get a break, practised on Santillana del Mar, pronouncing it 'the most beautiful village in Spain'. Sooner or later someone in town will remind you of this, and it's best not to argue. The tour buses disgorge their hundreds daily upon this tiny village (which despite the 'del Mar' is not on the sea), and in summer it can be a ghastly tourist inferno, with no place to put your car for a mile around. If you come at all, do it out of season, or spend the night after the day-trippers have all gone.

Santillana is both an evocative medieval town of grand palaces and a country village of dairy farmers, whose pastures lie on the hills just beyond the mellowed stone and

Getting Around

By Train

FEVE trainsfrom Santander go to Torrelavega, with frequent bus connections to Santillana. Another FEVE station is 3km from San Vicente – a lovely walk if you're not carrying a lot.

By Bus

Suances, Santillana, Comillas and San Vicente are linked around six times daily to Santander by La Cantábrica de Comillas or SA Continental buses, from Santander's main bus station.

Tourist Information

Suances: C/Ceballos 12, t 94 281 09 24.
Santillana del Mar, C/Jesús Otero 20, t 94 281 82 51, *santillana@cantabria.org*.
Comillas: C/Aldea 6, t 94 272 07 68.
San Vicente de la Barquera: Avda Generalísimo 20, t 94 271 07 97, *www.sanvicentedel barquera.org*.
Cabezón de la Sal: Pza de Ricardo Botín s/n, t 94 270 03 32, *turismosanvicente@ cantabria.org*.

In Suance, **market day** is Tuesday, in Torrelavega, Wednesday; Comillas, Thursday; and in San Vicente and Cabezón, it's Saturday.

Where to Stay and Eat

Santillana ✉ 39330

Ask at the tourist office for a list of *casas particulares*, though many of them are in the newer suburbs en route to Altamira; or head for C/Los Hornos or Avda Le Dorat, which have plenty of rooms.

*****Casa de Marqués, C/Canton 24, t/f 94 281 88 88 (*luxury–expensive*). Magnificent new hotel in a 15th-century building with stone and beam interior. *Closed mid-Dec–Mar*.

***Hotel Altamira, C/Cantón 1, t 94 281 80 25, *www.hotelaltamira.com* (*moderate*). A good choice, installed in a palace with a patio and garden; an elegant dining room serving big plates of roast meats (and some seafood) – possibly the best restaurant in town.

***La Casa de Güela, C/Los Hornos 9, t 94 281 8250 (*moderate*). A beautiful boutique-style hotel with just 10 rooms in a handsome old stone palace. With pool, tennis and gardens.

***Parador de Santillana Gil Blas, Pza Ramón Pelayo 11, t 94 281 80 25, *santillana@parador.es* (*moderate*). Wonderfully atmospheric with medieval rooms and an elegant dining room; reserve well in advance in season; request a room on the first or second floor.

La Casa del Organista, C/Los Hornos 4, t 94 284 03 52, *www.casadelorganista.com* (*moderate–inexpensive*). Gorgeous wood-panelled rooms with sloping ceilings, in a medieval mansion overlooking fields on the edge of town.

El Cantón, C/Cantón 3, t 94 284 02 74 (*inexpensive*). A lovel and welcoming *posada*, boasting the cheapest rooms with bath in Santillana's old quarter.

Posada La Cerrá de San Roque, t 94 284 0065, *www.posadadelcerra.com (budget)*. A charming inn set in lovely countryside half-way between Suances and Santillana del Mar. A good family option, with pool and gardens.

Camping Santillana, t 94 281 82 50 (*inexpensive*). Just north of the village, this is a more pricey campsite, but it has all amenities, including a pool and tennis courts.

La Joraca, C/Los Hornos 20, t 94 284 0137 (*moderate*). An atmospheric restaurant serving fine traditional cuisine prepared with flair: go for the *menú del degustación* (€32).

Los Blasones, Pza de la Gándara 8, t 94 281 80 70 (*moderate–budget*). Feast on local and mountain specialities here – from *fabada* to grilled *langostinos* (crayfish). *Closed Thurs*.

La Robleda, C/Revolgo, t 94 281 83 36 (*budget*). You pay even less for *fabada* and *langostinos* here. Otherwise the bar nearest the Colegiata offers good tapas and reasonable meals.

Suances ✉ 39340

Most rooms here go for about €40.

*Castillo de Suances, t 94 281 03 83, *www. turismosuances.com* (*inexpensive*).This 19th-century crenellated folly by the beaches offers interesting, individually decorated rooms, some with television.

Casa Sito, Pso de la Marina Española, t 94 281 15 08 (*budget*). This good seafood restaurant is as popular with the locals as the tourists; it offers a good-value menu and dishes like *paella* with lobster (*paella bogavante*) for a splurge.

half-timbered houses that line Santillana's patchwork of ancient streets and squares. Its past distinctions come from great wealth in medieval times, which was earned from wool and linen. By 1600 nearly every man in town was a noble, or *hidalgo* (from *hijo de algo*, 'son of somebody'), courtesy of easily purchased titles of nobility in the time of Charles V (1516–56) and his son, Philip II (1556–98). So they stopped doing any work, and Santillana has changed little since. In the 1920s Juan Antonio Güell López, grandson of the famous Marquis of Comillas (*see* box on p.191), became minister for tourism under the dictatorship of Primo de Rivera. He took a special interest in Santillana, and began the restoration of its old buildings.

The village is famous as the birthplace of Spain's favourite fictional rogue, Gil Blas, and home of the real Marqués de Santillana, Íñigo López de Mendoza, the Spanish Sir Philip Sidney, a warrior and poet and courtly lover whose house still stands on the Calle del Cantón. Other houses have equally noble pedigrees; an archduchess of Austria owned the one across from the **Colegiata** (*open 10–1 and 4–6; adm*). The latter is a 12th-century masterpiece, dedicated to St Juliana (or Iliana), an Anatolian martyr under Diocletian whose remains have lain here since the 6th century, and who gave her name to the town; the monks who built the cloister for themselves owned most of the town and ran its affairs until the 1400s.

The church has a fine weather-beaten façade, rebuilt in the 1700s with bits and pieces of the Romanesque original tacked on; inside, the impressive altar is made of silver from Mexico – plenty of the *hidalgos'* younger sons went off to America to make their fortune, and many of the family mansions in the village are *casas de indianos*. There is a beautiful, ivy-draped **cloister**, with capitals carved with biblical and hunting scenes.

The ticket to the cloister will also get you into the **Museo Diocesano** (*across town near the car park; open Tues–Sun 10–1 a nd 4–7, closed Feb*), which is installed in the 17th-century Convento de Regina Coeli. It is Gothic in style and displays an exceptional collection of ecclesiastical artefacts from all over Cantabria, some Templar in origin, and all perfectly restored by the nuns.

In the eloquent Plaza Ramón Pelayo, the tower house of Don Borja holds the **Fundación Santillana**, which organises temporary exhibitions on local themes – particularly on the region's seafaring past and its relationship with the Americas. This makes up in a way for the town's anomalous name 'del Mar' when it's 3km from the sea. On the same plaza stands the Ayuntamiento, rebuilt in 1770, and from the same century, the Palacio de Barreda-Bracho, now the Parador Gil Blas.

Twenty or so years ago, residents of Santillana still kept cattle on the ground floors of their homes and sold delicious rich milk by the glass and tasty *bizcocho* (cake) by the piece to tourists. You'll see less of that today, but there are still plenty of souvenirs to buy. If you're in a hurry to get to the promised Mar, the closest beaches are at **Suances**, just 5km away; it's a fishing village and a small resort. Although the sea here isn't the cleanest, people come her for water sports, including surfing. Suances began life as *Portus Blendium*, the chief Roman port on this part of the coast, though there's nothing Roman to be seen.

The Caves of Altamira

¡Mira, papa. Bueyes! (Look, papa. Oxen!)

María de Sautuola, discoverer of the paintings at Altamira

From Santillana you can walk up to Altamira in 20 minutes, though don't expect to get in unless you've written three years in advance (*Centro de Investigación de Altamira, Santillana del Mar, 39330 Santander*) and are one of the 20 chosen ones allowed the 15-minute glimpse at one of the sublime masterpieces of Upper Palaeolithic art. Still, an extraordinary number of people show up at the caves, pilgrim-like to pay homage to the genius of the artists of *c.* 12,000 BC, who covered the undulating ceiling with stunningly exuberant, vividly coloured paintings of bison, horses, boars and stags. Only at Lascaux, up at the northern end of the Franco-Cantabrian arc of Magdalenian cave painting, will you find such powerful, masterful technique; the movement and strength in the coiled, startled and galloping bisons, the attentive deer, the frisking horses are awesome. As they say, 'This is the infancy of art, not an art of infancy.'

The story of the discovery of Altamira, however, is a parable of perceptions. As at Lascaux, an ancient landslide sealed the entrance of the caves and tunnels (and more or less vacuum-packed the paintings) until it was rediscovered by a hunter and his dog in 1868. In 1875, Don Marcelino de Sautuola, an amateur prehistorian, was intrigued by the black drawings on the walls in the outer rooms and, over the years, explored them, in 1879 taking his nine-year-old daughter María along. The child wandered a little deeper into the caves, and lifted her eyes to the superb polychrome paintings. Although no one had ever seen the like, the Marquis at once recognized the ceiling for what it was: a ravishing work of genius from the Stone Age. Excited, he published a description of Altamira but, rather than receiving the expected response of awe and wonder from the 'experts' in the field, de Sautuola was mocked, ridiculed, viciously attacked, and even accused of forging the paintings; the scholars simply refused to believe that people who used stone axes were capable of painting, one of the 'civilized arts'.

Undaunted, the Marquis held his ground, insisting Altamira was for real and died heartbroken in 1888, vilified and as forgotten as the caves themselves. Fifteen years later, the discovery of a dozen painted caves in the Vézère Valley in the Dordogne led to a change of mind, beginning in 1902 with one expert, E Cartailhac, making a public apology to de Sautuola's memory in his *Mea Culpa d'un Sceptique*.

Although the 'white disease' caused by the moisture in the breath of visitors has restricted admission to the caves, you can do the next best thing at Altamira: visit an exact replica, including videos and a holographic tableaux explaining the history of the caves and explanations of the stunning reproductions of the paintings. Picasso, for one, would not have approved – he visited the caves back in the 1920s, declaring that 'not one of us is capable of painting like this' – but his posthumous hand-wringing is unlikely to deter the extra 400,000 tourists who show up annually to visit the fascinating **museum** (*open June–Sept Mon–Fri 9.30–7.30; Oct–May Mon–Fri 9.30–5, Sun 9.30–5; adm*). You can also explore a small stalactite cave which is prettily lit to emphasize nature's wonders as compensation for the inaccessibility of the more fragile works of man.

Comillas, with a Little Modernista Madness

Definitely *the* place to be on this stretch of the coast, the seaside resort of Comillas offers a bit of Catalan quirkiness in a gorgeous setting, framed by two endearing beaches – the Playa Comillas and the longer Playa de Oyambre. Comillas' old town, with its rough cobbled streets and arcaded mansions, has been a quiet watering hole for the Madrid and Barcelona aristocracy for a long time; the latter brought along their favourite architects in the 19th century to add a *modernista* flair.

The peculiar legacies of the robber barons are up on the hills to the west of the village centre. There you will see Gaudí's **El Capricho**, built for a relation of the Marquis', and subsequently restored and pressed into service as a restaurant (*see*

Where to Stay and Eat

Comillas ✉ 39520

Ask at the tourist office for a list of *casas particulares*.

★★★Marina de Campíos, C/General Piélago 14, t 94 272 27 54, *www.marinadecampios.com* (expensive–moderate). A handsomely renovated villa with elegant , individually styled rooms and suites and a piano-bar.

★★★Casa del Castro, San Jerónimo, t 94 272 00 36 (*moderate*). Right in the centre of town in a fine old building, with a pretty garden and comfortable rooms. *Closed Jan.*

★★Hs Esmeralda, C/Antonio López 7, t 94 272 00 97 (*inexpensive*). A good budget choice, which is close to the beach and has a pleasant bar/restaurant. *Closed Nov–Mar.*

★Fuente Real, Barrio de Sobrellano 19, t 94 272 01 55 (*budget*). A basic alternative behind El Capricho.

Adolfo, Avda Las Infantas 10, t 94 272 20 00 (*moderate*). A good choice, with traditional cooking for a few more euros.

El Capricho de Gaudí, Barrio de Sobrellano, t 94 272 03 65 (*moderate*). Comillas is the only place where you can dine in a building designed by Gaudí. The interior, if not entirely as he meant it to be, has been beautifully restored. The food is mostly seafood with a *nouvelle cuisine* touch; the set menu is a bargain. Ring ahead in season as it's usually booked solid. *Closed Sun eve and Mon in winter.*

Gurea, C/Ignacio Fernandez de Castro 11, t 94 272 24 46 (*moderate*). A good alternative to El Capricho, serving excellent and unusual Basque dishes like merluza in crayfish sauce and fig ice cream. *Closed Sun eve and Mon.*

Fuente Real, t 94 272 21 59 (*budget*). Just outside the grounds of El Capricho, this cheerful seafood haunt with its décor of *azulejo* tiles, has been a favourite for over a century.

San Vicente de la Barquera ✉ 39540

★★★Miramar, Pso de la Barquera 20, t/f 94 271 00 75 (*inexpensive*). Modern, with great views of the bay and the rising Picos de Europa; the restaurant allows you to enjoy the vista.

★★Luzón, Avda Miramar 1, t/f 94 271 00 50 (*inexpensive*). A solid, square stone inn smack in the centre of town facing the tidal basin.

★La Paz, C/del Mercado 2, t 94 271 01 80 (*inexpensive*). Has been remodelled and offers stylish, if bathless, rooms.

Camping El Rosal, Playas de San Vicente, t 94 271 01 65 (*budget*). Conveniently located near the beaches, on the main road just outside San Vicente.

Boga-Boga, Pza José Antonio, t 94 271 01 35 (*moderate*). Expect more seafood at this place, where the chef turns out delicious Cantabrian favourites along with a very good *solomillo con verduras*. The upstairs hotel is predictably good (*moderate*).

Maruja, Avda Generalísimo s/n, t 94 271 00 77 (*moderate*). For a less serious seafood attack, you can do well here for under €30, and there's a bargain menú for €16.

Bárcena Mayor ✉ 39500

Posada La Franca, C/La Franca, t 94 270 60 67, *www.lafrancaposadarural.com* (*moderate*). Come here for the village's famed mountain cuisine – stuffed haunch of venison and other game dishes in season. The comfortable rooms are *budget*.

The Instant Marquis

The Spain of the Industrial Revolution is a land not very well known, but if the nation's capitalists never could match the mills of the Midlands or Massachusetts in the 19th century they certainly produced some marvels, and some incredible robber-baron careers. Antonio López was a local boy who went off to Cuba and made a fortune in shipping and slaves (slavery wasn't abolished in Spanish-run Cuba until 1886), and then moved out and made another pile running a monopoly, the Philippine National Tobacco Company. He came back home, and purchased the title of Marquis of Comillas. The new Marquis' son married the daughter of Joan Güell, the richest man in Barcelona, who had also started in Cuba and ended up as Spain's biggest textile magnate. If the name is familiar, you're thinking of Antoni Gaudí's famous surreal Güell Park in Barcelona. Like Cosimo de' Medici in old Florence, this robber baron had a talented aesthete to succeed him, whose sponsorship of Gaudí sparked the golden age of *modernista* architecture in Catalunya. It was the Güell connection that brought Gaudí to Cantabria, where he helped with the López family palace in 1878 and came back to build El Capricho in 1883. The centre of the López interests was Barcelona, where they ran factories, banks and the Transatlántica shipping line (which later fell into the grasp of the greatest of all Spanish robber barons, Juan March, and still runs most of the Spanish island ferries). The Lópezes lived on the Ramblas in Barcelona, but they spent their summers here, bringing along their Catalan friends and making Comillas a genteel upper-class resort; locals called them the 'Transatlánticos'. López's castle-like summer mansion, on the hill overlooking the town, was one of the most spectacular private homes in its day, and the centre of the glittering social season Comillas knew at the turn of the century. But modern capitalist glories never seem to last more than a generation or two, and today López's palace stands as empty and weird and forlorn as *Citizen Kane*'s Xanadu.

below). If not one of the architect's more ambitious works, it is a delightful house, exciting the envy of the crowd of Spanish tourists usually milling about it. The main feature is an eccentric, perfectly non-functional tower, half-lighthouse and half-minaret. The decorative theme, held together by lovely ceramic tiles in green and gold and by extravagant wrought-iron balconies and cornices, has a repeated sunflower motif.

Next to El Capricho you can have a peek into the vanished lifestyle of Comillas' rich and shameless at the **summer palace of the Marqués de Comillas**, the Palacio de Sobrellano (*open daily in July–early Sept 10.30–1.30 and 4–7.30, closed Mon and Tues in winter; adm*). A work of another Catalan, Gaudí's friend Joan Martorell, this ponderous palace in a quirky *modernista* neo-Gothic style is protected by an imitation castle wall with oubliettes. It's worth taking the guided tour to see Gaudí's grinning *modernista* dragons, which adorn the walnut fireplace in the Marquis' old billiard room; more wicked specimens lurk on the arms of his fireside chairs. Next door, the Marquis' **chapel** adds the perfect touch of discreet surrealism to the ensemble. It's bigger than Comillas' parish church, and inside there are furnishings by Gaudí himself and marble sepulchres of the Marquis and his family.

The third member of this singular trio stands on the opposite hill, across the main road through Comillas, but it commands the views for miles around. Construction of the **Universidad Pontificia** began in 1883, with a plan by Martorell and some financial help from Antonio López. The pope's university moved to Madrid in 1964, leaving a huge complex of buildings with no specific use; still the people of Comillas maintain the site and give tours of the sumptuous main building (*times vary – check at tourist office*) containing decorations by a third major figure of Catalan modernism, Lluís Domènech i Montaner. There are frescoed rooms and a chapel, but the best features are the figures carved in wood over the main stairway in the form of gargoyles: fearsome monsters share space with, among others, a house cat, a chicken and a fly.

If you like Domènech i Montaner there's a wonderfully florid **Monument to Antonio López** by him near the beach, within sight of Comillas' peculiar **cemetery**, built in a Gothic ruin and topped with a huge marble angel. Domènech i Montaner is responsible for some of the funerary statues inside too, and it isn't difficult to guess which ones are his.

San Vicente de la Barquera

The next resort to the west, San Vicente de la Barquera is still as much a fishing port as a holiday retreat, though it's hugely popular with Madrileños in summer – you won't find a place to park your car. Marvellously sited on a hill in the last elbow-bend of the wide and marshy Río Escudo (arriving on the coastal road from the west provides the best view), it is linked by a long causeway to the eastern coast, near the town beach. The older, upper town is dominated by the rose-coloured parish church **Nuestra Señora de los Ángeles**, a 13th-century transitional work containing the finely sculpted Renaissance tomb of the Inquisitor Antonio Corro. Below, interwoven branches of plane trees add a French touch to the main plaza. Every quarter of an hour the bell tower of the church San Vicente booms out a recording of the first phrase of Schubert's *Ave María*, guaranteed to drive you nuts. The locals claim an enemy of their town had it installed – with any luck it will be a bad memory by the time you get there.

If you want to take a dip inland in this western end of Cantabria, the first town south of San Vicente is **Cabezón de la Sal**, a town where the *pozos de sal* – 'salt wells' – have been mined since before the Romans came. Cabezón is little more than an industrial centre, but nearby both the landscapes and the area's modest attraction remind you of Cantabria's more rural side: at **Carrejo**, the **Museo de la Naturaleza** has exhibits of local flora and fauna in an 18th-century *palacio* (*open Apr–Oct Tues–Sat 11–2 and 4–7, Sun 11–2, rest of the year Tues–Sat 11–2 anad 4–6*). Beyond that come two rather refined villages, each with a number of fine mansions and other works: **Ruente** and **Bárcena Mayor**. Bárcena especially, on a back road in the mountains, retains a medieval ambience, with arcaded streets, wooden balconies, and woodworkers' shops. Legend claims it as one of the first towns of Cantabria and a stronghold of the *foramontanos*, as they call the mountaineers who resisted the Moors in the Dark Ages; the village has a fountain that goes back to Visigothic times.

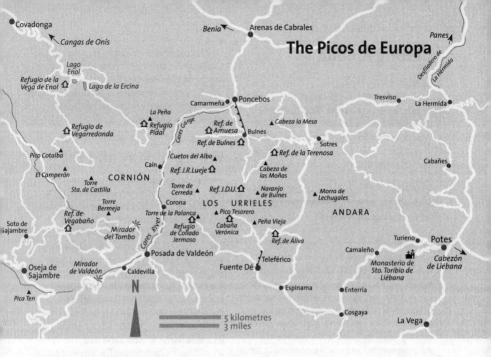

The Picos de Europa

The Picos de Europa

They are not the highest mountains in Spain, or even in the Cantabrian–Pyrenean *cordillera*, but the Picos de Europa have a certain cachet. So many peaks, closely packed in a small area, make a memorable landmark for Spain's northern coast. No one knows the origin of the name, though it may have been that they were the first sight of the continent for Atlantic sailors. To the Asturians they are known as the Urrieles.

Thank Asturian ecologists for their efforts in keeping Spain's most beautiful mountains enchanting and unspoiled: what development there is (ski resorts, hotels) is mostly in western Cantabria. The Picos are divided by rivers into three tremendous massifs – **Andara**, mostly in Cantabria, **Urrieles**, in the middle, and **Cornión**, to the west. The highest peak, **Torre de Cerredo**, stands 8,606ft. But for sheer beauty and rugged grandeur, for the contrast of tiny rural villages in fertile green valleys against a backdrop of sheer, twisted stone peaks snow-crested year round, the Picos de Europa are hard to beat.

The range seems to have been dropped from heaven, especially for hikers; there are trails for Sunday walkers and sheer cliffs for serious alpinists. Hiking boots, however, are universally recommended because of frequent patches of loose shale on the trails and slopes. If you're going for an extended holiday in the Picos, get the detailed maps published by the Federación Española de Montañismo, generally available at Potes, the main base for visiting the mountains. The guide *Picos de Europa* by Robin Collomb (West Col, Reading) is a great help, and up-to-date detailed information on guides, itineraries and mountain *refugios* (free overnight shelters) is available from the **Federación Asturiana de Montañismo**, C/Melquiades Álvarez 16, Oviedo, **t** 98 525 23 62, or online at *www.fempa.net*, the **Federación Cántabra de Montaña**, C/Sánchez Díaz 1,

Getting Around

By Bus

Palomera buses, **t** 94 288 06 11, *www.auto busespalomera.com*, serve Potes up to four times daily from Santander, via Unquera, San Vicente and Torrelavega. There are two buses (one in the winter) daily between Santander and León that stop at Potes and Lebeña. From Potes there are three buses in high season from the central square to Fuente Dé and the *teleférico* (times change according to the season, so check in advance).

By Jeep

Jeeps make the link between the upper station of the *teleférico* to the *refugio de Aliva*. Arenas de Cabrales (in Asturias) is the main hub in the northern Picos, with Land Rover services to Poncebos and Sotres and daily buses to Cangas de Onis and Panes. **4WD jeeps** can be hired in Potes for journeys deeper into the mountains with **Europicos**, *www.europicos.com*, **t** 94 273 07 24, or with **Picostur**, *www.picostur. com*, **t** 94 273 8091, two of several companies offering adventure activities in the region.

Also, a stable in Turieno next to Potes offers several guided riding excursions in the Picos. If you want to do it yourself, Viajes Wences and other firms in Potes rent **mountain bikes**.

Tourist Information

Unquera: (Val de San Vicente) Ctra N-639 Km 279, **t** 94 271 96 80, *turismounquera@ cantabria.org*.

Potes: C/Independencia 12, **t** 94 273 07 87, *turismopotes@cantabria.org*. Try Bustamante, C/Capitán Palacios 10, a photo- and bookshop specialising in the Picos de Europa with a wide range of maps and guides. You can also check out *www.liebanaypicosde europa.com*.

Turieno: National Park Office, Urb. La Molina, **t** 94 273 05 55. The National Park runs free

daily guided walks in summer in the Liébana valley and Cabrales, covering various routes.

Arenas de Cabrales: Ctra General, **t** 98 584 64 84, *turismo@cabrales.org (summer only)*.

There are **markets** in Unquera on Tuesdays and in Potes on Mondays.

Where to Stay and Eat

It may be paradise for hikers, but there's no need to rough it. Nearly every village in the Picos has at least one *casa particular* or *fonda* or a place to camp, and you can purchase supplies or dine out in a traditional restaurant. Every village has its specialities, and the shops under the arches on the main street of Potes are treasure-houses of the mountains' finest; you can buy local cheeses and charcuterie, honey in various original flavours and *orujo*, the clear Cantabrian firewater sold in dangerous-looking bottles all over town. It's made from the stems and pulp of grapes after the wine harvest, like French *marc* or Italian *grappa*.

Potes ✉ 39570

Potes has by far the most accommodation.

★★Infantado, Ojedo (1km from Potes), **t** 94 273 09 39 *(inexpensive)*. Modern, stone-built and one of the best here.

★★Picos de Europa, C/San Roque 6, **t** 94 273 00 05 *(inexpensive)*. A small place run by a friendly, knowledgeable fellow with an adjoining agency for advice on hiking and a range of outdoor activities.

★★Picos Valdecoro, C/Roscabao, **t** 94 273 00 25, *(inexpensive)*. At the top of the list.

★Casa Cayo, C/Cántabra 6, **t** 94 273 01 50 *(inexpensive)*. A modernized mountain hotel, with simple but comfortable rooms overlooking the river and a very popular *comedor* downstairs that serves huge portions.

★Hotel Rubio, C/San Roque 31, **t** 94 273 00 15 *(inexpensive)*. Slightly more expensive, but

Reinosa, **t** 94 275 52 94, *www.fcdme.com*, and the **Delegación Leonesa de Montaña**, Paseo de la Facultad 3, León, **t** 98 725 00 52.

Hiking in the high Picos is practical only from the end of May to October, but even then you may get a soaking – the Picos are only 32km from the rainy Atlantic has rooms in an attractively restored village house. Pets allowed.

★★Hs La Serna, C/La Serna 9, t 94 273 09 24 (*budget*). A budget choice, with good restaurant downstairs.

La Casa del Frama, Frama (8km from Potes), t 94 273 04 65 (*budget*). A lovely stone mountain house with just six pretty rooms and friendly owners.

Posada de Bistruey, La Vega (9km south of Potes), t 94 273 60 95 (*budget*). If Potes is too hectic, head for this peaceful roadside *posada*, run by a friendly family who provide a hearty breakfast, free sweets, and spotless rooms with bath at bargain prices.

Camping El Molino, La Vega, t 94 273 04 89, (*budget*). Offers sites and bungalows in a leafy setting.

El Fogon de Cus, C/Doctor Encinas, t 94 273 00 60 (*moderate*). Has the best name in town for local dishes and Basque cooking. It also has rooms (*budget*).

Paco Wences, C/Roscabao s/n, t 94 273 00 25 (*moderate*). A good place to try the local speciality, *cocido liebaniego*, a hearty stew of garbanzo beans, chorizo, black pudding and anything else that happens to be on hand.

Los Camachos, C/El Llano, t 94 273 0064 (*budget*). For dinner, this place has an honest menu with *fabada*, trout and other local treats.

Fuente Dé ✉ 39588

★★★Hotel del Oso, Cosgaya (12km from Fuente Dé), t 94 273 30 18, *www.hoteldeloso.com* (*moderate*). Amid stunning mountain scenery, this modern but traditionally stone-built place is owned by the famously welcoming Rivas family and the restaurant is perhaps the best in the area.

★★★Parador Río Deva, t 94 273 66 51 (*moderate*). Since 1965, this magnificently sited hotel has been a part of the Picos

experience. A modern building at the end of the *teleférico*, many of its rooms have grand views; the hotel organizes jeep excursions into the peaks, and its restaurant specializes in mountain and Castilian dishes. *Closed mid-Nov–Mar.*

Espinama ✉ 39500

Refugio de Áliva, about 7.5km up from Espinama, t 94 273 09 99 (*budget*). Has a restaurant and 24 rooms available on a first-come, first-served basis. Ring in advance; a Land Rover from Espinama will take you up (or take the *teleférico*). *Open 15 June–30 Sept.* (For other *refugios* in the Picos, ask at the Potes tourist office.)

Arenas de Cabrales ✉ 33554

★★Hotel Villa de Cabrales, Carretera General s/n t 98 584 67 19, *villacabrales@hotmail.com* (*moderate*). Large bright rooms with views of the picos.

★★★Picos de Europa, Ctra General s/n, t 98 584 64 91 (*inexpensive*). The poshest choice here, with smart rooms, a pool and a good restaurant.

La Casa del Chiflón, Bulnes, t 98 584 59 43, *www.casadelchiflon.com* (*inexpensive*). The only places to stay in Bulnes are in *casas rurales* or hostels – this traditional stone-built house has attractive, if simple, rooms and can arrange guided tours and excursions.

Pensión La Perdíz, at Sotres, t 98 594 50 11, (*inexpensive*). Has doubles with bath; two rooms have private balconies and fantastic mountain views.

Casa Cipriano, at Sotres, t 98 594 50 24, *www.casacipriano.com* (*budget*). Run by Cipriano López, the mountaineering mogul of Sotres, come to this simple *pensión* and hostel for information on outdoor activities; the staff can arrange Land Rover taxis and climbing guides. Good hearty stews and *raciones* are served in the bar.

seaboard. Low-level walks can be done at any time of year. Bring warm clothes and a lightweight plastic poncho, a sleeping bag and a food supply for any nights you may spend in the *refugios*, and a pair of binoculars to take in the wonderful array of wildlife and birds.

Potes and the Valley of Liébana

The eastern mountains of the Picos are the most visited and the most accessible. The main entrance from the coast begins at **Unquera** (a FEVE stop on the coast to the west of San Vicente de la Barquera); the N621 from here climbs up through the **Desfiladero de La Hermida**, a dramatic, high, narrow gorge walling in the River Deva, and the hamlet of **La Hermida**, famous in sunny Spain for not seeing *el sol* at all from 26 October to 8 March. The road climbs up from here into the idyllic little valley of the Liébana, more happily fated by geography to have an unusual 'Mediterranean' microclimate. Vines and even olives grow here, though you'll see mostly apple orchards with the vineyards around the first village, **Lebeña**, with its parish church – the 10th-century Mozarabic **Santa María** – signposted south of the village on the N621.

This is one of the finest pre-Romanesque churches, a little jewel in the middle of nowhere that is the perfect expression of the strange little mountainous state of Asturias and, perhaps, its dreams of future greatness. Built in 925 for a Count Alfonso, Santa María is as impressive a work as any of the more famous churches around Oviedo. Most of the exterior was restored a century ago, but the original roof corbels and decorated parts of the exterior are carved with originality, and inside the simple Greek-cross plan – with horseshoe Visigothic arches and not too much regard for precision – is a delight.

A few years ago, the stone step up to the altar was raised and found to be carved with geometric symbols, along with a human figure apparently painted on the stone in blood. The information card the caretaker hands out claims that the stone is 2,000 years old, and carved with Celtic sun symbols; the symbols may be that old, but the stone probably came as the original altar when the church was built. You'll see a photo of a lovely carved wood Virgin, the work of the great Renaissance sculptor Gil de Siloé. Unfortunately the picture is all Lebeña has left; someone nicked the icon in 1993. Two venerable companions, an olive and yew tree, stand next to the church; they were both planted at the time the church was built – over a thousand years ago. **Potes**, the capital of the Valley of Liébana, is the metropolis of the Picos, where you can garner information, catch buses, change travellers' cheques and stock up on supplies. For all the tourist traffic Potes is still a gracious town, with stone arcades to shelter the cafés on the main street and a warren of medieval lanes behind. There are also a number of jeep excursions on offer. The main monument in Potes itself is the 15th-century **Torre del Infantado**, a massive, square defensive-residential work in the centre of town.

The most popular excursions from Potes include the 4km trip up to the **Monasterio de Santo Toribio de Liébana**. Don't miss it, because this is the only place in Cantabria where a visit will earn you an indulgence – time off from purgatory. It is a long-established pilgrimage site, allegedly the home of the world's largest chunk of the True Cross. In the early days of the Kingdom of Asturias the Liébana was a kind of monastic preserve, and this monastery was its centre, founded early in the 8th century. What you see today, though, is mainly Romanesque and Gothic. The 'world's largest sliver of the True Cross' is kept in an ornate Baroque chapel where Masses are said daily. In its earliest days the monastery was ruled by the Abbot Beato de Liébana, whose *Commentaries on the Apocalypse* were popular in Spain throughout the Middle Ages.

Beato de Liébana Defends the Faith

Back in the grim 8th century, when the heathen Normans were attacking from the north, the godless Magyars from the east and the infidel Moors from the south, and the Faith was in gravest peril, just what were the Christians up to? Well, they were arguing amongst themselves as usual. Christian Spain in that age may not seem to have been really big enough to generate a proper theological controversy, but somehow it managed. At issue was something called Adoptionism, the doctrine that Jesus the man was only the 'adopted son' of God. In the far corner, wearing the black trunks, we see Bishop Helipandus of Toledo, then under Muslim rule, who argued for Adoptionism. In the near corner, in the white trunks, stands Beato of Liébana, who isn't about to let anybody say his Saviour does not participate fully in Godhood. Like all such controversies, this brouhaha masked some more mundane conflicts – between the mountaineer Asturians and the more sophisticated Mozarabic Christians of the south, over who was boss in matters of faith and politics. This particular conflict caught the attention of all Western Christianity though, and it found a solution not with the pope in Rome, surprisingly, but at the court of Charlemagne. In those days, if you were lucky enough to find someone with the necessary wisdom and erudition to decide on such a case, he would probably have been (another surprise) an Englishman. The King of the Franks was fortunate enough to have in his services the greatest doctor of Christendom, Alcuin of York, who was busy trying to reform the Carolingian educational system, and with less success to teach Charlemagne how to write his name. In 799 Alcuin pronounced that Adoptionism was just a rehash of the old Nestorian heresy, and awarded a clean decision to Beato, who thereupon retired from the ring of Church politics and went home to write about the End of the World.

Girona and El Burgo de Osma have beautiful 10th-century illuminated editions of the manuscript, but in the cloister here you can see a full set of copies of one of them – mad and brilliant pictorial prophecies from an age when people were convinced the world would soon be meeting its end.

The nearby **mirador de Santo Toribio** takes in splendid views over the Andara massif. Another longer walk south will take you through **Cabezón de Liébana**, where some of the houses have coats of arms, and two medieval bridges cross over to the lovely church of **Santa María de Piasca**, built in 1172 with fine Romanesque carvings on the capitals within. The monastery was shared by monks and nuns, which was typical for the mountains but unusual elsewhere.

From Fuente Dé to Arenas de Cabrales

The classic excursion from Potes is to take the bus west up to the stunning old village of **Espinama** and, 1.6km beyond, to **Fuente Dé**. Here you can catch the *teleférico* for an awesome, vertigo-inducing ride 2,568ft up the sheer cliff to the **mirador del Cable** (*the teleférico runs daily, July–Sept 9–8, rest of the year 10–6; adm; in peak season arrive very early or you'll get stuck waiting, maybe for hours*). Once at the top, walk 4km

(2½ miles) up to the **Hotel-Refugio Áliva**, a modern version of the old mountain refuge; a path from here leads down to Espinama – a pleasant day's circuit, and very popular with gnarly mountain bikers, who consider this one of the best rides in Europe.

From Espinama or the hotel, you can make a longer, more serious hike through the eastern and central massifs north to **Sotres**, a pleasant mountain village in spectacular scenery (jeep excursions also available from Espinama). Sotres has a couple of basic *pensiónes* and places to eat, and makes an excellent base for walks deeper into the mountains; a good one is the 11km (7-mile) haul up to **Tresviso** on the eastern edge of Andara massif, where there's a magnificent view 3,000ft down into the Desfiladero de la Hermida. Most people head west, though, across the Pass of Pandébano and into the majestic central cirque of Los Urriellos; the big landmark in this area is **Naranjo de Bulnes** (Pico Urriellu on some maps), a distinct sheer-sided, tower-like pinnacle, loved and hated by daredevil alpinists. Below the Naranjo, **Bulnes** is a classic mountain village, set in a steep green valley surrounded by towering cliffs; until recently, the only way to get there was to walk, but in 2001 a funicular was finally built – to the delight of locals and the despair of environmentalists – which links the village with Poncebos (*open daily, 10–12.30 and 2–6, until 8pm Easter Week, July–Sept, trains leave every 30 mins; adm*).

The most important village in the area is **Arenas de Cabrales**, connected by Land Rover with Poncebos and Sotres and the centre of an area renowned for its stinking mountain cheese – 'never matured in manure, never contains worms', the tourist literature boasts. *Raciones* of the stuff are served everywhere, and almost everyone finds themselves trying it before they can get out of town. Hikers will be more interested in the classic traverse of the Divine Gorge from Poncebos, more commonly approached from the south by way of Posada de Valdeón in León province (*see p.202*).

The Asturian Picos de Europa: Cangas and Covadonga

The salmon-filled Río Sella defines the west edge of the western Massif de Cornión. Most easily reached from Ribadesella on the Asturian coast, or through the stunning narrow gorge **Desfiladero de los Beyos** (N625) from León and Riaño, the region lacks the high drama of the mountains further east, but is nonetheless green and tranquil, and for Spaniards constitutes a pilgrimage.

Desperately Seeking Pelayo

Cangas de Onís claims to be the first capital of Christian Spain, where the Asturian kings set up shop right after their victory at nearby Covadonga. The most beautiful things in Cangas are the high **medieval bridge** (erroneously called 'Roman') with its great arch spanning the Río Sella, and the **Capilla de Santa Cruz** (*open Easter Week and June –Sept, Tues–Sun 10–2 and 4–7; closed the rest of the year, but contact the tourist office for guided visits t 98 584 80 05*), where the kings worshipped. It was built over a dolmen, and according to legend its founder was Favila, the successor of Pelayo. The original building may really be as early as the 5th century, though it was completely rebuilt in

Getting Around

By Bus and Taxi

ALSA buses, t 902 42 22 42, www.alsa.es, serve Cangas de Onis several times daily from Oviedo and Gijón with a less frequent service from Llanes and one daily from León. There's a direct bus from Oviedo to Covadonga, or change at Cangas de Onis for services to Covadonga and Arenas de Cabrales. The ALSA website lists seasonal timetables. ALSA also run buses from Arenas de Cabrales to the Bulnes funicular at Poncebos. There are no bus services to Ponga, where you will need your own transport to explore properly. Taxis can be hired in San Juan de Beleño on t 98 584 30 17.

Tourist Information

Cangas de Onís: Jardines del Ayuntamiento, t 98 584 80 05, www.cangasdeonis.com. National Park information at Casa Dago, t 98 584 86 14, in summer. Free guided walks daily from the car park at Lago de la Ercina to areas of the Peña Santa range. There is a Sunday **market**.

Where to Stay and Eat

Cangas de Onís ✉ 33550

★★★★★**Parador de Cangas de Onís**, in Villanueva (2km from Cangas), t 98 584 94 02, cangas@parador.es (*expensive–moderate*). The 12th-century **Monasterio de San Pedro de Villaneuva** is now one of Spain's most luxurious paradores, with palatial guest quarters. The views over the river and Picos are superb, as is the traditional Asturian cuisine.

★★★**Los Lagos**, Jardines del Ayuntamiento 3, t 98 584 92 77, www.loslagos.as (*moderate*). A good choice in the centre of Cangas, in a traditional building with friendly staff and an excellent restaurant 'Los Arcos' (*see below*).

★**Plaza**, La Plaza 7, t 98 584 83 08 (*budget*). Small, friendly, and well located in the middle of town. *Closed Oct–Feb.*

Piloña, San Pelayo 19, t 98 584 80 88 (*inexpensive– budget*). Cangas has pricey hotels and a score of *hostales* where the going rate is about €60 in high season, considerably less the rest of the year; this is one of the more central ones. *Closed Oct–Feb.*

Casa Juan, Avda de Covadonga 20, t 98 584 80 12 (*moderate*). *Fabada* and other Asturian dishes are to be had at this restaurant, open since 1943. *Closed Tues and Wed night and June.*

Los Arcos, Avda Covadonga 17, t 98 584 92 77 (*moderate*). This place is one of the very best in the region, and has established an enviable reputation for its imaginative interpretations of traditional Asturian cuisine.

Sidrería Polesu, C/Angel Tárano s/n, t 98 584 9248 (*budget*). A traditional old *chigre*, full of locals and easily identified by the stench of cider wafting from the doors, with good *raciones* of local meats and cheeses.

Covadonga ✉ 33589

Accommodation here is scarce. several bars and restaurants hang out *camas* (beds) signs along the main road.

★★★**Hotel Pelayo**, t 98 584 60 61, (*expensive in season; otherwise moderate*). Basic and perhaps a bit overpriced.

Casa Priena, Santuario de Covadonga, t 98 584 60 70 (*moderate–inexpensive*). A delightful B&B close to the Sanctuary, with four small, stylish rooms, hearty breakfasts and a decent traditional restaurant, open to the public.

El Colladín, in Llerices, t 98 584 9097 (*inexpensive–budget*). A traditional, antique-filled country house in a tiny village close to the Santuario de Covadonga. Simple rooms and lavish homecooked breakfasts.

El Huerto del Ermitaño, Cruce a los Lagos, t 98 584 61 12 (*moderate*). Surrounded by trees and mountains with a real Alpine feel. Excellent *fabada* and home-made desserts.

Hospedería del Peregrino, 200m below the sanctuary in Covadonga, t 98 5120 55 99 (*moderate*). Has a well-deserved name for its *fabada*, seafood and mountain dishes. Rooms are without bath.

Ponga ✉ 33557

La Casona de Con, Mestas de Con, t 98 594 40 74, www.lacasonadecon.com (*inexpensive*). A wonderful rural retreat in a tiny village 10km easy of Cangas de Onís, in a typical 18th-century farmhouse with stylishly furnished bedrooms and delicious breakfasts.

Fonda Ponga, San Juan de Beleño, t 98 584 30 04 (*budget*). A basic but funky *pensión* above a restaurant.

the 15th (get the key at the Ayuntamiento, and they might
also let you have the key for the cave of Buxu). On a pillar near the entrance, an old
relief shows a cross over a crescent moon, symbolizing the Christians' victories over
Islam. As for the dolmen, it is still clearly visible in the chapel's crypt, carved with
religious symbols.

From Cangas it's 3km north to **Villanueva**, where Alfonso I founded the **Monasterio
de San Pedro** in 746. Recently restored and converted into a parador, it has a 12th-century
doorway, with capitals carved with bear-hunting scenes. East of Cangas, the AS114
follows the narrow valley of the Río Güeña, providing the northern part of the circuit
around the Picos. In Cardes, the **Cave of Buxu** (*open Apr–Sept Wed–Sun 10–12.30 and
4–6.30; Oct–Mar Wed–Sun 9–1 and 3–5; maximum of 25 visitors per day; adm, free Wed*)
contains rare, very abstract paintings from the Solutrian era (20–15,000 BC).

From here it's 10km to **Covadonga**, dominated by an enormous, kitschy 19th-century
basilica. Here Pelayo, supposedly the son-in-law of Roderick, the last Visigothic king,
and 300 followers managed to ambush a small Moorish expedition and defeat them,
according to legend. The Moors, who didn't much care for the climate to begin with,
made the mistake of letting the Christians stay and consolidate their power, preferring
to seek richer spoils in France. Next to the basilica is the **cave** where Pelayo fought
with his back to the wall and now rests in peace in a sarcophagus next to his wife.

From Covadonga it's a beautiful 12km through the national park to the mountain lakes
of **La Ercina** and **Enol**, with the huge Peña Santa mountains as a backdrop. In response
to the huge summer traffic jams, a shuttle bus service (€6/€3 for children) now ferries
the endless surge of families up to the lakes. The bus runs from 10am–7pm from end-
July to mid-September; outside these times you can drive up. On sunny weekends the
lakes pack out with day-trippers, but a stroll around the shore of La Ercina should see
you well away from the picnicking throng, and surrounded instead by wild flowers.
There are plenty of longer walks from the lakes; try the four-hour descent into the
gorgeous **forest of Pome**, home to eagle owls and capercaillie.

A more serious proposition is to hike right across the Cornión massif to 6,340ft
Jultayu, beyond which the mountains collapse precipitously into the Garganta Divina.
In summer there is a frequent bus service from Cangas and Covadonga; the rest of
the year there's just one a day. Back on the AS114, the next village east is **Corao**; nearby
at a place called Abamia, the church of Santa Eulalia has parts going back to the 8th
century, along with fragments of medieval frescoes.

Ponga and the Desfiladero de Los Beyos

South of Cangas de Onís the N625 follows the crystalline Rio Sella towards León,
passing some hidden swimming holes that most people drive straight past; the best
one is near **Ceneya**, a deep ice-blue pool reached by way of a tiny bridge across the
gorge. A couple of miles before Ceneya, in the hamlet of Santillán, the AS261 turns off
to the west and makes its narrow and sinuous way through the *concejo* of **Ponga**, a
little-known and rarely visited land of sparkling brooks, enchanting green valleys and
tiny villages plastered to steep hillsides. A good overview of the area can be had from
the *mirador* of **Les Bedules**, a short walk off the main road 3km beyond Beleño; to the

east, the central ranges of the Picos heave their crests skyward in a crescendo of limestone extravagance; to the west the tranquil Valle de Ponga is dominated by massive, craggy **Tiatordos**. An easy trail continues from Les Bedules into the beautiful **forest of Peloño**; diehards can tackle the ascent of Tiatordos itself, a tough uphill grunt from the village of Taranes for which a guide must be hired. Beyond Les Bedules the road passes through raggle-taggle **Viego** before narrowing to a single lane and dropping steeply to rejoin the main road at Puente La Huera. This is the start of the **Desfiladero de los Beyos**, a narrow cleft through the mountains which Spain's engineers are pleased to announce is the narrowest motorable gorge in Europe. It's an exhilarating piece of highway, threading between cliffs that rise vertiginously to 3,000ft above the canyon floor, with plenty of pullouts and tantalizing views; snow finch and wallcreepers can be spotted flitting around the walls. After six twisting kilometres the road emerges into the wide open Valle de Sajambre, and León province.

The Leónese Picos de Europa

At the southern end of the *desfiladero*, pyramidal Pica Ten dominates the Sajambre valley and its main village, **Oseja de Sajambre**, a pretty place that sees few visitors. Most

Getting Around

By Bus and Taxi
Buses (about five weekly, more in high season) from Cangas de Onis to Madrid pass through Oseja de Sajambre, as does the summer-only service from Cangas to Posada de Valdeón; Posada is also served by daily buses from Riaño, where there is a twice-daily service to León. Beyond the main villages the only transport is by **taxi**; in Oseja **t** 98 774 03 59, or in Posada (for Land Rovers to Caín), **t** 98 774 26 09.

Tourist Information

Posada de Valdeón (National Park information office): Travesía Los Llanos, **t** 98 774 05 49. Free guided walks into the hills around Posada run daily in summer, courtesy of the National Park (call in advance for information).

Where to Stay and Eat

Oseja de Sajambre ✉ 24916
*Hs Pontón, Ctra Nacional 625, **t** 98 774 03 16 (*budget*). Has great views and a good value *menú del día*.

Soto de Sajambre ✉ 24916
*Hs Peña Santa, C/Principal s/n, **t** 98 774 03 95 (*budget*). A lovely traditional *hostal*, with flower on the balconies. The restaurant (for guests only) serves up slabs of *cabrito asado* (roast goat) for a minimum of 6 people, and Asturian stews; information about hiking trails is available next door in the *albergue*.

Posada de Valdeón ✉ 24915
Hs Abascal, El Salvador, **t 98 774 05 07 (*budget*). This offers the most comforts. Posada has several *casas particulares* and some fine *fondas*.
Hs Campo, Ctra Cordiñanes, **t/f 98 774 05 02 (*budget*). Has good-value modern rooms with bath, and wonderful views from the terrace. The cafeteria serves decent stews and *fabadas*.
Pensión Begoña, C/de los Llanos 2, **t** 98 774 05 16 (*budget*). Offers an authentic mountain experience – small and spartan rooms with goatskins on the floor, terrific meals and a warm welcome.
Camping El Cares, Santa Marina de Valdeón, **t** 98 774 26 76 (*budget*). Has 400 pitches and plenty of facilities, including horse-trekking. Open Mar–Oct.

people pass through on their way to the isolated mountain hamlet of **Soto de Sajambre**, high above Oseja and bang in the middle of the Picos' most pristine forest. Soto attracts plenty of hikers, who come to tackle the **Senda del Arcediano**, an epic high-altitude traverse of the Sierra de Beza. The trail can also be walked from its Asturian end in Amieva; this used to be the main route between Cangas de Onís and the *meseta*, and traces of the original paving remain. It takes less effort to wander out through densely wooded territory to **Vegabaño**, where a lonely *refugio* looks out over spectacular views of the central Picos.

Posada de Valdeón

From Oseja its a short drive across the Puerto de Pontón to Posada de Valdeón, chief village of the high Valley of Valdeón and a serenely magnificent place to rest up in before or after the Cares Gorge; here tiny farming villages and their rustic granaries, or *hórreos*, built on stilts to protect their contents from moisture and mice, look like mere toys under the loftiest mountains in the Picos. One of the most stupendous views of these is from the **Mirador del Tombo**, 1.6km from Posada de Valdeón towards Caín, framed by a statue to the chamois goat, an animal occasionally seen in the flesh frisking over the steep slopes. The **Chorco de los Lobos** nearby was used to trap the mountains' most fearsome predator, the now-rare wolf. Across the river is the tiny hermitage of **Corona**, according to Leónese legend the true site of Pelayo's coronation after the battle of Covadonga.

The Divine Gorge

Between Caín and Poncebos, the **Cares Gorge** (better known as simply the 'Garganta Divina') extends north to south across the Picos. It is a spectacular 12km (7-mile) walk over sheer drops down to the Río Cares, made relatively easy by a footpath sculpted into the mountainside (although 80 per cent of all accidents in the Picos de Europa happen here, so make sure you are well prepared for the trek). The classic approach is from **Caín** in the south, itself linked to Posada de Valdeón by a regular four-wheel-drive service. Walking south from **Poncebos** isn't much more strenuous – but you risk either spending the night in Caín, which has limited lodgings, or walking the 9km (5½ miles) further south to sleep in Posada de Valdeón.

Asturias

The Asturian 'Costa Verde': East to West 206
Gijón and Avilés **211**
Oviedo **214**
Southern Asturias 218
Asturias' Western Coast 224

Asturias

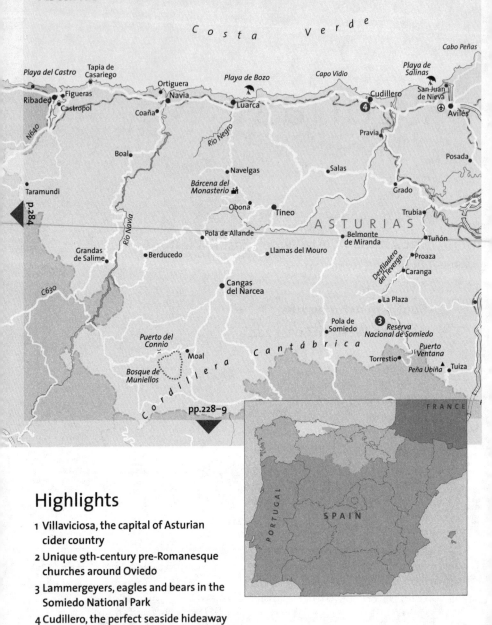

Highlights

1 Villaviciosa, the capital of Asturian cider country

2 Unique 9th-century pre-Romanesque churches around Oviedo

3 Lammergeyers, eagles and bears in the Somiedo National Park

4 Cudillero, the perfect seaside hideaway on Asturias' dramatic coast

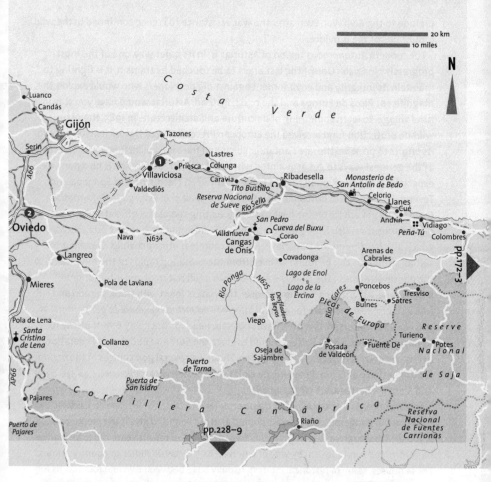

The Principality of Asturias is the Spanish Wales, a rugged country of stupendous mountains, mines and a romantically beautiful coastline. The inhabitants have traditionally been a hardy lot, beginning with the Iberian tribe of Astures, after whom the province is named, who defied both the Romans and Visigoths. Yet the proudest date in Asturian history is 718, when a band of Visigoths, led by the legendary Pelayo, defeated the Moors in the mountain glen of Covadonga, officially beginning the Reconquista and founding the first tiny Christian kingdom in Muslim Iberia. Their beautiful churches are Asturias's chief artistic patrimony; the language they spoke, *el Bable*, or 'Babel', survives only as a dialect against the modern dominance of Castilian, its direct descendant.

Since the 14th century, the Spanish heir-apparent has borne the title of 'Prince of Asturias', a practice initiated by John of Gaunt when his daughter married the son of Juan I. Not long after, Asturias fell into an obscurity that lasted centuries. The discovery of iron ore and coal in the 19th century rapidly transformed its traditional agricultural economy into a mining one with radical tendencies. These brought about the second great date in Asturian history: an epic miners' revolt in October 1934 that served as a prelude to the Civil War. Even after the war, resistance to Franco continued in the wild mountains of the province.

The modern autonomous region of Asturias is, in its quiet way, one of the most progressive in Spain. One of the last areas to be touched by tourism, it is fighting to maintain its integrity and environment against big developers who would exploit the magnificent Picos de Europa and the coast; instead, Asturias would have you stay in a rural village, to learn something of its culture and architecture. In 1985, the Asturian wildlife protection fund received the European Preservation of Nature (FAPAS) prize for its efforts to preserve the rare Cantabrian bear and the capercaillie from extinction. One of the gentlest ways to get acquainted with the Asturian countryside is on a pony trek, especially along the Roman road of Lamesa, between the districts of Somiedo and Teverga (*see www.cuadrosobia.com, or call* **t** *63 054 42 41 in Teverga for information*). Cyclists can get advice on the best routes by visiting the useful official website, *www. infoasturias.com (*also in English*) or calling their information line on* **t** *902 300 202,* which also has tips on the National Parks and countless other activities. Canoeing to suit all standards can be found all over, from the tumbling rapids of the mountains to the gentle streams in the valleys – Asturias has a full national and international programme. Asturias is a fishing paradise; the waters teem with trout, salmon and eel (*see www.infoasturias.com for general information including where to get permits*). If you like your watersports with a flavour of salt, head for the gusty Bay of Biscay for sailing and windsurfing. Surfers should contact the Surf and Bodyboard Federation (*www.costasurf.com/fsbpa*) based in Gijón. There are several golf courses in the region, including those at Gijón (Real Club de Golf Castiello, *www.castiello.com*, **t** *98 536 6313*) and Siero (La Barganiza, **t** *98 574 24 68*).

At least once, visit an old Asturian *chigre* or *sidrería* to taste the local poison, *sidra* (cider) – natural but dangerous stuff always poured at arm's length to give it the proper bounce. If you drink enough of it, it even begins to taste good. In recent years the principality has promoted rural tourism by way of a network of 'Casas de Aldea' or country homes. These houses, some of historical interest, usually have between two and four rooms for rent, with meals also available. An official guide to these homes is put out each year and is available at any tourist office.

The word *pola* in this chapter is the local Asturian word for *pueblo* (village).

Note that although the Picos de Europa are partly in Asturias, the whole range has been grouped together in **Cantabria and the Picos de Europa** *(see pp.198–202).*

The Asturian 'Costa Verde': East to West

Although the Picos de Europa attract mountaineers and hikers from all over the world, the very attractive coast of Asturias sees relatively few foreigners. There are over 50 sandy beaches, most of them on unmarked roads just off the main coastal highway; some have spectacular locations, and a few can offer relative peace and quiet even in the middle of August. It's a mountainous and rugged coast for the most part, and the lack of a good road along it (until recently) has kept development to a minimum.

Llanes

This eastern section of the coast is well endowed with beaches and quiet coves, especially around Llanes, the first sizeable town. Llanes gets busy in summer – in fact when this agreeably funky old town becomes loaded with *madrileños* it becomes charmingly anarchic. Llanes is so popular because the coast around it contains some of the best beaches in Asturias: the town beach, El Sablón, is a pretty arc of golden sand, but it's small and quickly fills up in summer. Head east for bigger beaches near two pretty villages. At **Cué**, signs point to the less frenetic Playa de Toró, set among pinnacle-like rock formations; at **Andrín**, 3km further, you can find two good beaches not yet crowded and commercialized: Playa de Andrín and Playa de Ballota. The area's two antiquities lie east of Llanes: near Vidiago and the Playa de France, there's a peculiar Bronze Age monument called **Peña-Tú** or the 'Cabeza del Gentil' (Gentile's Head). Even older are the cave drawings in the **Cueva del Pindal** near Colombres, featuring the only known painting of a mammoth in Spain (*open Wed–Sun 10–2 and 3.30–4.30; adm, a maximum of 200 people per day are allowed in; guided tours in Spanish*).

West of Llanes, at **Celorio**, the unspoiled Playa de Borizu faces a small islet you can swim to, and you can find another string of beaches, some ideal for children, around the charming village of **Niembro**, along with the ruins of a 12th-century monastery, San Antolín de Bedo. For more isolation, try the **Playa de Torimbia**, situated in a perfect crescent of cliffs and accessible from a path down the rock face.

Ribadesella

The next town, Ribadesella, at the mouth of the meandering Río Sella, makes an excellent base for forays along the coast or into the western Picos. Split in two by the river and bridge, with a picture-postcard backdrop of mountains, Ribadesella has a handful of old streets, a long protected beach, and plenty of chances for hiking, pony trekking, canoeing and fishing. The beaches lie just across the Sella to the west of town. Just outside town are the stalactitic **Tito Bustillo Caves**, where some 15–20,000 years ago the residents painted the walls with stylish animals and humans in the Altamira fashion, worth a visit although their sienna, purple and black tones have faded (*t 986 86 11 20, open end-Mar–early-Sept Wed–Sun 10–4.30; adm, free Wed*).

Farther west, into what is officially known as the 'Costa Verde', you'll find quiet beaches in the tiny hamlets of **Caravia** (Baja and Alta), and near **Colunga**: **La Isla**, **La Griega** and **Lastres**. You'll also find evidence of Asturias' Jurassic inhabitants – fossilized shells, tree trunks, and dinosaur tracks – all along the coast between Ribadesella and Villaviciosa. The best-preserved remains are around Playa de la Griega near Lastres, including footprints left in the coastal mud by giant sauropods. Overlooking the beach, you can find out more in the slick new **Museo del Jurásico de Asturias** (*www.museojurasicoasturias. com, open Easter Week, July–Sept daily 10.30–2.30 and 4–8, rest of the year Mon 10.30– 2.30, Wed–Sun 10.30–2.30 and 4–7; adm*), with huge bones and dinosaur skeletons, models and plenty of interactive exhibits. Equally renowned for its clams and *sidra*, Lastres's stack of red-tile-roofed houses and noble mansions overlooks one of Asturias' most picturesque fishing harbours.

Getting Around

By Train and Bus

FEVE trains along the coast take in much of the marvellous scenery. Two trains a day run between Santander and Oviedo, with stops at Unquera, Colombres, the beaches at Nueva and Villaharmes and Ribadesella; a further two a day go from Oviedo to Llanes.

To continue west up the coast from Ribadesella, you take a Gijón-bound bus. FEVE has frequent connections between Gijón and Avilés, and west to Cudillero, Luarca, Soto de Luiña and Ortigueiro. ALSA buses link all these towns with Oviedo as well, while RENFE links Gijón with Oviedo, Madrid, Barcelona and the rest of the peninsula.

FEVE timetables and information at *www.feve.es*, t 94 220 95 22 (Santander),t 98 534 2415 (Gijón) and t 98 529 7656 (Oviedo).

By Car

Turning the old N632 along the coast into the big A8 motorway has been the biggest road project in this region for some years. Most of it is already finished and driving is not a problem.

Tourist Information

Llanes: Alfonso IX, La Torre t 98 540 01 64, f 98 540 19 99, *www.venallanes.com*.
Ribadesella: El Muelle, t 98 586 00 38 (*summer only*), *www.ribadesella.com* .
Villaviciosa: Parque Vallina, t 98 589 17 59 (*summer only*), *www.villaviciosa.es*

There are **markets** in Llanes on Tuesday; in Ribadesella and Villaviciosa on Wednesday.

Where to Stay and Eat

Llanes ✉ 33500

★★★Don Paco, Parque Posada Herrera, t 98 540 01 50, *www.llaneshoteldonpaco.com* (*moderate*). In a graceful 17th-century palace; it's quiet, with a garden, and the main hall is now an elegant restaurant, serving mostly seafood. *Closed Nov–Mar.*
★★★Hotel Sablón, El Sablón, t 98 540 07 87, f 98 540 19 88 (*moderate*). Perched on the rocks above the Playa El Sablón, with comfortable rooms and a restaurant with panoramic terrace.
★★★Montemar, C/Genaro Riestra 8, t 98 540 01 00, *www.hotelesmontemar.com* (*moderate*). A classic 1960s' block overlooking the beach, with modern, comfortable rooms with TV and other amenities.
★★★Posada de Babel, La Pereda (4km from Llanes), t98 540 25 25 , *www.laposadadebabel. com* (*moderate*). An elegant country house in its own tree-filled grounds, with stylish rooms (including the glassy ultra-modern 'Cube') and a wonderful restaurant for hotel guests only.
★★★La Posada del Rey, C/Mayor 11, t 98 540 13 32, (*moderate*). One of the nicest places to stay in the old quarter, its stylish modern rooms occupy a converted 16th-century town house. Charles V stayed next door on his way to Santander, hence the 'del Rey'.
★★Hotel Quinta, in Cué, t 98 540 10 11, *www. laquintallanes.com* (*inexpensive*). Both Llanes and the villages near the beaches have lots of inexpensive accommodation, such as this good-value place in the pretty village of Cué.
★★Pensión La Guia, Pza de Parres Sobrino, t 98 540 25 77 (*inexpensive*). Has decent rooms in a lovely old building on a square in the centre of town.
Casa Moran, at Puente Nuevo (on the road from Posada to Robadella), t 98 540 6093 (*moderate*). In season there are some wonderful instant restaurants, nothing more than a roof and a few tables, where you can get anything finned at bargain rates.Not far from Llanes, try this popular place with a traditional menu featuring items like *fabada asturiana* and roast lamb. *Closed Tues.*
El Jornu, C/Cuetu Molín 43, Pancar (1km from Llanes) t 98 540 1615 (*moderate*). A much-loved local classic, with traditional dishes like rice with clams and freshly grilled fish of the day served out on the terrace. It also rents apartments. *Closed Sun eve, Mon, Nov.*
El Pescador, C/Manuel Cué 4, t 98 540 22 93 (*moderate*). Serves wonderfully unusual seafood dishes (for example, try the sea urchin omelette), with décor and music to match.
Mesón El Galeón, C/Mayor 28, t 98 540 16 50 (*moderate–budget*). It may look ordinary but the chef is superb and creative. Try the goat's cheese salad with pine nuts as a starter.

Ribadesella ✉ 33560

Ribadesella has more accommodation than most villages around the coast.

****Gran Hotel del Sella, La Playa, **t** 98 586 01 50, *www.granhoteldelsella.com* (*expensive–moderate*). A posh, air-conditioned, beachside hotel in a converted palace, once belonging to the Marquesses of Argüelles. With a pool, tennis courts and garden – a bit of Costa del Sol luxury on the Atlantic. *Open Apr–Sept.*

***Ribadesella Playa Hotel, C/Ricardo Congas 3, **t** 98 586 03 69, *wwww.ribadesellaplayahotel.com* (*moderate*). A grand residence from the turn of last century, this hotel has a lovely waterfront location on the peninsula and rooms with all modern luxuries. *Closed Nov–Mar.*

Casa de Paloma Castillo, La Playa, **t/f 98 586 08 63 (*moderate–inexpensive*). A charming seaside villa from 1910 set in gardens overlooking the beach, this is an exquisite little hotel with just a handful of rooms. *Closed mid-Jan to mid-Feb.*

*Boston, C/El Pico 7, **t** 98 586 09 66, *bostonasturias@eresmas.com* (*budget*). Good-value doubles with bath.

La Huertona, C/de la Piconera 2, **t** 98 586 05 53 (*expensive–moderate*). On the edge of town, this lovely restaurant sits on the banks of the river and serves superb local cuisine, including seafood and a fine *fabada*.

La Parrilla, Av Palacio Valdés 33, **t** 98 586 0288 (*moderate*). Ribadesella's favourite restaurant: wonderfully fresh fish and shellfish is served simply grilled. Reservations essential.

Sidrería Corroceu, facing the harbour (*budget*). The place to go for tapas and cider; noisy and convivial.

Lastres ✉ 33330

This growing resort can still be your best bet for a peaceful place to spend a few days. There are *casas particulares* and rooms over bars.

***Hotel Palacio de Vallados, C/Pedro Villarta s/n, **t** 98 585 04 44, *www.palaciodevallados.com* (*moderate–inexpensive*). A restored 16th-century palace with lovely lounge but somewhat spartan rooms overlooking the port.

Hotel Eutimio, C/San Antonio s/n, **t/f 98 585 00 12, *www.casaeutimio.com* (*moderate*).

This lovely old stone residence has individually decorated rooms with views over the sea.

Casa Eutimio, C/San Antonio s/n, **t** 98 585 00 12 (*moderate*). Something of a tradition round these parts, serving a marvellous *sopa de marisco* and other seafood delights.

Tazones ✉ 33330

*Hotel El Pescador, San Miguel 6, **t** 98 589 70 77 (*inexpensive*). Has pleasant rooms in an old harbourside house with views across the port; the restaurant serves the usual array of seafood, or you could try one of the myriad similar places along the main drag.

Villaviciosa ✉ 33300

It may be a couple of miles away from the beach, but this is an agreeable place to stay.

La Casona de Amandi, at Amandi, **t** 98 589 01 30 (*expensive*). A *casa de indiano* (a house built by a returned emigrant to the Americas); now a very charming nine-room hotel in a lovely formal garden. The owners dealt in antiques and the rooms are full of their finds.

****La Corte de Lugás, Lugás, **t** 98 589 0203, *www.lacortedelugas.com* (*expensive–moderate*). A beautiful stone country manor, with large, elegant rooms (some with four-poster beds) and a fine restaurant.

***Casa España, Pza Carlos I, **t** 98 589 20 30, *www.hcasaespana.com* (*inexpensive*). Occupies a converted *casa de indiano* in the monumental centre of town, with antique-furnished rooms and a pleasant café on the plaza.

Carlos I, Pza Carlos I, **t 98 589 01 21 (*inexpensive*). A handsome hotel in a 17th-century *palacio* in the centre. *Closed during the week Nov–Mar.*

*Manquín, Plaza Santa Carla 2, **t** 98 589 05 06, *www.hotelmanquin.com* (*inexpensive*). Has quiet rooms and a restaurant on a pretty square with a fountain; seafood and properly poured cider.

Sol, C/Sol 27, **t** 98 589 11 30 (*budget*). Pleasant rooms at bargain rates with spit'n'sawdust bar below.

Sidrería La Oliva, C/Eloisa Fernández 6 (*budget*). A friendly and atmospheric *sidrería* (one of many), full of local families, couples and friends knocking back cider and filling up on satisfying *raciones*.

There is a small beach at the village, but a better one just to the west at **Rodiles**, a half-mile of sand lined with eucalyptus trees, very popular in season. Some rare Asturian horses, descendants of the hardy creatures used by the Romans for mountain duty, survive in the **Reserva Nacional de Sueve**, 3km south of Colunga, where you'll also find the **Mirador del Fito** with splendid views of the Picos de Europa and the coast. There is a small pre-Romanesque church, built in 921, in the village of **Priesca**, off the N632 or the A8 12km west of Colunga.

Villaviciosa

Apple orchards line the coast around Villaviciosa, and as you enter the town you'll pass a sign welcoming you to the 'Apple Capital of Spain'. They grow every sort of apple around here, but most common are the ones that feed the town's dozen cider manufacturers. No town makes more of Asturias's favourite sauce, and none seems more devoted to drinking it – particularly during the Fiesta de la Manzana, held every year in mid-October. Every warm evening the tables go out from *chigres* (cider bars) onto the streets around the market, and the noise goes on half the night. Children run around; cider is splashed everywhere. You can visit El Gaitero (*t 98 589 01 00, www.gaitero.com; open June–Sept, Mon–Fri 10–12.30; tours include a tasting*), one of the most famous cider manufacturers. (The tourist information office has a list of others which also offer tours.)

O villa más viciosa, as an old drinking song chides it, is really a quite pleasant place, with a lively centre built around the Parque Vallina, and a small collection of old streets and palaces, including the attractive 13th-century **Santa María de la Oliva**. Not much has changed since 1517, when Villaviciosa became the first town in Spain to see the handsome but all-too-intense face of their new king, Charles V, who was sailing to Santander from his home in Flanders and was blown off course. There is a plaque on the house where the king stayed to mark the biggest surprise in Villaviciosa's history. If you want to swim, there are two beaches near Villaviciosa: long **Rodiles**, facing the sea and the *ría*, and, across the *ría*, **Tazones**, a picturesque fishing village on a little cove.

Villaviciosa was a more important town a thousand years ago than it is today, and though nothing from that time survives in the place, its surroundings have a number of early Asturian churches that can serve as an introduction to the better-known pre-Romanesque churches around Oviedo. One kilometre south, signposted off the O121, the Romanesque San Juan de Amandi (*open Tues–Sun 11.30–1.30 and 5.30–7.30*) is noted for its beautiful sculpture: graceful geometric patterns on the portal and the usual vigorous but mystifying scenes on the capitals. The lovely rounded portico was added in 1796. Other churches can be sought out in the nearby villages of Ambás and La Piñeda.

Valdediós was probably an ancient site from the earliest times, and in the days of the Kingdom of Asturias it was the religious centre of the region. Nine kilometres southwest of Villaviciosa, in the pretty Puelles valley, it contains two separate churches. The oldest is the oratory of **San Salvador** (*open Tues–Sun 11–1 and 4–6; adm*), built in 893 by Alfonso III. It's an interesting building, one that shows some of the influences behind Asturian architecture. The top still shows a memory of Roman times with its neat classical pediment, though below this has been amplified into a basilican-style three-aisled church. The windows have stone latticework and *ajimeces* (mullioned windows) derived from al-Andalus. A Cistercian monastery was later built nearby, around the 11th-century basilica of **Santa María** (better known as El Conventín); the glorious Romanesque portal and the apse survive from the original building, though most of the interior is much later. The monastery is still in use, and the church interior, usually shut off behind an iron *reja*, glitters like a cave of mystery with its gilt Baroque *retablo* and other furnishings – an effect heightened when the organist monk is practising.

Gijón and Avilés

With some 270,000 people, Gijón (pronounced Hee-Hon) is the largest city in Asturias and a major industrial centre and port, a salty, slightly gritty town with few sights but plenty of personality. Built on a rock projecting from the sea called the Cimadevilla, Gijón goes back to the Romans and possibly the Phoenicians – Cimadevilla is often referred to as the 'atalaya'. When coal began to boom it grew into one of Spain's biggest ports. It was the home of the Enlightenment reformer Jovellanos. Parts were almost totally rebuilt after the Nationalists devastated it in the Civil War. Lately, regionalists have painted over the road signs to remind us that the Asturian spelling, is *Xixón*.

What sets Gijón apart are the excellent beaches stretching east from the Cimadevilla. Lined with the slick *urbanizaciones* of the newer town, they give the industrial city a carnival air in the warm months – hordes of locals, mostly red as lobsters, decorate the beaches in a way reminiscent of Reginald Marsh's famous caricatures of Coney Island.

Almost everything worth seeing in Gijón is within walking distance of Cimadevilla, starting with the birthplace and home of the city's most famous reformer, the 16th-century **Museo Casa Natal Jovellanos** (*www.jovenallos.net, open July–Aug Tues–Sat 11–1.30 and 5–9, Sun 11–2 and 5–8; rest of the year Tues–Sat 10–1 and 5–8, Sun 11–2 and 5–7; free, audio guide €3.10*). As well as a collection of Jovellanos' belongings, the museum has a good cross section of 19th- and 20th-century Asturian painting and a selection of sculptures by José María Navascués. However, what everyone comes for is the *Retablo del Mar* by local woodcarver Sebastian Miranda, a misty-eyed evocation of a fishing port that takes up a whole wall. Old photographs next to the *retablo* suggest that Miranda mellowed with age – his original, carved in the 1930s and destroyed in the Civil War, was full of leering faces and grotesque posture, a stark contrast to his 1970s version.

There's not much else to see in Cimadevilla, which suffered greatly in the Civil War. The *atalaya*, also called the hill of Santa Catalina, has a park overlooking the sea, with the obligatory sculpture by Eduardo Chillida; this one's called *Elogio al Horizonte*, 'Tribute to the Horizon'. The rest of the hill is taken up with an abandoned cigar factory where *farias*, the most noxious of smokes, used to be made. The centre occupies the isthmus leading to the newer quarters; there you will find the enclosed and arcaded **Plaza Mayor**, surrounded with restaurants and cafés. Behind it, and cleverly landscaped underground, are the **Termas Romanas**, part of a 2nd-century baths complex notable for its underfloor hypocaustal central heating. Computer animations explain how the baths worked (*open July–Aug Tues–Sat 11–1.30 and 5–9, Sun 11–2; Oct–Feb Tues–Sat 10–1 and 5–7, Sun 11–2 and 5–7; Mar–June and Sept Tues–Sat 10–1 and 5–8, Sun 11–2 and 5–7; adm*).

Getting Around

By Air

There is an airport (the Aeropuerto de Asturias) 14km west of Avilés near Piedras Blancas, t 98 512 75 00; daily flights to Madrid, Barcelona and Malaga, and three weekly flights direct to London with Iberia, plus daily flights in summer (four times a week in winter) to London Stansted with easyJet. ALSA buses link the airport with Gijón, Avilés and Oviedo.

By Train and Bus

There are frequent FEVE trains to Avilés and Cudillero, t 98 552 57 13 or www.feve.es, hourly RENFE services to Oviedo and less frequent long-distance RENFE trains to León and Madrid (t 902 24 02 02 for timetables and reservations). The FEVE and RENFE stations are close together on the Avda de los Telares on the edge of town. The main bus station is also here, with services (ALSA is the main bus operator) to Oviedo, into the mountains of Asturias, and along the coast as far as San Sebastián and Galicia.

By Car

Finding a place to park can be a problem in the centre of Gijón. If your hotel doesn't have parking, there is a convenient garage under Plaza 6 de Agosto. For a taxi, t 98 514 11 11.

Tourist Information

Gijón: General information on Asturias at C/Marqués de San Esteban 1, t 98 534 60 46. Municipal information is available from InfoGijón, in the port, t 98 534 17 71, www.info gijon.com, who also have a series of booths scattered along the beaches and waterfront;

they organize free daily walking tours in summer. They also sell the Gijón Card (valid three days, €15) which offers free entrance to museums, plus unlimited local bus travel and discounts in some shops and restaurants. Avilés: C/Ruiz Gómez 21, t 98 554 43 25.

Gijón's post office is on Plaza 6 de Agosto; For Internet access, try Clickea, Avda Pablo Iglesias 39, or Ciber del Muelle, on the harbour.

There is a market daily in Gijón at La Camocha, C/La Camocha s/n and in Avilés on Mondays, and a Sunday morning flea market in the car park of Estadio El Moliñón, in Gijón's eastern suburbs.

Where to Stay and Eat

Gijón ✉ 33200

There are plenty places to stay in Gijón and also some of the best restaurants in Asturias.

★★★★Parador Molino Viejo, in the pretty Parque Isabel La Católica, t 98 537 05 11, gijon@parador.es (expensive–moderate). An old mill with a modern annexe, it has the best rooms in town and all the usual facilities (except a pool, but the beach is a 10 min walk). It serves Asturian food in its restaurant in the old mill.

★★★Asturias, Plaza Mayor 11, t 98 535 06 00, www.hotelasturiasgijon.com (moderate). A handsome old building with plain rooms but grand public spaces in the historic centre.

★★★Gran Hotel Jovellanos, Porceyo s/n, t 90 252 50 00, www.granhoteljovellanos.com (moderate). Offers history along with modern comforts: built to house the great reformer's Asturian Institute of Navigation and Mineralogy, renovation work turned up remains of Cimadevilla's original Roman walls, which can now be seen in the fancy restaurant. Next door is one of the city's

This is the start of the main beach, the **Playa de San Lorenzo**. At the other end, in the **Pueblo de Asturias** (Paseo Dr Fleming 877, bus no.10, Tues–Sat 10–1 and 5–8, until 9 in July and Aug, Sun and hols 11–2 and 5–7; adm) on the far side of the Río del Piles, there is a display of traditional Asturian architecture, from sidrerías and hórreos (raised granaries) to 18th-century farmhouses: one contains the **Museo de la Gaita**, which displays a host of bagpipes from Celtic northwestern Spain and around the world, as well as a workshop.

If you have children, you'll probably end up at the **Museo del Ferrocarril** (open July– Aug Tues–Sat 10–2 and 5–9, Sun 11–2 and 5–9; rest of the year Tues–Sat 10–2 and 4–8, Sun 11–2 most popular *chigres*, a good place to begin the evening's festivities.

**Hotel Miramar, C/Santa Lucía 9, t 98 535 10 08, *www.greencom.net/h.miramar* (*moderate*). Gracious town house bang in the centre with tasteful revamped décor.

**La Ermita de Deva, C/San Antonio, Deva (3km from Gijón), t 98 533 34 22, *www.hotel-laermita. gijon.com* (*moderate–inexpensive*). A lovely country hotel, with just a handful of pretty rooms, a café-bar and welcoming owners.

**Castilla, C/Corrida 50, t 98 534 62 00 (*inexpensive*). Has smart modern rooms with bath on the classiest street in Gijón; good out-of-season rates.

**Hs Manjón, Plaza del Marqués 1, t 98 535 23 78 (*budget*). Friendly but a bit run-down; some rooms overlook the harbour.

Casa Gerardo, Ctra Nacional in Prendes (8km from Gijón), t 98 588 77 97 (*expensive*). Breathes new life into traditional Asturian cooking, with innovative dishes like *rodaballo en aceite de canela* (turbot in cinnamon oil) accompanied by tomato marmalade happily sharing a menu with old favourites like *fabada*. *Closed Mon and eves from Sun–Thurs, plus three weeks in Jan.*

Las Delicias, Camino de las Dalias (in the suburb of Somió), t 98 536 73 78 (*expensive–moderate*). you'll find this long-established upmarket eaterie, which mixes surf and turf – *lubina al horno* (sea bass from the oven), *medallones de solomillo* (sole), *escalopines de ternera a la sidra* (veal in cider) – and very good service. *Closed Tues.*

La Colegiata, C/Melquiades Álvarez 3, t 98 535 44 35 (*moderate*). Fashionable restaurant and café, good for vegetarians, with an excellent *ensalada primavera* (spring salad). *Closed Sun.*

La Pondala, Avda Dionisio Cifuentes 27, Somió, t 98 536 11 60 (*moderate*). La Pondala has existed for nearly a century. Specialities are the rice and seafood dishes – try the *arroz con almejas* (rice with clams) and the delis *merluza rellena de mariscos* (hake filled with shellfish). There are also plainer options and a good wine list. You have a choice of three smart dining rooms and, in summer, dining on the garden terrace. *Closed Thurs.*

Torremar, C/Ezcurdia 120 (one block back from the beach), t 98 533 01 73 (*moderate*). Come here for something kinder on the pocket but just as interesting to the taste buds; offerings include seafood and Asturian dishes such as *fabes con almejas* (broad beans with clams).

La Galana, Plaza Mayor 10, t 98 517 24 29 (*moderate–budget*). A fine old *sidrería* and restaurant with dark wooden beams and huge barrels.

Sidrería Plaza Mayor, Travesía Jovellanos 10, t 98 535 0938 (*budget*). One of several convivial places around Plaza Mayor; good for a basic dinner.

Avilés ✉ 33400

This unlikely destination has a few good restaurants.

La Capilla, Plaza de España 9, t 98 512 90 80 (*moderate*). Inventive cuisine from an up-and-coming young chef is on offer at this stylish restaurant.

La Fragata, C/San Francisco 18, t 98 555 19 29 (*moderate–budget*). Pause at the bar with the locals, or head to comedor for a wide range of tasty local dishes.

***Hotel de la Villa-Arga, Plaza Domingo Álvarez Acebal 4, t 98 512 97 04 (*inexpensive*). A good, central option in a much-modernised old building.

and 4–8; *adm, free Sun*), in the old Estación del Norte, home to over 50 pieces of rolling stock and other memorabilia from the Steam Age. On Saturdays in July and August, it organises special trips with the FEVE narrow-gauge railway across the road, when an historic train chugs out along the old Langreo rail line to San Vicente and the Museo de la Mineria. Lunch on board is included (€30, reserve on t 98 517 89 29).

Up to Cabo Peñas and Down Again

Between the industrial centres of Gijón and Avilés the Asturian coast juts north-wards for a bit; the coastal road from Gijón may take hours to find, but eventually it will take you out beyond the new port district to **Candás**, an old tuna-fishing village famous for its *corridas marineras* – bullfights on the beach that were unique in Spain, but are no longer practised. **Luanco**, just up the coast, had similar beginnings, but has now become much more of a resort; acres of holiday cottages surround the tidy, small centre. Luanco is famous for lace and embroideries, which you will see in shops and even in the tourist office. There is a small **Museo Marítimo** (*open July and Aug daily 11–2 and 6–9, rest of the year Tues–Sat 11–2 and 5–8, Sun and hols 11–2; adm*) in Calle Gijón, with model ships and old maps. Luanco has two beaches close to the centre, but there are quieter ones around the tip of the peninsula, at **Cabo Peñas**: the prettiest, Playa de Ferrero and Playa de Llumere, are found on either side of the cape.

At the opposite side of the peninsula is **Avilés**, another large and friendly industrial town with disheartening sprawl that includes a dilapidated steel mill covered in red dust, right across the *ría*. But, unlike Gijón, Avilés has a beautiful and well-preserved historic centre worth exploring: this medieval town still has a copy of its *fueros*, its charter of rights, kept proudly in the Ayuntamiento. Look especially for the arcaded **Plaza de España**, and the expressively sculpted 16th-century fountain, **Caños de San Francisco**, in little Plaza San Nicolás, next to the 13th-century church of **San Nicolás de Bari**. Inside, note the tomb to favourite son Pedro Menéndez de Avilés, who founded St Augustine, Florida, the oldest city in the USA. Avilés can be a pretty lively place at night, especially in the *chigres* and clubs around Calle Galiana, on the western side of the lovely town park, the **Parque de Ferrera**. This was the garden of the Marqués de Ferrera, whose refined 17th-century palace still stands at the edge, across from the Ayuntamiento. Just north of Avilés, an old lighthouse guards the entrance to the *ría*, at **San Juan de Nieva**, and a long, gorgeous beach at **Salinas** (an otherwise nondescript modern resort).

Oviedo

The modern capital of Asturias, Oviedo is an elegant and delightful town wrapped around a charming old centre of crooked, tavern-lined streets opening into unexpected squares. Not long ago, the historic core was grimy and neglected, but a determined city council have cleaned it up beautifully, restricting traffic and restoring many of its graceful palaces and churches. It has a fine cathedral, a university almost 400 years old, and two of Europe's most exquisite pre-Romanesque churches, built when the rest of the continent was still living in the Dark Ages. Founded by Fruela I in 757 as a fortress guarding the key road over the mountains to the coast, Oviedo became the capital of Christian Spain when Alfonso II 'el Casto' (the Chaste) built himself a palace in 810, and stayed capital until the Asturian kings conquered León in 1002.

The city suffered terribly in the insurrection of 1934 and during the Civil War. It used to earn a living from the surrounding coal and iron mines, but today Oviedo has its sights firmly set on the tourist euro. It continues to take up a variety of causes – walls are covered with graffiti encouraging the revival of *el Bable*; a helter-skelter mix of pro-choice, 'Viva la Virgen' and 'Europa Blanca' rally posters are pasted side by side on the walls of the numerous *chigres*.

Getting There and Around

By Train

All trains leave from the station at the head of C/Uria in the centre of town. RENFE, t 90 224 02 02, has hourly connections to Gijón and fewer links to Barcelona, Zaragoza, Burgos, León, Pamplona, Madrid, Valladolid and Palencia. FEVE trains, t 90 210 08 18, run east to Santander and Bilbao, and west along the coast to Ferrol.

By Bus

The new Estación de Autobuses is next to the train station, info t 98 596 9696, *www. estaciodeautobusesdeoviedo.com*. ALSA, the biggest company, t 90 242 22 42, *www.alsa.es*, serves destinations throughout Asturias and Northern Spain, as well as Madrid, Sevilla, Barcelona, Valladolid and Valencia; international buses go as far as Paris, Geneva, Zürich and Brussels.

By Car

Parking and getting around can be a pain in Oviedo. Almost all of the old centre is closed to traffic; as a last resort there is a parking garage underneath the Campo de San Francisco.

Tourist Information

'El Escorialín', C/Marqués de Santa Cruz s/n, t 98 522 75 86, *www.ayto-oviedo.es*. The **post office** is on C/Alonso Quintanilla. Cheap **Internet** access is available at Laser, C/San Francisco 9; there are several other cyber cafés, including the Café Cultural, C/Jovellanas 8. There is a covered **market** on Plaza del Fontán. A flea market is held outside on Sundays.

Where to Stay

Oviedo ⊠ 33000

Luxury–Expensive

★★★★★**Hotel de la Reconquista**, C/Gil de Jaz 16, t 98 524 11 00, *www.hoteldelareconquista. com*. A couple of blocks from the Parque de San Francisco, this lovely 17th-century palace has been converted into a super-luxury hotel.

★★★★**Gran Hotel España**, C/Jovellanos 2, t 98 522 2343. Plush and comfortable, this classic hotel is in the heart of the old centre.

★★★★**Gran Hotel Regente**, C/Jovellanos 31, t 98 522 23 43, *www.granhotelregente.com*. Even pricier than La Reconquista, this offers

The Cathedral

The middle of Oviedo (take C/Uría, the main shopping street, from the station) is occupied by the tranquil, shady **Campo de San Francisco** – a typically lavish Spanish city park with fervent memorials to past literati, grand promenades, carefully labelled exotic trees, ducks to feed, and children getting ice cream all over their best clothes. From here C/San Francisco leads to the oldest part of the city, and the asymmetrical Cathedral, an attractive Gothic temple from the 14th century; its lovely tower with its delicate stone latticework is Oviedo's landmark. King Fruela began the first church on this site when he founded the city, and Alfonso el Casto enlarged it, but the current incarnation, recently restored, is a high Gothic work begun in 1388. In the Capilla Mayor look for an enormous florid 16th-century *retablo* of the Life of Christ sculpted by Giralte of Brussels.

Best of all, a door in the right transept leads to the original church of Alfonso el Casto, now known as the **Cámara Santa** (*open Mon–Fri July–Sept 10–8, Oct–June 10–1 and 4–6; Sat all year 10–6; adm to the Cámara Santa only, or combined adm to Cámara Santa, museum and cloister*), strange and semi-barbaric, with fine carvings of the Apostles attributed to Master Mateo on the capitals of the outer chamber and disembodied heads on the walls. The Capilla de San Miguel was built by Alfonso el Casto in 802 to traditional elegance opposite the Monastery de San Pelayo. It is geared towards business travellers, hence good website deals.

Moderate

****Libretto Hotel**, C/Marqués de Santa Cruz 12, **t** 98 520 2004, *www.librettohotel.com*. An elegant Modernista building, now a stylish hotel, with a chic mixture of the contemporary and antique at a very reasonable price.

****M Hotel**, C/Comandante Vallespín, **t** 98 527 40 60, *www.mhotel.es*. An ultra-modern hotel by the Palacio de Congresos, with quirky contemporary rooms and a spa.

***Hotel Vetusta**, C/Covadonga 2, **t** 98 522 22 29, *www.hotelvetusta.com*. An excellent central option, in a traditional building with slick, modern décor and Jacuzzis in some rooms.

Palacio de la Viñona, C/Julián Clavería 14, Barrio Colloto, **t** 98 579 33 99. A graceful 18th-century stone manor on the outskirts, with a garden and beautiful rooms (most with Jacuzzi).

Inexpensive

***Santa Clara**, C/Santa Clara 1, **t** 98 522 27 27. In the centre, this friendly, well-equipped place offers weekend discounts.

Hotel Favila, C/Uría 37, **t** 98 525 38 77. A good family-run option close to the bus and train stations, with immaculate rooms and a decent restaurant (*cheap*) downstairs.

El Ovetense, C/San Juan 6, **t** 98 522 08 40. A welcoming little hotel close to the cathedral, with its own *sidrería* and restaurant.

Budget

****Hs Arcos**, C/Magdalena 32 (just off the Pza de la Constitución), **t** 98 521 47 73. One of the cheapest central options, with rooms with or without bath and very friendly staff.

Hotel Alteza, C/Uría 25, **t** 98 524 04 04. Another reliable, if rather worn, option by the train station. All rooms with bath and TV.

Hs Belmonte, C/Uría 31, **t** 98 524 10 20, *calogon@teleline.es*. Family-run, one of the best of several *hostales* that cluster on and around C/Uría, near the RENFE station.

Pensión Riesgo, C/9 de Mayo 16, **t** 98 521 89 45. Cheap and cheerful rooms with shower, on a pedestrianized street near the centre.

Eating Out

Casa Fermín, San Francisco 8 (near the park), **t** 98 521 64 52 (*expensive*). Although there are plenty of restaurants and tapas bars in

house the relics of Visigothic Toledo rescued after its capture by the Moors, and largely rebuilt in the 12th century. Today it contains the cathedral's precious treasures: the *Cruz de la Victoria*, supposedly borne by Pelayo at Covadonga, and today on Asturias's coat of arms; the *Cruz de los Angeles* (808), a golden cross embedded with huge rubies and carved gems, reputedly made by the angels themselves and donated by Alfonso II; and a beautiful, silver-plated reliquary chest of 1073. Oviedo cathedral was always famous for its collection of relics – a phial of the Virgin Mary's milk and one of Judas's 30 pieces of silver; most of these are kept here too. The museum includes Romanesque sculptures and glittering liturgical plate, and the cloister is pale and lovely. Just off the cloister, the Crypt of Santa Leocadia contains the plain tomb of the 3rd-century, martyr-saint from Toledo. The crypt is part of the ancient cathedral under the Cámara Santa, with a pair of carved Visigothic stone reliefs.

Behind the cathedral the old convent of San Vicente houses the **Museo Arqueológico** (*closed indefinitely for restoration*), featuring finds from the Palaeolithic era to the days of the Asturian kingdom. There are a few attractive old streets to the south of the cathedral around the **Plaza del Fontan**, an enclosed square that was starting to fall down before restoration works were started.

Oviedo, this remains the oldest and the best, offering award-winning Asturian cuisine and seasonal Spanish regional dishes in a refined atmosphere. *Closed Sun.*

La Mar del Medio, C/Mon 18, t 98 522 55 75 (*expensive–moderate*). Has excellent fish and seafood in a suitably nautical ambience; arrive early as it fills up quickly during lunch times, or pop in and try the tasty *pinchos*. *Closed Sun night and Mon.*

El Cabroncin, Ctra Paredes 1 (in Lugones, 2km from Oviedo), t 98 526 63 80 (*moderate*). Drive out to this charmingly rustic *comedor*, and try the inventive interpretations of traditional Asturian cooking; kidney beans with rabbit cutlets and slivers of *calamari*, followed by truly decadent chocolate ravioli smothered in orange cream.

El Raitán, Plaza de Trascorrales 6, t 98 521 42 18 (*moderate*). A classic that specializes in grilled meats along with homemade desserts like the *carbayones* (made with almonds).

Cervantes, C/Jovellanos 4, t 98 522 00 11. (*moderate–inexpensive*). A good choice for traditional fare for forty years.

Villaviciosa, C/Gascona 7, t 98 520 44 12 (*budget*). Hearty Asturian stews and good *fabadas* bubble away at all the *sidrerías* around C/Gascona. This is one recommendation.

Entertainment and Nightlife

Oviedo is the centre of Asturian rock, and you can see what the local groups are getting up to in the desperate-looking clubs all along C/Rosal, one street south of the Campo de San Francisco. Otherwise, the action is on the nearby streets in the old town, with more clubs and bars for the younger set: Pza Riego, Pza del Fontan, C/Canóniga and C/Ildefonso Martínez. The best places for a simple drink are the informal bars around Fontan, where tables magically appear on the street at dusk.

Cervecería Asturianu, C/Carta Puebla 8, Serves every different kind of beer and whisky imaginable, with décor that includes pieces of the Berlin Wall.

Danny's Jazz, La Luna 11. Funky café/bar with live jazz.

El Pigüeña, C/Gascona 2. On this street of *sidrerías*, one of the best to start your evening.

La Real, C/Cervantes 19. A mythical, massive disco, with excellent DJs.

Salsipuedes. A lively disco-bar, which is good for an early evening drink on the outdoor terrace on Ildefonso Martínez. Busy later on.

The Asturian Pre-Romanesque Churches

Oviedo has the finest of Asturias's post-Visigothic pre-Romanesque churches. Enjoying the patronage of its kings, this little capital can claim the beginnings of sophisticated medieval architecture, at a time when most of Christian Europe was still scratching its carrot rows with a short stick. The two most important churches were built on Mount Naranco as part of the palace that Alfonso el Casto built for himself and Ramiro I (842–850) expanded, and it's fascinating to think of these pocket potentates throwing up a summer pleasure-dome in the hills in imitation of the great sultans of al-Andalus.

Some scholars have found a Carolingian influence in their structures, although this is hard to see. The major influence clearly comes from North Africa or the Middle East, via Christian refugees from those newly Islamized countries. The classical pediment common atop Asturian churches was also common there; it goes back to the origins of Christian building, to the basilicas of Constantine and Theodosius in the Greek east. Hints of later Byzantine elements can be seen in many of the details, but this is all – Byzantium was 2,700km away. The only building that has anything in common with Santa María de Naranco and its unusual plan is a unique, mysterious little chapel in central Italy called the Tempio del Clitunno, built a century earlier. Even with these influences, much in these provocative prototypes that never made it to the assembly line is original and beautiful. In 1985 UNESCO declared them the best architecture produced in 9th-century Christian Europe, to be protected as part of the 'Patrimony of Humanity'.

Alfonso el Casto built the oldest of these, **San Julián de Los Prados** (also called *Santullano*), northeast of the centre; C/de Martínez Vigil from the back of the cathedral takes you there (*open Mon–Fri 10–1 and 4–6, Sat 9.30–11.30 and 3.30–5.30; adm, free Mon*). This is a simple, solid building with three square apses, a secret compartment in the wall, and interesting murals by an artist influenced by Roman monuments.

If you're pressed for time, head in the opposite direction up the Cuesta de Naranco, a hill overlooking the town (facing the RENFE station, turn left to the sign at the bridge over the tracks and continue 3km (2 miles); city bus no.10 makes cameo appearances on the hour. Pick it up from C/Uría and get off by the car park at La Cruce). The two churches here, **Santa María de Naranco** (*currently closed for restoration, although you can still view the exterior*) and **San Miguel de Lillo** (*open Tues–Sat 9.30–1 and 3–7, Sun–Mon 9.30–1; adm, free Mon*), can be found halfway up the mountain with a view over Oviedo. Both of these churches were built by Alfonso el Casto's successor, Ramiro I; incredibly, the perfectly proportioned Santa María is believed to have been part of the king's summer palace. Built of a fair golden stone and set in a small clearing, it is an enchanting building, supported by unusual flat buttresses and flanked by two porches. The lower level is believed to have been a waiting chamber and bath; the upper, with a rough-hewn altar on the porch, was the main hall. Inside are blind arches of subtly decreasing height, topped by round medallions. An Interpretation Centre is nearby in an old schoolhouse, where you can organise guided visits and pick up information.

Just up the road, San Miguel is a more traditional cruciform church, although of stunted proportions after an ancient amputation removed two-thirds of the original length. Its round windows are adorned with beautiful stone traceries, and what the guides claim to be a circus scene is carved on the door jamb, along with some Visigothic arabesques.

Southern Asturias

The principality, beyond the coast and the Picos, is *terra incognita* for most foreigners a hilly, wooded land of small mining towns and agricultural villages, crisscrossed with walking paths. Much of it is protected, especially in the national hunting preserves that cover the northern slopes of the Cordillera Cantábrica. The coast is excellent – rugged cliffs, few tourists, and plenty of shellfish and beaches. Public transport is limited in the area, and you'd do well to rent a car – and pack a big lunch – before setting out. Be sure to pick up one of the large detailed maps at the tourist office in Oviedo.

Around Oviedo: Miners' Valleys and More Churches

Southeast of Oviedo, the AS17 passes **Langreo** and **Pola de Laviana**, both typical Asturian copper-mining towns. Langreo is home to the **Museo de Minería y Industria** (*www. mumi.es, open July–Aug Tues–Sat 10–8, Sun 10–2; rest of the year Tues–Sat 10–2 and 4–7, Sun 10–2; adm, see Gijón for information on days out by historic train [Train Museum]*),

Getting Around

By Train

The RENFE train between Oviedo and León stops at Pajares and Pola de Lena; Pola de Lena is linked by frequent *cercanías* (local trains. Call **t** 902 24 02 02 for information and reservations.

By Bus

All the main towns in southern Asturias can be reached by bus. ALSA buses from Oviedo's main bus station, **t** 90 242 22 42, *www.alsa.es*, go to Salas, Puerto de Somiedo, Cangas del Narcea, Tineo and Pola de Allande. Empresa Fernández, **t** 98 523 83 90, has buses to Mieres, Pola de Lena and Turón; there are also a half-dozen or so daily buses down the western coast to Cudillero and Luarca, and as many from Gijón. Alcotán, **t** 98 521 76 17, runs buses to Pola de Laviana.

By Car

If you're driving when the snow is flying, it's essential to call ahead for road conditions, **t** 98 525 46 11. To rent a car, the main companies in Oviedo are along C/Ventura Rodríguez.

Tourist Information

Salas: Pza de la Campa, **t** 98 583 09 88, *www.ayto-salas.es*.
Tuñón: t 98 576 15 34.
Pola de Somiedo: Centro de Recepción e Interpretación del Parque, **t** 98 576 37 58.
Tineo: Calle Mayor, **t** 98 580 01 87 (*summer only*).
Cangas del Narcea: C/Mayor 48, **t** 98 581 14 98, *www.narceaturismo.com*.

There are **markets** in Mieres on Sunday; in Pola de Somiedo on Tuesday; in Tineo on Thursday and in Cangas del Narcea on Saturday.

Where to Stay and Eat

Puerto de Pajares ✉ 33693

★★Puerto de Pajares, Puerto de Pajares, **t** 98 595 70 51 (*moderate*). A little further away from the slopes than La Rectoral de Tuiza, with comfortable basic rooms and central heating.
La Rectoral de Tuiza, in Tuiza de Arriba, **t** 98 545 14 20 (*moderate*). Groups tackling the heights of Peña Ubiña can try something a bit different: set up base in a complete *casa rural* with space for up to six people, in a beautiful setting high up in the mountains (between €90–110 per night for the whole house; only rented out whole).
Albergue Toribión de Llanos, in Brañillín, **t** 98 595 70 40, *www.toribiondellanos.com* (*inexpensive –budget*). Dormitories and some double, triple and quadruple rooms; you can step straight out of the hotel and into the ski lifts.

Mieres ✉ 33600

★★Hotel Rural Cenera, Cenera, **t** 98 542 63 50 (*inexpensive*). Traditional country inn in a tiny village close to Mieres, with comfy rooms and sturdy homecooking in the *mesón* below.
★★Hs Villa de Mieres, C/Teodoro Cuesta 33 (off the Oviedo–León road), **t** 98 546 11 08 (*budget*). Offers good home cooking in modern, smart surroundings.

Salas ✉ 33600

Salas is a convenient stopover on the N634, with a few inexpensive *hostales* over bars. There are basic campsites within the Somiedo Park at Valle de Lago and Saliencia.
★★Castillo de Valdés, Pza Campa, **t** 98 583 22 22, *www.castillovaldesalas.com* (*inexpensive*). A restored 16th-century palace (formerly a castle), with a popular restaurant. Servings include imaginative Asturian dishes, and local salmon.
Casa Soto, C/Arzobispo Valdés 9, **t** 98 583 00 37 (*budget*). Pleasant large rooms in an historic building in the centre.

Pola de Somiedo ✉ 33840

★★Casa Miño, C/Rafael Rey López, **t** 98 576 37 30, **f** 98 576 37 50, *www.hotelcasamino.com* (*moderate*). A comfortable traditional hotel, with nicely furnished spacious rooms and a friendly local bar.
★★Mierel, C/Fernández Álvarez s/n, **t** 98 576 39 93 (*moderate*). Small but perfectly formed, with individually decorated rooms and three apartments for longer stays. The restaurant serves hearty mountain meals and wicked *fabadas*.
Casa Cobrana, in Valle del Lago, **t** 98 576 37 48 (*budget*). A rural *hostal* which also offers good meals, at the head of the beautiful trail to Lago del Valle.

with exhibits on the history of mining; there are scale models of old machinery, a recreated explosives laboratory, and a replica of a copper mine.

Beyond Pola de Laviana the road continues to Reres National Reserve and the beautiful mountain pass, **Puerto de Tarna**. The next pass to the west, **Puerto San Isidro**, has a major ski installation (in the province of León, see *www.san-isidro.net* for information). Both passes can be reached by bus from Pueblo de Lillo in León province. **Coyanzo**, some 12km below the pass, is set near an idyllic little gorge, the **Hoces de Río Aller**.

Directly south of Oviedo, along the train route and recently built highway to León (an engineering feat Spain is not a little proud of), the views become increasingly magnificent as you ascend to the dramatic **Puerto de Pajares**, another ski spot on the border with Léon. But before you get there, look for the signs 6km south of the grim industrial town of **Pola de Lena** for another of Ramiro I's lovely churches, the hill-top **Santa Cristina de Lena** (*open Tues–Sun 11–1 and 4.30–6.30*), a cruciform temple built around 845, with blind arches similar to Santa María de Naranco, Visigothic decorations and an intricate iconostasis of Mozarabic inspiration.

The landmark in this part of the Cantabrian mountains is the jagged-peaked 7,855ft **Peña Ubiña**, which sturdy walkers can tackle in around four or five hours from **Tuiza de Arriba** for incomparable views over the Picos de Europa and Somiedo (to reach Tuiza, take the side road from the highway at Campomanes). From Pajares, you can make the much shorter climb up the 5,580ft **Pico de los Celleros**.

Up to the Cordillera, and Somiedo National Park

Southwest of Oviedo, in the highest part of the Cantabrian mountains, is the **Parque Natural de Somiedo**. This vast wild area stretches from Puerto de Pajares in the east to Pola de Somiedo in the west, encompassing 7,000ft peaks, dense beech and oak forests, and several *brañas*, ancient villages of straw-roofed huts built by the *vaqueros* (*see* p.224). Although not a true National Park – much of Somiedo is protected as a hunting reserve – this is the Cordillera Cantabrica's great wildlife stronghold; it has the healthiest population of brown bears in Spain, and the Iberian wolf is so successful it is considered common. For birdwatchers too it is a paradise: middle-spotted and black woodpeckers make their home in the forests, ultra-colourful bee eaters reach the northern limit of their range on the lower slopes, and wallcreepers flit around the vertical crags. The very fortunate may get a glimpse of the rare lammergeyer or bearded vulture, the largest bird of prey in Europe – a startling sight, with its black wings, fierce expression, and its habit of dropping bones on rocks to get access to the marrow inside. The Spanish call it *quebrantahuesos*, the 'bone-breaker'. There's a park information office in Pola de Somiedo (*t 98 576 37 58, open Easter Week and mid-June–mid-Sept 10–2 and 4–9, rest of the year, 10–2 and 4–7*).

One approach to Somiedo is by way of **Trubia**, a village known mostly for its enormous armament works. Ten kilometres south of Trubia on the road to the park you can stop at **Tuñón** for one of the last of the 'Asturian' churches, **Santo Adriano**, built by Alfonso III (866–910). Sombre in design and Mozarabic in style, it features clerestory windows and pretty latticework crosses. Inside are some of the oldest frescoes anywhere in Spain, traces of what seem to be sun symbols over the altar and zigzag motifs taken

The Dress Rehearsal

The event of the 20th century in Asturias was the epic miners' revolt of 1934, a full-scale battle that eerily prefigured the Spanish Civil War. Because of the large numbers of workers in mining and industry, Asturias was politically the odd man out, an island of belligerent Marxists in the middle of the arch-conservative northwest. Mining and metalworking go way back in Asturias, but really took off at the beginning of the 20th century, when *indianos* forced home by Spain's loss of Cuba and the Philippines began to invest their money here. In the First World War, Spanish neutrality made for a boom in the mining areas, one which collapsed in the 1920s, leaving Asturias with the angriest proletariat in Spain.

Along with the Basques and Catalans, Asturians were strong supporters of the Republic when it appeared in 1931 but, for many of their leaders, the new regime was only a stepping-stone to Socialism. The depression increased popular discontent, but what really set the workers boiling was the radical right-wing national government elected in 1934. Under Prime Minister Gil Robles, it began dismantling all the reforms of its leftist predecessors and openly postured for the restoration of the monarchy. On 4 October 1934 the trade unions declared a general strike in Asturias in protest. Barcelona and Madrid also rose up but failed to follow through, leaving the Asturians on their own and in a fighting mood. The main centres of the revolt were Mieres, Sama and Oviedo, but it was the munitions works at Trubia, near Somiedo, that turned the strike into a war. The workers occupied it and seized some 30,000 rifles inside. Soon there was a 30,000-man 'Red Army', and a revolutionary committee was formed to govern the province.

The government sent in a dependable general named Mola, leading a force made up mainly of Moroccan troops – northern Morocco was still a Spanish protectorate. The Moors were mercenaries who had fought against their own people, but they were fiercely loyal to their commander, a certain Francisco Franco. Franco, a Galician married to an Asturian woman, felt right at home. He had already led troops, using the Spanish Foreign Legion, to crush a general strike in Asturias in 1917. The Legion was also present in 1934. An outfit not much like the romantic French version, this one was now led by a fascist psychopath named Millan Astray, famous for his missing arm and eye-patch. As for the Moors, some of them must have enjoyed the irony of a Spanish commander, an heir to Pelayo, bringing them to a place where they hadn't set foot for a thousand years. The government had to make its point, and the revolt was crushed quickly and with the utmost ferocity. Many of the mining towns were thoroughly wrecked, and the troops slaughtered nearly 1,300 Asturians in reprisals after the surrender on 19 October. A year and a half later, after new elections brought the leftist Popular Front to power, the coup that began the Civil War started with the same cast of characters: General Mola, who was to be the new dictator, but who died in an air crash at the start; the Foreign Legion; and the inevitable Francisco Franco, whose Moroccans won him the title of *caudillo* (leader). The best-equipped and trained forces in Spain, they used their practice in Asturias to get the jump on the disorganized government and citizens' militias, and gained control of much of Spain within a month, an advantage that helped assure the Nationalists' final victory.

straight from the Grand Mosque of Córdoba. Paloma in the tobacco shop opposite has the key, but the only guide is the unusually friendly bat that lives in the choir.

Further south, **Proaza** has a number of medieval buildings; it is separated from the next village, **Caranga**, by a pretty gorge you can walk through, the **Desfiladero del Teverga**. The road continues south through **La Plaza**, site of the interesting 12th-century **Colegiata de San Pedro**, where elements of Asturian pre-Romanesque combine with early French Romanesque; on the capitals are sculpted local animals, and there are two 18th-century mummies.

From La Plaza, the road south cuts through a magnificent forest to the Puerto Ventana, perhaps the least-used Asturian mountain pass. Just on the other side of the pass, from the Leonese village of **Torrestío**, you can hike in three hours into the lovely heart of Somiedo and its mysterious lakes, where *xanas*, or mermaids, guard the sunken treasures they use to please their lovers on the night of St John. The first lake, **Lago de la Cueva**, is the source of the Río Sil; the third and largest is the eerie, dark **Lago Negro**.

A second approach to Somiedo is via the N634, the main road west from Oviedo. This will take you through the village of **Grado**, where everybody comes on Wednesday and Sunday for the markets, and lovely **Salas**, with its medieval monuments and palaces, as well as the fine Renaissance **Colegiata de Santa María**, home to the beautiful alabaster tomb of the Inquisitor Valdés-Salas. The surrounding countryside is rich in picturesque *hórreos* (granaries), and to the west are the lovely pasturelands and hills around **Navelgas** and **Bárcena del Monasterio**, where the *vaqueros* (*see* p.224) winter their herds.

From Salas head south and follow the valley of the Pigüeña towards Somiedo. The big village in this iron-mining area is **Belmonte de Miranda** (C633); a curiosity in the region is the **Machuco de Alvariza** (near Belmonte village), an oak-built hydraulic hammer used in the 18th-century iron works. Many *vaqueros* still live here – some of their conical-roofed *pallozas* (huts), along with several Celtic *castros* (hill forts) lie towards **Pola de Somiedo**, the district's major town (where the Natural Park information office, *see* p.219, is located).

One of the best excursions in this area is to **Lago del Valle**, an easy four-hour ramble through a fantasy valley plucked from the pages of Tolkien; eagles soar above twisted peaks, a dusty road winds through wild flower meadows, and dogs as big as horses stand guard over the livestock. There are a few scattered *pallozas* along the way; a better collection can be found west of Pola de Somiedo in the ancient *braña* of **La Pornacal**, Somiedo's largest and best-preserved *vaquero* hamlet, reached by a farm track from Villar de Vildas. Two kilometres beyond La Pornacal lies the much older **Braña de los Cuartos**, its circular walls in a state of poetic semi-dereliction at the head of the valley.

West of Oviedo: Ancient Pottery and Primeval Forests

Back on the main route west from Oviedo, after Salas the next village is **Tineo**, a great trout-fishing area crossed by a branch of the Santiago pilgrimage route. Several medieval churches survive from that era – Tineo's 13th-century parish church and the ruined monastery and church of San Miguel in nearby **Obona**. Further south, a dirt road leads up to the tiny borough of **Llamas del Mouro**, where potters, isolated from the rest of the world, still create the shiny black ceramic jugs and bowls made by their Celtiberian ancestors. The pieces are fired in the ancient style, in circular ovens buried in the

Where to Stay and Eat

Cangas del Narcea ✉ 33800

Cangas has the widest range of choices in this region.

**Hotel La Casilla, Limés, t 985 81 26 80, *www. hotellacasilla.com (inexpensive)*. A traditional, pretty hotel in a small village just outside Cangas del Narcea plus good local restaurant.

*Peña Grande, Ctra Leitariegos (1km from the centre), t 98 581 23 92 *(inexpensive)*. A comfortable place to stay, with lovely views, flouncy rooms and a large restaurant.

**Pensión Virgen del Carmen, C/Mayor 46, t 98 581 15 02 *(budget)*. Small, with seven good rooms with heating and air conditioning.

*Hotel La Pista, Vega de Rengos (20km south), t 98 591 10 04, *www.hotellapista.com (budget)*. Near the entrance to Bosque de Muniellos, this is a cosy place to stay, with immaculate, bright rooms, a *budget* restaurant and an extremely welcoming owner.

*Hs Acebo, C/Hermanos Flórez 1, t 98 581 05 46 *(budget)*. Has rooms without bath.

Casa Pasarón, C/Moal 12, t 985911247, *www. casapasaron.com (budget)*. Three rustically furnished apartments, each sleeping two, with stone walls and wooden beams.

Tineo ✉ 33870

*Hotel Don Miguel, El Viso, t 98 580 03 25 *(inexpensive)*. Pleasant hotel with good rooms.

**Hs Casa Sole, on the main road, t 98 580 60 44 *(budget)*. Simple and old-fashioned, offering pleasant rooms with or without bath above a café-bar.

*Casa Lula, El Crucero, t 98 580 16 00 *(budget)*. A cosy spot with rooms for around €45.

Where to Ski

Valgrande Pajares, 3km from the Busdongo train station. Offers 15 slopes from the very difficult to the very easy, 10 lifts and two chairlifts. Info at *www.valgrande-pajares.com*.

San Isidro, near Puebla de Lillo (León province). With a total of 23 ski-runs, of which about half are difficult, three chair-lifts and several ski lifts. There are a couple of hotels at Puebla de Lillo (you can book accommodation online), but no public transport. Info at *www.san-isidro.net*.

Lietariegos Pass, San Emiliano. A small ski installation on the slopes of Peña Ubiña. Info at *www.leitariagos.com*.

earth. Only the family of Jesús Rodríguez Garrido continues to make and fire pottery; they sell it too, at very good prices, in a little shop adjacent to the workshop.

Cangas del Narcea, the largest town in southwest Asturias, is modern and has little to waylay you; head instead further south to **Pico de la Masa** (near Puerto del Connio) for the view over the magnificent 5,000-hectare **Bosque de Muniellos**, one of Europe's last and most extensive forests of primeval oak and beech. A strictly protected wildlife preserve, the forest is home to rare species like capercaillie, otter and pine marten, while larger mammals and predators inhabit the area's higher regions; chamois, wolves, and a few itinerant brown bears. There's only one trail through the forest, beginning at **Tablizas**, a short hike from Moal; from here it's a delightful scramble up a ferny green canyon to the edge of the woods, beyond which lie three glorious subalpine lakes. The whole hike takes about five-and-a-half hours and will leave you mourning for the ancient times, when (they say) a squirrel could cross the whole of Iberia without ever touching the ground. Like Altamira, Muniellos is accounted such a threatened treasure that only 20 people a day are allowed inside the forest; make sure you call well in advance (t 98 527 91 00), or submit a petición del permiso de acceso through the website *www.princast.es* (Spanish only), or you can write in advance to the Agencia de Medio Ambiente del Principado de Asturias, 1 Plaza General Ordóñez, Oviedo 33007. East of Muniellos lies the **Reserva Nacional de**

Degaña, another lovely, wooded area, with pretty meadows and small lakes formed by glaciers. In the Roman era Degaña was heavily mined for its gold.

Gold was also mined in the most westerly zone of the province, around **Pola de Allande** and **Grandas de Salime**, both enchanting, seldom visited villages. Grandas has a partially Romanesque church, San Salvador, and a **Museo Etnográfico y Escuela de Artesanía**, with exhibits on country life in old Asturias and craftworkers there in person weaving, making baskets and carving wood. In **Celón**, 5km from Pola, there's a fine 12th-century church, **Santa María**, with impressive frescoes and carvings. One of Asturias' best-preserved Celtic castros is up on **Pico San Chuis** to the west near Berducedo, whose ancient inhabitants, like the modern, exploited the region for its supply of minerals.

Asturias' Western Coast

The Asturian coast west of Avilés could be the best chance in this book for a peaceful and agreeable seaside holiday. The shoreline does not seem dramatic until you see it close up – wild cliffs of jumbled, glittering metamorphic rock, mixed with long stretches of beach where you can find uncrowded spots even on August weekends. Cudillero in particular happens to be one of the most delightful seaside villages on earth, and there are plenty of isolated beaches all along the rugged coast between them.

Cudillero and Luarca

The first resort west of Avilés, **Cudillero** was for many years well protected from the tourist hordes by its geography; the only way into this fishing village was along its narrow, cobbled main street, which snakes down almost vertically for around three kilometres. The hordes can now sweep down to Cudillero on a smooth new road, into

The Vaqueros

The territory around Luarca is the land of the *vaqueros*, one of Iberia's marginal peoples, first mentioned in Middle Ages. The *vaqueros* were cowherds who spent half of the year in the mountain pastures with their cattle, transporting all of their worldly goods in ox carts and building *pallozas* (huts with conical thatched roofs), which you can still see in rural regions further inland. Although ostracized from society (in most parishes they weren't even allowed to hear Mass inside a church or be buried in holy ground), they themselves claimed to be far older than God, and returned disdain for disdain. Recent research based on their dialect places them as 1st-century AD immigrants from Italy. Those still living around Luarca have traded in their ox carts for pick-ups though, curiously enough Franco, abolisher of so many ancient Spanish festivals, inaugurated a new one, ostensibly to preserve their customs in the form of a 'vaquero wedding' in La Braña de Aristébano, six kilometres south of Luarca. On the last Sunday in July, prominent citizens are chosen to play the parts of the *vaqueros*, who are duly married and escorted home with a procession that includes the neatly made matrimonial bed pulled by oxen.

Tourist Information

Cudillero: Puerte del Oeste, t 98 559 13 77, *www.cudillero.org*. Fri Market at the harbour.
Luarca: Olavarrieta 27, t 98 564 00 83 (*summer only*).
Navia: Pza del Ayuntamiento, t 98 547 37 95, *www.ayto-navia.es*.
Tapia de Casariego: Pza de la Iglesia, t 98 547 29 68, *www.ayuntamientodetapia.com* (*summer only*).
Castropol: C/La Fuente 15, t 98 563 51 13.
Taramundi: Avda de Galicia, t 98 564 68 77, *www.taramundi.net*.

There are **markets** in Cudillero and Navia on Fridays; in Tapia de Casariego on Mondays and Fridays.

Where to Stay and Eat

Cudillero ✉ 33150

★★Azpiazu, Playa de Aguilar, t 98 558 32 10, *www.azpiazu.com* (*moderate*). Well-known hotel at Playa de Aguilar; the restaurant specializes in seafood and has a breezy terrace where you can tuck into shellfish soup, hake and cider-marinated dishes.
★★Hotel Casona Selgas, Avda Selgas s/n, El Pito, t 98 559 01 13 (*moderate*). A charming hotel with a pretty sky-blue façade, set 1.5km from the port. The friendly owners offer a wealth of activities.

★★La Casona de la Paca, El Pito, t 98 559 1303, *www.lacasonadelapaca.com* (*moderate– inexpensive*). A charming hotel in a converted Indiano mansion, surrounded by flower-filled gardens. Choose from stylish rooms and suites or equally elegant self-catering apartments.
★★La Casona de Pio, C/Río Frío 3, t 98 559 15 12, *www.arrakis.es/~casonadepio* (*inexpensive*). Sympathetically designed to fit into the old port, this traditional establishment provides style and comfort, right in the centre of Cudillero. Great restaurant.
★La Lupa, in San Juan de la Piñera (2km east of the village), t 98 559 09 73 (*inexpensive*). A modest hotel with a good restaurant.
Pensión Alver, C/Garcia de la Concha 8, t 98 559 00 05 (*budget*). Colourful paintings adorn the breezy rooms in this welcoming and central *pensión*.
Pensión El Camarote, C/Garcia de la Concha 4, t 98 559 12 02 (*budget*). Has impressively large rooms with bath, and is run by a friendly family.
Casa Mariño, t 98 559 01 86 (*moderate*). In a lovely setting with a view of the sea and mountains, Concha de Artedo has one of the many pretty beaches in the area (off the coastal road west of Cudillero). This restaurant, which serves top-class seafood, and a memorable *zarzuela de mariscos y pescados* (shellfish and fish casserole).

the picturesque little harbour with its Portofino-style coloured houses at the bottom of the cliffs. Except for the summer days when it fills up with Madrileño day-trippers, Cudillero is a perfect place to hide away for a few days. If you have your own car you can find plenty of good beaches nearby, especially the broad **Playa de la Cueva** (visible from a high viaduct on the coast highway, though in fact it is many miles away).

Asturias has no shortage of souvenirs. The most common things you'll see are traditional wooden clogs, or *madreñas*, but recently the hot item seems to be whole cow hides; the roadside stand by the viaduct has a wide selection. Just to the west, a road branches off to Soto de Luiña and **Cabo Vidio**, from where there are views of the coastal mountains; on a clear day it's possible to see as far as the Estaca de Bares, the northernmost point in Spain, an incredible 112km away in Galicia.

Luarca, with its sheltered harbour at the mouth of the Río Negro, is a little more tourist-orientated, but it is still a satisfactory place for a stay on Spain's northern coast. The village was an important place in medieval times, first as a whaling port and then from trade with the Americas. The best way to see it is to follow the first signposted

Taberna del Puerto, t 98 559 04 77 (*moderate*). Excellent seafood is served at this restaurant, one of many that line the tiny harbour.

Los Arcos, Plaza de la Marina, **t** 98 559 00 86 (*budget*). Popular restaurant with scrubbed wooden tables overlooking the harbour, and offering an excellent seafood tapas (and menu) choice.

Luarca ✉ 33700

★**Hs Rico**, Pza Alfonso X, **t** 98 570 05 59 (*moderate*). A pleasant, comfortable choice.

★★★**Gayoso**, Paseo Gómez, **t** 98 564 00 50, **f** 98 547 02 71 (*moderate–budget*). Actually, this is two hotels: the older one-star frontage is cheaper, while the modern annexe is bland, but undeniably more comfortable.

Villa La Argentina, Villar de Luarca s/n, **t** 98 564 01 02, *www.villalargentina.com* (*moderate–inexpensive*). A charmingly, if eccentrically, refurbished *Indiano* villa, with cosy rooms and suites (some with Jacuzzi) plus an outdoor swimming pool and gardens.

★★**Casa Consuelo**, at Otur (6km west of town on the N634), **t** 98 547 07 67, *www.casa consuelo.com* (*inexpensive*). One of the best hotel-restaurants in the area, where the food attracts people from miles around with classic Asturian *fabada* and cider. The wine list is exceptional.

La Colmena, C/Uría 2, **t** 98 564 02 78, **f** 98 547 04 34, *www.lacolmena.com* (*inexpensive*). Newly refurbished with warm earth colours and plenty of wood and tile; offers internet access.

La Mesón del Mar, t 98 564 09 94 (*moderate*). As at Cudillero, for dinner in Luarca you need look no further than the row of seafood restaurants on the harbour; nearly all of them have outside tables, allowing you to enjoy the view. This restaurant on the far end offers a wonderful seafood *menú gastronómico* with a bit of everything that was landed in the day's catch.

Los Cantiles, at Villar (on the cliffs above Luarca), **t** 98 564 09 38 (*budget*). The closest campsite, open year-round.

La Dársena, **t** 8 564 11 60 (*budget*). The least expensive restaurant on the harbour (with a tiny terrace) and a good one for fish and seafood. *Closed in winter*.

Figueras del Mar ✉ 33793

★★★**Palacete Peñalba**, El Cotarelo, **t** 98 563 61 25, **f** 98 563 62 47, *www.hotelpalace tepenalba.com* (*moderate*). At the farthest western limit of Asturias, near Castropol, you'll find the region's loveliest hotel. Set in a pair of glorious Art Nouveau mansions designed by a follower of Gaudí, it is a listed monument, and retains its gardens and much of its original furnishings; all rooms have TV and minibar.

road in from the east – a back road that will take you to the cemetery, high on a cliff with a stunning view over the village below. Luarca is still an important fishing port, mostly for tuna, and the harbourfront ensemble makes a pretty photograph. Old Luarca stretches inland from there, with some stately palaces from the 17th and 18th centuries, and some old quarters with narrow alleys climbing up the steep hills.

There is a quite acceptable beach right in the centre of Luarca, but for something special head for **Playa del Barayo**, a beautiful natural area to the west of Luarca.

Continuing westwards, **Navia** is the next fishing village. Southwest of here at **Coaña** you can visit the extensive remains of another Celtic *castro* – foundations of stone walls, paved streets and the foundations of houses. The similarity between these and the *vaquero* huts led some to believe that the *vaqueros* were a lost Celtic tribe.

The Asturian coast ends with Figueras del Mar and then **Castropol**, another attractive fishing port sheltered on the broad Ría de Ribadeo. Inland, south beyond Vegadeo, tiny **Taramundi** up in the mountains has long been famous for the manufacture of knives which have become popular Asturian souvenirs.

Old Castile and León

Approaches to Burgos 230
Along the Camino, from Redecilla to Burgos **230**
To Burgos from Bilbao: the Gate of Pancorbo **233**
Northeast Approaches **234**
Burgos 238
Southeast of Burgos **245**
Along the Pilgrim Route:
  Burgos to Carrión de los Condes 251
Frómista **253**
North of Frómista: the Románico Palentino **254**
Along the Carrión River **257**
Along the Pilgrims' Road to León 260
León 263
North of León **272**
West of León 272
El Bierzo **277**

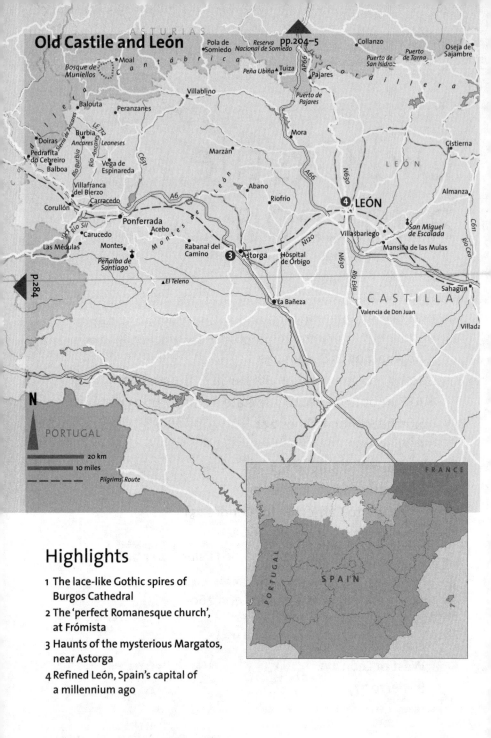

Old Castile and León

pp.204–5

p.284

ASTURIAS

Pola de Somiedo · Reserva Nacional de Somiedo · Collanzo · Puerto de San Isidro · Puerto de Tarna · Oseja de Sajambre

Bosque de Muniellos · Moal · Peña Ubiña · Tuiza · Pajares

Balouta · Peranzanes · Villablino · Puerto de Pajares

Doiras · Burbia · Ancares Leoneses · Mora · Cistierna

Pedrafita do Cebreiro · Balboa · Vega de Espinareda · Marzán · LEÓN · Almanza

Villafranca del Bierzo · Carracedo · Abano · Riofrío · ④ LEÓN

Corullón · Ponferrada · Acebo · San Miguel de Escalada

Carucedo · Villasbariego · Mansilla de las Mulas

Las Médulas · Montes · Rabanal del Camino · ③ Astorga · Hospital de Órbigo

Peñalba de Santiago · El Teleno · La Bañeza · CASTILLA · Sahagún

Valencia de Don Juan · Villada

Montes de León

Río Sil · Río Burbia · Río Ancares · Río Esla · Río Cea

A6 · A66 · N630 · N120

PORTUGAL

N

20 km
10 miles
- - - Pilgrims' Route

FRANCE

PORTUGAL · SPAIN

Highlights

1 The lace-like Gothic spires of Burgos Cathedral

2 The 'perfect Romanesque church', at Frómista

3 Haunts of the mysterious Margatos, near Astorga

4 Refined León, Spain's capital of a millennium ago

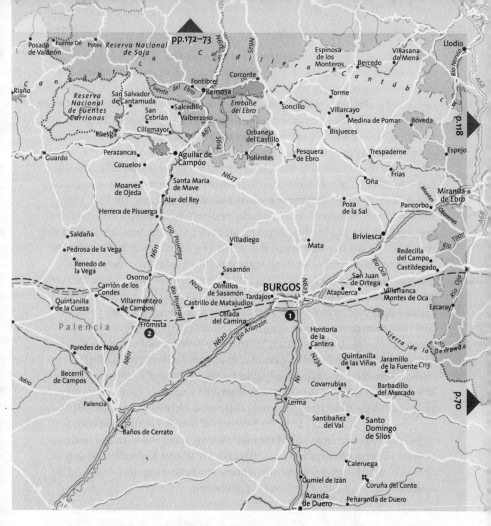

pp.172–73

Old Castile and León encompasses two ancient kingdoms of Spain and the *meseta* – a flat, semi-arid table-top 2,300–3,300 feet above sea level, where the climate, summed up in an old Castilian proverb, is nine months of winter and three months of hell. It looks like no other place in Europe: endless rolling dun-coloured plains, spotted with scrub and patches of mountains, but few trees; during the mindless free-for-all of the Reconquista nearly all of the forests were axed. Depending on your mood you will find the *meseta* romantic and picturesque, or brooding and eerie, but you'll never forget it. From this unlikely land, however, came the culture, language and people who would dominate in their day not only the nations of Iberia, but a good part of two continents. Even today Burgos, seat of the first counts of Castile, is the headquarters of all that is pure Castilian and *castizo*, down to the proper lisping pronunciation of the name of Castile's hero, the Cid, or 'El Theed'.

In early times Castile not only resembled America's Far West, but played the same kind of frontier role twice in European history. After the Romans whipped the native

Iberians, retired legionaries were given land to raise wheat (any place named Quintanilla recalls one of their settlements, as in *quinta*, a rural villa or farm). The Visigoths followed in their tracks, but the Moors found little to like in Old Castile and conquered it without settling it. The Christian kingdoms to the north erected a string of border fortifications that gave the region its name Castile ('Land of Castles') sometime around 800. In 882 the first part of Castile was reconquered by Alfonso III of Asturias; two years later, Diego Porcelos founded Burgos and became the first count of Castile. According to the medieval Romance de Fernán González, the Good Count Fernán González obtained Castile's independence from Asturias–León in the 10th century by selling the king of Asturias a horse and goshawk. The king, lacking any handy cash, promised Fernán González he'd pay him double the price for every day that he didn't pay. The king forgot his promise, and by the time Fernán González reminded him, the sum was so vast that all the king could do was give him Castile.

Fernán González formed his fledging state politically into seven counties, the Antiguas Merindades de Castilla. Unlike the feudal Christian kingdoms to the north, where the land was owned by great lords, or the Church, or the military orders, Castile was settled by free men or *hidalgos*, each of whom owned their farms and bore the responsibility for defending them. The difficulties in repopulating vast expanses of empty land was greatly eased by the development of the *camino de Santiago* (the medieval road equivalent of the Union-Pacific, America's first transcontinental railroad), especially after Castile was 'tamed' by the reconquest of Toledo by Alfonso VI and the Cid in 1085. It set off a medieval boom: settlers moved in and towns sprouted all along the length of the road. Northwest Spain includes only the oldest parts of Castilla y León, the provinces of Burgos, Palencia, and León, a region that encompasses some of the most striking, weird and unknown landscapes in Spain. In between are picturesque little towns that have been collecting dust since Charles V sucked them dry in the 16th century; others have changed little since the medieval pilgrims wended their way to Compostela.

Approaches to Burgos

This section covers the approaches to Burgos from the east and north, whether you're coming in slowly along the pilgrims' road from La Rioja, quickly on the *autopista* from Bilbao, or through the magnificent mountain scenery of the Cantabrian range from Santander.

Along the Camino, from Redecilla to Burgos

The pilgrimage road follows the N120 from Santo Domingo de la Calzada (*see* p.113) and enters Castile at medieval **Redecilla del Campo**, built like an old strip frontier town along the road. Houses still bear their *hidalgos'* crests, but as usual the main focus is the church, Virgen de la Calle, not much in itself but notable for its sublime 12th-century baptismal font, intricately carved with the towers and windows of a city

Around Burgos

Reserva Nacional de Saja

CANTABRIA

Cordillera Cantábrica

Reserva Nacional

Alto Campoo
Fuente del Ebro
Reinosa

Neila

Espinosa de los Monteros
Bercedo
Vallejo de Mena
Villasana de Mena
Amurrio

Corconte

Ojo Guareña

Torme

Salcedillo

San Salvador de Cantamuda
San Cebrián
Cervera de Pisuerga
Cillamayor
Valberzoso

Embalse del Ebro

Soncillo

Villarcayo
Medina de Pomar

Villaláin
Bisjueces

Bóveda

Espejo

Aguilar de Campóo
Orbaneja del Castillo
Polientes
San Martín de Elines
Pesquera de Ebro

Perazanca

Vallespinosa de Aguilar
Cozuelos de Ojeda

N627

Trespaderne

Frías

Becerril del Carpio
Moarves
Santa María de Mave
San Andrés de Aguilar
Alar del Rey

Poza de la Sal

Oña

Miranda de Ebro

Pancorbo

Montes Obarenes

Herrera de Pisuerga

Rio Pisuerga

Briviesca

Río Tirón

Redecilla del Campo
Santo Domingo de la Calzada

Villadiego

Mata

Monasterio de Rodilla

Rio Oca

Viloria de Rioja
Belorado
Castildelgado

Osorno

Grijalba
Sasamón
Olmillos

N120

CASTILLA

N623

San Juan de Ortega
Atapuerca

Villafranca
Montes de Oca
Santa de Oca

Río Oja

Ezcaray

San Lorenzo

n de los Condes
illalcázar de Sirga

Rio Pisuerga

Castrillo de Matajudios
Hornillos del Camino
Tardajos
Las Huelgas Reales

BURGOS

Miraflores

Villarmentero de Campos
Frómista

Castrojeriz

Celada del Camino
Rio Arlanzón

Sierra de la Demanda

Boadilla del Camino

N620

Hontoria de la Cantera

Palencia

N234

Nuestra Señora de las Viñas
Mazariegos
Quintanilla de las Viñas

Jaramillo de la Fuente

C113

Reserva Nacional de Cameros

Covarrubias

Barbadillo del Mercado

Lerma

Ermita San Pedro de Arlanza
Salas de los Infantes

Santibáñez del Val
Santo Domingo de Silos
Garganta de la Yecla

Baños de Cerrato

N

Caleruega
Peñalba de Castro

Gumiel de Izán

Clunia
Coruña del Conte

Rio Duero

Aranda de Duero

Peñaranda de Duero

20 km
10 miles
Pilgrims' Route

presumed to be Jerusalem. The church in the next town, **Castildelgado**, has interesting
Gothic *retablos*; while beyond, **Viloria de Rioja** conserves the font where Santo
Domingo de la Calzada was baptized. Further west, the much larger, leather-making
town of **Belorado** (the Belfuratus of the *Codex Calixtinus*) attracts a different kind of
pilgrim these days with its factory outlets. Ruins of a monastery and a hospital recall
its former vocation, along with two churches, San Pedro and Santa María, built in the
1500s in the wide, airy Catalan Gothic style. Hermits lived in the caves by Tosantos,
around the church of the Virgen de la Peña, built into a cliff, while to the west in

Getting Around

There are four or five **buses** a day from Burgos to Belorado, fewer to Miranda de Ebro, a major rail junction. At least one bus a day goes to Oña and Briviesca; services are less frequent to Frías, Espinosa de los Monteros and Poza de la Sal.

Tourist Information

Miranda de Ebro: C/Río Ebro 31, t 94 732 03 03, *www.mirandadeebro.es*.
Medina de Pomar: C/Mayor 14, t 94 714 72 28, *www.medinadepomar.org*.
Villarcayo: C/Lain Calvo 22, t 94 713 04 57.
    There is a **market** in Oña on Fridays; in Medina de Pomar on Thursdays; and in Espinosa de los Monteros on Tuesdays.

Where to Stay and Eat

Villafranca Montes de Oca ✉ 09240
La Alpargatería, C/Mayor 2, t 94 758 20 29 (*budget*). A sweet little *casa rural* in the centre; B&B or rent out the whole place.
El Pájaro, Ctra Logroño–Burgos, t 94 758 20 29 (*budget*). Your best bet for a simple room and meal along this stretch of the pilgrims' route.

Pancorbo/Briviesca ✉ 09240
★★Hotel Isabel, C/Santa María Encimera 2, Briviesca, t 94 759 29 59, *www.hotel-isabel.com* (*budget*). A modern, central hotel with comfy rooms.
Casa Rural El Ferial, C/San Nicolás 59, Pancorbo, t 94 735 42 02, or t 94 735 42 76 (after 9pm) (*budget*). This place, lying on the edge of the old town, is the best lodging choice. Fronted by a gallery, it's really a cheap bed and breakfast overlooking a garden, but the best thing about it is the charming owners, Vicente Cardiñanos and his wife, who must be the most hospitable people in the whole of Castile.
El Concejo, Pza Mayor 14, Briviesca, t 94 759 16 86 (*expensive–moderate*). Prettily set in a 15th-century mansion in town, this restaurant serves a tasty leek and prawn *pastel* in cheese sauce and imaginative desserts; good value menú del día (€12).

Medina de Pomar ✉ 09500
★★★Ciudad de Medina, Pza Somovilla, t 94 719 08 22, *www.ciudaddemedina.com* (*moderate*). Located in a pretty, historical building with the village's best, moderately priced restaurant downstairs.

Espinosa del Camino, you can see the 9th-century ruins of the Mozarab monastery of San Félix de Oca, where the first count of Castile, Diego Porcelos, was buried.

Just west of the Sierra de la Demanda, the deeply forested Montes de Oca (Mountains of the Goose) mark the traditional border of Castile. At their foot, **Villafranca Montes de Oca**, a town settled by Franks, was once a major pilgrims' halt; today both Franks and pilgrims have gone, leaving a church and the 14th-century Hospital de San Antón (currently undergoing restoration) to recall its glory days. A path leads up to the hermitage of the **Virgen de Oca**, a pretty, leafy place with plenty of picnic tables. At Villafranca the N120 and the walking path split; the latter, heading up the pine-forested slopes (enjoy it: it's the last shade before the mountains west of León) eventually emerges at **San Juan de Ortega**.

San Juan de Ortega is named after Santo Domingo's architecturally minded sidekick, who, after a pilgrimage to Jerusalem, came back to Spain determined to build chapels, bridges and hostels along the *camino*, especially in places like this, where wolves devoured more than a few pilgrims. A couple of miles from the N120, the hamlet he founded is all but abandoned, although unlike the hostel (now *parador*) built by Santo Domingo de la Calzada, San Juan's still serves its original purpose, thanks to the local priest who feeds and lodges pilgrims. In 1142 the saint designed the church, of which most notably the apse survives, an original, elegant design of slender round columns and three receding arches around alabaster windows. Inside, San Juan is buried in a magnificent tomb, with an effigy and delightful cartoon-like scenes from his life carved in the base and crowned by an Isabelline Gothic baldachin, paid for by Isabel the Catholic herself, who got pregnant for the first time in 1477 after praying by the saint's Romanesque tomb (now down in the crypt). At 5pm, on the day of the spring and autumn equinoxes (21 March and 22 September), pilgrims come to see the *Milagro de la Luz*, when a sunbeam illuminates the womb of the Virgin of the Annunciation, carved on a triple capital in the crossing. Isabel also paid for the chapel of San Nicolás, designed to hold the tomb now removed to the old church; in exchange the Renaissance grille from the old church has been installed in the chapel. Just to the west, the walking path continues to one of San Juan de Ortega's bridges in the tiny hamlet of **Agés**. In **Atapuerca**, the next town (13km from Burgos), excavations threw up incredibly important paleontological finds which can be visited by guided tour (*www.atapuerca.com; tours Sat, Sun and hols 10am, 12pm, extra tours July–Sept, for weekday tours, consult the tourist office in Burgos; adm, a guided tour is included with the Burgos Card, see p.240*). Unique bones found here may have solved the missing link in the evolutionary chain (connecting the Neanderthals with modern human beings) and will be displayed in the new Museo de la Evolución Humana, currently being built in Burgos. A new visitor's centre in Atapuerca is also under construction.

Beyond the Sierra of Atapuerca are the sprawling eastern suburbs of Burgos (*see* p.238).

To Burgos from Bilbao: the Gate of Pancorbo

The Bilbao–Madrid motorway A1 runs into Castile near **Miranda de Ebro**, a major town surrounded by dreary industrial suburbs with little to see besides the glass balconies of its old houses hanging over the river. It grew up around a medieval bridge, which was replaced in 1777 by the Puente de Carlos III. The 16th-century church of Santa María is Miranda's most beautiful monument, while the Ebro itself sculpted the stunning gorge, the **Hoces del Sobrón**, through the nearby Montes Obarenes.

The road, the *autopista*, and train funnel dramatically through the pass at **Pancorbo**, for VS Pritchett 'a place of horror, for the rock crowds in, comes down in precipitous, yellow shafts, and at the top has been tortured into frightening animal shapes by the climate'. A ruined Moorish castle and an 18th-century fort that played a role when Wellington's army chased the French through the gorge in 1813 survive above the homely old town. Most of the Pancorbans work in the big truck stops, where drivers tuck into a bowl of *sopa castellano* to prepare themselves for their long ride in the night to beat the heat of the *meseta* beyond. Or, as Pritchett put it: 'Pancorbo is the moment of conversion. Now one meets Spain, the indifferent enemy.'

Between Pancorbo and Burgos, **Briviesca** on the River Oca was on the *camino francés* until the 11th century, before Sancho the Great prompted a change of route through Nájera. The regular rectangular plan of Briviesca, with its pleasant Plaza

Mayor, was the model for several towns founded in South America; its octagonal church, **Santa Clara** (1565), has star vaulting and a florid carved *retablo mayor* (a rare, unpolychromed one, with a central figure dreaming off the tree of Jesse); another fine 16th-century *retablo* is in the Capilla de Santa Casilda in the **Colegiata de Santa María**. In 1388, the Cortes Generales of King Juan I were held in Briviesca, and here he bestowed on his eldest son, Enrique, the title of 'Prince of Asturias' for his wedding to Catherine of Lancaster, a title, like the Prince of Wales, that has been held ever since by the heir to the Spanish throne.

Farther west towards Burgos, the Benedictine Monasterio de Rodilla has vanished, leaving only its lovely Romanesque church, **Nuestra Señora del Valle**, set in a meadow with picnic tables.

Northeast Approaches

Oña

Briviesca is the chief town of the Bureba, where the foothills of the Cantabrian mountains begin. This bulge of the map in northeast Burgos province, the cradle of Old Castile, is full of curiosities and remarkable scenery; a good place to start is medieval Oña, 'La Villa Condal', north of Briviesca. Founded by the Romans on the River Oca, Oña had one of the first castles of Castile and was granted its *fueros* or privileges in 950 by Fernán González, Castile's first king. In the early days, the king's travelling court often stayed here; in 1033, Sancho the Great of Navarra, heir of Castile, ordered the old royal stronghold replaced by the Benedictine Monasterio de San Salvador. He meant this to serve as a royal pantheon, a status he encouraged by spending his dying days in Oña.

Oña's main plaza is picturesquely laid out on three different levels. Behind an old pilgrims' cross the monastery, rebuilt in 1640 and decorated with four squat kings who would look perfectly at home on a deck of cards, is now used as a psychiatric hospital. However, the town offers guided tours of its **church**, atop a flight of steps (*tours Tues–Fri 10.30, 11.30, 12.45, 4, 5, 6.15, Sat–Sun 10.30, 11.30, 12.30, 1.15, 4, 5, 6.15; adm*). The entrance is through the 15th-century Pórtico de los Reyes, carved with figures of kings and counts, leading into an open atrium; beyond is the oldest Romanesque façade in Castile (1072), with Flemish-Gothic paintings just inside, and a *mudéjar* door. Although the walls of the long narrow church date from the 11th century, the interior was redone in the 15th by Fernando Díaz. The second Baroque *retablo* on the right marks the tomb of Santa Tigridia, San Salvador's first abbess; its expressive Romanesque *Cristo de Santa Tigridia* is attributed to sculptors from the Toulouse school.

Further up, charming 14th-century Gothic frescoes depict the legend of St Mary of Egypt (really Isis, they say, dressed in Christian clothing). Fernando Díaz's starry dome measures 4,300sq ft and is the second largest in Spain after Tarragona; below are filigree choir stalls in walnut, and flanking the ultra-florid 18th-century Baroque *retablo* is the magnificent **Panteón Real**. Sancho the Great (d.1035) and his wife are here, among others, their tombs arranged by Fernando Díaz into charming little temples, richly carved and decorated with elaborate tracery and Hispano-Flemish paintings by Fray Alonso de Zamora. Behind the *retablo*, the **Capilla de San Íñigo** contains the 16th-century silver reliquary of Íñigo (Eneco), persuaded to be first abbot of Oña by Sancho the Great and whose death, they say, grieved Christian, Jew and Saracen alike. The **museum** in the sacristy contains the alabaster tomb of Bishop López de Mendoza, by Italian Mannerist master Leone Leoni, a fragment of 10th-century cloth once belonging to Sancho the Great, with Arabic writing, the figures of an alchemist and the horse and goshawk of Castile's independence.

The **cloister**, built by Simón de Colonia in 1508, is a rich piece of Isabelline Gothic. Presiding over the door is the Gothic statue of Santa María de Oña, whom the poet-king Alfonso the Wise praised in his *Cantiga 221*; when his son Fernando, the future saint, was given up for dead by his doctors, the statue, brought into his presence, restored him. She was also known as sovereign against worms in Infantes. One wing of the cloister holds the tombs of the counts of Bureba, cousins to the counts of Castile and the granddaughters of the Cid. One of their epitaphs translates:

> *Gómez, who defended the Spanish coasts*
> *Like Hector you guarded them, while your faithful wife Urraca*
> *Remained here, and contemplated how the cold winters*
> *and pleasant springs passed*
> *And how nothing under heaven endures.*

Down towards the river, you can see a little more of Oña's past: the last of its medieval gates, the **Arco de la Estrella**, and the Gothic church of **San Juan**, with a carved portal under the porch.

Up the Ebro: Frías and Medina de Pomar

East of Oña, built high over the banks of the Ebro, medieval **Frías** looks beautiful on postcards: a ruined 12th-century castle spirals up a rocky outcrop known as 'the Molar' high above the hanging whitewashed houses, arcaded lanes and intimate vegetable gardens. Because it's on the way to nowhere, few people ever visit, and if it's hot you can join the locals for a dip in the Ebro in the shadow of Frías' magnificent **medieval bridge**, complete with its mighty gate and central guard tower. Between Oña and Frías, turn north 16km at Trespaderne for 12th-century **San Pantaleón de Losa**, site of a curious hermitage set over the village on a boulder resembling a capsized boat. Odd carvings decorate the capitals (dragons' heads, masks and a speak-no-evil figure). Further up the valley, by the Orduña pass, is one of the highest waterfalls in Europe.

Another road north of Trespaderne leads to **Medina de Pomar**, site of a powerful, two-towered castle (*museum open Oct–May Tues–Sat 12.30–2 and 5.30–7.30, Sun 12–2; June–Sept Mon–Sat 12–2 and 6–8.30, Sun 12–2; adm*) built in the 14th century by the Velasco family, the hereditary Constables of Castile; a *mudéjar* stucco frieze in the main hall is decorated with inscriptions in Gothic and Arabic letters. The Constables founded the **Monasterio de Santa Clara** in 1313 (*open daily 11.30–1.30 and 6–8; adm*), and lie buried in tombs with alabaster effigies in its early Gothic church with an octagonal star-vault; Santa Clara's lovely 16th-century Capilla de la Concepción has a

Renaissance grille and *retablo* by Diego de Siloé and Felipe de Vigarni. In the convent museum, you'll find paintings attributed to Rogier van der Weyden, an ivory Christ of Lepanto, a dead Christ by Gregorio Fernández, and goldwork. Medina de Pomar is also proud of Juan de Salazar, who went to the New World in 1547 and founded Asunción, the capital of Paraguay.

The Canyons of the Ebro

Up the Ebro from Oña, just outside Puentearenas, **San Pedro de Tejada** (*visits by appointment only; t 94 730 32 00*) is one of the province's finest Romanesque churches, its portal carved with a Last Supper and Ascension of Christ. Its other carvings are flagrantly erotic, in the same vein as the church at Cervatos, just over the mountains in Cantabria (*see* p.208). Further up, above Incinillas, **Villarcayo** (due west of Medina de Pomar) was the capital of the Merindad de Castilla la Vieja, one of Fernán González's original counties, but it was burned in the First Carlist War. Only bits of its medieval past survive, especially in the **Museo-Monasterio de Santa María la Real de Vileña** (*open daily 10–12 and 4–6*), founded to hold the treasures and fragments of the 13th-century Cistercian monastery that burned down in 1970.

Villarcayo is in easy striking distance of a pair of sites associated with the archaic judges of Castile who, in this isolated pocket in the 8th and 9th centuries, played a role somewhere between chieftain, lawmaker and general sage. One of them, *juez* Laín Calvo, was buried in the Romanesque hermitage of the Virgen de la Torrentera in **Villalaín**; when disinterred, the chronicles write, all were amazed at the giant stature of his body, which turned to dust on contact with the air. The church, with a square apse and inscription dated 1130, has a lovely portal and interesting murals inside. Sculptures of the five judges of Castile decorate the elegant doorway of the large Renaissance church in nearby **Bisjueces**; one judge, Nuño Rasura, wears a striking Chinese hat. North of Villarcayo in **Torme**, the 12th-century Romanesque church of Butrera is one of the best preserved in the province, with fascinating capitals and an excellent relief of the Three Magi.

To the northwest, you can pick up the 6318 into the mountains (*see* p.237). For the Ebro Canyons, however, cut over to **Soncillo**, then drive southwest through the Puerta de Carrales towards Rúerrero (along the CA 274), at the beginning of the Canyons of the Ebro. The cliffs grow increasingly majestic and fantastical as you drive towards **Orbaneja del Castillo**: vultures and eagles circle high over the ruddy canyon walls, sculpted by aeons of wind and rain to form a bizarre natural roof line of soaring bridges, castle walls, haunted towers or hollow snaggle-toothed caves. In Orbaneja an enchanting, lush waterfall cascades, even in August; from here the road does a semicircle through the canyon before climbing up to the N623, the main Santander–Burgos highway. The main highway is not an unattractive route, but for something even better, pass it by and cross the Ebro at **Pesquera de Ebro**, make your way east to Pesadas de Burgos and turn right onto the CL629.

For the next 14km the road is surreal – perfectly straight, in the middle of absolutely nowhere, yet each kilometre is systematically marked off with an impressive 10-ft monument in stone, all identical, all bearing no identification whatsoever. The sensation of wandering across the middle of a bizarre games table for giants is confirmed when, after the last monument, you turn east and it's as if the world has suddenly dropped out beneath your feet, leaving you to wind down the edge of the table, with tremendous views across to the **Castillo de las Rojas**, an impressive ruin piled high on a rocky outcrop. The castle, where Charles V imprisoned the ambassadors of Pope Clement in 1528, defends **Poza de la Sal**, a town founded by the Romans, who first extracted salt from its marshes along the Río Torca Salada. Fortified in the 10th century, the town and its salt were so important that in 1530 its lord was made Marqués de Poza. In its web of tiny lanes there's a Gothic church with a Baroque façade, the 18th-century salt administration offices, a pair of old gateways and a panoramic view from Plaza Nueva; along the river, the old salt works, abandoned in the mid-19th century, are near an interesting Roman aqueduct that supplied the village wash basin. From here the road continues south towards Briviesca.

The Far Northeast Corner: in the Cordillera Cantábrica

Near Soncillo the 6318 leads into the secret corner of Burgos province; if you're coming from the north, the N629 from Laredo will take you straight there. Some day, perhaps, the most extraordinary attraction, the massive karstic cave complex of **Ojo Guareña** by Quintanilla-Sotoscueva, with its prehistoric paintings and Upper Palaeolithic footprints, will be open to visitors. The caves extend some 40km underground (still not fully explored). For now you can only get as far as the subterranean **Hermitages of SS. Bernabé and Tirso**, set on a panoramic esplanade with their façades built into the cliffs; inside are 17th- and 18th-century paintings and wax *ex votos* (*open mid–Sept–July Fri–Sun and hols 11–1.30 and 5–7.30; July–mid-Sept Tues–Sun 11-1.30 and 5–7.30;adm*).

The 6318 continues east to medieval **Espinosa de los Monteros**, the local market town, with its 14th-century Castillo de Los Condestables on the far bank of the river Trueba, and the constable's elegant Baroque palace in town; there are several tower houses, and a good 15th-century *retablo* by Fray Alonso de Zamora in the church of San Nicolás. 5 August is the best time to come, when the citizenry indulge in what the tourist office describes with some trepidation as 'strange dances of pagan origin'.

Some 15km north there's a small ski station at **Portillo de Lunada** (ski info at *www.lunada.es.vg*), where the old Roman road once passed between the *meseta* to Cantabria; the incredible views down the valley of the Miera are well worth the trouble of visiting at any time of year. On the other hand, if you venture east, interesting Romanesque churches are your reward: San Miguel at **Bercedo**, with a good portal and beams carved into animals; a 12th-century Templar church of Santa María at **Siones**, with an elegant double archway in the apse, strange and beautiful capitals and other carvings, a 12th-century statue of the Virgin and a Visigothic baptismal font; and the church of San Lorenzo at **Vallejo de Mena**, founded by the Knights of St John with a gallery of arcades along the top of the south façade and a handsome apse. The parish church of the big town in these parts, medieval **Villasana de Mena**, has a good relief of the Three Magi.

Burgos

First it must be said that Burgos is a genteel and pleasant town, its river, the Arlanzón, so filled with frogs in the spring and early summer that they drown out the traffic with their croaking; and that the favourite promenade, the Paseo del Espolón, is one of Spain's prettiest, adorned with amazing topiary hedges. Burgos contains one of the greatest collections of Gothic art and monuments in southern Europe, and it is the city in Spain where you are most likely to see a nun riding a bicycle. Yet throughout much of its history, Burgos' role has been that of a stern military camp, from the day of El Cid Campeador to Franco el Caudillo who, during the Civil War, made it his temporary capital, the city where, it was said, 'the very stones are Nationalist'. Here, in 1970, Franco held the infamous Burgos trials in which 16 Basque separatists (two of them priests) were tried in a kangaroo court. Six of them were sentenced to death, though outraged world opinion convinced Franco to commute the sentences.

The Kingdom of Castile was born in Burgos, and it is fitting that the city itself began as a castle erected on the Moorish frontier in 884. In 926 it took its first step away from Leónese rule, electing its own judges; in 950, one of the judges' successors, Fernán González, declared his independence as Count of Castile. His descendant, Ferdinand I, elevated the title to king and married the heiress of León. Burgos remained sole capital of Castile until 1087, when Alfonso VI moved to Toledo (perhaps to put some distance between himself and the overbearing Cid). The frontier was moving south and this city that had done so much to create the ethos of Spain now found itself a backwater. But Burgos has always remained true to the cause. It is still Spain's most aristocratic, pious, polite and reactionary city. Franco rewarded it with a programme of state-financed expansion, an attempt to drag it into the 20th century that may well succeed some day.

Arco de Santa María

Burgos' glistening white, fairy-tale front door, the **Arco de Santa María**, was originally part of the medieval walls, but after the Comunero revolt it was embellished to appease Charles V; triumphal arches like this were a Renaissance conceit (the first one was made at Naples for a Spanish king), and they were especially favoured by the vainglorious and ambitious Charles. The Emperor himself is portrayed in a Burgos pantheon that includes its first judges, King Fernán González, and El Cid. The arch was designed by Francisco de Colonia and Juan de Vallejo, two artists you are going to know well before you leave Burgos – along with Francisco's father Juan, responsible for the great openwork spires of the cathedral, looming just behind the arch.

The Cathedral

Along with León and Toledo, Burgos has one of Spain's greatest Gothic cathedrals (*main entrance for mass only on Plaza Santa María, visitor entrance and ticket office on Plaza Rey San Fernando; open spring and autumn daily 9.30–1.15 and 4–7.15; winter daily 10–1.15 and 4–6.45; summer daily 9.30–7.15, closed Sun 3.3.30pm; adm, audio guide €3.50*). Yet while León has an instant, sublime appeal, Burgos' power lies in its awesome number of masterworks and details from the tiniest carving in the choir stalls to its beautiful star-vaulted domes. In 1221, in honour of his marriage to Beatrice of Swabia, Ferdinand III and the English bishop Maurice laid the first cornerstone. On the north side, a stair leads up to the **Puerta del Sarmental**, its 13th-century tympanum showing Christ and the four Evangelists (sitting studiously at their desk, writing the Gospels). The first portal to be finished, the south-side **Puerta Alta de la Coronería** (1257) is the most interesting, with its Apostles, Almighty, and a peculiar row of mere mortals, the Blessed and the Damned, in between. Around the corner of the transept, the **Puerta de la Pellejería** is part of the original 13th-century work. These doors are rarely opened; Burgos is prey to a biting wind in the late afternoon, and the cross-current would blow the congregation away. From up here, though, you can get a good view of the forest of spires, especially on the lantern, adorned with scores of figures. Three generations of the Colonia family devoted themselves to moulding the soft grey stone of Burgos into

Getting There

By Train

RENFE is on Avda Conde Guadalhorce, across the river from the cathedral, t 90 224 02 02; tickets are also sold at the office at C/Moneda 21, t 94 720 91 31. Burgos is on the main rail line from Irún to Madrid (connections to Pamplona, Vitoria, Bilbao, Valladolid, etc.), with less frequent links with Zaragoza, Palencia, León, and La Coruña; also to Salamanca, Barcelona, Málaga, Madrid, Córdoba and Vigo on various Talgos.

By Bus

The bus terminal is on C/Miranda, across the river from the Arco de Sta María, t 94 728 88 55. There are daily buses to León (1), Santander (at least 3), Madrid (12), San Sebastián, Soria, Bilbao and Vitoria (4 or more), and the provincial villages. Even if there may be only one bus a day to places not on a main route, such as Frías, they're often conveniently timed for a day trip but check in advance to avoid getting stranded.

Tourist Information

Municial offices, both t 94 728 88 74, in the Teatro Principal, Paseo del Espolón s/n and at Plaza del Rey de San Fernando; provincial office at Plaza Alonso Martínez 7, t 94 720 31 25, www.aytoburgos.es and www.jcyl.es/turismo. The tourist office can sell you a Burgos Card (one day €10, two days €16), which will give you free entry to many local attractions.

The **post office** is on Plaza Conde de Castro, across the river from Paseo del Espolon; Ciber Café Cabaret, C/La Puebla 21, has **Internet access**, at €4/hr (open 12pm–2am, weekends 5pm–2am).

Where to Stay

Burgos ✉ 09000

Luxury–Expensive

★★★★★Landa Palace, just outside Burgos on the Madrid road (N1), t 94 725 77 77, www.landa palace.es (luxury). A member of the prestigious Relais et Châteaux, offering a memorable stay in an over-the-top pseudo-medieval tower full of antiques, an indoor atrium and swimming pool, and beautiful all-mod-con rooms. A meal in the equally palatial restaurant, the region's finest, will set you back some €50.

★★★★Abba Burgos, C/Fernán González 72, t 94 700 11 00, www.abbahoteles. com (expensive). Luxury hotel in a converted palace with all the extras, including a gym and swimming pool.

★★★★Hotel Almirante Bonifaz, C/Vitoria 22/24, t 94 720 69 43, www.almirante.com (expensive). A luxurious choice in the centre of town.

★★★Del Cid, Pza Santa María 8, t 94 720 87 15, www.mesondelcid.es (expensive–moderate). Magnificent location opposite the cathedral, with well-equipped modern doubles, garage space and a secret tunnel to their excellent restaurant next door. They have opened a new four-star hotel, Del Cid II, which is more luxurious, but has a little less character.

the cathedral's intricate towers and pinnacles. Colonia is Cologne, in Germany; Hans of Cologne began the works in the late 1400s, and his son Simón and grandson Francisco carried on, followed by Juan de Vallejo, who built the Plateresque crossing tower. These, and the Arco de Santo María, are illuminated at night for a dazzling tour de force.

The west façade incorporates two Stars of David, an unintentional reminder that more than one of Burgos' bishops hailed from a Jewish family before 1492, as did the city's greatest sculptors, Diego and Gil de Siloé, the undisputed masters of Isabelline Gothic. Their work inside is one of the cathedral's main attractions. Tragically, the three portals of the west façade were 'improved' in the 'Age of Enlightenment' of the 18th century, and replaced with pallid substitutes. But around the back, another monument of late Gothic excess survives, the huge Capilla del Condestable (see below), attached to the apse.

Along with the cathedral of Santiago, this is one of the two great treasure-houses of Spain. De Vigarni, who also designed the choir, carved the tomb of Don Gonzalo de

Moderate

***Cordón**, La Puebla 6, t 94 726 50 00, www.hotelcordon.com. A classic Spanish hotel with glass balconies on a quiet street. It has triples and rooms with private sitting room (*expensive*). It's geared towards business people and offers good deals at weekends.

***La Puebla**, La Puebla 20, t 94 720 00 11, www.hotellapuebla.com. A truly delightful little boutique hotel in the centre with chic decor and all comforts.

Inexpensive

****Norte y Londres**, Pza Alonso Martínez 10, t 94 726 41 25, www.hotelnorteylondres.com. Charmingly old-fashioned hotel, offering a whiff of elegance right in the middle of town.

***Hotel España**, Paseo de Espolón 32, t 94 720 63 40, f 94 720 13 30, www.hotelespana.net. Pleasant, good-value hotel on a tree-lined pedestrian street.

Cheap

****Hs Manjón**, Conde Jordana 1–7, t 94 720 86 89. Has good *budget* rooms close to the river; most have private bath. Run by two friendly sisters.

***Hs Hidalgo**, t 94 720 34 81. A well-kept, old-fashioned *hostal* on a relatively quiet street . off the Plaza Mayor. Shared baths only.

Pensión 196, Avda Vitoria 196, t 94 722 94 74. This *pensión* has spotless rooms with ensuite baths at bargain rates, though it's a trek from the centre; take the bus marked 'Gamonal' from Avenida Arlanzon.

Residencia Juvenil Gil de Siloé, Avda General Vigón, t 94 722 03 62. The town's youth hostel. *Open July–Aug.*

Eating Out

El Ángel, C/La Paloma 24, t 94 720 8608 (*expensive*). Perhaps the best in town: highly creative cuisine in the elegant dining room upstairs, and a popular tapas bar downstairs.

Casa Ojeda, Vitoria 5, t 94 720 90 52 (*expensive–moderate)* The most popular place in town, with the best tapas in its bar and good local cuisine in its dining room, including several veggie options.

Mesón del Cid, Pza Santa María 8, t 94 720 87 15 (*expensive–moderate*). For a medieval atmosphere in a 15th-century building facing the cathedral, and delicious roast suckling-lamb, this is the place to go.

Mesón de los Infantes, just inside the Arco de Santa María, t 94 720 59 82 (*moderate*). Offers Castilian specialities like *olla podrida* and 'medieval lentils'; outdoor summer dining.

Gaona, C/La Paloma 41 (near the cathedral), t 94 720 40 32 (*moderate–budget*). Has Basque cooking in a glassed-in terrace; peppers stuffed with cod is a treat.

Mesón de Los Herreros, C/San Lorenzo 20, t 94 720 24 48 (*budget*). Fill up on delicious tapas and raciones at this popular local favourite.

Tapa, Avda del Cid 22 (*budget*). A wide range of tasty tapas including some of the best patatas bravas in town.

Lerma in the 16th-century **Capilla de la Presentación**, the largest and most beautiful of the chapels on the southern aisle. Look out for the famous 15th-century mechanical clock across the nave (look up in the dim corner by the rose window), the **Papamoscas** ('Fly-catcher'), a grinning devil who pops out of a hole in the wall to strike the hour. The extravagantly Baroque Capilla de Santa Tecla on the northern aisle can be glimpsed through glass doors – it, like the celebrated Capilla de Santo Cristo (*see* below) is reserved for services. Next, is the lovely **Chapel of Santa Ana**, has a *retablo* of the Tree of Jesse by Gil de Siloé and a fine bishop's tomb by his son Diego. One of Diego de Siloé's masterpieces, the diamond-shaped, drippingly Plateresque **Golden Stair** (1523), is the most strikingly original feature of the interior, the perfectly proportioned solution to the Puerta Alta, 30ft above the floor of the cathedral. The idea of stairways as architectural showpieces was just beginning in 1523; Michelangelo was working on his famous one at the Laurentian Library in Florence at the same time.

A Building Trying to Disappear

If you have the time, take a good, long look at the exterior of this cathedral (preferably from up the stairs on the edge of the plaza). This is the Gothic idea stretched to its wildest extreme – in its day it must have looked as outrageous as Gaudí's Sagrada Familia when its first parabolic towers went up in the 1900s.

In the first blossoming of Gothic building in the Île-de-France, they concentrated on the interior – soaring arches and acres of stained glass to make the walls disappear and create a kind of spiritual union of inside and outside. Spain, the land of extremes, naturally had to take the principle a step further. The virtuoso stone lace spires, finished to Juan de Colonia's design in the 19th century, are only the crowning glory of the most diaphanous church ever built. Note how the windows in the bell towers were made so wide that from most points of view you can actually see through the towers. Hundreds of pinnacles, as electric as any of Gaudí's, pattern out the sky, while between the towers hangs an equally transparent, thoroughly over-the-top gallery of statues of Spanish kings, under the biggest, most delicate stone traceries ever perched over a façade. Imagine the master mason directing the works in the 1200s, dreaming of a building that would be built half of stone, half of light and air.

The enclosed **choir** is almost entirely shut off from the rest of the church, but nonetheless acessible on the visitor. Lift your gaze above the grill work to see the magnificent gold-trimmed star vault of Juan de Vallejo's **lantern**, under the central tower, which Felipe II declared couldn't have been built by men, but only by angels. Four stately round piers support a profusion of intricate carved decoration – a Spanish twist on Renaissance styles, married harmoniously into a Gothic building. Underneath its majestic beauty a simple slab marks the **tomb of the Cid and his wife Ximena**, their bones relocated here with great pomp in 1921. The other tomb in the *coro* belongs to Bishop Maurice, topped by his enamelled copper effigy; try to get in to see the magnificent carving on the wood and inlaid stalls – unabashed pagan figures on the seats, New Testament scenes above. They were done by Felipe de Vigarni, who also sculpted the dramatic scene on the ambulatory behind the main altar.

The most spectacular chapel, the octagonal **Chapel of the High Constable of Castile** (*Capilla del Condestable*), was built by Simón de Colonia for Pedro Hernández de Velasco in 1482–94. The tomb, accompanied by that of the Constable's wife, Doña Mencía de Mendoza, faces the elaborate altar by Vigarni and Diego de Siloé. The constable, the head of the Castilian army, clutches his sword even after death; his lady's little dog sleeps at her feet. Velasco was constable during the conquest of Granada, whose Moorish craftsmen inspired the great, geometric star-vaulting that crowns the chapel. Among the works of art within the chapel is a wonderfully voluptuous auburn-haired *Magdalen* by Giampetrino, a pupil of Leonardo da Vinci.

The nearby **Sacristía Mayor** – the cathedral's sacristy – is adorned with one of the cathedral's lighter scenes, a Baroque bubble bath of a heaven. Off the cloister, the **Museo Diocesano** (*adm included in ticket to cathedral*) is housed in a series of Gothic chapels: the Capilla de Corpus Christi contains the famous leather-bound coffer the Cid filled with sand and locked tight, then passed off as gold as security to Raquel and

Vidas, two Jewish money lenders, who made him a sizeable loan; another prized possession is the Cid's marriage agreement in the next door chapel of Santa Catalina. The most prized possessions, including a series of vivid paintings from a medieval reliquary, are gathered in the adjoining chapels of San Juan and San Diego.

The cathedral's main draw, however, is just inside the west door, in the part of the cathedral kept separate for religious services only. To the right, is the glass-doored **Capilla del Santo Cristo**, where ladies gathered to worship one of the strangest cult idols of any religion – the 13th-century **Cristo de Burgos**, a figure made of buffalo hide (long reputed to be human skin), real hair and fingernails (according to an old tale, both had to be trimmed regularly), in a green frock and warm to the touch. The head and arms can move, like a doll; these were probably somehow manipulated to impress the faithful, back in the golden age of miracles. Still the focus of enormous veneration, the only way to get a glimpse is to re-enter the cathedral via the west door and peer through the chapel's glass doors, or else attend a service.

Around the Cathedral

Just to the northwest of the cathedral on Calle Fernán González, **San Nicolás de Bari** (*open July–Sept Mon–Sat 11–2 and 4–8, rest of the year Mon–Fri 9.30–2 and 5–7; adm*) contains an incredible wall-sized alabaster *retablo* by Francisco de Colonia (1505), depicting 36 scenes from the Bible and more angels than could dance on a head of a pin. **Santa Águeda** (*open only before and after mass*) a plain 15th-century church on Calle Santa Águeda, is the successor of the church where the Cid forced Alfonso VI to swear on a silver lock that he had nothing to do with the assassination of his brother Sancho – an iron copy of the lock is hung over the door inside. The Cid's ancestral mansion, the **Solar del Cid**, was demolished in 1771, though two obelisks mark the site. Between his two banishments and innumerable campaigns, he probably had little leisure to enjoy it anyway.

The **castle** was blown up by the French in 1813 – an explosion that shattered most of the cathedral's stained glass, and little remains to be seen up here besides the fine view of the city. In its day, however, the castle saw many important events – Edward I of England and Leonora of Castile were married here. It is reached through the horseshoe **Arco de San Esteban**; also near the arch are two 14th-century Gothic churches: **San Esteban** and **San Gil**, both with fine interiors. San Esteban also houses a museum of altarpieces (*Museo de Retablos, open summer 10.30–2 and 4.30–7, rest of the year Sat 10.30–2 and 4.30–7; adm*). Near San Gil, in Plaza Alonso Martínez, you'll notice a grim little building called the **Capitanería**, guarded by military police and adorned with commemorative plaques dedicated to Franco and Mola. This was the Nationalist capital during the Civil War; here Franco assumed total power among the rebels and directed his campaigns in the north. Calle Santander is Burgos' main shopping street; at its head is the **Casa del Cordón**, named after the rope (really a Franciscan monk's belt) carved over the door in honour of St Francis. This palace was built by the Condestable de Velasco in 1485. Ferdinand and Isabel received Columbus here after his second voyage, and 18 years later, an ageing Ferdinand sent Ponce de León off to discover the Fountain of Youth.

Nearby, the attractive, arcaded **Plaza Mayor** has been refurbished and pedestrianized, although the shady **Paseo del Espolón** along the riverfront is the city's real centre; at the far end, a mighty equestrian **statue of the Cid** seems ready to fly off its base and attack any enemy crossing **San Pablo Bridge** towards the Plaza Primo de Rivera. The bridge is embellished with stone figures of the Cid's wife, his companions and a Moorish king. Across the bridge (and past the site of the new Museum of Evolution, due to open in 2008) the lovely **Casa Miranda** (1545) houses the archaeological collection of the **Museo de Burgos** (*open Tues–Fri 10–2 and 4–7, Sat 10–2 and 5–8, 4–7 in winter, Sun 10–2; adm, free Sat and Sun*). In the adjoining Casa de iñigo Angulo is the **Museo de Bellas Artes** (*same opening times, adm with same ticket*), with four floors of local art from the 12th–20th centuries. The best is the medieval art in the first gallery, which includes some exquisite treasures from the Monasterio de Santo Domingo de los Silos (*see* below).

Monasterio de Las Huelgas

On the outskirts of Burgos lie two of Spain's richest monasteries, both well worth a visit. A 20-minute walk to the west will take you to the Cistercian convent of **Las Huelgas** (*open Tues–Sat 10–1 and 3.45–5.30, Sun 10.30–2; adm, free Wed for EU citizens*), founded by Alfonso VIII in 1187 at the behest of his wife Leanor, daughter of England's Henry II (*huelga* in Spanish means a strike now, but, back then *Las Huelgas Reales*, the monastery's true name, meant 'The Royal Repose'). The abbess of Las Huelgas had more power and influence than any other woman in Spain except the queen herself, until her powers were revoked in the 19th century. In 1219 San Ferdinand III began the custom of Castilian kings going to Las Huelgas to be knighted into the Order of Santiago by Santiago himself; in the cloister you can see the statue of the saint with a moveable arm holding out a sword made for this purpose. Guided tours (in Spanish) will take you through the English-Gothic church: statues of Alfonso VIII and Leanor kneel before the altar, and there's a curious painted iron pulpit of 1560 that gyrated to allow the priest to address the nuns in the choir or congregation. The church also serves as a royal pantheon of Castilian kings and royal ladies. The French, as usual, desecrated the tombs, though the one they missed, that of Alfonso X's son Ferdinand de la Cerda, produced such a fine collection of goods as to form the nucleus of Las Huelgas' **Museo de Ricas Telas**, a fascinating collection of fabrics and medieval dress, showing considerable Eastern influences (*currently undergoing expansion and closed until late 2006*).

These are not the only Moorish touches in Las Huelgas: note the geometric tomb of the Infanta Doña Blanca, the peacock and stars in the *mudéjar* **cloister**, and the **Capilla de Santiago**. The grandest chamber, the **Sala Capitular**, contains a trophy from Alfonso VIII's great Battle of Las Navas de Tolosa – the silk flap of the Moorish commander's tent – and Don Juan's banner from Lepanto, which he gave to his daughter Ana, abbess of Las Huelgas. If the guide's in a good mood, he'll play a scale on the well-tuned columns in the halls. Some 44 nuns still live at Las Huelgas, painting porcelain and baking cookies. Noble and wealthy pilgrims would receive a fair welcome at Las Huelgas, but for the needs of poor pilgrims Alfonso VIII also built the **Hospital del Rey**, a short walk from Las Huelgas, facing the road to León. Most impressive here are the 16th-century Plateresque gateway and the court.

La Cartuja de Miraflores

Burgos' second great monastery, a 3.5km walk to the east, through a lovely park of shady trees. **Miraflores** (*open daily 10.15–3 and 4–6, Sun 11–3 and 4–6*), was founded by Juan II in 1441 and is still in use so you can see only the church, built by the Colonia family; yet this alone contains more great art than many cathedrals. Here Isabel la Católica commissioned the great Gil de Siloé to sculpt the **tomb of Juan II and Isabel of Portugal** as a memorial to her parents and, after four years' work, he created the most elaborate, detailed tomb of all time, 'imprisoning Death inside an alabaster star' as a local guide-book poetically put it. Instead of a chisel, it looks as if Siloé used a needle to sew the robes of the effigies – Juan pensive, his wife reading a book. Isabella owed her succession to her brother's death and, as a posthumous thank you, had Siloé carve his memorial too. The tomb of the Infante Don Alfonso shows the young prince (1453–68) kneeling at prayer among a playful menagerie of animals, putti and birds entwined in vines. Master Siloé also did most of the gilt *retablo* of the high altar, said to be made with the gold that Columbus had presented to the Catholic kings at the Casa de Cordón.

Other works of art include a lovely painting of the Annunciation by Pedro Berruguete; carvings on the stalls of the lay brothers' choir (the middle section of the Carthusian church's traditional three divisions – the monks' choir is in the front, the general public at the back), a painting of the Virgin sending the infernal spirits packing and a wooden polychrome **statue of St Bruno** in the side chapel by the Portuguese Manuel Pereira, so lifelike 'it would speak if it weren't a Carthusian monk', as the *burgaleses* like to say.

Below Miraflores, 10km further down the road is the **Abbey of San Pedro de Cardeña**, founded in 899 and now a Trappist monastery (*open Apr–Oct Mon–Sat 10–1 and 4–6, Sun 12–1.30 and 4–6; Nov–Mar Mon–Sat 10–1.30 and 3.30–5.30, Sun 12–1.30 and 3.30–5.30; adm*). Here the Cid left his family when banished by Alfonso VI, and here he was buried beside his wife Ximena. The French stole the bones and when the Spanish government finally got them back it was to inter them in the more secure precincts of the cathedral. You can visit the tombs with their effigies in a chapel off the **Cloister of Martyrs**, where 200 Benedictines were beheaded in a 10th-century Moorish raid. The Cid's faithful charger Babieca is buried just outside the gate.

Southeast of Burgos

The most popular corner for a day out from Burgos is the mountainous region to the southeast, on or off the N234 towards Soria where it's hard to tell where one sierra begins and another ends. Covarrubias and Santo Domingo de Silos are firmly marked on the tourist map, but you'll need a car to take in the prizes just off the beaten track such as San Quirce or the Visigothic church of Quintanilla de las Viñas.

A Scatological Abbey and a Visigothic Beauty

The **Abadía de San Quirce** is not easy to find; signposts guide you from **Hontoria de la Cantera**. Set in a quiet wooded valley, it was founded by Count Fernán González after his defeat of the Saracens on this spot in 929. Abandoned in 1835, the church

Getting Around

Transport here is sketchy. There are several **buses** daily from Burgos to Aranda de Duero, and usually one a day to Santo Domingo de Silos (except on Sundays) and Caleruega, and about three a day to Lerma and to Covarrubias. Services are reduced at weekends. Otherwise you'll need to hire a car or a taxi to get around.

Tourist Information

Covarrubias: t 94 740 64 61. *Open Mar–Dec.*
Santo Domingo de Silos: C/Cuatro Cantones 10, t 94 739 00 70. *Open Apr–Oct.*
Lerma: C/Audiencia 6, t 94 717 70 02.
Aranda de Duero: Plaza Mayor s/n, t 94 751 04 76.

Where to Stay and Eat

Covarrubias ✉ 09346

★★★**Arlanza**, Pza Mayor 11, t 94 740 64 41, *www.hotelarlanza.com* (*inexpensive*). Occupies a handsome old mansion in the town centre; its restaurant serves medieval banquets on Saturday nights with music and ancient Castilian dances; book ahead.
★★**Doña Sancha**, Avda Victor Barbadillo 31, t 94 740 64 00 (*budget*). A welcoming rural hotel, built in traditional style. Every room has a balcony offering lovely views.
Restaurante de Galo, C/Monseñor Vargas 10, t 94 740 63 93 (*moderate*). Atmospheric restaurant with medieval open chimney, serving typical Castilian fare. *Closed Mon eve and Wed.*

Santo Domingo de Silos ✉ 09610

★★★**Tres Coronas**, Pza Mayor 6, t 94 739 00 47, f 94 739 00 65 (*moderate*). Located in a charming 18th-century stone house, with 16 intimate rooms. There's a classic restaurant which serves a filling *menú del día*.

★★★**Santo Domingo de Silos**, C/Santo Domingo 14, t 94 739 0053 (*moderate–budget*). Choose from the 3★ hotel or the hostel; all rooms are flouncy in classic Spanish style, but those in the hotel are better equipped. The restaurant serves hearty Castillian classics and a good value lunch *menú*.
★★**Arco de San Juan**, Pradera de San Juan 1, t/f 94 739 00 74 (*inexpensive*). Near the famous cloister, this is a quiet place with a delightful garden.
Hospederia de Monasterio, t 94 739 00 49 (*budget*). Men 'in need of spiritual exercise' can eat and sleep for a song (well, almost) in the monastery; ring in advance.

Aranda de Duero ✉ 09400

Aranda gets plenty of business travellers en route to Madrid and concentrates its functional hotels near the highway; most have cheap weekend rates.
★★★★**Torremilanos**, Ctra N122 km 274, t 94 751 2852, *www.torremilanos.com* (*expensive*). A pretty, pastel-painted bodega-hotel in its own gardens just outside the centre. Elegant, well-equipped rooms and a fine restaurant featuring their own highly respected wines.
★★**Hotel Julia**, Plaza de la Virgencilla s/n, t 94 750 12 50 (*inexpensive*). A modest, but conveniently central hotel, with comfy rooms and a decent old-fashioned restaurant.
Mesón de la Villa, C/La Sal 3, t 94 750 10 25 (*expensive*). Serves some of the best food around, including poultry and garden vegetables raised on owner Eugenio Herrero's own farm, accompanied by the finest bottles of Rioja. *Closed Mon.*
Rafael Corrales, C/Carrequemada 2, t 94 750 02 77 (*moderate*). An *asador* that opened in 1902, serving baby lamb baked in a wood oven, washed down with Ribera del Duero. *Closed Thurs eve.*

conserves its original structure, with a stout fortified tower in the centre; the west door has 11 modillions showing the Creator, Adam and Eve, Cain and Abel and, in between, earthy reliefs of men squatting and defecating, with inscriptions reading *io cago* and *mal cago* (I shit, and I shit badly); one thinks of the anarchical shitting figure, the *caganer*, that accompanies every Catalan Christmas crib. Other reliefs decorate the north door and modillions supporting the charming bubble of an apse, unusually illuminated by two round bull's-eye windows and a regular Romanesque window, which was probably originally a bull's eye as well; inside (*open only the first Tues of each month, 9.30–6*) the capitals are carved with the legend of San Quirce and a naked woman who suckles serpents, with lions on either side.

Further south on the N234, there's an unusual corridor-dolmen at the ghost town of **Mazariegos**, where the big stones are engraved with what could be horses. Aim your next stop for **Quintanilla de las Viñas**, where 4km up under the steel-toned Montes de Lara and the ruins of the Castilla de Lara, the gold-stoned Visigothic **Nuestra Señora de las Viñas** drinks up the sun (*open Oct–Mar 10–5; Apr 10–2 and 4–6; May–June 10–2 and 4–7; July–Sept 10–2 and 4–8; closed Mon, Tues and the last weekend of each month; t 652 649 6215*). This is the last Visigothic basilica in Spain, dated 7th century or just before the invasion of the Moors. Made of large blocks incised with Christian graffiti, only the square apse and part of the transept have survived the past 1,300 years. The exterior of the former is beautifully girdled with three friezes, the lowest band of vines and grapes, the middle band decorated with plants and birds – ducks, peacocks, doves, and what are thought to be the monograms of the founders, in round medallions of curling tendrils. The upper band has a Persian air with griffons, leopards, lions, deer, bulls and rams. Inside, on the triumphal arch, there's another bird frieze and a rare example of Visigothic syncretism: angels with rocket wings, Byzantine in style or perhaps even more like the winged figures on Roman tombs, holding up portraits identifying Christ with the moon (a bearded figure, with a crescent moon LVNA on his head like horns) and the Virgin (or Church) with the sun SOL, topped by a Latin inscription: 'I, modest Flammola, I offer this modest gift.' Blocks in the apse show heavily coiffed, symmetrical but inexplicable 'astral' figures, sculpted by another artist who had trouble getting the arms and hands right.

Fernán González Country: San Pedro de Arlanza and Covarrubias

South of Quintanilla de las Viñas, the Arlanza river runs east–west through a valley known in the 10th century as the Valley of Towers, the frontier of old Castile, pushed this far south by 'the Good Count' Fernán González, the founder of the realm. His exploits are described in an epic poem, written in the 13th century by a monk in the large, now romantically ruined, abbey of **San Pedro de Arlanza** (*open Oct–Mar 10–5; Apr–June 10–2 and 4–7; July–Sept 10–2 and 4–8; closed Mon, Tues and last weekend of every month, t 689 596 064*) founded by the count's father, Gonzalo Fernández in 912, below a cave where the hermit Pelagio predicted the illustrious destiny of his line. The guardian will let you in to see what's left of the church, its tower, cloister and nave.

Medieval **Covarrubias** is Old Castile's half-timbered showcase of porticoed squares and lanes, guarded by the only surviving 10th-century Mozarab tower in the Valley of Towers, the sturdy **Torreón de Doña Urraca**, whose countess was walled up inside in 965 and left to die. The Ayuntamiento has a Romanesque doorway that once belonged to Fernán González's palace. Behind this, the ex-Colegiata, **San Cosme y San Damián** (*open Wed–Sat 10.30–2 and 4–7, Sun 10.30-12 and 4–7; adm*) was rebuilt in 1474 as the pantheon for the count's descendants, the Infantes de Covarrubias, whose tombs line the nave; in 1848, the remains of Fernán González and his wife Sancha were brought from San Pedro de Arlanza and placed next to the altar in a 4th-century Roman sarcophagus. The 17th-century organ, one of the most beautiful in Spain, still works, although you'll

The Bloody Cucumber of Vengeance

East of Santo Domingo de Silos, Salas de los Infantes is named after the legend of the Siete Infantes de Lara, a favourite subject of Spanish ballad and romance. The seven sons of Gonzalo Gustios, the Lord of Salas, were known for their chivalry and prowess, in no small thanks to their tutor, the judge Nuño Rasura. In 986 their troubles began at the splendid wedding of their uncle Ruy Velázquez to Doña Lambra, when the youngest of the seven brothers quarrelled with a kinsman of the bride. Doña Lambra took the quarrel as a personal insult and, as the brothers rode away, she ordered her slave to heave a bloody cucumber at them. This was the ultimate deadly insult in 10th-century Castile (discretion forbade the romancers to explain exactly why); the outraged brothers slew the slave, even though he tried to 'hide even in the folds of her garment'.

Now it was Ruy Velázquez's turn to feel insulted by the brothers, and he schemed to avenge himself on the whole family. First he sent the father to Córdoba with a message in Arabic for the king, asking him to slay the bearer; but the Moorish king took pity on Gustios and merely put him in prison, where the king's sister fell in love with him and bore him a son named Mudarra. Meanwhile, Ruy Velázquez plotted an ambuscade with another Moorish king, so that when he sent the seven brothers and Nuño Rasura out to fight the Moors they were headed off at the pass by a far superior force and killed. The Moorish king sent Velázquez their eight heads, and he forwarded them to Gustios as a homecoming present. After 14 years, Mudarra came north to find his father and promised to avenge the deaths of his seven brothers. When Ruy Velázquez heard of Mudarra, he thumpingly declared, in Lockhart's translation of the Spanish Ballads:

Oh, in vain have I slaughter'd the Infants of Lara,
There's an heir in his halls – there's the bastard Mudara.
There's the son of the renegade – spawn of Mahoun:
If I meet with Mudara, my spear brings him down.

Of course it was Mudarra who brought down Velázquez instead. He then stoned and burned Doña Lambra at the stake for the bloody cucumber insult, and became lord of Salas. The parish church of Salas de los Infantes keeps the heads of the Seven Infantes and Nuño Rasura in a reliquary; their trunks are stored in the weird old tombs at San Millán de la Cogolla (see p.110).

have to attend Mass to hear its sweet antique sound. The cloister contains the tomb of a 13th-century Norwegian princess, promised to Alfonso the Wise but married to his ex-bishop brother Ferdinand (see p.254). The prize in the museum is the Flemish-inspired *Triptych of the Magi*, by an unknown 16th-century sculptor.

Santo Domingo de Silos and its Sublime Cloister

South of Covarrubias at **Santibáñez del Val**, the road to Barrious leads 2km to the River Ura and the 10th-century Mozarabic hermitage of **Santa Cecilia de Barriosuso**, with a square apse and window made of five rings and a horseshoe arch inside. The attraction in these parts, though, one that brings many pilgrims down on a special detour, is **Santo Domingo de Silos** (*www.silos.arrakis.es, open for guided visits only Tues–Sat 10–1 and 4.30–6, Sun, Mon and hols 4.30–6; adm*), a Benedictine monastery founded in 954 by Fernán González and ruled in the 10th century by the abbot who gave it its name. Rebuilt after al-Mansur razed it to the ground, the monastery was re-founded in the 19th century by French Benedictines from Solesmes, who have made it famous for Gregorian chant (*sung six times a day: times on the website, or call* t *94 739 00 49*). They inherited the most beautiful Romanesque **cloister** in Spain, elegant, two-tiered and ivory coloured, built around an ancient cypress tree. The lower section dates from the late 11th–early 12th centuries and has fascinating capitals on twin columns carved by a sculptor so well versed in animals and other motifs of the Córdoba caliphate and Middle East that he may have been a Moor. On the corners of the cloister, eight large reliefs on the life of Jesus are in a similar style; one shows the only known representation of Christ in pilgrim's garb. The cloister's *mudéjar* **ceiling**, painted with scenes of everyday life in the Middle Ages, has been restored. Off the cloister, the **museum** houses Mozarabic illuminations (Santo Domingo is a study centre of Mozarabic art, liturgies and manuscripts), the Romanesque tympanum from the first church, a 12th-century paten with Roman cameos, an 11th-century chalice and the 18th-century **pharmacy** (*botica*) with big jars. After all this, the **church**, rebuilt in the neoclassical style in the 18th century, seems dull.

A mere 2.5km from Santo Domingo towards Caleruega, a narrow gorge, the **Desfiladero de la Yecla**, has been fitted with some rather battered wooden walkways , making for an easy and spectacular walk; the stair descends just before the tunnel and the end of the walkway emerges just after it. The gorge is part of a nature park with colonies of vultures, hawks and buzzards, the largest *sabina* (shrubby juniper) forest in the world, and remains of a Celtic *castro*. Beyond attractive hill-top **Hinojar de Cervera**, the Cueva de San García has even older traces of civilization, dating back to the Upper Palaeolithic era. **Caleruega**, further south, was the birthplace in 1170 of yet another canonized Domingo, the one who went into the heavenly big time, Santo Domingo de Guzmán. It was his theological battles against the heretical Cathars in Toulouse that led, in 1216, to Domingo's founding of his preaching order, the Dominicans or Black Friars, who took on the job of the Inquisition. The Guzmán tower house is still intact, and the exact spot of the saint's birth is marked in the crypt of the church of Dominican Madres.

There are some strange things around Salas, including a Visigothic hermitage covered with weird symbols on a hill just south of **Barbadillo del Mercado** (on the N234), under cliffs where you can see lammergeyers. East, in **Palacios de la Sierra**, the parish church has a collection of indecipherable Palaeochristian tombstones. **Jaramillo de la Fuente**, towards the Sierra de la Demanda, has a fine 12th-century Romanesque church.

Way Down South in Burgos Province

The N1 south of Burgos to Madrid passes through **Lerma**, another town on the Arlanza river, founded by the son of Fernán González in 978. It owes its impressive appearance to the unusually successful Dukes of Lerma, one of whom (Francisco Gómez de Sandoval y Rojas) ruled Spain between 1598 and 1618 for Felipe III. It was the duke's idea to expel the *moriscos*, and devote a part of the proceeds from their expropriated property into making Lerma (effectively, the capital of Spain during his lifetime) a unique monumental complex, with at least six monasteries and a four-towered **Palacio Ducal**, recently converted into a luxurious parador. This is linked by a flying walkway (so the duke could attend mass without mingling with the commoners) to the **Colegiata de San Pedro**, bearing the duke's crest over the door. Inside, the church contains its original organ of 1616 and a statue in bronze of the archbishop of Seville, the uncle of the duke. The tourist office (*see* p.246) offers daily guided tours of the town.

Much further south, **Gumiel de Izán** has a fine 15th-century parish church with monumental stairs and a beautiful Renaissance *retablo* by an unknown master; the adjacent museum, open when the priest is around, has Romanesque capitals salvaged from its long-gone monastery. Gumiel marks the northern limits of DO Ribera del Duero, the largest and finest wine region in Castile, producing a variety of reds, especially from a local grape known as *tinto del país*; mixed with garnacha, malbec, merlot and cabernet sauvignon, it becomes a fresh rosé, a purplish young wine or a mellow well-aged wine; '95, '96, '99 and 2001 are excellent; Vega Sicilia is the most illustrious name. **Aranda de Duero**, the third town of the province, has a number of old *bodegas* and a pair of good churches: Santa María has a beautiful portal attributed to Simón de Colonia and an excellent Renaissance *retablo*.

Downriver, the Augustinian **Monasterio de la Vid**, 'of the vine' (*open Tues–Sun 10–1 and 4–7.30*), boasts an 18th-century Baroque façade with spiralling leaves and roses on the sides of the elegant belfry and octagonal dome. East of Aranda, picturesque **Peñaranda de Duero** is built around the sprawling castle of its medieval lords, the Avellaneda, who in the safer 16th century decided to move down into the arcaded Plaza Mayor. A fine Plateresque portal marks their **Palacio de los Zúñiga y Avellaneda** (*open Tues–Sun 11–1 and 3–5*), built around an elegant two-storey patio; rooms are adorned with superb *artesonado* ceilings and plasterwork. Around the corner, the 17th-century **Botica de Jimeno** is the second-oldest pharmacy in Spain, and has been in the same family for seven generations; of its original fittings, there are some 230 pharmaceutical jars, stills and books.

North of Peñaranda, the half-ruined silhouette of a castle tops **Coruña del Conde**, where in the 18th century a local inventor named Diego Marín made the first manned flight in Spain. The equally isolated 11th-century **Ermita del Santo Cristo** is made out of stones cannibalized from the Roman city of **Clunia**, just north, near Peñalba de Castro, where the guardian lives (*www.arqueoturismoclunia.com, open summer Tues–Sun 10–2 and 4–8; winter Tues–Sun 11–2 and 3–6*). Founded under the reign of Augustus, it counted 30,000 inhabitants at its peak. In AD 69 Galba, Governor of Nearer Spain, rose up here against Nero and was proclaimed emperor by his legionaries; the Senate concurred, leaving Nero to run himself through. He was the first ruler to come from outside the Julian and Claudian families, although he adopted the names Caesar and Augustus. Managing to displease nearly everybody by the time he got to Rome, he was brutally murdered the next year by Otho, his successor – another, more ominous, precedent. Clunia was abandoned with the fall of Rome, leaving the forum, a large if eroded rock-cut theatre, baths, temples, and houses with mosaics dusty and mute.

Getting Around

By Bus

Daily buses run from Burgos to Aguilar de Campóo and Cervera de Pisuerga (twice a day on Thurs and Sat), to Palencia, Frómista, Sahagún, Saldaña and Carrión (on the Burgos–León route), to Sasamón and Grijalba.

By Train

Frómista can also be reached by train on the Palencia–Santander line .

Tourist Information

Frómista: Plaza del Tui 11, t 97 981 07 63, www.fromista.com.

Where to Stay and Eat

Castrojeriz ✉ 34440
★★Mesón de Castrojeriz, C/Cordón 1, t 94 737 86 10 (*inexpensive*). Offers a handful of rooms in a lovely old stone building, a peaceful setting. Simple traditional fare in the dining room (*moderate–inexpensive*)

Frómista ✉ 34440
★Hotel San Martín, Plaza San Martín 7, t 97 981 00 00 (*budget*). Modern, but built in traditional style, this is a friendly, central spot.
Fonda Marisa, t 97 981 00 23 (*budget*). Costs even less and cooks up good *menús*.
Hostelería de Los Palmeros, Pza San Telmo, t 97 981 00 67 (*expensive–moderate*). Fine restaurant that began as a *hostal* for pilgrims, although the medieval décor has undergone several styles since; furnished with antiques; the set lunch is €18. *Closed Tues in winter.*

Villalcázar de Sirga ✉ 34440
There's limited accommodation here, besides a pilgrims' shelter behind the town hall and a couple of *casas rurales* nearby.
Hostal Infanta Doña Leonor, C/Condes de Toreno 1, t 97 988 80 15 (*budget*). A delightful little hostal with café-bar in the centre. They also run the cosy and simpler hostal Los Cantigos (*budget*) geared towards pilgrims.
Mesón Los Templarios, Pza Mayor, t 97 988 80 22 (*moderate*). This popular, charming former grainhouse offers Castilian favourites, including baked suckling-pig with almonds. *Closed eves in winter, exc Fri–Sun.*

Along the Pilgrim Route: Burgos to Carrión de los Condes

Those rayes that do but warm you in England, do roast you here; those beams that irridate onely, and gild your honey-suckled fields, do here scorch and parch the chinky gaping soyle, and put too many wrinkles on the face of your common mother.

Howell

If the medieval pilgrim survived the storms, cut-throats and wolves at Roncesvalles, the Navarrese who exposed themselves when excited, and the dupers and fleshpots of Burgos, then they faced the dustiest, flattest, hottest and most monotonous landscape in Europe. The idea is that with nothing to look at one becomes introspective and meditative, altogether in a proper state to receive enlightenment. On the other hand, nearly all the route between Burgos and León is off the highways, on paths and lonely backroads where 20th-century intrusions are rare; their straggling hamlets of humble adobe houses, church towers crowned with storks and huge dovecotes (pigeon was the only meat the country folk could afford) evoke the Middle Ages as powerfully as any cathedral.

From Burgos to the Puente de Fitero

After Burgos, the pilgrim's path goes straight to Castrojeriz, leaving the N120 in Tardajos; by car the first important stop is **Sasamón**, 33km west of the capital. This was the Celtiberian Segisamo, where Augustus camped with his Macedonian legions, en route to pummel the Cantabrians. The town's pride is its church of **Santa María la Real**, with an exact 12th-century copy of the Sarmental door on the cathedral of Burgos (*see* p.239); it has a good, if damaged, cloister and a statue of St Michael attributed to Diego de Siloé. The **Ermita de San Isidro Labrador** has a superb 16th-century cross, the Cruz del Humilladero. Of the third church, the 15th-century **San Miguel**, only the portal survives with its seven archivaults isolated in a field like a lost triumphal arch.

In nearby **Olmillos**, the stately 15th-century castle belonged to the Leví, a noble family of Conversos; the current owner plans to convert it into a pilgrims' guesthouse. A few kilometres northwest, at **Grijalba**, the 13th-century Gothic church of **Santa María de los Reyes** has plenty of gargoyles and carved capitals with New Testament themes; inside, the ribs of the vaults are painted with alligators with sharp teeth. The font is a pretty 12th-century work carved with interlacings, and supported by a lion and a serpent.

The main road, however, heads south of Tardajos, passing through the village of **Hornillos del Camino**, home to an old pilgims' hospital, the Espíritu Santo. After Hornillos the road passes through the haunting, ravaged remains of the 14th-century **Monasterio de San Antón**, its once magnificent vaults hanging miraculously in the void. Its monks were famous for treating pilgrims afflicted with 'St Anthony's fire' or erysipelas, inflammations on the body, associated with leprosy. What really went on is a medieval mystery. The Order of St Anthony was founded in France in 1093, named after a 5th-century anchorite in the Egyptian desert, often depicted holding fire in his hands, symbolic of spiritual force and energy. His followers went about dressed in blue with the Greek **T** or *tau*, the cross of St Anthony, sewn on their habits, bearing a staff and bell; they would not only give passing pilgrims a meal but little *tau*-shaped amulets holding 'St Anthony's fire'. As St Anthony was also the patron of domestic animals (when not shown with fiery hands, he is accompanied by his pet pig), his monks kept pigs, or rather let them run wild, a practice that ended when one jaywalking porker in Paris tripped up the horse bearing the dauphin and caused him to break his neck.

West is the medieval castle and village of **Castrojeriz**, an old Iberian settlement that once had seven hospitals and a residence of Pedro the Cruel along its long Calle de los Peregrinos. In 974 Fernán González wrote down its privileges in a charter, giving equal rights to Christians and Jews. Its finest monument is at the village entrance: the Gothic church of **Santa María del Manzano**, named after the apple tree trunk where its statue of the Virgin was found when Santiago on his white horse, leapt from the castle to the tree; note the horseshoes on the door. Inside there are 16th-century tapestries and a *retablo* by Mengs; other tapestries, 17th-century and Flemish, are displayed in the parish museum of **Santo Domingo**; **San Juan**, built next to a 12th-century tower, conserves a half-ruined 14th-century cloister with an *artesonado mudéjar* ceiling.

An 8km detour to the south leads to **Celada del Camino**, which recalls a former pilgrimage role in its name and in its late Romanesque church, with striking Gothic tombs. Closer to Castrojeriz, **Castrillo de Matajudíos** (apparently not 'Kill Jews' but 'Hill of Jews') was the birthplace of the great Spanish composer of the Renaissance, Antonio de Cabezón.

West of Castrojeriz the ruthless horizons of the *meseta* come into their own. The last hill for miles, the windswept **Alto de Mostelares** (2,950ft), looks over the Pisuerga river, the traditional frontier between Castile and León, although these days it just delimits the dotted line between Burgos and Palencia provinces. It is spanned by the handsome **Puente de Fitero** with 11 arches, built in the 11th century by pilgrimage-promoter Alfonso IV. Just before the bridge are the ruins of a 13th-century hospital of San Nicolás; just across it begins the Tierra de Campos, the high plains of the Visigoths. Little **Boadilla del Camino**, the first village (9km), has a beautiful 15th-century Gothic column in its plaza decorated with scallops. The parish church has a curious Romanesque baptismal font on 12 baby columns and decorated with swastikas and solar symbols.

Frómista

Six kilometres west, Frómista has been a key pilgrims' stop since the days of the *Codex Calixtinus* for its 'perfect Romanesque church', golden **San Martín** (*open summer 10–2 and 4.30–8, winter 3.30–6.30; adm*), founded in 1035 by the widow of Sancho the Great. Restored in 1893 with no little controversy by the arch-restorer of France, Viollet-le-Duc, San Martín is now a national monument stripped of all its trappings. Two slender turrets buttress the west door; inside, the proportions of the three-aisled, three-apsed, barrel-vaulted interior crowned by an octagonal tower satisfy the soul, and delight every architect who has ever entered. But just as noteworthy is the extraordinary amount of sculpted detail inside and out, on the modillions and capitals; the original 11th-century carvings are superb and easy to distinguish from the fond fancies of the restorers, who based their work on medieval sarcophagi and marked their work with an R. The whole is a tantalizing, but ultimately inaccessible, book of hundreds of medieval symbols and occult messages; a pair of binoculars comes in handy and a crick in the neck is probably unavoidable. The dedication to Martin, the 4th-century bishop of Tours, is also meaningful for he was a strong defender of the Priscillianists when they were persecuted and their leader, Prisciliano executed for heresy (*see* p.296); not that he supported their gnostic-Celtic beliefs as much as he fought the Church's use of civil means and persecutions to put down heresies. Of Frómista's other churches, note the 16th-century Santa María del Castillo with its elaborate painted Hispano-Flemish *retablo* with 29 panels. Near Frómista, you can visit four sets of locks of the Castilian Canal, dug in the 18th and 19th century and the inspiration for Lesseps' bigger ditch in Panama.

Beyond Frómista, the tawny little villages of Palencia merge into the tawny earth. **Villarmentero de Campos** has a delightful picnic ground, with a lawn for a siesta to prepare yourself for the next stop at **Villalcázar de Sirga**, once a thriving town and key Templar possession. The Knights, at the start of the 13th century, built the enormous church of **Santa María la Blanca** (*open 10.30–2 and 4.30–7.30, until 6.30 in winter*) with what must be the tallest porch in Spain, to shelter a richly decorated double portal

Richard Ford's Recipe for Roadkill

Richard Ford's *Handbook for Travellers in Spain* (1845), was the first serious guide to Spain and is perhaps the best guide written to any country – ever. No subject daunted him, not even Spanish cuisine. He diplomatically advises his readers never to let mine host's cat out of sight during the making of a meal, then quotes the old Spanish saying, 'A prudent diner will never look too closely into the things of the kitchen if he wishes to live a quiet life'; after all, Ford reasonably adds: 'it is the knowledge of the cheat that kills, not the cat', simmering away in the *olla podrida*.

Ford then suggests that if you really want to be sure of the ingredients in your supper, the only thing to do is have your own valet cook it for you, and offers a fine recipe for a *guisado*: 'Take hare, partridge, rabbit, chicken, or whatever you may have foraged on the road; it is also capital with pheasant...cut it up, save the blood, the liver and the giblets; do not wash the pieces, but dry them on a cloth; fry them with onions in a teacup of oil till browned; take an *olla* (pot), put in the bits with oil, equal portions of wine and water, but stock is far better than water; claret answers well, Valdepeñas better; add a bit of bacon, onions, garlic, salt, pepper pimientos, a bunch of thyme or herbs; let it simmer, carefully skimming it. Half an hour before serving, add the giblets; when done, which can be tested by feeling with a fork, serve hot. The stew should be constantly stirred with a wooden spoon, and grease, the ruin of all cookery, carefully skimmed off as it rises to the surface. When made with proper care and with a good salad, it forms a supper for a cardinal, or for Santiago himself.'

with a double frieze. Pilgrims made a beeline for the Capilla de Santiago and its miraculous Virgin (now a little the worse for wear), to whom Alfonso X the Wise dedicated his *Cantigas*, but modern visitors tend to head to the beautifully carved tombs sculpted by Antón Pérez de Carrión of the Infante Don Felipe (son of Ferdinand III the Saint) and his second wife, Leonor Ruiz de Castro, curiously gagged. Don Felipe, fifth of 14 children, was pursuing a meteoric ecclesiastical career and had just been made archbishop of Seville when he reversed course and married the Norwegian princess promised to his brother, the future Alfonso X. The princess died after four years and is buried in Covarrubias; Felipe soon remarried, but not long after, in 1271, was murdered by Alfonso, the next in line to the throne, who got away with it (no wonder he celebrated the Virgin's miracles). Here too is the tomb of a Knight Templar, with his hawk and sleeping lion: a rare burial, as most Templars were buried face down in the earth without a casket. The magnificent *retablo mayor* was painted by the school of Berruguete.

North of Frómista: the Románico Palentino

If you've the time or inclination, you could wander off the beaten track into the northern part of Palencia province, into the foothills of the Cantabrian mountains, known as the Románico Palentino for its rare collection of some 200, mostly untouched, never remodelled Romanesque churches (nothing less than the greatest concentration in Europe). It seems that the masons who built churches along the *camino* came up here to build churches in the new villages, founded to repopulate the region. Aguilar de Campóo, linked by bus from Burgos or Palencia, or train from Santander, makes the best base for exploring, although you really need a car and patience, and that most elusive object of desire: a good map of Spain.

North to Aguilar

Northwest of Alar del Rey (on the Santander–Palencia N611) you can easily see two of the finest Romanesque works in the region. **San Andrés de Arroyo** (*open summer 10–1 and 4–6.45, winter 10–12.30 and 3.15–6; adm*) is a Bernardine convent founded in 1190 with an small, interesting museum; the chapterhouse entrance is beautiful and the cloister has extraordinary twin columns and capitals, decorated with fretwork, zigzags and exotic flora. The second church, the golden-stone Iglesia de San Juan at **Moarves de Ojeda** (*get the key from the warden across from the entrance*) has a superb portal, with a Christ in a mandorla, four Evangelists and 12 Apostles; the capitals are crowded with people and inside there's a 13th-century baptismal font and a Gothic Virgin and Child. Other prime stops on the Romanesque trail are north of Moarves: **Cozuelos**, with a simple early 12th-century church; **Vallespinoso de Aguilar**, home to a fortified 12th-century hermitage on a rock with a cylindrical tower and pretty door; and **Barrio de Santa María**, a handsome village where the Ermita de Santa Eulalia is a pristine example of a 13th-century church with a lovely apse, the narrowest windows in Spain and murals. Its parish church underwent a Renaissance remodelling and has good 15th-century paintings inside and a finely carved Renaissance *retablo mayor*. From Vallespinoso the road skirts the Aguilar reservoir to Aguilar de Campóo (*see* below).

Tourist Information

Cervera de Pisuerga, Plaza Modesto Lafuente, t 97 987 06 95.
Aguilar de Campóo: Pza de España 30, t 97 912 36 41, *www.aguilardecampoo.com*

Where to Stay and Eat

Aguilar de Campóo ✉ 34800

***Valentin, Avda Ronda 23, t 97 912 21 25, *www.hotelvalentin.com* (*moderate*). A classic mountain hotel with chintzy rooms, a pleasant garden and good restaurant.
**Posada El Convento, in Santa María de Mave (12km from Aguilar de Campóo), t 97 912 36 11 (*moderate*). Serene and part of a lovingly restored Benedictine monastery. Its restaurant (*moderate*) is one of the best in the region.
Posada Santa María La Real, Avda de Cervera s/n, t 97 912 20 00 (*inexpensive*). Part of the 11th-century monastery buildings have been transformed to house this charming posada, with a lovely garden.
**Villa de Aguilar, C/José Antonio 15, t 97 912 22 25 (*budget*). For those on a tighter budget; all rooms with bath.
Cortés Poza, C/El Puente 39, t 97 912 30 55 (*budget*). Simple rooms and satisfying food awaits here: try the *caldereta de pescados y mariscos* (a huge seafood stew for two).

Cervera de Pisuerga ✉ 34840

***Parador de Cervera Pisuerga, Ctra de Resoba, t 97 987 00 75, *cervera@paradors.es* (*moderate*). On the edge of the Picos, this modern place is a plush spot for nature-lovers, with a good restaurant.
**El Roble, C/San Roque 6, t 97 987 44 29, *www.hotelelroble.com* (*inexpensive*). Stylish, modern hotel with individually decorated rooms and a bright café-bar.
Asador Gasolina, by Plaza Mayor, t 97 987 07 13 (*budget*). Tasty grilled meats at this popular restaurant; fills up at weekends.

Alternatively, if you stick to the N611, north of Alar del Rey, you'll find (just to the left) **Becerril del Carpio** with two Romanesque churches: one in Barrio de San Pedro with a fine portal; one in Barrio de Santa María, amid the Baroque mansions, where they had enough *pesetas* to remodel the church and give it some fancy *retablos*. In nearby **Santa María de Mave**, the monastery founded in 1208 has a fine portal, an octagonal lantern and some Renaissance murals in one of its three apses; the monastery building itself has been converted into a charming hotel (*see* p.255). The church in **Olleros de Pisuerga** to the west is some 300 years older, a rare example of a Spanish church carved into the living rock, with two naves. Further north, only a kilometre from Aguilar, **Lomilla** has a pretty Romanesque church with a 14th-century calvary.

Aguilar de Campóo

Set in the green mountain valley of the Río Pisuerga and next to a large man-made lake, Aguilar de Campóo is a picturesque town of cookie-bakers and leaning, medieval houses with big bold coats of arms, founded in the 10th century during the Reconquista resettlement scheme. The Aguilar, or eagle, of its name refers to its rocky limestone outcrop, its eagle's nest, crowned by a ruined but still mighty five-towered **castle** built in the 11th century. At the foot of the castle, the **Hermitage of Santa Cecilia** (get the key in the *casa rectoral*) was founded in 1041, and has a fine 12th-century tower and excellent capitals: one shows the Massacre of the Innocents, by 11th-century knights in fishscale armour. The town walls were built in the 1300s by Pedro I of Castile; one of the surviving six gates has an inscription in Hebrew and Spanish, a unique souvenir of Aguilar's once sizeable Jewish population. On the arcaded Plaza de España, Charles V once spent a week at the Palacio de los Marqueses; the Gothic **Colegiata de San Miguel** has the Renaissance mausoleum of the Marquesses of Aguilar and a **museum** (*open summer only 10.30–1 and 5–8; adm*) full of tombs, *retablos* and sculptures. Another square is named after Aguilar native Juan Martín, one of the 18 sailors to return from Magellan's trip around the world.

Two kilometres west of Aguilar, the Cistercian monastery of **Santa María la Real** (1213) has more excellent capitals and a good cloister; in 1988 it won a Europa Nostra award for its restoration and now shelters a **Museo del Romántico** (*open July–Aug daily 10.30–2 and 4–8, Sept–June Tues–Fri 4–7, Sat and Sun 110.30–2 and 4.30–7.30*), with plenty of information on, and a unique collection of, models of the region's churches. Tradition has it that Bernardo de Carpio is buried in a cave nearby; offended by Charlemagne's invasion of Spain in the *Chanson de Roland*, Castilian troubadours invented Bernardo as their own hero, a doughty warrior who along with the Castilians joined up with the Saracens and personally slew Roland, the brutish Frank invader. But after the battle of Roncesvalles Bernardo was betrayed by his own king and joined the Moors for good.

Romanesque Routes North of Aguilar

The road directly north of Aguilar takes in more Romanesque charmers: the 12th-century church at **Matalbaniega**, with two decorated portals, carved modillions and unusual caryatids. **Cillamayor**'s Romanesque church has a funerary hypogeum; at **Revilla de Santullán**, the church has a handsome portal with 15 figures, sitting at desks like members of the board, and other sculptures that verge on the pornographic.

Further along, **Valberzoso**'s church has 15th-century frescoes; the village of **Brañosera** claims to be one of Spain's oldest municipalities, with its charter dating back to 824; its Romanesque church has a good 12th-century portal. **Salcedillo**'s church also has a 12th-century portal; medieval **Villanueva de la Torre** has a 14th-century tower and church. **San Cebrián de Muda**'s 12th-century church has Renaissance paintings and murals.

West of Aguilar, **Cervera de Pisuerga** was once an important frontier settlement, but has retired to its meadows and old family manors, proud of its recently restored 16th-century Gothic church, **Santa María del Castillo** (*open June–Sept daily 10.30–1.30 and 5–8, rest of the year Sat–Sun 10.30–1.30 and 5–8; adm*), built on the medieval citadel, with a fine Hispano-Flemish *retablo* by Felipe de Vigarni and a beautiful painting of the *Adoration of the Magi* by Juan de Flandres, both in the Capilla de Santa Ana.

Three kilometres away, at **Ruesga**, there's a *parador* from which to enjoy the huge views across the mountains. At the northernmost point of Palencia province, **San Salvador de Cantamuda** is a graceful church with a pretty steeple and altar table. Southeast of Cervera de Pisuerga, **Perazancas de Ojeda** has a Romanesque parish church, and the 12th-century Lombard Romanesque hermitage of San Pelayo with contemporary murals.

Along the Carrión River

West of Frómista, into the *campos góticos*, the Visigothic plains, the pilgrims' route continues to Carrión de los Condes, whichoccupies one of Old Castile's chief north–south arteries. Palencia and environs were more important in Roman and Visigothic times than now; among things to see are two Roman villas and Spain's oldest dated church.

Back on the Pilgrim Track: Carrión de los Condes

West of Villalcázar de Sirga, Carrión de los Condes is named after the River Carrión and not for putrefying nobility, although it can't be denied that the Infantes or Counts of Carrión, who married the Cid's two daughters, were genuinely rotten villains; after picking up their big, glittering dowries, they beat their wives and tied them to oaks and left them for dead. The outraged Cid gathered up a posse, killed the Counts, and found his daughters new, even more princely husbands. The wicked Infantes are buried in the lovely Renaissance cloister of **San Zoilo**, a Benedictine monastery (now a luxury hotel) by the river, founded in 1047, when the Emir of Córdoba sent the 4th-century relics of Zoilo to the Count of Carrión. The lower gallery of the cloister is the work of Juan de Badajoz, who began in 1537; the upper bit was added in 1604.

Over the 16th-century bridge from San Zoilo, the heart of Carrión has two worn 12th-century Romanesque churches that preserve interesting portals. **Santiago**, in the Plaza Mayor, has a fine Christ in Majesty and apostles and representatives of 22 medieval guilds, including an armourer, scholar, musicians, cooks, tailor, smith, soldiers bashing each other, and contortionists (*information and tickets to church and museum from the church of Santa María, or by calling t 97 988 00 72*). On the edge of town, **Santa María del Camino** has a capital on the portal depicting the Tribute of 100 Maidens that the Castilians sent yearly to the Moors (probably because they had nothing else

Getting Around

By Train

There are frequent trains from Palenica to Burgos, Valladolid, Ávila, Madrid and Santander (via Frómista and Aguilar de Campóo); trains to León call at Paredes de Nava. The RENFE station is at Plaza de los Jardinillos, t 90 224 02 02.

By Bus

Carrión de los Condes is connected by bus with Frómista and Palencia; there are at least two buses a day. Palencia's bus station is next to the train station, on Plaza de los Jardinillos, t 97 974 32 22.

Tourist Information

Palencia: provincial tourist office at Plaza Abilio Calderón s/n, t 97 971 51 30, municipal office at C/Mayor 105, t 97 974 00 68.

Carrión de los Condes: Pza Santa María, t 97 988 09 32. *Open weekends only May and June, daily July, August and Easter Week.*

Where to Stay and Eat

Carrión de los Condes ✉ 34120

★★★**San Zoilo**, C/Obispo Souto, t 97 988 00 50, *www.sanzoilo.com* (*moderate*). Monastery providing attractive rooms (the nicest are in the original building) and a decent restaurant.

★★**Estrella del Bajo Carrión**, Ctra Palencia-Riaño (south of Carrión in Villoldo), t 97 982 70 05 (*inexpensive*). A comfortable, modern hotel

with a garden; the restaurant is fabulous (*moderate*), offering classic Castilian cuisine and wonderful desserts.

★**Hs La Corte**, C/Santa María 34, t 97 988 01 38 (*budget*). Rooms with or without bath are available along with a decent restaurant.

★**El Resbalón**, C/Fernán Gómez 19, t 97 988 04 33 (*budget*). Reasonable rooms. Its restaurant serves *menús* for around €8, including wine.

Convento de Santa Clara, C/Sta Clara 1, t 97 988 0134 (*budget*). The nuns at this ancient convent offer austere rooms with bath.

Palencia ✉ 34000

★★★★**AC Palencia**, Avda de Cuba 25, t 97 916 57 01, *www.ac-hotels.com* (*moderate*). Stylish, modern hotel on the outskirts of town.

★★★**Castilla Vieja**, Avda Casado del Alisal 26, t 97 974 90 44, *www.hotelessuco.com* (*moderate*). Similar to the Rey Sancho but with no pool, this is a sound choice with a good restaurant.

★★★**Rey Sancho de Castilla**, Avda Ponce de León, t 97 972 53 00, *www.reysancho.com* (*moderate*). Modern hotel offering swimming, tennis, football and activities for children.

Asador La Encina, C/Casañé 2, t 979710936 (*expensive–moderate*). Offers traditional Castillian dishes such as suckling pig, hearty stews, wild mushrooms plus a good selection of fish. Their tortilla has been awarded the prize for the best in Spain.

La Fragata, C/Pedro Fernandez del Pulgar 4–6, t 97 974 95 91 (*moderate–inexpensive*). Delicious, affordable contemporary cuisine in a slick modern restaurant in an old building.

Aparicio, C/Gaspar Arroyo 6, t 97 974 12 39. Local favourite; good range of tapas and *raciones*.

the Moors could possibly want); other figures are of Samson fighting the lion and women riding beasts. The interior is out of kilter, although whether it was done so intentionally (like Getaria, for instance) is hard to fathom; it could just be falling over. Lastly, the **Convent of Santa Clara** has a small **museum**, with religious art and a 17th-century organ (*open Tues–Sun 10.30–1 and 4.30–7.30; adm*). During the great days of the pilgrimage, the town produced two men of genius: Rabbi Shem Tov Ardutiel (Sem Tob), author of the *Danza General de la Muerte*, who died in 1370, and Íñigo López de Mendoza, the Marqués de Santillana, the Renaissance poet, not to be confused with the tycoon who bought the title (*see* p.191). Lastly, just off the road before the province of León, you can visit the 3rd-century AD Roman villa at **Quintanilla de la Cueza** (*open Apr –mid-Oct 10–1.30, 4.30–8; adm*) for its colourful mosaic floors and the heating system or hypocausts, protected by a shelter; there's a small museum on the site with finds.

South along the Carrión to Palencia

Paredes de Nava was the birthplace of two influential Castilian artists, painter Pedro Berruguete (d.1504) who worked in Urbino and introduced the Renaissance style to Spain as court painter to Ferdinand and Isabella, and his son Alonso (d. 1561), a pupil of Michelangelo, who brought Mannerism back with him and served as court painter to Charles V, although sculpture was his real love.

A few of the Berruguetes' paintings, including a *retablo mayor* by Pedro, remain in **Santa Eulalia**. The adjacent **museum** (*open 11–1 and 4–6, Sun am only*) has an impressive collection of works by other Renaissance masters (Gil de Siloé, Juan de Valmaseda, Juan de Flandres, Juan de Juni, among others) brought in from little churches in artsy Paredes de Nava. If you can't get enough, you'll find more paintings by Pedro Berruguete inside the church of Santa María in **Becerril de Campos**, 10km south (*closed Jan–Feb*).

Palencia

Once a thriving centre, Palencia remains one of the bigger wallflowers in the garden of Spain's provincial capitals; in 1185 Alfonso VIII made it the site of Spain's first university (though in 1239 it was removed to Salamanca). Charles V is partly responsible for Palencia's failure to thrive in later centuries, having not only sucked the city dry to pay the bribes he gave to be elected as Holy Roman Emperor, but also rubbed out the city's prospects and privileges in revenge for its leading role in the Comunero revolt.

The one thing they couldn't take away from Palencia is its Gothic **cathedral**, nicknamed *La Bella Desconocida* ('The Unknown Beauty'), in Plaza San Antolín (*open 9–1.30 and 4–6.30; adm to crypt and museum*). The exterior is magnificent. Don't miss the gargoyles. Juan de Flandres' Renaissance *retablo mayor* is the prize in an interior that has remained more or less unchanged – a lack of Baroque curlicues and rolling eyeballs is a tell-tale sign of decline in a Spanish town. The oldest part of the crypt (673) is the only known surviving example of a Visigothic martyrium, built by King Wamba before he was shuttled off to a monastery (in the 7th century, the Visigothic kings lived in nearby Pampliega, a little village that time forgot). Among the museum's highlights are an early San Sebastián by El Greco and a fine Virgin and Child by Pedro Berruguete. Don't miss the clock in the transept, where a lion and knight strike the hours with gusto.

The bridge over the Carrión, the Puentecillas, is contemporary with the cathedral; 11th-century **San Miguel**, further south, is a fine little ogival Romanesque church, where the Cid married his Ximena. Around the corner, the **Museo de Palencia** (*open Sept–June Tues–Sat 10–2 and 4–7 Sun 10–2; July and Aug 10–2 and 4–7, Sun 10–2; adm, free at weekends*) occupies the 16th-century **Casa del Cordón**, containing archaeological souvenirs of Palencia's illustrious past – Bronze Age weapons, Celtiberian goldwork and ceramics, and funerary stelae from the Roman era. There are also some well-preserved mosaics. East of Calle Mayor, the 16th-century **Santa Clara** has a famous Cristo Yacente that elicited the comment from the ultra-pious Felipe II: 'If I had faith, I would believe that this was the real body of Christ.' Nearby, the 13th-century **Convento de San Francisco** has a magnificent *mudéjar* coffered ceiling in the sacristy.

If you're feeling a little churched-out, Palencia offers something a bit different, in the shape of the privately run **Museo de la Calzada**, just off C/Mayor on C/Barrio y Mier 10 (*open Mon–Wed and Fri 10–2 and 4–8*), where Juan Carlos's personal cobbler displays pairs of His Majesty's shoes, along with other celebrities' footwear.

Ten kilometres south of Palencia in the village of **Baños de Cerrato** (2km from Venta de Baños), the Visigothic King Recesvinto (he of the famous golden crown with dangling letters spelling his name) founded the church of **San Juan de Baños** back in 661 (*open summer Tues–Sun 10–1.30 and 4.30–8, winter Tues–Sun 10.30–1.30 and 4–6; adm, free Wed to EU citizens*), the purest extant example of Visigothic architecture. Fretwork windows like impossible key holes and a carved doorway (and a belfry, added by restorers) relieve the simple stone exterior. Inside, the nave is divided by rows of horseshoe arches, and the capitals, doorways and the apse are decorated with finely carved eight-pointed crosses (*croix pattées*), leaves, scallop shells, solar spirals and palms. Recesvinto's rather complex dedicatory inscription survives on the triumphal arch, framed by modillions decorated with diving eagles. In its use of pleasing, robust architectural volumes and the concentration of intricate detail in a few places, San Juan has been called the first Spanish church. Recent excavations uncovered 58 7th-century tombs and the original plan of the church, with its three apses standing out separately like prongs on a fork; in the Middle Ages it was converted into a more ordinary rectangle. The Baños of its name refers to a nearby curative spring, closed in by two Visigothic arches and restored in 1941.

North of Carrión de los Condes: Saldaña and a Roman Villa

From Carrión de los Condes, the CL615 follows the River Carrión up to **Renedo de la Vega** and the ruins of the monastery of Santa María de la Vega, a *mudéjar* work of 1215; the parish church has a fine Renaissance cross. Further north, towards Lobera, a sign points the way to **Pedrosa de la Vega** (1.5km), where the 3rd–4th-century Roman **Villa of Olmeda** was discovered in 1968 (*open summer Tues–Sun 10–1.30 and 4.30–8, winter Tues–Sun 10.30–1 and 4–6; adm, includes adm to Saldaña museum*) with its perfectly preserved polychrome mosaic floors, including not only geometric designs, but also mythological and hunting scenes. Nearby, in the pretty medieval village of **Saldaña**, the church of San Pedro houses finds from the ongoing excavations.

Saldaña's ruined 11th-century castle was the residence of Doña Urraca, sister and advisor of Alfonso VI; the 15th-century Gothic **San Miguel** has a *retablo* attributed to Gil de Siloé and effigy tombs of the Counts of Saldaña. The holy of holies in these parts is an 8th-century statue of the Virgin in the neoclassical **Ermita de la Virgen del Valle**.

Along the Pilgrims' Road to León

The *camino de Santiago* continues its flat way towards León, imperceptibly rising as it crosses 236km of the largest province in Castile. Framed by the Cordillera Cantábrica to the north and the lower, softer Montes de León to the west, the province was a refuge for Mozarabs from Andalucía in the first days of the Reconquista, and what remains of their monasteries are among the finest monuments along the whole road.

Sahagún and its Mudéjar Bricks

Sahagún started out as the site of a Roman villa and an early Christian basilica dedicated to San Facundo, a martyred legionary. During the 12th century, when it was the seventh official stop of the *Codex Calixtinus*, it had a population of 12,000 and artificially concentrated so much wealth in the middle of nowhere that it subsequently earned the nickname 'the Las Vegas of the Middle Ages'. Today a mere 3,000 souls try to fill up the dusty Plaza Mayor, the darkened old porticoes and forlorn houses. Sahagún's rise and fall went hand in hand with that of Spain's most powerful Benedictine abbey, **San Benito**. In 904, the old Roman road had just begun its transformation into the pilgrims' way when the site was purchased by Alfonso III the Great of Asturias for a community of Mozarab refugees from Andalucía. Although it was twice burned by the Moors, the seeds of its future glory were sown in the 11th century when Sancho III of Castile snatched León, the inheritance of his brother Alfonso, and locked Alfonso up in the abbey. He was about to tear out Alfonso's eyes for good measure when their sister Urraca intervened. Urraca had always liked Alfonso better, and managed to save his eyes by promising nasty Sancho to become a nun. With both siblings locked away, Sancho felt safe on the throne. But Alfonso made a secret pact with the abbot of San Benito, who helped him escape and take refuge with the Moors in Toledo.

In 1072 Sancho was assassinated and Alfonso was crowned king of Castile and León. Like Henry VIII, Alfonso VI married his way through six wives; those from Aquitaine and Burgundy put him into contact with Cluny – the great promoter of the Santiago pilgrimage. Never forgetting the help he received at Sahagún, the king refounded San Benito in 1080 under the new Cluniac reforms and made his personal confessor, Bernard de Sédirac (the future primate of Spain), its first abbot. Alfonso poured money into

Getting Around

Sahagún is linked by **trains** between Palencia and León and less frequently by **buses** between León and Carrión de los Condes.

Tourist Information

Valencia de Don Juan: Avda Carlos Pinilla, t 98 775 07 01, *www.aytovalenciade-donjuan.org*. Open July–Sept only.

Where to Stay and Eat

Sahagún ✉ 24320
**Hs La Codorniz, Avda de la Constitución 97, t 98 778 02 76 (*inexpensive*). One of the smarter choices, with a good restaurant.
*Hs Hospedería Benedictina, Santa Cruz, t 98 778 00 78 (*budget*). Has sparkling rooms with bath.

*Hospedería Monástica, C/Mayor 12, t 98 778 01 50 (*budget*). In summer, the Benedictine nuns at San Pedro de las Dueñas (5km from Sahagún) offer tasty meals at this place over the weekends.
Fonda Asturiana, C/Lesmes Franco 12, t 98 778 00 73 (*budget*). Colourful place with good *budget* food.

Valencia de Don Juan ✉ 24200
**Hs El Palacio, C/Palacio 3, t 98 775 04 74, *www.hostalelpalacio.com* (*inexpensive*). This charming little inn, decorated with antiques and a document saying that King Philip III once slept here (in the bed of the missus) is the oldest house in town, is. Run by Asturians, it also has an excellent *sidrería* and good home cooking. *Open Easter to mid-Sept.*
**Villegas II, C/Palacio 17, t 98 775 01 61 (*inexpensive*). Family hotel with just five rooms and a garden in the centre of town.

the abbey, gave it vast estates and founded a huge pilgrims' hospital. In its heyday San Benito even minted its own coins; in 1534 its theological school had the status of a university. Philip II brought it low by moving the school to Navarra's Monasterio de Irache in 1596 and constraining the abbey to pay nearly all of its rents to the crown.

In the 18th century two fires finished off what remained, leaving only a 17th-century portal by Felipe Berrojo, now a decorative city gate at the west end of town, an ungainly clock tower and the adjacent ruins of the 12th-century Gothic **Capilla de San Mancio** with its brick arches. Smaller bits of San Benito are in the museum in the **Monasterio Santa Cruz** (*open Tues–Sat 9.45–12.45 and 4–6.35; closed Nov–Easter; adm*): the tombs of Alfonso VI and some of his wives and the great silver custodia by master Enrique de Arfe, which makes appearances only for Corpus Christi although the nuns will show it if you ask (especially with a donation). They also run a pilgrims' hostal.

What Sahagún never had was a ready supply of building stone, which led the craftsmen who immigrated here from the Moorish lands to develop an architecture in brick, a medium that permitted new decorative patterns and delicacy. The first example, **San Tirso** (*currently closed for restoration*) was built near the monastery in the first decade of the 12th century, with its squat, tapering skyscraper tower rising out of three round apses; recent restoration work unearthed two sculpted Mozarab imposts with floral reliefs from the original monastery. **San Lorenzo** is just a little later and more obviously Moorish in design, but has suffered more changes over time, its interior redone in the 18th century (the chapel has Renaissance reliefs by Juan de Juni); both churches have porticoes along their sides for the famous markets Sahagún held in its boom period. In 1259 the Franciscans founded another monastery and the much-damaged **Santuario de La Peregrina** (*open Tues–Sat 10.30–1.30 and 4–6, Sun 10–1.30*), just outside the town on the N620, the third and latest *mudéjar* church, applying the new brick techniques to Gothic; inside some lovely bits of the original stucco work survive.

Near the medieval bridge that crosses the Río Cea stands a grove of poplars. According to the *Codex Calixtinus*, these are the lances of Charlemagne's paladins who, awaiting battle with the Moor Aigolando, planted them in the ground before going to sleep. Overnight some of the lances took root and flowered, a sign of impending martyrdom. Thinking to spare the men whose lances had taken root, Charlemagne let them stay in camp when he went off to fight the Moors. But when he returned, victorious, he found that all the men he had left behind had been massacred by a Moorish raiding party.

Five kilometres south, on the Cea's bank, two sisters founded **San Pedro de las Dueñas** in the 10th century, which has a beautiful Renaissance crucifix by Gregorio Fernández and 18 top-notch Romanesque capitals from the church's 1109 rebuilding, begun in stone and continued in brick by *mudéjar* craftsmen. Another road from Sahagún, the LE613, leads in 6km to the mighty, well-preserved 16th-century castle (private, no adm) at **Grajal de Campos**.

San Miguel de Escalada

After Sahagún the pedestrian *camino* parts from the highway, to meet again at **Mansilla de las Mulas** on the River Esla, which has preserved only atmospheric ruins of its 12th-century walls, monasteries and *hostales*. Nearby, between Villamoros and

Villasbariego, **Lancia** started out as an *oppidum* (fortified settlement) of the Astures; in 25 BC they were soundly defeated by the Romans after a fierce resistance: a few ruins remain and to this day farmers uncover antiquities in the surrounding fields.

This was the new frontier back in the early days of the Reconquista, when the kings of Oviedo had just added León to their title. Among the first pioneers on the scene were Abad Adefonso and his companions, refugees from Córdoba, who in 913 founded the beautiful church of **San Miguel de Escalada** (*just before Mansilla, take the road northeast 8km; open summer Wed–Sat 10–2 and 4.30–8, Sun 10–2; winter Wed–Sat 10–2 and 4.30–6, Sun 10–2*). The site, a gentle hill overlooking a valley, previously had a Palaeochristian church dedicated to the archangel. A lovely portico of horseshoe arches, an *ajímez* window and a heavy 11th-century tower mark the exterior, while the interior is proof in golden limestone that the Cordovans never forgot the classic symmetrical Roman basilica form and its proportions. Delicate horseshoe arches divide the three aisles, and separate the transept and triple apse from the main body of the basilica (like the Byzantines, the Mozarab liturgy called for a screen between the holy precinct and the parishioners). The capitals have simple palmette designs; luxuriant floral and geometric reliefs with lions and peacocks eating grapes decorate the chancels and friezes; over the door you can make out the highly elaborate if faint dedicatory inscription. The ceiling, a later *mudéjar* addition, bears the arms of León and Castile.

Valencia de Don Juan

Southwest of Mansilla, **Valencia de Don Juan** was named after its first duke, son of Alfonso the Wise, and is worth a detour for a theatrical 15th-century **castle** that rises from the banks of the Río Esla and is featured on all León's tourist brochures, with its massive walls (on one side only, like a stage set) broken by a series of turrets and crenellations.

The surrounding Esla *vega* is one of the most fertile swathes of the province, producer of Valdevimbre-Los Oteros, a light, fruity rosé with an orangeish rose colour, fermented in curious bunker-like *bodegas*. Its gentle sparkle comes from a technique called *madreo*. Only small quantities are produced; Valencia de Don Juan or Villamañán to the west provide your best chances to hunt down a bottle.

León

León tuvo veinticuatro reyes
antes que Castilla leyes
(León had 24 kings before Castile even had laws)

Radiant under the famous spires of its cathedral, León is a singularly happy city of clean boulevards shaded by horse-chestnut trees: one of the few places in Spain to achieve modern *urbanización* with grace and elegance. Part of the credit for this must go to its hyperactive City Hall (*Ayuntamiento*), which blankets the city with posters depicting itself as a friendly lion, advising the Leonese to ride the bus, recycle their glass and not to blaspheme in front of the children. The founding of a university has given the old city a transfusion of young blood and keeps the bars full until the wee hours of the morning.

History

Although the lion has long been the city's symbol, its name actually comes from *Legio Septima Gemina*, the Roman Seventh Legion, established here in AD 68 when Galba built a fort to guard the plain and the Roman road from Zaragoza. Reconquered from the Moors in the 850s by Ordoño I of Asturias (850–66), León changed hands several times more before King Ordoño II (914–24) moved his capital here. Even then, factionalism in the royal family left the city weak and prey to Moorish re-reconquests; in 981 the pious iconoclast al-Mansur grabbed it and his son reoccupied it from 996 until Alfonso V's victory at the Battle of Calatañazor in 1002.

After this last Moorish hurrah, León, rebuilt and refortified, reconquered Castile. But just as León eclipsed Asturias, Castile – first a county, then a separate kingdom – eclipsed León. In 1252, under Ferdinand III el Santo, the on-again off-again union of the two kingdoms was finalized. Castile never looked back, but for León, then one of the largest cities in Spain, the marriage spelt nothing but decline and marginalization: the nobles went off to the court in Burgos and the people left to settle the new frontiers gained by the Reconquista.

Into this vacuum of power and influence stepped the Church: the pilgrims' road became the chief source of income. Medieval pilgrims eagerly looked forward to León, with its Hilton of a *hostal*, where they could shake the dust off their wide-brimmed hats and catch their breath for the last leg of their journey. Broken and crushed during the Comunero revolt against Charles V, León sank into oblivion until the invention of the railway made its mines viable once again. These in turn declined, leaving León its share of modern autonomy atavists who, remembering the good old days of the 10th and 11th centuries, preach '*León sin Castilla*' ('León without Castile'). As yet their movement has little support – it's too much like a mother rejecting her own child.

The Cathedral

Open Oct–June Mon–Sat 8.30–1.30 and 4–7, Sun and hols 8.30–2.30 and 5–7; July–Sept Mon–Sat 8.30–1.30 and 4–8, Sun 8.30–2.30, www.catedraldeleon.org; free, guided visits (adm €4.50, inc adm to choir and cloisters) depart 12pm Tues–Sat and 4pm Mon–Sat from the tourist office. Separate adm to cloister and museum, see below.

The Spaniards call this the most splendid articulation of French Gothic in Spain, *La Pulchra Leonina* ('Belle of León'), a cathedral so remarkable that it would stand out even in France for its daring and superb walls of stained glass. A like amount of glass caused Beauvais, its closest rival in window-acreage, to collapse, a disaster León has managed to avert so far by increasing support to the walls and by maintaining a continual campaign to keep it vertical in the face of subsidence; expect some scaffolding. Although Calahorra in La Rioja claims the most storks' nests, León comes in a close second with some 100 families, to the extent that droppings on the stone have become a problem.

Getting There and Around

By Train

The RENFE station is at Avda de Astorga 11, (**t** 90 224 02 02 for the centralized information and timetable service, and to make reservations for any RENFE trains). There are frequent trains to Burgos, Palencia, Medina del Campo, Madrid, Astorga, Ponferrada, Ourense and Lugo; regular trains depart for Oviedo and Gijón nine times a day, travelling through some magnificent mountain scenery and at least 500 tunnels.

The Transcantábrico makes the journey to Santiago de Compostela from May to October (plus holidays during the rest of the year). It's a seven-day trip, which costs from €3000. Info at *www.transcantabrico.feve.es*. There are also regular FEVE trains from León to Bilbao (journey time 7½ hours), which take in the magnificent scenery of the Picos de Europa. More information from the FEVE station, Avda Padre Isla 48, **t** 98 727 12 10, or at *www.feve.es*.

By Bus

Buses (**t** 98 721 10 00 for information) depart from the bus terminal just south of the RENFE station, on Pso Ingeniero Sáenz de Miera, for the villages in the province and Oviedo, Burgos, Santander, Salamanca and Madrid.

Tourist Information

Plaza de Regla 4, **t** 98 723 70 82, *www.aytoleon.com*.

The **post office** is on Avda de la Independencia; the **Locutório La Rúa**, C/de la Rua 6, has public telephone and **Internet** facilities.

Where to Stay

León ✉ 24000

★★★★★**Parador San Marcos**, Pza San Marcos 7, **t** 98 723 73 00, *leon@parador.es* (*luxury*). This is not only Spain's best hotel, it is a veritable antiques museum. There are less expensive rooms in the modern building behind, with views over the river and pretty gardens.

★★★★**Alfonso V**, C/Padre Isla 1, **t** 98 722 09 00, *www.lesein.es/alfonsov* (*expensive*). Despite the austere exterior, this relatively new hotel is well equipped and decorated in severe, classic style.

★★★★**NH Plaza Mayor**, Plaza Mayor 15, **t** 98 734 43 57 (*moderate*). Part of a reliable chain, this is a crisp, modern hotel behind a neoclassical facade in the Barrio Húmedo. Excellent facilities for the price.

★★★**La Posada Regia**, C/Regidores 9–11, **t** 98 721 31 73, *www.regialeon.com* (*moderate*). Perhaps the most charming choice in the old city, this lovely inn has original wooden beams, quirky artwork, a great restaurant and delightful staff. Highly recommended.

★★★**Quindós**, Gran Via de San Marcos 38, **t** 98 723 62 00, *www.hotel quindos.com* (*moderate*). Situated in the new part of town, very modern and arty; comes with excellent service.

★★★**Paris**, C/Ancha 18, **t** 98 723 86 00, *www.hotel parisleon.com* (*moderate–inexpensive*). A good little hotel with all the usual facilities, including internet; situated close to the Cathedral. Good weekend deals.

★★**Hs Boccalino**, Plaza San Isidoro 9, **t** 98 720 30 60 (*inexpensive*). Sunny rooms in a peaceful location overlooking the Real Basílica de San Isidoro; the restaurant downstairs serves decent Italian meals.

The first church was built by Ordoño II, who donated part of his estates for the construction of Santa María de la Regla. It was twice destroyed before 1204, when Alfonso IX began a new church of warm golden stone in unheard-of dimensions, modelled on the soaring Gothic cathedrals of Chartres and Rheims. His successor, Ferdinand III, worried by the expense, tried to limit its size, but the Leonese responded by putting up their own money for the construction. The cathedral was more or less completed by the 15th century – the date of the openwork tower of the west façade by Joosken van Utrecht, linked rather oddly to the main body of the cathedral with visible buttresses.

★Hs Gúzman El Bueno, C/López Castrillon 6, t/f 98 723 64 12. One of the best *inexpensive* choices in León – brightly painted rooms with bath in a restored old house, around the corner from Los Botines.

★Pensión Blanca, C/Villafranca 2, t 98 725 19 91 (*budget*). Excellent new budget option, in a turn-of-the-20th-century building with bright, modern rooms and Internet access.

Eating Out

León is famous for sweetbreads and black puddings (*morcilla*), game dishes and garlic soup with trout. In the Barrio Húmedo, Plaza San Martín is the bopping headquarters for bars, tapas and inexpensive restaurants.

Vivaldi, C/Platerías 4, t 98 726 07 60 (*expensive*). Award-winning, elaborate cuisine plus marvellous wine list at what is generally considered the finest restaurant in the region.

El Faisán Dorado, C/Cantareros 2, t 98 725 66 09 (*expensive–moderate*). Has a good name for excellent Mediterreanan rice dishes, including paella and fideuás, along with classic Castillian fare; good wine list too. *Closed Sun eve and Mon.*

Restaurante Zuloaga, Sierra Pambley 3, t 98 723 78 14 (*expensive–moderate*). Fabulous must-see former palace skilfully redesigned as bar and restaurant with an interior courtyard. Come for a drink at least.

Adonías Pozo, C/Santa Nonia 16, t 98 720 67 68 (*moderate*). Elegantly decorated in hacienda style, this fine restaurant specialises in fish but also serves local meat dishes. Traditional favourites like *merluza en salsa verde* are cooked to perfection, or you can try exotica like swordfish *a la brasa. Closed Sun.*

Palacio Jabalquinto, C/Juan de Arfe, t 98 721 53 22 (*moderate*). Refined cuisine and stylish surroundings in a 17th-century palace in the Barrio Húmedo. *Closed Sun eve and Mon.*

Bodega Regia, C/Regidores 9-11, t 98 721 31 73 (*moderate–budget*). Specializes in well-cooked traditional dishes at reasonable prices. *Closed Sun and Feb.*

Casa Pozo, Pza San Marcelo 15 (near the Ayuntamiento), t 98 722 30 39 (*moderate–budget*). Specialises in both trout and salmon and prime fresh ingredients. *Closed Sun eve.*

El Besugo, C/Azabachería 10, t 98 725 69 95 (*budget*). An old-fashioned spot with good tapas and *raciones* including delicious grilled sardines. The slightly pricer restaurant upstairs serves classic Leonese dishes like roast lamb.

La Competencia, C/Conde Rebolledo 17, just off Plaza San Martín, t 98 721 23 12, (*budget*). Very popular for good pizza. There are three more Competencias in town.

El Gaucho, C/Plegarías 16 (*budget*). Just off Plaza San Martín, the *patatas bravas* at this bar are worth stopping off for.

El Llar, Plaza San Martín 9 (*budget*). One of the very best tapas bars on the popular Plaza San Martín; try the delicious potatoes with alioli.

El Nuevo Racimo de Oro, Pza San Martin 8, t 98 721 47 67 (*budget*). Great Leonese cuisine is served in this 12th-century building; there's a good bar as well and plenty of atmosphere.

La Poveda, C/Ramiro Valbuena 9, t 98 722 71 55 (*budget*). Track this place down for home cooking at the best price. *Closed Sun.*

La Ruta Jacobea, C/del Cid, t 98 723 28 07 (*budget*). Campo-style brick and stone bar fronting restaurant specialising in innovative seafood, like *sopa de truta* (trout soup). *Closed Sun.*

Outstanding 13th-century sculptures decorate the north, south, and especially the **west portal** with its three finely carved tympana – the one in the centre illustrates a lively scene of the Last Judgement, the devils boiling the sinners. In between the doors a pillar with a statue of Solomon was where the king or his representative sat in judgement.

The exterior, however, pales before the soaring **interior**, stripped of its Baroque frosting, leaving it bare and breathtaking, especially when the sun streams in igniting the 19,400 sq ft of vivid greens, reds and golds of the richest stained glass imaginable. The oldest glass, in the chapels around the apse and the great rose window of the 12 Apostles, dates from the 13th century; the latest is 19th-century and made by Spanish artists.

If you can draw your eyes away from the soaring walls of glass, note the choir in the centre of the nave, set behind an ornate triumphal arch of a façade and embellished with 15th-century alabaster carvings by Juan de Badajoz the elder; its midsection of glass was added fairly recently so you can see straight through to the altar, swimming in reflections of the windows. The *retablo mayor* contains an excellent Renaissance painting of Christ's Burial by Nicolás Francés. The chapels in the ambulatory house beautiful Gothic tombs, and there's an altar to Nuestra Señora del Dado, at which a disgruntled gambler allegedly once flung his dice, hitting the Christ Child on the nose and making it bleed.

Through the Plateresque Puerta del Dado, the **cathedral museum and cloister** (*open July–Sept Mon–Fri 9.30–2 and 4–7.30, Sat 9.30–2 and 4–7; Oct–Mar Mon–Fri 9.30–1.30 and 4–7, Sat 9.30–1.30 and 4–7; adm €1 for cloister only, €2.50 for cloister plus one level of the museum, €3.50 for admission to the cloister and a guided visit to the whole museum*) has one of the largest collections of Romanesque Virgin Marys in Europe; also a Crucifixion by Juan de Juni and a Mozarabic Bible. The beautiful cloister itself was damaged in the 14th century and reworked with classical motifs by Juan de Badajoz the elder.

Around the Cathedral: the Barrio Húmedo

Alongside the cathedral run León's **walls**, built by Alfonso XI in 1324 over the Roman and early medieval fortifications; nearly half of the original 80 bastions remain intact. To the east extend the narrow lanes of the old town, where so many Leonese come to wet their whistles that everyone calls it the **Barrio Húmedo**, the 'Humid Quarter'. The elegant **Old Consistorio** (1677) presides in the arcaded **Plaza Mayor**, where Roman walls have been unearthed. A tower here belonged to the Ponce family, one of whom went to Florida seeking the Fountain of Youth; the adjacent **Plaza de San Martín** is the most humid corner of the humid quarter. By the market in Regidores, another famous family, the Quiñoneses, had their 14th-century **Palace of the Condes de Luna**, of which only the tower and fine façade remain. The best church is Romanesque **Nuestra Señora del Mercado** (*open daily 11–12 and 7–8*) in the serene and lovely Plaza Santa María del Camino.

A Spanish Legend Past its Sell-by Date

An earlier Guzmán palace on the site of Gaudí's Los Botines saw the birth of Guzmán el Bueno, the knight who in 1292 defended the citadel of Tarifa at the southernmost point of Spain against a Moorish army. Fighting with the Moors was the renegade Infante Don Juan, brother of Sancho IV, who captured Guzmán's young son, took him beneath the walls of Tarifa, and threatened to kill him if Guzmán refused to surrender. Guzmán's response was to toss him a dagger. His son was killed but Tarifa did not fall. During the Spanish Civil War, the Nationalists recycled this legend for the 1936 siege of the Alcázar in Toledo, with the Republicans playing the villain's role. It was a splendid piece of Francoist propaganda – in the war that first used the very word propaganda (from the Church's *Propaganda Fide*, or Propagation of the Faith) as we use it today.

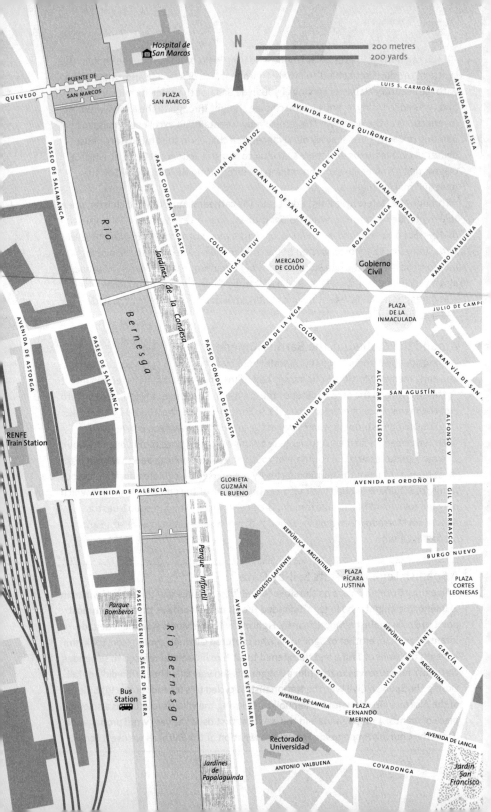

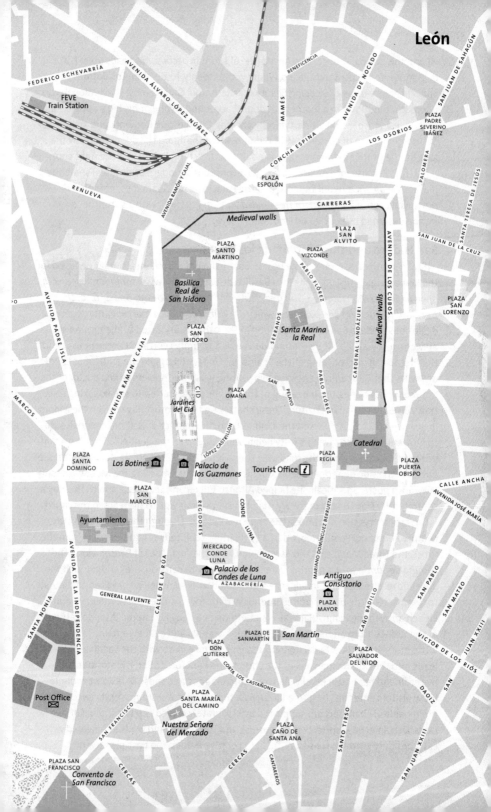

León

FEDERICO ECHEVARRÍA

AVENIDA ÁLVARO LÓPEZ NÚÑEZ

FEVE
Train Station

MAMÉS

BENEFICENCIA

AVENIDA DE NOCEDO

AVENIDA DE NOCEDO

SAN JUAN DE SAHAGÚN

LOS OSORIOS

PLAZA
PADRE
SEVERINO
IBÁÑEZ

PALOMERA

SANTA TERESA DE JESÚS

RENUEVA

AVENIDA RAMÓN Y CAJAL

CONCHA ESPINA

PLAZA
ESPOLÓN

CARRERAS

Medieval walls

PLAZA
SANTO
MARTINO

PLAZA
VIZCONDE

PLAZA
SAN
ALVITO

SAN JUAN DE LA CRUZ

AVENIDA DE LOS CUBOS

AVENIDA PADRE ISLA

**Basílica
Real de
San Isidoro**

PABLO FLÓREZ

*Santa Marina
la Real*

SERRANOS

PLAZA
SAN
LORENZO

PLAZA
SAN
ISIDORO

AVENIDA RAMÓN Y CAJAL

CID

PLAZA
OMAÑA

SAN

PELAYO

PABLO FLÓREZ

CARDENAL LANDÁZURI

Medieval walls

MARCOS

*Jardines
del Cid*

LÓPEZ CASTRILLÓN

Catedral

PLAZA
SANTA
DOMINGO

Los Botines 🏛

🏛 **Palacio de
los Guzmanes**

Tourist Office ℹ

PLAZA
REGIA

PLAZA
PUERTA
OBISPO

CALLE ANCHA

AVENIDA JOSÉ MARÍA

PLAZA
SAN
MARCELO

RECIDORES

CONDE

LUNA

POZO

MARIANO DOMÍNGUEZ BERRUETA

SAN PABLO

Ayuntamiento

AVENIDA DE LA INDEPENDENCIA

GENERAL LAFUENTE

CALLE DE LA RÚA

MERCADO
CONDE
LUNA

🏛 **Palacio de los
Condes de Luna**
AZABACHERÍA

*Antiguo
Consistorio*

CAÑO BADILLO

SAN MATEO

VÍCTOR DE LOS RÍOS

SANTA NONIA

PLAZA
MAYOR

PLAZA DE
SANMARTÍN *San Martín*

PLAZA
DON
GUTIERRE

PLAZA
SALVADOR
DEL NIDO

SAN JUAN XXIII

DAOIZ

Post Office ✉

SAN FRANCISCO

PLAZA
SANTA MARÍA
DEL CAMINO

CORTA LOS CASTAÑONES

*Nuestra Señora
del Mercado*

PLAZA
CAÑO DE
SANTA ANA

SANTO TIRSO

CANTAREROS

PLAZA SAN
FRANCISCO

CERCAS

CERCAS

CERCAS

SAN JUAN XXIII

*Convento de
San Francisco*

From the cathedral, busy Calle Ancha (the old Roman *decumanus*) leads up to Plaza de Botines and Plaza San Marcelo, where you suddenly come upon **Los Botines** ('The Spats'), León's version of Sleeping Beauty's castle. Antoni Gaudí's most conventional work, it was built in 1891 – 'in a moment of doubt', according to one of his biographers – as a private residence, with turrets, typically swirling Gaudíesque ironwork and a statue of St George (patron of Gaudí's native Catalunya) overhanging the door, where, by the look on the grinning dragon's face, the saint is scratching him in just the right spot.

Two fine Renaissance palaces (and two incongruous modern sculptures) share the plazas: the arcaded **Ayuntamiento** and the **Palacio de los Guzmanes** (now the provincial Diputación, *open for free guided visits, ask within*), with a sumptuous façade designed by Rodrigo de Hontañón in 1559.

San Isidoro and the Panteón de los Reyes

If León's cathedral is one of the best in Spain, the city can claim a similar pedestal for the Romanesque frescoes in its **Real Basílica de San Isidoro** (*www.sanisidorodeleon.org, open July–Aug Mon–Sat 9–8, Sun 9–2; Sept–June Mon–Sat 10–1.30 and 4–6.30; church free, adm to museum and pantheon which are visited by guided tour only*), north of Plaza de Botines in Plaza San Isidoro. Founded in the 9th century, razed to the ground by al-Mansur, it was rebuilt by Ferdinand I, the first to unify León and Castile in 1037 and the first to call himself 'King of the Spains'. In 1063 León bagged the relics of St Isidoro of Seville, that 6th-century, encyclopedia-writing Visigothic nobleman and doctor of the Church whose bones, upon hearing of the Reconquista, started to speak, asking to be transferred to Christian territory. These chattering bones must have driven the Moors in Seville crazy, so they packed them off to León; the basilica was at once rededicated to him, enlarged and given its lofty bell tower. Once here, the gentle Isidoro, like a half-dozen other saints along the road, was conscripted into Reconquista duty; you can see him over the side door, on horseback in his bishop's gear, whacking the Moor with John Wayneish gusto. Specifically, he helped Alfonso VIII reconquer Baeza, and to this day a confraternity from Baeza, in theory, maintains a 24-hour vigil by his relics in the church.

The façade has two entrances; the church is entered through the right-hand, 11th-century Puerta del Perdón topped by a tympanum sculpted with the Descent from the Cross, the Three Marys and the Ascension. This is the first Door of Pardon along the *camino de Santiago*; if a pilgrim were too ill or weak to carry on, they could touch the door and receive the same indulgence and absolution as someone who walked all the way to Compostela. The barrel-vaulted interior with its foiled arches, desecrated by Soult's French army in the Peninsular War, is something of a heavily restored disappointment; of the 12th-century original only the transept capitals and chapel remain.

The more ornate Puerta del Cordero, its tympanum carved with the Sacrifice of Isaac, leads into the original narthex of the church, the **Panteón de San Isidoro**, founded by Ferdinand I to house his simple stone sarcophagus and those of his descendants (now visitors enter on the guided tour via a tiny stone spiral staircase). Its two small groin-vaulted chambers are supported by elaborately carved capitals (*Daniel in the Lions' Den* and the *Resurrection of Lazarus*), and the ceiling and walls are covered with extraordinary vivid frescoes from the 12th century, among the best-preserved

Romanesque paintings anywhere still in their original setting. Stylistically similar to the 5th-century frescoes and mosaics in Santa Costanza (which all the pilgrims on their way to Rome would have visited), Christ Pantocrator and the Evangelists, with human bodies and animal heads (Luke looks like the Minotaur) reign over scenes of the shepherds, the Flight to Egypt, the Last Supper, the Tears of St Peter, the Seven Cities and Seven Lamps of the Apocalypse. Best of all, there's an allegory of the months, beginning with the two-headed Janus, Roman god of the door, who looks both backward and ahead at the 'hinge' of the old and new years.

Although the French desecrated the tombs and burned the library, they somehow missed the treasures displayed in the Pantheon's **museum** (*adm included in entrance ticket*) on the first floor, which originally formed part of Ferdinand I's palace: St Isidoro's original silver reliquary, the gem-studded chalice of Doña Urraca (made from two Roman cups), and lovely Mozarab caskets covered with ivories and enamels. The library, rebuilt in the 16th century by Juan de Badajoz, has an illuminated Bible of 960 that somehow escaped the French firebugs.

The Hospital de San Marcos and the Archaeology Museum

León's third great monument lies at the end of the garden along the riverside Paseo Condesa de Sagasta. The **Hospital de San Marcos** was built in 1173 as headquarters for the Order of the Knights of Santiago, charged with the pilgrims' protection; at their hospital the weary, blistered pilgrim could rest and prepare for the rigours ahead. In 1514, when the powerful knights were more devoted to their own pleasure and status, they set about rebuilding their headquarters thanks to an enormous donation by Ferdinand the Catholic – something of a payoff for electing him to the post of Grand Master and surrendering their semi-autonomy to the Crown. Over the 16th to 18th centuries the monastery was given its superb 330ft Plateresque façade, first designed by Pedro de Larrea but altered by many hands afterwards, including those of Juan de Badajoz the younger; its frieze of busts, niches (the statues were never completed), swags and garlands, scallop shells, pinnacles, and intricate lacy reliefs culminating in the portal topped by Santiago Matamoros and the arms of Charles V, who inherited the title of Grand Master from his grandfather Ferdinand. Used after 1837 as a barracks, the building went quickly to rack and ruin and was several times condemned by the city until 1961, when the government purchased it and invested a fortune to create Spain's most beautiful luxury hotel. Non-guests as usual can partake at the bar, and visit the upper choir of the adjacent church of **San Marcos** with its cockleshell façade as part of daily guided tours (ask in the parador). The chapterhouse and sacristy by Juan de Badajoz the younger contain the **Provincial Archaeology Museum** (*open Oct–June Tues–Sat 10–2 and 4–7, Sun 10–2; July–Sept Mon–Sat 10–2 and 5–8 and Sun 10–2; adm. The museum will be moving to new, larger premises by the Plaza Santo Domingo in mid-2006.*), with a small but prize collection: the 11th-century ivory Carrizo crucifix, enamels from Limoges, a Mozarab cross given by King Ramiro II in 940 to Santiago de Peñalba, the Corullón calvary, three pairs of beautiful capitals from the first Mozarab church at Sahagún, made by the same craftsmen as at Escalada, medieval weapons and mementoes of the Roman Seventh Legion, portraits of the knights of Santiago, and artefacts discovered in a Punic necropolis near the Maragato village of Santa Colomba de Somoza – a key discovery in unravelling the origins of the Maragatos (*see* p.275). The museum – which currently has space for only a tiny percentage of its treasures - is moving to an elegant new building in mid-2006. Visitors will still be able to visit the Hospital San Marcos, which will house a new museum dedicated to the cult of Santiago and the pilgrim's road.

To prove it isn't a city stuck in the past, León established the glossy MUSAC (*Museo de Arte Contempóraneo de Castilla y León; Avda de los Reyes Leoneses 24, open Tues–Thurs 11–8, Fri 11–9, Sat–Sun 10–9, free, buses 7, 11,12*) in a remarkable block of multicoloured cubes. There is an excellent programme of temporary exhibitions: check the website, *www.musac.es*, to find out what's on.

North of León

Northern León encompasses the southern slopes of the Cordillera Cantábrica and the Picos de Europa and one of Spain's best caves, the **Cueva de Valporquero**, 46km from León through the spectacular gorges of the Torio river (*open daily 10–2 and 4–7; adm; bring non-skid shoes and a jacket*). The caves have no prehistoric art, but 4km of colourful galleries with little lakes, esplanades, a stalactite 'cemetery', and a chamber of wonders. Another beauty spot is the **Puerto de Pajares** (4,525ft), the lofty pass in the Cordillera Cantábrica used since antiquity as the main gate between León and Oviedo. The Leonese gateway to the Picos de Europa is **Riaño**, from where you can visit the **Valle de Valdeón** and **Valle de Sajambre** (*see* pp.201–2).

West of León

Two distinct regions fill the area between León and Galicia: between Astorga and Ponferrada is **La Maragatería**, the homeland of the Maragatos, one of Spain's marginal peoples, and west of Ponferrada is **El Bierzo**, a unique mountainous region, with some of the province's prettiest wooded valleys, distorted and eroded by mining and a favourite abode for contemplative 10th-century hermits.

Don Quixote's Prototype

Back in July 1434, Don Suero de Quiñones, a knight from León, vowed to hold the Puente del Paso Honroso with his nine companions for the 13 days preceeding 25 July, the feast day of Santiago, and challenge every passer-by to declare his lady, Leonor de Tovar, the fairest in the land. If they refused to admit it, they had to joust. As it was a Holy Year, the road was crowded with pilgrims. The bishop of León condemned the enterprise and refused burial in sacred ground for anyone killed, but not even that deterred 727 men from taking up the challenge. Don Suero and his companions broke over 300 lances, wounded a score and killed one, but at the end of the month retired undefeated. The incident, the last hurrah of Spanish romantic chivalry, has gone down in history as the *Paso Honroso*; many scholars believe the story was an inspiration for Cervantes' *Don Quixote*.

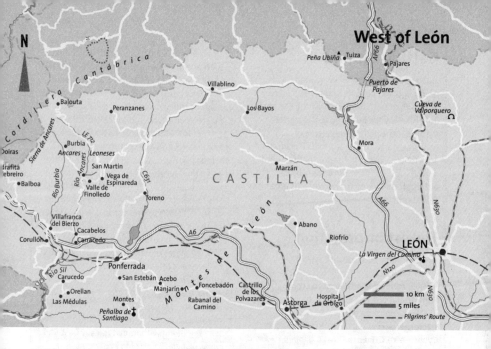

Along the Pilgrimage Road to Hospital de Órbigo

On the N120, not far from the industrial sprawl west of León, is, for better or worse, the only modern chapel along the *camino de Santiago*: **La Virgen del Camino**, a concrete box built in 1961 by Brother Coello de Portugal which houses a much-venerated 16th-century statue of the Virgin, set in a Baroque *retablo*; the stained-glass workshop at Chartres produced the ugly windows and Catalan sculptor Subirachs contributed the weird emaciated bronze figures of the Virgin and the Apostles that cover the front. One of the bridges the pilgrims crossed, the 13th-century Puente del Paso Honroso (*see* box opposite), still stands parallel to the N120, 23km west of León, not far from the long-gone *hostal* that gave its name to Hospital de Órbigo.

Astorga, Gaudí and the Maragatos

Astúrica Augusta was an important administrative centre for the Romans, close to the mines and a main station along their *Vía de la Plata*, the 'Silver Road' that ran down to Zamora and Sevilla and across to Galicia, to transport the gold of the Bierzo, the silver of Galicia and the copper of Asturias. Like León, Astorga had its own bishopric by the 3rd century; like León it was important in the Middle Ages because of the pilgrimage. It has declined genteelly ever since, helped along by a bit of sacking in the Peninsular War.

The best way to approach Astorga is to circle the centre, still belted by half of its robust Roman-medieval **walls**, and enter on the northwest side of town, where the **Catedral de Santa María** (*open daily summer 9–12 and 5–6.30; winter 9.30–12 and 4.30–6*) and Bishop's Palace looming over the walls make a startling impression. Begun in 1451, the cathedral was not completed until the 18th century, with too many cooks along the way; even the colour of the stone in the towers doesn't match. The façade with its flying

Getting Around

RENFE links Astorga and Ponferrada with León, Lugo and beyond, four times a day – although note that for Astorga the station is a long hike – while **buses** go to the centre. Astorga is the point of departure of buses for La Maragatería; Ponferrada for El Bierzo; and León for the villages in the south. The Cueva de Valporquero is accessible only by **car**, although there are often excursions organized from León.

Tourist Information

Astorga: Plaza Eduardo de Castro 5,
t 98 761 82 22,
www.ayuntamientodeastorga.com.
Ponferrada: C/Gil y Carrasco 4, t 98 742 42 36, *www.ponferrada.org.*
Internet access is available in Astorga at Cybercentro, C/Puerta Obispo 9 (*open 11–2 and 5–11*). There is a **market** in Astorga on Tues, and in Ponferrada on Wed and Sat.

Where to Stay and Eat

Astorga ✉ **24700**
Viejo Molino Cela, Nistal (5km from Astorga), t 98 760 05 02, *www.viejomolinocela.com* (*moderate*). A lovely riverside mill, exquisitely converted into a romantic rural hotel with a garden with white geese and elegant dining room (guests only, book in advance).
★★★Astur Plaza, Plaza de España 2, t 98 761 89 00, *www.asturplaza.com* (*inexpensive*). A smart and well-equipped, if rather bland, hotel, with an enjoyable tavern serving local dishes.
★★★HR Gaudí, Pza Eduardo de Castro 6, t 98 761 56 54 (*inexpensive*). A comfortable and elegant choice, across from the Palacio Episcopal; its good, moderately priced restaurant with a fancy marble floor features several Maragato dishes and fish.
★★Hostal Gallego, Avda Ponferrada 78, t 98 761 54 50 (*inexpensive*). Has rooms with bath in a new building on the way out of town.
★★Hs La Peseta, Pza San Bartolomé 3, t 98 761 72 75 (*moderate*). Central and boasting to be the best restaurant in Astorga; you can sample the generous wines of El Bierzo with heaped plates of hake baked with rosemary or ox stew. *Closed Sun eve, fortnight in Oct and in Feb.*
Serrano, C/Portería 2, t 98 761 78 66 (*moderate*). Has an unusually good selection of salads and exotic treats like *langostinos al whiskey*, along with more typically Castilian meat dishes. *Closed Mon eve.*
Guts Muths, C/Matanzas s/n, Santiago Millas, t 98 769 11 23, *www.guts-muths.com* (*inexpensive*). There can't be many places in the world called Guts Muths, and there are certainly few places to stay that can claim to be as characterful. A cosy living room and warming, succulent stews in the restaurant help to ward off night-time chills.
Casa Maragata I, C/Húsar Tiburcio 2, t 98 761 88 80 (*budget*). Dedicated purely to serving the local staple *cocido de maragato* in its *menú del día*. There is an equally good branch at Redentonstas 6. *Closed eves, last week in June and first week of July.*

buttresses between the towers was inspired by the cathedral in León, only here the ornamentation on the façade is floridly Baroque: intricate garlands, cherubs, columns with plump rings of vegetation and reliefs of the Descent from the Cross, the Adulterous Woman, and the Expulsion of the Merchants from the Temple. The interior suffers from a clammy ecclesiastical anomie, with all the interest concentrated in the *retablo mayor*, in marble high relief, by Gaspar Becerra (1520–70), an Andalucian who studied with Michelangelo. Off the neglected, classical cloister, the **Museo Diocesano** (*open summer daily 10–2 and 4–8; winter daily 11–2 and 3.30–6.30; adm, combined adm with Palacio Episcopal available*) houses some fine medieval pieces, including a 10th-century casket of gold and silver that belonged to Alfonso III, a figure of Santo Toribio by Gaspar Becerra and a 12th-century painted tomb.

Astorga seemed like a dusty, declining nowhere to Juan Bautista Grau y Vallespinós when he arrived as its new bishop. In 1887, hoping to give his see a dynamic jump start into the 20th century, he commissioned the most imaginative architect he knew, his good friend and fellow Catalan, Antoni Gaudí of Barcelona, to build him a new **Palacio Episcopal**. The rest of Astorga had deep reservations about the *modernista* fairy-tale castle that began to sprout on the edge of town and, once the bishop died in 1893, the public's hostility to the project burst open so violently that Gaudí quit and refused ever to return to Astorga. Without his input, this pale

Maragato Mysteries

Before leaving, look at the top of the cathedral apse, decorated with the figure of a Maragato named Pero Mato, who fought with Santiago at the legendary battle of Clavijo in 844. Astorga is the 'capital' of the Maragatos, who have lived here and in the villages to the west for as long as anyone can remember. Until the 19th century, they were muleteers and carriers, transporting nearly all the goods between Castile and Galicia, a line of work forced on them by their stubborn, almost uncultivatable land; their name has been traced back to the Latin *mercator*, or merchant. Grave and dry in manner, their honesty and industry were proverbial and no one hesitated to trust them with huge sums of money. Until recently they still wore their ancient costumes: huge slouched hats, very broad-bottomed breeches called *zaraguelles* (from the Arabic word for kilts) and red garters for the men; for the women, a crescent-shaped cap covered with a mantle and heavy earrings. They kept very much to themselves, marrying only other Maragatos. Twice a year, at Corpus Christi and the Ascension, they would gather in Astorga, and at exactly 2pm all would begin a dance called 'El Canizo', finishing at exactly 3; if any non-Maragatos attempted to join in, the dance would stop immediately. In the kitchen, they are known for their cakes called *mantecadas* (available in every Astorga pastry shop) and for the odd custom of eating their Maragato stew backwards: first they would eat the meat, then the vegetables, then the soup.

Who were the Maragatos? Common beliefs that they were Celts, Visigoths or Berbers, who came over in the 8th century and managed to hold on to this enclave after converting to Christianity, have been called into question by Dr Julio Carro, who in the late 1950s discovered a Punic necropolis near the village of Santa Colomba de Somoza, west of Astorga – hardly where you'd expect to find one, because the Phoenicians were sailors and León isn't exactly on the coast. Among the finds were figurines nearly identical to those found at Punic sites in Ibiza and dressed in a style very similar to the Maragatos. Carro's conclusion, based on his discoveries and on Maragato cultural traditions, was that the Maragatos were descended from Phoenicians and Iberians enslaved by the Romans to work the gold mines of El Bierzo. The Maragatos themselves agree, and to thank Carro for discovering their true origins, they put up a stone plaque to him in the village of Quintanilla de Somoza. These days the Maragato traditions and insularity have practically vanished, although you can still recognize a Maragata at once by her lime-green stretch slacks and horn-rimmed glasses.

asymmetrical castle (completed only in 1963), lacks the extraordinary detail and colour that characterize the works of Gaudí, who usually designed everything down to the furniture. Instead of a bishop, the palace now houses the **Museo de los Caminos** (*open summer Tues–Sat 10–2 and 4–8, Sun 10–2; winter Tues–Sat 11–2 and 4–6, Sun 11–2; adm*), a collection of pilgrimage paraphernalia, maps of the routes, Roman remains, art from various churches (note especially the mean-looking she-devil and Santiago in the Renaissance altarpiece from Bécares) along with some glowering examples of contemporary provincial art. For a hint of Gaudí's intentions, don't miss the magnificent atmospheric throne room with its discreet stained glass and chapels.

The only Maragatos you're likely to notice, other than those carved into the cathedral apse (*see* p.275), are the two figures, Zancudo and Colasa, who bang the hour atop the attractive 17th-century **Ayuntamiento** at the east end of Astorga; in front of it you can descend into the Roman slaves' prison, the Ergástula, where the Maragatos' ancestors languished.

The top two floors have been converted to house the **Museo Romano**, Plaza de San Bartolomé 2 (*open July–Sept Tues–Sun 10–1.30 and 4–8; Oct–June Tues–Sun 10–1.30 and 4.30–7; adm, combined adm with Museo de Chocolate available*); inside are ceramics and bronze artefacts from archaeological sites around Astorga, and some spectacular murals from the second century BC. In Plaza Roma you'll find ruins of Roman houses, some with pretty mosaics. The tourist office organizes a walking tour of Astorga's Roman heritage.

Chocoholics will be more interested in the **Museo de Chocolate**, C/Jose Maria Goy 5 (*open Tues–Sat 10.30–2 and 4.30–7, Sun 11–2; adm, combined adm with Museo Romano available*), a thinly veiled excuse to sell some of Astorga's finest product. An impressive collection of wrappers and antique machinery used in the production of what the Aztecs considered 'the food of the Gods' complete the illusion of education. If you're buying, the dark chocolate is tooth-rottingly delicious.

West of Astorga: Villages of the Maragatería

The mostly ruined villages of the Maragatería have been in decline ever since the railway took over the Maragatos' ancestral occupation, but **Castrillo de los Polvazares** (6km from Astorga, just off the *camino de Santiago*) has been restored to the verge of being twee, with old stone houses now mostly holiday homes, a score of roadside crosses and a main cobbled street built wide for mule trains. Further west, only a handful of people remain at **Santa Catalina de Somoza**, with its monument to a Maragato musician, while up from El Ganso ('The Goose'), down-at-heel **Rabanal del Camino** was the ninth stop on the pilgrimage in the *Codex Calixtinus*, a spot safeguarded by the Templars: now only a few people remain to tend its little Romanesque church.

After Rabanal, pilgrims tackled the wild Montes de León, climbing up to **Foncebadón**: 'Who hasn't passed by way of Foncebadón doesn't know solitude or sadness,' is an old saying, especially true now that the village is abandoned. Just beyond, at the top of the 4,935ft pass, stands the spindly **Iron Cross**, planted by a pilgrim untold years ago. Later pilgrims have added, one by one, the huge mound of slate stones at its foot, just as the Celts would 'give' stones to roadside shrines to placate the dangers ahead. To the left rises **El Teleno** (7,179ft), one of the two holy mountains of the Celts in El Bierzo.

El Bierzo

In the old days the Romans dug for gold in these hills; the modern Leonese extract the iron and cobalt. El Bierzo has bleak mining towns, lovely mountain scenery, vineyards, orchards and tobacco fields, charming villages that time forgot, and ancient hermitages – its isolation and warm climate (the mountains shield it from the worst of the *meseta* and Atlantic) – attracted so many anchorites early on that it was known as the Thebaid of Spain. Its inhabitants feel closer to their neighbours in Galicia than to León, and make half-serious murmurs about autonomy, mostly expressed in the venerable Spanish spraypaint tradition of changing the spelling on signs. After the Iron Cross the pilgrims' road descends into the fertile valleys of El Bierzo by way of **Manjarín**, another abandoned hamlet, and **Acebo**, with its still flowing pilgrims' Fountain of the Trout along its one street.

From Acebo it's 5km south to **Compludo**, a tiny isolated hamlet, where San Fructuoso, the first holy man in El Bierzo, founded his first monastery in 614. Although this is now long gone, San Fructuoso's forge, the remarkable **Herrería de Compludo** (now a national monument) still works as well as it did in the 7th century, using the stream to turn its great wheel.

Ponferrada

Both the easy A6 and the dramatic, lonely (but well-signed) pilgrims' track over the Montes de León lead to Ponferrada, originally a Roman mouthful known as Interamnium Flavium. It is the largest town of El Bierzo, and sums up the region's split personality, part of it mine-blackened, slag-heaped and shabby, the other half medievally pretty. The town's name comes from a long-gone bridge with iron balustrades, erected over the Río Sil for the pilgrims by the local 11th-century pontifex, Bishop Osmundo.

Where to Stay and Eat

Ponferrada ✉ 24400

****Temple Ponferrada**, Avda de Portugal 2, t 98 741 00 58 (*moderate*). The largest, best-endowed hotel in town, set in a pseudo-Templar castle; it can be noisy though.

***Bérgidum**, Avda de la Plata 4, t 98 740 15 12, *www.hotelbergidum.com* (*inexpensive*). A modern, central place offering contemporary comforts at a surprisingly good price.

****Hotel el Castillo**, Avda del Castillo 115, t 98 745 62 27, *www.hotel–elcastillo.com* (*moderate–inexpensive*). Castle-gaze from your room at this modern marble-clad hotel across the way.

****Madrid**, Avda de la Puebla 44, t 98 741 15 50, *www.hotelmadridponferrada.com* (*inexpensive*). In the new town, with superior restaurant. Bland but good value.

***Hs La Madrileña**, Avda A López Peláez 4, t 98 741 28 57 (*budget*). Very basic but clean; rooms with shared bath for around 20 euros.

La Fonda, Pza Ayuntamiento 10, t 98 742 57 94 (*moderate–budget*). Uses local ingredients to create interesting dishes. *Closed Sun eve*.

Las Cuadras, Tras la Cava 2, t 98 741 93 73 (*budget*). Located right by the castle walls. and serving tasty tapas and excellent fish dishes.

Taberna los Arcos, Plaza del Ayuntamiento 4, t 98 740 90 01, *www.hotelbierzoplaza.com* (*restaurant budget, hotel moderate*). A converted 17th-century bodega is the setting for this charming and good-value restaurant with smart modern rooms above. Look out for good Internet deals.

DO El Bierzo

After Ponferrada the pilgrimage route enters the Valley of Bierzo, the bed of a dried-up lake, surrounded by a ring of mountains and crisscrossed by trout streams. Its microclimate is warm and damp, with few frosts – ideal for cultivating vines, both on steep slopes and on the riverbanks. The finest, DO El Bierzo reds, are made entirely from the native Mencía grape and have a personality all their own, although this is diluted when Prieto Picudo and Garnacha are added. The less interesting whites are made from Malvasia and Valenciana. Three of the top producers are Valdeobispo, Casar de Valdaiga and Palacio de Arganza (try their Almena del Bierzo).

On the east bank of the Río Sil stands Ponferrada's proudest monument, the 12th-century **Castillo de los Templarios** (*open Oct–Apr Tues–Sat 10.30–2 and 4–6, Sun 10.30–2; May–Sept Tues–Sat 10.30–2 and 5–9, Sun 11–4; adm*), its triple ramparts built to defend the pilgrims from the Moors; its fairy-tale gate and towers were added later, in 1340. In 1811 the French went out of their way to vandalize it, resulting in heavy restoration. Here and there you can see Templar crosses and *taus* carved on the walls. While building the castle, the Templars discovered a statue of the Virgin in the heart of a holm oak tree, now enshrined in the **Basilica de Nuestra Señora de la Encina** (1577), with a good *retablo mayor* by the school of Gregorio Fernández. Elsewhere in the old town, look for the medieval gate, the **Puerta del Reloj**, and the early 17th-century **Ayuntamiento**. Nearby is the **Museo del Bierzo** (*open summer Tues–Sat 11–2 and 5–8.30, Sun 11–2; winter Tues–Sat 11–2 and 4–7; adm*), which displays bronzes retrieved from the mountain castros in Los Ancares and the original workings of Ponferrada's clock tower. Sitting on a hill, 2km south on the Madrid road, the minute church of **Santo Tomás de las Ollas** ('St Tom of the Pots' – there used to be a pottery workshop next door) is a curious Mozarabic church built by the monks of San Pedro de Montes, with horseshoe arches and, best of all, an elliptical 10-sided apse encircled with blind arcading.

Into the Valley of Silence

South of Ponferrada, the Oza river winds through the beautiful **Valle del Silencio** where, from the 7th century to the 10th, hermits took up their abode under the dramatic white flanks of Monte Aquiana, a mountain sacred to the Celts. Most of the hermits were Visigoths from Andalucía, come to spread the writings of San Isidoro of Seville. One of these was San Fructuoso, founder of the monastery of **San Pedro de Monte** in the village of **Montes**. To get there, take the road to San Esteban de Valdueza for 8km, then turn left for 14km on a narrow, hairpinning road that follows the River Oza; at the end of the road, it's a steep 500m walk up. Reinhabited in 890 by St Genadio of Andalucía and his monks, the ruins are mostly 12th century, although Genadio's 919 dedication is still embedded in the wall and some of the original Asturian style capitals are intact. Despite an 18th-century restoration, the whole complex is on the verge of collapse. The real jewel of El Bierzo, the recently restored little Mozarabic church of **Peñalba de Santiago** (*open Oct–Apr Tues–Sat 10–2 and 4.30–8, Sun and hols 10–2; May–Sept Tues–Sat 10–2 and 5–7, Sun and hols 10–2*) is a bit farther on in a spectacular setting at the head of the valley (take the left turning over the river, and leave your car at the entrance of the little medieval hamlet). Founded by Saint Genadio and dedicated in 913, its perfect proportions are reminiscent of Palaeochristian basilicas in Africa, as is its shape: rectangular with three cupolas and two apses rather oddly facing one another. The rough stone and slate exterior doesn't prepare you for the refinement and fine craftsmanship inside, beginning with a pretty double-arched portal crowned by two horseshoe arches. A track leads up to the hermit's cave of **San Genadio** for the magnificent view down onto the church and its tower, surrounded by a huddle of slate roofs.

Las Médulas

Fifteen kilometres southwest of Ponferrada, the ruined **Castillo de Cornatel** was built in the 12th century by Ferdinand II to protect the pilgrim route between Ponferrada and Villafranca del Bierzo. The castle itself looks more impressive from the valley than it does close-up, but its dominant position affords wonderful sunset views across the Lago de Carucedo to the mountains of Galicia.

Just beyond, **Carucedo** is the point of departure for an unusual journey through an ancient ecological disaster, **Las Médulas**. In the 1st century AD, the Romans noted the soft red soil was sprinkled with gold and minium (or red lead, used for painting), but to extract it meant sifting through thousands of tons of earth. Labour back then was no problem: some 60,000 slaves were brought in to dig a complex network of galleries, wells, dams and canals – one over 40km long – to erode the soil. The work was gruelling and dangerous, and thousands died over the next two centuries in moving an estimated 300 million tons of earth to extract 90 tons of gold. Whole hills collapsed in the process, and new ones of left-over tailings were piled up by the slaves, leaving behind a landscape like a row of jagged red spinal cords – or medullas. There's a natural balcony over Las Médulas from Orellán; from the village of Las Médulas, 4km from Carucedo, you can take a stroll (bring sturdy shoes) past the ancient canals, galleries, rock needles and surreal caves – a natural disaster perhaps, but a strangely beautiful one. It was recognised as a World Heritage Site in 1998.

Northwest of Ponferrada: the Ancares Leoneses

North of Ponferrada, a lonely road heads north to Vega de Espinareda and the beautiful, densely forested, mountainous **Ancares Leoneses**, now under the jurisdiction of the Reserva Nacional. Although sections are reserved for hunting, the park also protects a number of endangered species – a few brown bears, Iberian wolves, roe deer and capercaillie – as well as a dying way of life in its 27 remote mountain hamlets, with their traditional architecture and *pallozas*, straw-topped round stone huts first built by the Celts. The best examples are along the tiny roads up the Ancares river valley.

Vega de Espinareda

Nestled snugly at the confluence of three valleys, Vega de Espinareda is the modern metropolis of Los Ancares; many of the emigrants from tiny mountain villages get their first taste of urban life here. The action is centred around a narrow pedestrian

Puente Romano, but Vega's proudest monument is the 16th-century **Monasterio de San Andrés**, which presides over a large and dusty car park on the western outskirts of town. Founded in 923 by El Bierzo's home-grown saint, San Genadio, it burnt down in 1270 and again in 1500, before the monks were thrown out and their order disbanded under new anti-monastic laws in 1835. After its treasures had been looted the monastery was abandoned, and there it sits, empty and forlorn, overgrown with ivy and populated only by a few storks. The attached church, built in 1778 in neoclassical style, contains a 13th-century crucifix, while behind the monastery the Fuente de la Vida offers a lifetime of good health to anyone who drinks seven draughts of its water.

North and west of Vega the Ancares begin in earnest, rising steeply above the villages of Valle de Finolledo and San Martín, before dropping smoothly into the wide green valley of **Burbia**, and, simultaneously, into the Middle Ages. Although the name suggests parallel streets lined with identical houses, Burbia couldn't be much further from the reach of 21st-century standardization. The majority of the people continue to live in rough stone huts, tend their rows of beans, herd sheep through the dirt streets, and regale visitors at great length with intimate family histories.

From Burbia a dirt track leads to the abandoned village of **Campo del Agua**, which conserves the best collection of straw-roofed *pallozas* anywhere in Los Ancares. Serious hikers can tackle the full-day ascent of 5,880ft **Pico de los Tres Obispos**, one of the tallest mountains in the region, offering magnificent views across Galicia, Asturias and León.

More *pallozas* can be found in the next valley to the west, Valle de los Ancares, although there's no direct way across the mountains other than to walk (take LE712 north from Vega if you're driving). The best-preserved are in **Balouta**, and include what is believed to be the only permanently inhabited example in León, stuck in the kind of bleak location that only the Celts would have chosen to set up shop in. Roads lead onwards from Balouta through gorgeous mountain scenery to the Galician village of Doiras, from where it's possible to descend back into León via Balboa, or press on west to the main NVI, or the fast A6 highway, at Becerreá.

Further east, the **Castro de Chano** is a superbly preserved Celtiberian hill fort, just outside Peranzanes in the Valle de Fornela. The *castro* consists of 13 circular turrets, spectacularly positioned on a long spur, and is considered so valuable that access is restricted to archaeologists and dignitaries; a replica has been constructed nearby to satisfy lesser mortals (*open winter Tues–Sun and hols 10–2 and 3–6, summer Tues, Thurs–Sun and hols 10.30–1 and 4–8, Thurs 4–8*).

Carracedo

Cacabelos, 12km west of Ponferrada, was another important stop on the *camino*, although these days it's best known for its wines and its Santuario de las Angustias, where there's a famous scene of baby Jesus floating on a cloud playing cards with St Anthony. Don't miss a brief detour 3km south to the **Monastery of Santa María de Carracedo** (*open winter Tues–Sun 10–2 and 4–6, summer Tues–Sun 10–2 and 5–8; adm*), founded in 990 in a pastoral setting, this time by Bermudo II the Gouty of León. In 1138 it came under the patronage of Doña Sancha, sister of Alfonso VII, who built a

Getting Around

ALSA has frequent **buses** to Cacabelos and Villafranca del Bierzo from León and Ponferrada; a less regular service calls in at Villafranca on the way to Galicia. AUPSA serve Vega de Espinareda from Ponferrada and Cacabelos. To continue into Los Ancares from here you'll need to have transport, hitch, or take a **taxi**.

Tourist Information

Vega de Espinareda: in the Casa Consistorial, t 98 756 47 47.
Villafranca del Bierzo: Avda Diaz Ovelar 10, t 98 754 00 28, www.villafrancadelbierzo.org.

Where to Stay and Eat

Vega de Espinareda ✉ 24430
Casa Rural Valle de Ancares, Pereda de Ancares (30km north), t 98 756 42 84 (*moderate–inexpensive*). Has a few comfortably rustic rooms in a traditional house, with heavy wooden shutters on the windows. Meals are served, and mountain bikes can be rented.
HR Piñera, C/La Conchera 18, t 98 756 46 12 (*budget*). Pleasant and modern, it makes a good base for exploring the valleys – the owners can help to arrange 4WD rental. Next door, **El Jardín serves an excellent and reasonable *menú del día*.
Camping-Albergue Burbia, in Burbia (25km northwest), t 98 756 60 27 (*budget*). Has dormitories for up to six, and two big bathless doubles in a solid, stone-built hostel near the river. The *comedor* downstairs cooks up good honest meals at bargain prices.

Villafranca del Bierzo ✉ 24500
***Parador de Villafranca del Bierzo, Avda de Calvo Sotelo, t 98 754 01 75, villafranca@parador.es (*moderate*). Modern, comfortable *parador* on the outskirts of town.
*Hospederia Convento San Nicolás El Real, C/Travesía San Nicolás 4, t 98 754 04 83, www.hospederiasannicolas.com (*inexpensive*). Occupies the wonderful old convent; the guest areas have been remodelled to modern standards, but original frescoes and paintings remain in the halls. Out in the cloister a restaurant serves food with a religious theme – 'Archbishop's Salad', and to finish up 'Cherries of Perdition'. *Open only at weekends during winter.*
*Hs Casa Méndez, C/Espiritu Santo,1, t 98 754 24 08 (*budget*). Family-run with good home cooking, to go with its well-priced rooms with bath.
*Hs Comercio, C/Puente Nuevo 2, t 98 754 00 08 (*budget*). Offers few luxuries but plenty of character – this rambling old mansion can't have changed much since the 15th century. The huge, high-ceilinged rooms may have seen better days, but this is still the best bargain in town. Shared bath.
La Escalinata, Plaza de Prim 4, t 98 754 07 06 (*moderate*). Bright décor and friendly service accompany a menu of ever-changing delights, in a lovely location opposite the castle. If it's on the menu, try the nest of *langostinos* with smoked peppers and quail eggs, or the home-grown pears stewed in wine and cinnamon. *Open daily July–Sept; rest of the year Fri eve, Sat–Sun lunchtimes.*
Mesón Don Nacho, C/Truqueles, t 98 754 00 76 (*moderate*). Welcoming place with good menu. Try the *solomillo a la pimiento* (fillet steak with pepper sauce). Great desserts.

new church and monastery. At the end of the 18th century the monks decided it was time for a change and began a large neoclassical church. It was only partially finished in 1811 when the French marched through and effectively put an end to the project, leaving half of a new church and much of the old intact, pieced together, restored and roofed over for the monastery's 1,000th birthday. By the church are the remains of a little **palace** built by Alfonso IX in the early 1200s to house his wife and two daughters when the pope annulled his marriage. The claims of the princesses to the throne were a powerful reason behind the union of León and Castile declared by Ferdinand III el Santo – Alfonso IX's son from his second marriage. The palace has a fancy Gothic room known as the 'Queen's Kitchen', the Queen's Mirador, and a relief of a mysterious woman on a bed surrounded by attendants, including the Virgin.

Villafranca del Bierzo

The *Codex Calixtinus*'10th stop on the *camino de Santiago*, Villafranca del Bierzo, is one of the most attractive small towns along the whole road, embraced on all sides by mountains, built at the confluence of the Burbia and Valcarce rivers. As its name suggests, the town was founded by the French in the 11th century and in its heyday it had eight monasteries and six pilgrims' hospitals; today it makes wine and lodges visitors to the region.

On the hill where pilgrims entered Villafranca is the well-preserved 16th-century **Castillo de Villafranca** (*private, no adm*) and the 12th-century **Santiago**, a simple Romanesque church but an important one, with the second Puerta del Perdón along the road. Pilgrims too weary or ill to continue had only to touch the door to achieve the same indulgences as they would at Compostela. Some then keeled over dead and were buried in the adjacent cemetery. All of the church's unfortunately eroded decoration is concentrated around the Puerta del Perdón; you can see three kings on horseback, a Crucifixion and Christ in Majesty. The pilgrims would descend from the church and castle to walk along wide, atmospheric **Calle del Agua**, 'Water Street', lined with blazoned 16th- and 17th-century palaces with iron balconies that often looked over a real street of water, so frequently has the Burbia flooded it. The Plaza Mayor was set higher up away from danger, and near this you'll find the 13th-century church of **San Francisco**, all that remains of a monastery founded by St Francis himself during his pilgrimage. It has a magnificent 15th-century *mudéjar artesonado* ceiling, much of which has been recently restored. Down on the banks of the Burbia, **La Colegiata de Santa María** (*open for mass only; the tourist office organises guided visits at weekends*) stands on the site of the 11th-century monastery founded by the monks of Cluny. It fell into ruins and was rebuilt from scratch in 1544 to designs by Rodrigo Gil de Hontañón. Construction continued into the 18th century, when the money ran out, leaving the nave cut short and the west façade closed by a simple wall, although what was completed of the part-Gothic and part-Renaissance interior is uncommonly grand; note especially the chapel of the Trinity and a reliquary by Juan de Juni.

Just to the south of Villafranca, the 13th-century **San Juan de San Fiz** was built over a Roman cistern; the walls can still be seen under the raised presbytery. **Corullón** has two more lovely Romanesque churches: San Esteban and the recently restored San Miguel, adorned with leering and grinning faces. Corullón's ivy-smothered castle affords a lovely view of the Bierzo valley. West of Villafranca, the pilgrims' road passes through the narrow valley of the Valcarce dotted with tiny villages. At **Herrerías**, with its old Hospital de los Ingleses (English Hostel), the road and pilgrims' route divide; the latter, rising to the pass at Cebreiro and hence into Galicia, was as dangerous and dreaded as it is beautiful.

Galicia

The Coast West of Asturias: As Mariñas de Lugo **286**

The Galician Interior: the Road to Santiago **290**

Lugo: a Detour off the *Camino* **293**

Santiago de Compostela 297

Back to the Rías: the Golfo Ártabro **310**

A Coruña **314**

West of A Coruña: A Costa da Morte **317**

Into the Rías Baixas 320

The Ría de Pontevedra **326**

Pontevedra **327**

The Ría de Vigo **330**

Vigo **331**

Up the Minho to Ourense **336**

Ourense (Orense) **338**

12

Galicia

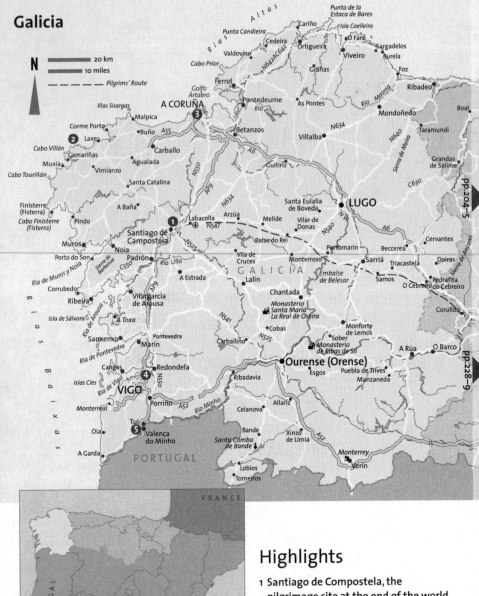

N 20 km / 10 miles

- - - Pilgrims' Route

Rías Altas

Punta de la Estaca de Bares
Punta Candieira
Cariño
Isla Coelleira
Cedeira
Ortigueira
O Faro
Punta Prior
Valdovino
Viveiro
Sargadelos
Burela
Ferrol
Grañas
Foz
Golfo Ártabro
Pontedeume
As Pontes
Ribadeo
Illas Sisargas
A CORUÑA
Río Eume
Mondoñedo
Boal
Malpica
Betanzos
Río Masma
Corme Porto
Buño
A55
Villalba
N634
Taramundi
Laxes
Carballo
A6
Santa Eulalia
Grandas de Salime
Cabo Villán
Agualada
Guitiriz
N640
Camariñas
Muxia
Vimianzo
Santa Catalina
C630
Cabo Touriñán
A Baña
Arzúa
LUGO
Finisterre (Fisterra)
Labacolla
Melide
A6
Cervantes
Cabo Finisterre (Fisterra)
Pindo
Santiago de Compostela
N547
Vilar de Donas
N540
Doiras
Muros
Noia
Palas do Rei
Portomarín
Beccerea
Porto do Son
Padrón
Río Ulla
Vila de Cruces
Monterroso
Sarriá
Triacastela
Ribeira
Corrubedo
A Estrada
Lalín
Embalse de Belesar
Samos
O Cebreiro
Redrafita do Cebreiro
Isla de Sálvora
Chantada
Corullón
Vilagarcía de Arousa
Monasterio Santa María La Real de Oseira
Sanxenxo
Toxa
Cobas
Monforte de Lemos
A Rúa
Pontevedra
Carballiño
N525
Sober
O Barco
Marín
Monasterio de Ribas de Sil
Cangas
Redondela
Ribadavia
Ourense (Orense)
Islas Cíes
Ría de Vigo
Esgos
Puebla de Trives
Manzaneda
Monterreal
VIGO
Porriño
A52
Río Miño
Celanova
Allariz
Oia
Tui
Valença do Minho
Bande
Xinzo de Limia
A52
A Garda
Santa Comba de Bande
Monterrey
PORTUGAL
Lobios
Verín
Torneiros

Rías Baixas

FRANCE
PORTUGAL
SPAIN

Highlights

1 Santiago de Compostela, the pilgrimage site at the end of the world
2 The rough and rugged cliffs of the Costa da Morte
3 The glass balconies of maritime A Coruña, the 'Crystal City'
4 Seafood dining in Vigo, Spain's largest fishing port
5 The lovely granite border town of Tui

If Asturias is Spain's Wales, then Galicia is in many ways its Ireland, for many years so far removed from the mainstream of Spanish life and history it might just as well have been an island. Here the Celtic invaders of 1000 BC found their cosiest niche, in the same kind of rain-swept, green land facing the setting sun that their brethren had settled farther north in Brittany and Cornwall. The Moors left no mark in Galicia, having been expelled in the 8th century by the kings of Asturias – who promptly turned their attention to the richer spoils of the south.

While the rest of the north expanded into the newly won lands of the Reconquista, the Galicians, or *Gallegos*, were hemmed in by Portugal and forced to turn inwards, dividing their land into ever smaller holdings with every generation. Famines were common and, as soon as the New World was discovered, they emigrated in droves – there are more Gallegos in Buenos Aires alone than in all of Galicia. Even today Galicia is one of the poorest regions in Spain. Yet few places in Spain have such a lasting charm. The coastline is pierced by a dozen estuaries, or *rías*, wild and scenic in the north, and in the south, sheltering serene beaches (Galicia has some 772 of these) and tiny coves, perfect for the smuggling that has long been a mainstay of the economy. Rivers in deep, narrow valleys with fantasy names – the Éo, the Ulla, the Lor, the Sil and Jallas – spill down wild mountains on their way to the sea. Bright green gardens cover every inch of cultivable land, although a third of the acreage is wasted by the granite walls each Gallego has erected around his own little plot. Each farm, however small, has a sturdy, self-sufficient air, with its cow and conical hayrack, its trellis of vines (producing excellent white wines similar to Portugal's 'green' wines) and tiny plots of turnips, peppers, maize, cabbage, peas and Spain's finest potatoes. Many cottages have granaries (*hórreos*), monumental pieces of granite set up on pillars to protect the grain from rodents and wet, with window-like vents to permit air to circulate, topped by a gabled roof with crosses. Early travellers mistook them for hermitages.

Because of the endless division of land, much of Galicia is covered higgledy-piggledy with farms and houses in some 31,000 'villages' (most with populations of 100–200), sprinkled with the showy bungalows of the *Americanos* who made their fortunes in Argentina. Many older houses, especially in A Coruña, have balconies closed in by glass 'crystal galleries', adorned with elaborate white mullions. Another distinctive feature of Galicia is the sculpted granite crosses at the crossroads. Some seem to have guided pilgrims, or marked out the high roads, or fulfilled vows, or perhaps even served the same geomantic organization as Neolithic menhirs and dolmens, only carved into Christian forms. In the Rías Baixas, especially along the rivers leading into them, you'll see the stately manor country villas the Gallegos call *pazos*, from the Roman *palatio*.

Galicia's language, Gallego, is chock-full of x's (pronounced 'sh') and closely related to Portuguese, and spoken by a greater percentage of the population than Basque or Catalan are in their respective regions. This, although it's hard to find out exactly, is true now: gallego is in decline among young people, while it's on the rise in the Basque Lands and Catalunya (where 90 per cent of 18–29 year olds speak it). Even García Lorca penned verses in Gallego, inspired by the language of Alfonso the Wise's masterpiece, the *Cantigas de Santa María* and the evocative poetry, reminiscent of Emily Dickinson's, by Rosalía de Castro (1837–85, especially her *Cantares Gallegos*). Rosalía was a key figure in the *Rexurdimento* (literary renaissance), inspired by the Catalans and, like theirs, a forerunner of Spain's nationalist movements.

Culturally, Galicia has always looked to its ancient roots. The national instrument, the *gaita*, is very similar to Breton or Irish bagpipes, and Gallegos like nothing better than to blow it at festivals. Celtic influences are also strong in Galicia's festivals (many associated with death, witches and evil spirits); you can buy a 400-page book that lists every one of them. Irish immigrants in the 16th century introduced lace-making (*camarinhas*), still done by older women all along the coast.

In November 2002, the Bahamas-registered oil tanker, *Prestige*, ran into heavy seas off Cape Fisterra in Galicia. The hull ruptured and she drifted to within 16km of the coast, releasing 3,000 tonnes of oil, before being towed further out to sea by the Spanish, where she broke in two and sank. The spill devastated wildlife in the region and the fishing industry along a 400km-stretch of coast was entirely shut down, devastating communities dependent on the sea for their livelihood. After a massive (and ongoing) two billion-euro clean-up Galicia now boasts more Blue Flag beaches than ever before, but the long-term effects of the disaster remain a cause for concern. The Galician fishing industry is still in crisis, and the highly toxic chemicals in oil (*polyaromatic hydrocarbons*) are expected to affect plankton and the eggs of fish and shellfish, causing a chronic knock-on effect in the food chain, for up to ten years.

Don't let this put you off trying Galician cuisine (*see* p.35, **Food and Drink**). Strict food controls are in place, and Galician seafood is considered by some to be the best in the world and should not be missed.

The Coast West of Asturias: As Mariñas de Lugo

In the Spanish drive to leave no coast unchristened, this wild Atlantic-thundered northernmost stretch of Galicia is known as As Mariñas de Lugo after the provincial capital Lugo. It surrenders every so often to admit sandy beaches decorated with storm-chiselled cliffs and rocks; until very recently, deplorably slow roads conspired to keep it a secret.

As Mariñas de Lugo

Getting Around

Besides **buses** originating from Lugo, Gijón and A Coruña, the slow **FEVE** train from Oviedo at Pravia for Gijón goes along the coast to Ferrol, stopping at Ribadeo, Foz, Burela, Viveiro, Covas, O Barqueiro and Ortigueira. See *www.feve.es*.

Tourist Information

Ribadeo: Plaza de España, t 98 212 86 89, *www.ribadeo.org*.
Viveiro: Avda Ramón Canosa, t 98 256 08 79.
   There are **markets** in Mondoñedo on Thursdays and Sundays; in Foz on Tuesdays; in Viveiro on Mondays, Thursdays and Saturdays; there is a daily fish market in Cedeira and a food market on Wednesdays and Saturdays.

Where to Stay and Eat

Ribadeo ✉ 27700

★★★★**Parador de Ribadeo**, C/Amador Fernández, t 98 212 88 25, *ribadeo@parador.es* (*expensive–moderate*). Lacks atmosphere but comfortable and in a scenic, spot overlooking the *ría*, with views over the harbour; the restaurant offers the day's catch.
★★**Hotel Balastrera**, C/Carlos III, t 98 212 00 21, *www. balastrera.com (moderate–inexpensive)*. A delightful blue-and-white *Indiano* villa with pretty rooms, garden and excellent restaurant.
Huerta de Obe, Ctra Santa Cruz, t 98 212 87 15 (*moderate–inexpensive*). The beaches west towards Foz are well supplied with camp sites, but if you prefer a *casa de campo*, this is a charming choice, with gardens and pool.
★**HR Ros Mary**, C/San Francisco 3, t/f 98 212 86 78 (*inexpensive*). Modern and bland, but rooms are clean and well-equipped and there's a handy cafetería downstairs.
★**Hs Galicia**, C/Virgen del Camino 1, t 98 212 87 77 (*budget*). The cheapest decent place in Ribadeo.
San Miguel, Puerto Deportivo s/n, t 98 212 97 17 (*moderate*). Dine on wonderful fresh seafood overlooking the port.

Mondoñedo ✉ 27740

★**Montero**, Avda San Lázaro 7, t 98 252 17 51 (*budget*). Has pleasant doubles.

★**Montero II**, C/Cándido Martínez 8 (across from the cathedral), t 98 252 10 41 (*budget*). For character, opt for this old-fashioned place decorated with antiques.
★**Hs Padornelo**, C/Buenos Aires 1, t 98 252 18 92 (*budget*). Small and simple, providing room with bath.

Viveiro ✉ 27850

Most places offer big discounts off season. Also, check out internet deals.
Pazo da Trave, in Galdo, t 98 259 81 63, *www.pazodatrave.com* (*expensive– moderate*). A luxurious 15th-century stately home in the countryside, with pools, gardens and an excellent dining room, which serves marine exotica (restaurant open to the public). Highly recommended.
★★★**Ego**, Playa de Area (3km from the centre), t 98 256 09 87 (*moderate*). Modern, over-looking the beach, and comfortable, this hotel contains the region's best restaurant (*see* below).
★★**Las Sirenas**, t 98 256 02 00 (*moderate*). Among a clutch of hotels along Covas beach; this one is smart and offers rooms, flats and studios sleeping up to four. *Open all year.*
★★★**Orfeo**, C/J. García Navia Castrillón 2, t 98 256 21 01, f 98 256 04 53 (*inexpensive*). Respectable, if characterless, rooms near the centre.
★★**Hotel Alameda**, C/Brieiro 67, Área (4km from Viveiro), t 98 255 10 88 (*inexpensive*). A new, simple beachside hotel, good for families.
★★**Hs Vila**, C/N.Montenegro 57, t 98 256 13 31 (*budget*). An unremarkable option with the advantage of being central.
Nito (in the Hotel Ego), Playa de Área, t 98 256 09 87 (*expensive–moderate*). This attractive and welcoming hotel-restaurant offers exquisitely fresh seafood prepared to traditional local recipes and is justly famous throughout the region.
O Muro, C/Margarita Pardo de Cela 28, t 98 256 08 23 (*moderate*). Just inside the old walls, serving up steaming plates of *pulpo* and delicately grilled fish and meat dishes. Great lunch menú for under 10 euros.
El Laurel, C/Melintón Cortiñas, t 98 256 0023 (*moderate–budget*). Try the dining room tucked behind this friendly wine bar, where you'll find more excellent seafood.

Ribadeo and Foz

Galician *rías*, or estuaries, are usually named after their largest towns. The first *ría* west of Asturias, **Ribadeo**, is named after a piquant old fishing town that staggers up to a dusty main **Praza de España**, where palm trees and the delightfully eclectic **Casa Morena** of 1905 lend it a lost Californian air. The 18th-century town hall was built as the home of the Marqués de Sargadelos, a liberal-minded reformer and philanthropist who was tied to the tail of a horse and dragged to his death for his beliefs. The hermitage atop **Monte de Santa Cruz**, 2km south of Ribadeo on LU133, offers splendid views of the Galician-Asturian coastline, guarded by a folksy monument to the Galician bagpiper; in early August Santa Cruz pipers from across Galicia gather here in an ear-splitting eisteddfod called the *Xira a Santa Cruz*. West, the tiny lobster-fishing village of **Rinlo** is the gateway to the long sandy beach known either as the **Playa del Castro**, or **As Catedrais,** after its spectacular rock formations in the sea. Other pretty beaches dwarfed by towering cliffs, **Playa de Rapadoira** and **Playa de Llas**, lie further west by **Foz**, an industrial fishing port at the mouth of the Río Masma. Only a lonely pile of stones, the Peña do Altar, recalls Foz's illustrious Celtiberian origins.

Inland: Mondoñedo

If Foz is no prize, Mondoñedo, 18km to the south up the Masma valley offers some consolation. Mondoñedo was founded in 1117, when the diocese of San Martín de Mondoñedo (*see* opposite) was relocated inland; it received a second boost in its fortunes in the 15th century, when it became capital of its own little province, a distinction that lasted until 1834 and witnessed the construction of many proud houses of provincial barons, some with the glassed-in balconies or *solanas* typical of Galicia. Mondoñedo's granite **Cathedral** was begun in 1219 and when the time came to add a Baroque façade, it was done with surgical discretion, preserving the Romanesque portal and Gothic rose window in harmonious blind arches. The interior is still late Romanesque and decorated with remarkable 14th-century frescoes of the Massacre of the Innocents; there's a wonderful organ with trumpets (1710), and a painted Gothic statue known as the Virgen Inglesa, brought over from St Paul's in London for safekeeping during the Reformation.

The 17th-century cloister's **Museo Diocesano** (*open daily 11–1.30 and 4.30–7.30; adm*) displays paintings from Sevilla, furniture, and fancy liturgical bric-a-brac. The cathedral square is Mondoñedo's best, particularly colourful during the Sunday morning market, and there's a pretty Alameda before the Baroque church **Os Remedios**, decorated with grand Churrigueresque *retablos*, 'that sculpture of emblazoned tripes' as Pritchett calls it, and lots of candles, too, for the remedies in its name are said usually to be granted. Between Mondoñedo and Foz, the Benedictine **Monasterio de Vilanova de Lourenzá** (*open daily 11–1 and 4–7; adm*) dates from the 10th century, but became wealthy enough in the 17th and 18th centuries to finance a major rebuilding programme so ambitious that the fancy façade of the church by granite wizard Fernando de las Casas y Novoa was never quite finished. The graceful interior gives the lie to the idea that Spanish Baroque means dark, gloomy and heavy. Don't miss the exquisitely carved altarpiece in the sacristy (1680); in the chapel of Santa María de Valdeflores you can make a wish while stroking the bones of the monastery's founder, Conde Gutierre Osorio.

Las Rías Altas: West of Foz to Viveiro, O Barqueiro and Ortigueira

From Foz, a brief inland detour will take you to the impressive, mightily buttressed 11th-century **San Martín de Mondoñedo** (*open 11–1 and 4–7*), a rare Romanesque church left untampered with over the centuries, mainly because it was abandoned by its parishioners, leaving intact and uncovered fine 13th-century murals and the original capitals and the tomb of San Gonzalo, who sank a belligerent Norman fleet with a single prayer. Heading west on the coast, you can pay your respects to the **Citania de Fazouro**, a well-preserved Celtic *castro*; the similar Castro do Chan, near the pretty fishing port of **Burela**, yielded the unique golden torques in the Lugo museum.

Just inland from Cervo, **Sargadelos** had one of Spain's earliest ironworks and a famous Royal Ceramics Factory. The latter closed in 1860, but reopened in 1970 as the **Antigua Fábrica de Cerámica de Sargadelos** (*call t 98 255 79 22 for opening hours*) manufacturing traditional blue and white jugs and avant-garde works (*see www.sargadelos.com for for information on the ceramics courses held in summer*).

Beyond Cervo and Sargadelos, the Rías Altas, or Upper Estuaries, begin in earnest, offering some of the best wild and windy coastal scenery in Iberia. Fragrant eucalyptus groves dot the coast around **Viveiro**, at the head of its lovely *ría*. Viveiro is the choice place to stay in the Rías Altas, sheltered by its partly ruined medieval walls from the ravages of the Atlantic, automobiles, and time itself. In the 18th century it imported linen from the Baltic in exchange for Galician agricultural goods but these days its outer fishing port **Celeiro**, on the opposite side of the estuary, deals mostly in sardines. Three medieval gates survive, along with the fancy **Puerta de Carlos V** (1548) on Avda Galicia, erected to curry favour with Charles V. Inside, the narrow lanes and pretty **Praza de Pastor Díaz** are paved in granite and lined with medieval houses sucking in light through their *solanas*, while the austere but pure 12th-century Romanesque **Santa María del Campo** provides a town centrepiece. Viveiro has some ravishing beaches: the sand plain of **Covas** sweeping out to a treetop rock 'castle', **O Faro** facing the ocean, and **Xilloi** and **Ares** near Celeiro, where legend has it an ancient city sank into the sea for refusing to hear the preaching of St James. You can get a good overview from the mirador atop **San Roque**, the mountain just behind Viveiro. To the west, the rugged **Isla Coelleira** – 'Rabbit Island' – has been forlorn and desolate ever since the Templars, who took refuge there from the pope's pogrom, were massacred one night in 1307 by the lord of Viveiro.

The next estuary west, the Ría do Barqueiro, provides a magnificent setting for the hamlet of **Vicedo** and its pretty azalea gardens, the wide beach at **Arealonga** and, over the *ría*, for **O Barqueiro**, a picture-postcard amphitheatre of white, slate-roofed houses cupped around a lobster port, in a landscape of piney fjords. A road leads down the *ría* to more beaches and to the tiny fishing hamlet and fabulous curling sandy beach of **Bares**, the northernmost settlement in Spain, marked by a lighthouse and blocks of walls from the days when it was a port for Phoenician ships en route to the tin mines of Cornwall.

The next estuary, Ría de Santa María de Ortigueira, takes a veritable network of rivers. **Ortigueira**, on the pine-wooded east bank is a peaceful, unremarkable town (except during its annual Festival del Mundo Celta, *www.festivaldeortigueira.com*, held in July) with narrow streets running down to the waterfront and white sandy beaches that never get too crowded. On the west bank of the *ría* (cross the river at

Mera) the long toes of the Sierra de Capelada extend down to Cape Ortegal, where the fishing village of **Cariño** is the last to look over the Cantabrian sea.

Cliffs, Lizards and Cedeira

West of Cariño the road takes in spectacular views of the 2,008ft cliffs of the **Garita de Herbeira** en route to the village and tiny sanctuary of **San Andrés de Teixido**, perched on savage, wave-battered cliffs. Wild horses roam here, and pilgrims flow in year round for, as the saying goes, '*A San Andrés de Teixido, vai de morto o que no foi de vivo*' ('If you don't go while alive, you'll go dead') – reincarnated as a lizard or toad, creatures that are never harmed in the village. On 8 September, the dead are given a formal invitation to the festival, when colourful, archaic dough figures are baked to be consumed before Mass, and pilgrims who over the past year had a close brush with the Grim Reaper are carried to the church in coffins. Buy an amulet or *santera* of the saint, or enquire about San Andrés' famous love herb, which in the good old days was consumed in large quantities after Mass as a prelude to a general orgy. A corniche road continues to the lovely town and port of **Cedeira**, which marks a series of stunning beaches, dunes and lagoons that stretch all the way to Ferrol. The Ría de Cedeira is lined with beauty spots: the lofty **Mirador de Peña Edrosa**, the lighthouse at **Punta Candelaria** and, to the west, the gorgeous setting of the hermitage of **San Antonio de Corveiro**.

The Galician Interior: the Road to Santiago

Pilgrims who made it as far as Villafranca del Bierzo (*see* p.282) had to gird their loins for one last trial: the Puerto Pedrafita in the Sierra de Ancares. This is Galicia at its wildest, driest and bleakest, deceptively covered with blooms in the spring, but the haunt of werewolves and witches in the evening – a zone apart, bound in dreams and legends. The regional government, the Xunta de Galicia, has restored the atmospheric old *camino francés* and placed yellow scallop-shell markers every 500m. The *camino* itself rarely coincides with the highways, making this last leg of the journey especially pleasant for walkers; to maintain the medieval mood, Galicia's fierce sheepdogs are still in place with medieval sheepdog attitudes, just asking for a buffet from a stout pilgrim's staff.

O Cebreiro, Os Ancares, and the Pilgrim's Road

After Villafranca, the *camino* (and the road) pass through the narrow valley of the River Valcarce, ascending to the 3,609ft pass at **Pedrafita**, the boundary between Léon and Galicia. Here, in 1809, Sir John Moore's troops – fleeing to A Coruña, with Marshal Soult's terrible army in hot pursuit – nearly rebelled. Discipline had vanished in Villafranca, where the soldiers had sacked, raped and looted the homes of their Spanish allies; at Pedrafita and at **O Cebreiro**, another 650ft up and a famous brunt of blizzards, hundreds of men froze to death. Such was their haste that the soldiers threw thousands of pounds in gold – the army's pay – over the cliff, along with hundreds of horses, while the women and children camp followers were abandoned in the icy wilderness. It was one of the blackest pages in the history of the British army, and it was almost miraculous that Moore was able to restore order and continue to the coast.

Getting Around

By Bus

Lugo's bus station is on Praza de Constitución, **t** 98 222 39 85; buses from Lugo to León pass through Becerreá and Pedrafita.

By Train

Lugo and the junction at Monforte de Lemos are linked by train to León, A Coruña, Ourense and Vigo, with speedy Talgos to Zaragoza, Barcelona, Bilbao and Irún. Lugo's station is on Pza Conde de Fontao, **t** 98 222 21 41. There's a RENFE office at Pza Maior 27, **t** 98 222 55 03.

Tourist Information

Lugo: Praza Maior 27, **t** 98 223 13 61, *www.concellodelugo.org.*

Lugo's **post office** is at Rúa San Pedro 5; **Internet cafés** ('cibers' in Spain) congregate around Rúa Vilalba, just outside the walls.

Where to Stay and Eat

O Cebreiro and Becerreá ✉ 27600

Hs Piornedo, in Cervantes, **t 98 216 15 87 (*inexpensive*). A stone building with reasonable rooms and lovely views over the mountain.

Hs Rivera, Avda Madrid 86, **t 98 236 01 85 (*budget*). A roadside *hostal* outside Becerreá, with café, pool and parking. *Open all year.*

Hs San Giraldo de Aurillac, near the *pallozas*, **t 98 236 71 25 (*budget*). Now a *mesón* and hostal in a former convent founded by French monks in the 11th century. You will find several other places to stay in the Os Ancares area in Becerreá. There are a couple of bars in town that serve decent meals as well.

*Hs Herbón, G Jiménez 8 (in Becerreá), **t** 98 236 01 34 (*budget*). Basic and clean. *Open all year.*

Casa Catuxa, Ouselle (6.5km from Becerreá), **t** 98 236 03 15 (*budget*). A lovely old stone house offering simple B&B.

Sarriá ✉ 27600

***NH Alfonso IX, Rua do Peregrino 29, **t** 98 253 00 05, *www.nh-hoteles.es* (*inexpensive*). Sarriá has lots of choices, starting with this modern chain hotel, well placed for the old town.

Casa A Rectoral de Goián, C/Cabezares 8, **t** 98 253 3813, *www.rectoraldegoian.com* (*inexpensive*). An 18th-century rectory houses this tranquil rural hotel, with gardens, restaurant and delicious breakfasts. It's 10km from Sarriá.

Casa Nova de Rente, Barbadelo, **t** 98 218 78 54 (*budget*). Simple rooms in an old stone house in lovely countryside; a cheap home-cooked dinner is available on request. There's also a camping area.

Today O Cebreiro has a huge parking lot to allow everyone to enjoy the tremendous views (in good weather) and have a look at the village's Celtic *pallozas*, oval stone huts topped with conical straw roofs where man and beast lived side by side. Two have been set aside as a Spartan pilgrim's refuge, while another pair house a small ethnographic museum (*usually open daily 12–2 and 5–7*). A Benedictine monastery, **Santa María del Cebreiro**, contemporary with the Asturian churches of the 9th century, was built over an old Celtic temple (note the carved stone reused in the entrance). Pilgrims never failed to pay their respects in its squat slate church, where one of the greatest miracles of the road took place: in the late 13th century, an old priest, tired of celebrating Mass for just one shepherd in the winter, was grumbling away during the Transfiguration when he and his parishioner were astonished to see the host transformed into flesh and the wine into blood. The chalice in which this miracle happened is a fine example of Romanesque gold work and displayed in the right aisle; legend identifies it with the Holy Grail, left here by a pilgrim (compare it to other Grails in the cathedrals of Genoa and Valencia); next to it in the case are the miraculous paten and a silver reliquary for the blood and flesh donated by celebrity pilgrims Ferdinand V and Isabel I in 1489.

O Cebreiro and the mighty mountains to the north form part of the **Reserva Nacional de Os Ancares**, part refuge of the rare capercaillie (especially around Degrada) and part hunting reserve of roebuck and boar. Several of the tiny villages lost in the range also have *pallozas*, a few still inhabited by diehards – **Villarello**, **Cervantes**, **Doiras** and, best of all, **Piornedo**, at the top of a twisting mountain road. **Becerreá**, on the Lugo road, is the main base for excursions into Os Ancares. From O Cebreiro, the *camino* ascends vertiginously to **O Poio** pass (4,387ft), but from here it's all downhill through mountain meadows, chestnut groves and tiny hamlets, where most of the pilgrims' chapels and *hostales* have survived only in name. The exception, **Triacastela**, huddled under an old *castro*, still has its Romanesque church of Santiago, with a simple Baroque tower, and by the River Ouribio a pilgrims' fountain and monument. During the construction of the cathedral of Santiago at Compostela, every medieval pilgrim would pick up a chunk of limestone in the quarries outside Triacastela, and carry it 100km to the Castañeda kilns to be melted into mortar. Modern pilgrims sometimes continue the custom, but now that the cathedral is finished they leave their stone atop Monte de Gozo.

At San Xil, the *camino* splits, the right branch heading prettily over hill and dale, while the other, longer, passes down the narrow wooded Ouribio valley to the huge Benedictine **Abadía de San Xulián** at Samos (*adm by guided tour only, tours every 30 mins Mon–Sat 10–12.30 and 4.30–6.30, Sun 11.30–12.30; adm*), where the hospitable old monks seem glad to see visitors. Founded in 655, abandoned with the arrival of the Moors but rebuilt a few years later, the abbey had a famous library in the Middle Ages. The intellectual tradition continued in the 1700s, when Samos was the home of Padre Feijóo, the 'Spanish Voltaire', a major figure in the Spanish Enlightenment. The tiny slate chapel of San Salvador is from the 9th century, but the medieval monastery burned down in the 16th century and its replacement in 1951, leading to the reconstruction of the two cloisters, one late Gothic and the other, larger, very strict and buttoned-down Spanish Baroque, decorated with frescoes of St Benedict (as truly awful as only modern religious art can be). In the centre flows the lovely Fountain of the Nereids, said to be the work of Velázquez. There's a recent statue of Padre Feijóo, who founded the monastic church with profits from his essays. Designed by monk Juan Vázquez, the west façade is elegant, even minus its planned towers. The interior is austere and virtuous, the only sign of playfulness – *trompe l'oeil* doctors of the church – tucked in the pendentives of the dome.

The two branches of the *camino* meet in **Sarria**, a cement-making town on the rail line. In its quietly aloof medieval core there's a ruined castle, the little Romanesque church of San Salvador and a pilgrims' hostel in the **Convento de los Mercedarios**, where the church has Isabelline Gothic frills. Ten kilometres west, **Portomarín** was a pilgrims' halt protected by the Templars, but even they couldn't have fended off the waters of the Minho, when the river was dammed in the 1960s to form the Embalse de Belesar, submerging the medieval bridge and village. However, old Portomarín's porticoed main street plan was salvaged in a new Portomarín, along with the pretty façade of **San Pedro** and the Romanesque tower church of **San Nicolás**. The latter has a rose window like a telephone dial and Romanesque portals so fine that they were long attributed to Master Mateo, one decorated with the 24 Elders playing their rebecs and the other with a charming scene of the Annunciation; step inside to see the stately single-aisled interior. The adjacent monument is to the electrical engineer who helped the villagers with their request to relocate rather than simply receive an indemnity for their property. And they continue to do what they've always done best: supply Galicia with excellent *aguardiente* – firewater which they not only distil but drain during the nightly *marcha*.

And the Last Leg of the *Camino*

At **Vilar de Donas**, 'Ladyville' (just off the pilgrim's road, 15km west of Portomarín), the 13th-century granite church of **San Salvador** merits a detour. From the exterior you can see the ruined Gothic cloister of the long-gone monastery and the pretty Romanesque-Gothic portal, decorated with reading and praying monks; inside, the tall granite walls are emerald green from the damp, while those in the rounded apse are embellished with 15th-century paintings: the Resurrection, Annunciation, the queen of heaven and the noble ladies who gave their name to the village. The altar stone is carved with the miracle at O Cebreiro, with Jesus in person emerging out of the chalice; the 15th-century baldachin in the transept is one of the few to survive intact in Galicia. San Salvador was once the seat of the Knights of Santiago in Galicia (note the crossed swords, the symbol of the order, on the tombs).

If it weren't for the proximity of Santiago itself, the last two days' march along the *camino* would be disappointing, especially for the modern pilgrim. The *Códice Calixtino* advised pilgrims to say the rosary at **Palas do Rei**, the penultimate stop, although only a few medieval traces remain in its church. The old road passes over a medieval bridge at **Furelos**, before arriving in **Melide**, where the church of Sancti Spiritus decorates the endearing Praza do Convento, and the roadside cross, marking the geographic centre of Galicia, is one of the oldest. Just outside Melide, you'll find a dolmen, the **Pedra de Raposo**, and the crumbling church Santa María with 15th-century murals in the apse, perhaps by the same artist as Vilar de Donas. **Arzúa** was the traditional last overnight stop, 30km (19 miles) from Compostela.

These days Santiago's airport is the dominant feature of **Labacolla** ('Wash Arse'), 8km (5 miles) from Compostela, where 'for the love of the Apostle' the pilgrims bathed in the stream flowing by the church. Sentries were posted to ensure they did this, as much against lice as for the sensibilities of St James. Another 5km (3 miles) would take them up to the now rather desolate hill (km 717 along the *autopista*), **Monte del Gozo** or Mountjoy, and the tremendous, long-awaited sight of the towers of Santiago. The first member of each pilgrimage band to sight the cathedral towers was called the 'King', a proud title that was passed down as a surname; if yours is King, Leroy or Rey, chances are you had a sharp-eyed ancestor. These days you barely make them out; Santiago's sprawl and traffic make the last few kilometres a hellish welcome to a heavenly goal (*see* p.297).

Lugo: a Detour off the *Camino*

Many pilgrims made the detour to Lugo, the capital of Spain's poorest province but happily dozing away in cosy retirement on the banks of the Minho after a career of some consequence, the kind of town 'where an ill poet would feel happy', according to one French observer. Its Celtic name *lug* means either the sun god or sacred forest, and when the Romans took it over in the 2nd century AD, they renamed it Lucus Augusti, made it the capital of their province of Gallaecia and endowed it with a remarkable dark slate corset of walls, the best-preserved ancient fortifications in Spain, just over 2km long and 28ft high and interspersed with 85 rounded towers. For all that, Lugo was grabbed by the Suevi in the 5th century, the Visigoths in 585, and the Moors in the 8th century. The bastions now defend historic Lugo from its own modern sprawl; for a good view, take a walk on the promenade along the top of the walls.

Four ancient gates (and six modern ones) pierce the dark fastness of Lugo's fortifications. Pilgrims would enter the southern Santiago gate to visit Lugo's **cathedral**, built in 1177 and encased in a Baroque skin that offers a modest prelude to the great façade and three towers at Santiago de Compostela. On the west front note the figure of Lugo's patron San Froilán with his wolf: the story goes that the saint was travelling with a well-laden mule when a ferocious wolf ambushed him and killed the mule. The angry saint scolded until the beast repented and agreed to bear the mule's load himself. Only the north, 14th-century, Gothic portal survived the Baroquers, with its fine Romanesque Christ in Majesty and a capital carved with a Last Supper. Inside there are fittings from every century: a Romanesque chapel and another from 1735, lavish and Baroque in the shape of a rounded Greek cross, dedicated to the Virgen de los Ojos Grandes, 'Our Lady of the Big Eyes', designed by Fernando de las Casas, master of the Obradoiro façade at Compostela. Glass protects a beautiful walnut *coro* carved with a proto Art Nouveau flair by Francisco Moure (1590–1621), whose detailed scenes include an anatomy lesson. The Renaissance *retablo mayor* survives in two bits, filling the transepts; there's a pretty Baroque cloister off the south transept. Since the miracle of O Cebreiro, the cathedral has had the rare privilege of *manifestado* (having the Host on permanent display), an honour depicted on Galicia's crest.

Next to the cathedral, elegant Praza Santa María holds the handsome 17th-century **Bishop's Palace**, built in the style of a typical *Gallego pazo*. Just west, **Praza do Campo** with its fountain was the Roman forum; Lugo's medieval neighbourhood, **La Tinería**, extends here around Rúa Cruz and Rúanova. Just north of Prazo do Campo, the formal Alameda gardens give onto the Praza Maior, site of Lugo's rococo Ayuntamiento. Rúa da Raiña heads north to busy **Praza de Santo Domingo**, dominated by an eagle on a column, dedicated to Augustus. The square has two Gothic churches: 14th-century **Santo Domingo** and 16th-century, *mudéjar*-influenced **San Francisco**, formerly part of a 12th-century monastery founded by St Francis on his return from pilgrimage to Santiago. The delicate cloister and refectory house the interesting **Provincial Museum** (*open July–Aug Mon–Fri 10.30–2 and 4.30–20.30, Sat 10.30–2 and 4.30–8, Sun 11–2, Sept–June Mon–Fri 11–2 and 5–8, Sat 10–2*) containing Celtic and Roman finds – a 2nd-century-BC, golden, winged ram , gold torques, jet figures from Compostela, the biggest collection of sundials in Galicia, ceramics and folk art; if you like what you see, don't miss Sargadelos shop in the square.

Lugo's beauty-spots are along the Río Minho, the most beautiful of Galicia's rivers; in the **Parque Rosalía de Castro**, outside the Santiago gate and popular during the evening *paseo*, the *mirador* has magnificent views of the valley. Nearby are the brick vaults of the **Termas Romanas**, or Roman hot baths, now part of a modern hotel-spa complex.

Where to Stay and Eat

Lugo ✉ 27000

★★★★Gran Hotel Lugo, Avda Ramón Ferreiro 21, t 98 222 41 52, *www.gh-hoteles.com* (*moderate*). Top of the scale: a pool, piano bar, spa and a good seafood restaurant (**Os Marisqueiros**).

★★★Méndez Núñez, C/de la Reina 1, t 98 223 07 11 (*inexpensive*). Large, comfortable and well located within the walls; recently renovated rooms.

★★Hs Mar de Plata, Ronda Muralla 5, t 98 222 89 10 (*inexpensive*). You can have a view of the walls here – one of several budget choices just outside the walls, not far fro, the bus station.

★★Hs San Roque, Plaza Comandante Manso 11, t 98 222 27 00 (*budget*). One of the better budget choices outside the walls, in a quiet location set back from the main road.

★España, Rúa Vilalba 2, t 98 223 15 40 (*budget*). Good value, functional rooms with views over to the cathedral, private bath and TV.

★Hs Parames, Rúa do Progreso 28, t 98 222 62 51 (*budget*). Decent and central, with a popular restaurant.

Although Lugo boasts of quirky delicacies such as pancakes with pig's blood, it also has good seafood restaurants:

Casa Grande de Nadela, Nadela (6km from Lugo), t 98 230 5915 (*restaurant and hotel, moderate*). One of the area's best restaurants, serving elaborate contemporary cuisine. It also has ten very comfortable guestrooms.

Campos, Rúa Nova 4, t 98 222 97 43 (*moderate*). Has traditional Gallego sucking-pig, octopus and seasonal game dishes. *Closed Mon.*

Mesón de Alberto, Rúa da Cruz, t 98 222 85 72 (*moderate*). The best in town, offering classic and modern Galician dishes. Excellent wine. Good tapas at the bar downstairs. *Closed Sun.*

Restaurante La Barra, San Marcos 27, t 98 225 29 20 (*moderate*). Mouthwatering meat and fish dishes in an Art Deco-meets-Starbucks ambience. *Closed Sun.*

Verruga, Rúa da Cruz 12, t 98 222 98 55 (*moderate*). Seafood restaurant with a good value lunch *menú*. *Closed Sun eve and Mon.*

Pulpería Palmira, Plaza Comandante Manso 17, t 98 225 39 22 (*budget*). Share a table and feast on octopus at this basic but friendly *comedor*.

Villalba ✉ 27400

★★★Parador Condes de Villalba, Valeriano Valdesuso, t 98 251 00 11, *vilalba@parador.es* (*expensive–moderate*). A crenellated fortress with 3m-thick walls and slit windows. Book early for one of the six rooms in the old tower. The modern annexe is comfortable. Baronial dining in the restaurant.

★★★Villamartín, Avda Tierra Llana, t 98 251 12 15 (*inexpensive*). For half as much, you could check into this modern, functional place complete with disco.

Monforte de Lemos ✉ 27400

★★★★Parador de Monforte de Lemos, Praza Luis de Góngora, t 98 241 8484, *monforte@parador.es* (*expensive–moderate*). Plush parador, with a fine restaurant, formerly an 11th-century monastery and the 16th-century palace of the Counts of Lerma.

★★Hs Puente Romano, Paseo del Malecón, t 98 241 11 68, *hotelpromano@ interbook.net* (*budget*). Just beyond the bridge; pleasant accommodation with busy bar downstairs.

★★Hs Río, Rúa da Baamonde 30 (near the centre), t 98 241 13 02 (*budget*). Basic but fine.

O Grelo, Campo da Virxe s/n, t 98 240 47 01 (*moderate*). Offers delicious Gallego cuisine.

Castroverde ✉ 49110

Pazo de Vilabade, t 98 231 30 00 (*moderate*). One of the nicest *pazos* in Galicia, with antiques and a lovely garden.

Santa Eulalia de Bóveda, and a Mystery

Some 16km southwest of Lugo (take the Ourense road for 4km, then bear right to Friol and follow the signs) is the extraordinary 4th-century subterranean chapel of **Santa Eulalia de Bóveda** (*open for guided tours in Spanish, summer Tues–Sat 10.30–2 and 4.30–8.30, winter Tues–Sat 10.30–2 and 3.30–5.30*), built over a Celtic temple as a Roman nymphaeum, and later as a mausoleum. Discovered in 1962, steps lead down to what must have been an antechamber. A horseshoe arch with mysterious reliefs of female dancers on one side and the healing of a man on the other leads into a vaulted room with a shallow pool (perhaps used for immersion baptisms by the early Christians), decorated with colourful winsome murals of birds and trees, dated 4th and 8th century – just predating the pre-Romanesque churches of Asturias. The columns by the pool were found nearby and re-erected; under the pavement, a drainage system kept the water clear. The only similar known building is in the Ukraine, and just as mysterious.

Another rewarding excursion from Lugo and a popular detour for pilgrims is north-west to the evocative ruins of **Sobrado dos Monxes** (*open daily 10.30–1 and 4.15–6.15*), Galicia's greatest monastery, founded by the Cistercians in 1142. Although the original building (by an architect from Clairvaux specially sent over by St Bernard) hasn't survived, efforts are being made with government funds to preserve the massive towered Baroque church, the lovely, if rotting, choir stalls, originally in the cathedral of Santiago, and the monumental, ogival kitchen where pilgrims once cadged meals; also intact are the 13th-century chapel dedicated to the Magdalen, a sacristy (1571) by Juan de Herrera, a 12th-century chapterhouse or Sala Capitular, and three 17th- and 18th-century cloisters, wreathed in lichens and wild flowers. The monks now run a livestock breeding centre and their own milk business as well as a basic pilgrim's hostal.

Villalba, farther north, was the capital of the Terra Cha, ruled by the Andrade family, who left behind their powerful 15th-century octagonal castle, now an extremely nice *parador*.

A Detour South: Monforte de Lemos

If you're driving, consider a detour south to **Monforte de Lemos**, dominated by a Homage tower, all that remains of the medieval castle of the counts of Lemos. It had two important monasteries: Benedictine **San Vicente del Pino**, founded in the 10th century, with a late Romanesque church sheltering a 15th-century statue of St Anne; and, near the medieval bridge, the huge 16th-century Jesuit **Colegio de la Compañía**, inspired by the geometric Baroque of Herrera. Look in the chapel for a lovely Renaissance

Heresy, Galician Style

According to popular belief, the right wall of Santa Eulalia once contained the tomb of Galicia's first 'saint', Prisciliano, whose doctrines, a syncretism of old Celtic and Christian beliefs, attracted many followers in Galicia and León but upset the Church. For one thing, Prisciliano believed works of the spirit obliterated sexual differences, and that monks and nuns should live together. His followers walked barefoot to stay in contact with the earth's forces, were vegetarians, did a bit of sun-worshipping on the side and retreated to hermitages (alone or with their families and servants) in the holy mountains of the Celts. The counsel of Zaragoza (380) interdicted him, and when that had no effect, the bishop of Triers had him beheaded five years later – making Prisciliano one of the first holy men to be martyred by the Church instead of by the Romans. His death only increased the popularity of what became known as Priscillianism in Galicia until the early 9th century, when, by an extraordinary coincidence, the head and body of St James were discovered in Santiago. Galician nationalists know they really belonged to Prisciliano, and that the holy heretic now has the last laugh in the venerated crypt in Compostela.

retablo in walnut carved with the life of the Virgin by de Moure, two El Grecos painted before the Cretan reached the summit of his style, and a lovely triptych attributed to Hugo van der Goes. The area south of here towards the River Sil contains the vineyards of Amandi, one of Galicia's finest reds, grown in a village named, of all things, **Sober**.

Santiago de Compostela

The original European tourist destination, Santiago de Compostela still comes up with the goods. Not only does it boast a great cathedral where pilgrims are promised 50 per cent off their time in purgatory, but the moss-stained Baroque city is pure granite magic, a rich grey palette of a hundred moods crowned with curlicues. Any tendency towards atrophy into a Euro-tourist museum shrine is thwarted by the university, which keeps the ancient streets and especially the bars full of life year round and fuels the raw *urbanización* that engulfs the perimeters, swelling the population to more than 90,000.

Expect rain – the city, the 'Urinal of Spain', never fails gently to remind you that the showers are good for granite, fostering the elegant patina on its monuments and the micro-gardens that sprout out of the stone, an especially appropriate flourish to the Competelan Baroque of Simón Rodríguez and Fernando de Casas y Novoa with its 'vegetative impulse of verticality'. But on a cold winter's twilight you may see it stripped as bare as García Lorca did in one of his Galician poems:

See the rain on the streets,
a moan of glass and stone,
See in the failing wind
The dust and ashes of your sea.

History

The story goes that in the year 813, a bright star led Pelayo, a hermit shepherd of Iria Flavia (Padrón), to the forgotten tomb of St James the Greater, the legendary Apostle of Spain. The place was named Compostela, a corruption of the Latin *Campus stellae* 'Field of the star', although some say that Pelayo's discovery merely happened in the Roman cemetery, or *compostum*, where bodies decomposed. This theory was given a boost in the late 1940s when excavations in the cathedral's foundation revealed Roman graves over a Celtic *castro*. Of course apostles don't compost like everyone else, and the remains of James were just what Christian Spain required at the dawn of the Reconquista. Local bishop Theodomir confirmed the relics' authenticity and built a chapel; in 829 Alfonso II the Chaste of Asturias built a much larger chapel over the tomb. So many pilgrims began to arrive that an even larger church was needed and supplied by Alfonso III the Great in 896. This in turn fell to al-Mansur and his Moorish armies when they swept through in 997; al-Mansur took the bells as a souvenir for the Great Mosque at Córdoba, where they were turned upside down to hold oil, but he left the Apostle's tomb alone, awed, they say, by the piety of a single monk, who fearlessly knelt there and prayed during the battle.

CORR DAS ARREPENTIDAS

DO CARME DE ABAIXO

RÚA DE ENTREGALERAS

RÚA DE GALERAS

RÚA DE ENTRERRÍOS

RÚA POZA DE BAR

CRUZEIRO DO GAIO

CAMPO DAS HORTAS

RÚA DAS CARRETAS

RÚA DE SAN FRANCISCO

Hospital Real/
Hostal de los
Reyes Católicos
H

Pazo de
Gelmírez/
Xelmírez

AV DE COMPOSTELA

RÚA DO POMBAL

RÚA DAS HORTAS

San Fructuoso

Pazo
de Rajoy

PRAZA DO OBRADOIRO

Cathedral

Carballeira de Santa Susana

RÚA DA TRINIDADE

RÚA DE RAJOY

Colegio de
San Jerónimo

Santa Susana

CAMPO DE SAN CLEMENTE

TRAVESÍA DE FONSECA

Colegio
Mayor de
Fonseca

PRAZA DAS
PRATERÍAS

RÚA DE GELMÍREZ

RÚA DE RODRIGO DE PADRÓN

Oficina
do
Peregrino

RÚA DA RAIÑA

Post Office ✉

i

Colegio de S.
Clemenzo

RÚA DO FRANCO

RÚA DO VILAR

Iglesia del Pilar

AVENIDA DE FIGUEROA

i
Tourist
Information

RÚA NOVA

AV DE ROSALÍA DE CASTRO

CARREIRA DO CONDE

RÚA DA SENRA

PRAZO
TOURAL

Santa María
Salomé

RÚA DE CALDERERÍA

RÚA DAS ORFAS

RÚA XENERAL PARDIÑAS

PRAZO
DE GALICIA

RÚA DE MONTERO RÍOS

PRAZA DE
GALICIA

FONTE DE SANTO ANTONIO

Convento de las
Mercedarias

CONCEPCIÓN ARENAL

RÚA DO PATIO DE MADRES

↓ Train Station

RÚA DE GARCÍA BLANCO

↓ Santa María
del Sar

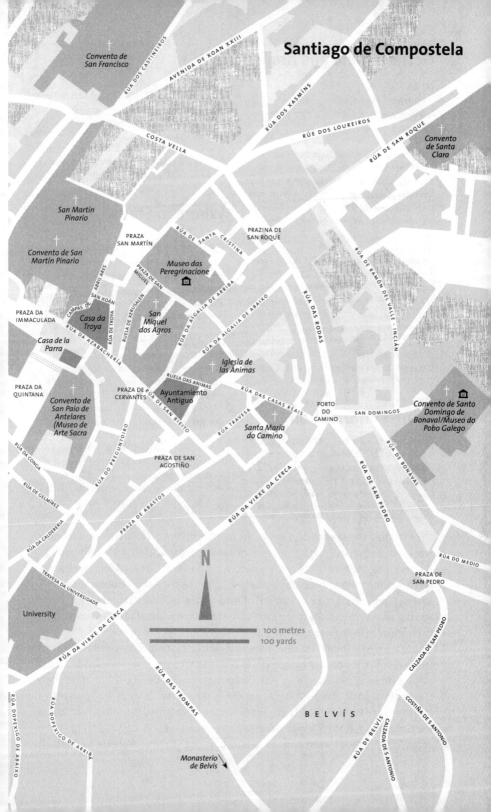

Getting There and Around

By Air

Santiago's airport, **t** 98 154 75 00, *www.aena.es*, is at Labacolla, 11km to the east. It has regular flights to Barcelona, Madrid, Sevilla, Santa Cruz de Tenerife, Bilbao, Santander and San Sebastián, as well as direct flights to London, Paris, Amsterdam, Geneva and Frankfurt. Iberia's office is at Gral. Pardiñas 36, **t** 90 240 0 5 00, *www.iberia.com*, there are buses to the airport from the bus station roughly every 60– 90 mins, **t** 98 158 81 11.

By Train

Santiago's train station is a 15-minute walk from the centre at the end of Rúa do Hórreo, **t** 902 24 02 02, with daily connections to Madrid, Ourense, A Coruña, Vigo, Zamora and other points. More inconveniently, the bus station is way out on Rúa de Rodríguez de Viguri, **t** 98 154 24 16, north of the old centre; city bus nos. 5 and 10 link it to Praza de Galicia. **Buses** go to nearly all points in Galicia, especially the Rías Altas.

Tourist Information

Municipal: Rúa de Vilar 63, **t** 98 155 51 29, *www.santiagoturismo.com*. Walking tours in Spanish (*daily*) and English (*three times a week in summer*) can be booked here (€8 per person). They offer a wide range of activities, from city audio guides to hop-on hop-off tourist bus tickets. Full info at Santiago Reservas, **t** 902 19 01 60, *www.santiagoreservas.com*.
Provincial: Rúa de Vilar 63, **t** 98 158 40 81. The Galician tourist board.
The **post office** is on Travesía de Fonseca, near the Praza do Obradoiro; a good central **ciber** is Cyber Nova 50, Rúa Nova 50.
There is a **market** from Monday to Saturday in the covered market in Praza de San Félix.

Where to Stay

Santiago ✉ 15705

Finding a place to stay at any price is easy; even during the high holy day of 25 July you may be met at the bus or train station by landladies luring you to their *hostales* or *casas particulares* for around €15 a head.

Luxury–Expensive

★★★★★Hs de Los Reyes Católicos, Praza del Obradoiro, **t** 98 158 22 00 *santiago@parador.es* (*luxury*). Poor pilgrims used to stay in this magnificent 15th-century building, but since 1954 it has been the luxurious *nec plus ultra* of Spanish *hostales* and one of Europe's best hotels. Most rooms look onto one of four shady patios and the bridal suites have been enjoyed by VIPs from Franco on up – but it's probably the priciest *parador* in Spain.
★★★★★AC Palacio del Carmen, Oblatas s/n, **t** 98 155 24 44/98 155 24 45, *www.ac-hotels.com*

Sometime in these early days James the humble fisherman with a voice of thunder was given a new posthumous role as Santiago Matamoros, a fierce Moor-thumping *Generalísimo*, the hero of the entirely apocryphal Battle of Clavijo of 844. This legend was 'confirmed' in a 12th-century document known as the *Privilegio de los Votos de Santiago*, purporting to be by Ramiro I of Asturias, the grateful victor of Clavijo, vowing a tax in perpetuity to the saint's church in Compostela (a tax that continued to be imposed in Spain until 1834).

After al-Mansur, church and town were soon rebuilt, this time with walls. In 1075, thanks to the new tax, the present cathedral was begun to accommodate the massive flow of pilgrims from all over Europe. By 1104, Compostela was made an archbishopric, under the feisty Diego Gelmírez; in 1189, Alexander III decreed it a Holy City, on a par with Jerusalem and Rome. In 1236, Ferdinand III the Saint brought back Santiago's bells from the Great Mosque. In 1589, with Drake (a pirate and worse, a Protestant) ravaging the coast, Santiago was tucked away for safekeeping but, in a fit of amnesia, no one could (*expensive*). A much-restored convent outside the centre, but with every amenity including a heated pool, fine restaurant and gardens.

****Hesperia Compostela**, Hórreo 1, t 98 158 57 00 (*expensive*). A grand old granite hotel with a touch of class and all the comforts.

***Rua Villar**, Rúa do Villar 8–10, t 98 151 98 58, *www.hotelruavillar.com* (*expensive*). A new hotel in an ancient building; the stone walls and wooden beams ooze charm, while the contemporary art and designer gadgets add pizazz. Smaller rooms are *moderate*.

Moderate

***Virxe da Cerca**, Rúa Virxe da Cerca 27, t 98 156 93 50, *www.pousadasdecompostela.com*. Stylish serenity and beautiful gardens in an 18th-century Jesuit residence. The sympathetically built extension is slightly cheaper.

Hotel Airas Nunes, Rúa do Vilar 17, t 98 155 47 06. An elegant *pousada* in an early 18th-century building. The interior is fabulous, all honey-coloured stone with warm fabrics and attractive finishing touches.

Hotel San Clemente, Rúa San Clemente 28, t 98 156 92 60. Another listed building with original stone and polished wood interior. Parking is available next door.

Hotel Sino, Algalia de Abaixo 5, t 981554436, *www.sino-compostela.com*. The historic buildings have been nicely restored. Also offers a gourmet restaurant.

As Artes, Trav. de Dos Puertas 2, t 98 155 52 54, *www.asartes.com*. A charming old stone house, with seven individually decorated rooms. It's next to the parador, a stone's throw from the cathedral, and extras include a massage room and tiny sauna.

Inexpensive

Costa Vella, Rúa Porta da Peña 17, t 98 156 95 30, *www.costavella.com*. A beautiful, very peaceful place, located on a traffic-free street above the Convento de San Francisco. It's worth paying more for a sunny room overlooking the city; part of Santiago's old walls can be seen in the lovely garden. Their glossy new sister hotel, **Altair** (*moderate*), is nearby, with chic urban décor, WiFi and café-bar.

Hs Mapoula, Entremurallas 10, t 98 158 01 24. Just inside the *casco viejo*, this *hostal* has nice airy rooms with baths.

Libredón Hostal, Praza de Fonseca 5, t 98 157 65 20. Good views of the square and *palacio* from sparkling pine and white rooms.

Budget

Hs Suso, Rúa del Vilar 65, t 98 158 66 11. Located on Santiago's prettiest street, this pilgrims' favourite is run by a jovial fellow who knows everything and probably has something to do with the tasty tapas in the excellent bar downstairs.

Hospedaje Mera, Rúa Porta da Pena 15, t 98 158 38 67. Perfectly located, this peaceful *pensión* offers functional rooms with or without bath; those with private terraces enjoy wonderful views across the city.

remember where. Still, the pilgrims came, and only in the 19th century, when numbers declined drastically, did a cathedral workman stumble across the most important relics in Spain (1879). How to make sure they were genuine? An authenticated apostolic bone chip from Pistoia was sent over and fitted the notch in the skull like a hand in a glove.

On years when the 25th of July, Santiago's feast day, happens to land on a Sunday, a Holy Year is proclaimed and the city launches into a year's worth of festivities. The last one was in 2004, when hundreds of thousands of visitors enjoyed music, dance and street activities celebrating all things Gallego – both traditional and contemporary. For the next one, you'll have to wait until 2010. Santiago de Compostela was also named a European City of Culture for the year 2000. Along with the generous funding for a wide range of cultural events, the city has gained some significant public works out of the deal, including a new communications port on Monte Pedroso designed by Norman Foster, and a generous park by the architect JP Kleihues.

*Hotel Oca Avenida, Fonte de San Antonio 4, t 98 157 80 07. Provides more character and comfort than usual in this category, with polished wooden floors in a restored 18th-century house.

*Hs La Estela, Raxoi 1 (by the cathedral), t 98 158 27 96. A friendly, charming *hostal*, with a lovely patina of age and authentic character.

*Pensión da Estrela, Praza San Martín Pinario 5, t 98 157 69 24, *www.pensiondaestrela.com*. A simple, immaculate little *pensión*: book early for a room with views over the old city.

Eating Out

Eating in Santiago is a pleasure – competition is keen and the food has to be good to succeed. Rúa do Hórreo has the biggest concentration of restaurants – one window of tempting seafood after another.

Don Gaiferos, Rúa Nova 23, t 98 158 38 94 (*expensive*). For tradition mixed with international, seasonal dishes, try this beautiful vaulted dining room. *Closed eves Sun and Mon, except in summer.*

Roberto, San Xulián de Sales, t 98 151 17 69 (*expensive*). For a special treat, drive out 8km to Vedra in the Valle de Ulla, where Roberto prepares some of the most delicious, imaginative dishes in all Galicia in a lovely country villa. *Closed Sun eve and Mon.*

Tacita d'Juan, Rúa Hórreo 31, t 98 156 32 55 (*expensive*). Offers nouvelle cuisine made from fresh Galician ingredients. *Closed Sun.*

Toñi Vicente, Rúa Rosalía de Castro 24, t 98 159 41 00 (*expensive*). Toñi Vicente's breathtakingly original take on Gallego cuisine has picked up awards and accolades from all quarters of the cookery world. Try the *lubina braseada en fondo de buey* (grilled sea bass on a bed of ox), a thoughtful combination of rich flavours and delicate herbs, or the delicious mango ravioli. *Closed Sun, two weeks in May and in mid-Dec–early Jan.*

Casa Marcelo, Rúa Hortas 1, t 98 155 8580 (*expensive–moderate*). An utterly charming restaurant on a pretty old street, serving exquisite cuisine from the hand of master chef Marcelo Tejedor. There are no menus: the daily offerings vary according to what's in season and Tejedor's remarkable imagination. The *menú de degustación* is a very reasonable €33.

Moncho Vilas, Avda de Villagarcía 21 (on the outskirts), t 98 159 83 87 (*moderate*). One of the classic eateries where an informal tapas bar serves delicious seafood and *empanadas*, while a dining room upstairs produces simple fresh food. *Closed Sun eves and Mon.*

Nobis, Rúa do Villar 47, t 98 158 28 03 (*moderate*). East meets West fusion favourites make a change from seafood at this fancy new restaurant near the tourist office.

San Nicolás, Rúa Sar 1, t 98 157 07 92 (*moderate*). A chic new restaurant in an old converted factory, serving creative Gallego cuisine at reasonable prices.

The Praza do Obradoiro

Irresistibly all roads in Compostela lead up to the towering granite magnet of the Cathedral of Santiago, the town's *raison d'être* and culmination of the pilgrim's journey. Approach it from the huge Praza do Obradoiro, the 'Square of Works', also known as Praza de España, where for centuries the cathedral's stonemasons liberated the soul of Galicia's stone and made it sing and blaze like a Baroque bonfire. In the rain and mists, at morning or sunset or the heat of the day, the cathedral façade changes its tune; it cries out for a new Monet to paint its moods or, perhaps even better, a composer.

Before going in, pause for a look over the Praza do Obradoiro itself, where a colourful carnival of pilgrims, students, Gallegos holding demonstrations, vendors of postcards and plastic birds with flapping wings all play out their roles before a prize collection of civic monuments, erected over the last six centuries. Left, and adjacent to the cathedral, the rather plain Pazo de Gelmírez was built in the 12th and 13th centuries by the two

Vilas, Rosalía de Castro 88, t 98 159 10 00 (*moderate*). Another brother runs this even better bastion of Gallego cuisine in a turn-of-the-century house. *Closed Sat eve and Sun.*

Belgo Mejillones, Rúa Travesa 22, t 98 158 72 35 (*budget*). A big local favourite, serving Galician mussels from the owners' own mussel farm prepared in myriad ways.

Casa Manolo, Rúa San Bieto, t 98 158 29 50 (*budget*). Roomy restaurant, where a colossal *menú* drags in the crowds every lunch time and evening. *Closed Sun eve.*

O Cabaliño do Demo, Rúa Aller Ulloa, t 98 158 81 46 (*budget*). A relaxing little vegetarian haunt with a wide range of wholefood goodies, including some reasonable Mexican and Eastern dishes. The bar downstairs is a good place to ask for information on Santiago's gay scene. *Closed Sun.*

Bars and Nightlife

Santiago's lively bars offer a great way to eat and drink a rainy night away. The area around Rúa Franco is the focus of the evening *marcha*.

Bodeguilla de San Roque, San Roque 13 (near Santa Clara). Serves good wine with plates of delicious *tetilla* cheese and ham, and scrumptious home-made *croquetas*.

La Borriquita de Belém, San Paio. For jazz with your drinks, try this place, which is not far from the cathedral.

Café Casino, Rúa do Villar 35. This 150-year-old café provides sink-into sofas and armchairs,

piles of newspapers and a vast sitting-room space for drinking coffees and cocktails.

Café Jacobus, Rúa Azevacheria 5. Claims the widest selection of exotic coffees, infusions, and sinful chocolate concoctions. One of a chain of three in town.

Café Literarios, Praza Quintana 1. With a perfect terrace at the top of the steps of this lovely square, this is a charming spot to relax.

Casa das Crechas, Via Sacra 3, t 98 156 07 51. Live music and other happenings can be taken in here. When you can't eat or drink any more, you can dance it off.

Dado Dada, Alfredo Brañas 19, t 98 159 15 74. Santiago's classic jazz joint, with occasional live gigs.

El Franco, Rúa Franco 28, t 98 158 1234. A typical place to start the evening's revelry with your first *aperitivo*. Cheap Gallego favourites on the menu too.

Garigolo Café-Teatro, Praza Algalia de Arriba 1. All kinds of performances – film screenings, cabaret, theatre, etc. – take place in this relaxed gay-friendly café.

Liberty, Alfredo Brañas 4. A popular place with plenty of action.

Metate, Colexón de San Paio. If you are an *aficionado* of chocolate, don't miss the hot chocolate and chocolate cocktails served at this former chocolate factory.

Tupperware Café, Frai Rosendo Salvado 28. A hip hang-out, with tongue-in-cheek retro décor and good music.

archbishops whose worldly aplomb helped make Santiago great: Diego Gelmírez, the first to hold the job, who received a licence to mint money when he oversaw the forgery of the *Votos de Santiago* and used the funds to build the cathedral, and Arias, reputedly 'one of the great ecclesiastical pirates of 13th-century Spain'. They didn't build their own palace as well as they might have: new walls had to be added between the 16th and 18th centuries to keep it from collapsing. Although the upper section is still the archbishop's palace, you can visit the lower medieval rooms (*adm included with Museo da Catedral ticket, see below, same opening times*), especially the huge Romanesque dining hall, where the corbels under the vaults are carved with delicious scenes of a medieval feast, complete with musicians; one trencherman is tucking into an *empanada*. For sublime close-up views of the cathedral spires and across the whole city, the cathedral's rooftop has recently been opened to visitors (*access through the left door in the Pazo de Gelmírez, open Tues–Sun 10–2 and 4–8 by guided tour only; adm exp*).

Continuing around the square, the Plateresque **Hospital Real** (1501–9) was built for poor pilgrims by Ferdinand and Isabel with the booty from taking Granada in 1492. Based on Enrique de Egas on Filarete's design for the Ospedale Maggiore in Milan, its façade, typical of Plateresque, concentrates its embellishments in a few key spots, in its long Baroque balconies added in 1678 and especially in the crowded triumphal Gothic Renaissance altarpiece of a doorway. Medallions of the founders glower at each other in the corners of the arch, while a Christian's *Who's Who* from Adam and Eve on up fill the chiselled niches. The building was used as a hospital until 1953, when it was converted into a five-star *parador*: at least have a drink down in the bar (the former hospital morgue!) and try to visit the four elegant courtyards and beautiful late Gothic chapel.

Tucked at the bottom of the stairway to the left of the hospital, the little church of **San Fructuoso** by Lucus Caaveiro (1757) is a good introduction to Compostela's special Baroque and its fondness for heavy geometrical forms. The enormous 18th-century **Pazo de Rajoy**, designed as a seminary and now the town hall, is pure Parisian neoclassicism, by French architect Charles Lemaur; on top note the proud figure of Santiago Matamoros.

Next, the 16th-century **Colegio de San Jerónimo** was founded as a university, where priests learnt languages to hear the pilgrims' confessions; its curious portal was reused from a 15th-century *hostal* and is often pointed out as an example of Renaissance retro. Classes were held just behind in the **Colegio Mayor de Fonseca**, built by Juan de Álava (1546) around a lovely, peaceful cloister with a beautiful *mudéjar* ceiling, still a favourite place for scholars to enjoy a breath of fresh air; the college is now used as a library.

The Cathedral of Santiago

Back to that Baroque firecracker, the Obradoiro façade of the cathedral where the two towers shoot like huge flames to heaven. On the right, the Tower of the Bells was built by José Peña de Toro in the 1600s, while the left-hand one was added by Fernando Casas y Novoa in the 1750s, when he tackled the main façade. A lively triple-ramp stair leads to a pair of doors, arranged to form a cross in stonework; stacked above are two calm windows in a shallow arch like the eye of a hurricane just before the front peaks in a flickering crest of granite fire. At the foot of the steps a door leads into the delightful **crypt of Master Mateo** or 'Catedral Vieja' (*open June–Sept Mon–Sat 10–2 and 4–8, Sun 10–2; winter Mon–Sat 10–1.30 and 4–6.30; adm, keep your ticket for the treasury, cloister, museum and Pozo de Gelmírez*), built by the great master builder to distribute the weight of his Romanesque façade, but so elaborately, with ancient columns, capitals, and fine sculpture under the vaults that people used to think this was the first cathedral.

Inside the Cathedral: the Pórtico de la Gloria

Perhaps the most startling surprise awaits just within the busy Baroque doors up the staircase, where the original 12th-century façade of the cathedral survives perfectly intact. This is the sublime **Pórtico de la Gloria**, the greatest single piece of Romanesque sculpture, anywhere. Sculpted in warm brown granite between 1168 and 1188 by Master Mateo (dated and signed on the lintel of the central arch) its three doorways are dedicated to the Triumph of the Apocalypse, a theme that decorated many churches along the *camino*, but here, at the very end of the road, it reaches an apogee of joy and mirth, full of movement, life and rhythm; if the end of the world is like this, you want to be there. Nearly all the 200 or so figures are smiling or laughing, beginning with St James himself, welcoming you from his perch on the central pillar, carved with the Tree of Jesse, showing the genealogy of Christ from Adam to the Virgin Mary; so many pilgrims have touched the pillar while bending to kiss the base in thanksgiving that the stone has five worn indentations from their fingers. It was originally brightly painted and traces of a 17th-century touch-up remain.

Above St James in the central arch, Christ in Majesty appears 'like jasper and carnelian' according to the text in Revelations, raising both hands in blessing, surrounded by the four Evangelists, Apostles and angels. 'And round the throne was a rainbow that looked like an emerald', an ogival rainbow of musicians – the 24 Elders of the Apocalypse (plus a few stand-ins), each with a different instrument on his lap. On the two side pillars apostles and prophets chat pleasantly, among them the famous laughing Daniel, who is said to owe his good humour to the loveliness of Queen Esther, whom he eyes across the way; Chinese monsters grimace on the lowest frieze. The door on the right is dedicated to heaven and hell, mostly, and depicts children suffering the torments of the damned with their parents – on the surface a powerful psychological trick to make parents toe the line – while the scenes above the left door are more elusive and food for all kinds of interpretations; note the benign portrayal of Jews waiting for the Messiah and the twins, recalling the tradition that St James was Jesus' mortal twin (*see* p.327). After drinking in this eloquent draught of medieval happiness, pilgrims – then as now – lined up behind the central pillar before the curly-haired figure of Master Mateo, who is humbly kneeling to offer the cathedral to God; his nickname, '*O Santo dos Croques*', 'Saint Bump-on-the-Head', comes from the millions who have bowed their heads to touch Mateo's in the hope that some of his genius would rub off.

The **Romanesque interior** of the cathedral is essentially as Master Mateo left it, a long, majestic, barrel-vaulted nave lined with galleries; it takes a while to get used to the gloom, the cathedral's Baroque additions blocking out much of the light that once poured through an unusual nine-sided rose window over the Pórtico de la Gloria. The huge, silver high altar glimmers, visible since the 1940s when the enclosed Baroque choir was removed. Of the chapels along the nave the most important is the first on the right, the 16th-century **reliquary chapel** and Royal Pantheon, with medieval tombs of Galicia's royal family, and reliquaries containing bits of the True Cross and the head of St James the Lesser, who was occasionally purposefully confused with James the Greater for propaganda ends. Next on the right is the cathedral **Treasury**, aglitter with the silver hammer used to pound open the Holy Door in Holy Years, silver scallop shells, a score of other showy religious trappings and a celebrated 16th-century monstrance decorated with scenes from the lives of Jesus and St James.

Thou shield of that faith which in Spain we revere
Thou Scourge of each foeman who dares to draw near
Whom the Son of the God whom the elements tames,
Called Child of the Thunder, Immortal Saint James!

Pilgrims' hymn, translated by George Burrows

Actually, when you get close up, the glow-in-the-dark 17th-century high altar, lavishly covered with Mexican silver, turns out to be a piece of tomfoolery, its cast of knick-knack characters borrowed from a giant's Christmas tree. On top Santiago Matamoros cuts down the Moors. Just over the altar itself sits a stiff idol, a 12th-century statue of Santiago, the patron saint of Spain, his clothes and throne later tricked out lavishly by a Mexican archbishop. The thing to do is climb the narrow stairway behind the altar, kiss the statue's robe and receive a holy card (for the certificate of indulgence, the *compostellana*, pilgrims should apply with their documents to the *Oficina arzobispal*, in the back of the cathedral). Below the altar you can pay your respects to the saint's bones in the 19th-century silver crypt; the outer, rounded wall here survives from Alfonso III's 9th-century church, while the inner wall is believed to be Roman.

In front of the high altar, notice the ropes and pulleys suspended from the octagonal dome or *cimborio*, from which, on high feast days, the **Botafumeiro**, the world's largest censer, is suspended and swung with terrifying force across the entire length of the transept in a comet-like arc of perfumed smoke and sparks. Weighing in at 119lb, the Botafumeiro is a smaller brass version of the original silver model made in 1602 and pilfered by Napoleon's troops: it takes eight men, the *tiraboleiros*, to swing it on a system invented in the Middle Ages. Don't miss it if you're in town on a holy day, and try not to think about the time when Catherine of Aragón attended Mass and the Botafumeiro broke loose and flew out of the window. The Botafumeiro sweetened the air in the cathedral, where many medieval pilgrims slept at night (until a few behaved scandalously and doors were added to the previously wide-open Pórtico de la Gloria); others say the Botafumeiro was invented as a public-relations gimmick to upstage the pilgrimage to Rome. The ten chapels radiating like petals from the ambulatory are all worth a look, especially the one straight behind the altar, the Romanesque **Capilla de San Salvador**, where pilgrims received Communion. Off the north transept, a doorway topped with a 13th-century relief of the Magi leads into the church-sized three-aisled Romanesque **Capilla de la Corticela**. Off the south transept, a 16th-century Gothic-vaulted **cloister** (*part of the Museo da Catedral, and included in a single admission ticket; see above [crypt] for times*) big enough for a football match was designed by Juan de Álava and Gil de Hontañón to replace Master Mateo's Romanesque original, and holds the **Cathedral Museum** and **Library**.

The highlight here is a faithful but incomplete restoration of Master Mateo's original granite *coro*, torn down in the overenthusiastic spring-clean of the late 16th century. The carvings show the new Zion descending from heaven, but the computer-designed modern facsimiles can't match the delicacy of the few original pieces that survive.

Elsewhere, the museum has an illuminated 12th-century *Codex Calixtinus*, while the library contains the Botafumeiro when it's not in use. The archaeological section is of special interest for the fragments of Master Mateo's cloister, while the lavish 18th-century **Sala Capitular** contains some of the cathedral's impressive collection of tapestries. Most of them are in the upper rooms, including 17th-century Flemish scenes of Hannibal crossing the Alps and Scipio with his Romans, along with others, some remarkably insipid even if designed by the likes of Rubens and Goya. There are pretty views from the gallery off the upper rooms across the Praza do Obradoiro.

Around the Cathedral

Although low key after the Obradoiro façade, the cathedral's other entrances each deserve a look. Circumnavigating the Pazo de Gelmírez, you'll come first to the split-level **Praza das Praterías**, named after the silversmiths whose shops once filled the arcades of this jewel-like square. The double **Puerta de las Praterías** is the only one to remain essentially unchanged from the Romanesque cathedral: the tympanum on the right has scenes from the Life of Christ and the Passion, and the one on the left features winged monkeys and a woman giving birth to a skull; below, King David plays the fiddle. Some of the figures were salvaged from the demolished French door and the cathedral's stone Romanesque choir. Locals use the doors as a short cut across town, as their ancestors did in the Middle Ages, when cathedrals were covered public squares as much as religious shrines. From here you can gaze up the Cathedral's highest tower, the ornament-laden 26oft **Berenguel** designed by Galician humanist Domingo de Andrade in the 1710s to hold the town clock. The *praza*'s geometric Baroque **Chapterhouse** and the fountain of the horse were both designed by Fernández Sarela.

Continuing past the bulk of the Berenguel is the enclosed Praza da Quintana, an inviting place to sit on the steps and linger; the upper level is named 'of the living' and the lower 'of the dead', recalling the Roman cemetery that once occupied the spot. In the Middle Ages this was the square of cheap food, ladled out from the stalls. Alongside the square runs the stern façade of the **Convento de San Paio de Antelares**, 'Pelayo before the Altars', containing a **Museo de Arte Sacra** (*entrance at rear, open Apr–Dec Mon–Sat 10.30–1.30 and 4–7; adm*), where the Virgin holds the Child in one hand and thumps a devil with the other. The cloistered nuns keep up the square's culinary tradition with their famous almond and coconut tarts. In the lower square is the Puerta Santa, opened only during a Holy Year, or *Año Xacobeo*, when St James' Day – 25 July – falls on a Sunday; 2010 is the next. The doorway of 1611 consists of 24 compartments, each pigeonholing a carved figure from the Romanesque choir, which may have been the work of Master Mateo. In the upper level of the square, the handsome 17th-century Casa de la Parra is one of the prettiest in Santiago, decorated with stylized bunches of grapes.

The north façade faces **Praza de la Azabachería** ('of the Jet-makers'), where pilgrims bought souvenirs such as little a black figure of the St James with you praying at his feet. The use of jet (hard, black, polished lignite) is said to be in memory of a local coal-worker, Contolay, who helped St Francis of Assisi on his pilgrimage. Two jet-makers are still in business, although they now specialize in jewellery and works of art: Regueira, at Azabachería 9, and Mayer, Platerías 6. In the Middle Ages, the square was the favourite rendezvous for French pilgrims, who would bathe in the long-gone Fountain of Paradise, before entering the Cathedral for the first time through the French Door, unfortunately obliterated by the dullest of the 18th-century facelifts the cathedral underwent.

San Martín Pinario

Another attraction in Praza de la Azabachería was the chance for destitute pilgrims to hang their rags on an iron cross, the *Crus d'os farrapos*, and pick up new clothes from the Benedictines around the corner at San Martín Pinario. San Martín, one of the most venerable monastic institutions in the city, was founded in 912 as the special

The Gallop to the Scallop

The very first thing a medieval pilgrim did upon arriving in the city was stop in the Barrio de los Conchieros, buy a scallop, eat it (this is where French pilgrims learned to make *coquilles St Jacques*, after all) and stick the shell on the turned-up brim of his or her hat – visible proof that they had made it at last; strict laws forbade the selling of scallops anywhere else along the *camino*. By the 16th century, the real shell was replaced by a fancy souvenir replica, either in silver or in jet (*see* below).

The scallop, that tasty bivalve that thrives in the *rías* of Galicia, has been associated with the Santiago pilgrimage since the early Middle Ages. In Compostela, as usual, they can explain it with a miracle: a young Gallego, on the eve of his wedding, was spirited into the sea by his wayward horse and believed drowned, although in truth the horse was running along the waves to meet the stone boat bringing the body of St James to Galicia. When the bridegroom returned, escorting the boat, his body was covered with an armour of milk-white shells, so amazing the locals that they converted at once to the new faith. Its Spanish name, *venera*, calls up associations with the vagina and Venus, the goddess of love, who was born of the seafoam and surfed ashore on a giant scallop shell. For pilgrims, the shell also symbolized the end of the journey, the resurrection and unity in the world – the sea from which it came, the earth in its stony hardness, and the sun in its radiant lines. It's hard to think of another symbol so polyvalent, embracing sex, death, dinner and spiritual wholeness – not to mention a multinational company peddling the Super or Unleaded souls of the dead dinosaurs that fuel the way.

protector of the Apostle's tomb. In the 1400s, the two other Benedictine houses in Santiago joined San Martín to form an institution powerful enough to challenge the Inquisition. In spite of complaints that it would compete with the cathedral, they commissioned an elaborate top-heavy façade by Gabriel Casas in the 18th century; note on top the monks' vocation reflected in the statue of St Martin of Tours sharing his cloak with a poor man. Inside, the vast Claustro de la Portería with its elegant fountain was completed by Casas' more famous follower, Casas y Novoa, while just beyond is an extraordinary, floating 17th-century staircase with Aztec decorations under a Baroque dome. Beyond, the huge barrel-vaulted church is the stage for Casas y Novoa's *retablo mayor*, one of the most over-ripe pieces of flummery ever produced, a feverish blast of intricate gilded detail, a nightmarish vision of total paradise marked by the merciless destiny of the unbelieving Moors stage left and stage right. Casas y Novoa was also responsible for the Capilla del Socorro on the right side of the nave, and the rather more restrained sacristy; the elaborate 17th-century choir stalls are also well worth a look. The stately, colonnaded 18th-century façade facing Praza San Martín grows like an altarpiece above a sunken Baroque staircase designed by a Dominican named Manuel de los Mártires, all granite ribbons squirming below the level of the pavement, like nothing else in Spain.

In Praza San Miguel (in front of Praza San Martín) the 14th-century Gothic Pazo de Don Pedro contains the **Museo das Peregrinacións** (*open Tues–Fri 10–8, Sat 10.30–1.30* *and 5–8, Sun and hols 10.30–1.30; adm*); opposite, San Miquel dos Agros is another product of Santiago's 18th-century boom. But for a real eyeful of local Baroque, continue along to Rúa da Algalía de Arriba and walk north to Rúa de San Roque, where the startling façade of **Santa Clara** by Simón Rodríguez almost jumps out at you, its fat, abstract almost mechanical-looking volutes culminating in a trio of huge unadorned cylinders that look as if they could roll off the roof any second, altogether more 1930s in effect than 1730s.

Elsewhere in Santiago

Like any natural, organic medieval city, Santiago is a delight to wander in, its narrow, arcaded streets and intimate squares paved with granite flagstones, lined with old palaces, churches, and monasteries, tinged with green and gold from moss and lichens. The founders of the two great mendicant orders of the 13th century both made pilgrimages and personally founded monasteries. In 1214, St Francis founded the **Convento de San Francisco**, in Rúa de San Francisco, under the Hospital de los Reyes Católicos; the Benedictines were impressed enough with Francis' preaching to give him the land, in return for an annual basket of fish. Rebuilt in the 18th century, the convent has a fine granite cross sculpted by Caaveiro with scenes of Francis' life.

St Dominic's rather larger **Convento de Santo Domingo de Bonaval**, founded during his pilgrimage in 1220, is due east on the Puerto del Camino at the end of Rúa das Casas Reais. Behind the Baroque façade hides a handsome Gothic church from the 1300s and the chapel of the Pantheon of Illustrious Gallegos, last resting-place of poet Rosalía de Castro and the caricaturist Castelao (d. 1950), the Goya of the Civil War. The convent and cloister house the **Museo do Pobo Galego** (*open Tues–Sat 10–1 and 4–7; adm*) with a good collection of folk items, rural tools and other odds and ends, although most memorable of all is the triple spiral staircase, a stunning architectural tour de force by Domingo de Andrade, where three different, unsupported granite stairways interlace almost as if by magic in a single tower, each leading to different doors.

Off the Azabachería, Rúa de Troya is named after the venerable **Casa-Museo da Troia** (*open Easter–end-Sept Tues–Sat 11–2 and 4–8, Sun 11–2; adm*), base for the local *tunas*, not fish but bands of student minstrels in capes and ribbons, who play Galician-Celtic music around the Praza da Immaculada. The Azabachería leads into Praza Cervantes and a street called Preguntoiro ('Questioning') after all the pilgrims who asked for directions here. This curves around to arcaded Rúa Nova, site of the little church of **Santa María Salomé** with a Romanesque door under a Gothic arcade. Parallel extends **Rúa do Vilar**, Santiago's delightful, arcaded main shopping street, where the **Casa do Dean** has a fine Baroque portal; at the Confitería Mora (No.60), pick up a delicious *tarta de Compostela*, made with chocolate bumps in honour of the Santo dos Croques.

For the classic view of Santiago's towers and roofs, walk along the **Paseo da Ferradura** just east to the cathedral, a leafy 19th-century park where old men will take your photo with cameras nearly as old as themselves. The ornate iron pavilion on the Alameda where bands often play on Sunday afternoons is all that survives of the 1909 **Exposicíon Regional Gallega**.

Santa María del Sar

After all the Baroque in the centre of Santiago, take a break at the Romanesque 12th-century Santa María del Sar, a mile south of the **Convento de las Mercedarias**, another stately Baroque confection. Set alone in its meadow, Santa María is an architectural jewel, with a different slant – literally. The piers and arches along the high barrel-vaulted nave have leant back from time immemorial; although the common explanation it is the result of subsidence, it may have been done intentionally – like the *campanile* of Pisa or the leaning towers of Bologna, along with other pieces of crooked bravura of the same period. A rakish tilt would be in the imaginative and often outlandish spirit of the brilliant 12th century. The buttresses were added after the Lisbon earthquake of 1755.

Don't miss the remarkable carvings by Master Mateo along one gallery in the **cloister** (*open Mon–Sat 10–1 and 4–6, summer till 10pm*).

Back to the Rías: the Golfo Ártabro

Two of Galicia's most important ports, Ferrol and A Coruña, occupy either end of the 20km Golfo Ártabro, savagely bitten out of the northwest coast, with four teeth marking the four estuaries that flow into it. You can get there by dawdling west along the Rías Altas (*see p.289*) or by racing up the A9 motorway from Santiago.

Ferrol and Pontedeume

Plump on the big fat Ría de Betanzos, swollen by four rivers, the salty city of Ferrol was named after its lighthouse (*faro*) and counts some 80,000 souls, many of whom work for or depend on the Spanish navy. Gently, slowly, the port city has dropped the article 'El' from the front of its name and the 'del Caudillo' stuck on the back in honour of Francisco Franco, born here in 1892, son of a naval supply officer who grew up to be the youngest general in Spanish history before his career as dictator, never losing his Gallego roots in his maddening stubbornness and inscrutability – earning himself the nickname 'the Sphinx without a secret'. Besides the enormous docks, navy yards and sailors' red-light gauntlet, Ferrol has a pretty enough medieval core, a large planned 18th-century geometric, neoclassical quarter, the legacy of Philip V who greatly boosted Ferol's fortunes, and a modern quarter that looks like SimCity. The best thing is to just wander among the pretty houses with 'crystal galleries' and the casino and gardens. A pair of castles on the slender waist of the ría defend the naval base. Five kilometres from Ferrol, at the bottom of the estuary, San Martín de Xubia was founded as a monastery in the 9th century. It was the only one in Galicia adopted by Cluny (1113) but all that survives is the Cluniac church with its three apses and excellent carved capitals.

South of Ferrol, the charming medieval town of **Pontedeume** was once the preserve of the Counts of Andrade, who built and collected the tolls from their great bridge over the Ría Eume, once supported by 58 arches; some 15 arches still remain, as well as a 14th-century palace and tower emblazoned with the family's huge crest. The tolls financed the Andrades' hunts; note the weathered stone boars standing guard by the bridge. The parish church, the late-Gothic Santiago, is a trove of minor art.

N

```
━━━━━━━ 20 km
━━━━━ 10 miles
─ ─ ─ ─  Pilgrims' Route
```

Golfo Ártabro

Ría de la Coruña

Ría de Betanzos

Río Eume

Ferrol

Caaveiro

A CORUÑA

Pontedeume

Illas Sisargas

Santa Cruz

Sada

Monasterio de Monfero

Malpica

Mens

Buño

A55

Cambre

Betanzos

A6

Corme Porto Playa de Balarés

Laxe

Ponteceso

Carballo

A9

Praia de Traba

Cabo Vilán

Camariñas

Ría de Camariñas

Muxía

Agualada

Vimianzo

N550

Cabo Touriñán

Berdoias

Santa Catalina

Sobrado dos Monxes

Praia do Rostro

Corcubión

Cée

Embalise de Fervenza

A Baña

GALICIA

Ezaro

Finisterre (Fisterra)

Pindo

N634

N547

Arzúa

Melide

Cabo Finisterre (Fisterra)

Río Tambre

Santiago de Compostela

Labacolla

Playa de Carnota

There are a couple of beaches along the *ría* (the Praia Perbes is a good one) and off the NVI to Betanzos, **San Miguel de Breamo** (1137), with its façade pierced by a window in the shape of an 11-point star and capitals to warm the cockles of any Romanesque diehard's heart.

If you have a car, two ruined monasteries beckon inland from Pontedeume, as much for their architecture as for their lovely settings. Up the Eume river, the Benedictine **Monasterio de Caaveiro** was founded in 934 by San Rosendo, who became a bishop at 18 and defended Compostela from the Normans and Saracens. Although renowned as a stickler for the rules, Rosendo could hardly have founded Caaveiro in a more evocative place, and to this day the ruined, overgrown 12th-century church perched over the river is exceedingly romantic. Twenty kilometres south of Pontedeume, the 12th-century Cistercian **Monasterio de Monfero** with its two cloisters is equally derelict, even if more recently rebuilt in the 17th century, unabashedly grandiose for its remote rustic setting; only the church, with a singular chequerboard façade of granite and slate blocks, is still in use.

Betanzos

Rising steeply over the head of yet another small estuary, lovely Betanzos is a far more ancient place, a Celtic village that grew into the Roman port of Brigantium Flavium. It thrived into the 18th century, when the Mandeo and Mendo rivers washed in so much silt that they stole Betanzos' seacoast. Progress stopped, leaving a time capsule: houses and mansions of all sizes with wrought-iron balconies, or *solanas*, line the narrow lanes that wind up the hill from the harbour's medieval gates. Life revolves around the charming, monumental **Praza de García Hermanos**, its central ornament a statue of two Indianos and a replica of Versailles' Fountain of Diana. Most of the surrounding buildings are from the 18th century, including a neoclassical palace now used as the National Archives of Galicia; this runs a small but interesting

Getting Around

By Air

A Coruña's airport is 9km away at Alvedro, t 98 118 73 15, www.aena.es, with connections to Madrid, Barcelona and Sevilla. There's an airport bus to the main bus station in town (departures are timed to meet flights).

By Boat

Three boats daily ply the *ría* between Ferrol and A Coruña, arriving next to Coruña's tourist office; from the same spot, summer-only launches go to Playa de Santa Cristina.

By Train

RENFE connects Ferrol and A Coruña with Pontedeume and the main junctions at Betanzos, Santiago, Ferrol, Lugo, Vigo, Padrón and Villagarcía de Arousa.

In A Coruña the station San Cristóbal is a bit out of the way on Avda Joaquín Planelles, t 90 224 02 02 – best to take bus no.1 from the nearby bus station to the historic centre.

There's also a RENFE travel office on Fontán 3, t 98 122 19 48. In Ferrol, RENFE and FEVE share the same station, t 98 137 04 01.

By Bus

A Coruña's bus station is on C/Caballeros, t 98 118 43 35 (near the RENFE station), with connections to the Costa da Morte and all major points in Galicia; Alsa provide services to Madrid, León, and the Basque country.

Ferrol's buses depart from next to the train station, t 98 132 47 51, and go to Betanzos, Viveiro, Foz, Ribadeo and Lugo.

Tourist Information

Ferrol: Praza Camilo José Cela, t 98 131 11 79, *www.ferrol-concello.es*.

Pontedeume: Avda Saavedra Meneses 2, t 98 143 02 70.

A Coruña: Regional office on Avda de la Marina s/n, t 98 122 18 22, *www.turgalicia.es*. Municipal information is available in Jardines de Méndez Núñez, t 98 118 43 44, *www.turismocoruna.com*.

A Coruña's **post office** is at Alcalde Manuel Casas s/n, by the Marina; Net Print Center,

Plaza María Pita 4, is the most central of the city's **cibers**.

There are **markets** in Pontedeume on Saturdays; in Betanzos on Tuesdays, Thursdays and Saturdays; in A Coruña from Monday to Friday (Mercado San Agustín).

Where to Stay and Eat

Ferrol ✉ 15400

****Pazo Libunca**, Lugar de Castro, Castro (10km from Ferrol), t 98 138 3540, *www.libunca. com* (*expensive*). A small, romantic hotel in a sumptuous Modernista villa surrounded by gardens. Excellent restaurant (*expensive*).

***Parador do Ferrol**, Almirante Fernández Martín, t 98 135 67 20, *ferrol@parador.es* (*moderate*). The ageing nautically decorated rooms have handsome views over the *ría*.

***Pazo da Merced**, Camiño da Merced, Neda, t 98 138 22 00 (*moderate*). If you're driving, this is a prettier little place to stay, a 17th- and 18th-century manor with *ría* views and a pool. *Closed Oct–Easter week*.

***Hotel Suizo**, Dolores 17, t 98 130 04 00, *www.hotelsuizo.net* (*moderate–inexpensive*). In a modernist building with a pleasant café.

Casa do Castelo de Andrade, Lugar do Castelo de Andrade s/n, 7km from Pontedeume, t 98 143 38 39 *www.castelodeandrade.com* (*moderate–inexpensive*). A handsome stone mansion, with just ten elegant, individually decorated rooms (some with Jacuzzi) and a pretty garden.

**Hs Almendra, Almendra 4, t 98 135 81 90 (*inexpensive*). A good choice; cheaper rooms are on Pardo Bajo near the station.

O'Parrulo, Avda Catabois 401, t 98 131 86 53 (*moderate*). A classic, serving delicious local seafood like grilled clams from the ría, along with succulent meat dishes. There's a garden in summer, and a good wine selection.

Casa Rivera, Galiano 57, t 98 135 07 59 (*budget*). A popular local favourite, with traditional dishes like caldeirada de pescados (a sturdy fish stew) and a great value lunch *menú*.

Pataquiña, Dolores 35, t 98 135 23 11 (*budget*). Offers heaps of good, well-prepared Gallego specialities; try their *salsa Pataquiña*, a delectable mixture of shrimp and crab cooked in brandy and garlic.

Sur, C/Magdalena 50, **t** 98 135 08 70 (*budget*). Trad bar with great tapas and good wine.

Betanzos ✉ 15300

*Los Ángeles, Los Ángeles 11, **t** 98 177 15 11 (*inexpensive*). Modest but well-equipped rooms, an excellent local restaurant downstairs and private parking.

La Casilla, Ctra de Castilla 90, **t** 98 177 01 61 (*budget*). Packs out, especially at weekends, with crowds enjoying the famous local tortilla cooked and other traditional dishes.

Casanova, Pza García Hermanos 15, **t** 98 177 06 03 (*moderate*). Rustically romantic; serves tasty salmon and lamprey dishes for the bold upstairs, with a lively tapas bar downstairs.

San Andrés, Los Ángeles 4, **t** 98 177 20 44 (*moderate*). Another good, traditional choice with fabulous seafood (try the turbot if it's on the menu) and local desserts.

A Coruña ✉ 15000

A Coruña fills up in the summer. The bar area around Rúa Franja and Praza María Pita goes on well into dawn when the fishing fleet pulls in and everyone watches the Muro, the auctioning of the catch, a ritual featuring fast-talking Gallegos and fish you've never seen before.

*****Finisterre, Pso del Parrote 2, **t** 98 120 54 00, *www.hesperia-finisterre.com* (*luxury*). The best-located and most luxurious hotel in A Coruña, overlooking the sea, with pools, tennis courts, a nursery, playground and a health and wellness centre.

***Ciudad de La Coruña, Polígono Adormideras, **t** 98 121 11 00 (*expensive*). Near the Torre de Hércules, with frequent buses into the centre; has modern rooms, all with sea views.

***Riazor, Avda Pedro Barrié de la Maza 29, **t** 98 125 34 00 (*expensive*). A pleasant, less costly alternative to the Finisterre, with a fine beachside location and modern rooms.

Hotel Maycar, C/San Andrés 159, **t 98 122 60 00, *www.hotelmaycar.com* (*budget*). This modern hotel is centrally located and offers excellent value for money. Parking available.

El Pescador, Avda Che Guevara 81c (Ctra Santa Cruz), **t 98 163 95 02 (*inexpensive*). A pebble's throw from the sandy beach of Santa Cristina.

Hs Alborán, Ruego de Agua 14, **t 98 122 65 79 (*budget*). Near the main *praza* with adequate rooms, perhaps not as distinguished inside as they look from the outside.

Sol, Sol 10, **t 98 121 00 19 (*budget*). Pleasant welcoming *hostal* despite the disconcerting flashing sign.

*Hs Centro Gallego, Rúa Estrella 2, **t** 98 122 22 36 (*budget*). One of the best budget options: central, welcoming and spick and span. All rooms with private bath.

*Hs El Parador, Olmos 15, **t** 98 122 21 21 (*budget*). Well kept; among the cheaper central places.

*Hs Las Rias, San Andrés 141, **t** 98 122 68 79 (*budget*). Functional and friendly, offering all the necessary facilities.

*Hs Palacio, Pza de Galicia 2, **t** 98 112 23 38 (*budget*). Clean and welcoming.

A La Brasa, Juan Flórez 38, **t** 98 127 07 27 (*expensive*). True to its name, this place specialises in meat and fish sizzling from the grill; if there are two of you, order the *punta trasera de ternera a la parrilla*, a huge dish of succulent steak with baked potatoes.

Coral, Callejón de la Estacada 9 (near the port), **t** 98 120 05 69 (*expensive*). Seafood rules the menus round here and this is one of the best places; exceptional, delicate shellfish dishes are served in a classy setting. *Closed Sun.*

Casa Pardo, Novoa Santos 15, **t** 98 128 00 21 (*moderate*). Currently considered the best in town, this long-established place offers lovely seafood and grilled meats and is famous for monkfish dishes. It has opened a stylish new branch (where the son is chef) in the Domus, with wonderful views over the bay. *Casa Pardo closed Sun; Domus Pardo open for lunch Tues–Sun, dinner Fri and Sat.*

La Penela, Praza María Pita 12, **t** 98 120 92 00 (*moderate–budget*). A reliable and popular place on the main square, serving delicious local specialities out on terrace in summer.

Taberna Pil Pil, Pelamios 7, **t** 98 121 27 12 (*budget*). A wonderful spot, with a well chosen wine list to accompany its tasty local dishes. Try the house speciality, *bacalao al pil-pil*.

Bánia, Cordelería 7, **t** 98 122 13 01 (*budget*). Serves a range of elaborate and unusual vegetarian dishes and organic wines.

There are dozens of atmospheric cafés, *mesones*, and tapas bars on and around Rúa La Franja, heading off the Praza María Pita.

historical **Museo das Mariñas** (*open Mon–Fri 10–2 and 4–7, Sat 10.20–1; adm*). The three attractive churches are just off the square: the 14th-century **Santa María del Azogue**; 15th-century **Santiago**, with a figure of Santiago Matamoros on the tympanum; and Gothic **San Francisco**, inspired by the basilica at Assisi and its door topped with a bizarre figure of a boar with a cross rising out of its back. Inside, don't miss the delightful 14th-century tomb of Fernán Pérez de Andrade O Boo (the Good), who paid for the church and whose sarcophagus, supported on the backs of a boar and a bear, is covered with hunting scenes, perhaps in the hope that there'd be plenty of game in heaven. Take time to walk along the Ría Mandeo, one of Galicia's prettiest.

Rather than take the NVI or the AP9/E1 motorway directly to A Coruña, follow the pretty scenery along the Ría de Betanzos up to the local resort of **Sada**, to see its boardwalk and **La Terraza**, the finest *modernista* building in Galicia, designed by López Hernández, a curious pavilion made of glass and giant music stands. The road to A Coruña passes the **Pazo de Meirás**, residence of Galicia's greatest novelist, Countess Emilia Pardo Bazán, and later Franco, whose descendants still own it; further along, offshore on a wooded islet, the 17th-century **Castillo de Santa Cruz** once defended A Coruña. Inland, south of the AP9, **Cambre**'s late 12th-century Romanesque church of Santa María has five sweet little chapels around its apse, decorated with good carvings and sculpted columns.

A Coruña

Occupying the length of the Ría da Coruña and the southwest fringe of the Golfo Ártabro, A Coruña is the liveliest city in Galicia, a big (pop. 243,000), exuberant, commercial capital with character to spare. Sprawling over a peninsula and attached to the mainland by a thin neck of land, it has beautiful windswept beaches facing the Atlantic and a magnificent sheltered harbour in the estuary that has made its fortune and paid for all of its hypnotic wall of windowed balconies or *solanas* that gave A Coruña its nickname, 'Crystal City'.

A Coruña's relationship with Britain goes back to its first settlers, Phoenician merchants who imported tin from Cornwall. The Romans called it *Ardobicum Corunium*, and tenuously associated it with Hercules, who performed one of his Twelve Labours (stealing the cattle of Geryon) in Cádiz on the other side of Spain and reputedly had a hand in building the lighthouse. The Suevians and the Moors took turns running the show until 1002; in the Middle Ages, English pilgrims to Santiago often landed here, among them Chaucer's Wife of Bath and his patron John of Gaunt, who arrived in 1386, though unsuccessfully, to claim the Spanish throne for his wife, daughter of Pedro the Cruel.

In the 'Groyne'

The classic view of A Coruña is of its harbour along Avenida de la Marina, lined with a solid wall of crystal galleries set in white balconies, a window cleaner's vision of hell. It is magical to sail into, just as Drake fearlessly did in 1589, swooping down in the night with 30 ships to rub salt in Philip's wounds. Only a young girl named María Pita stood in the way, not only raising the alarm to save the city but somehow swiping

Philip II and the Invincible Armada

Some 200 years later it was Spain's turn to invade England. The pious royal bureaucrat Philip II had more than one bone to pick with Queen Elizabeth's England in the 1580s: Elizabeth had recently invented the Bloody Mary by lopping off the head of Mary Queen of Scots, Philip's favourite candidate for the English throne, and England was helping the Protestants of the Netherlands in their revolt against Spain; Spanish trade routes were threatened but, worst of all, Elizabeth had confirmed the country's Protestant orientation. To solve all of his problems and force England back into the Catholic fold, Philip decided on what seemed to be a foolproof plan: to build up the biggest fleet of warships in Spanish history, and coordinate this invincible armada with an invasion of England by his army in the Netherlands. Francis Drake got wind of Philip's plans and in 1587 sailed into Cádiz 'to singe the king's beard' by burning the parked fleet and setting the invasion date back by a year.

Finally, on 22 July 1588, an Armada of 130 enormous galleons, manned by 10,000 sailors and 19,000 soldiers set sail from A Coruña. The great mastodons were intercepted near Plymouth by the faster ships of Lord Howard, who continued to hound Philip's majestic fleet for the next week in various sea battles, without inflicting much damage or causing any fissures to the Armada's formation. England's stroke of luck came when the Armada set anchor near Calais, where it was to meet with the invasion fleet from the Netherlands. Howard sent fireships against the Armada, which panicked the Spaniards into breaking up their formation; soon after, on 8 August, in a battle that raged along the Channel, the quick English defeated the lumbering Armada at Gravelines, the score one English ship to two Spanish. When the Spaniards tried to sail home to regroup, the wind and luck against them, the English forced them home the long way around Scotland, where appalling storms wreaked havoc; by the time the Invincible Armada limped back to Spain, only 76 half-wrecked galleons pulled into port, minus 15,000 soldiers. Although the war between England and Spain dragged on until 1604, the repercussions of the defeat of the Armada endured for centuries. Spain was demoralized, Philip's treasury was empty, but in cocky Elizabethan England the party had just begun.

Drake's flag in the process. In gratitude A Coruña gave her name to its biggest, busiest square, Praza María Pita, where the bars under its porticoes stay packed until the wee hours of the morning. One side is taken up with the city hall, the eclectic *modernista* **Palacio Municipal** (1907) by Pedro Mariño, decorated with symbols of A Coruña.

The older part of A Coruña – what old British seadogs called 'the Groyne' – begins at Praza María Pita, a labyrinth of winding streets squeezed around a hill. Near the harbour at Rúa Tabernas 13, Countess Emilia Pardo Bazán was born in 1851; the mansion now houses the **Casa Museo de Emilia Pardo-Bazán** and a small **museum** dedicated to the novelist (*open Mon–Fri 10–2 and 4–7*). Nearby Rúa Santiago leads into little Praza A Fariña (or de Azcárraga), its bright flowerbeds covering the spot where gallows once stood. For pilgrims who sailed into A Coruña, the over-restored 12th-century Romanesque church of **Santiago** was their first stop; one door has a carving of Santiago Matamoros at Clavijo, another the Lamb of God; its 16th-century tower once defended the city from English pirates. The **Colegiata de Santa María del Campo**, begun in the 1210s and finished in the 1400s, stands at the top of the square. Its sculptors were star-struck: star decorations run along the roof and on the west façade; the triple portal has a carving of the Three Magi. Over the north door two angels stand by as someone seems to fall out of the sky with star symbols, or perhaps Ezekiel's wheel of fire, whirling up in the cosmos. Inside are some fine Romanesque tombs, polychrome statues and just to the left of the altar, another star, carved on a capital.

Just down from here, the little Plazuela de Santa Bárbara is A Coruña's most charming, site of the **Convento de Santa Barbara** (1613), where cloistered Poor Clares live behind the portal, carved with SS. Barbara, Catherine, and the Virgin, while over the door there's St Michael, God holding a pilgrim in his hand and a sun and another star. Behind this, the **Convento de Santo Domingo** has two excellent Baroque chapels from the 17th century, especially the Capilla de la Virgen del Rosario, sheltering the City's patroness.

Santo Domingo stands on the edge of the evocative little **Jardín de San Carlos**, set in the walls of the old fortress of San Carlos. It contains the granite tomb of Sir John Moore, who in 1809 led the routed, dispirited British army across Galicia with the French on his tail. At Elviña, just before A Coruña, he sent most of his troops ahead to board ships for home, just as Marshal Soult launched into a vicious attack; Moore managed to stall the French long enough for 15,000 of his men to embark under Soult's nose, an operation that has been called a precursor to Dunkirk. Casualties were high on both sides (Moore died pierced by a cannonball) and the British lost at Elviña, only to return under a new commander, the Duke of Wellington. Moore earned some verses in Gallego by Rosalía de Castro and some in a more Kiplingesque vein from Rev. Charles Wolfe:

> Lightly, they'll talk of the spirit that's gone,
> And o'er his cold ashes upbraid him –
> But little he'll reck, if they let him sleep on
> In the grave where a Briton has laid him.

Just opposite, A Coruña's busy military history is remembered in the **Museo Militar** (*open Mon–Sat 10–2 and 4–7, Sun and hols 10–2; adm*) in the old church of San Francisco. From here, bus no.3 will take you out 2km to the northernmost tip of the peninsula and the 431ft **Torre de Hércules**, A Coruña's proudest symbol (*open Apr–May and June–Sept daily 20–6.45, July and Aug 10–8.45, Oct–Mar 10–5.45; adm*). Built in the 2nd century AD in the time of Trajan, it's the oldest continuous working Roman lighthouse, but with an external skin from 1791. Bring a pep pill: you'll have to climb the 242 steps to the top for the splendid view of the city and ocean. Within walking distance from the Jardin de San Carlos, the Paseo do Parrote leads out to **Castillo de San Antón**, last rebuilt in 1779. It now defends artefacts from the Iron Age, the Celtic castros, Romans, and Middle Ages in the **Museo Arqueológico** (*open July–Aug Tues–Sat 10–9, Sun and hols 10–3; Sept–June Tues–Sat 10–7, Sun and hols 10–2.30; adm*).

In the newer part of A Coruña (beyond Praza de María Pita) the ex-Maritime Consulate in Praza do Pintor Sotomayor (off the Rúa Panaderas) houses the **Museo de Bellas Artes** (*open Tues–Fri 10–8, Sat 10–2 and 4.30–8, Sun 10–2; adm*), with a collection of European paintings, sculptures, ceramics and coins dating from the 17th century. Near the Mercado San Agustín, the old Plaza dos Ovos has been converted into a charmingly goofy square devoted to comedians. A completely different atmosphere reigns in spooky Praza de España a block up from the market, with its soldiers and monument to José Millán Astray, the one-armed, one-eyed psychopath who led the Spanish Foreign Legion and taught his troops to cry '¡Viva la Muerte!' in the Civil War. The **Casa de las Ciencias** (open July and Aug daily 11–9, Sept–June daily 10–7; adm, combined adm with the Aquarium and Domus available) in Parque de Santa Margarita has a planetarium and museum dedicated to the world of science, technology and nature. On the other side of the isthmus lie A Coruña's beaches: the **Praias de Ríazor** and **Orzán** fill up in summer and are backed the Paseo Marítimo. Heading up towards the headland, is the ultra-modern **Domus**, or **Museum of Man** (open summer daily 11–9, winter daily 10–7), designed by Arata Isozaki to look like an upturned boat and dedicated to the human body. A little further up, just below the Torre de Hércules, is the immensely entertaining **Aquárium**, with a vast subterranean tank of wheeling fish (including small sharks), a pool with six friendly seals, and an Octopus Garden (www.casaciencias.org, open Mon–Fri 10–7, Sat–Sun and hols 10–8; July and Aug daily 10–9; adm, combined adm with Domus and Casa de las Ciencias available).

If the summertime crush along the city beaches is unappealing, there are quieter, cleaner and prettier strands are outside the city at **Santa Cristina**, **Bastiagueiro**, **Santa Cruz**, **Mera** and **Lorbe** (this last is the farthest from town, 16km away).

West of A Coruña: A Costa da Morte

Before tourism invented the Costa del Sol and the Costa Blanca, the Galicians dubbed this region down to Finisterre the 'Coast of Death' after its number of drownings, shipwrecks and ancient Celtic memories; from the end of the west, from the end of the Milky Way, Celtic warriors would sail out to their reward in the seven-towered castle of Arianhrod. The scenery along this wild land of the setting sun is romantic, the waves are dramatic and the beaches pale and inviting, only the water is icy cold.

Ría de Corme e Laxe

Heading west of A Coruña and Carballo, **Buño** is Galicia's traditional pottery town par excellence, manufacturing yellow and brown earthenware plates and crocks in the shape of pigs for as long as anyone can remember, readily purchasable along the main street. The road north of Buño ends up at **Malpica**, where the granite cliffs west of A Coruña first relax their vigilance. A former whaling port, Malpica is partly sheltered by the windswept Sisargas islets, populated only by a large seabird nursery (boteros, marine taxis, will take you out for a small fee). Appropriately enough, the Costa da Morte has some fine dolmens, or Neolithic tombs, beginning with Malpica's **Pedra de Arca**. Malpica has a beach, pounded with surf, or you can head to the sheltered **Praia de Niñons**, passing by way of the romantic little ivy-shrouded castle known as the **Torres de Mens**, next to a tiny Romanesque chapel decorated with erotic figures.

Corme Porto, a picturesque fishing village to the west, has a reputation for being a law unto itself, a nest of resistance to Franco's Guardia Civil goons even into the 1950s, perhaps because they tried to get in the way of Corme's main industry: smuggling. Ask directions to the **Pedra da Serpe** at Gondomil, a snake carved in the stone believed to date from the Phoenicians and connected to the legend of St Adrian, the local St Patrick, who is said to have gathered all the snakes in Galicia here and given them a mighty kick into the ground, where they disappeared. It has a fine white beach and dunes and a more sheltered strand, the **Praia de Balarés** just before the medieval bridge to **Ponteceso**, birthplace of poet Eduardo Pondal (1835–1917). **Laxe**, a pleasant fishing village across the estuary from Corme, has a white beach, safe even for children; for something more remote, continue south along the coast past Pedreira to the enormous **Praia de Traba** (one of the worst affected beaches after the Prestige disaster, but now cleaned up). There's a 14th-century church dedicated to Santiago and two intriguing dolmens on the road to Bayo, 5km inland: signs point the way to the **Dolmen of Dombate**, with engravings of a ship inside on the right and the **Pedra Cuberta**, another kilometre south, with a 20ft chamber.

Ría de Camariñas

After some rugged coast, the rocks relent to admit another *ría* shared by the remote fishing hamlets of **Camariñas** and **Muxía**, both renowned for intricate bobbin lace (Camariñas has a little museum dedicated to the art). From little, white and increasingly trendy Camariñas you can walk 5km (3 miles) to **Cabo Vilán** and its lighthouse, a wild piece of savage, torn coast, which makes you feel small and far away from civilization, although perhaps less so now that a set of experimental windmills have been erected to harness the wild winds that whip the cape. **Muxía** has always been a bit more important, as the proud escutcheons on the houses testify. It is also the holy city of the Costa da Morte, with its seaside sanctuary of **Nostra Señora de la Barca**, where the Virgin Mary herself is said to have sailed in a stone ship when Santiago was preaching in these parts (it wasn't her only Spanish holiday: she made a similar appearance riding a stone pillar in Zaragoza). Ship-shaped votive offerings dangle in the church. Parts of the Virgin's own magic boat may be seen around the church, including the hull, the Pedra de Abalar, which moves whenever someone completely free of sin stands on it. If you suffer from colic or gastritis, a walk under the stone keel, the Pedra dos Cadrises (the stone that looks like a stylized dinosaur) should fix you up nicely. Four kilometres from Muxía, in Moraime, the Benedictine church of **San Xián** (Julian) is mostly from the 12th century, but was founded in the 900s as a shelter for pilgrims; although humidity has destroyed most of the frescoes, 26 (again, two extra) Elders of the Apocalypse survive on the main portal. Inland, along the AC432, the 16th-century **Castillo de Vimianzo** (*open Tues–Sat 10–1 and 4–7*), once home to the cruel Álvaro Pérez de Moscoso, has been restored to house a collection of paintings, photos and crafts.

Ría de Corcubión and the End of the World

Further south, a byroad off the AC432 leads up to the lighthouse at **Cabo Touriñán**, where, as the plaque states, and notwithstanding Finisterre, you are standing on the

Getting Around

A Coruña and Santiago are the main bases for transport to the Costa da Morte, but **buses** are not very frequent. If you plan to visit more than one place in a day, study the bus schedules first. Carballo, 35km southwest of A Coruña, is the main bus junction for the coastal villages.

Where to Stay and Eat

The gastronomic prize of the the Death Coast is barnacles, or *percebes*, which cost a fortune; people who gather them are washed away so often that they can't buy insurance.

Malpica ✉ 15113

***Fonte de Fraile, Playa de Canido s/n, t 98 172 07 32, *www.fontedofraile.com* (*moderate–inexpensive*). A pretty seaside hotel on the beach, with airy rooms, Jacuzzi and café-bar.

*Hostal As Garzas, in Barizo, t 98 172 17 65 (*inexpensive*). In a fine location, this also has a restaurant.

*Hs Panchito, Pza Villar Amigo 6, t 98 172 03 07 (*inexpensive*). A good little *hostal* in the centre.

**Hs JB, by the beach, t 98 172 19 06 (*budget*). Comfy, with a bar. *Open all year.*

San Francisco, t 98 172 04 89 (*budget*). Good for reasonable fresh seafood.

Camariñas ✉ 15123

4 Ventos, C/Molino de Viento 81, t 98 173 60 64 (*inexpensive*). Come here for comfortable, basic rooms and a down-to-earth restaurant.

*Hs Scala, Paseo Marítimo, t 98 173 71 09 (*budget*). On the seafront, with frilly rooms (some with terraces), and a friendly family.

Corcubión ✉ 15100

***El Hórreo, Sta Isabel, t 98 174 55 00 (*moderate*). Bland, modern hotel with more facilities than most on the Costa da Morte, including pool and garden. Beautifully located near the sea.

*HR Las Hortensias, Playa de Quenxe, t 98 174 50 29 (*inexpensive*). A simpler alternative on the beachfront.

Casa Lestón, Ctra Finisterre (at Sardiñeiro), t 98 174 35 99 (*moderate*). Can't be beaten for fresh fish and simple good food.

Finisterre/Fisterra ✉ 15155

**O Semáforo, Faro s/n, t 98 172 58 69 (*moderate*). The famous lighthouse at Cabo Finisterre is a delightful little hotel, where you can enjoy the spectacular sunsets.

**Insula Finesterrae, t 98 171 22 11, *www.insulafinisterrae.com* (*inexpensive*). Rusticity and contemporary style are combined in this charming hotel by the lighthouse. With pool.

*Finisterre, Federico Ávila 8, t 98 174 00 00, *www.finisterreae.com* (*inexpensive*). At the end of the world, this is a large, modern hotel. They also run the simple hostal opposite (*budget*), with a good, lively restaurant.

*Hs Rivas, Ctra Faro, t 98 174 00 27 (*budget*). Cheapest of all – but only just.

Pensión Casa Velay, C/La Cerca 1, t 98 174 01 27 (*budget*). Just off main square; good value basic doubles with bath.

Tira do Cordel, Playa de San Roque s/n, t 98 174 06 97 (*moderate*).Some of the best seafood on this stretch of coast, famous for *navajas a la plancha* (razor clams from the ría).

Los Tres Golpes, C/Huertas 9, t 98 174 00 47 (*moderate–budget*). A good simple restaurant, serving excellent shellfish.

Don Percebe, Ctra Faro, t 98 174 05 12 (*budget*). Try this place for bountiful seafood.

westernmost point of continental Europe. Another branch of the road leads to the huge (and hugely exposed) beach, the **Praia do Rostro**, before continuing south to the little industrial port of **Cée**, defended by the 18th-century Castillo de Cardenal.

Cée has practically merged with **Corcubión**, an old fishing village sprinkled with manor houses and *solanas*. The parish church has a curious statue of St Mark, brought from Venice by a ship that refused to budge until the saint was taken ashore. White beaches are sprinkled under the pines, among them **Praia Sardiñeiro** with a few bars and restaurants.

Finisterre (Fisterra)

Beyond lies the traditional westernmost point of Europe, the granite houses of Finisterre huddled on the rocks around the church of the miracle-working Christ of the Golden Beard, who came out of the sea. According to tradition, these same waters contain the city of Duyo (or Dugium), which sank beneath the waves at the same time as Pompeii went under the lava; but sunken cities are a wide-ranging Celtic conceit, like Ys in Brittany, that hark back to the Hesperides, the Blessed Isles beyond the West.

Two kilometres beyond is **Cabo Finisterre** with its lighthouse, the World's End, where the Roman legions and pilgrims from Santiago came to gaze at the sun setting. Often at other times the cape is bleak and wrapped in fog, when it's easy to imagine wandering souls flitting mournfully along the savage coast before taking their last step into the Beyond. At the foot of the cape, pilgrims would visit the Romanesque church and the **Ara Solís**, evoking the mysteries of life, death and resurrection. For the best overviews, take the road up to **Vista Monte do Facho** where sterile women used to rub up against a menhir until an 18th-century bishop ordered it destroyed.

From Cée, the AC550 follows the coast around to **Ezaro**, a wild, picturesque place where massive granite boulders on Mount Pindo (1968ft), 'the Celtic Olympus', have mysterious engravings and ruins of ancient shrines. Unable to erode an estuary of its own through the mountain, the Río Xallas instead tumbles down in a dozen shimmering waterfalls to the sea, polishing the multicoloured stones as it flows over them. Some of its wild charm has been sacrificed to a ugly hydroelectric plant, but a wander upstream reveals the tumbling Xallas in a more pristine state. South, beyond the cute granite port of **Pindo**, the dune-backed beach of **Carnota** is the longest in Galicia (it also holds a more gloomy record for drownings: even if you think you're a strong swimmer, beware). Carnota also claims Galicia's largest *hórreo*, about 100ft long and made entirely of granite. Although the surrounding valley is fertile, this 18th-century *hórreo* was moved here from elsewhere and extended to win the title, which doesn't seem quite fair.

Into the Rías Baixas

The Lower Estuaries, or Rías Baixas/Bajas, almost at once have tamer, greener scenery than their wild cousins to the north; here the ocean is predictably warm enough to maintain a regular holiday trade. These less exposed, less continuously 'flushed' *rías* can, however, get a bit dirty if you swim in the innermost coves.

The Ría de Muros e Noia

Under Monte Costiños on the north edge of the *ría*, **Muros** is a fine, old-fashioned, granite town, with narrow, arcaded lanes, a market, and a fountain with a stone turtle, all stacked under its Gothic church. This contains a startling crucifix that was found in the sea, the Cristo de la Agonía, with long, flowing hair like that of his counterpart in Burgos; and a stone serpent coiled in the basin of the holy water stoup. There's a good beach at **Louro**, 'the golden', 1.6km from Muros on the tip of the cape. Inland, past Ponte-Outes, **Entines** has the shrine of miracle-working **San Campio**. After making the ritual walk round the crucifix (six times clockwise, three times anti-clockwise) you can pay a visit to Campio, or so it seems – the skeleton of an Christian martyr brought from Rome in the 18th century by a bishop of Santiago, has been lovingly covered with wax and dressed in a centurion's costume and a garland so that he looks as if he is sleeping.

To reach Noia, cross the medieval **Ponte Nafonso**, named after its master builder who lies buried under the 14th-century cross at the end, having laboured 30 years without seeing it completed. **Noia** (or Noya) is full of legends, beginning with its name, after Noah, whose dove is said to have found the olive branch here – a scene depicted on the town's arms – while his ark came to rest on the holy Celtic mountain of Barbanza just south. This local Mt Ararat is adorned with dolmens and in Noia you can visit the mysterious cemetery next to the Gothic **Santa María a Nova** (1327) where guildsmen between the 10th and 16th centuries left headstones carved with symbols more pagan than Christian; some 200 have designs relating to the trades of the deceased. Others are a total enigma. Another church, early 15th-century **San Martín**, has a good rose window carved into its fortress-like façade, and fine carvings on the portal; opposite, the **Pazo de Tapal** dates from the same period.

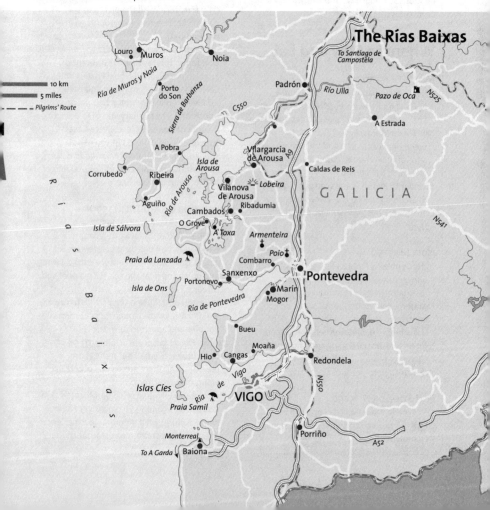

Getting Around

RENFE **trains** between A Coruña and Vigo pass through Padrón and Vilagarcía. There are hourly **buses** (7am–9pm) from Santiago to Noia, from where connections can be made to Porto do Son and beyond. From Vilagarcía buses leave for Isla de Arousa.

Tourist Information

Vilagarcía de Arousa: Avda Juan Carlos I, 37, t 98 651 01 44.
Cambados: Praza do Concello, t 98 652 07 86.
O Grove: Praza de O Corgo, t 98 673 14 15, www.turismogrove.com.
    There are **markets** in Noia on Thursdays; in Rúa do Mercado on Sundays; in Vilagarcía de Arousa on Tuesdays and Saturdays; in Cambados on Thursdays.

Where to Stay and Eat

Muros ✉ 15250
**Hs La Muradana, Avda Castelao 99, t 98 182 68 85, www.hotelmuradana.com (*inexpensive*). A good place to eat and sleep.
*Hs Ría de Muros, Avda Calvo Sotelo, t 98 182 60 56 (*inexpensive*). Good, charming owner and value for money. Popular with repeat guests, so call ahead.
*Convento Padres Franciscanos, t/f 98 182 61 46 (*budget*). The Franciscan brothers run an austere but atmospheric *hostal* (*June–Sept*).

Noia ✉ 15250
**Hs Ceboleiro, Avda Galicia 15, t 98 182 44 97 (*inexpensive*). Friendly, with a decent restaurant; meals at around €15-20.
Pesquería del Tambre, Santa María de Roo (4km from Noia), t 98 105 16 20, www.pesqueriadeltambre.com (*inexpensive*). An unsual and charming rural hotel, in a cluster of Modernista buildings used a century ago to produce electricity.

Porto do Son ✉ 15250
*Hs Arneda, Travesía 13 de Septiembre 4, t 98 176 73 44 (*inexpensive*). Modern and friendly, with baths in all rooms.

Padrón ✉ 15900
Casa Antiga do Monte, Dodro, t 981 81 24 00, www.susavilaocio.es (*expensive–moderate*). An elegant stone hotel in charming grounds just outside Padrón, with an 18th-century *hórreo* and stylishly decorated rooms. Also offers pool, gym and all kinds of outdoor activities.
***Escala, Pazos, t 98 181 13 12 (*moderate*). The fanciest place in Padrón.
La Casa Grande de Cornide, in Cornide, t 98 180 55 99, www.casagrandedecornide.com (*moderate*). A *pazo-hostería* from the 18th century with suites, a library and a museum of Gallego painting.
***Pensión Jardín, Salgado Araujo 3-1, t 981810950 (*budget*). A sweet little stone house, with fussy but cosy rooms.
**Hs Casa Cuco, Avda de Compostela, t 98 181 05 11 (*budget*). Of all the places to stay, this has the best name going; rooms with or without bath.
Casa Ramallo, in Rois, t 98 181 12 10 (*moderate*). Don't miss this favourite restaurant of Spanish novelist and Nobel Prize-winner, Camilo José Cela. Family-run and rustic.
Chef Rivera, Enlace Parque 7, t 98 181 04 13 (*moderate*). The culinary star of Padrón, this is your chance to try José Rivera Casal's superb, seasonal dishes (if you're not squeamish, the lamprey *empanada* is exquisite) and a mix of traditional Gallego and international cuisine.

Vilagarcía de Arousa ✉ 15900
Prices here are over the odds.
****Pazo O Rial, O Rial 1, Ctra Vilagarcía-Cambados, t 98 650 70 11 (*moderate*). Set in a pine wood, this 17th-century *pazo* is sweet and quiet and near the sea, with a pool and satellite TV.
***Castelao, Arzobispo Lago 5, t 98 651 24 26, www.hcastelao.com (*moderate*). Comfortable doubles and apartments in the centre.
*Hs 82, Pza de la Constitución 13, t/f 98 650 62 22 (*budget*). Small but more than pleasant; and there are several others like it along the waterfront.
Chocolate, in Villajuán (Vilaxoán, located 2km away), t 98 650 11 99 (*inexpensive*). For dinner, splurge on a memorable experience at Galicia's most famous restaurant, where

good grilled fish or tender Texas-sized steaks are prepared by the flamboyant owner, accompanied by famously bad service; tributes to the restaurant from celebrities and VIPs line the walls. There are also 18 simple rooms that will set you back around €40 each.

Loliña, Alameda 1 in Carril, t 98 650 12 81 (*moderate*). The day's catch gets the home-cooked treatment here, served in a sun-baked courtyard. *Closed Sun eve, Mon and Nov.*

Cambados ✉ 36630

★★★Parador de Cambados, Paseo de Cervantes, t 98 654 22 50, *cambados@parador.es* (*expensive–moderate*). Occupies an old country *pazo* (manor house) with a beautiful garden and a restaurant featuring seafood.

★Europa, Ourense 12, t 98 654 37 25 (*inexpensive*). Simple, modern hotel with neat rooms with bath.

★El Duende, Ourense 10, t 98 654 30 75 (*budget*). Offers a nice, cheaper alternative by the sea. Rooms with or without bath.

Pazos Feijoo, Rúa Curros Enríquez 1, t 98 654 29 10 (*budget*). Spick'n'span hostal in the centre of town.

Maria José, Rúa San Gregorio 2, t 98 654 22 81 (*budget*). Surrender to the tender loving culinary care of Maria José, who makes a mean *sopa de mariscos*.

Ribadumia ✉ 36980

Pazo Carrasqueira, in Sisán, t 98 671 00 32, (*moderate–inexpensive*). A lovely 18th-century manor, with nine comfortable rooms, and a pool and gardens.

O Grove/A Toxa ✉ 36980

★★★★★Gran Hotel La Toja, Isla A Toxa, t 98 673 00 25, *www.granhotehesperia-latoja.com* (*luxury*). In summer, in a park setting, you can enjoy golf, tennis, a spa, and a heated pool, while rubbing shoulders with the likes of Julio Iglesias, all in a park setting.

★★★★Louxo, t 98 673 02 00, *www.louxolatoja. com* (*expensive, luxury in high season*). For somewhat less than at La Toja, you can bask here in almost as much luxury.

★★★Mar Atlántico, Pedras Negras San Vicente do Mar, t 98 673 80 61, *www.hotel maratlantico.com* (*expensive*). On the other side of town; similarly well equipped, with tennis courts.

★★★Bosque Mar, Reboredo 93, t 98 673 10 55, *www.bosquemar.com* (*moderate*). In O Grove proper, a pleasant family place with a garden and a swimming pool.

★★La Lanzada, Playa de la Lanzada , t 98 674 32 32 (*inexpensive*). Has lovely views over the ocean from its breezy rooms. The Nueva Lanzada nearby is more upmarket (*moderate*).

★El Besugo, González Besada 102, t 98 673 02 11 (*inexpensive–budget*). On the road to A Toxa, offering simple, clean rooms with or without bath. *Closed Oct–Apr.*

★Hs Isolino, Avda Castelao 30, t 98 673 02 36 (*budget*). One of the best deals in town, offering good-value modern rooms at the heart of O Grove's night-time scene.

Beira Mar, Avda Beiramar 30, t 98 673 07 41 (*expensive*). Serves delicious oysters plucked straight from the *ría*, in elegantly modern surroundings with views of the port.

O Crisol, Rúa Hospitál 10, t 98 673 00 99 (*expensive*). A long-time favourite for its excellent seafood and fine service. *Closed Mon.*

Casa Pepe, Rúa Castelao 149, t 98 673 02 35 (*moderate*). Slightly cheaper than O Crisol, though with a similar pedigree, again specializing in locally caught seafood.

Posada del Mar, Rúa Castelao 202, t 98 673 01 06 (*moderate*). Has fine views from its dining room and good seafood croquettes, now served by its third generation.

Caldas de Reis ✉ 36650

★★Acuña, Herrería 2, t 98 654 00 10 (*moderate*). Attached to the spa, this hotel has a charming *modernista* air, with *solanas* overhanging the river. *Closed Oct–Apr.*

Sena, Juan Fuentes 99, t 98 654 05 96, *www.hotelsena.com* (*inexpensive*). A cheaper option just on the outskirts of the centre, with a decent restaurant.

Casa Baltar, Alhóndiga 9, t 98 654 00 41 (*budget*). An attractive dining room with a lovely summer terrace serving surprisingly contemporary local cuisine.

Often windy beaches and lagoons dot the coast of the *ría* south from Noia. The main village, **Porto do Son**, lies between the state-of the-art defensive outpost of NATO atop Mount Iroite and its rather more picturesque Celtic equivalent at the **Castro de Baroña**, located on an outcrop over the sea. From **Oleiros** you can drive up to a pair of miradors (1,633ft) on the Montes Barbanza, for great views from Cabo Finisterre to Vigo on a clear day. Oleiros also has an exceptional dolmen, **Axeitos** – an enormous rock measuring nearly 172 sq ft, supported by eight smaller ones. At the tip of the headland, **Corrubedo** has a proud set of dunes, the highest in all Galicia, constantly sculpted by the wind.

Ría de Arousa to Pádron

The shore-hugging AC550 first runs into the Ría de Arousa, touristically the most developed of all Galicia's estuaries, although this hardly means anything remotely like Benidorm or Torremolinos. The first town you come to, **Santa Uxia** (or Eugenia) **de Ribeira** (often known simply as Ribeira), combines tourism with its status as Spain's top coastal and underwater fishing port. Remains of a Phoenician port are nearby at Aguiño, while further south, the **Isla de Sálvora** is a haunt of mermaids; a 16th-century *hidalgo* married one, and gave birth to a dynasty named Mariños de Lobeira. Locally a whole science has evolved to distinguish mermaids in case of doubt: they have smooth soles on their feet and no belly buttons. The rest of this shore has quiet beaches; **A Póboa do Camaniñal** has some stately homes.

At the head of the estuary, at the mouth of the blood-sucking lamprey-rich River Ulla, **Padrón** is the raggle-taggle capital of Galicia's favourite vegetable tapa, midget green *pimientas de Padrón*, roasted in oil and salted and astonishingly tasty, although occasionally one packs the same wallop as a *jalapeño*.

Padrón has plenty of legendary baggage to accompany its peppers: it is ancient *Iria Flavia*, the port where Santiago's disciples sailed with their precious cargo, anchoring their stone boat to a stone 'memorial pillar' (*pedrón*), now displayed under the altar in the 17th-century church of **Santiago**. The stone boat was met by a pagan queen, Lupa, who mockingly gave the Christians two wild bulls to transport the coffin. When yoked the bulls became peaceful oxen; astonished, Lupa converted at once and was baptized by Saint James himself, who popped out of his coffin in the ox cart to do the job.

On the Carretera de Herbón on the fringes of town, the **Casa-Museo de Rosalía de Castro** (*open Tues–Sat 10–1.30 and 4–7, Sun 10–1.30; adm*) was the home of Galicia's favourite poet Rosalía de Castro (1837–85), the illegitimate daughter of a priest, who unhappily married historian Manuel Murguía, had six children, wrote beautiful poetry in Gallego and died young of cancer. Another house nearby is covered from top to bottom in bleached scallop shells. The bridge over the Ulla to Puentecesures is attributed to Master Mateo.

Vilagarcía to Isla A Toxa

From Padrón the AC550 continues south past **Catoira** and the romantic remains of Alfonso V's Towers of the West, part of the front line defences of Santiago against the Normans (and scene of the annual Fiesta Vikinga). The big town on the south bank is

The Perfect Accompaniment to Fish

As if seafood lovers didn't have enough to rave about in Galicia, the *rías* also supply Albariño, the ideal dry, fruity white wine to go with their heaving plates of *mariscos*. Cambados is the capital of Albariño, and the first Sunday of every August the lovely gardens of its *parador* hosts a wine festival.

Burgundian monks at the Cistercian monastery of Armenteira (*see* p.326) introduced Albariño vines in the 12th century and they thrived; if most other vineyards in dry hot Spain produce red wines, the humid Atlantic coast and sunnier sheltered slopes of the *rías* provide the ideal climate for aromatic whites. In 1988, the growing region DO Rías Baixas was given its demarcation status, divided into the subzones of O Rosal, Val do Salnés (around Cambados), Condado de Tea (which also produces some reds) and the Zona del Albariño. Like its cousin, Portuguese Vinho Verde, Albariño is ever so slightly sparkling, sending a gentle trail of bubbles to the top of your glass (for lots of suds, go for the Albariño del Palacio). Although usually best drunk as young as possible, Cambados' Albariño Fefiñanes is stored in oak barrels for a few months to give it more flavour. Other recommended Albariños are Lagar de Cervera, Castelo de Fornos (from Bodegas Chaves) and Martín Codax, from Valariño-Cambados. Nothing goes to waste: the stems, seeds, and other leftovers (*oruja*) are distilled into fiery *aguardiente*.

Galicia has two other demarcated wine regions: DO Ribeiro, the largest, is just west of Ourense, where production is dominated by the large Bodega Cooperativa do Ribeiro, producer of whites (light Viña Costeira, or the rare celebrated Brandomín) and some reds; the newly popular Armandi and Telura reds come from Ribeiro's new Bodegas Lapatena. The third region, do Valdeorras, is out east of Ourense and produces as many red wines as whites. The latter are of interest for their recent revival of the native *godella* grapes (Viña Guiran and Viña Abad are two leading labels). The best reds probably come from Bodegas Jesús Nazareno, with Valdoura its most reputed wine.

Vilagarcía de Arousa, the glossy base for Galicia's drug-smuggling barons. After a drink and a look at all the suspicious types in a fancy pants café, perhaps the best thing to do is leave and drive up to the home of the pagan queen, Castro Lupario, atop **Monte Lobeira** (5km from Vilagarcía) for the extraordinary views, or visit the woodsy, sand-fringed **Isla de Arousa**, reputedly the chief drop-off point for Colombian cocaine in Europe.

All this nefarious underworld activity seems far away in charming **Cambados**, an atmospheric noble town with plenty of old family crests and a lovely granite paved square; note the Italianate details on the balconies around the 17th-century Praza de Fefiñanes. The cemetery church, **Santa Mariña Dozo**, on Camino de la Pastora has carvings on its vault of the allegory of the man who ate his own excrement; if you know where that comes from, please drop us a line.

From Cambados, the AC550 circles down to the overblown family resort of **O Grove**, linked by a bridge to **Isla A Toxa** (de la Toja), a sand-rimmed, pine-clad islet that first became famous when a donkey left for dead was miraculously restored after a few days. Now adorned with a casino (one that Franco always turned a blind eye to), shell-coated church, spa, nouveau-riche estates, sports complex, nine-hole golf course and watched by security guards, A Toxa is designed for people with bags of money, leaving O Grove for those who don't, but know how to have a good time. There is also the excellent **Acquariumgalicia** (*www.acquariumgalicia.com, open Oct–Mar Fri–Sun and hols 10–8, call for times on other days, Apr–Sept daily 10–9; adm*).

An Excursion Inland from Vilagarcía to the Manor of the Goose

From Vilagarcía, the N640 leads in 12km to the old spa town of **Caldas de Reis**, founded by the Romans. If you decide to forgo drinking the waters, which promise marriage within a year, at least take a walk through the charming *alameda* and botanical gardens. Farther along, 8km east of the centre of **A Estrada** (the largest rural municipality in Spain), you can visit the exterior of the most lavish country villa in all Galicia, the sumptuous 18th-century **Pazo da Oca** (*gardens open daily 9am–dusk;adm*) with its ancient trees, arcaded patio, pond and chapel, an enchanting mix of granite, lichens and greenery.

The Ría de Pontevedra

Although nothing in the southern Rías Baixas is as tourist-orientated as the Ría de Arousa, the hotels of the Ría de Pontevedra fill up fast enough in the summer with vacationing Spaniards and Portuguese. The scenery is domesticated, green and pretty, while most of the beaches are safe even for the kids. Pontevedra, the provincial capital, is a handsome confection of granite, the best urban architecture in Galicia after Santiago itself.

The end of the Salnés peninsula, dividing the Arousa and Pontevedra estuaries, is occupied by the great sweep of the **Praia da Lanzada**, one of Galicia's finest beaches, the delight of windsurfers and, in the old days, of family planners: hoping to get pregnant, women would flock to Lanzada and wade into the sea, lifting up their skirts and letting nine waves (one for each month of gestation) rush against their privates.

Nearby **Portonovo** and its neighbour **Sanxenxo** are jumping little resorts, with beaches like sugar and a chamber-of-commerce claim that they get more sun than the rest of Galicia; on summer evenings everyone for miles around descends on its clubs for a bop. Sanxenxo is also the departure point for ferries to the **Isla de Ons** (which, along with the Islas Cíes, the Isla Sálvora, and the Isla Cortega, forms part of the Parque Nacional de las Islas Atlánticas de Galicia), whose romantic gorse-covered hills and immaculate beaches suggest a lost Scilly Isle, stranded off Galicia. Aside from the gorgeous sand and crystalline water of **Playa de Melide**, the big attraction here is the **Buraco del Infierno**, a blowhole 16ft across and 130ft deep, through which the ocean explodes when conditions are right.

Continuing along the *ría*, pretty little **Combarro** has a famous view of its *hórreos* lined up along the shores of the *ría*. Roads from Sanxenxo or Combarro go up to the abandoned medieval **Monasterio de Armenteira**, where the Virgin favoured a monk named Ero: one morning, while listening to the song of a bird, he was granted a look into eternity. To him the ecstasy lasted but a few minutes, but upon returning to the monastery he found that centuries had passed (if the story sounds familiar *see* Leyre, in Navarra, pp.90–91). The story is the subject of King Alfonso the Wise's *Cantiga CIII*, and of the carvings on the entrance to Armenteira. The rose window on the main façade of the church is believed to have been a mandala for meditation, the carved archivaults around the door are *mudéjar*, and the guardian will show you the unusual octagonal cupola inspired by Islamic architecture. Look for the peculiar masons' marks left on the walls.

Just before Pontevedra, the **Monasterio de Poio** (*www.mercedarios.com; although still home to a community of Mercedarian monks, it is open for visits Apr–Oct Mon–Sat 10–1 and 4.30–8, Sun 4.30–8; Nov–Mar 10–1 and 4–6; adm*) was founded in the 7th century by San Fructuoso, a member of the Visigothic royal family, who caused a sensation by walking across the water to the islet of Tambo to rescue a sinking boat. In the oldest part of the church is the tomb of yet another unorthodox Galician saint, Santa Trahamunda, whose body floated to Galicia in a stone boat from Córdoba; note her statue, clutching an Andalucían palm tree. The modern annexe is a hostel (open Easter–mid-Oct, **t** 98 677 00 00) and the orchards contain an enormous 18th-century hórreo ever built - the monks say it's the oldest ever built.

Pontevedra

Pontevedra is nothing less than the perfect genteel granite Gallego town. Its streets are shaded with arcades, its squares marked with stone crosses. Ancient tradition states that it was first called *Helenes*, founded by Teucer (Teucro), who fought at Troy. *Teucro* means 'Trojan' in Castilian, and there is, in fact, a Teucro who fits the bill, a son of Scamander and a nephew of Priam, who is recorded as leading a band of Cretans to western Spain to found a colony.

It's also significant that Teucro named the city after Helen, the sister of the twins Castor and Pollux, the favourite gods of Roman warriors. The cult of the warrior twins inspired the soldiers of the Reconquista in the apocryphal tradition that St James was the twin brother of Jesus. As if this weren't enough, Pontevedra (along with Mallorca, Barcelona and Corsica) also claims to be the birthplace of Columbus; there's a statue to him at the west end of the Alameda looking towards the ocean and the distant Americas.

Pontevedra's promising mythological progress was stymied back in the Middle Ages, when the Río Lérez silted up the port. By the time of Columbus, all the marine business had moved south to Vigo, leaving a compact, endearing and exceptionally vibrant **Zona Monumental**, its showcases all within a stone's throw of the Praza da Peregrina. Here is the tall, twin-towered 18th-century **Virgen La Peregrina** church, built in the shape of a scallop, to house a statue of the city's patroness. It was one of the few instances where the Virgin had any role at all to play in the pilgrimages (Pontevedra lies on the *camino* from Portugal); during our most recent visit in August

Getting Around

By Train and Bus

In Pontevedra the RENFE station, t 90 224 02 02, and bus station, t 98 685 24 08, are next to each other, but a long walk along Alféreces Provisionales; buses C1 and C2 can take you into town, except on Sundays. Frequent buses serve the main *ría* villages.

By Boat

Up to eight **ferries** a day run from Portonovo and Sanxenxo to the Isla de Ons, from July to mid-September. Three boats make the longer journey out from Marin.

Tourist Information

Sanxenxo: Avda Generalísimo, t 98 672 02 85, *www.sanxenxo.org.*

Pontevedra: Gutiérrez Mellado s/n, t 98 685 08 14, *www.concellopontevedra.es.*

Municipal tourist **information booths** are located in the Alameda and the Jardínes de Castro Sampedro. **Walking tours** (only in Spanish) are available during July, August and September. Pontevedra's **post office** is on Hermanos Vázquez, down the road from the Capilla de la Peregrina; **Internet** facilities are available at Santa Clara 2, just outside the *casco viejo*. There is a **market** in Pontevedra in the Mercado by the river (*daily except Sunday*).

Where to Stay and Eat

Sanxenxo/Sangenjo ✉ 36000

There are scores of places, but just try to get one in the summer without a reservation.

★★★**Hotel Minso**, Avda do Porto 1, t 98 672 01 50, *www.hotelminso.com* (*moderate*). Modern, central, and attractively renovated. *Closed Oct–Mar.*

★★★**Montalvo**, Praia Montalvo, t 98 672 30 28 (*moderate*). A reasonable if unremarkable place, although the restaurant is certainly more than adequate.

★★★**Pazo el Revel**, Revel 15, Villalonga (5km from Sanxenxo), t 98 674 30 00 (*moderate*). An ivy-clad 18th-century *pazo*, with gardens, pool and restaurant.

★★★**Rotilio**, Progreso 140, t 98 672 02 00, *www.hotelrotilio.com* (*moderate*). Some of the best are along Praia de Silgar, such as this modern place (with a superb seafood restaurant).

Antigua Casa de Reis, Reis 39, Padriñán, t 98 669 05 50, (2km from Sanxenxo), *www.antiguacasadereis.com* (*moderate*). A beautiful 19th-century stone house in lovely gardens, with rooms furnished with antiques, offering complete tranquility. Wonderful breakfasts with home-made jam and a genuine welcome from the owners.

★**Hostal San Roque**, Anebados 6, t 98 672 40 82 (*budget*). A good, central budget option – near the beach and the marina at Portonovo.

her feast day was celebrated with folk dances and a procession of hundreds of revellers before a crowd so thick you could scarcely breathe, while the 18- to 30-year-olds indulged in an all-out red wine war. And this was just one of Pontevedra's minor holidays.

Behind the Virgen La Peregrina, there's a lovely 16th-century fountain in a small garden and the 13th- and 14th-century church of **San Francisco** with some good tombs, while across the street arcaded Praza da Ferrería is a favourite hangout for Pontevedrans. From here, Calle Pasantería descends to Pontevedra's most perfect little granite square, the **Praza da Leña**, with its granite porticoes and an ancient cross as its centrepiece. On one side two old houses have been joined to form the main body of the charming **Museo de Pontevedra** (with three other locations around the town, *open Tues–Sat summer 10–2.15 and 5–8.45, winter 10–1.30 and 4.30–8, closed Mon*), which holds an excellent collection of jet figures from Santiago, Celtic gold work, ancient headstones, paintings (by the likes of Zurbarán and Murillo) and works by the talented Gallego caricaturist Alfonso Castelao. The buildings are joined by an enchanting little stone courtyard, with trailing roses and ancient fountains. Almost next door, another section of the

Pontevedra ✉ 36000

★★★**Parador Casa do Barón**, Barón 19, t 98 685 58 00, *pontevedra@parador.es* (*expensive*). Prices are only a tad higher here, and you can sleep in an 11th-century, Gallego *pazo* with a magnificent stone staircase and a garden.

★★★★**Galicia Palace**, Avda de Vigo 3, t 98 686 44 11, *www.galaciapalace.com* (*moderate*). A central chain hotel, but not that luxurious.

★★★**Virgen del Camino**, Virgen del Camino, t 98 685 59 04, *www.hotelvirgendelcamino. com* (*moderate*). Modern, comfortable business hotel.

★**Madrid**, Andrés Mellado 5, t 98 186 51 80 (*moderate*). Near the centre, but rooms are on the dingy side.

★**Comercio**, Avda González Besada 3, t 98 685 12 17 (*inexpensive*). Adequate and central; better-than-average restaurant.

★**Hotel Rúas**, Sarmiento 37, t 98 684 64 16 (*inexpensive*). Perfectly located in the Zona Monumental, has good rooms with bath, some with balconies overlooking the pretty Praza da Verdura.

Casa Maruja, Avda Santa María 12, t 98 685 49 01 (*budget*). Very, very basic and very, very cheap, but rooms have bath and TV.

Monasterio de Poio, 2km from Pontevedra, t 98 677 00 00 (*budget*). The Mercedarian monks up here run a guesthouse (*see* p.327).

Casa Solla, at San Salvador de Poio (2km out of town), t 98 685 26 78 (*expensive*). One of the best and prettiest restaurants in Galicia;

famous for its traditional recipes, freshest seafood and meat dishes and excellent service. *Closed Thurs and Sun eve, and Mon.*

Casa Filgueira, Praza da Lená 2, t 98 685 88 14 (*moderate*). Eat and drink well at this charming restaurant and bar on the town's prettiest square. The award-winning wine selection is superb. *Closed Sun eve and Mon, dinner only Nov–Mar.*

Casa Román, Avda Augusto García Sánchez (south of the centre), t 98 684 35 60 (*moderate*). Prides itself on select ingredients, especially shellfish. *Closed Sun eve.*

Doña Antonia, Soportales Herrería 4-1 (on the first floor), t 98 684 72 74 (*moderate*). Has a well-deserved reputation for imaginative dishes – including duck breasts, baked honeyed lamb and seafood salads; also a delicious chocolate *tarta de trufa* with coffee cream. *Closed Sun.*

Bar El Pitillo, Rúa Alta 3 (*budget*). This popular spot is always full, and offers delicious simple meals cooked in garlic (try the heavenly *zamburiñas* (bay scallops), and mop up the sauce with fresh bread). Good local wines, too.

La Navarra, Princesa 13 (*budget*). Evocative old *bodega* where locals help themselves to wine from the barrels, accompanied by thick slices of *chorizo* and cheese.

A Picota, Rúa de la Peregrina 4 (*budget*). Serves tasty *charcuterie* and cheese.

O Merlo, Santa María 2, t 98 684 43 43 (*budget*). Great tapas. *Closed Mon.*

museum is housed in the Férnando López building, with a gallery of 19h-century painters, including works by Goya, and a temporary exhibition space. The fourth section is the Sermiento, around the corner (closed for restoration).

There are other pretty little squares tucked in the streets to the northwest, among them **Praza de Teucro** with its crystal galleries, named after the city's putative father. Just below, where Rúa Isabel II intersects with four other streets, there's a fine stone cross portraying Adam, Eve and the serpent – the numerous tapas bars in the vicinity are also tempting. Rúa Isabel II cuts across the Zona Monumental to the **Basílica de Santa María la Mayor**, constructed in the 16th century by the local Seafarers' Guild, with a Plateresque façade by Cornelis of Holland, with scenes of the Assumption and Death of the Virgin; two cannons still defend the church from incursions up the river. Inside there's a wooden Gothic *retablo* and some relief comic-strip-like carvings on the back wall. On the corner with Praza de España and the Alameda are the romantic, ivy-draped late 13th-century ruins of the **Convento de Santo Domingo** (also part of the Museo de Pontevedra, *open Tues–Sat summer 10–2.15 and 5–8.45, winter 10–1.30* and *4.30–8, closed Mon*); the leafy Alameda and adjacent **Jardines de Vincenti** are favourite spots for the evening's *paseo*.

Out on a little promontory, a granite statue called the 'Emigrant's Wife', looking out forever across the *ría*, was put up by the people, for the people, honouring the earthy, independent, hardworking women who ran families and farms on their own for years.

Along the South Bank of the Ría de Pontevedra

If Pontevedra has a drawback it tends to be olfactory, a strong pong that wafts in when the wind's up from the massive paper mill to the south. Usually it doesn't hit you until you start down the *ría*, and usually it puts people off from exploring further; this coast, in spite of its garden charm and sandy coves, has scarcely any tourist facilities. Persevere. One of the chief curiosities is just past **Marín** and its naval academy, by the newish fishing hamlet and beach of **Mogor**: here are some of the most important petroglyphs in Spain, a labyrinth and spirals carved by the Celts. They inspired a local retiree to carve his own petroglyphs, some less than perfect spirals and symbols of God and Country.

Another 15km further south along the C550 you'll find **Bueu**, a sleepy fishing village with a couple or so *hostales*, a great base from which to explore the surrounding beaches (it's also one of the departure points for boats to the Illa de Ons). The sands continue 12km west, down towards the tip of the cape, **Hio**, site of Galicia's most elaborate stone crucifix, sculpted out of a single block of granite in the 19th century by José Cerviño of Pontevedra, with a Descent from the Cross and souls in Purgatory.

The Ría de Vigo

The Ría de Vigo is the economic star of Galicia's estuaries: where all the others get narrower and shallower as they cut into land, the Ría de Vigo narrows at Rande (site of a huge suspension bridge), then widens again to form the sheltered inlet of San Simón, site of one of Europe's largest oyster beds. At the mouth of the estuary, the enchanting Cíes islets (part of the national park of Atlantic Islands, see above) protect the port from tempests off the Atlantic and enable mussel farmers to moor their wooden platforms or *bateas* safely in the estuary, where the little molluscs incubate on long ropes suspended in the water. Vigo itself has grown to become the largest city in Galicia, with a population of 280,000.

The North Bank of the Ría and the Islas Cíes

From Hio (*see* above) the road crosses the dolmen-dotted promontory for the pleasant small resort of **Cangas**, stretching along the coast with a lively port in its centre and a pleasant beach at the end. In a pirate raid in the 17th century, nearly the entire male population was massacred, leaving the women, they say, to go mad, slowly; accused of witchcraft, they would meet on Areas Gordas beach on St John's Eve, and get into trouble; many ended up in the Inquisition's dungeons, including María Soliña, the subject of a famous Gallego nationalist song. Five kilometres east, **Moaña** is another if quieter resort in the Cangas mould, with an even better beach.

From Cangas, Vigo, or Baiona the summer-only excursion to the two **Islas Cíes** (the third is off limits as a bird sanctuary) is a delight. Linked by a lick of sand that forms a sheltered lagoon of calm crystal water, the islands offer a perfect lazy day out on the beach, with a couple of cafés and restaurants; or take a picnic and wander along the oceanside paths. As it is a national park, the only place to stay is a campsite with limited space (*open Easter Week and summer only*); ring ahead to book (*t 98 668 70 50 or 98 643 83 58*) and buy a voucher in the booth at Vigo's port before getting your boat ticket.

Vigo

Nothing less than Spain's premier fishing port, bringing in more fish than anywhere in the world except Tokyo, Vigo occupies a privileged hillside spot that attracted both ancient Phoenician and Greek seamen. Its name comes from the Roman *Vicus Spacorum*, but the city claims that its true founder was an early 12th-century troubador, Martín Codax, who, as he describes in his most famous poem, liked to hang out with the boys where Vigo stands today and watch their lady-loves bathe in the estuary. The city's history is full of unwanted English visits; two by Sir Francis Drake (1585 and 1589) and in 1702, when the English surprised a joint Spanish and French treasure fleet just back from the New World, in the Battle of Rande. The English captured some of the ships but 11 were sunk or run aground near the tiny islets by the suspension bridge, the Puente de Rande; some sources say the silver had already been unloaded, but they haven't stopped treasure-seekers from looking. If they found any, they haven't told.

For all that, there's not much to 'see' in Vigo beyond the fine views towards the sea, although the old part of town hugging the fishing port, the **Barrio del Berbés**, is thick with atmosphere and rough, cobbled streets. As in A Coruña, there's a lively fish auction by the waterside at the crack of dawn; if you've had a rough night you'll have no problem finding a dozen supremely fresh oysters on the half-shell from the fishwives along Rúa Teófilo Llorente or in the **Rúa da Pescadería** morning market. Look at the noblemen's palaces in López Puigcerver (**Calle Real**); from **Parque del Castro**, on top of the city, enjoy a great view of the *ría* from the modern monument to the Galeones de Rande: the Celts had their settlement in this commanding position.

The **municipal museum** Quiñones de León is in the 17th-century **Pazo de Castrelos** (*open Tues–Sat 10–1.30 and 5–8, Sun 10–1.30, closed Mon*) in the southwest of town, in the geometric gardens of the **Parque Quiñones de León**. The museum contains antique furniture and paintings by some of Galicia's most important artists, and funerary stelae from archaeological excavations around the city. Vigo also has a magnificent new **Contemporary Art Museum** (*www.marcovigo.com, open Tues–Sat 11–9, Sun 11–3; adm*) on Rúa Príncipe with excellent temporary exhibitions and a wide-ranging programme of events from talks to film-screenings. Overlooking the Ría at the Punta de Muíño, the sleek new **Museo da Mar de Galicia** (*open Tues–Sun 9–9; adm*) offers an interesting glimpse into the region's maritime history. Vigo is home to Galicia's sole **zoo** (*open summer 9–1.30 and 2.30–8; winter 9–1.30 and 2.30–6.30; adm*), situated along the road to the airport.

Getting Around

By Air

Vigo's airport is 9km away, with connections to major Spanish cities and Lisbon, t 98 626 82 00, *www.aena.es*.

By Bus and Train

There are plenty of buses, and several trains daily between Vigo and Pontevedra and beyond. A regular regional train plies between Vigo and A Coruña. The **train station** is at the top of Rúa Alfonso XIII, a 15-min walk uphill from the port, t 90 224 02 02. **Buses** (to Tui, A Garda, Baiona, Pontevedra, O Grove, Vilagarcía, Santiago and A Coruña) depart frequently from the bus station near Praza de España, a few blocks from the train station; for information, t 98 637 34 11. Bus C4C links the centre with the bus station.

By Boat

Weekdays from 6am–10pm and Sundays from 9am–10.30pm, **ferries** (foot passengers only) sail every 30mins to Cangas, every hour to Moaña and up to 10 times daily from mid-June to mid-Sept to the Islas Cíes from Vigo's Estación Marítima near El Berbés (*port information t 98 622 52 72*). For the Cíes, buy your ticket early in the day so you can choose your return boat – the latest sailings fill up first. The islands are also accessible from Cangas and Baiona in summer.

Tourist Information

Cangas: Paseo Castelao, t 98 639 20 23.
Vigo: Rúa Teófilo Llorente 5, t 98 622 47 57, *www.turis modevigo.org* and Rúa Cánovas del Castillo (in the port, regional) t 98 643 05 77. There are summer booths in the city centre.
Tui: Edif. Área Panorámica, t 98 660 17 89.

The **post office** in Vigo is at Reconquista 2, off Praza de Compostela; **Internet access** is available a few blocks away at República de Argentina 24. The tourist office in Vigo has a guide book In English of walking tours in the surrounding countryside. There are **markets** in Cangas on Fridays; in Baiona on Mondays; and in Tui there is a Gallego/Portuguese market on Thursdays.

Where to Stay and Eat

Vigo ✉ 36200

★★★★Gran Hotel Samil, Playa de Samil 15, t 98 624 00 00 (*luxury*). Big, modern resort hotel for luxuriating beside the beach; extensive facilities include a swimming pool and tennis courts.

★★★★Bahía de Vigo, Canovas del Castillo 24, t 98 622 67 00 (*expensive*). A tall, modern block with great views of the port and the *ria*; its restaurant, claimed to be the biggest *marisquería* in Spain, serves up colossal *parrilladas* of grilled seafood.

South of Vigo to the Ría de Baiona

Vigo's main beaches, white **Praia de Canido** and **Praia Samil**, are just west and often crowded, but the main lure here is **Baiona** (Bayona), down the coast, one of Galicia's choice resorts, topped by the walls of the medieval **Castillo de Monterreal**. The grounds are occupied by a ravishing *parador*; fork out to tour the grounds and walls. The coast is embellished with little beaches of soft sand, namely Ladeira, Santa María and the magnificent crescent of Praia América; the latter named after the fact that Baiona was the first place in Europe to learn that Columbus had discovered a New World, on 10 March 1493, when the little *Pinta* sailed into its port. A replica sits on a floating jetty in the harbour, complete with ship's cat, ropes of garlic, and dummy sailors.

The 13th-century church of **Santa María** (*open daily 10–1 and 4–8*) is a good example of transitional architecture; more contemporary religious art is 1km south of town in the form of a huge granite sculpture of 1910, a sailors' *ex voto* to the **Virgen de la Roca**. Wild horses have a free rein in the hills here, rounded up once a year in a *rapa das Bestas*, or *curros*, when Gallego cowboys tame them, run a race or two, and let them

***Ensenada**, Alfonso XIII 7, **t** 98 644 74 40, **f** 98 644 74 14 (*moderate*). Modern and in the centre with fine views across the bay.

****Dinastía**, Progreso 13, **t** 98 622 78 60 (*inexpensive*). Excellent facilities for the price, including gym, jacuzzi and satellite TV.

****Hs Puerta del Sol**, Puerta del Sol 14, **t** 98 622 23 64, *www.alojamientosvigo.com* (*inexpensive*). Stylish and charming, in a solid old stone building with glassed-in balconies in the upper floors. Also offers apartments.

***Hotel Águila**, C/Victoria 6, **t** 986431398, *www.hotelaguila.com* (*inexpensive*). A change from Vigo's endless modern blocks, this pretty hotel is in an historic building by the Plaza da Compostela.

****Hs La Nueva Colegiata**, Praza da Iglesia 2, **t** 98 622 09 52 (*budget*). All rooms have bath, and double glazing to counter the wake-the-dead tolling of the bells across the plaza.

Eating out is an excellent reason for staying in Vigo. To every kind of seafood and shellfish add the delicacies from the River Minho: salmon, lamprey and baby eels (*anguillas*), the latter two favourite stuffings for *empanadas*.

El Mosquito, Pza da Pedra 4 (near the port), **t** 98 622 44 41 (*expensive*). For seafood or roast leg of lamb, the people's choice in Vigo, is a classic place with a familiar atmosphere.

Sibaris, Avda García Barbón 122, **t** 98 622 15 26 (*expensive*). Gets kudos for its first-rate land and sea cuisine in an upmarket, intimate setting. *Closed Sun.*

Timón Playa, Cánido 8, Corujo, **t** 98 649 08 15 (*expensive*). Perfectly prepared seafood, rice dishes and empanadas at this attractive beachfront restaurant, with views of the Cíes islands. *Closed Sun.*

El Castillo, Monte do Castro, **t** 98 642 11 11 (*moderate*). Up here you can dine with a superb view; exquisitely grilled fish and meat are the specialities. *Closed Sun eve and Mon.*

Cíes, Canido 8, **t** 98 649 01 01 (*moderate*). A pretty place by the beach, with deliciously fresh shellfish and tasty *empanadas*. Good lunch menú for around €10. *Closed Sun.*

La Oca, Av. Purificación Saavedra 8, **t** 98 637 12 55 (*moderate*). Award-winning cuisine at very reasonable prices, prepared with whatever's freshest at the Teis market nearby. Book well ahead.

Puesto Piloto Alcabre, Avda Atlántida 194, **t** 98 624 15 24 (*budget*). For piles of good old-fashioned seafood (and some beef dishes), come to this place overlooking the sea. *Closed Sun eve.*

Marisqueria Bahía, Avda Cánovas Castillo, **t** 98 644 96 55 (*moderate–budget*). Another catch of the day restaurant – but one of the best, with outside tables on seafood street and oysters hawked by fishermen's wives.

---

go again. In **Oia**, 16km south along the pretty and wild coastline, there's a lonely 18th-century Baroque monastery, where the monks run a charming little *hostel*.

To the south, **A Guarda**, at the mouth of the Río Minho, may look more intriguing on the map than it does in reality, with its clutch of nouveau-riches *Americanos'* bungalows. However, a 40-minute walk (or shorter drive) up in the excavated Celtic *castro* on Monte Santa Tegra, is one of Spain's most important *citanías*, or fortified hill settlements, inhabited from the 7th century BC up to the Roman period. It has over 100 houses, some reconstructed, others mere foundations, linked by cobbled lanes and encircled by walls.

From the top of Monte Tegra there are fine views over the Valley of the Minho into Portugal. Farther up there's a cromlech, or Neolithic stone circle, and at the very top a church with a small **museum** (*open Tues–Sun 11–2 and 4–7.30*) where you can find out about the strange carving discovered on the site, believed to be a map; if so, one of the oldest found in the West. The nearest beach is at Camposancos, 3km from A Guarda, overlooking the mouth of the wooded Río Minho, Galicia's prettiest river and the frontier between Spain and Portugal.

Cocedero Bar La Piedra, Pescadería 3, t 98 643 12 04. A classic in A Pedra, with stalls of oysters to eat on the street or on the terrace.

Although El Berbés is generally tucked up in bed before midnight (except at weekends), there's normally plenty going on in the streets surrounding the old port. Regular open-air concerts are held in summer in the Parque Quiñones de Léon; the programme ranges from classical music to big-name rock artists.

La Iguana, Churraca 14, t 98 622 01 90. Celebrated club in a warehouse-style space, with nightly live acts (mainly rock and pop).

Café Concierto Joker, Rúa Carral 3. This place has a regular programme of live blues, jazz and swing bands, and a large dance floor.

Redondela ✉ 39800

Pazo Torres de Agrelo, t 98 640 80 21 (*moderate*). A handsome 19th-century pazo, with gardens and a classic restaurant and all kinds of facilities including pool, tennis, gym and sauna.

Baiona ✉ 36300

★★★★Parador Conde de Gondomar, Monte Real, t 98 635 50 00, baiona@ parador.es (*expensive*). Galicia's finest, housed in a modern reconstruction of a typical Galician *pazo* within the medieval walls of Monterreal, in a lovely park; it offers a pool, tennis, children's recreation, and a short walk to the beach.

★★La Anunciada, Ventura Misa 58, t 98 635 55 90, f 98 635 55 34 (*moderate*). A moderate choice worth a try.

★★Pazo de Mendoza, Elduayen 1, t 98 638 50 14, www.pazodemendoza.es (*moderate*). A tastefully restored 18th-century *casona*, with a restaurant (*expensive*) considered Baiona's finest, where the best Gallego traditions and ingredients are combined with the finest elements of *nouvelle* sensibility. The monumental *menú degustación* (€32) offers such delights as cuttlefish brochette in *Albariño tempura*.

Pazo da Touza, Rúa dos Pazos 119, Nigrán (8km from Baiona), t 98 636 69 89, www.pazodatouza.com (*moderate*). A beautiful 18th-century pazo surrounded by orchards and gardens. Spacious rooms and wonderful breakfasts.

★★Hs Tres Carabelas, Ventura Misa 61, t 98 635 51 33, www.hoteltrescarabelas.com (*inexpensive*). A fine old inn on a narrow cobbled lane right in the middle of town.

★Hs Cais, Alférez Barreiro 3, t 98 635 56 43. A good *inexpensive* option, with some rooms overlooking the bay.

★Hs Mesón del Burgo, Barrio del Burgo, t 98 635 53 09 (*budget*). One of a wide range of budget options in Baiona with sea views from most rooms.

Pedro Madruga, Ramón y Cajal 1, t 98 635 68 22 (*expensive*). Renowned as one of Baiona's finest *marisquerias*; its ample selection of

Tui

From A Guarda the best thing to do is follow the course of the River Minho up to Tui (or Tuy, pronounced *twee*), a rare frontier town worth visiting in its own right. One of the seven ancient capitals of Galicia, Tui is picturesquely piled upon its acropolis; like Pontevedra, it claims to have been founded by wandering Greeks after the Trojan War. It was the capital of the Visigoth King Witiza in 700, and has seen many battles and border skirmishes with Portugal, defended by the walled city of Valença.

Tui's granite lanes and houses are crowned by the military profile of the **Catedral de Santa María** with its powerful walls and keep; until the 13th century it did double duty as Tui's castle. Construction began in 1120 but not completed until much later; the stone has mellowed into a grey, vertical garden of wild flowers. There is a fine Romanesque porch and a portal from 1225, carved with the Adoration of the Magi by French-trained sculptors, one of the first and finest Gothic works in Galicia; be sure to note the lovely but strange coat-of-arms on the side wall, which has five stars and a crescent moon, said to symbolize the burning of the town by al-Mansur. The inside of the cathedral is (mostly live) crustaceous goodies decorates an outside counter and provides pre-dinner entertainment for the crowds, who are invariably waiting for a table; remember to book in advance.

Mesón El Candil, San Juan 46, t 98 635 74 93 (*moderate*). In the centre, with good home cooking.

O Moscón, Alférez Barreiro 2, t 98 635 50 08 (*moderate*). One of the best around; known for its fine lobster (*bogavante*).

El Túnel, Ventura Misa 21 (*moderate*). Attractive stone seafood restaurant on an old street in the centre.

A Garda ✉ 01300

**Convento de San Benito, Pza de San Benito, t 98 661 11 66, *www.hotelsanbenito.com* (*moderate–inexpensive*). Set in a 16th-century monastery with a lovely garden, antique-furnished rooms, and a wonderful collection of old *azulejos* in the cloister.

*Hs Martirrey, José Antonio 8, t 98 661 03 49 (*inexpensive*). A harbourside *hostal* with rooms with or without bath.

*Pazo Santa Tecla, t 98 661 00 02 (*budget*). A delightful place near the top of Monte Tecla with views in every direction. *Open Apr–Sept.*

Marisquería Olga, Malteses 24, t 98 661 15 16 (*budget*). Good fish soups and seafood wait at this friendly family-run *taberna*. *Closed Sun.*

Tui ✉ 36700

***Parador San Telmo, Avda Portugal, t 98 660 03 00, *tui@.parador.es* (*moderate*). Overlooking the Minho, and located in a large reproduction of a typical Gallego *pazo* 1km below town, with a garden, tennis and pool; very refined.

Abadía do Pelouro Axeito, at Caldelas de Tui (12 km from Tui), t 98 662 90 24 (*moderate*). If you're looking for something special, this is a delightful rural hotel with rooms and apartments to rent. With pool and bikes to rent.

***Colón Tuy, Colón 11, t 98 660 02 23, *www.galinor.es/hotelcolontuy* (*moderate–inexpensive*). Modern and rather charmless, but offers excellent facilities (pool, tennis, and garden) for very reasonable prices.

*Hs San Telmo 91, Avda de la Concordia 88, t 98 660 30 11 (*inexpensive*). A basic cheapie, but all rooms have bath.

Hostal Cruceiro do Monte, Carretera de Baiona 23, t 98 660 09 53 (*budget*). Simple and family run, in a country setting; good home-cooked food.

O Cabalo Furado, Pza do Concello, t 98 660 12 15 (*moderate*). Offers good home cooking. *Closed Sun eve.*

Meson Taqueyui, Pza do Concello (*budget*). Makes up for everyone else's marine obsession by serving *raciones* of ham and *queso de tetilla*.

Bodegón O Conde, Circus 9 (*budget*). Tasty and inexpensive tapas.

also heavily fortified – against earthquakes – and contains the relics of San Telmo, also known as Pedro González of Astorga (confessor of King Saint Ferdinand of Castile), who also worked among the seafolk of Galicia in 1246. He is the patron saint of Spanish sailors, who confused his name with their first patron St Elmo (or Erasmus), who sends them his lucky fire to light upon their masts, igniting even their fingers without burning them. His tomb, accredited with miracles, oozes a vinegary gunk prized as a cure-all.

Among Tui's smaller churches are **Santo Domingo** (1415), inside is a mix of Gothic and pre-Romanesque with finely carved effigies on the tombs and the stone pulpit; and the circular **San Telmo** (1803), the only example of Portuguese Baroque in Galicia. In 30 mins, you can walk from the centre of Tui to the lovely Portuguese walled town of **Valença do Minho**, crossing an iron bridge built by Gustave Eiffel. The views from Valença to Tui are lovely, as is Valença, blanketed in bright towels that Spaniards flock to buy. On the other hand, the Portuguese, seem to come to Tui for salt cod and toys, especially during the Thursday market. If it's hot, there are a couple of small river beaches perfect for a dip.

Up the Minho to Ourense

Galicia's least known and only landlocked province is an introspective place, with more valleys, they say, than towns, descending from the great tableland of Castile to form the frayed coastline of *rías*. The province is famous for wine (Do Valdeorras, Do Ribeiro, Verín and Monterrey), hot springs, and Julio Iglesias.

From Tui to Ribadavia

Both the train and road follow the wooded banks of the Minho, offering one more chance to cross into Portugal on the ferry from Salvaterra do Minho to the delightful walled city of Monção. To the east, past the first dam, the river becomes wider and more elegiac, around the start of the wine-growing region of Ribeiro. Ribeiro's charming 15th-century capital, **Ribadavia**, has the best-preserved Jewish *barrio* in Galicia, a web of narrow lanes around the church of Santiago; even after the expulsion of the Jews by the Catholic kings, many remained here, hidden with the help of the Christian population.

Ribadavia has a beautiful **Praza Maior** and some interesting Romanesque churches: a tree grows out of the bell tower of the **Oliveira** church, **San Juan** has a 13th-century *cruceiro*, while the **Convento de Santo Domingo**, occasional residence of the kings of Galicia, has a fine Gothic church and a cloister. The **Museo del Ribeiro** (*open Mon–Fri 9.30–2*) offers information on local wines and the ruined **Castillo de los Condes de Ribadavia** is an impressive pile of walls, gates, towers, and tombs carved into the rock.

From Ribadavia, it's 5km to the curious hill-top **Monumento de Beade** (or **Calvario**), with three granite crosses, overlooking a cluster of *hórreos*, and a bit further to the 8th-century, Asturian-style church of **San Ginés (Xens) de Francelos** with a unique decorative programme by the entrance arch, a mix of Mozarabic and Visigothic elements: rude scenes on the capitals, reliefs of the Flight from Egypt and Christ's entrance into Jerusalem and silhouettes of birds inside.

The Minho and its tributary, the Sil, are the 'holy rivers' of Galicia, their banks thick with churches and hermitages. South of Ribadavia, the village of **Celanova** is built around a vast **Praza Maior**, with a fountain in the middle (where you mustn't drink from the north spout, because of the risk of going mad) and a Cecil-B.-De-Mille Baroque façade of 1681, pasted on the venerable Benedictine monastery of **San Salvador**. The church's Capilla Mayor holds a gargantuan *retablo* of 1697 and the choir is a masterpiece of Gothic carving. Although the monastery itself is occupied by a school (it was a prison in the Civil War), you can pick up the key to see the elegant Renaissance cloister, a Baroque cloister, and the garden at the back, the setting for the diminutive (25ft by 10ft) chapel of **San Miguel**, a Mozarabic jewel with a roof that looks like a Chinese hat. Founded by St Rosendo in 936 in memory of his brother Froila, the chapel to this day bears an inscription over the door, asking visitors to pray for Froila's soul.

An even older church is further south on the OU540 near **Bande**: the rural Visigothic chapel of **Santa Comba**, overlooking the reservoir of Limia. Built with a Byzantine plan around the year 700, Santa Comba is remarkably well preserved with its borrowed late Corinthian marble columns supporting a horseshoe arch. The rest of the decoration is quite sober, but there are traces of frescoes, including a man in the moon.

Getting Around

By Train
Ourense is the main hub here, with trains to Santiago, Lugo, A Coruña, Vigo, Ribadavia, León and elsewhere. RENFE's Estación Empalme is across the river, **t** 90 224 02 02; tickets are also on sale at Rúa do Paseo 15, **t** 98 821 46 04 .

By Bus
The bus station is 1km from the centre on the Vigo road, **t** 98 821 60 27, with frequent services to Vigo and all major points in Galicia.

Tourist Information

Ribadavia: Praza Maior, **t** 98 847 12 75, *www.ribadavia.com*.

Ourense: Burgas 12, Bajo, **t** 98 837 20 20, *www.ourense.es*, and Ponte Romana (regional), **t** 98 837 20 20, *www.turismourense.es*.

Verín: Casa del Escudo, **t** 98 841 16 14, *www.verin.net*.

There are **markets** in Ourense on the 7th and 17th of each month; in Allariz on the 1st and 15th of each month; in Ribadavia on the 10th and 25th of each month; and in Verín on Wednesdays and Fridays.

Where to Stay and Eat

Ribadavia ✉ 32000

****Mosteiro de San Clodio**, Plaza Eladio Rodríguez 1, Leiro (10km from Ribadavia) **t** 98 848 56 01, *www.eurostarshotels.com* (*expensive–moderate*). A beautiful, luxurious hotel in a lovingly restored 16th-century monastery; four-poster beds, gardens, pool and fine restaurant.

Hotel Rural Doña Blanca, San Clodio, Leiro (10km from Ribadavia) **t** 98 848 56 88 (*moderate*). A stylish fusion of old and new characterise this chic rural hotel in Leiro, with an outdoor pool for summer and tiny spa for winter.

Hs Plaza, Plaza Mayor 15, **t 98 847 05 76 (*inexpensive*). Well restored and well run, right in the heart of the old quarter; its restaurant is one of the better choices in town.

Hs Oasis, Ctra N 120, **t 98 847 16 13 (*budget*). Modern place a couple of kilometres out of town, with pleasant rooms, views and a no-frills but perfectly acceptable *budget* restaurant.

*Hs Evencio, Avda R. Valcárcel 30, **t** 98 847 10 45 (*budget*). Has a swimming pool and garden to delight its guests.

Lobios ✉ 32868

****Lobios Caldaria**, Riocalco s/n, **t** 98 801 00 50 (*expensive*). Modern spa hotel, with all kinds of treatments and good amenities.

*Lusitano, Ctra Concejal 312 (Mayeta Portela), **t** 98 844 80 28 (*budget*). This is the only other hotel in this area; all rooms with bath and breakfast included.

Ourense ✉ 32000

Ourense has plenty of business hotels but nothing with much charm.

****Gran Hotel San Martín**, Curros Enríquez 1, **t** 98 837 18 11 (*expensive*). Modern, business-orientated hotel with large, air-conditioned rooms in the centre.

***Auriense**, El Cumial, **t** 98 823 49 00 (*moderate*). Another modern business hotel a few minutes from the centre, with pool, tennis and disco.

***Hotel Princess**, Avda de la Habana 4, **t** 98 826 95 38 (*moderate*). Central new hotel off the main square.

Martín Fierro (Casa Ovidio), Sáenz Diez 17, **t** 98 837 20 26 (*expensive–moderate*). Choose one of three dining rooms and tuck in to the surf or turf delicacies from the grill, or try the tasty pilgrims' menu. *Closed Sun*.

San Miguel, San Miguel 12, **t** 98 822 12 45 (*expensive*). One of Ourense's best restaurants, specialising in seafood fresh from the coast, accompanied by Galicia's finest wines, served in the traditional *taza*. *Closed Tues*.

Pena Vixía, Hernán Cortés 29, **t** 98 824 69 69 (*moderate–budget*). A traditional *tasca*, which has been renovated and offers delicious gourmet tapas and raciones.

A few kilometres further south around **Lobios** are monuments that predate Santa Comba; monolithic Roman *miliarios*, or milestones, standing from the days when this was the main Roman route between Astorga and the newly conquered territory of *Gallaecia*. The best can be found way up in the hills on the Portuguese frontier, south of **Torneiros**. The surrounding glacial valleys and granitic peaks are home to wolves and wild boar, and enjoy protection as the **Parque Natural Baixa Limia-Serra do Xurés**.

East of Celanova (and south of Ourense just off the A52 motorway) the medieval town of **Allariz** is a monument in itself and site of two more Romanesque churches: **Santiago** with an unusual round apse and **San Esteban**, on the way to the ruins of the castle. The **Convento de Santa Clara** was founded in 1282 by Violante, the wife of Alfonso X, who is buried in the huge Baroque cloister. Between Allariz and Ourense, the ruined 12th-century **Santa Mariña das Aguas Santas** (a 15-minute walk from the village; bring a flashlight) has steps down to its crypt – actually a corridor dolmen, constructed of boulders.

Ourense (Orense)

Continuing up the Río Minho, Ourense greets visitors with a graceful **Ponte Romano**, its seven ogival arches striding over 100ft above the Minho. The footbridge – the biggest stone bridge in Spain – was built by the Romans and rebuilt on the ancient piers in the 13th century. It's now been upstaged by a vast, modern bridge, built for the Millennium. Traffic is Ourense's day-in day-out nightmare, funnelled down the discouraging main street, Rúa do Progreso, cut through the city in the 19th century. Equally discouraging *urbanizaciones* housing Ourense's 100,000 souls take up most of the rest of the space.

If you can find a place to park, or don't mind walking a mile in from the bus or train stations, you can see what first attracted the Romans: the steaming hot springs, *Aquae Urentes*, known by the Visigoths and Suevi as Warm Sea (hence *Ourense*). The main source, **As Burgas**, still steams out of the neoclassical fountain at a constant, nearly boiling temperature midway down Rúa do Progreso. The locals have invented a many uses for the hot water – put a dead chicken in it, they say, and you can pluck it in two minutes. During 1386–7, when Ourense was John of Gaunt's capital when he tried to claim the throne of Castile, many Englishmen here had the first hot baths of their lives.

Up from here, the arcaded **Praza Maior** and its charming little annex, **Praza de la Magdalena**, is Ourense's historic core and hub of its social life. The old episcopal palace in Praza Maior houses the **Museo Arqueológico Provincial** (*open Tues–Fri 9–2 and 4–8, Sat 9–2*), with a collection of finds spanning from the Neolithic era to the Bronze Age, as well as *retablos* and other bits of art salvaged from the province's numerous churches.

In the Praza Maior, the **Cathedral** was begun in the 12th century and is entered through the **Pórtico del Paraíso**, a 13th-century (and rather naïve) brightly painted reproduction of Santiago's great Pórtico de la Gloria. The high altar contains the reliquary of St Martin of Tours, while the florid Baroque chapel by Francisco Castro Canseco houses Ourense's oddest attraction, the Santísimo Cristo who, like the Christ of Burgos, has real hair and a beard and a wood and fabric body; according to legend it was made by Nicodemus and floated ashore near Finisterre. The **Museo Catedraliceo** (*open daily 12–1 and 4.30–7;*

adm) off the 12th-century cloister has one of the first books printed in Galicia and the 'Treasure of San Rosendo' – rare 10th-century chesspieces carved from rock crystal.

Around Ourense

From Ourense, take the N525 north to the turn-off to Cobas, and continue beyond to the monumental Cistercian monastery of **Oseira** (*open daily 9.30–12.30 and 3.30–5, until 6 in summer; adm, guided visit only*), where the late Graham Greene spent time with his heretical thoughts on Catholicism and wrote *Monsignor Quixote* (1982). He came to the right spot; founded in 1137 by four hermits, Oseira was famous for monks who dallied in alchemy and magic cures. The monastery façade has a gigantic Churrigueresque doorway and the odd crest of two bones with the tree of knowledge. The massive church dates from the 12th century, and has seven chapels around its altar, with the Virgen de la Leche, supposedly an alchemist's idol, in the main one. Don't miss the curious faces carved in the Claustro de los Medallones.

The most majestic scenery in these parts begins just east of Ourense, heading up the Minho along the N120, where the cliffs over the river rise ever steeper. At **San Esteban**, dominated by its Romanesque **Monasterio de Ribas de Sil** (and its three atmospheric cloisters) the Sil flows into the Minho, and along the latter are wild gorges to walk along.

The nearly as dramatic OU536 east of Ourense goes up to **Esgos**, where a small byroad leads to the ruined monastery and church of **San Pedro de Rocas**, founded by followers of Prisciliano (*see* p.318) in 573, its three apses excavated in the rock. Abandoned in the Muslim invasion, the spot was rediscovered in the 10th century; there are some curious old tombs and a little monolithic Mozarabic altar in the centre apse. The road continues to rise up higher and higher to **Puebla de Trives (Pobra de Trives)**, where there's a ski resort, **Manzaneda** with 10 different pistes of all degrees of difficulty, served by a chairlift and three other ski lifts (more information at *www.manzaneda.com*). If you're heading southeast from Ourense towards Bragança or Zamora, consider stopping in the old walled town of **Verín**, capital of the wine-growing Monterrey valley; high on one side of the valley looms the **Castle of Monterrey**, built in the 16th century, part of it converted into a *parador*. Don't pass up the chance to try a bottle of Verín red – as long as you aren't driving anywhere; this Galician wine can pack 14 per cent alcohol.

Where to Stay and Eat

Offers pool, sauna, gym, horse-riding and much more. Book.

Puebla de Trives/Pobra de Trives
✉ 32600

★★★**Pazo Casa Grande**, Marqués de Trives, t/f 98 833 20 66 (*moderate–inexpensive*). Set in a lovely 18th-century building with seven rooms plus private chapel. Warm, family welcome.

★★★**Pazo Paradela**, Ctra de Barrio km 2, t 98 833 07 14 (*inexpensive*). Another, equally charming, *pazo*, in a lovely rural setting.

★★**As Maceiras**, Manzaneda (ski resort), t 98 833 00 34, *www.asmaceiras.net* (*inexpensive*).

Verín ✉ 32600

★★★**Parador de Verín**, 4km outside Verín, t 98 841 00 75, *verin@ parador.es* (*expensive*). Part of the 16th-century Castle of Monterrey has been converted into this *parador*, with lovely views across the valley; its restaurant offers seafood and Gallego dishes.

★**Dos Hermanas**, Avda de Sousas 106, t 98 841 02 80 (*budget*). Literally, a lower range option from where you can look up at the castle.

Language

Castellano, as Spanish is properly called, was the first modern language to have a grammar written for it. When a copy was presented to Queen Isabel in 1492, she understandably asked what it was for. 'Your majesty', replied a perceptive bishop, 'language is the perfect instrument of empire'. In the centuries to come, this concise, flexible and expressive language would prove just that: an instrument that would contribute more to Spanish unity than any laws or institutions, while spreading itself effortlessly over much of the New World.

Spanish may have the simplest grammar of any Romance language, and if you know a little of any one of these, you will find much of the vocabulary looks familiar. It's quite easy to pick up a working knowledge of Spanish; but Spaniards speak colloquially and fast, sometimes leaving out half the consonants and adding some strange sounds so expressing yourself may prove a little easier than understanding the replies. Spaniards will appreciate your efforts, though.

If you already speak Spanish, note that the Spaniards increasingly use the familiar *tú* instead of *usted* when addressing even complete strangers.

Pronunciation

Pronunciation is phonetic, though a few of the consonants are somewhat difficult for English speakers.

Vowels

a   short *a* as in 'pat'
e   short *e* as in 'set'
i   as *e* in 'be'
o   between long *o* of 'note' and short *o* of 'hot'
u   silent after q and gue- and gui-; otherwise long u as in 'flute'
ü   *w* sound, as in 'dwell'
y   at end of word, or meaning *and*, as i

Diphthongs

ai/ay   as *i* in 'side'
ei/ey   as *ey* in 'they'
au   as *ou* in 'sound'
oi/oy   as *oy* of 'boy'

Consonants

c   before the vowels i and e, it's a castellano tradition to pronounce it as th; many Spaniards and all Latin Americans pronounce it in this case as an s
ch   like *ch* in 'church'
d   often becomes th, or is almost silent, at end of word
g   before *i* or *e*, pronounced as *j* (*see* below)
h   silent
j   the *ch* in loch – a guttural, throat-clearing *h*
ll   *y* or *ly* as in million
ñ   *ny* as in canyon (the ~ is called a tilde)
q   *k*
r   usually rolled, which takes practice
v   often pronounced as *b*
z   *th*, but *s* in parts of Andalucía

Stress

If the word ends in a vowel, an *n* or an *s*, then the stress falls on the penultimate syllable; if the word ends in any other consonant, the last syllable is stressed. Exceptions are marked with an accent.

General

hello *hola*
good evening/night *buenas tardes/noches*
goodbye *adiós*
please *por favor*
thank you (very much) *(muchas) gracias*
yes/no *si/no*
excuse me *disculpe*
I don't understand *No entiendo*
doctor *el doctor*
emergency room *la sala de emergencias*
pharmacy *la farmacia*
police station *la comisaría de policía*

Time and Days

What time is it? *¿Qué hora es?*
It is 2 o'clock *Son las dos*
... half past 2 ... *las dos y media*
... a quarter past 2 ... *las dos y cuarto*
... a quarter to 3 ... *las tres menos cuarto*
month/week/day *mes/semana/día*
morning/afternoon/evening *mañana/tarde/
  noche*
yesterday/today/tomorrow *ayer/hoy/
  mañana*
it is early/late *es temprano/tarde*
Monday/Tuesday/Wednesday/Thursday/
  Friday/Saturday/Sunday *lunes/martes/
  miércoles/jueves/viernes/sábado/domingo*

Shopping and Sightseeing

Do you have...? *¿Tiene usted...?*
I would like... *Quisiera...*
How much is it? *¿Cuánto vale eso?*
open/closed *abierto/cerrado*
It's cheap/expensive *es barato/caro*
bank/post office *banco/correos*
beach *playa*
church *iglesia*
museum *museo*
postage stamp *sello*
sea *mar*
shop *tienda*
telephone *teléfono*
theatre *teatro*
toilet/toilets *servicios/aseos*
men *señores/hombres/caballeros*
women *señoras/damas*

Hotels and Restaurants

Do you have a room/a table for two? *¿Tiene
  usted una habitación/una mesa para dos?*
How much is the room per night? *¿Cuánto
  cuesta la habitación por noche?*
... with 2 beds *con dos camas*
... with double bed *con una cama grande*
... with a shower/bath *con ducha/baño*
Can I see the menu, please? *¿Me puede dar la
  carta del menú, por favor?*
wine list *la lista de vinos*
Can I have the bill (check)? *La cuenta, por favor*
Can I pay by credit card? *¿Puedo pagar con
  tarjeta de crédito?*

Driving and Transport

rent *alquiler*
car/bicycle *coche/bicicleta*
motorbike/moped *moto/ciclomotor*
petrol *gasolina*
This doesn't work *Esto no funciona*
road *carretera*
breakdown *avería*
driving licence *carnet de conducir*
driver *conductor/chófer*
exit/entrance *salida/entrada*
no parking *estacionamento prohibido*
give way/yield *ceda el paso*
road works *obras*
I want to go to... *Deseo ir a...*
How can I get to...? *¿Cómo puedo llegar a...?*
What time does it leave/arrive? *¿A qué hora
  sale/llega?*
How long does the trip take? *¿Cuánto tiempo
  dura el viaje?*
I want a (return) ticket to... *Quiero un billete
  (de ida y vuelta) a...*
aeroplane/flight *avión/vuelo*
airport *aeropuerto*
bus/coach *autobús/autocar*
bus/railway station *estación*
bus stop *parada*
on foot *a pié*
platform *andén*
port *puerto*
seat *asiento*
ship *buque/barco*
dock *embarcadero*
subway *el metro*
ticket *billete*
train *tren*
timetable *el horario*
ticket office *la taquilla*
on time *puntual*
left-luggage locker *la consigna automática*

Directions

Where is ...? *Dónde está?*
here/there *aquí/allí*
close/far *cerca/lejos*
left/right *izquierda/derecha*
straight on *todo recto*
up/down *arriba/abajo*
corner *esquina*
square *plaza*
street *calle*

Glossary

ajimez: in Moorish architecture, an arched double window.

alameda: park or promenade.

ayuntamiento: city hall.

azulejo: painted glazed tiles, popular in Moorish and *mudéjar* work and later architecture.

baldachin: canopy on posts over an altar or throne.

barrio: city quarter or neighbourhood.

Calvario: Calvary, or outdoor Stations of the Cross.

Castizo: anything purely Spanish (from the Castilian point of view).

castrum: Roman military camp.

churrigueresque: florid Baroque style of the late 17th and early 18th centuries in the style of José Churriguera (1650–1725), Spanish architect and sculptor.

converso: Jew who converted to Christianity.

coro: walled-in choir in the centre of a Spanish cathedral.

corregidor: royal magistrate.

Cortes: Spanish Parliament.

fueros: exemptions, or privileges of a region under medieval Spanish law.

hidalgo: literally 'son of somebody' – the lowest level of the nobility, just good enough for a coat-of-arms.

torre del homenaje: the tallest tower of a fortification, sometimes detached from the wall.

hórreo: Asturian or Galician granary or corn crib.

Isabelline Gothic: late 15th-century style, roughly corresponding to the English Perpendicular.

judería: Jewish quarter.

mirador: a scenic overlook or belvedere.

Modernista: Catalan Art Nouveau.

Morisco: Muslims who submitted to Christianization to remain in Spain after the Reconquista.

Mozarabic: referring to Christians under Muslim rule in Moorish Spain.

mudéjar: Moorish-influenced architecture; Spain's 'National style' in the 12th to 16th centuries.

ogival: pointed (arches).

pallazo: circular, conical-roofed shepherd's hut in Asturias and Galicia.

pazo: Galician manor house.

Plateresque: 16th-century style; heavily ornamented Gothic.

plaza de toros: bullring.

pronunciamiento: a military coup.

reja: iron grilles, either decorative ones in churches or those covering the exterior windows of buildings.

retablo: carved or painted altarpiece.

Transitional: in northern Spanish churches, referring to the transition between Romanesque and Gothic.

Further Reading

Atxaga, Bernardo, *Obabakoak* (Pantheon, 1993). Collection of stories by the best-known living Basque author, the first to be translated into English.

Borrow, **George**, *The Bible in Spain* (various editions, first written in 1843). A jolly travel account by a preposterous Protestant Bible salesman in 19th-century Spain.

Brenan, **Gerald**, *Spanish Labyrinth* (Cambridge, 1943). Origins of the Civil War; *The Literature of the Spanish People* (Cambridge, 1976).

Carr, **Raymond** (editor), *Spain: A History* (OUP, 2000). Probably the best concise history of Spain available.

Casas, **Penelope**, *The Foods and Wines of Spain* (Penguin). The best Spanish cookbook in English, with great regional recipes.

Castro, **Américo**, *The Structure of Spanish History* (E. L. King, 1954). A remarkable interpretation of Spain's history, published in exile during the Franco years.

Collins, **Roger**, *The Basques* (Blackwell,1990). A good general introduction to the Basques.**Elliot**, **J. H.**, *Imperial Spain 1469–1714* (Pelican, 1983). Elegant proof that much of the best writing these days is in the field of history.

Epton, **Nina**, *Navarre: the Flea between Two Monkeys*, and *Grapes and Granite* (on Galicia); good reads but out of print, available only in libraries.

Ford, **Richard**, *Gatherings from Spain* (Everyman). A boiled-down version of the all-time classic travel-book *A Handbook for Travellers in Spain*, written in 1845. Hard to find but worth the trouble.

Harnilton, **R. and Janet Perry**, translators, *The Poem of the Cid* (Penguin).

Hemingway, **Ernest**, *The Sun Also Rises*, (*Fiesta* in the UK) and *Death in the Afternoon* (various editions). The former put Pamplona on the map, the latter is his book on bullfighting.

Hooper, **John**, *The New Spaniards* (Penguin 1995). A comprehensive and enjoyable account of contemporary Spanish life and politics.

Lee, **Laurie**, *As I Walked Out One Midsummer Morning* and *A Rose for Winter*. Very well-written adventures of a young man in Spain in 1936, walking from Vigo to Málaga and his return 20 years later.

Lojendio, **Louis**, *Navarre Romaine* (Zodiaque, 1967). One of the excellent illustrated volumes in the French Zodiaque series on medieval art; other pertinent volumes for northern Spain are *Le Pré-Romaine Hispanique* (on the Visigoths and Asturian churches) and *Le Mozarabe*.

Kurlansky, **Mark**, *The Basque History of the World* (Penguin Books, 2001). Wonderful, wide-ranging and simpatico account of the Basques; history, cuisine and much more.

MacLaine, **Shirley**, *The Camino* (Simon & Schuster, 2000). The Hollywood star's spiritual memoir of her own pilgrimage to Santiago de Compostela.

Michener, **James A.**, *Iberia* (Fawcett, 1984). A 950-page compendium of windy bosh, but full of fascinating sidelights just the same.

Morris, **Jan**, *Spain* (Penguin, 1982). A little disappointing considering the author; careless generalizations and dubious ideas sustained by crystalline prose.

Mitchell, **David**, *The Spanish Civil War* (Granada, 1982). Anecdotal; wonderful photographs.

Mullins, **Edwin**, *The Pilgrimage to Santiago* (Secker & Warburg/Taplinger). Perhaps the most colourful and wide-ranging account of the journey.

Reilly, **Bernard F.**, *The Medieval Spains* (Cambridge University Press, 1993). Dry but painstakingly detailed account of the origins of Spain.

Richardson, **Paul**, *Our Lady of the Sewers* (Abacus, 1999). An engaging collection of stories about almost forgotten corners and customs of Spain, including a description of Lekeitio's gruesome goose rodeo.

Index

Main page references are in **bold**. Page references to maps are in *italics*.

A Coruña 313, 314–17
A Guarda **333**, 335
A Póboa do Camaniñal 324
A Toxa 323, **325–6**
accommodation 65–8
  see also individual places
Acebo 277
Adoptionism 197
Agés 233
Agoitz 87–8
agotes 24, 89
Aguilar de Campóo 255, **256**
Aguilar del Río Alhama 106
Aizkomendi 170
Alaisa 170
Álava province 168–70
Alfaro 106
Algorta 162
Alhama valley 106
Allariz 338
Altamira 189
Alto Campóo 185
Ancares Leoneses 279–80
al-Andalus 10–12
Andara 193
Andrín 207
Aoiz 87–8
Arabs 9–12
Aralar 94–5
Aranda de Duero 246, 250
Arantzazu 137
Arealonga 289
Arenas de Cabrales 195, **198**
Argómaniz 169
Arizcun 78
Armada 315
Arnedillo 106–7
Arnedo 105, **106**
Arrasate 137
art and architecture 30–2
Arúza 293
As Mariñas de Lugo *286*, 286–90
asadores 40
Astorga 273–6
Asturias 4, 204–5, *205–26*
  food and drink 34
  Picos de Europa 198–201
Atapuerca 233
Auritz 77
Auritzberri 77
Avilés 213, **214**

Axeitos 324
Azpegi I 73
Azpeitia 136, **138**

Baiona **332**, 334
Bakio 143, 147
Balouta 280
Baños de Cerrato 260
Barbadillo del Mercado 249
Bárcena Mayor 190, **192**
Bárdenas Reales 94
Bares 289
Barrio de Santa María 255
Basque Lands (Euskadi) 4,
  118–71, *118*, *139*
  ETA 16–18, 122
  folklore 124–5
  food and drink **34**, 37, 125
  history 9, 10–11, 15–16, **120–2**
  language 123–4
  people 119–20
  sports 125–6
Beato de Liébana 197
Becerreá 291, 292
Becerril de Campos 259
Becerril del Carpio 256
Belorado 231–2
Bergara 137
Bermeo 146
Betanzos 311–14
Betelu 95
Bilbao (Bilbo) 148–61, *150–1*
Bisjueces 236
Boadilla del Camino 253
Bolívar 148
Bolmir 186
Brañosera 257
Briñas 115–16
Briones 116
Briviesca 232, **233–4**
Bueu 330
bullfighting 63
Bulnes 198
Buño 317
Burbia 280
Burela 289
Burgos *231*, *238*, 238–45
Burguete 77
Burgui 73
buses and coaches 48, 50–1
Butrón 147

Caaveiro 311
Cabezón de Liébana 197
Cabezón de la Sal 192
Cabo Finisterre 319, **320**
Cabo Peñas 214
Cabo Touriñán 318–19
Cabo Vidio 225
Cabo Villán 318
Calahorra 104–6
Caldas de Reis 323, **326**
Caleruega 249
Camariñas **318**, 319
Cambados 323, **325**
Cambre 314
Camino de Santiago **20–3**, 62,
  74, 96–7
Campo del Agua 280
Canales de la Sierra 112
Candás 214
Cangas 330
Cangas del Narcea 223
Cangas de Onis 198–200
Cantabria 4, *172–3*, **173–202**
  food and drink 34
Caracedo 280–2
Caravia 207
Cares Gorge 202
Carlist Wars 16
Carnota 320
Carraspio 142
Carrejo 192
Carrión de los Condes 257–8
Carrión River 257–60
Carthaginians 7
Carucedo 279
Casalarreina 116
Cascante 94
Castildelgado 231
Castile *see* Old Castile
Castillo de Butrón 147
Castillo de Cornatel 279
Castillo de las Rojas 237
Castillo de Santa Cruz 314
Castillo de Vimianzo 318
Castrillo de Matajudios 253
Castrillo de los Polvazares 276
Castro de Chano 280
Castro, Rosalia de 324
Castro Urdiales 174–6
Castrojeriz 251, **252**
Castropol 226

Castroverde 295
Catoira 324
caves
  Altamira 189
  Buxu 200
  Covalanas 177
  Ekain 141
  Ojo Guareña 237
  Pindal 207
  Puente Viesgo **184**, 185
  Santimamiñe 146
  Tito Bustillo 207
  Urdax 78
  Valporquero 272
  Zugarramurdi 78
Cedeira 290
Celada del Camino 252–3
Celanova 336
Celeiro 289
Cellórigo 116
Celón 224
Celorio 207
Cenciero 116
Ceneya 200
Cervatos 186
Cervera de Pisuerga 255, **257**
Cervera del Río Alhama 106
Charlemagne, Emperor 71
Charles V, Emperor 14–15
Chorco de los Lobos 202
cider 37–8, 42
Cihuri 116
Cillamayor 256
Cintruénigo 93, **94**
Ciraúqui 97
Citanía de Fazouro 289
Civil War 16, 221
Clavijo 107
Clunia 250
Coaña 226
Codex Calixtinus 23
Colunga 207
Combarro 326–7
comedores 40
Comillas 190–2
Compludo 277
comunes 13
Contrebia Leucada 106
Corao 200
Corconte 185
Corcubión 319
Corella 94
Corme e Laxe 318
Cornago 107
Cornión 193
Corona 202
Corrubedo 324
Corullón 282
Coruña del Conde 250

Costa Esmerelda 174–7
Costa da Morte 311, 317–20
Costa Verde 206–18
Covadonga 9, 199, 200
Covarrubias 246, **247–8**
Coyanzo 220
Cozuelos 255
crime 62
cromlechs 78
Cudillero 224–5
Cué 207
cultural tours 46
customs formalities 49

Deba 141
Desfiladero de La Hermida 196
Desfiladero de los Beyos 198, 201
Desfiladero del Teverga 222
Desfiladero de la Yecla 249
dinosaur tracks 106–7
disabled travellers 54–5
Divine Gorge 202
dolmens 73, 293, 317–18
Domingo, Saint 113
Donostia (San Sebastián)
  127–35, *130–1*, *139*
Durango 146, **147**
duty-free allowances 49

Eibar 147
El Bierzo 272, 277
  wine 278
El Cid Campeador 11, **28–9**, 108
El Pocillo 176
Elantxobe 144
Elcano, Juan Sebastián 139, **142**
Elciego 116
Elizondo 78
Elorrio 147
Embalse del Ebro 185
embassies, consulates 48, 55
emergencies 64
Enciso 105, **107**
Enol 200
entertainment 55–6
Entines 320–1
Ermita de la Virgen de Allende 114
Esgos 339
Espinal 77
Espinama 195, 197
Espinosa de los Monteros 237
Estella 97–9
ETA 16–18, 122
Ezaro 320
Ezcaray 109, **114**

Ferdinand of Aragon 14
Ferrol **310**, 312
festivals 56–7, 84–5

Figueras del Mar 226
Finisterre 319, **320**
Fitero 94
folklore 124–5
Foncebadón 276
Fontibre 184–5
food and drink **34–42**
  bars 55–6
  cafés 55–6
  drinks 36–8
  menu reader 40–1
  regional specialities 34–6
  restaurants 38–9, 40, 55
  tapas bars 39
  vegetarians 40–1
Ford, Richard 254
Forest of Irati 73
Forest of Oma 146
Forest of Peloño 201
Forest of Pome 200
Foz de Arbayún 73, 91
Foz de Lumbier 91
Franco, Francisco 16–17
frescoes 27
Frias 235
Frómista 251, 253
frontón 126
Fuente Dé 195, 197–8
fueros 13, 14, 71
Furelos 293

Gaceo 27, 168–70
Galicia 4, 284, **285–339**
  food and drink 34, 325
Garita de Herbeira 290
Gasteiz (Vitoria) 162–8, *163*
Gaudí, Antoni 190–1, 275–6
Gayarre, Julián 73
Getaria 139, 141
Getxo 161–2
Gijón 211–13
Golfo Ártabro 310–14, 311
Gómez, Garcia 29–30
Grajal de Campos 262
Grandas de Salime 224
Gregory of Ostia, Saint 100
Grijalba 252
Guernica (Gernika) 143, 144–5
Guernica (Picasso) 145
Guetaria 139, 141
Guggenheim museum 158–61
Gumiel de Izán 250
Guzmán el Bueno 267

Haro 114–15
health **57–9**, 64
Herrería de Compludo 277
Herrerías 282
hiking 64, 194–5

Hinojar de Cervera 249
Hoces de Río Aller 220
Hoces del Sobrón 233
Hondarribia 126, **128**
Hontoria de la Cantera 245
Hornillos del Camino 252

Igea 107
Ignatius, Saint 138
Inestrillas 106
insurance 57–9
Irache 99–100
Iranzu 100
Irati forest 73
Iregua 107
Irún 128
Iruña oppidum 168
Iruña (Pamplona) 79–87, *80*
Isaba 72–3
Isabel of Castile 14
Isla A Toxa 323, **325–6**
Isla de Arousa 325
Isla Coelleira 289
Isla de la Conferencia 127
Isla de Ons 326
Isla de Sálvora 324
Islares 175, **176**
Islas Cies 331
Isuntza 142
Izpegui pass 78

James the fisherman 20, 297, 300
Jaramillo de la Fuente 249
Javier 88, **90**
Jesuits 138
Jews 25
Julióbriga 186
Knights Templars 96

La Cartuja de Miraflores 245
La Ercina 200
La Hermida 196
La Maragatería 272
La Plaza 222
La Pornacal 219, **222**
La Rioja 4, **101–16**, *102*
  wine 36–7, 104, 114–16
La Rioja Alavesa 170
La Terraza 314
Labacolla 293
Laga 146
Lago del Valle 219, 222
Laguardia 169, **170**
Laida 146
Lancia 263
Langreo 218
language **340–1**
  Basque 123–4
  Castilian 111

Gallego 285–6
  menu reader 40–1
Laredo 175, **176**
Las Améscoas 95
Las Huelgas 244
Las Médulas 279
Lastres 209
Laxe 318
Lebeña 196
Leitza 95
Lekeitio 142–4
Lekunberri 95
León 4, 228–9, 229–30, **263–72**, *268–9, 273*
  food and drink 34
  Picos de Europa 201–2
Lerma 249–50
Les Bedules 200–1
Leyre 88, **90–1**
Liérganes 177–8
Lizarra 97–9
Llamas del Mouro 222
Llanes **207**, 208
Lobios 337, **338**
Lodosa 100
Logroño 102–4
Loiola 138
Lomilla 256
Los Arcos 98, **100**
Los Sanfermines 84–5
Louro 320
Luanco 214
Luarca 224–6
Lugo 293–5

Magellan, Ferdinand 142
Mairuillarrieta 78
Malpica **317**, 319
Manjarín 277
Mansilla 112
Mansilla de las Mulas 262
al-Mansur 11
Manzaneda 339
Maragatos 272, **275**
Marín 330
Markina 146, **148**
Marqués de Murrieta 104
Marquis of Comillas 191
Matalbaniega 256
Mazzariegos 247
Medina de Pomar 232, **235–6**
Melide 293
Michael, Saint 95–6
Mieres 219
Millán, Saint 110, 111–12
Mirador del Fito 210
Mirador del Tombo 202
Miraflores 245
Miranda de Ebro 233

Moaña 330
Moarves de Ojeda 255
Mogor 330
Monasterio de la Vid 250
Mondoñedo 287, **288**
money 61
Monfero 311
Monforte de Lemos 295, 296–7
Monte Artxandamendia 162
Monte del Gozo 293
Monte San Marcial 126
Monterrey 339
Montes 278
Moors 9–12
Moraime 318
moriscos 25–6
Mundaka 143, **146**
Munila 107
Muros 320, 322
Mutriku 141
Muxía 318

Nacimiento del Ebro 184
Nájera 108–10
Napoleonic Wars 15
Naranjo de Bulnes 198
Navarra 4, **70–101**, *70*, *72*
  Pyrenees 72, *72–9*
Navarrete 108
Navia 226
Niembro 207
Noia 321, 322
Noja 176–7
Nuestra Señora de la Bien
  Aparecida 177
Nuestra Señora del Valle 234

O Barqueiro 289
O Cebreiro 290–1
O Grove 323, **325**
Obanos 96
Obona 222
Obregón 184
Ochagavía **73**, 74, 75
Oia 333
Old Castile 4, 228–9, **229–63**, *231*
  food and drink 34
Oleiros 324
Olite **91–2**, 92–3
Olleros de Pisuerga 256
Olmeda 260
Olmillos 252
Oma 146
Oña 234–5
Oñati 136–7
Ondárroa 142–4
oppidum of Iruña 168
Orbaitzeta **73**, 75
Orbaneja del Castillo 236

Oriñón 176
Orio **138**, 140
Ortigueira 289–90
Os Ancares 292
Oseira 339
Oseja de Sajambre 201
Otxandio 170
Ourense 337, **338–9**
Oviedo 214–18

Padrón 322, 324
Palacios de la Sierra 249
Palas do Rei 293
Palencia 258, **259–60**
Pamplona (Iruña) 79–87, 80
Pancorbo 232, **233**
Paredes de Nava 259
Parque Natural del Señorío de
　　Bértiz 79
Parque Natural de Somiedo
　　220–2
Parque Natural Urkiola 147–8
Parque de la Naturaleza de
　　Cabárceno 184
Parque de Pagoeta 138
Pasajes de San Juan 126–7
Pasajes de San Pedro 127
passports 48–9
Pazo da Oca 326
Pedernales 146
Pedra de Raposo 293
Pedrafita 90
Pedrosa de la Vega 260
Pelayo 200
Peloño 201
Peña-Tú 207
Peñalba de Sntiago 278–9
Peñaranda de Duero 250
Peninsular War 15
Perazancas de Ojeda 257
Pesquera de Ebro 236
Philip II 15, 315
Phoenicians 6–7
Picasso, Pablo 145
Picaud, Aymery 21, 23
Pico San Chuis 224
Picos de Europa 4, *193*, 193–202
　　Asturia 198–201
　　Cantabria 193–8
　　Leónese 201–2
Pindo 320
Piornedo 292
Playa Brazomar 176
Playa de Ostende 176
Playa de Torimbia 207
Playa Zuloaga 141
Playas de Arnuero 177
Playas de Barayo 177
Población de Suso 185

Poblado de la Hoya 170
Poio 327
Pola de Allande 224
Pola de Laviana 218
Pola de Lena 220
Pola de Somiedo 219, 222
police 62
Polientes 186
Pome 200
Poncebos 202
Ponferrada 277–8
Ponga 199, **200**
Ponteceso 318
Pontedeume 310
Pontevedra 327–30
Portillo de Lunada 237
Porto do Son 322, **324**
Portomarín 292–3
Portonovo 326
Posada de Valdeón 201, **202**
Potes 194–5, **196**
Poza de la Sal 237
Préjano 107
Priesca 210
Prisciliano, Saint 296
Proaza 222
Puebla de Trives 339
Puente Arce 185
Puente Colgante 162
Puente la Reina **96–7**, 98
Puerto Ibañeta 77
Puerto de Pajares 219, **220**
Puerto San Isidro 220
Puerto de Tarna 220
Puppy (Koons) 159
Pyrenees 72, 72–9

Quintanilla de la Cueza 258
Quintanilla de las Viñas 247

Rabanal del Camino 276
racial purity doctrine 25–6
railways 46–8, 49–50
rainfall 54
Ramales de la Victoria 177
Reconquista 11–12, 27–8
Redecilla del Campo 230–1
Redondela 334
Reinosa **184**, 185
Renedo de la Vega 260
Reserva Nacional de Degaña 223
Reserva Nacional de Os Ancares
　　292
Reserva Nacional de Sueve 210
restaurants 38–9, 40, 55
　　menu reader 40–1
　　see also individual places
Retortillo 186
Revilla de Santullán 256

Ría de Arousa 324
Ría de Camariñas 318
Ría de Corcubión 318–19
Ría de Corme e Laxe 317–18
Ría de Muros e Noia 320–4
Ría de Pontevedra 326–30
Ría de Vigo 330–5
Riaño 272
Rías Baixas 320–6, *321*
Ribadavia **336**, 337
Ribadeo 287, **288**
Ribadesella 207–10
Ribadumia 323
Ribas de Sil 339
Rinlo 288
Río Bidasoa 127
Rioja *see* La Rioja
Rodiles 210
Roland and Oliver legend 9, 76
Romanesque art and
　　architecture 30–2
Románico Palentino 254–7
Romans 7
Roncal 73
Roncesvalles 9, 22, **73–7**
Ruente 192
Ruesga 257

Sada 314
Sahagún 261–2
Saja National Reserve 185
Sajazarra 116
Salas 219, **222**
Salas de los Infantes 248
Salcedillo 257
Saldaña 260
Salinas 214
Salvatierra 170
San Adrián de Argiñeta 147
San Andrés de Arroyo 255
San Cebrián de Muda 257
San Esteban 339
San Estéban hermitage 107
San Genadio 279
San Juan de Gaztelugatxa 147
San Juan de Ortega 232–3
San Juan de San Fiz 282
San Martín de Elines 186
San Martín de Mondoñedo 289
San Martín de Unx 92
San Miguel de Escalada 263
San Miguel in Excelsis 94–5
San Millán de la Cogolla 110–12
San Pedro de Arlanza 247
San Pedro de Cardeña 245
San Pedro de las Dueñas 262
San Pedro monastery 200
San Pedro de Tejada 236
San Quirce 245–7

San Salvador de Cantamuda 257
San Salvador de Leyre 90–1
San Sebastián (Donostia)
128–35, *130–1, 139*
San Telmo monastery 133
San Vicente de la Barquera 190,
192
San Xulián 292
Sancho the Strong 75, 77
Sanctuary of Arantzazu 137
Sanctuary of St Ignatius 138
Sanctuary of San Miguel in
Excelsis 94–5
Sangüesa 88–90
Santa Catalina de Somoza 276
Santa Eulalia de Bóveda 295–6
Santa María de Cañas 112
Santa María de Caracedo 280–2
Santa María del Cebreiro 291
Santa María de Eunate 96
Santa María de Mave 256
Santa María la Real 94
Santa Uxia de Ribeira 324
Santander 178–84, *182–3*
Santiago de Compostela
297–310, *298–9*
pilgrimage 20–3, 62, 74, 96–7
Santibáñez del Val 248–9
Santillana del Mar 186–8
Santo Domingo de la Calzada
109, **113**
Santo Domingo de Silos 249
Santo Toribio de Liébana 196–7
Santoña 176
Sanxenxo **326**, 328
Sargadelos 289
Sarriá 291, **292**
Sasamón 252
Saturrarán 141
scallops 308
Segura 136–7
Senda del Arcediano 202
sherry 37
shopping
duty-free allowances 49
opening hours 61
sidra 37–8, 42
Sierra de Leyre 90–1
Siones 237
Smoking 63
Sober 297
Sobrado dos Monxes 296
Somiedo National Park 220–2
Soncillo 236
Sonsierra 115–16
Sorginetxe 170
Sorlada 100
Sorzano 107
Soto de Sajambre 201

Sotres 198
special-interest holidays 47
sports and activities 63–4
Suances 187, **188**
Suano 185
Suero de Quiñones, Don 272
Suevi 8
Suso 110–112

Tablizas 223
Tafalla **91**, 92
Taramundi 226
Tazones 209, **210**
Templars 96
Teodosio de Goñi 95
Tiatordos 201
Tineo **222**, 223
Tolosa 135–6
Torme 236
Torneiros 338
Torre de Cerredo 193
Torrecilla en Cameros 107
Torres del Río 100
Torrestio 222
tour operators 46–7
travel **44–52**
disabled travellers 54–5
entry formalities 48–9
getting around 49–52
getting there 44–8
insurance 57–9
when to go 54
women travellers 68
Trespuentes 168
Treviso 198
Triacastela 292
Tricio 100
Trubia 220
Tudela 92–4
Tui 334–5
Tuiza de Arriba 220
Tuñón 220

Ujué **92**, 93
Ullivarri 170
Unquera 196
Urdaibai Biosphere Reserve 145–6
Urkiola 147–8
Urrieles 193
Urrunaga 170

Valberzoso 257
Valcarlos 74–5
Valdearenas 184
Valdediós 210–11
Valdezcaray 114
Valença do Minho 335
Valencia de Don Juan 261, **263**
Valle de Baztán 77–8

Valle de Bidasoa 78–9
Valle del Roncal 74–5
Valle de Roncal 72–3
Valle de Salazar 73
Valle del Silencio 278
Vallejo de Mena 237
Vallespinoso de Aguilar 255
Valley of Iregua 107
Valporquero 272
Valvanera 112
Vandals 8
vaqueros 224
Vega Casar, Francisco de la 178
Vega de Espinareda 279–81
Vegabaño 202
Vera de Bidasoa 78–9
Vercedo 237
Verín 339
Viana 98, **100–1**
Vicendo 289
Vid 250
Viego 201
Vigo 331, 332–4
Viguera 107
Vilagarcía de Arousa 322–3, 325
Vilanova de Lourenzá 288
Vilar de Donas 293
Villa of Olmeda 260
Villa Zuloaga 141
Villafranca del Bierzo 282
Villafranca Montes de Oca 232
Villalaín 236
Villalba 295, **296**
Villalcázar de Sirga 251, **253–4**
Villanueva 200
Villanueva de la Torre 257
Villarcayo 236
Villarmentero de Campos 253
Villasana de Mena 237
Villaviciosa 209, **210**
Viloria de Rioja 231
Vimianzo 318
Virgen de Oca 232
Visigoths 8–9
Vitoria (Gasteiz) 162–8, *163*
Viveiro 287, **289**

walking tours 46–7
wine 36–7, 41–2, 325, 278, 325
La Rioja 36–7, 104, 114–16
women travellers 68

Yesa 90
Yuso 112

Zarautz **138–9**, 140
Zudaire 95
Zuloaga 141
Zumaia **140**, 141
Zumárraga 137

Northern Spain
touring atlas

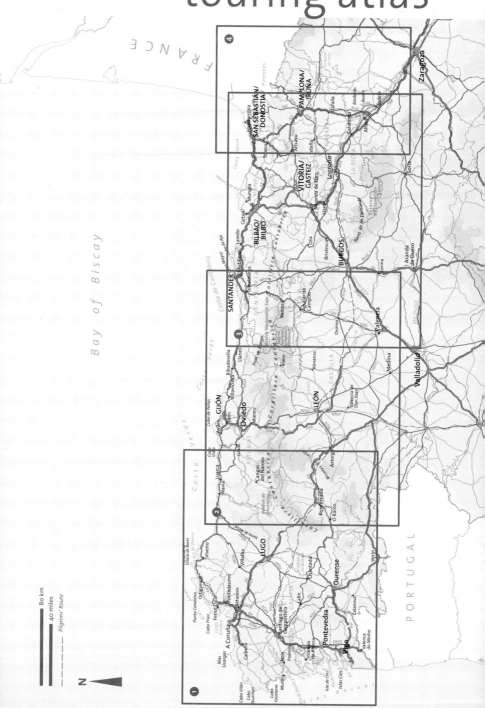

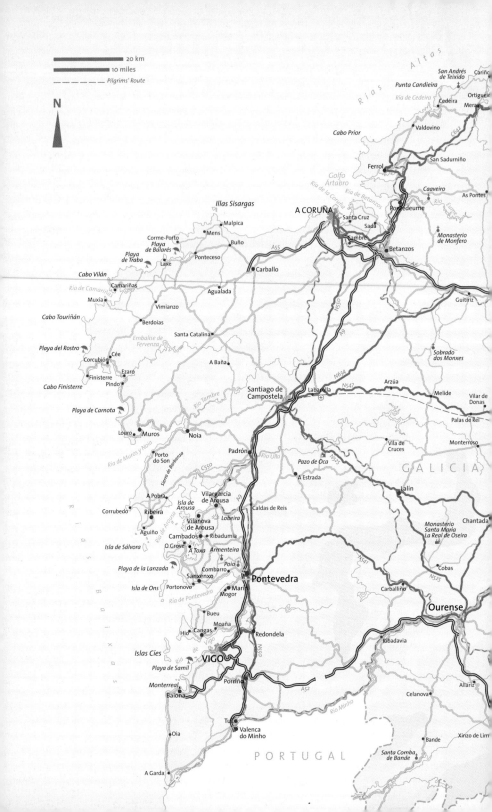

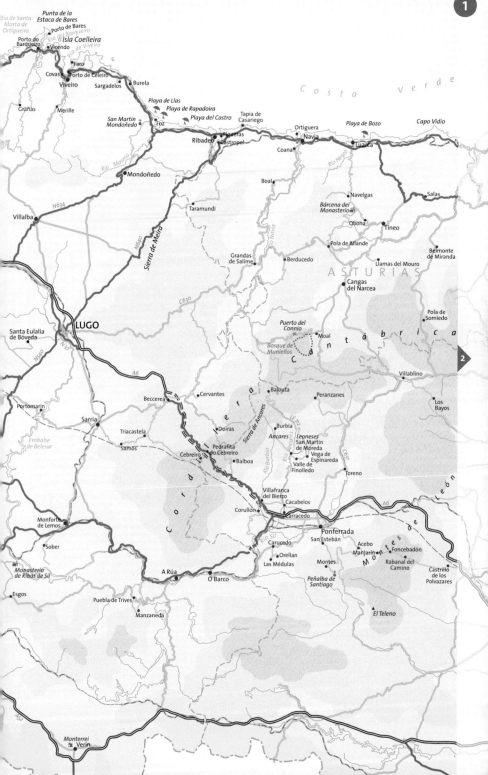

Ría de Santa Marta de Ortigueira

Punta de la Estaca de Bares
Porto de Bares
Porto del Barquero
Isla Coelleira
Porto do Barqueiro
Vicendo
Ría de Viveiro

Costa Verde

Faro
Covas
Porto de Celeiro
Viveiro
Burela
Sargadelos
Grañas
Merille

Playa de Llas
Playa de Rapadoira
Playa del Castro
San Martín Mondoñedo
Foz

Tapia de Casariego
Figueras
Castropol
Ribadeo

Ortiguera
Coaña
Navia
Playa de Bozo
Capo Vidio
Luarca

Río Mayru

Mondoñedo

Boal

Navelgas
Salas

Bárcena del Monasterio
Obona
Tineo

Villalba
N634

Taramundi

Pola de Allande

Belmonte de Miranda
Llamas del Mouro

Río Navia

Grandas de Salime
Berducedo

ASTURIAS
Cangas del Narcea

Sierra de Meira
N540

C630

Santa Eulalia de Bóveda

LUGO

Puerto del Connio
Moal
Bosque de Muniellos
Cantábrica

Pola de Somiedo

N540

A6

2

Portomarín

Becerreá
Cervantes
Balouta
Peranzanes
Villablino

Los Bayos

Sarria
Triacastela
Samos
Doiras
Burbia
Ancares
Sierra de Ancares
Leoneses
San Martín de Moreda
Vega de Espinareda
Valle de Finolledo
Toreno

Embalse de Belesar

Pedrafita do Cebreiro
Cebreiro
Balboa

Corial
de
llera

Robunbia
Río Ancares
LE-712
C631

Villafranca del Bierzo
Cacabelos
A6

Monforte de Lemos
Sober

Corullón
Carracedo
Ponferrada

Montes de León

Monasterio de Ribas de Sil
Esgos

A Rúa
O Barco

Río Sil
Carucedo
Orellan
Las Médulas
Montes

San Esteban
Acebo
Manjarín
Foncebadón
Rabanal del Camino
Castrillo de los Polvazares

Peñalba de Santiago

El Teleno

Puebla de Trives
Manzaneda

Monterrei
Verín

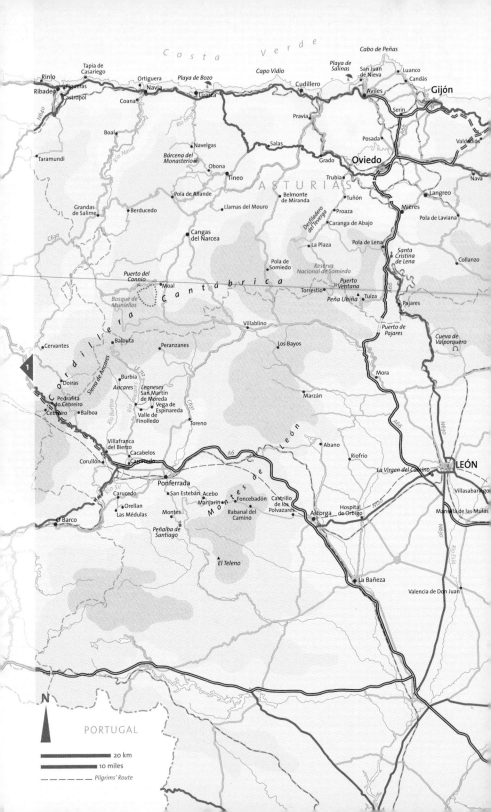